American Cars,
Trucks and Motorcycles
of World War I

ALSO BY ALBERT MROZ
AND FROM MCFARLAND

American Military Vehicles of World War I:
An Illustrated History of Armored Cars, Staff Cars,
Motorcycles, Ambulances, Trucks, Tractors and Tanks (2009)

American Cars, Trucks and Motorcycles of World War I

Illustrated Histories of 225 Manufacturers

ALBERT MROZ

McFarland & Company, Inc., Publishers
Jefferson, North Carolina, and London

Table of Contents

Credits and Acknowledgments

American Truck Historical Society, Art Archives at Imperial War Museum, Autolit.com, Tom Berndt, Cadillac Factory Literature, Fred Crismon, Bev Davis, Peter Debski, Paul DeLucchi, Ralph Dunwoodie, Ford Factory Literature, FWD Museum, David Gallagher, Al Garcia, General Motors Factory Literature, Bryan Goodman, A. W. Hays, Don Hays, Elayne Hurd at Autopaper, Johnson's Auto Literature, Arthur Jones, James V. Lee, Library of Congress, Jacques Littlefield, Mack Factory Literature, McLellan's Auto Literature, Medical College of Pennsylvania, Military Vehicle Preservation Association, Edward Mroz, Nash Factory Literature, National Archives, National Automotive Museum, Pacific Northwest Truck Museum, Bill Powk, Dirk Roberts, Ed Roberts, Peter Roberts, Randy Shapiro, Society of Automotive Engineers, Society of Automotive Historians, Stanford Hoover Library, U.S. Patent Office, Roger Viollet, Western Front Association, White Factory Literature, Geoffrey Wintrup, Greg Wintrup, World War I Museum at Kansas City, Peterr Zappel.

Published articles by the author of this book used in part throughout the text, including some photographs and illustrations, have appeared in the following magazines: *American History, American Iron, Antique Power, Army Motors, Auto Moto, Autoweek, Automotive History Review, Hard Hat, Militaria International, Old Time Trucks, Old Truck Town News, SAH Journal, Steam Traction, Tractor and Machinery, Transport Topics, Turning Wheels, Vintage Truck, VTFE Monthly*, and *Wheels*.

Preface

At the turn of the twentieth century the Industrial Revolution had become an incubator of machine development to such a degree that the birth of the motor vehicle was a normal and natural outcome, even if self-propelled personal transport was not welcomed by those who were perfectly comfortable with horse-drawn conveyances and steam-powered locomotives. However, as the 1900s progressed, the motor vehicle industry in America began to grow exponentially, and entrepreneurs, designers and inventors jumped at the chance to become a part of the industry that would define a new era.

Less than two decades into the mass production of cars, trucks and motorcycles, motor vehicle technology was thrust into the arsenals of war, and new vehicles in the form of armored cars, motor ambulances and tanks were invented. This evolution of design and manufacturing is addressed in my earlier book *American Military Vehicles of World War I* (McFarland, 2009).

The present work portrays the complex American civilian motor vehicle industry within the specific time frame of World War I. The Great War, as it was called, began in 1914 in Europe, spread to other continents, and finally entangled the United States directly in 1917 when this country mobilized its military-industrial complex to come to the aid of the Allied nations in Europe and those standing with them around the globe.

Even as huge sections of American industry and population were drawn or conscripted into military service and arms production, a large portion of manufacturing continued producing what was needed for the civilian market. At least 225 private American enterprises produced motor vehicles in the form of cars, trucks and motorcycles which were built not for military use but for the non-military home market. A number of these firms produced vehicles for civilian use as well as military hardware, and this overlap is duly noted. (The Liberty truck, which is listed, was built by a collaboration of private companies under the auspices of the Society of Automotive Engineers and the U.S. Army, and can be considered the only exception in this book.)

Each of these 225 manufacturers is catalogued herein, with a profile consisting of a brief history of the company and an illustration and specifications of at least one representative model built in 1917–1918, including cars, trucks and motorcycles. The illustrations and specifications have been selected from catalogs of the Great War era. That there were 225 such companies may be remarkable, but there are also no doubt some omissions, since a few very small firms which built prototypes or experimental vehicles made too slight an impact in the marketplace to be included in this collection. For nearly all the makes, the specifications shown below the illustrations are in addition to the company history, so that neither the prose nor the numbers stand alone at representing the entire picture for each company's production during the two years in which the United States was directly involved in World War I overseas.

As with my earlier effort, *The Illustrated Encyclopedia of American Trucks and Commercial Vehicles* (Krause, 1996), this book is organized simply by vehicle name in alphabetical

1

order, not necessarily by company name order — e.g., Acme Trucks are listed under Acme, though they were made by the Cadillac Auto Truck Company. These company histories are overviews of the genesis of firms organized for actual manufacturing of autos, trucks and motorcycles in the United States, and this discussion is intended to serve as a basic perspective on the marketplace in America.

What was available to the general public sometimes overlapped with what the military used in battle or behind the lines in the very first war that involved motor vehicles of any type (considering that the Punitive Expedition of 1916–1917, in which General John Pershing and his troops chased Pancho Villa and his men into Mexico, was considered a skirmish, or more precisely an expedition, rather than a war).

The difficulty for private companies to survive during wartime, when material and labor shortages and the diversion of production facilities for the war effort were looming obstacles, is addressed in this succinct discussion, along with brief mention of the postwar recession, labor strikes, competition during the Roaring '20s, and the disaster of the 1929 Wall Street stock market crash and the Great Depression, which saw the demise of so many companies in America.

Of the companies that did survive the Depression, a full history is beyond the scope of this work. Each firm deserves entire chapters or even whole books. The lessons told by the histories within are those of the adverse effects of war and postwar economics; the gargantuan effects of fiscal mismanagement, both governmental and private; and the reluctance to progress with market demands and innovation, all of which have been repeated. There are certain cases which make it seem as if history is truly repeating itself, such as the Woods Dual Power gasoline-electric hybrid of 1917.

With only a few exceptions as to precise dates, the illustrations and specifications published here reflect a sampling of each company's product offerings and do not necessarily cover all models or body styles produced in 1917 and 1918, although every illustration in this book is from either one of these two years. Moreover, they were chosen as largely the best representatives of the elaborately diverse American motor vehicle industry and the 225 American companies that built cars, trucks and motorcycles during the era of the Great War.

THE HISTORIES

Acason

As World War I exploded in Europe, Acason Motor Truck Company began building ½-ton trucks in 1915 in Detroit, Michigan. Perhaps it is fortuitous to begin this historical review of American motor vehicle manufacturing during this specific era with a company located in Detroit, Michigan, which would become the metonym for the American auto industry, eventually being dubbed Motown, where a highly regarded style of music eventually also became known worldwide.

Detroit was founded in 1701 by Antoine Laumet de la Mothe, Sieur de Cadillac, a name destined to become famous for another one of its numerous motor vehicle manufacturers. Famous as the City of Detroit would become, the Acason Motor Truck Company would not rise to that level of recognition, just as numerous other small companies of this re-gion would not for various reasons, which included cutthroat competition and various economic fluctuations of the region and of the entire nation largely as a result of World War I.

Acason's model line for 1916 would also include a 2-ton model, which was powered by a Waukesha four-cylinder engine using a four-speed transmission. The standard, assembled Acason trucks also used Timken worm-drive rear axles.

By 1917 Acason added a 1½-ton, and in 1918 a 5-ton model was also developed. An effort was made to begin building a model line of Acason tractors. However, shortages during the war and the economic downturn directly afterwards brought a slow demise to the company. By 1921 only a 2½-ton truck and a 3½-ton truck were available, and by 1925 the end of all manufacturing arrived for this small company.

ACASON TRUCKS
Manufactured by
ACASON MOTOR TRUCK CO., Detroit, Mich.

S P E C I F I C A T I O N S

Model	3½	2	1½	5
Capacity	3½ tons	2 tons	1½ tons	5 tons
Drive	Worm	Worm	Worm	Worm
Chassis Price	On application	On application	On application	On application
Motor				
H. P. (S.A.E.)	28.9	28.9	19.6	36.1
H. P. (Actual)	36	36	32	52
Cylinders	4 in pairs	4 in pairs	4 in pairs	4 in pairs
Bore	4¼″	4¼″	3½″	4¾″
Stroke	5¾″	5¾″	5¼″	6¾″
Wheel Base	165″	150″	150″	172″
Tread Front	66½″	58¼″	58¼″	66½″
Tread Rear	67¾″	59″	59″	72″
Tires Front	36x5″	34x4″	34x3½″	36x6″
Tires Rear	38x5″ dual	36x6″	36x5″	40x6″ dual

Frame—Pressed steel.
Front Axle—Drop forged.
Rear Axle—Timken worm axle.
Springs Front—Semi-elliptic.
Springs Rear—Semi-elliptic.
Carburetor—Schebler "R."
Cooling System—Pump.
Oiling System—Circular splash.
Ignition—Eisemann magneto.
Control—Right drive, center control.
Clutch—Dry disc.
Transmission—Selective, four speeds forward and one reverse. Model 5, constant mesh.
Brakes—On rear drums, expanding.
Steering Gear—Ross gear.
Equipment—Driver's seat, oil lamps, horn, tools, etc. Chassis in the prime.

Acme

Like Acason, Acme got its start in 1915 in Michigan. The first Acme trucks from this firm, not to be confused with Acme of Pennsylvania, were built by the Cadillac Auto Truck Company of Cadillac, Michigan.

Like many truck builders of the era, the company built standard, assembled trucks using original equipment manufacturer components that included engines, axles, transmissions, steering gear, et cetera, offering a model line that at first consisted of 1-ton, 2-ton and 3½-ton vehicles. Continental four-cylinder engines were used in the case of Acme, a word meaning "pinnacle" and at one time used very widely by countless companies, partly because the word conveyed high status and partly because it came early in any alphabetical listing.

By 1917 Acme offered a 40 hp Continental engine using a 148-inch wheelbase and full-floating Timken rear axle. At this point the Cadillac Motor Company sued the Cadillac Auto Truck Company for name infringement, and did so successfully, having been in business a dozen years earlier. Acme became the name of the truck and the manufacturer itself. Production of models A through D was only in the hundreds per year, but Acme built ambulances during World War I, as factory literature illustrated.

Acme survived the postwar recession and began building the Flyer, which was rated at 1 ton. The company grew and expanded its model line numbered 40, 40L, 60, 60L, 90, 90L and 125. In 1927 Acme was acquired by United Truck Company of Grand Rapids, Michigan. At that time a 7½-ton truck was offered with a six-cylinder Continental motor. During the 1920s smaller components such as carburetors, ignition, lights and radiators were provided by a wide selection of suppliers. Acme built small buses during the decade after World War I but finally succumbed to the Great Depression in 1931.

Allen

Brothers E.W. Allen and W.O. Allen decided to start an auto manufacturing business at Fostoria in northern Ohio during 1913. Fostoria was a small city, but as in many towns in this region, industry and industriousness abounded there. The brothers bought the factory of the Peabody Buggy Company and subsequently the factory of the Columbia Buggy Company in Columbus, Ohio.

The first Allen car was designed by L.A. Sommer, who had left the Hammer-Sommer Auto Carriage Company of Detroit. The Allen used a 221 cid four-cylinder engine and had a full-floating rear axle, which was quite ahead of its time. After buying out Sommer, who was building the engines for Allen in Bucyrus, Ohio, Allen output ramped up during the two years of American involvement in World War I, when 7150 cars were built.

The Allen brothers insisted on continuing with a formula that worked, so that by 1920 the Allen cars were still essentially the same cars of 1913 and 1914. In 1921 styling was upgraded as Allen's decision-makers got a sense of foreboding when finances looked dismal. The bodies of the higher-end Allen cars, which were called Artcraft, were painted with exotic colors such as amethyst, garnet, sapphire or turquoise, all gemstones, yet buyers did not clearly see the need to shell out an extra $300-$400 for an Allen Artcraft Touring or Artcraft Roadster. The company was $2,000,000 in debt by 1920, forcing the sale of its Fostoria factory to John North Willys. After producing some 20,000 cars in slightly less than a decade the company finally folded in 1922.

This company should not be confused with a handful of other small ventures by the name of Allen, including ones at Hueneme, California; New York City; Adams, Massachusetts; New Bedford, Massachusetts; Philadelphia, Pennsylvania; Allen & Clark of Toledo,

ACME TRUCKS
Manufactured by
CADILLAC AUTO TRUCK CO., Cadillac, Mich.

S P E C I F I C A T I O N S

Model	A	B	C
Capacity	2 tons	1 ton	3½ tons
Drive	Worm	Worm	Worm
Chassis Price	$2,200	$1,575	$3,000
Motor			
H. P. (S.A.E.)	27.23	19.60	32.40
H. P. (Actual)	40	30	48
Cylinders	4 en bloc	4 en bloc	4 in pairs
Bore	4⅛″	3½″	4½″
Stroke	5¼″	5″	5½″
Wheel Base	148″	130″	168″
Tread Front	58½″	56″	66¼″
Tread Rear	58½″	56″	65¼″
Tires Front	36x4″	34x3″	36x5″
Tires Rear	36x6″ or 36x4″ dual	34x4″	40x5″ dual
Frame	Heat treated pressed steel 6″ section	Heat treated pressed steel 4½″ section	Rolled channel steel 8″ section

Front Axle—Solid drop forged, I-beam section.
Rear Axle—Timken full-floating worm drive.
Springs Front—Detroit self-lubricating, semi-elliptic, bronzed bush.
Springs Rear—Detroit self-lubricating, semi-elliptic, bronzed bush.
Carburetor—Rayfield.

Cooling System	Water centrifugal pump	Thermo-syphon	Water centrifugal pump

Oiling System—Constant level splash (oil circulated by pump).
Ignition—Eisemann magneto.
Control—Left drive, center control.
Clutch—Dry plate.
Transmission—Selective, three speeds forward and one reverse.
Brakes—Internal service and emergency brakes on real wheels.

Steering Gear	Worm and gear	Worm and gear	Screw and nut

Equipment—Seats, lamps, horns, jack and tools.

ALLEN MOTOR
C O M P A N Y

FOSTORIA, OHIO

Price $1095
Sedan 1395

ALLEN TOURING—41

COLOR	Body, brown or green; running gear, black	BORE AND STROKE .	3¾ x 5 inches
		LUBRICATION	Splash with circulating pump
SEATING CAPACITY. .	Five	RADIATOR	Cellular
POSITION OF DRIVER .	Left side	COOLING	Thermo-syphon
WHEELBASE	112 inches	IGNITION	Storage battery
GAUGE	56 inches	STARTING SYSTEM . .	Two unit
WHEELS	Wood	STARTER OPERATED .	Gear to fly wheel
FRONT TIRES	32 x 3½ inches	LIGHTING SYSTEM . .	Electric
REAR TIRES	32 x 3½ inches, anti-skid	VOLTAGES	Six
SERVICE BRAKE . . .	Contracting on rear wheels	WIRING SYSTEM . . .	Single
		GASOLINE SYSTEM . .	Vacuum
EMERGENCY BRAKE .	Expanding on rear wheels	CLUTCH	Plate
		TRANSMISSION . . .	Selective sliding
CYLINDERS	Four	GEAR CHANGES . . .	Three forward, one reverse
ARRANGED	Vertically		
CAST.	En bloc	DRIVE	Spiral bevel
HORSEPOWER . . . . 22.5 (N.A.C.C. Rating)		REAR AXLE.	Full floating
		STEERING GEAR . . .	Worm and gear

In addition to above specifications, price includes top, top hood, windshield, speedometer, ammeter, electric horn and demountable rim.

Ohio, and Allen-Kingston of Kingston, New York — all of them predecessors.

American–La France

As one may imagine, there were numerous motor vehicle companies which were named American (with variations such as American Underslung, American Balanced Six, American Six, American Fiat, American Gas, American Mercedes, American Motors, American Mors, et cetera). This one in particular, known for its fire trucks, also built a few passenger cars from 1907 to 1914.

The American–La France Company of Elmira, New York, had always built fire engines, but in the early days there was an "extracurricular" effort to build "chief's cars" and other passenger cars in the form of roadsters also used for training. Simplex four-cylinder engines were used in building the few such cars, which were designed to be very fast inasmuch as they were meant to be used by fire department chiefs and executives.

When the American Fire Engine Company of Seneca Falls, New York, merged with the La France Fire Engine Company of Elmira, the resulting model line consisted of horse-drawn steam engines for firefighting. It was not until 1907 that a chemical truck was built using a Packard chassis for the City of Boston. By 1909 American–La France began building its own motorized apparatus using Simplex motors. In 1910 the company delivered a Register No. 1 Type 5 (model name) combination chemical and hose truck.

The following year Type 10 and Type 12 trucks were offered with rotary-gear pumps, and by 1913 the Type 16 and Type 30 were offered, each one with increasing size of pumping capacity, although model numbers did not sequentially reflect larger vehicles, such as the Type 15. Another example was the Type 40, which was the smallest rotary-gear pumper, and it was offered into the 1920s on Brockway chassis as well.

American–La France Type 16 and Type 30 were out of the ordinary in that they were hybrid gasoline-electric vehicles. In addition, the Type 31 was a front-drive tractor used to retrofit horse-drawn fire apparatus at a time when full conversion was too expensive, especially as pumpers and aerial hook-and-ladder units were still new and in excellent operating condition, yet to be relegated to the museum or scrap heap. American–La France competed with several companies building retrofit tractors for mechanizing fire apparatus, including A&B, Christie and Couple-Gear. Entire new trucks were also built.

AMERICAN-
LA FRANCE
FIRE ENGINE
COMPANY

ELMIRA
NEW YORK

Price, 85-foot, 6-C $12750
       75-foot, 6-C 12250
       65-foot, 6-C 11750
       55-foot, 6-C 11250
       85-foot, 4-C 12250
       75-foot, 4-C 11750
       65-foot, 4-C 11250
       55-foot, 4-C 10750

AMERICAN-LA FRANCE AERIAL HOOK AND LADDER TRUCK

COLOR	Optional
POSITION OF DRIVER .	Right side
WHEELBASE.	19 ft. 9 in. to 31 ft. 9 in.
GAUGE	Front, 76¾ inches; rear, 62 inches
WHEELS	Front, solid cast steel; rear, wood
FRONT TIRES	38 x 4 inches, dual solid
REAR TIRES	42 x 4 inches, single solid
SERVICE BRAKE . . .	Expanding on front wheels
EMERGENCY BRAKE .	Expanding on front wheels
CYLINDERS	Four or six
ARRANGED	Vertically
CAST.	In pairs
HORSEPOWER . . .	48.4 or 72.6 (N.A.C.C. Rating)
BORE AND STROKE .	5½ x 6 inches
LUBRICATION	Force feed and splash
RADIATOR	Cellular
COOLING	Water pump
IGNITION	High tension magneto and storage battery
STARTING SYSTEM . .	Two unit
STARTER OPERATED .	Gear to fly wheel
LIGHTING SYSTEM . .	Electric
VOLTAGES	Six
WIRING SYSTEM . . .	Single
GASOLINE SYSTEM . .	Gravity
CLUTCH	Dry multiple disc
TRANSMISSION . . .	Selective sliding
GEAR CHANGES . . .	Three forward, one reverse
DRIVE	To front wheels
REAR AXLE	Dead
STEERING GEAR . . .	Planetary

In addition to above specifications, price includes
speedometer, voltmeter, horn and demountable rims.

From 1913 to 1929 American–La France also built commercial trucks ranging in capacity from 2-ton to 7½-ton. American–La France fire trucks and fire engines were used in World War I by the military, mostly in the United States, but some were shipped overseas as well. Trucks for commercial use were built primarily at the new Bloomfield, New Jersey, factory after its construction in 1923. American–La France operated almost as a national institution until 1985, when it delivered its last fire engine. Some small component manufacturing continued until 1994, when the company finally closed its doors permanently.

Apperson

Good repair mechanics were often inspired to begin a manufacturing company back in the late 1800s when it was not unreasonable to expect that a small operation could build motor vehicles and do so for a profit. Such was the case of Elmer and his brother Edgar Apperson of Kokomo, Indiana, who opened their Riverside Machine Works after a neighbor named Elwood Haynes hired them to help him build a car in 1894. By 1898 the brothers, along with Haynes, claimed they had been the first ones to build an automobile in America when they founded their Haynes-Apperson Automobile Company.

By 1902 the first Apperson car appeared, powered by a Sintz two-cylinder engine, the same make as in the earlier prototype. The following year a four-cylinder engine was offered, and by 1908 a six-cylinder engine was available, although it did not become standard equipment until 1914.

The early Apperson is best known for a model called the Jack Rabbit, which appeared first in 1907. It was easily recognizable by its round gasoline tank at the rear, but most significantly it was known for its top speed of 75 mph despite the fact that it continued to use chain drive as late as 1914. Although not a race car *per se*, the Jack Rabbit (sometimes spelled Jackrabbit in advertising) appeared at various contests such as the Vanderbilt, and by 1916 the four-cylinder engine was superseded by a V-8 built by Apperson, the year 2000 vehicles were sold by the company.

Speed was the image the company wanted to promote, and in 1917 the model line of the Apperson was called Roadplane, available in different body styles. Along those lines was the Chummy Roadster of 1918. In 1920 Elmer Apperson suddenly died of a heart attack at age 58 during a race in Los Angeles, which had a severe impact on his brother and the rest of the entire company, with an ensuing downturn in business.

A Falls six-cylinder engine was offered by 1923, and a Lycoming straight-eight engine was included in the 1925 lineup. Priced at $7000 to $9000 by 1910, the Apperson came down during World War I, and by 1925 could be bought for $1,700 to $3,000. However, not enough buyers could be found at any price, and by 1926 the company was bankrupt.

Armleder

Otto Armleder was a successful wagon builder in the 1890s in the area of Cincinnati, Ohio, where he supplied beer brewers with horse-drawn conveyances. By 1910 he realized the future was in mechanized transportation, and his six-story factory began building trucks.

The first model line from O. Armleder, as the company was called, consisted of standard, assembled trucks starting at ¾-ton and up to 3-ton capacity. The large brewing industry around Northern Ohio kept Armleder in business.

In 1917 the company offered its heaviest truck built thus far, which was 3½-ton capacity either as a short wheelbase tractor or long

**APPERSON
BROTHERS
AUTOMOBILE
COMPANY**

**K O K O M O
I N D I A N A**

Price, $2550

APPERSON CHUMMY ROADSTER—8-18-4

COLOR	Imperial wine, motor car gray, or Brunswick green	BORE AND STROKE	3¼ x 5 inches
		LUBRICATION	Full force feed
		RADIATOR	Cellular
SEATING CAPACITY.	Four	COOLING	Thermo-syphon
POSITION OF DRIVER	Left side	IGNITION	Storage battery
WHEELBASE	130 inches	STARTING SYSTEM	Two unit
GAUGE	56 inches	STARTER OPERATED	Gear to fly wheel
WHEELS	Wood	LIGHTING SYSTEM	Electric
FRONT TIRES	34 x 4 inches	VOLTAGES	Six
REAR TIRES	34 x 4 inches	WIRING SYSTEM	Double
SERVICE BRAKE	Contracting on rear wheels	GASOLINE SYSTEM	Vacuum
EMERGENCY BRAKE	Expanding on rear wheels	CLUTCH	Single dry plate
		TRANSMISSION	Selective sliding
CYLINDERS	Eight	GEAR CHANGES	Three forward, one reverse
ARRANGED	V type 90 degrees		
CAST	In fours	DRIVE	Spiral bevel
HORSEPOWER	33.8	REAR AXLE	Semi-floating
(N.A.C.C. Rating)		STEERING GEAR	Worm and gear

In addition to above specifications, price includes top, top hood, windshield, speedometer, ammeter, clock, tire pump, electric horn and demountable rims.

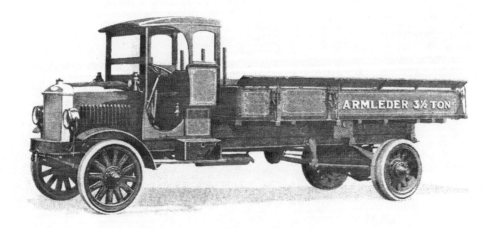

ARMLEDER TRUCKS

Manufactured by

THE O. ARMLEDER TRUCK CO., Cincinnati, O.
Plum, Charles and Twelfth Sts.

Model	H.W.	K.W	H.W.	K.W.
Capacity	2-ton Truck	3½-ton Truck	2-ton Tractor	3½-ton Tractor
Drive	Worm	Worm	Worm	Worm
Chassis Weight	4,500 lbs.	6,600 lbs.	4,350 lbs.	6,100 lbs.
Chassis Price	$2,750	$3,600	$2,750	$3,600
Engine	Continental C-4	Continental E-4	Continental	Continental
H. P. (S.A.E.)	27.23	32.7	27.23	32.7
H. P. (Actual)	30 at 1200 R.P.M.	42 at 1200 R.P.M	30 at 1200 R.P.M.	42 at 1200 R.P.M.
Cylinders	4 en bloc	4 in pairs	4 en bloc	4 in pairs
Bore	4⅛"	4½"	4⅛"	4½"
Stroke	5¼"	5¼"	5¼"	5½"
Wheel Base	148" and 166"	156" and 186"	108"	113"
Tread Front	60"	66"	60"	65¾"
Tread Rear	60"	69"	60"	69"
Tires Front	36x4"	36x5"	36x4"	36x5"
Tires Rear	36x7" or 36x4" dual	36x5" dual	36x7" or 36x4" dual	36x5" dual
Frame	Pressed	Rolled	Pressed	Rolled
Front Axle	Timken	Timken	Timken	Timken

Rear Axle—Timken full floating.
Springs Front—Armleder semi-elliptic.
Springs Rear—Armleder semi-elliptic.

Carburetor	Schebler	Schebler	Schebler	Schebler

Cooling System—Pump.
Oiling System—Constant level splash and force feed combination.
Ignition—Eisemann G-4.
Control—Center.
Clutch—Dry plate.
Transmission—Brown-Lipe selective type.
Brakes—Internal expanding on rear axle.

Steering Gear	Screw and nut	Worm	Screw and nut	Worm

Equipment—Seat, oil lamps, front fenders, tail lamp, speedometer, bumper, governor and large tool box with full kit of tools.

wheelbase truck . This model line continued after World War I using engines from Buda, Continental and Hercules.

A truck tractor for articulated trailer work appeared in 1920. Following the industry trend, Armleder stepped up to six-cylinder engines in 1927. The company advertised that it used structural steel beams for its chassis, which made for good promotional value, but it was not necessarily the best material due to its weight. However, once wood was abandoned for structure of motor vehicle chassis, every manufacturer prided itself on producing its own frames and chassis, and in effect was required to do so. The forming of the metal, which required very heavy equipment, as well as the design of the chassis pattern, differentiated one company from another.

LeBlond-Schacht Truck Company of Cincinnati absorbed Armleder in 1928, but the Great Depression put an end to the whole enterprise by 1937, with the Armleder name dropped a year earlier.

Atlantic

The Atlantic Vehicle Company of Newark, New Jersey, was the builder of battery-powered trucks from 1-ton to 5-ton capacity starting in 1912. The trucks were designed by Arthur J. Slade, who was chief engineer and was formerly from the Commercial Motor Car Company of New York. The Atlantic electric trucks were built in the former Royal Machine Company in Newark after a year and a half had been spent on experimentation and prototyping.

At the time lead-acid batteries were ubiquitous among electric vehicle manufacturers, and Atlantic was no exception in its model line of five different capacity trucks. They were limited to run at 15 mph and had a basic range of 50 miles. Although the year the Atlantic company began production was also the advent of electric starting for internal com-

bustion engines, specifically at Cadillac once Charles Kettering perfected the electric self-starter, commercial delivery vehicles had the distinct advantage of being shut off and restarted simply by flipping an electrical switch. This saved energy as the vehicle stood idly while goods were loaded and unloaded, instead of sitting at the curb while belching exhaust fumes at a time when horse manure was something more commonly tolerated by many people than thick, acrid smoke and the clatter of loud motors.

The replacement of two carbon brushes for the commutator and two bearings at each end of the motor shaft was all that was required to rebuild most DC electric motors, as opposed to the numerous parts in an internal combustion engine, its transmission, clutch and differential. But range, speed and quick "refueling" would soon be the undoing of electric vehicles, even though Atlantic sold its 1-ton for $2,665 and its 2-ton for $3,215, which were very reasonable prices for electric trucks during this period.

In 1914 Atlantic also offered a ½-ton model, but this was the year the company went into receivership under the control of A.P. Osborn and H.L. Davisson, who blamed the financial trouble on liberties taken by the sales department. Atlantic adopted General Electric motors and experimented with taxi design but never went beyond the prototype stages.

In its reorganized form it was now called the Atlantic Electric Vehicle Company by 1916, offering six new models. By 1918 the model line consisted of ½-ton to 3½-ton capacity trucks. In its last year of production in 1921 Hycap batteries were adopted, but nothing could prevent the manufacturer from closing its doors permanently.

Atterbury

The Atterbury Motor Truck Company began building the Buffalo truck in 1910 in

ATLANTIC TRUCKS
Manufactured by
ATLANTIC ELECTRIC VEHICLE COMPANY, Newark, N. J.
893-897 Frelinghuysen Ave.

Model	10-B	1-C	2-C	3-C
Capacity	½ ton	1 ton	2 tons	3½ tons
Drive	Bevel gear	Chain	Chain	Chain
Chassis Weight	4,325 lbs.	4,530 lbs.	5,890 lbs.	8,000 lbs.
Chassis Price	$1,950	$2,400	$2,950	$3,500
Wheel Base	102″	103″	115½″	135″
Tread Front	56″	60¾″	61″	65″
Tread Rear	56″	61″	62″	71″
Tires Front	36x3″	34x3½″	34x4″	36x5″
Tires Rear	36x3″	34x4″	36x3″ dual	40x4″ dual
Frame	Pressed steel	Rolled	Rolled	Rolled
Speed	15 M.P.H.	10 M.P.H.	9 M.P.H.	8 M.P.H.
Miles	60	45	45	45
Front Axle	146-C	No. 1531	No. 1631	No. 1731
Rear Axle	Timken 547	Timken No. 4500	Timken No. 4605	Timken No. 4770
Springs Front—Semi-elliptic.				
Springs Rear—Semi-elliptic.				
Battery Equip.	13 Hycap Exide 44 cells	13 Hycap Exide 44 cells	17 Hycap Exide 44 cells	21 Hycap Exide 44 cells
Motor	G. E. 1026	G. E. 1039	G. E. 1039	G. E. 1022

Steering Gear—Ross irreversible.

Transmission—General Electric controller, four speeds forward and two reverse.

Brakes—Two sets.

Equipment—Dashboards, footboard, driver's seat box in which controller is mounted and
tool space provided; Sangamo ampere hour meter, Veeder hub cap odometer, main
circuit switch, charging receptacle, charging plug and six feet of cable, two electric
dash lamps, one tail lamp mounted on combined license plate bracket, mechanical
horn, bolster bars over battery compartment, which form guides for curved sliding
metal covers which permit of flushing the battery through a trap door in the floor of
the body, a suitable tool kit, driver's seat upholstered with back cushion and re-
versible cushion using the best leather, the seat being of sufficient size to accom-
modate two men.

ATTERBURY TRUCKS

Manufactured by

ATTERBURY MOTOR CAR CO., Buffalo, N. Y.

Model	7R	7C	7D	7C Long
Capacity	1½ tons	2 tons	3½ tons	2 tons
Drive	Worm	Worm	Worm	Worm
Chassis Weight	4,770 lbs.	5,260 lbs.	6,910 lbs.	5,410 lbs.
Chassis Price	$2,475	$2,875	$3,775	$2,975
Engine	Continental	Continental	Continental	Continental
H. P. (S.A.E.)	27.2	27.2	32.4	27.2
H. P. (Actual)	32.5	32.5	41	32.5
Cylinders	4 en bloc	4 en bloc	4 in pairs	4 en bloc
Bore	4⅛"	4⅛"	4½"	4⅛"
Stroke	5¼"	5¼"	5½"	5¼"
Wheel Base	140½"	153½"	167½"	171½"
Tread Front	58"	58"	66"	58"
Tread Rear	60½"	60½"	67¼"	60½"
Tires Front	36x3½"	36x4"	36x5"	36x4"
Tires Rear	36x5"	36x4" dual	40x5" dual	36x4" dual

Frame—Pressed.

Front Axle   I-beam 2x2¾"   I-beam 2x2¾"   I-beam 2¼x3⅜"   I-beam 2x2¾"

Rear Axle—Timken full-floating.

Springs Front—Semi-elliptic.

Springs Rear—Semi-elliptic.

Carburetor—Zenith 0-5.

Cooling System—Pump.

Oiling System—Force and splash.

Ignition—Eisemann magneto.

Control—Right hand.

Clutch—Dry plate.

Transmission—Brown-Lipe selective, four speeds.

Brakes—Internal, rear wheels.

Steering Gear—Worm and sector.

Equipment—Two locomotive type dash lamps, one tail lamp, complete set of tools, jack, hand horn, cab or plain seat.

Buffalo, New York. It was a line of trucks designed by George C. Atterbury, who started out as an electrical engineer for Westinghouse and left in 1902. Henry Brunn, a Buffalo carriage builder, became his business partner, and in 1903 they received an order for 50 electric buses and a few two-cylinder trucks for the St. Louis Exposition.

Subsequently, George Atterbury joined the Conrad Carriage Company as general manager, and he started the Auto-Car Equipment Company, which changed its name to Atterbury in 1909. The company chose to issue Model 100 in 1910. In 1911 a large 10-passenger jitney was built, but this model had a very limited market. Two-ton, 3-ton and 5-ton models with chain drive were also offered until 1917, when Atterbury switched to worm drive across the board for all its trucks.

As with those who survived the postwar financially troubled times, Atterbury did continue to build quality vehicles and exported a large percentage across the border to Ontario, Canada. By mid-decade the company offered 1½-ton to 5-ton trucks which ranged in price from $2,450 up to $5,500. As previously, Buda and Continental four-cylinder engines were offered, but prices were high in comparison to other builders, of which there were dozens in the region.

One of the reasons that there were so many manufacturers across America was that customers bought cars and trucks regionally and had regional loyalties. Sales, marketing, distribution as well as maintenance, parts and repair facilities were regionally concentrated. Except for very large manufacturers such as Chevrolet, Dodge, GMC, Mack, White and a few others, dealerships were not easily established in cities that tried to protect their own products and their own employers. Atterbury was not one of the large companies. Even before the stock market crash of 1929, total production for that year was 141 vehicles. By 1935, in the throes of the Great Depression,

even going to the extent of using other truck makers' cabs and sheet metal, the company went out of business.

Auburn

Naming the company was simple for Frank and Morris Eckhart, who lived in Auburn, Indiana, with their father Charles, a former wheelwright who had gained experience as a wagon builder for the Studebaker brothers earlier in South Bend. By 1900 the Eckhart brothers built their first car, which had a one-cylinder motor and was tiller-steered. After experimenting for another two years the Eckharts showed a car at the Chicago Auto Show in 1903, and sales took off for certain.

The first chain-driven runabout was soon followed by a touring version, and in 1905 a two-cylinder motor was introduced. By 1909 the company offered a four-cylinder engine which was rated up to 40 hp in the 1910 Model X. A half dozen models were available in the years preceding the Great War, but body styles remained as roadsters or touring cars, which were offered with winter tops. A six-cylinder motor appeared in 1912.

The Auburn car was popular around the Midwest, but once the war ended, the Eckhart brothers were forced financially to sell controlling interest, and one new investor was the chewing gum magnate William Wrigley, Jr. The new influx of capital resulted in the Auburn Beauty-Six which appeared in 1919. However, the postwar recession hurt the Auburn Company, and the press noted later that about 4,000 autos were sold per year between 1920 and 1924, a considerable reduction in sales compared to the years during and in spite of World War I.

Errett Lobban Cord became general manager of Auburn in 1924. With some of his own money he upgraded hundreds of unsold Auburns by applying some cosmetic changes to cars that were waiting to be purchased, and

AUBURN
AUTOMOBILE
COMPANY

A U B U R N
I N D I A N A

Price $1985
Touring 1685
Chummy Roadster 1685
Seven-Passenger Sedan 2450

AUBURN TOURING WITH WINTER TOP—6-44

COLOR	Royal blue, purple lake or gray	LUBRICATION	Force feed and splash
SEATING CAPACITY. .	Seven	RADIATOR	Cellular
POSITION OF DRIVER .	Left side	COOLING	Water pump
WHEELBASE	131 inches	IGNITION	Storage battery
GAUGE	56 inches	STARTING SYSTEM . .	Single unit
WHEELS	Wood	STARTER OPERATED .	Gear to fly wheel
FRONT TIRES	35 x 4½ inches	LIGHTING SYSTEM . .	Electric
REAR TIRES	35 x 4½ inches, anti-skid	VOLTAGES	Six to eight
SERVICE BRAKE . . .	Contracting on rear wheels	WIRING SYSTEM . . .	Single
		GASOLINE SYSTEM . .	Vacuum
EMERGENCY BRAKE .	Expanding on rear wheels	CLUTCH	Dry disc
CYLINDERS	Six	TRANSMISSION . . .	Selective sliding
ARRANGED	Vertically	GEAR CHANGES . . .	Three forward, one reverse
CAST	En bloc		
HORSEPOWER	29.4	DRIVE	Spiral bevel
(N.A.C.C. Rating)		REAR AXLE	Full floating
BORE AND STROKE .	3½ x 5¼ inches	STEERING GEAR . . .	Screw and nut

In addition to above specifications, price includes windshield, speedometer, ammeter, tire pump, electric horn and demountable rims.

the gimmick worked. With the help of chief engineer James Crawford the new manager incorporated Lycoming straight-eight motors in 1925, along with two-tone paint, and the resulting models 8-63 and 8-88 doubled sales, helping Errett Cord to assume presidency of the company.

By 1928 Auburn was setting new records, such as 108.4 mph at Daytona Beach, and new records at Atlantic City and Pikes Peak. A bobtail speedster was introduced, and along with new models and new dealership distribution, Auburn continued to stay in business through the early 1930s, but the story of the Great Depression would grip Errett Cord's automobile empire to such an extent that by 1937 his Auburn, Cord and Duesenberg companies were out of business altogether.

tled in July of 1913. During the war Austin experimented with a model line of smaller cars, but in 1917 the company management instead went on with a lavish V-12 on a 142-inch wheelbase. Called the Austin Highway King, the line included limousines.

Among those who bought such extravagant automobiles were boxing star Jack Johnson and newspaper magnate William Randolph Hearst. The long Touring car allowed passengers to sit between axles for a very comfortable ride, albeit at prices ranging up to $5000 or $6000. In the postwar recession demand fell for the hand-built Austins, production of which only amounted to a few dozen per year. By 1920 Austin met its demise as a company, but father and son continued to collaborate in real estate until James Austin died in 1936.

Austin

Located in Grand Rapids, Michigan, this company began doing business in America completely independently of Austin in England after James E. Austin of Grand Rapids bought the Michigan Iron Works in 1900. James E. Austin was a successful lumberman and his son, Walter S. Austin, was the one who built a car by December of the following year he sold thirteen of his 25 hp two-cylinder Model XXV cars, and Austins grew to 50 hp four-cylinder cars on a 100-inch wheelbase in 1904, then to 109-inch wheelbase and 60 hp for 1906 with the Model LX limousine. By 1907 there was six-cylinder 90 hp Touring and Limousine on a 116-inch and 130-inch wheelbase chassis, respectively.

For the era these were grand cars, and by 1911 they featured electric lighting, left-hand steering (in appearance British), and a two-speed rear axle for country and urban driving. Just before World War I began in Europe a court found in favor of Austin regarding the two-speed axle, which was challenged as an exclusive patent by Cadillac; the case was set-

Autocar

Not affiliated with the earlier Auto-Car of Buffalo, New York, the Autocar Company of Pittsburgh, Pennsylvania, became one of the largest and longest-living truck builders in the United States. The company started out as the Pittsburgh Motor Car Company, which was founded in 1897 by Louis S. Clark and his brother John C. Clark. Their first vehicle was an experimental three-wheeler and a small car called the Pittsburgher.

In 1899 they changed the company's name to Autocar, and at the turn of the century they moved to Ardmore, Pennsylvania, still close to America's steel industry. From 1908 onward until 1953 Autocar was a large, successful manufacturer of trucks before being absorbed by White, even though the Autocar name would continue under other owners.

In 1900 Autocar was building passenger cars. At a time when motor vehicles were rather primitive and most light cars were not designed for carrying much weight, the transition from building a passenger car to a commercial car was sometimes only a matter of

A U S T I N
AUTOMOBILE
C O M P A N Y

GRAND RAPIDS
M I C H I G A N

Price	$5250
Touring	3750
Roadster	3750
Sedan	4950

AUSTIN HIGHWAY KING TWELVE LIMOUSINE

COLOR	Body, Brewster green; running gear, black	BORE AND STROKE	2⅞ x 5 inches
		LUBRICATION	Full force feed
SEATING CAPACITY	Seven	RADIATOR	Cellular
POSITION OF DRIVER	Left side	COOLING	Water pump
WHEELBASE	142 inches	IGNITION	Storage battery
GAUGE	56 inches	STARTING SYSTEM	Single unit
WHEELS	Wood	STARTER OPERATED	Gear to fly wheel
FRONT TIRES	34 x 4½ inches	LIGHTING SYSTEM	Electric
REAR TIRES	34 x 4½ inches	VOLTAGES	Six
SERVICE BRAKE	Expanding on rear wheels	WIRING SYSTEM	Single
		GASOLINE SYSTEM	Vacuum
EMERGENCY BRAKE	Contracting on rear wheels	CLUTCH	Dry multiple disc
		TRANSMISSION	Selective sliding
CYLINDERS	Twelve	GEAR CHANGES	Six forward, two reverse
ARRANGED	V type, 90 degrees		
CAST	In threes	DRIVE	Spiral bevel
HORSEPOWER	39.68 (N.A.C.C. Rating)	REAR AXLE	Two-speed three-quarters floating
		STEERING GEAR	Worm and nut

In addition to above specifications, price includes windshield, speedometer, ammeter, voltmeter, clock, tire pump, electric horn and demountable rims.

THE AUTOCAR TRUCK

Manufactured by

THE AUTOCAR COMPANY, Ardmore, Pa.

Model	XXI-F
Capacity	1½—2 tons
Drive	Compound bevel and spur
Chassis Weight	3,700 lbs.
Chassis Price	$2,050, subject to change without notice
Engine	Autocar Company
H. P. (S.A.E.)	18
H. P. (Actual)	18
Cylinders	Double opposed cast singly
Bore	4¾"
Stroke	4½"
Wheel Base	97"
Tread Front	59"
Tread Rear	58"
Tires Front	34x4" solid or 36x5" pneumatic
Tires Rear	34x5" solid or 36x5" pneumatic

Frame—Double channel pressed steel, reinforced.
Front Axle—I-beam.
Rear Axle—Autocar full-floating.
Springs Front—Semi-elliptic.
Springs Rear—Semi-elliptic, platform cross.
Carburetor—Stromberg M-2.
Cooling System—Pump.
Oiling System—Splash from mechanical oiler.
Ignition—High tension magneto.
Control—Steering wheel right hand, control right hand.
Clutch—Triple dry plate.
Transmission—Autocar Progressive, three speeds forward.
Brakes—Service, contracting; emergency, expanding. Rear wheels.
Steering Gear—Bevel pinion and sector.
Equipment—Storm apron, tools, jack, gas headlight, oil side and tail lamp.

exchanging seats for a flatbed. Such was the case with Autocar when the company first offered a commercial vehicle that was tested in 1907. Its 85-inch wheelbase belied its 1-ton capacity, but the chassis and suspension were stiffened so that the vehicle could carry more than the weight of four stout passengers. The same two-cylinder, horizontally-opposed "boxer" motor, which produced 18 hp, was also used in passenger vehicles.

The next model, called the Type XXI-F, had the same two-cylinder motor and three-speed transmission with shaft drive but was built on a 97-inch wheelbase. The two-cylinder motor remained in production through World War I, and the all-purpose Autocar was exported to Canada and Great Britain.

After the war Autocar greatly expanded its model line up to 5-ton capacity. A pair of the new Autocar trucks made a coast-to-coast transcontinental journey, stopping in Yosemite and climbing Pikes Peak. But in addition to the gasoline trucks, Autocar also offered 1-, 2- and 3-ton electric trucks, which were built in limited numbers. It was the gasoline-powered Autocar trucks that became popular during the 1920s, and a whole new range up to 7½-ton appeared in 1926. The following year Robert P. Page became company president, keeping the company together beyond the stock market crash.

Having used the design in the early years as the "engine-under-seat" design, Autocar reintroduced a cab-over-engine (COE) truck type called the U Series in 1933, setting a precedent for GMC, International, Mack, White and others who followed suit with their own COE models in the following years. The rich history of Autocar continued for many decades even after being absorbed by other manufacturers such as White and subsequently General Motors, but the oldest builder of trucks in the U.S. finally became only a footnote as its model line was eliminated in 1995 at GMC-Volvo-Autocar.

Available

Founders of companies in the early 1900s often looked for clever names for their motor vehicles, and since many of the regional and personal names had already been taken, the name "Available" was still available in 1910. It does not appear that anyone affiliated with the founding of the company had that last name.

Chicago was a large market, and that's where the first model line was locally built with ¾-ton capacity using "engine-under-driver-seat" design. The Available truck was offered with a 22 hp two-cylinder "flat" motor. Such a designation nearly always signified a horizontally-opposed motor as there was almost no reason to lay down an inline motor on its side. There was a resemblance in outward appearance to the Autocar XXI, but underneath the sheet metal, Available used a two-speed planetary transmission similar to that used in the Ford Model T, quite different from the Autocar's three-speed gearbox.

As the trucking industry grew rapidly and increasing numbers of businessmen accepted that motor vehicles were superior to horses, despite claims by such groups as the American Horse Association, Available became yet another manufacturer to fill the supply in the demand. As World War I unraveled in Europe, the company introduced a new model line of trucks powered by a 32 hp four-cylinder motor which was once again located under the driver's seat. This was not a fully accepted design by many in the industry, where the horsepower was expected to be up front ahead of the driver, just as it would be with a team of horses. In 1915 Available switched back to the standard truck design with 1-ton and 2-ton trucks using three-speed transmissions and shaft worm drive.

AVAILABLE TRUCKS

Manufactured by

AVAILABLE TRUCK CO., Chicago, Ill.

Model	1	2	3	5
Capacity	1 ton	2 tons	3½ tons	5 tons
Drive	Worm	Worm	Worm	Worm
Chassis Weight	3,200 lbs.	4,500 lbs.	6,300 lbs.	8,000 lbs.
Chassis Price	$1,950	$2,650	$3,650	$4,600
Engine	Continental	Continental	Continental	Continental
H. P. (S.A.E.)	22½	27.6	32.4	32.4
H. P. (Actual)	30	35	40	40
Cylinders	4 en bloc	4 en bloc	4 en bloc	4 en bloc
Bore	3¾″	4⅛″	4½″	4½″
Stroke	5″	5¼″	5½″	5½″
Wheel Base	132″	144″	156″	156″
Tread Front	56″	56″	66½″	71¾″
Tread Rear	58″	58″	65¼″	69¼″
Tires Front	36x3½″	36x4″	36x5″	36x6″
Tires Rear	36x5″	36x7″	40x5″ dual	40x6″ dual

Frame—Rolled.

Front Axle—I-beam.

Rear Axle—Timken floating.

Springs Front—Semi-elliptic.

Springs Rear—Semi-elliptic.

Carburetor—Stromberg.

Cooling System   Thermo   Pump   Pump   Pump

Oiling System—Forced.

Ignition—Magneto.

Control—Left drive, center control.

Clutch—Dry plate.

Transmission—Brown-Lipe Selective, three speeds forward and one reverse.

Brakes—Internal rear wheels.

Steering Gear—Screw and nut.

Equipment—Three oil lamps, hand horn, tools, hubodometer, gasoline tank, front fenders
       and governor.

By 1917, when America was entering the war, Available offered trucks up to 5-ton capacity, a standard at the high end of any model line with only a few exceptions. These Available trucks were powered by four-cylinder Continental motors and four-speed transmissions with either Timken or Wisconsin rear axles.

As in other large cities of the Great Lakes, Midwest and East Coast, just about every truck that drove by was of a different make. Such "diversity" required a new industry of parts manufacturers, distributors and mechanics, but at the cost of high expense and lack of interchangeability of parts. Standardization was not a concern at a time when competition among new companies was at its height in a climate of revved-up production primarily due to the war. Standardized trucks, tractors and other types of vehicles became a pinnacle of achievement in the U.S. as a result of the lessons of the Great War.

During the Great War, Available trucks were available from 1-ton to 5-ton capacity. It wasn't until 1920 that Available offered a 7-ton capacity truck powered by a 50 hp Waukesha motor, but heavy-duty trucks were not as high in demand as light- and medium-duty trucks, and the line was soon dropped. One- to three-ton capacity was the most desirable for use in local city distribution or for trips to and from the farm. Heavy, efficient cross-country hauling was yet to be a truly feasible concept in light of competition from railroads and ship companies. For distribution with limited range around a city, slow, but quiet and efficient electric trucks were still being used even if their manufactured numbers continued to dwindle.

By the time of the stock market crash at the end of 1929, American industry was in trouble due to banking policies gone awry; there was no FDIC to prop up those institutions about to keel over, and Available was no exception in terms of financial trouble. Like other companies, they advertised numerous models but built only a partial list in reality.

As an exception to the rule, Available survived during the beginning of the Great Depression, building specialized trucks that included 6-ton capacity tankers and some COE six-wheel tractor trucks for pulling trailers. The company was engaged in building trucks for the military during the Second World War, and lasted until 1957 when Crane Carrier Corporation took over. Over the 47 years in operation it has been estimated that only 2,500 trucks were ever built with the Available emblem.

Avery

After the company's organization in 1874 with the intent to sell agricultural implements, the Avery Company settled in Peoria, Illinois, to become a tractor and farm equipment manufacturer. By 1910 the firm also entered truck manufacturing, akin to International Harvester in nearby Chicago and a few other companies at a time when autos, trucks and tractors were all quite similar in their overall design and construction and used the same motors in most instances. The trucks were also primarily intended for the agricultural market.

The first Avery truck was a 1-ton capacity model powered by a four-cylinder motor producing 36 hp at 1000 RPM. The tractor and truck were nearly interchangeable, with steel wheels for the tractor and solid rubber tires and a bed for the truck, both capable of 15 mph.

As was most common at the time, the truck had chain drive and used an open cab. However, in 1911 Avery introduced what was called a vestibule cab, which could also mean an enclosed passage between passenger cars of a train or enclosed porch or foyer. This was a large square cab with windows, protecting the driver from the elements at a time when such

AVERY TRUCKS

Manufactured by

AVERY CO., Peoria, Ill.

S P E C I F I C A T I O N S

Model	2-Ton Type B	3-Ton Type B	5-Ton Type B
Capacity	2 tons	3 tons	5 tons
Drive	Chain	Chain	Chain
Chassis Price	$2,700	$3,200	$4,500
Motor			
H. P. (S.A.E.)	36.1	36.1	44.1
H. P. (Actual)	45	45	55
Cylinders	4 single	4 single	4 in pairs
Bore	$4\frac{3}{4}''$	$4\frac{3}{4}''$	$5\frac{1}{4}''$
Stroke	5″	5″	$5\frac{3}{4}''$
Wheel Base	128″	128″	140″
Tread Front	62″	63″	64″
Tread Rear	68″	70″	72″
Tires Front	36x4″	38x5″	38x6″
Tires Rear	36x3½″ dual	38x4″ dual	38x5″ dual
Frame—Channel section.			
Front Axle	Flat bars	Flat bars	I-beam section
Rear Axle—Fixed, round.			
Springs Front—Semi-elliptic.			
Springs Rear—Semi-elliptic.			
Carburetor—Schebler.			
Cooling System—Pump.			
Oiling System—Forced feed and splash.			
Ignition—Dual system with magneto.			
Control—Right drive, center control.			
Clutch	Disc	Disc	Hele-Shaw

Transmission—Selective, three speeds forward and one reverse.

Brakes—Service brake on jackshaft, internal expanding; emergency brakes on rear wheels.

Steering Gear—Sector.

Equipment—Side oil lamp, tail lamp, tools, jack, and horn.

luxury was unusual and out-of-the-ordinary. Usually, drivers of tractors and trucks were expected to suffer through whatever the weather presented them, especially if they were involved in farming. Only gradually over decades, did fully enclosed cabs with adequate visibility and ventilation come into acceptance and common use.

Starting in 1912 Avery introduced a 2-ton and a 3-ton capacity truck. All models used three-speed transmissions. For 1917 a 5-ton model called the Type B was added to the lineup, powered by a 44.1 hp four-cylinder engine which featured a dual ignition system with magneto, something fairly unusual for truck engines. Front axles were rather primitive, using a "flat bar" design as late as World War I. Enclosed chain drive was an option at this time in order to protect and lubricate the chain in an oil bath.

After building trucks which were all forward-control, later called cab-over-engine (COE), in 1921 Avery switched to conventional truck design with a hood in front of the cab. One reason was that a six-cylinder engine was introduced that year, which did not fit well under the seat. Nevertheless, the widespread economic downturn of the early 1920s would force Avery out of business by 1923.

Beck, Beck/Hawkeye

As obscure as the name Beck might be today in truck manufacturing, there were a few incarnations of manufacturers to use this name. The first was located in Cedar Rapids, Iowa. A truck built on a 120-inch chassis and an 18-passenger bus were the first vehicles built by this company in 1911, both very similar basically and powered by a 40 hp engine.

When the Cedar Rapids Auto Works became Beck & Sons in 1914 as World War I began in Europe, the model line was expanded with a 2-ton and 3-ton commercial chassis, and these could be built up as trucks or as buses. The following year a ½-ton truck was offered, and later the same year a 1½-ton truck appeared on a 134-inch wheelbase chassis, powered by a four-cylinder engine using a three-speed transmission and double reduction drive. None of the design factors of the Beck were unusual or extraordinary, but Cedar Rapids did not have many competitors at the time.

For 1917 the company was reorganized and changed names to the Beck Motor Truck Works before merging with Hawkeye Truck Company of Sioux City, Iowa. The model line was simply designated as A, B and C, ranging from 1-ton to 2-ton capacity. The 1½-ton and 2-ton shared a 144-inch wheelbase chassis, but each of the three models had a different size Continental four-cylinder engine. Cabs had a distinctive oval porthole, which was one of the few unique features of a standard, assembled truck.

Some records show that as World War I ended Beck/Hawkeye also offered Herschell-Spillman and Buda motors, with a price of $3,700 for the 2-ton chassis with all running gear and cowl. But no matter what OEM motor was available, postwar financial troubles were unforgiving for Beck. Truck production using the name Hawkeye continued, and another Beck emerged in 1934 when C.D. Beck began building buses in nearby Sidney, Ohio. That separate company with the same name lasted until 1957.

Bessemer

The Bessemer Truck Company was located in Grove City, Pennsylvania, borrowing the name from one of the most famous inventors of steel manufacturing. The Bessemer name is more famously associated with the metallurgical processes invented by Henry Bessemer, which included the technique of blowing air through molten iron. This resulted in a more pure metal and therefore better steel, which at the time was used to make cannon for the

BECK TRUCKS

Manufactured by

BECK-HAWKEYE MOTOR TRUCK WORKS, Cedar Rapids, Iowa

Model	A	B	C
Capacity	1 ton	1½ tons	2 tons
Drive	Internal gear	Internal gear	Internal gear
Chassis Weight	2,800 lbs.	3,200 lbs.	4,000 lbs.
Chassis Price	$1,180	$1,440	$1,860
Engine	Continental	Continental	Continental
H. P. (S.A.E.)	19.6	22.5	28.9
H. P. (Actual)	24 at 2000 R.P.M.	34 at 2000 R.P.M.	42 at 1500 R.P.M.
Cylinders	4 en bloc	4 en bloc	4 en bloc
Bore	3¼"	3¾"	4⅛"
Stroke	5"	5"	5¼"
Wheel Base	124"	144"	144"
Tread Front	56"	56"	56"
Tread Rear	56"	56"	56"
Tires Front	34x3"	34x3"	36x3½"
Tires Rear	34x3½"	34x5"	36x6"

Frame—Pressed.

Front Axle—I-beam, ball and joint.

Rear Axle—Clark semi-floating.

Springs Front—Semi-elliptic.

Springs Rear—Semi-elliptic.

Carburetor	Stromberg KL	Stromberg KL	Stromberg 2-M
Cooling System	Thermo-syphon	Thermo-syphon	Pump

Oiling System—Splash.

Ignition—Bosch high tension magneto.

Control—Left-hand drive, center control.

Clutch—Dry plate.

Transmission—Fuller Selective.

Brakes—Internal and external rear.

Steering Gear—Screw and nut.

Equipment—Tools, lamps, tool box, wrenches, jack and governor.

BESSEMER TRUCKS

Manufactured by

THE BESSEMER MOTOR TRUCK CO., Grove City, Pa.

Model	G	J	D	E
Capacity	1 ton	2 tons	2 tons	3½ tons
Drive	Internal gear	Internal gear	Worm	Worm
Chassis Weight	2,850 lbs.	4,000 lbs.	4,280 lbs.	6,260 lbs.
Chassis Price	$1,225	$2,200	$2,550	$3,450
Engine	Continental	Continental	Continental	Continental
H. P. (S.A.E.)	25	36	36	42
H. P. (Actual)	25	36	36	45
Cylinders	4 en bloc	4 en bloc	4 en bloc	4 in pairs
Bore	3½"	4⅛"	4⅛"	4⅛"
Stroke	5"	5¼"	5¼"	5¼"
Wheel Base	124"	158"	146" and 171"	150" and 175"
Tread Front	56"	60"	60"	66"
Tread Rear	56"	60"	60"	66"
Tires Front	34x3"	36x4"	36x4"	36x5"
Tires Rear	34x4"	36x4" dual	36x4" dual	36x5" dual
Frame—Channel, pressed.				
Front Axle—I-beam, ball and socket.				
Rear Axle	Torbensen fixed I-beam	Torbensen fixed I-beam	Timken full-floating, round	Timken full-floating, round
Springs Front	Semi-elliptic.			
Springs Rear	Semi-elliptic.			
Carburetor	Zenith—Jet	Rayfield	Rayfield	Rayfield
Cooling System	Thermo-Syphon	Pump	Pump	Pump
Oiling System—Combination force and splash.				
Ignition—Magneto.				
Control—Left drive, center control.				
Clutch	Dry plate	Cone	Cone	Cone
Transmission	Fuller Selective, three speeds	Brown-Lipe Selective, three speeds	Brown-Lipe Selective, three speeds	Brown-Lipe Selective, three speeds
Brakes	Expanding and contracting on rear wheels	Expanding and contracting on rear wheels	Two expanding on rear wheels	Two expanding on rear wheels
Steering Gear—Worm.				
Equipment—Jack, tool kit, wheel puller, three oil lamps.				

Crimean War in 1855. Even though Bessemer Trucks were built in the steel-producing heartland of America, it had nothing to do directly with Sir Henry of that surname over a half century earlier.

Bessemer trucks began rolling off the assembly line in 1911, along with several other American companies that year. But this was the era of the sudden burgeoning of the motor transport industry, and anyone with some capital, a bit of know-how and the desire to enter into the competitive field could open a small factory, or even a modest shop, purchase major components off the shelf, and assemble a truck or two, a few dozen, or even a few hundred. Assembly was done manually one and two at a time. The assembly line was still a high-tech innovation reserved for large-scale operations such as at GM and Ford. For the individual "mom-and-pop" operation there was a lot of pride in building a motor vehicle with the company's name prominently cast into the top front of the radiator. Profitability was a hopeful consideration.

The first model line consisted of 1-ton and 2-ton trucks. What was unusual about Bessemer trucks was that they had used a cone clutch, as well as a three-speed transmission along with standard chain drive. For 1913 the model line was expanded to include ¾-ton, 2-ton and 2½-ton priced at $1,250, $1,800 and $2,100, respectively. Axles were from Timken and engines were bought from Continental and were advertised as long-stroke at a time when this seemed like a superior feature, but it turned out long stroke was less than optimum and an equal bore and stroke were most often the best ratio. Piston diameter and stroke would eventually be equalized for maximum efficiency and long life, but in the early days torque was of primary consideration, not RPM, and durability was poorly defined by comparison among manufacturers. An engine that lasted 30,000 miles without repair was considered reliable.

Left-side drive was adopted during World War I when motor vehicle manufacturers were still trying to make up their minds where to place the steering wheel, even though right-hand traffic had been adopted decades before the advent of cars and trucks in America. For delivery work having the driver nearer to the roadside had its advantages, and some vehicles such as for postal delivery would have the steering wheel on the right side even in right-hand traffic up to modern times. Center controls were also adopted when some builders still placed the gear shifter and brake to the outside on the running board, precluding enclosed cabs.

In 1916 a selective three-speed transmission was introduced with a new internal-gear drive 1-ton model. Chain drive was still used for a 1½-ton model for those who still swore by the articulated steel link, but the 2-, 3½- and 5-ton models now had shaft worm drive. The lightest truck chassis was priced at $975, with the 5-ton going up to $4,295. By 1918 chain drive was discontinued altogether, and a standard dry-plate clutch was adopted. The model line now consisted of 1-ton to 3½-ton capacity.

In 1920 prices had risen to $1,835 and as much as $4,295 for the 5-ton model. A new factory was built in Philadelphia, but in 1923, for financial reasons, Bessemer merged with the American Motors Corporation (not related to the later company) of Plainfield, New Jersey. The press announced another merger with Northway and Winther in 1924 which did not transpire, and although Bessemer listed at least three models for 1925, the following year doors were permanently shut at the factory.

Bethlehem

Bethlehem Motors Corporation should not be confused with the Bethlehem Automobile Company, the latter being located in

BETHLEHEM TRUCKS

Manufactured by

BETHLEHEM MOTORS CORP., Allentown, Pa.

Model	A1	B1
Capacity	1¼ tons	2¼ tons
Drive	Internal gear	Internal gear
Chassis Weight	2,650 lbs.	3,700 lbs.
Chassis Price	$1,245	$1,775
Engine	Golden, Belknap & Swartz	North American
H. P. (S.A.E.)	22.5	25.6
H. P. (Actual)	32.5	39
Cylinders	4 en bloc	4 in pairs
Bore	3¾"	4"
Stroke	4¼"	4½"
Wheel Base	126"	144"
Tread Front	55.625"	56"
Tread Rear	56"	60.312"
Tires Front	34x3"	34x4"
Tires Rear	34x4"	34x6"

Frame—Pressed steel channel.
Front Axle—I-beam, Sheldon Type.
Rear Axle—Russell full-floating, round.
Springs Front—Semi-elliptic.
Springs Rear—Semi-elliptic.
Carburetor—Schebler Model R.
Cooling System—Thermo-syphon.
Oiling System—Comb. Splash and force Splash
Ignition—Magneto.
Control—Left-hand drive, center control.
Clutch   Disc in oil   Dry disc
Transmission—Detroit Selective, three speeds.
Brakes—Foot, external rear wheels; hand, internal rear wheels.
Steering Gear—Screw and nut.
Equipment—Tool kit, jack, front and rear axle wrench, horn, oil side and tail lights, parts price list, oiling instruction diagram and governor.

Bethlehem, Pennsylvania. Bethlehem Motors, which built trucks, was actually located in Allentown, Pennsylvania, but both companies were not far from the heart of American steel production (across the state of Pennsylvania) and next door to the second largest steel producer, Bethlehem Steel, which was founded in 1857 (bankrupt in 2001). In naming their city, the Moravian founders of the City of Bethlehem in 1741 had the birthplace of Jesus Christ in mind for whatever good reasons they had at the time.

Bethlehem trucks first appeared in 1917 just as the United States was entering World War I, and this may have been a propitious time to start a truck manufacturing enterprise. Bethlehem Steel was in its peak of forged steel production, and shipbuilding had become a successful enterprise of the region. The very first Bethlehem trucks rated at 1¼-ton used Golden, Belnap & Swartz engines rated 22.5 hp. This was not a small engine manufacturer but filled orders for the time being before Bethlehem switched to a North American engine rated at 26 hp for its 2¼-ton model. Both models used internal-gear shaft drive and prices were $1,245 and $1,775, respectively. Whatever was the company's strategy, it worked, and by the end of World War I Bethlehem was building ten trucks per day. In 1919 the company produced 3,500 trucks, which was considered mass production at a time when many small companies were building one or two per day.

By 1920 Bethlehem Motors absorbed North American Motors in Pottsdown, Pennsylvania, acquiring an important supplier and its factory for its engine manufacturing. Four models were offered that year from 1-ton to 4-ton capacity. Within three years grand plans to build a passenger car called the Ideal and a line of buses were quickly followed by receivership. Even though optimism was promulgated by company officials and a new seven-speed "California Special" was offered, Lehigh Company merged with Bethlehem in 1925, and the following year the company was closed. Hahn and Company bought the factory in 1927.

Blair

Blair Manufacturing shared the Blair name with other motor vehicle manufacturers, but this was the Blair of Newark, Ohio, which got its start in 1911. Duplication of names, both of company names and city names (such as Newark and many others) across the United States, could complicate sales and marketing in the years of actual production, as well as decades later when research has attempted to untangle the details of company history and unravel confusion regarding product lines.

Luckily, enough information has been left extant that it is clear this company was organized by Frank M. Blair along with investors Harold H. Baird, John R. McCune, Willis A. Robbins and Edwin C. Wright. It should be noted that between 1908 and 1914 at least four motor vehicle companies by the name of Blair existed in the Midwest and on the East Coast. And there are at least three substantial cities in America called Newark.

By 1914 the truck builder changed its name to the Blair Motor Truck Company. The designers of the Blair truck chose a somewhat unusual configuration in that a three-point frame held the engine, transmission, driveshaft and rear axle, while the main frame held the body, front axle, steering and controls. The patented drive system allowed the engine and driveline to flex with the rear axle and wheels. This was intended to eliminate U-joints, which in the early days were considered the weak link of any drive system.

The three early Blair truck models used a four-cylinder Continental engine and these trucks were rated at 1½-ton, 2½-ton and 3½-ton. The running chassis were priced $3,000, $3,250 and $3,750, respectively, and a

BLAIR TRUCKS

Manufactured by

BLAIR MOTOR TRUCK CO., Newark, Ohio

Model	C	D	F
Capacity	2 tons	3 tons	5 tons
Drive	Worm	Worm	Worm
Chassis Weight	5,100 lbs.	5,750 lbs.	7,350 lbs.
Chassis Price	$2,850	$3,250	$4,250
Engine	Waukesha	Waukesha	Waukesha
H. P. (S.A.E.)	28.9	28.9	32.4
H. P. (Actual)	35	35	40
Cylinders	4 en bloc	4 en bloc	4 en bloc
Bore	$4\frac{1}{4}''$	$4\frac{1}{4}''$	$4\frac{1}{2}''$
Stroke	$5\frac{3}{4}''$	$5\frac{3}{4}''$	$6\frac{3}{4}''$
Wheel Base	121″—144″	121″—144″	135″—144″
Tread Front	$64\frac{3}{4}''$	$65\frac{1}{4}''$	67″
Tread Rear	$64\frac{1}{4}''$	$64\frac{1}{4}''$	67″
Tires Front	34x4″	36x5″	36x6″
Tires Rear	$34x3\frac{1}{2}''$ dual	36x5″ dual	36x6″ dual

Frame—Pressed steel.
Front Axle—Timken.
Rear Axle—Full-floating worm drive.
Springs Front—Semi-elliptic.
Springs Rear—Semi-elliptic.
Carburetor—Zenith L-5.
Cooling System—Pump.
Oiling System—Splash and forced.
Ignition—Eisemann automatic.
Control—Right drive, right control.
Clutch—Cone.
Transmission—Cotta Selective, three speeds.
Brakes—Service on worm shaft, emergency on rear wheels.
Steering Gear—Screw and nut.
Equipment—Lamps, gas tank, tools, jack and governor.

standard stake body was priced at $150. These were designed as a forward-control type with a seat noticeably lower on each side of the covered motor, predating some of the trucks and vans built decades later with the engine behind the front axle and covered by a semi-soundproof "doghouse."

By 1918 Waukesha motors were adopted with capacity ratings of 2-ton, 3-ton and 5-ton on models C, D and F, respectively. But the company could not stay in the market, and this was the last year of manufacture for Blair Trucks.

Brewster

At the beginning of 1915 there were two Brewster companies in America that were organized to produce automobiles. The one started in Birmingham, Alabama, built only a few prototypes and closed down the same year. The one founded at Long Island, New York, lasted for a full decade, with a restart another decade later that also lasted about one year.

Brewster began as a company a century earlier as a horse-drawn carriage builder, but joining the ranks of many such enterprises in the early 1900s, the company built a motor vehicle prototype in 1915 which went into production for the following year.

The outstanding feature of the Brewster was the Knight Sleeve-Valve engine that was adopted for the make. After the Knight engine had been accepted in Europe and England first, American companies finally warmed up to the design, and Brewster was one of many companies to begin building expensive cars using this type of motor, which varied basically in valve and cylinder configuration from the standard poppet-valve design. Among autos first offered from Brewster was a Limousine for $6650 and a Glass-Quarter Brougham for $8300, which was considered very exclusive pricing at the time.

Brewster subcontracted to Rolls-Royce when the British company began assembling its cars in Springfield, Massachusetts, using Brewster coachwork. However, Brewster continued to build its own motorcars in twelve body styles through 1918, gradually reducing that number as prices grew to $11,000 in 1921. In 1925 Brewster was absorbed by Rolls-Royce of America with a brief re-emergence in 1934 and 1935 using Ford running gear.

Brinton

Brinton trucks were first offered in 1913 in Coatesville, Pennsylvania. The allure for starting a truck manufacturing company in the small town of Coatesville was that it was the home of the Lukens Steel Corporation. Coatesville was known as "The Pittsburgh of the East" as it was the easternmost city of what became known as the Rust Belt, a swath of steel and manufacturing centers from Minnesota running to the Atlantic. Most of the people living in Coatesville worked for Lukens Steel, except for a few that built Brinton trucks.

The very first Brintons were rated at ¾-ton and resembled Kelly and IHC in that they had the radiator behind the engine, allowing for a distinctive tapered hood which had nothing to do with aerodynamics at speeds of 15 mph. However, demand for locally-built trucks was not high around Coatesville, and in the first three years of existence Brinton built a total of 76 chain-drive vehicles. In 1916 the company moved to Philadelphia, where a conventional 2-ton model was built using a four-cylinder Rutenber engine. For 1918 the company offered a 1-ton called Model H and 2½-ton capacity Model F.

The Roaring '20s may have been good for business if a manufacturer could stay competitive, which meant mass production. By the last year of production at Brinton the Model C, which was rated at 1½-ton, was priced at

**BREWSTER &
COMPANY**

LONG ISLAND CITY
N E W   Y O R K

Price	. . . .	.$8300
Open Phaeton	. . . .	7700
Town Brougham	. . . . . .	8300
Town Landaulet	. . . . . .	8450
Touring Landaulet	. . . . .	8800
Enclosed Drive	. . . .	8400
Limousine	. . . .	8500
Runabout	. . . .	7200

BREWSTER COUNTRY BROUGHAM

COLOR	Optional		LUBRICATION	Force feed
SEATING CAPACITY. .	Four		RADIATOR	Cellular
POSITION OF DRIVER .	Right or left side		COOLING	Water pump
WHEELBASE	125 inches		IGNITION	High tension magneto
GAUGE	56 inches			
WHEELS	Wood		STARTING SYSTEM . .	Single unit
FRONT TIRES	34 x 4½ inches		STARTER OPERATED .	Fly wheel generator
REAR TIRES	34 x 4½ inches, anti-skid		LIGHTING SYSTEM . .	Electric
			VOLTAGES	Twelve
SERVICE BRAKE . . .	Expanding on rear wheels		WIRING SYSTEM . . .	Single
EMERGENCY BRAKE .	Expanding on rear wheels		GASOLINE SYSTEM . .	Vacuum
			CLUTCH	Cone
CYLINDERS	Four		TRANSMISSION . . .	Selective sliding
ARRANGED	Vertically		GEAR CHANGES . . .	Three forward, one reverse
CAST.	En bloc			
HORSEPOWER	25.6 (N.A.C.C. Rating)		DRIVE	Spiral bevel
			REAR AXLE.	Full floating
BORE AND STROKE .	4 x 5½ inches		STEERING GEAR . . .	Worm and nut

In addition to above specifications, price includes windshield, speedometer, ammeter, voltmeter, clock, tire pump, electric horn and demountable rims.

BRINTON TRUCKS
Manufactured by
THE BRINTON MOTOR TRUCK COMPANY, Philadelphia, Pa.
5740-42 Cherry Street

Model	H	F
Capacity	1 ton	2½ tons
Drive	Worm	Timken worm
Chassis Weight	2,800 lbs.	4,900 lbs.
Chassis Price	$1,250	$2,500
Engine	Wisconsin	Continental
H. P. (S.A.E.)	25	35
H. P. (Actual)	25	35
Cylinders	4 en bloc	4 en bloc
Bore	3¼"	4¼"
Stroke	5"	5¼"
Wheel Base	125"	139"
Tread Front	56"	56"
Tread Rear	56"	58"
Tires Front	33x4½" Pneu.	36x4"
Tires Rear	33x4½" Pneu.	36x6"

Frame---Built up.
Front Axle—I-beam fore and aft.

Rear Axle	Special full-floating	Timken full-floating

Springs Front—Semi-elliptic.
Springs Rear---Semi-elliptic.

Carburetor	Rayfield	Stromberg
Cooling System	Thermo-syphon	Pump

Ciling System—Pump.

Ignition	High tension	Bosch high tension

Control—Left side drive, gear levers center.
Clutch—Dry plate.

Transmission	Muncie Selective	Brown-Lipe Selective

Brakes—Internal Duplex.
Steering Gear—Worm.
Equipment—Governor.

$2,500. The Model D, rated at 2½-ton, was $2,975. Brinton was offering Continental engines and used Timken front and rear axles along with standard Ross steering. Listings for both models stated that the ignition system was not supplied, allowing the buyer more flexibility, but this was rather unusual and added a hidden cost. In the final analysis, over a twelve-year period Brinton had built 287 trucks. There was just no way the company could stay competitive and it closed in 1926.

Briscoe

Benjamin Briscoe had one advantage when he got into automobile manufacturing in 1903 in that he was already in the sheet-metal business, but he had no faith in his partner, David Dunbar Buick. So he sold his investment in what would be one of the most successful makes of motor vehicles in the world and instead sank his money into the Maxwell-Briscoe Company in 1905 and then the United States Motor Company, the latter of which was notably unsuccessful. He then sallied forth in an attempt to build the Argo, a cyclecar that was only one of an entire fad just before World War I that would go nowhere. But he wasn't about to surrender to bad fortune, and so in 1914 he embarked on yet another venture, this time named after himself: Briscoe Motor Corporation of Jackson, Michigan, which was largely financed by the Swift family of meat-packing notoriety in Chicago at that time.

The first Briscoe was shown at the New York Auto Show in early January of 1914, and what would otherwise be an average car at an average price powered by a 22 hp L-head four-cylinder motor stood out from the hordes of other auto builders and assemblers in that the Briscoe was a cyclops of a car with one large headlight in the upper center of its rounded radiator. As non-conformist as the car was, which on one hand may have been a

marketing ploy to stand out from the rest, a single headlight did not conform to regulations in many states. Moreover, the Cloverleaf Roadster, as the Briscoe was dubbed, had a body made of compressed papier-mâché.

These out-of-the-ordinary features were quickly abandoned, and for 1916 Briscoe reached out to the potential buyers with a Ferro V-8 engine option that could be purchased as a retrofit even after buying a four-cylinder Briscoe, upgrading from a 4-38 Model to an 8-38 Model in case the customer thought the 33 hp four-cylinder was inadequate to power his new Briscoe Cloverleaf Roadster or Touring car.

The V-8 gimmick, along with a choice of five body styles including one called Coachair as well as a Delivery Car, was good enough to survive World War I, with some 8100 Briscoe vehicles sold for 1917 and 1918 alone. The Briscoe B4-24 was especially popular. Following the war Briscoe sold 11,000 cars in 1919 with only three body styles: Roadster, Touring and Delivery Car, the latter of which was cut from the lineup in 1920 and 1921.

After trying various schemes, such as selling assembly franchises to small cities and greatly simplifying production (which was quickly recognized as vast oversimplification), Benjamin Briscoe sold his company to Clarence A. Earl, former vice president of Willys-Overland. Earl renamed the car for himself, lasting only through 1923 while selling slightly warmed-up leftover Briscoes.

Brockway

Among the lesser known truck manufacturing companies in America that became what could be called "long-lasting giants" would be Brockway. Founded by William Brockway, who was a carriage maker, the company opened in 1851 in Homer, New York. Following in his father's footsteps but moving on with technological progress, his

**B R I S C O E
M O T O R
CORPORATION**

**J A C K S O N
M I C H I G A N**

Price $725
Two-Passenger Runabout . . 725
Delivery 725

BRISCOE TOURING—B4-24

COLOR	Body, green; wheels, cream; chassis and fenders, black	BORE AND STROKE .	$3\frac{3}{16}$ x $5\frac{1}{8}$ inches
		LUBRICATION	Pump over and splash
SEATING CAPACITY. .	Five		
POSITION OF DRIVER .	Left side	RADIATOR	Tubular
WHEELBASE	104 inches	COOLING	Thermo-syphon
GAUGE	55¼ inches	IGNITION	Storage battery
WHEELS	Wood	STARTING SYSTEM . .	Two unit
FRONT TIRES	30 x 3½ inches	STARTER OPERATED .	Gear to fly wheel
REAR TIRES	30 x 3½ inches, anti-skid	LIGHTING SYSTEM . .	Electric
		VOLTAGES	Six
SERVICE BRAKE . . .	Contracting on rear wheels	WIRING SYSTEM . . .	Single
		GASOLINE SYSTEM . .	Gravity
EMERGENCY BRAKE .	Expanding on rear wheels	CLUTCH	Cone
		TRANSMISSION . . .	Selective sliding
CYLINDERS	Four	GEAR CHANGES . . .	Three forward, one reverse
ARRANGED	Vertically		
CAST.	En bloc	DRIVE	Plain bevel
HORSEPOWER	16.3	REAR AXLE.	Live
(N.A.C.C. Rating)		STEERING GEAR . . .	Worm and gear

In addition to above specifications, price includes top, top hood, windshield, speedometer, ammeter, tire pump, electric horn and demountable rims.

BROCKWAY TRUCKS

Manufactured by

BROCKWAY MOTOR TRUCK CO., Cortland, N. Y.

Model	J-2	K-3	R
Capacity	1½ tons	2 tons	3¼ tons
Drive	Worm	Worm	Worm
Chassis Weight	4,000 lbs.	4,800 lbs.	6,700 lbs.
Chassis Price	$2,450	$2,850	$3,750
Engine	Continental	Continental	Continental
H. P. (S.A.E.)	22.5	27.2	32.4
H. P. (Actual)	30	35	40
Cylinders	4 en bloc	4 en bloc	4 in pairs
Bore	3¾"	4⅛"	4½"
Stroke	5"	5¼"	5½"
Wheel Base	124"—140"—156"	113"—148"	120"—164"
Tread Front	58"	61"	61"
Tread Rear	58"	61"	65¼"
Tires Front	36x3½"	36x4"	36x5"
Tires Rear	36x5	36x7"	36x5" dual

Frame—Pressed.
Front Axle—I-beam, Elliott.

Rear Axle	Sheldon semi-floating	Timken full-floating	Timken full-floating

Springs Front—Semi-elliptic.
Springs Rear—Semi-elliptic.
Carburetor—Schebler "R".

Cooling System	Thermo-syphon	Pump	Pump

Oiling System—Combination Splash and Force Feed.
Ignition—Magneto—Eisemann.
Control—Left hand steer, center control.

Clutch	Cone	Cone	Dry plate

Transmission—Brown-Lipe Selective, three speeds.
Brakes—Internal expanding, rear wheels.
Steering Gear—Worm and wheel.
Equipment—Seat, front fenders, three oil lamps, jack, horn, oil can, tool box and complete set of tools, chassis painted any color desired.

son George Brockway founded the Brockway Motor Truck Company in Cortland, New York, during 1912 with capital announced at $100,000.

Unlike many light trucks built just before World War I, Brockway followed the lead of International Harvester Corporation with its version of what has been called a "high-wheeler." The truck was very much in appearance a horse-drawn wagon with a motor under the front hood, similar to the IHC, but even more so to the 1912 Chase in that it was powered by a three-cylinder, two-cycle, air-cooled motor and used a two-speed planetary transmission. Simplicity was the theme, even if two-stroke motors had their quirkiness and difficult-to-manage torque curve, meaning very high idling RPM or the necessity of revving the motor to attain desired vehicle speed.

The 1913 Model B rated at ¾-ton sold for $1,450, Model C Van for $1,400 and the 2-ton Model D stake body was priced at $1,925. For 1915 two 2-ton models were offered with a four-cycle, four-cylinder Continental engine along with three-speed selective gear transmission as buyers quickly learned to distinguish the pros and cons of two-stroke and four-stroke motors at a time when simplicity did not always translate to mean reliability.

Having gotten into state-of-the-art technology of the day, Brockway was contracted to build Liberty B trucks for the military during World War I. The company built 587 such vehicles before the contract was canceled at the time of the Armistice. Brockway also built numerous fire engines for the protection of military camps, ports and explosives factories. Cancellation of the Liberty contract hurt the finances of the company, but it was large enough to withstand the hit.

As the war ended, Brockway reentered the civilian market with conventional models such as the 1½-ton Model J-2, 2-ton Model K-3 and 3½-ton Model R. The following year

models ranged from the 1½-ton Model S2 priced at $2,100, 2½-ton Model K-4 for $3,000, 3½-ton Model R2 for $3,900 and 5-ton Model T for $5,000. Some models were hyphenated, some were not, and some had single letter designations, which continued to stay the same even as capacity ratings changed. Continental engines were offered throughout the line, as were Brown-Lipe transmissions and clutches as well as Timken front and rear axles and Gemmer steering assemblies.

Brockway survived the Depression, and surprisingly, built electric trucks after 1933 from ¼-ton to 7-ton capacity. Most of the electric trucks were delivery vans used in large cities. The long history of Brockway is beyond the scope of this review, but it's important to note that Mack acquired Brockway in 1956, and by 1977, despite local community efforts to save the last major truck manufacturer of New York, the Brockway name was dropped entirely, along with subsequent mergers of Mack with Renault and Volvo.

Buick

David Dunbar Buick arrived in America from Scotland as a boy, and by the early 1890s he had become successful in the plumbing business. His dream, like that of hundreds of other people, was to build a motor vehicle with his own name affixed to it, and after selling his plumbing equipment manufacturing business, Buick embarked on manufacturing engines with the help of Walter L. Marr, a talented mechanical designer, along with a business partner named William Sherwood and another engineer named Eugene Richard who had worked for Ransom Olds.

Generally overlooked by historians until now, their first actual Buick automobile was built by 1901 under the auspices of the Buick Auto-Vim and Power Company of Flint, Michigan, but the overhead-valve engine

BUICK MOTOR
C O M P A N Y

F L I N T
M I C H I G A N

Price, $790

BUICK LIGHT DELIVERY—E-4

COLOR	Body, green; running gear, black	LUBRICATION	Splash with circulating pump
CARRYING CAPACITY .	500 pounds	RADIATOR	Cellular
POSITION OF DRIVER .	Left side	COOLING	Water pump
WHEELBASE	106 inches	IGNITION	High tension generator and storage battery
GAUGE	56 inches		
WHEELS	Wood		
FRONT TIRES	31 x 4 inches, anti-skid	STARTING SYSTEM . .	Single unit
		STARTER OPERATED .	Gear to fly wheel
REAR TIRES	31 x 4 inches, anti-skid	LIGHTING SYSTEM . .	Electric
		VOLTAGES	Six
SERVICE BRAKE . . .	Contracting on rear wheels	WIRING SYSTEM . . .	Single
		GASOLINE SYSTEM . .	Vacuum
EMERGENCY BRAKE .	Expanding on rear wheels	CLUTCH	Cone
		TRANSMISSION . . .	Selective sliding
CYLINDERS	Four	GEAR CHANGES . . .	Three forward, one reverse
ARRANGED.	Vertically		
CAST	En bloc	DRIVE	Plain bevel
HORSEPOWER	18.23	REAR AXLE	Three-quarters floating
(N.A.C.C. Rating)			
BORE AND STROKE .	3⅜ x 4¾ inches	STEERING GEAR . . .	Screw and nut

In addition to above specifications, price includes top, windshield,
speedometer, ammeter, electric horn and demountable rims.

("valve-in-head" as they called it), which was manufactured in two-cylinder form, was also sold to the Reid Manufacturing Company that was building the Wolverine automobile in Detroit.

With the help of another brilliant engineer, Gilbert Albaugh, Buick manufactured a few dozen of his small but powerful motors for Reid, whom he had to sue to receive payment for the series of engines that were purchased and installed in the Wolverine cars. The lawsuit against Reid, only uncovered recently, illustrates the difficulty of finding working capital for early auto makers, and the fact that a lawsuit had to be filed for payment on goods shipped exonerates, at least in part, David Buick as a businessman, who has been up until now called inept at financial dealings in his auto manufacturing venture by various journalists and auto historians.

By 1903 with the help of sheet-metal manufacturer Benjamin Briscoe, who would later have his own car, Buick founded the Buick Motor Company, which was soon bought by Flint businessman James H. Whiting. By mid–1904 sixteen Buick cars had been sold as Buick stayed on to continue improving the engine and other design aspects of the car with his name on it. By November of 1904 Whiting sold out to William Crapo Durant, who was owner of the Durant-Dort Carriage Company in Flint. Durant was beginning to build his auto empire, and Buick was one of the first major acquisitions, which Durant capitalized with $1,500,000 by selling stock within one year mostly to his own neighbors.

In 1905 Walter DeWaters of Cadillac joined Buick, but the man himself had disappeared by 1908 to try his hand at building the Dunbar auto and the Lorraine, both without success. Under Durant, Buick manufacturing took off quickly with production of the Model C up to 750 for 1905 alone, which nearly doubled the following year with the Model G and Model F, and was up to 4,640 by 1907 when a four-cylinder motor was added. Both a two-speed planetary or a three-speed selective sliding gear transmission were offered. A small number of commercial vehicles were built by Buick using four-cylinder motors and special chassis, which newly discovered photos show began as early as 1906. These went on in production until at least 1918, when Chevrolet was appointed as the light commercial vehicle builder for GM, in addition to Oldsmobile's output for a few years in the 1920s, as well as the continual production of GMC trucks.

Early on Durant had formed a racing partnership with Louis Chevrolet, who became one of the most famous men in the world (even before a car was named after him) by

winning dozens of racing events in a Buick. But just before World War I began in Europe, Buick discontinued racing. For 1914 the company introduced an OHV six-cylinder engine and a new model that was noticeably longer and more luxurious than previous Buicks, using a 130-inch wheelbase.

Buick was also a shining example of mass production by 1915 with 43,940 vehicles built, but for 1916 that number jumped up to 124,830. Under Richard H. Collins, Buick was now selling cars by the trainload, literally. Each train of flatcars that was traveling across the country was also announced to the press, making delivery of vehicles a public relations marketing show in itself.

Collins became president of Cadillac in 1917, which had also been absorbed into General Motors earlier before Durant's removal from the very company he had founded. But he returned as Henry Leland and his son departed from Cadillac, at the same time bumping out Charles Nash and Walter Chrysler, both of whom went on to start their own automobile companies.

During the Great War, Buick supplied ambulances, which were first built privately on various commercial and passenger chassis, then by the factory itself. Spotlight trucks were also built by Buick for the war effort, and Buick experimented with a "caterpillar" type tractor which did not go into production. The Buick Six Touring sold well in the civilian market. Buick continued building light trucks, called the E-4 Series, in 1918.

After World War I Buick built a light truck series for 1922 and 1923 called SD4, which was based on the inexpensive four-cylinder Buick passenger car named Series 22-Four and may well have appeared as a reaction to the recession of 1920–21. By 1920 Durant had been removed from GM again, this time permanently. Four-wheel brakes were introduced in 1924. Harry H. Bassett, who had been president of the company since Walter Chrysler's

departure, died suddenly in 1926. For 1929 Buick's new styling was called "pregnant" and as the Great Depression began, many changes took Buick into the new tumultuous decade of the 1930s. David Buick himself was discovered to be working at the information desk at the School of Trades in 1928, still trying to make ends meet at the age of 73, passing away impoverished the following year. But the rich history of the Buick marque has continued successfully to the day of this writing.

Bulley Tractor

M. Bulley was the president of the Mercury Manufacturing Company, which was located in Chicago, Illinois. There were more than half a dozen motor vehicle manufacturing companies by the name of Mercury, although this company was the only one that resided in Chicago.

Beginning in 1910 the company built ½-ton highwheelers which were very similar to International Harvester highwheelers. These were essentially motorized wagons which were forward control with open cabs, engine under seat and chain drive. Motors were two-cylinder two-cycle air-cooled type using a planetary two-speed transmission up to 1912.

At about this time Mercury Manufacturing began building the Bulley Tractor, which was a chain-driven three-wheel vehicle for use off-road in warehouses and in construction work. The tractor could be single wheel in front and two in back or two wheels in front and single wheel in back for various applications. It was powered by a four-cylinder motor with a three-speed transmission and had tire chains for traction when used as a tow vehicle.

Although tractors are not covered in this book, this vehicle was crossover between trucks and tractors and was not used in agricultural work. As an industrial vehicle it serves as an example of the type of tractor built by a

THE BULLEY TRACTOR
Manufactured by
MERCURY MFG. CO., Chicago, Ill.

SPECIFICATIONS

Model	**A**
Capacity	
Drive	Double Chain
Chassis Price	$3,400
Motor	
H. P. (S.A.E.)	28.9
H. P. (Actual)	40 at 800 R. P. M.
Cylinders	4 in pairs
Bore	$4\frac{1}{2}''$
Stroke	5''
Wheel Base	70''
Tread Front	None
Tread Rear	61''
Tires Front	34x4''
Tires Rear	38x4'' dual

Frame—Single piece channel, U shape.

Rear Axle—Fixed, round.

Springs Front—Special design.

Springs Rear—Semi-elliptic.

Carburetor—Stromberg.

Cooling System—Pump.

Oiling System—Forced feed.

Ignition—Bosch magneto.

Control—Right drive, right control.

Clutch—Dry plate.

Transmission—Sliding gear, three speeds forward and one reverse.

Brakes—Service, expanding on rear wheels; emergency, contracting on jack shaft.

Steering Gear—Sector.

Equipment—Tools, lamp, horn, special skid chains.

few companies both as gasoline-powered and electric in the years to come when many other industrial vehicles were developed, such as fork lifts and prime movers, which were in overlapping categories of vehicle type.

Burford

The H.G. Burford Company built trucks both in Fremont, Ohio, and in Kensington, England. H.G. Burford had gotten his start in 1905 with Milnes-Daimler Limited as director and by 1914 had developed a truck using his own name.

The truck was actually a Fremont-Mais originally built in Fremont, Ohio, and at first sold under that name. It was powered by a Buda four-cylinder engine and used a three-speed transmission with internal gear drive. The name was changed to Burford within the first year of importing and was sold in both countries. The illustration here is from 1917.

In 1918 the Taylor Truck Company bought the H.G. Burford Company and the Burford name continued only in England until the war ended. In the U.S. the Burford, which was now called Taylor, continued to be built with four-cylinder Continental engines and internal gear drive. The 1-ton chassis was also used to build passenger cars in England.

By 1921 four-wheel brakes were introduced for the passenger cars, and this was one of the earliest such innovations in the industry. Forward control was introduced in 1923, and the following year a ¾-ton van was offered. It was powered by a two-cylinder horizontally-opposed engine, built by Anzani in England, which did not gain any acceptance in the United States.

Burford attempted to get into the half-track market with a collaboration with Kegresse after Cletrac crawlers were imported into England. A few Burford/Kegresse half-tracks were sold to the War Office before Burford was liquidated in 1926.

Cadillac

Cadillac was founded in 1903 at Detroit by Henry Leland and his son, Wilfred, who named their company after French explorer Antoine de la Mothe Cadillac, discoverer of the Detroit area. The company began building passenger cars after Henry Leland had already gained considerable experience in producing precision gears and steam engines, then gasoline engines for Ransom Olds, albeit the contract's not being fulfilled due to cost and time overruns as a result of the factory fire at Olds in 1901.

Getting William Murphy and Lemuel Bowen in as investors, who were disillusioned with Henry Ford's racing car tinkering at that time, Cadillac quickly built a reliable, handsome little car by the end of 1902 under the engineering wing of Alanson P. Brush, who was to build his own car five years later.

Shown in January of 1903 at the New York Auto Show, the first Cadillac had a 10 hp single-cylinder motor (9 hp in 1905 by N.A.C.C. and S.A.E. standards, which finally became consistently measured also by A.L.A.M. in 1908) and two-speed planetary transmission with center chain drive. Salesman *extraordinaire* William Metzger, formerly of Olds Motor Works, who would also build his own car, received orders for 2,286 autos at the January show and announced the company was "sold out" for 1903 orders.

What Cadillac called the Model A in 1904 was improved in a number of details, but it was essentially the same car with a Touring model added to the Runabout. By 1905 the popularity of the luxurious-looking Cadillac had evolved into Model B, C and D. A four-cylinder motor was introduced, as were Model E and F, preceding alphabetical order models which continued until 1909. What set apart Cadillac from most other motorcars of the time was styling, which was exemplary from the beginning, and also at a price. The Model

BURFORD TRUCKS
Manufactured by
THE H. G. BURFORD CO., Fremont, Ohio

S P E C I F I C A T I O N S

Model	O-3	D-3
Capacity	2 tons	4 tons
Drive	Internal gear	Worm
Chassis Price	$2,250	$3,600
Motor		
H. P. (S.A.E.)	24½	34
H. P. (Actual)	35	45
Cylinders	4 en bloc	4 en bloc
Bore	3¾″	4½″
Stroke	5½″	6½″
Wheel Base	144″ Std.—132″ short	175″ Std.—144″ short
Tread Front	58″	58″
Tread Rear	62″	66″
Tires Front	36x3½″	38x5″
Tires Rear	36x3½″ dual	38x5″ dual
Frame—Pressed steel.		
Front Axle	I-section	Semi-floating
Rear Axle—Burford, I-section.		
Springs Front—Semi-elliptic.		
Springs Rear—Semi-elliptic.		
Carburetor	Zenith 1¼″, Model L-5	Zenith 1¼″, Model L-6
Cooling System—Pump.		
Oiling System—Splash.		
Ignition—Magneto.		
Control	Right drive, center control	Right drive, right control
Clutch—Cone		
Transmission	Selective, three speeds forward, one reverse	Selective, four speeds forward, one reverse
Brakes	Ext. service, contracting on rear wheels; Emergency, contracting on drive pinion shaft at axle end	Equalizing on rear wheels

Steering Gear—Nut and screw.

Equipment—Two 4-C. P. electric side lamps, one 4-C. P. electric tail lamp, one 6-80 Willard storage battery, jack and tool kit.

**CADILLAC
MOTOR CAR
COMPANY**

**DETROIT
MICHIGAN**

Price	**$4295**
Limousine	4145
Imperial	4345
Town Limousine	4160
Town Landaulet	4310

CADILLAC LANDAULET—TYPE 57

COLOR	Calumet green with black trimmings	LUBRICATION	Force feed
		RADIATOR	Tubular
SEATING CAPACITY .	Seven	COOLING	Water pump
POSITION OF DRIVER .	Left side	IGNITION	High tension generator and storage battery
WHEELBASE	132 inches		
GAUGE	56 inches		
WHEELS	Wood	STARTING SYSTEM . .	Single unit
FRONT TIRES	35 x 5 inches	STARTER OPERATED .	Gear to fly wheel
REAR TIRES	35 x 5 inches, anti-skid	LIGHTING SYSTEM . .	Electric
		VOLTAGES	Six
SERVICE BRAKE . . .	Contracting on rear wheels	WIRING SYSTEM . . .	Single
		GASOLINE SYSTEM . .	Pressure
EMERGENCY BRAKE .	Expanding on rear wheels	CLUTCH	Dry multiple disc
		TRANSMISSION . . .	Selective sliding
CYLINDERS	Eight	GEAR CHANGES . . .	Three forward, one reverse
ARRANGED	V type, 90 degrees		
CAST	In fours	DRIVE	Spiral bevel
HORSEPOWER	31.25 (N.A.C.C. Rating)	REAR AXLE	Full floating
BORE AND STROKE .	3⅛ x 5⅛ inches	STEERING GEAR . . .	Worm and sector

In addition to above specifications, price includes windshield, speedometer, ammeter, clock, tire pump, electric horn and demountable rims.

L two-door limousine of 1905 had a $5,000 price tag, for example. In comparison, the most expensive four-passenger touring car built by Ford for that year was priced at $2,000 (before the advent of the Model T).

A C-cab Delivery Van based on the Model B was introduced already in 1904. The following year the van was mounted on a Model F chassis, and from 1906 to 1908 it was based on the Model M. The small vans had 45 cubic feet of cargo area and could carry no more than half a ton. Commercial vehicles were not built after 1909, but during World War I, Cadillac manufactured spotlight trucks, officers' cars in the form of touring and limousines, 2½-ton artillery tractor V-8 motors, as well as tools, gauges, instruments and other materiel for the war effort. Late in 1911 Cadillac introduced the first electric self-starter, points-type ignition and battery-generator lighting system for model year 1912.

Cadillac became one of the first auto makers to offer a series-built V-8 motor, which appeared for 1915 in its Type 51 Model. This was ninety-degree 312 cid L-head engine rated at 70 hp, which was increased to 77 hp in 1916 for the Type 53 Model, the latter of which was showed off with a Los Angeles-to-New York, 7-day, 11-hour stunt drive by Erwin "Cannonball" Baker and William Sturm. For the year 1917 Cadillac's series was now called Type 55, and many if not most of the military cars for the AEF and Army which were shipped overseas were the Type 57 of 1918. These were built for the civilian market in at least ten body styles.

As early as 1916 the Cadillac factory listed a number of body styles: Touring, Salon, Roadster, Victoria, Coupe, Brougham, Limousine, and Berline, as well as Ambulance, Police Patrol and Hearse. The latter three were no longer listed by 1920, but Cadillac "professional" cars were built on extended factory chassis afterwards. Such problems as the recession, railway strikes and the building of a new factory resulted in a noticeable decrease in production for Cadillac in 1920 and 1922. Cadillac continued to improve its styling and technical prowess as the top-of-the-line General Motors marque, and its colorful and successful history has continued up to this writing.

Case

More than a century and a half after its beginnings, the J.I. Case Company of Racine, Wisconsin, may well be better known for producing threshers, steam traction engines and gasoline tractors, the latter of which appeared as early as 1895. But the inspiration of a local doctor named J.M. Carhart, and an already established ownership in the factory that built Pierce-Racine autos, propelled the J.I. Case Company to build its own motorcar by 1911.

The new auto was offered with a 30 hp four-cylinder motor in "Fore-Door Touring, Torpedo, Limousine, Roadster and Suburban" body styles, which became the Model L along with the longer, more powerful Model M for 1912.

From the beginning Case promoted its cars through racing, which was managed by sports impresario J. Alex Sloan, and even in the first year of manufacture, Case entered a number of races, albeit at the cost of one driver's death: Lewis Strang. Nevertheless, after the firm's half a century of producing farm equipment, the rural customer was well familiar with the Case name, and sales reflected the brand recognition as far away as Russia, where at least 100 Case cars were shipped.

A Continental four-cylinder engine rated at 50 hp was offered for 1918 when the automobile wing of the company was organized as the Case Motor Car Division. By 1920 only six-cylinder motors were offered and the cars were called Jay-Eye-See, which was the phonetic pronunciation of the parent company's initials. Much as customers wished Case autos

J. I. CASE T. M.
C O M P A N Y

R A C I N E
W I S C O N S I N

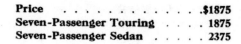

Price	. . . .	.$1875
Seven-Passenger Touring	. . . .	1875
Seven-Passenger Sedan	. . . . .	2375

CASE SPORT—U

COLOR	. . . .	Periscope green	LUBRICATION	Forcefeed and splash
SEATING CAPACITY	. .	Four	RADIATOR	Tubular
POSITION OF DRIVER	.	Left side	COOLING	Water pump
WHEELBASE	125 inches	IGNITION	High tension distributor and storage battery
GAUGE	56 inches		
WHEELS	Wood		
FRONT TIRES . . .	35 x 4½ inches	STARTING SYSTEM . .	Single unit
REAR TIRES	35 x 4½ inches, anti-skid	STARTER OPERATED .	Gear to fly wheel
		LIGHTING SYSTEM . .	Electric
SERVICE BRAKE . . .	Contracting on rear wheels	VOLTAGES	Six
		WIRING SYSTEM . . .	Single
EMERGENCY BRAKE .	Expanding on rear wheels	GASOLINE SYSTEM . .	Vacuum
		CLUTCH	Dry plate
CYLINDERS	Six	TRANSMISSION . . .	Selective sliding
ARRANGED	Vertically	GEAR CHANGES . . .	Three forward, one reverse
CAST.	En bloc		
HORSEPOWER	29.4	DRIVE	Spiral bevel
(N.A.C.C. Rating)		REAR AXLE.	Three-quarters floating
BORE AND STROKE .	3½ x 5¼ inches	STEERING GEAR . . .	Screw and split nut

In addition to above specifications, price includes top, top hood, windshield, speedometer, ammeter, tire pump, electric horn and demountable rims.

could live up to the company's tractor reputation of durability, such was not the case, and the division was closed by the end of 1927, with Case surviving to build other products.

Chalmers

Starting out as the Thomas-Detroit, to sponsor their automobile in 1908, Howard Coffin and Roy Chapin got a new investor by the name of Hugh Chalmers, who was vice president of the National Cash Register Company. He resigned his well-paying position with the ambition, like so many others at the time, to go into automobile manufacturing, especially if they had his name on it. That came into reality in August/September of 1908 when the Chalmers-Detroit Motor Car Company produced its first vehicle for model year 1909. It was powered by a 24 hp four-cylinder motor as the Model F at around $1500, or the 40 hp Model E which sold around $2800.

Chapin and Coffin were more interested in building lower-priced cars for a larger customer base, and Coffin designed a smaller car that would sell for under $1000 with a 20 hp four-cylinder motor, perhaps keeping an eye on the new Ford Model T that had just been introduced and was selling very well for $825. But Chalmers wasn't interested in the mass market on that level, so Chapin and Coffin sold their interest in the Chalmers-Detroit to Chalmers himself while also getting department store magnate J.L. Hudson to foot the bill for a new car. The Hudson automobile went on to distinguish itself until World War II, while Hugh Chalmers was perfectly pleased to start out with his own car, which had already won five first places in auto racing before the end of 1909.

In the following year the company was reorganized as the Chalmers Motor Car Company, adding people like the Rockefellers and Vanderbilts to their list of customers. The car

was simply called Chalmers from then on, and also in 1910 a Chalmers won the Glidden Trophy. Within two years a six-cylinder engine was offered, and once World War I began in Europe the company only produced cars with these larger engines in six different models from 30 hp on a 115-inch wheelbase to 54 hp on a 130-inch wheelbase, including body styles such as Touring, Duplex, Limousine, Victoria Cabriolet and Planquin Sedan (Touring Sedan).

Model types were reduced in number down to just one as World War I ended and the postwar recession set in, so that the volume of 20,000 vehicles that were being sold annually by Chalmers was now reduced by about half. The nearby Maxwell company bought out Chalmers in 1922 as creditor lawsuits were looming, and the whole enterprise was obtained for just under $2,000,000. Walter Chrysler would soon purchase the new Maxwell-Chalmers, but cars by the name of Chalmers were only marketed until 1923, when the new owner would name a car after himself that would last up to this writing.

Chandler

Former organizers of the Lozier Motor Company founded the Emise Motor Car Company, named after Lozier's successful sales manager, but by the end of 1913 the company name was changed to Chandler. A factory in Cleveland, Ohio, was soon churning out six-cylinder cars under that name, after another investor who was known as F.C. Chandler. The combination of capital and expertise quickly resulted in a well-regarded automobile that sold very well almost from the outset.

By 1915 the Chandler 120-inch wheelbase chassis with 27 hp six-cylinder motor could be purchased as a Touring, Sedan, Runabout, Coupe or Limousine. The following year the wheelbase was extended two inches and the

CHALMERS
MOTOR
COMPANY
────────────
DETROIT
MICHIGAN

Price	$1485
Four-Passenger Duplex	1485
Three-Passenger Cabriolet . . .	1775
Three-Passenger Roadster . . .	1485
Seven-Passenger Touring	1535
Seven-Passenger Touring Sedan	1950
Seven-Passenger Limousine . . .	3025

CHALMERS TOURING

COLOR	Optional		LUBRICATION	Force feed and splash
SEATING CAPACITY. .	Five		RADIATOR	Cellular
POSITION OF DRIVER	Left side		COOLING	Water pump
WHEELBASE	117 inches		IGNITION	High tension magneto and distributor
GAUGE	56 inches			
WHEELS	Wood		STARTING SYSTEM . .	Two unit
FRONT TIRES	32 x 4 inches		STARTER OPERATED .	Gear to fly wheel
REAR TIRES	32 x 4 inches, anti-skid		LIGHTING SYSTEM . .	Electric
SERVICE BRAKE . . .	Contracting on rear wheels		VOLTAGES	Six
			WIRING SYSTEM . . .	Single
EMERGENCY BRAKE .	Expanding on rear wheels		GASOLINE SYSTEM . .	Vacuum
			CLUTCH	Dry multiple disc
CYLINDERS	Six		TRANSMISSION . . .	Selective sliding
ARRANGED	Vertically		GEAR CHANGES . . .	Three forward, one reverse
CAST	En bloc			
HORSEPOWER	25.35		DRIVE	Spiral bevel
(N.A.C.C. Rating)			REAR AXLE	Full floating
BORE AND STROKE .	3¼ x 4½ inches		STEERING GEAR . . .	Worm and gear

In addition to above specifications, price includes top, top hood, windshield, speedometer, ammeter, electric horn and demountable rims.

**CHANDLER
MOTOR CAR
COMPANY**

CLEVELAND, OHIO

Price	.$1595
Roadster . . .	1595
Sport	1675
Coupe	2195
Sedan	2295
Limousine . . .	2895

CHANDLER TOURING

COLOR	Chandler blue and black	LUBRICATION	Pump over and splash
SEATING CAPACITY . .	Seven	RADIATOR	Cellular
POSITION OF DRIVER .	Optional	COOLING	Water pump
WHEELBASE	123 inches	IGNITION	High tension magneto
GAUGE	56 inches	STARTING SYSTEM . .	Two unit
WHEELS	Wood	STARTER OPERATED .	Gear to fly wheel
FRONT TIRES	34 x 4 inches	LIGHTING SYSTEM . .	Electric
REAR TIRES	34 x 4 inches, anti-skid	VOLTAGES	Six to eight
SERVICE BRAKE . . .	Contracting on rear wheels	WIRING SYSTEM . . .	Single
		GASOLINE SYSTEM . .	Vacuum
EMERGENCY BRAKE .	Expanding on rear wheels	CLUTCH	Dry plate
CYLINDERS	Six	TRANSMISSION . . .	Selective sliding
ARRANGED	Vertically	GEAR CHANGES . . .	Three forward, one reverse
CAST	In threes	DRIVE	Spiral bevel
HORSEPOWER . . . . 29.4 (N.A.C.C. Rating)		REAR AXLE	Three-quarters floating
BORE AND STROKE .	3½ x 5 inches	STEERING GEAR . . .	Worm and gear

In addition to above specifications, price includes top, top hood, windshield, speedometer, electric horn and demountable rims.

next year another inch was added as prices also grew from $1295 in 1916 to $1795 for the Touring, while the Chandler Limousine had attained a price tag of $2895 by war's end.

Chandler cars were also proven to be reliable with a few publicity stunts, such as the 2000-mile run from Tijuana, Mexico, to Vancouver, Canada, without repair work. In 1919 a subsidiary called Cleveland Automobile Company was organized to produce a cheaper car, logically called the Cleveland. However, the six-cylinder was proven in wins at Pikes Peak to the extent that the company began using the slogan "The Pike's Peak Engine" in its advertising. The marketing seemed to work as sales went up, and while other auto companies struggled during the early 1920s in what was called the postwar recession, Chandler's sales increased from 5000 in 1921 to 10,000 in 1922.

Improvements such as the constant-mesh transmission and central chassis lubrication appealed to customers. At the end of 1926 the Cleveland Automobile Company was absorbed and vanished, while the parent company became Chandler-Cleveland. For 1927 a straight-eight motor was offered, but somehow business slipped away, and Hupp Motor Car Corporation bought out Chandler-Cleveland, which was almost immediately discontinued as a marque.

Chase

Of the numerous motor vehicle builders from the beginning of the last century, the Chase Motor Truck Company of Syracuse, New York, lasted only a decade. Prior to starting his own company, Aurin Chase had been the vice president of the Syracuse Chilled Plow Company.

Chase and his crew built a highwheeler that resembled the contemporary International Harvester as well as the previously mentioned early Brockway. This was essentially a horse-drawn wagon with a motor in front which could be easily transformed from a light, open passenger jitney to a light truck with a 100-inch wheelbase. All the operator needed to do was to remove the benches of the five-passenger surrey and quickly turn it into a 700-pound capacity express. The first engines that were offered were all two-, three- or four-cylinder in-line two-stroke type. The most common engine at first was the 20 hp 160 cid three-cylinder with Bosch ignition.

Suspension was full-elliptic leaf springs in the front, with semi-elliptic transverse auxiliary spring at the rear. Wagon-type wood spoke wheels carried hard rubber tires. The 1912 1-ton Model H, which had a 106-inch wheelbase, was priced at $1,250. Top speed was 12 mph. This was the last year of the passenger-type vehicle. It probably occurred to most farmers that their passengers could sit on the floor and they could save some money that way by forgetting about the hard bench seats. Or they built their own. However, the passenger version would most often be fitted with a two-speed planetary transmission, although some of the lighter trucks also used this simpler gear box.

The heaviest Chase truck was a 3-ton model and used the 30 hp four-cylinder two-cycle engine, which was air-cooled just as the other versions, and this model also had a three-speed transmission. It sold for $3,500 in 1912. Unusual as it may seem, the three-cylinder two-cycle air-cooled motor design was commonly used as late as in the 1960s to power Saab and Trabant passenger cars and in the 1970s to propel Kawasaki motorcycles, among many other vehicles outside the United States.

Chase trucks were sold in Great Britain during World War I by Henry Spurrier of Leyland. By 1914 Chase had adopted conventional four-cycle motors from Continental with four-speed transmission and shaft worm drive. Models ranged from 1- to 3-ton

CHASE TRUCKS
Manufactured by
CHASE MOTOR TRUCK CO., Syracuse, N. Y.

S P E C I F I C A T I O N S

Model	O	B	A
Capacity	3¼ tons	2¼ tons	1 ton
Drive	Worm	Worm	Worm
Chassis Price	$3,300	$2,475	$1,725
Motor			
H. P. (S.A.E.)	28.9	27.2	19.6
H. P. (Actual)	45	36	23
Cylinders	4 en bloc	4 en bloc	4 en bloc
Bore	4¼″	4½″	3¾″
Stroke	6″	5½″	5¼″
Wheel Base	148-175″	146-160″	138″
Tread Front	62″	58″	56″
Tread Rear	66″	62″	56″
Tires Front	36x5″	36x4″	36x3½″
Tires Rear	36x5″ dual	36x4″ dual	36x5″

Frame—Pressed.

Front Axle—I-beam.

Rear Axle—Semi-floating.

Springs Front—Semi-elliptic.

Springs Rear—Semi-elliptic.

Carburetor—Standard.

Cooling System—Centrifugal pump.

Oiling System	Forced feed	Circulating splash	Circulating splash

Ignition—Magneto.

Control—Right drive, center control.

Clutch—Dry plate.

Transmission	Selective, 4 speeds forward, 1 reverse	Selective, 3 speeds forward, 1 reverse	Selective, 3 speeds forward, 1 reverse
Brakes	Internal on rear wheels	Internal and external rear wheels	Internal on rear wheels

Steering Gear—Screw and nut.

Equipment—Lamps, regular tool equipment, horn, cab, storm curtains, etc.

capacity, and by 1917 the line was expanded to include a ¾-ton and a 3½-ton truck.

Chase was listed for 1918 with four models which were named, somewhat incongruously, the 1-ton Model A, 1½-ton Model C, 2½-ton Model B and 3½-ton Model O. The lighter two used Waukesha engines and the heavier two had Buda engines. There was a mix of Brown-Lipe and Cotta transmissions and prices varied from $1,725 up to $3,600. The heaviest Model O had a 175-inch wheelbase. The year 1918 was the last year of manufacturing for this company.

Chevrolet

Out of all the automobile companies that got their start before the United States entered World War I, Chevrolet had one of the most unusual beginnings. It was William Crapo Durant's creation after he had control of General Motors taken away from him in 1910 by investment bankers. He had spent wildly on new acquisitions after founding GM and was still connected to GM through his own investments when he hired Louis Chevrolet, the famous French-born racing car driver who had taken Buick to many victories, to build a new car. Durant poured his own money into a project that was to be Louis Chevrolet's design of a "light French type auto" for the American public which would compete with other mass-produced cars of the day such as Dodge and Ford. In turn Chevrolet hired Etienne Planche, who was an experienced French engineer.

When the finished prototype finally arrived in mid–1912 it turned out to be anything but a "light French type." It was solidly designed and built, but it had a 299 cid motor and a wheelbase of 120 inches. Durant was not on great terms with Louis Chevrolet by this time, detesting his cigarette habit among other things, and soon the two men parted ways, with Durant not only having ownership of

the prototype but also of the Chevrolet name itself. The automobile went on without the name to whom it belonged, and what would be a coup of sorts was an illustration of how Durant had manipulated those around him in the auto industry.

While no longer in a decision-making position at General Motors, Billy Durant had helped start a few other independent automotive ventures, including the Little Motor Car Company and the Mason Motor Company in addition to the Chevrolet venture. The Chevrolet now became the car with which Durant wanted to give Ford a run for his money. But the car that was to be marketed was not what Durant had envisioned. Nevertheless, nearly 3,000 of the first design Model C Chevrolet were built in five-passenger, four-door touring form.

Having simultaneously started the Little Motor Car Company turned out to be fortuitous in a completely unexpected way. Durant's rejection of the initial Chevrolet was quickly rectified by using the Little car's best features combined with the Chevrolet's most salient ones, and the resulting auto was the new Chevrolet of 1913. The whole Detroit operation of Little Motors was moved to Flint, and the famous "bow-tie" emblem was adopted. The same motor was continued, which was a T-head, twin-cam six-cylinder cast iron in banks of three pairs which produced 40 hp, or 30 net according to N.A.C.C. Nearly 6000 of these Chevys were sold that year.

For 1914 Chevrolet introduced an OHV four-cylinder engine in addition to the six-cylinder motor. The smaller series H had a shorter wheelbase of 104 inches. Instead of the previous air-starter, a Gray & Davis electric starter was introduced. Durant opened a sales office on the West Coast in Oakland, California, and the Chevrolet launched into grand success.

For 1915 the Model 490 was introduced,

**CHEVROLET
MOTOR
COMPANY**

**BROADWAY
AT 57th STREET
NEW YORK CITY**

Price **$1385**
Four-Passenger Roadster 1385

CHEVROLET TOURING—D-5

COLOR	Green		LUBRICATION	Splash with circulating pump
SEATING CAPACITY. .	Five		RADIATOR	Cellular
POSITION OF DRIVER .	Left side		COOLING	Water pump
WHEELBASE	120 inches		IGNITION	Storage battery
GAUGE	56 inches		STARTING SYSTEM . .	Two unit
WHEELS	Wood		STARTER OPERATED .	Gear to fly wheel
FRONT TIRES	34 x 4 inches		LIGHTING SYSTEM . .	Electric
REAR TIRES	34 x 4 inches		VOLTAGES	Six
SERVICE BRAKE . . .	Contracting on rear wheels		WIRING SYSTEM . . .	Double
			GASOLINE SYSTEM . .	Vacuum
EMERGENCY BRAKE .	Expanding on rear wheels		CLUTCH	Cone
			TRANSMISSION . . .	Selective sliding
CYLINDERS	Eight		GEAR CHANGES . . .	Three forward, one reverse
ARRANGED.	V type, 90 degrees			
CAST	In fours		DRIVE	Spiral bevel
HORSEPOWER . . . . 36.45 (N.A.C.C. Rating)			REAR AXLE	Three-quarters floating
BORE AND STROKE .	3⅜ x 4 inches		STEERING GEAR . . .	Worm and gear

In addition to above specifications, price includes top, top hood, windshield, speedometer, ammeter, tire pump, electric horn and demountable rims.

named for its price of $490 in order to compete with the Ford Model T. Meanwhile, Durant had used Chevrolet to buy GM stock secretly, and before anyone knew it at the end of 1915, Chevrolet had controlling interest in General Motors. The press called it "Jonah swallowing the whale."

In 1917 a V-8 was introduced, but it was incongruous with Chevrolet's marketing strategy and lasted only through 1918 before being discontinued. Chevrolet Model T trucks, perhaps named as such to goad Ford, appeared in 1918 but too late to be useful in World War I.

In 1920 the postwar recession affected General Motors, as it did nearly all businesses in America, and Billy Durant was removed by the GM board of directors and investment bankers once again. He would go on to found a company under his own name. Pierre Du Pont, who had invested heavily in GM and Chevrolet, at first wanted to discontinue the latter make altogether. He hired Alfred Sloan, Jr., to sort out the complex network of semi-independent companies which GM comprised. Sloan brought in K.W. Zimmerschied as Chevrolet's president and general manager.

Chevrolet was placed one tier up from the Ford Model T in the marketplace regarding price and corresponding accouterments. One blunder that Sloan and du Pont made was trying to develop a copper-cooled engine for Chevrolet, which Charles Kettering insisted he could make functional, but after a pilot run of a little more than 750 copper-cooled Chevrolets, all of them ended up being scrapped or recalled. Chevrolet would go on under Alfred Sloan to become one of the most successful auto manufacturers in the world and is still producing motor vehicles as of this writing.

Cleveland (motorcycle)

The American Cycle Manufacturing Company was the enterprise that first built Cleveland Motorcycles in Hartford, Connecticut. The company began in 1902, the same year Indian motorcycles began sharing the same design configuration, along with some the other of the first bicycle-turned-motorcycle two-wheel vehicles during the birth of the industry.

More true to its origins, the second series of Cleveland motorcycles was built by the Cleveland Motorcycle Manufacturing Company in Cleveland, Ohio. This second company building bikes by the same name began in 1915. The engine was a two-stroke 220 cc displacement and was mounted transversely on the frame. The right-angle drive was accomplished through worm gear, and a two-speed transmission also drove the magneto in-line independently of the sprocket for the chain to the rear wheel.

Although Cleveland motorcycles were not used in World War I, sales to private citizens were increased by the lack of availability of other motorcycles sold to the military. In 1920 Cleveland sported a larger oil and gasoline tank, wider fenders and footboards. The single-cylinder model grew in displacement to 270 cc of the two-stroke motor as the motorcycle got heavier with the addition of a battery and larger tank.

In 1923 the sport Model E had electric lights using a battery. It wasn't unusual for endurance runs of 100 miles and 200 miles to be won on a Cleveland. The Cleveland Light was a single-cylinder 220 cc motorcycle that sold for $150 and weighed 150 pounds. This competed with the two-stroke Indian Model K at the same price, which was taller and heavier and therefore less popular with women. However, by 1925 the two-stroke was discontinued by Cleveland and the 350 cc four-stroke Model F-25 took its place.

The F-25 was heavier and slower, and so Cleveland got ambitious by hiring engineer L.E. Fowler to design a four-stroke four-cylinder bike. This was a complete departure

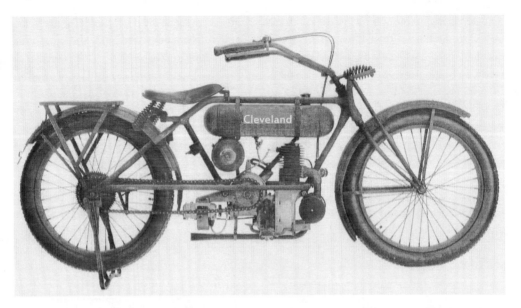

from the previous Cleveland offerings. The in-line four hung longitudinally in the perimeter cradle-type frame. The sprung front fork used a leading link design. The engine was patterned on a Pierce four-cylinder of the period, though it was not a direct copy. However, the side-valve four was replaced by a more powerful F-head four designed by Henderson engineer Everett DeLong.

The 750 cc motor produced 18 hp and made the 1926 Cleveland Four capable of 75 mph. For 1927 the engine was enlarged to 1000 cc with the price at $400. Then in 1929 the Cleveland Tornado appeared, capable of 100 mph, but the ensuing stock market crash put an end to the plans to build a yet more powerful Century model for 1930, and Cleveland simply went out of business.

Clydesdale

Because Clydesdale began manufacturing during World War I, one of the first and most notable advertising slogans the company used was "Tested in the Crucible of War — and Found Fit." The company was named in honor of the city where it was located: Clyde, Ohio, and it was originally known as Clyde

Cars Company when it changed names to Clyde Motor Truck Company in 1916.

It was no coincidence that the company named its trucks "Clydesdale," which also referred to the strong draft horses for hauling heavy loads, bred and developed in the 1700s around the Clyde River in Scotland. To help fulfill that image and duty, Clydesdale trucks of the heavier capacities up to 6-ton used deep, tapered, pressed-frame side-rails for added strength, as well as chrome vanadium springs pivoting on bronze bushings for the suspension.

For the years during World War I, Clydesdale trucks featured a Krebs Patented Automatic Controller, which was an engine governor to keep speed and rpm down in order to prevent burning out the bearings and valves. Using governors was a very common practice, and they would be used throughout trucking history so that durability was ensured. Top speeds for commercial vehicles was kept down to 15 to 20 mph during this era. The Krebs governor was manufactured by another truck builder, the Krebs Commercial Car Company that was located in Clyde, Ohio.

Clydesdale trucks had radiators that intentionally resembled those of the London Omnibus. Styling was not always a strong suit for

CLYDESDALE TRUCKS

Manufactured by

THE CLYDE CARS CO., Clyde, Ohio

Model	30	45	65	90
Capacity	1¼ tons	1½ tons	2 tons	3½ tons
Drive	Worm	Worm	Worm	Worm
Chassis Weight	2,900 lbs.	4,300 lbs.	4,900 lbs.	6,500 lbs.
Chassis Price	On application	On application	On application	On application
Engine	Continental	Continental	Continental	Continental
H. P. (S.A.E.)	19.6	27.2	27.2	32.4
H. P. (Actual)	Not governed	33	33	40
Cylinders	4 en bloc	4 en bloc	4 en bloc	4 in pairs
Bore	3½"	4⅛"	4½"	4½"
Stroke	5"	5¼"	5¼"	5½"
Wheel Base	134"	146"	163"—180"	180"—170"
Tread Front	56"	58"	58"	66½"
Tread Rear	56"	58½"	58½"	66¾"
Tires Front	34x3½" Solid	36x3½"	36x4"	36x5"
Tires Rear	34x4" Solid	36x5"	36x6" or 4" dual	36x5" dual
Frame—Pressed.				
Front Axle—Elliott I-beam.				
Rear Axle	Wisconsin semi-floating	Timken full-floating	Timken full-floating	Timken full-floating
Springs Front—Semi-elliptic.				
Springs Rear—Semi-elliptic.				
Carburetor	Zenith O-4	Zenith O-5	Zenith O-5	Zenith L-6
Cooling System	Thermo-syphon	Pump	Pump	Pump
Oiling System—Splash circulating.				
Ignition—Magneto.				
Control	Right drive, center control	Right drive, center control	Right drive, right control	Right drive, right control
Clutch	Cone	Dry plate	Dry plate	Dry plate
Transmission	Detroit Selective, 3 speeds	Brown-Lipe Selective, 4 speeds	Brown-Lipe Selective, 4 speeds	Brown-Lipe Selective, 4 speeds
Brakes	Internal and external rear wheel	Duplex expanding rear wheels	Duplex expanding rear wheels	Duplex expanding rear wheels
Steering Gear—Ross screw and nut.				
Equipment—Side and tail oil lamps, horn and seat.				

truck manufacturers, but Clydesdale made an attempt at distinguishing their truck model line from others, and after the war the company adopted pyramid-shaped headlights with an octagonal mount on the radiator.

As attractive as the company tried to make its trucks look, Clydesdales were another standard, assembled set of trucks using Continental engines with Detroit or Brown-Lipe clutches and transmissions and Timken axles during the war and into the 1920s. After 1925, following industry standards, Clydesdale introduced more powerful six-cylinder engines.

After the stock market crash of 1929 the next half-decade was brutal for Clydesdale, with only a few trucks going for export and the company hanging on with repair work and spare parts manufacturing. In 1936 the company tried to revive itself, offering Buda motors and early Hercules diesel engines as well as Waukesha-Hesselman diesel engines. The U.S. Army bought a few of the 6 × 6 trucks with up to 15-ton capacity, and numerous models were available, including truck tractors, COE and conventional models using Fuller and Clark transmissions as well as Timken and Wisconsin axles. But the company expansion was not successful and 1938 was the last year of the Clydesdale truck.

Cole

Joseph J. Cole was the man behind the car named after himself in Indianapolis, Indiana, and which first appeared in 1909. Having been in the business of agriculture, by the time Cole was 40 years old he yearned, as did many others, to get into buggy and subsequently into horseless buggy manufacturing. He bought out the Gates-Osborne Carriage Company in Indianapolis, and built his first self-propelled vehicle in 1908, a highwheeler with solid rubber tires. A modicum of success followed in that once he had installed brakes into the car he was able to sell 170 of them.

In 1909 he reorganized as the Cole Motor Car Company and began building runabouts called Model 30, which were powered by a 2-cylinder 14 hp motor; 100 were sold that year. In 1910 he found the right formula for building a roadster when his new four-cylinder car, now slightly renamed as the Series 30 Cole Flyer, received the Massapequa Trophy at the Vanderbilt Cup Race. Various races, including Brighton Beach with driver Wild Bill Endicott at the wheel, brought considerable fame to Cole at that time.

By 1913 Cole was installing a six-cylinder engine and adding electric lighting and starting, the latter of which had just been developed for the first time at Cadillac the previous year. As World War I began Cole adopted a V-8 engine in 1915, again following Cadillac's lead, where the V-8 had just appeared. This was more than a coincidence, due to the fact that the Cole V-8 was the same Northway engine that Cadillac was using. The four- and six-cylinder motors were discontinued altogether at Cole by 1916.

Cole avoided using or even acknowledging the term "assembled car" for his autos, even if it were true. He employed the term "standardized car" in order to deflect the notion that most of his components were bought from original equipment manufacturers (OEM companies) and not produced at his own factory. Aside from the overly regarded prestige of building all components under one name, there were advantages of buying parts from well-established manufacturers which produced the major subassemblies such as motors, transmissions, axles, steering gear, electrical system, carburetors, et cetera.

Apparently, the strategy worked well enough to the point that Billy Durant made Cole an offer to become a subsidiary of General Motors instead of competing with Cadillac. Cole declined the offer.

In 1918, before the war ended, Cole introduced the Aero-Eight, which was considered

**COLE MOTOR
CAR COMPANY**

**INDIANAPOLIS
INDIANA**

Price **$2395**
Touring **2395**
Roadster **2395**

COLE EIGHT SPORTSTER—872

COLOR	Dust-proof gray	LUBRICATION	Force feed
SEATING CAPACITY. .	Four	RADIATOR	Cellular
POSITION OF DRIVER	Left side	COOLING	Water pump
WHEELBASE	127 inches	IGNITION	Storage battery
GAUGE	56 inches	STARTING SYSTEM . .	Two unit
WHEELS	Wood	STARTER OPERATED .	Gear to fly wheel
FRONT TIRES	33 x 5 inches	LIGHTING SYSTEM . .	Electric
REAR TIRES	33 x 5 inches	VOLTAGES	Six
SERVICE BRAKE . . .	Contracting on rear wheels	WIRING SYSTEM . .	Single
EMERGENCY BRAKE .	Expanding on rear wheels	GASOLINE SYSTEM . .	Vacuum
		CLUTCH	Cone
CYLINDERS	Eight	TRANSMISSION . . .	Selective sliding
ARRANGED	V type, 90 degrees	GEAR CHANGES . . .	Three forward, one reverse
CAST	In fours		
HORSEPOWER	39.2	DRIVE	Spiral bevel
(N.A.C.C. Rating)		REAR AXLE	Full floating
BORE AND STROKE .	3½ x 4½ inches	STEERING GEAR . .	Worm and gear

In addition to above specifications, price includes top, top hood, windshield, speedometer, ammeter, voltmeter, clock, tire pump, electric horn and demountable rims.

the height of styling and performance. The Series 870 series Runabout, Roadster and Sportster were each powered by the Northway V-8 and rode on a 127-inch wheelbase. After the war Cole introduced a Tourster, Toursedan, Tourcoupe and a Towncar, using the amalgamated names for effect. Cole was one of the first auto builders to adopt balloon tires at that time. In 1919 the company sold 6225 vehicles, only second to Cadillac in that class of automobile.

The postwar recession hit Cole severely, and by 1922 only 1720 cars were sold, with 1520 the following year. Cole himself decided to close down his business rather than lose his own fortune, but by the time he had suspended manufacturing in 1925 he became ill suddenly and died at age 56.

Columbia (auto)

Columbia Motors of Detroit, Michigan, was yet another motor vehicle manufacturer using this name which was not affiliated with the commercial vehicle builders called Columbia, whether they were electric or gasoline powered. This company distinguished itself from all the other "Columbia" vehicles by calling itself Columbia Six, which got its start in 1916 as a manufacturer.

J.G. Bayerline, Walter L. Daly and T.A. Bollinger were executives who defected from the King Motor Car Company, also in Detroit. William E. Metzger, who was a founder of the E-M-F company, as well as A.T. O'Conner who left Olds, also cooperated to form this Columbia Six, which was an assembled car using Continental six-cylinder motors with Borg & Beck clutches as well Timken axles and Warner transmissions.

The press of the period praised the appearance and finish of the Columbia Six, with its disc wheels, radiator shutters that were thermostatically controlled, walnut dashboards,

and beveled windows, selling for under $2000 during the Great War.

The Columbia Six Shooter was a clever name, and sales had reached 6000 by 1923. The company overreached that year when it bought the Liberty Motor Car Company in Detroit, which so stressed both firms that they were closed down the following year.

Columbia (truck)

The Columbia Motor Truck and Trailer Company of Pontiac, Michigan, was not affiliated with the earlier Columbia which built electric vehicles under the ownership of Colonel Albert Pope. This company, formerly the Kalamazoo, which began manufacturing in 1916 during the war in Europe, was among ten other companies by the name of Columbia that built vehicles in the U.S.

By 1917, as America entered the war, the Columbia truck was available as a 2-ton capacity model, and the following year a 2-ton tractor model was added to the lineup. These were conventional, assembled trucks using Buda four-cylinder motors and three-speed Covert transmissions as well as Russell internal-gear rear axles. Continental engines were adopted for 1918 and price was the same for the tractor and the truck models at $1990.

After World War I, Columbia built trucks which were 1½-ton, 2½-ton and 3-ton capacity. In the three years following the war, Hinkley engines were used as the market slowed and fewer vehicles were built by Columbia. The company survived the market downturn of the early 1920s and by 1925 the same three capacity trucks were still offered. Specializing in local market penetration, for which early truck manufacturers were known, Columbia had the added burden of competing with General Motors Trucks, which were manufactured in Pontiac. By 1926, this Columbia, among others, closed its doors for the last time.

COLUMBIA
MOTORS
COMPANY

DETROIT
MICHIGAN

Price $1350
Four-Passenger Sport 1495
Five-Passenger Sedan 1995

COLUMBIA SIX TOURING—C

COLOR	Body, Columbia blue or maroon; running gear, black	BORE AND STROKE .	3¼ x 4½ inches
		LUBRICATION	Force feed and splash
SEATING CAPACITY. .	Five	RADIATOR	Cellular
POSITION OF DRIVER .	Left side	COOLING	Water pump
WHEELBASE	115 inches	IGNITION	Storage battery
GAUGE	56 inches	STARTING SYSTEM . .	Two unit
WHEELS	Wood	STARTER OPERATED .	Gear to fly wheel
FRONT TIRES	32 x 4 inches	LIGHTING SYSTEM . .	Electric
REAR TIRES	32 x 4 inches	VOLTAGES	Six
SERVICE BRAKE . . .	Contracting on rear wheels	WIRING SYSTEM . . .	Single
EMERGENCY BRAKE .	Expanding on rear wheels	GASOLINE SYSTEM . .	Vacuum
		CLUTCH	Dry plate
CYLINDERS	Six	TRANSMISSION . . .	Selective sliding
ARRANGED	Vertically	GEAR CHANGES . . .	Three forward, one reverse
CAST.	En bloc	DRIVE	Spiral bevel
HORSEPOWER	25.35	REAR AXLE.	Semi-floating
(N.A.C.C. Rating)		STEERING GEAR . . .	Worm and gear

In addition to above specifications, price includes top, top hood, windshield, speedometer, ammeter, voltmeter, tire pump, electric horn and demountable rims.

COLUMBIA TRUCKS

Manufactured by

COLUMBIA MOTOR TRUCK AND TRAILER CO., Pontiac, Mich.

Model	E	T
Capacity	2 tons	2-ton Tractor Truck
Drive	Internal gear	Internal gear
Chassis Weight	4,000 lbs.	3,600 lbs.
Chassis Price	$1,990	$1,990
Engine	Continental	Continental
H. P. (S.A.E.)	27	27
H. P. (Actual)	40	40
Cylinders	4 en bloc	4 en bloc
Bore	$4\frac{1}{8}''$	$4\frac{1}{8}''$
Stroke	$5\frac{1}{4}''$	$5\frac{1}{4}''$
Wheel Base	114", 134", 144", 164"	114'
Tread Front	56"	56"
Tread Rear	60"	60"
Tires Front	36x4"	36x4"
Tires Rear	36x6" or 36x4" dual	36x6" or 36x4" dual

Frame—Rolled steel.
Front Axle—I-beam.
Rear Axle—Russell internal gear, O section.
Springs Front—Semi-elliptic.
Springs Rear—Semi-elliptic.
Carburetor—Shakespeare.
Cooling System—Pump.
Oiling System—Forced feed.
Ignition—Dixie magneto.
Control—Left-hand drive, center levers.
Clutch—Cone.
Transmission—Covert Selective, three speeds forward and one reverse.
Brakes—Foot, internal; hand, external rear wheels.
Steering Gear—Worm and worm wheel.
Equipment—Seat, three oil lamps, jack, set of tools, painted in primer only. All body prices on application. Electric lighting extra.

Commerce

The Commerce Motor Car Company began manufacturing trucks in Detroit, Michigan, during 1911. The cleverly-named Commerce truck was at first a ½-ton model which was powered by a 16.9 hp L-head four-cylinder engine using single chain drive. The steering wheel was still on the right side before Commerce switched to left-side steering in 1912. At the time right-hand traffic had already been adopted a century earlier in the United States, but many motor vehicle manufacturers around the world vacillated between right-side and left-side steering. For commercial vehicles this was for the practical purpose of seating the driver for easy entry and exit of the vehicle in delivery work. Such design has been used for postal vehicles to this day.

Commerce adopted Northway engines in 1913, and the steering wheel was moved to the left side, as was gradually becoming the industry standard for general purpose trucks. By this time Commerce had built 800 trucks. For 1914 capacity was increased to ¾-ton. In 1917 Commerce introduced a 1-ton capacity Model E, which superseded the other models.

The truck used shaft drive and was now fitted with an electrical system, including starter, lights and ammeter, which was a considerable modernization of the earlier design, although a cone clutch was still employed. The cone clutch contact surface was lined with leather or fabric and was not considered very durable by World War I.

Having survived the exigencies of the Great War, and the postwar economic downturn that included labor strikes, by 1922 Commerce was still doing business manufacturing a line of trucks. By now four-cylinder engines from Continental were adopted, made by an independent engine manufacturer also located in Detroit.

In 1924 the company introduced several bus chassis, from 18-passenger to 28-passenger. There was also a funeral coach, a special "powermatic" lumber truck, oil tanker and dump truck model at that time. The 1-ton Model 11 was powered by a 22.5 hp four-cylinder Continental engine. The 1¼-ton Commerce Super 11 had a longer wheelbase at 142 inches and was powered by a 28.9 hp Continental four-cylinder S4 engine. There was also a 1½-ton Model 14B with a 22.5 hp Continental engine. The Model 25B and 25D were both rated at 2½-ton but had different wheelbases. Both used Brown-Lipe clutch and transmission.

It was in 1926 that Commerce adopted six-cylinder engines, following an industry trend as more and more customers accepted the idea of additional expense for more power. Spiral bevel gear was also adopted; it was becoming another industry standard as chain drive was a rarity by this time, and worm drive considered more expensive.

In 1927 Relay Motors of Wabash, Indiana, bought out Commerce and moved the operations into the factory of Service Motors, also of Wabash, which had also been purchased almost at the same time. The manufacturing would again be moved, this time to the Garford Truck plant in Lima, Ohio.

The Relay engineering department, which was now in charge, redesigned Commerce trucks and adopted worm drive, the overall design being very similar to the Relay trucks which were badged separately. Under the umbrella company, by this time there were essentially eight models from 1-ton to 4-ton capacity, and all used four-wheel hydraulic brakes. Garford, Service and Relay trucks kept their individual emblems, but were "badge engineered."

Only 85 trucks with Commerce emblems were sold in 1928, and just 16 were sold the following year, even before the Wall Street stock market crash. As with so many companies in this listing that survived the war and

COMMERCE
MOTOR CAR
COMPANY

DETROIT
MICHIGAN

Price, Chassis	. . . .	.$1340
With Express Body	. . . .	1375
With Covered Express Body	. . .	1450
With Stake Body	. . . .	1490

COMMERCE ONE-TON TRUCK—E

COLOR	Body, green with gold stripe; running gear, orange with black stripe	HORSEPOWER	19.6 (N.A.C.C. Rating)	
CARRYING CAPACITY	2000 pounds	BORE AND STROKE	3½ x 5 inches	
POSITION OF DRIVER	Left side	LUBRICATION	Splash with circulating pump	
WHEELBASE	126 inches	RADIATOR	Tubular	
GAUGE	56 inches	COOLING	Thermo-syphon	
WHEELS	Wood	IGNITION	Storage battery	
FRONT TIRES	34 x 3 inches, single solid	STARTING SYSTEM	Two unit	
		STARTER OPERATED	Gear to fly wheel	
REAR TIRES	34 x 4 inches, single solid	LIGHTING SYSTEM	Electric	
		VOLTAGES	Six	
SERVICE BRAKE	Contracting on rear wheels	WIRING SYSTEM	Single	
		GASOLINE SYSTEM	Vacuum	
EMERGENCY BRAKE	Expanding on rear wheels	CLUTCH	Cone	
		TRANSMISSION	Selective sliding	
		GEAR CHANGES	Three forward, one reverse	
CYLINDERS	Four	DRIVE	Internal gear	
ARRANGED	Vertically	REAR AXLE	Semi-floating	
CAST	En bloc	STEERING GEAR	Worm and nut	

In addition to above specifications, price includes windshield, ammeter and horn.

postwar economic and labor troubles, Commerce succumbed to the Great Depression by 1932. Relay and Garford survived as makes for only another year.

Commercial Truck (C.T.) (electric)

Starting out during 1907 in Philadelphia and using the abbreviation C.T., the company also known as Commercial Truck was one of the more successful builders of electric vehicles, as well as gasoline-electric hybrids, which now may seem ahead of its time over a full century later.

The first year a 3-ton and a 5-ton truck chassis was available, both of which were usually built up as flatbed or box van trucks. Appearing in 1908, other commercial vehicles the company also built included a 30-seat sightseeing coach and 35-passenger omnibus, the latter of which had six rows of open-sided overstuffed benches with a flat roof and a separate seat for the driver in front.

C.T. vehicles relied on a proven design using a General Electric D.C. motor independently geared and attached to each wheel, although G.E. motors were not used exclusively. A large lead-acid battery pack was hung under the high floor. Within three years of the company's start-up, models from ½-ton to 5-ton capacity were offered, with a price tag of $2,200 for the lightest model.

As World War I erupted in Europe, C.T. introduced a gasoline-electric hybrid commercial vehicle for 1915 and 1916. There are no records that any of the battery-powered or hybrid vehicles were ever shipped to Europe, but they were used in many cities on the East Coast. For example, in Philadelphia the Curtis Publishing Company bought a fleet of C.T. electrics in order to deliver *Jack and Jill, Holiday* and *Ladies' Home Journal* around the city. Out of twenty-two 5-ton flatbed trucks, two were used to bring coal to the power plant, while twenty were used for door-to-door delivery. Loaded with five tons of paper and traveling at a top speed of 10 mph, the trucks silently plied the streets early in the morning without making a racket or a cloud of exhaust. They were shut off during actual delivery and re-started with the flip of a switch, at the time considered a great convenience over hand-cranked starters for gasoline vehicles. The 85-volt 10-amp systems were very durable, since there was very little to break or replace except bearings and brushes, and using hard rubber tires with add-on cabs for poor weather, this fleet of trucks lasted until 1962.

During World War I the model line was reduced in number from ½-ton capacity to 3½-ton capacity. General Electric batteries were used to obtain speeds from nine to thirteen mph with a range of about 50 miles.

C.T. continued its success as other electric vehicle manufacturers went under, and by 1928 the company offered a dozen different battery-powered chassis. But C.T. was an exception rather than the rule, and even the short-range delivery business began drying up. By the Great Depression, Walker Vehicle Company, another battery-powered vehicle builder, absorbed C.T. That enterprise went out of business early in 1942.

Corbitt

Among the companies that started out as wagon builders was the Corbitt Company, which was founded by Richard J. Corbitt in 1899. By 1907 his wagon company, which was located in Henderson, North Carolina, began building highwheeler passenger cars resembling horse-drawn conveyances. These vehicles resembled IHC highwheelers, but gradually got more sophisticated; inasmuch as such early vehicles used horse-drawn wagon wheels and wooden chassis, they were considered fairly primitive, as so-called horseless wagons were. By 1910 Corbitt introduced its first

C. T. TRUCKS
Manufactured by
COMMERCIAL TRUCK CO. OF AMERICA, Philadelphia, Pa.
27th and Brown Streets

S P E C I F I C A T I O N S

Model	B	C	D	E
Capacity	½ ton	1 ton	2 tons	3½ tons
Drive	Spur gear	Spur gear	Spur gear	Spur gear
Chassis Price	$1,500	$1,800	$2,200	$3,100
Wheel Base	90″ or 100″	100″	116″	115″
Tread Front	56½″ or 62″	56½″ or 62″	66″	66″
Tread Rear	56½″ or 62″	56½″ or 62″	66″	66″
Tires Front	36x3″	36x3½″	36x5″	36x3½″ dual
Tires Rear	36x3″	36x4″	36x3½″ dual	36x4″ dual

Frame—Rolled channel.

Speed	13 M.P.H.	12 M.P.H.	10 M.P.H.	9 M.P.H.

Miles—Depending on battery equipment.

Front Axle	Rectangular box trunion	Rectangular box trunion	Rectangular box trunion	Special trunion
Rear Axle	Full-floating double I-beam	Full-floating double I-beam	Full-floating double I-beam	Special
Springs Front	¾-elliptic	Semi-elliptic	Semi-elliptic	Semi-elliptic

Springs Rear—Semi-elliptic.

Battery Equipment—42 cells improved lead, 60 cells Edison.

Motor	Two G. E. 1065	Two G. E. 1033	Two G. E. 1032	Four G. E. 1033

Steering Gear—Worm and sector.

Transmission	Concentric, enclosed	Concentric, enclosed	Concentric, enclosed	Double reduction, enclosed

Control—Four speeds forward and two reverse.

Brakes	Expanding and electric	Expanding and electric	Expanding and electric	Contracting and electric

Equipment—Head lights, tail light, hand-operated mechanical horn, running switch, charging plug and receptacle, full set of tools, Sangamo ampere-hour meter, odometer and automatic cut-out.

CORBITT TRUCKS
Manufactured by
CORBITT AUTOMOBILE CO., Henderson, N. C.

S P E C I F I C A T I O N S

Model	A	B	D	E
Capacity	3½ tons	2½ tons	1½ tons	¾ ton
Drive	Worm	Worm	Worm	Worm
Chassis Price	$2,900	$2,650	$2,150	$1,600
Motor				
H P. (S.A.E.)	32.4	27.2	22.5	22.5
H. P. (Actual)	45 at 1500 R.P.M.	40 at 1500 R.P.M.	34	34
Cylinders	4 in pairs	4 en bloc	4 en bloc	4 en bloc
Bore	4½"	4¼"	3¾"	3¾"
Stroke	5½"	5¼"	5¼"	5"
Wheel Base	168"	148"	138"	130"
Tread Front	58"	58"	58"	56"
Tread Rear	62"	62"	62"	58"
Tires Front	36x5"	36x4"	36x3½"	34x3"
Tires Rear	36x5" dual	36x7	36x5"	34x4"
Frame	Channel steel	Pressed steel	Pressed steel	Channel steel

Front Axle—I-ball.
Rear Axle—Semi-floating, round.
Springs Front—Semi-elliptic.
Springs Rear—Semi-elliptic.

Carburetor	Stromberg G2	Stromberg B4	Stromberg B4	Stromberg B4
Cooling System	Pump	Pump	Pump	Thermo-syphon

Oiling System—Forced feed and splash.
Ignition—Eisemann magneto.
Control—Left drive, center control.

Clutch	Multiple disc, oil plate	Multiple disc, dry plate	Multiple disc, dry plate	Multiple disc, dry plate
Transmission	Constant mesh, three speeds forward, one reverse	Selective, three speeds forward, one reverse	Selective, three speeds forward, one reverse	Selective, three speeds forward, one reverse

Brakes—External expanding of brake drum.
Steering Gear—Worm and sector.
Equipment—Horn, tool kit, jack, hubcap wrench, two side oil lamps, oil tail lamp and wheel puller.

truck, an idea which kept the business enterprise open for more than four decades, and passenger cars were abandoned entirely.

The first Corbitt truck was a standard, conventional assembled model with 1½-ton capacity powered by a four-cylinder engine using chain drive. The market for school buses and urban transit buses opened up for the company throughout North Carolina by 1915, and the Corbitt sales department worked diligently to also open an export market, selling trucks and buses in 23 countries around the world. By the time America entered the war the press called Corbitt "the South's largest truck builder." It was true, since most manufacturers were further north and west than North Carolina.

Corbitt continued to expand its manufacturing during the 1920s with a truck model line ranging from 1-ton to 5-ton capacity, along with its buses. The company survived the stock market crash and entered the Great Depression with a truck model line that included six-wheel truck tractors rated up to 15-ton. What greatly helped the company survive the 1930s was a series of contracts with the U.S. Army, which continued into World War II. After World War II Richard Corbitt finally retired, and the company faded out by 1952.

Couple Gear

Of the electric vehicle manufacturers at the turn of the previous century, Couple Gear built some of the more sophisticated vehicles and was one of the longest surviving companies. The manufacturing plant was located in Grand Rapids, Michigan.

The first model line beginning in 1904 consisted of 1-, 2- and 5-ton battery-powered trucks with an electric motor in each wheel. Two years later the company built a four-wheel-drive four-wheel-steer electric truck which could move directly sideways without rolling forward or backward. This was achieved by wheel/motor assemblies mounted on vertical shafts that could pivot at 90 degrees or more. How useful this type of steering was in actuality for use in warehouses and tight areas may have been overshadowed by the top speed of six mph, not much quicker than a rapid walking pace.

In 1908 Couple Gear introduced a gasoline-electric hybrid commercial vehicle. These were available up to 5-ton capacity and were used as tankers. The gasoline motor powered a generator to extend the range, which would otherwise be limited to only a few dozen miles. The name of the company derived from the design of the drive system, which used electric motors directly geared to each wheel. The lighter models were capable of nine mph.

Controversy over efficiency and range already abounded even in 1910, so the company performed a public relations test run with one of its heavy gasoline-electric hybrid trucks from Buffalo to Tonawanda, New York. Owned by the Dold Company, the truck carried a seven-ton load and traveled a total of 38 miles with 28 stops. Average speed was 8.14 mph and the engine used 11 gallons of gasoline and a quart of oil. Total time running was 7 hours and 32 minutes, which amounted to 3.45 miles per gallon in fuel consumption. Numbers of this sort may have been acceptable in 1910 but not after World War I.

Before the war Couple Gear transformed a few horse-drawn ambulances to gas-electric power, including one for the S.P.C.A., but more often it was horse-drawn fire apparatus that was converted to hybrid motive power. The companies that had built horse-drawn steam pumpers included Ahrens-Fox, Boyd, Peter Pirsch, Seagrave and Webb. One of the largest such retrofits involved a Seagrave combination unit which was sold to the City of Springfield, Massachusetts. It weighed 20,000 pounds, carried ten ladders and was fifty-two feet in length. Bedford, Massachusetts, also

COUPLE GEAR TRUCKS

Manufactured by

COUPLE GEAR FREIGHT WHEEL CO., Grand Rapids, Mich.

Model	ACS	LDS
Capacity	5 tons	7 tons
Drive	Bevel gear in wheels	Bevel gear in wheels
Chassis Weight	10,000 lbs.	12,000 lbs.
Chassis Price	$6,400	$7,000
Engine	Wisconsin	Wisconsin
H. P. (S.A.E.)	42	42
H. P. (Actual)	60	60
Cylinders	4 in pairs	4 in pairs
Bore	$5\frac{1}{4}''$	$5\frac{1}{4}''$
Stroke	7"	7"
Wheel Base	144"	144"
Tread Front	68"	68"
Tread Rear	68"	68"
Tires Front	36x5" dual	36x5" dual
Tires Rear	36x5" dual	36x6" dual

Frame—Built-up.
Front Axle—Bridged.
Rear Axle—Couple Gear bridged.
Springs Front—Semi-elliptic.
Springs Rear—Semi-elliptic.
Carburetor—Stromberg.
Cooling System—Pump.
Oiling System—Forced feed and splash.
Ignition—Eisemann magneto.
Control—Right side.
Clutch—None used.
Transmission—Couple Gear Electric, five speeds.
Brakes—Four wheels contracting.
Steering Gear—Worm and sector.
Equipment—Lamps, signal meter and tools. Governor furnished at extra cost.

used such retrofit fire apparatus for three decades before they were replaced with standard motorized fire trucks and fire engines.

As World War I erupted in Europe, Couple Gear began building trucks and truck tractors which were exclusively powered by a gasoline motor. Four-wheel drive was still a main feature, along with five-speed forward and backward control. The company also built tram-car trailer controls. But the competition was too tough, and in the economic slump after the war Couple Gear built only a few vehicles, closing its doors permanently in 1922.

Croce

Named for Francis Asbury, the first American Bishop of the Methodist Episcopal Church, Asbury Park, New Jersey, was established in 1871 by brush manufacturer James A, Bradley as a residential resort on the Atlantic Coast. By the 1890s the new town was connected to New York and Philadelphia by rail lines already in place since the 1830s. Asbury quickly became a place where people could relax at the "country by the sea" and housing sprang up in 1904 and 1905.

Such was the beginning of a town where a little-known truck manufacturer by the name of Croce would try its fortunes in 1914, but not for long despite its good location and available workforce. Scant records exist of the Croce Automobile Company, which purportedly built some passenger cars before offering a line of delivery trucks. The Model A of this type of vehicle was priced at $1,700 as an open-cab van, with a closed-cab van available the following year for a hundred dollars more.

For 1915 a Model C Croce was rated at 1-ton and priced at $1,850, although there was also Model A-1 which was apparently also rated at 1-ton but slightly cheaper.

Production was interrupted in 1916 when the company was reorganized. In 1917 the model line was named 17, and the ½-ton Croce truck was powered by a four-cylinder engine using three-speed transmission and sold for $825. The new model line for 1918 was dubbed 18, 19 and 20 with open- and closed-cab versions of the same vehicle. Production did not resume after 1918. Material, labor and sales deficiencies were all culprits in the company's expiration.

Crow-Elkhart

Two early pioneers of auto manufacturing were Dr. E.C. Crow and his son Martin E. Crow of Elkhart, Indiana. After going into some experimentation with a starter motor for Albert Menges and a car built at the Sterling-Hudson Whip Company of Elkhart, the two Crow men found themselves on their own and organized the Crow Motor Car Company in 1909.

At this factory the two men manufactured a car called the Black Crow under license with the Black Manufacturing Company of Chicago. In 1910 that business relationship was terminated by Crow, and they subsequently began building their own car under their own name, which was a roadster called the Model 10 that appeared for 1911.

For 1912 the Crow-Elkhart men decided to provide commercial vehicles in parallel with their passenger cars, which was common practice among many motor vehicle manufacturers at the time, using the same chassis and motor in most cases. The Crow-Elhart ¾-ton van was offered with the same four-cylinder motor that powered the passenger cars and the six-cylinder motor that appeared for model year 1913.

Commercial vehicles were only a small part of the overall business with which Crow-Elkhart was involved, and one of the marketing strategies was to offer a multitude of body styles designated as eleven separate models. Ads sometimes used "Elk-hart" as another

THE CROCE TRUCK
Manufactured by
CROCE AUTOMOBILE CO., Asbury Park, N. J.

S P E C I F I C A T I O N S

Model   17
Capacity   ¼ ton
Drive   Bevel gear
Chassis Price $825
Motor
  H. P. (S.A.E.)   17.5
  H. P. (Actual)   30
  Cylinders   4 en bloc
  Bore   3¼"
  Stroke   5"
Wheel Base   102"
Tread Front   56"
Tread Rear   56"
Tires Front   32x4"
Tires Rear   32x4"
Frame—Pressed.
Front Axle—Timken, No. 1212.
Rear Axle—Full-floating.
Springs Front—Semi-elliptic.
Springs Rear—Semi-elliptic.
Carburetor—Zenith, O4.
Cooling System—Thermo-syphon.
Oiling System—Forced feed.
Ignition—Magneto.
Control—Left drive, center control.
Clutch—Borg & Beck, dry plate.
Transmission—Selective, three speeds forward and one reverse.
Brakes—On rear wheels.
Steering Gear—Screw and nut.
Equipment—Three oil lamps, kit of tools, pump.

**CROW-ELK-
HART MOTOR
COMPANY**

**ELKHART
INDIANA**

Price $935
Four-Passenger Cloverleaf Road-
  ster   995
Convertible Sedan 1275

CROW-ELKHART TOURING

COLOR	Optional		LUBRICATION	Splash
SEATING CAPACITY. .	Five		RADIATOR	Cellular
POSITION OF DRIVER	Left side		COOLING	Thermo-syphon
WHEELBASE	114 inches		IGNITION	High tension magneto
GAUGE	56 inches			
WHEELS	Wood		STARTING SYSTEM . .	Two unit
FRONT TIRES . . .	32 x 3½ inches		STARTER OPERATED .	Gear to fly wheel
REAR TIRES . . .	32 x 3½ inches		LIGHTING SYSTEM . .	Electric
SERVICE BRAKE . . .	Contracting on rear wheels		VOLTAGES	Six
			WIRING SYSTEM . . .	Single
EMERGENCY BRAKE .	Expanding on rear wheels		GASOLINE SYSTEM . .	Vacuum
			CLUTCH	Dry multiple disc
CYLINDERS	Four		TRANSMISSION . . .	Selective sliding
ARRANGED	Vertically		GEAR CHANGES . . .	Four forward, one reverse
CAST	In pairs			
HORSEPOWER . . . 19.6 (N.A.C.C. Rating)			DRIVE	Selective sliding
			REAR AXLE	Full floating
BORE AND STROKE .	3½ x 5 inches		STEERING GEAR . . .	Worm and sector

form of the name, and the four- and six-cylinder engines during World War I were from a multitude of sources including Atlas, Gray, Herschell-Spillman, Lycoming and Rutenber. The "9-Year Chassis" was used as an advertising slogan in 1917 when 3800 vehicles were sold with a choice of ten colors, more than most makes offered.

At the end of World War I in 1918 Crow-Elkhart was in serious financial trouble due to material shortages, production limits, labor problems and lack of sales. The company went into receivership. The Crow family was bought out in 1919, and the postwar recession only hurt the company even more. By 1921 output was down to 600 cars, and by 1923 the company folded.

Cunningham

James Cunningham, Son & Company of Rochester, New York, was incorporated as a company in 1882, having already been in the business of building a multitude of horse-drawn conveyances with such names as Vis-à-Vis, Tally-Ho, Sleigh, Berlin, Cutters and Victoria. In 1886 James Sr. passed away and his son Joseph took over the reins.

The younger Cunningham was more interested in self-propelled vehicles, as many young men were at the time, and he spent some time experimenting with an electric vehicle in the late 1890s. It was marketed at the turn of the century without much success, although a number were sold to local customers.

By 1907 Joseph Cunningham got more serious about building a motorcar, and adopting Buffalo and Continental engines from the manufacturers, he sold a few custom-built cars through 1910 before offering a model line of manufactured cars. For 1911 the first Cunningham Model J was available as a Touring, Runabout, Landaulet and Limousine, each powered by a 40 hp four-cylinder engine on a 124-inch wheelbase chassis. The latter two body styles were each priced at $4500, which would be considered close to exorbitant, but the company did a steady business selling custom-built funeral cars and ambulances in a market that could count on a steady clientele.

Just before America entered the Great War, Cunningham introduced its own 442 cid V-8 engine, and right after the war the famous Ralph De Palma proved out a Cunningham Roadster at 98 mph in an elaborate trial at Sheepshead Bay. Specially-built coachwork on a Cunningham toward the end of the war and into the early 1920s would reach a $9000 price tag. Design and workmanship were considered top of the line by any standards, especially when riding on a wheelbase of 142 inches.

The celebrities of the day, and perhaps still known today, bought Cunninghams. People such as Fatty Arbuckle, William Randolph Hearst, Cecil B. De Mille, Mary Pickford and Philip Wrigley were proud owners of Cunningham motorcars, easily in the realm of the Brewster or Duesenberg during the 1920s. However, once the Great Depression entered the picture, Cunningham tried to rely on its hearse business.

By 1931 Cunningham was fading away as a car builder. A few leftover cars were sold as new until 1933, and then the company adopted Continental straight-eight motors building professional cars on Cadillac, Ford, Lincoln and Packard chassis and occasionally using Ford V-8 running gear. Cunningham built a few Cadillac-based half-tracks and after World War II stayed alive building garden tractors and other equipment.

Dart

In the 1890s numerous motor vehicle manufacturers started out closely associated with building horse-drawn wagons. Such was the

**J A M E S
CUNNINGHAM
SON & COMPANY**

**R O C H E S T E R
N E W   Y O R K**

Price	$4250
Seven-Passenger Touring	4250
Four-Passenger Roadster	4250
Landaulet	5750
Limousine	5500

CUNNINGHAM TOURING—"V"

COLOR	Optional		BORE AND STROKE .	3¾ x 5 inches
SEATING CAPACITY. .	Four		LUBRICATION	Full force feed
POSITION OF DRIVER	Left side		RADIATOR	Cellular
WHEELBASE	132 inches		COOLING	Water pump
GAUGE	56 inches		IGNITION	Storage battery
WHEELS	Wire or wood		STARTING SYSTEM . .	Two unit
FRONT TIRES	35 x 5 inches		STARTER OPERATED .	Gear to transmission
REAR TIRES	35 x 5 inches, anti-skid		LIGHTING SYSTEM . .	Electric
SERVICE BRAKE . . .	Contracting on rear wheels		VOLTAGES	Six
			WIRING SYSTEM . .	Single
EMERGENCY BRAKE .	Expanding on rear wheels		GASOLINE SYSTEM . .	Vacuum
			CLUTCH	Dry multiple disc
CYLINDERS	Eight		TRANSMISSION . . .	Selective sliding
ARRANGED	V type, 90 degrees		GEAR CHANGES . . .	Three forward, one reverse
CAST	In fours		DRIVE	Spiral bevel
HORSEPOWER . . . . 45 (N.A.C.C. Rating)			REAR AXLE	Full floating
			STEERING GEAR . .	Worm and gear

In addition to above specifications, price includes top, top hood, windshield, speedometer, ammeter, voltmeter, clock, tire pump, electric horn and demountable rims.

DART TRUCKS

Manufactured by

DART MOTOR TRUCK CO., Waterloo, Iowa

Model	E	CC-4	L
Capacity	1 ton	2 tons	3½ tons
Drive	Worm	Worm	Worm
Chassis Weight	3,200 lbs.	4,780 lbs.	6,450 lbs.
Chassis Price	$1,850	$2,600	$3,600
Engine	Buda	Buda	Buda
H. P. (S.A.E.)	22.5	28.9	32.5
H. P. (Actual)	29 at 1200 R.P.M.	40 at 1200 R.P.M.	52.5 at 1200 R.P.M.
Cylinders	4 en bloc	4 en bloc	4 en bloc
Bore	3¾″	4¼″	4½″
Stroke	5⅛″	5¼″	6″
Wheel Base	130″	150″	160″ and optional
Tread Front	58″	58″	65″
Tread Rear	58″	58″	65″
Tires Front	34x3½″	36x4″	36x5″
Tires Rear	34x5″	36x7″	36x10″
Frame	Pressed	Pressed	Rolled
Front Axle	I-beam, plain knuckle	I-beam with taper bearings	I-beam with taper bearings

Rear Axle—Timken full floating.
Springs Front—Semi-elliptic.
Springs Rear—Semi-elliptic.
Carburetor—Master.

Cooling System	Thermo-syphon	Pump	Pump
Oiling System	Pump and splash	Full pressure feed	Full pressure feed

Ignition—Magneto.
Control—Left side, center levers.
Clutch—Dry plate.

Transmission	Fuller Selective, three speeds	Muncie Selective, four speeds	Warner Selective, four speeds

Brakes—Duplex rear axle.
Steering Gear—Screw and nut.
Equipment—Hand horn, side and tail lights, hub cap wrench and tool kit, tool box, and governor on Models CC4 and L.

case with the Dart Company of Anderson, Indiana, which began manufacturing trucks in 1903. As with other companies of the period, Dart began building light-duty ½-ton capacity highwheelers with a 20 hp two-cylinder engine under the floor, and wagon-type full-elliptic suspension on all four wheels. A simple but rugged two-speed planetary transmission with multiple-disc clutch was incorporated into the design, which also used a motor-driven jackshaft that transferred power to the rear wheels using chain on both sides. Thirty-four-inch diameter pneumatic tires were offered, but were only two inches wide.

Up until 1907 a light delivery and an open-body model were offered, the former weighing only 1800 pounds. A panel van body was also available, and the eye-popping standard color combination, which could not be recognized in black-and-white photos and ads, was Brewster green body with maroon chassis. Optional were blue body with yellow or maroon chassis, all of which made the Dart truck stand out from the crowd. The light trucks were capable of 20 mph, claimed to get 20 mpg and started out with a price tag of $650 for the express model and $690 for the panel body.

In 1907 the company changed its name to Dart Manufacturing and moved to Waterloo, Iowa. There the trucks were completely technically redesigned, and following function, form also changed in terms of appearance. Four-cylinder engines were mounted using a conventional layout with dual chain drive, but by 1912 shaft drive was adopted. That year ½-, 1- and 1½-ton models were offered, and the name was now the Dart Motor Truck Company. This name continued through 1918 to the end of the war, in which Dart trucks were used in different capacities within the United States. Moreover, the U.S. Army purchased 325 two-ton Model CC-4s before the war ended. These were conventional trucks powered by a four-cylinder Buda engine, but the heavier capacity appeared to be specifically built for the military. Buda engines were also used in the lighter model designated 1-ton Model E, as well as in the 3½-ton Model L.

Directly after the war the company's name changed to the Dart Motor Truck and Tractor Corporation, but it stayed in the same location in Iowa. There is little doubt that with every name change a financial reorganization also took place, and the company continued to try to reinvent itself to the extent that by 1922 an attempt was made to enter the passenger car market with a prototype called the Dartmobile. This brief marketing excursion was not successful, and the company refocused on commercial vehicles.

Once oil executive A.H. Howard bought the company in 1925 it became the Hawkeye-Dart Truck Company, being now affiliated through mutual assets with Hawkeye Trucks of Sioux City, Iowa. However, Howard died later that year, and the company was bought by Max W. Cline. Truck building continued under his ownership at Kansas City, Missouri, and manufacturing expanded quite successfully. Dart built 40-ton 6x6 trucks for the U.S. Army during World War II. The company changed hands once again in 1947 when the George Ohrstrom Company of New York took over Dart, and again in 1950 when the Carlisle Company of Carlisle, Pennsylvania, bought out Dart.

Then in 1958 the Pacific Car and Foundry Corporation (PACCAR) of Renton, Washington, took over Dart, and production shifted to huge, off-highway mining and construction trucks up to 100-ton capacity. In 1970 the company's name went back to just Dart, and by this time off-highway dump trucks the size of two-story houses with a capacity of 150 tons were manufactured. PACCAR sold Dart in 1984 to Unit Rig & Equipment of Tulsa, Oklahoma, and diesel-electric dump trucks of enormous capacity were continued.

TEREX Corporation purchased Unit Rig/ Dart in 1988, continuing to build wheeled loaders and mechanical drive haulers up to 160-ton capacity. TEREX continued to use the Unit Rig/Dart name for its rear dump haulage trucks up to 260-ton capacity and bottom dump coal haulers up to 270-ton capacity. The Dart name has survived over several acquisitions and buy-outs for over a century as the model line also changed dramatically over the decades.

Davis

Among the many horse-drawn wagon builders that made the transition into motor vehicle production was the company started by George W. Davis in Richmond, Indiana. He first assembled motorized carriages in 1908 which he called Motor Buggy, and by 1911 a Torpedo and Fore-Door Touring were offered with a 35 hp or 50 hp four-cylinder engine using two wheelbase chassis of 112-inch or 120-inch. This motor, along with a very similar six-cylinder engine that appeared as World War I began in Europe, were provided by Continental without interruption as America stayed out of the conflict for the first three years.

That was pertinent in that Davis exported cars to Europe, including Spain, which largely stayed out of the overall conflict. Nevertheless, Davis participated in a hill climb near Madrid in 1917 at about the time terrorism and strikes rocked Spain.

The styling of Davis cars was what caught the eye of a few thousand customers per year. The cars were built in a variety of body styles and two-tone color schemes which were considered ahead of their time. Davis chose names such as Fleetaway, Legionaire and Man o'War for some of its sport roadsters, which also featured disc wheels and impressive paint combinations. All Davis cars were powered by six-cylinder motors starting in 1917 when

the four-cylinder Continental engine was discontinued.

Money troubles in the early 1920s saw a new owner, Villor P. Williams, who used some Davis cars to sell his Parkmobile device that could move a car sideways. The Great Depression finally killed the entire operation.

Dayton Motor Bicycle

Not related to the herein listed Dayton Auto Truck Company or Dayton Electric Car Company, Dayton motorcycles, motor bicycles and bicycles were actually built by the Davis Sewing Machine Company between 1911 and 1917, located at Dayton, Ohio. Dayton motorcycles had a V-Twin motor as large as 1190 cc which was built by Deluxe in Chicago, Illinois. However, the company was much better known for its motor bicycles.

Unlike some other companies that built "motor wheels" for adding or attaching to bicycles, the Dayton was a complete machine. It included the motor, which was a four-cycle engine with 165 cc displacement, along with the drive mechanism and footboards on each side. Top speed was given as 25 mph.

The front fender acted as a leaf spring and also held the motor on two aluminum tubes, one on each side, with the motor on the left side. The disc-type front wheel was driven by a reduction gear and wheelbase was 43 inches with a total weight of 120 pounds. Price was $100.

By 1917, which was the last year of manufacture, both a man's and woman's version of the Dayton motor bicycle was offered with or without clutch, the latter having a $10 extra cost. It represented one of the lightest motorcycles or motorized bicycles of the era, but it should be noted that every motorcycle manufacturer began building very light machines based on the modern bicycle that had been developed in the 1890s.

It is pertinent to add that motorized

**GEORGE W.
DAVIS MOTOR
CAR COMPANY**

**RICHMOND
INDIANA**

Price	.$1485
Five-Passenger Club Roadster	. . 1485
Seven-Passenger Sedan	 1850
Four-Passenger	 1485

DAVIS TOURING—SIX H-'18

COLOR	Body and hood, cobalt blue; fenders black; wheels white	BORE AND STROKE .	$3\frac{1}{4}$ x $4\frac{1}{2}$ inches	
		LUBRICATION	Splash with circulating pump	
SEATING CAPACITY. .	Seven	RADIATOR	Cellular	
POSITION OF DRIVER .	Left side	COOLING	Water pump	
WHEELBASE	119 inches	IGNITION	Storage battery	
GUAGE	56 inches	STARTING SYSTEM . .	Two unit	
WHEELS	Wood	STARTER OPERATED .	Gear to fly wheel	
FRONT TIRES	34 x 4 inches,	LIGHTING SYSTEM . .	Electric	
REAR TIRES	34 x 4 inches, anti-skid	VOLTAGES	Six	
		WIRING SYSTEM . . .	Single	
SERVICE BRAKE . . .	Contracting on rear wheels	GASOLINE SYSTEM . .	Vacuum	
		CLUTCH	Plate	
EMERGENCY BRAKE .	Expanding on rear wheels	TRANSMISSION . . .	Selective sliding	
		GEAR CHANGES . . .	Three forward, one reverse	
CYLINDERS	Six			
ARRANGED	Vertically	DRIVE	Spiral bevel	
CAST.	En bloc	REAR AXLE.	Three-quarters floating	
HORSEPOWER	25.35 (N.A.C.C. Rating)	STEERING GEAR . . .	Worm and gear	

In addition to above specifications, price includes top, top hood, windshield, speedometer, ammeter, electric horn and demountable rims.

attachment wheels were briefly popular during the Great War era. They were built by A.O. Smith of Milwaukee, Wisconsin, from 1914 until 1924. There were also the Davis and a wheel built by Crocker that were attached to front and rear wheel respectively. The A.O. Smith wheel attached to the frame next to the rear wheel and it could be removed relatively easily to use the bicycle in its stock form without being motorized.

"Every girl who cares for the outdoors can see the logic," was a slogan used in advertising aimed at female riders who may have been less inclined to ride a heavier motorcycle. The Smith Motor Wheel, as it was officially called, was 197 ccd and produced 1½ hp, giving the bicycle the ability to travel at 30 mph on a good day. Price was $80.

Another similar two-wheeler was the Autoped, built in New York City between 1915 and 1921. It was classified as a scooter with small wheels and a folding steering-control bar for storage and transporting. The Autoped used a single-cylinder 155 cid motor that produced 1.5 hp and was part of the front wheel assembly attached to a flat footboard scooter frame that had a 36.5-inch wheelbase.

All of these companies ceased to exist as heavier motorcycles became popular at the same time as bicycling increased in popularity, and other light two- and three-wheel motorized vehicles entered the market which did not use an engine mounted on the front wheel that impeded steering, maneuverability and performance. The Dayton Company, building two-wheel vehicles, went out of business in 1917.

Dayton (truck)

The Dayton Motor Truck Company, which built trucks also known as Durable Dayton, started out in Dayton, Ohio, and was first called Dayton Auto Truck Company. Starting out just before World War I began, the company offered models H, K and M in 1912, with capacities of 2-, 3- and 5-ton, respectively.

This company should not be confused with two other companies that built electric cars: the Dayton Electric Car Company of Dayton, Ohio, and the Dayton Autoelectric Company of Jersey City, New Jersey, the former of which coexisted with the truck

DAYTON TRUCKS
Manufactured by
DAYTON MOTOR TRUCK CO., Dayton, Ohio

Model	E	M	D	K
Capacity	7½ tons	5 tons	3½ tons	3½ tons
Drive	Chain	Chain	Worm	Chain
Chassis Weight	9,200 lbs.	9,000 lbs.	7,000 lbs.	7,100 lbs.
Chassis Price	On application	On application	On application	On application
Engine	Wisconsin	Wisconsin	Continental	Wisconsin
H. P. (S.A.E.)	53	44.2	32.4	36.1
H. P. (Actual)	95	80	40	60
Cylinders	4 in pairs	4 in pairs	4 in pairs	4 in pairs
Bore	5¾″	5¼″	4½″	4¾″
Stroke	7″	7″	5½″	5¼″
Wheel Base	148″	148″	160″	136″
Tread Front	65″	65″	67″	65″
Tread Rear	70″	70″	70¼″	66″
Tires Front	36x7″	36x6″	36x5″	36x5″
Tires Rear	42x6″ dual	42x5″ dual	36x5″ dual	36x5″ dual

Frame—Channel.
Front Axle—I-beam section.

Rear Axle	Timken fixed rectangular	Timken fixed rectangular	Sheldon semi-floating	Timken fixed rectangular

Springs Front—Semi-elliptic.

Springs Rear	Platform	Platform	Semi-elliptic	Platform

Carburetor—Zenith or Schebler.
Cooling System—Pump.
Oiling System—Splash and force.
Ignition—Magneto.

Control	Left-hand drive, center control	Left-hand drive, center control	Left-hand or right-hand drive, center control	Left-hand drive, center control
Clutch	Wet plate	Wet plate	Dry plate	Wet plate
Transmission	Rochester Selective, 3 speeds	Rochester Selective, 3 speeds	Cotta constant mesh	Rochester Selective, 3 speeds
Brakes	External and internal	External and internal	Internal	External and internal

Steering Gear—Screw and nut.
Equipment—Oil side and tail lamps, hand horn, tool box and tools, jack.
    NOTE: Prices and specifications of 2-ton chain and worm drive trucks furnished on application.

manufacturer in Ohio for at least two years. There was also a Dayton Steam vehicle built at the turn of the century, and three other Dayton companies were organized to build vehicles but never actually did so according to any records. The builder of motor bicycles and motorcycles listed here was also not affiliated.

The City of Dayton was connected to Lake Erie, so commerce was a viable form of business from the time the Dayton Erie Canal was built in 1830. However, it is not clear how the Great Dayton Flood of 1913 affected the Dayton Auto Truck Company. Another company with a similar name was Reliable Dayton, which built cars and trucks in Chicago starting in 1906. There was also the Dayton Wheel Company, and various companies building components and equipment.

Most of the Dayton trucks were sold locally as stake or express bodies with prices ranging from $2,500 to $4,500. Dayton built its own T-head four-cylinder engines rated at 35, 45 and 60 hp. Cylinders were cast in pairs and a water pump was used for cooling instead of thermo-syphoning, which was more common at that time.

The fact that Dayton built its own engines indicated it was a fairly large concern, yet very little history remains about the company. It was in 1914 that the name of the trucks was actually changed from Dayton to Durable Dayton when the firm was reorganized, possibly because it may have been affected by the great flood of March 1913.

The Dayton truck designers used different types of brakes for each of the early models: transmission brake, expanding shoes on the rear wheels, and jackshaft brake, respectively. It offered trucks as late as 1918 from all evidence, yet a number of books place the date of the company's demise as 1917. That year the company offered models H, K, D and M, which were 2-ton chain-drive, 3½-ton chain-drive, 3½-ton worm drive and 5-ton chain-drive.

For some reason, towards the end of production, models got a partially reverse order of designation: E, K, M, and U, with the heaviest being the E model, which was designated out of sequence and rated at 7½-ton. The worm drive model used a Sheldon semi-floating rear axle. But it appears that neither the worm drive nor the chain-drive trucks could compete in the market, and by the time World War I was over the company was also done with manufacturing trucks.

Day-Elder (D.E.)

Many American truck builders began manufacturing before World War I, but Day-Elder first offered trucks for the 1918 catalog, despite previously-published erroneous information that the company began the following year. The company was located in Irvington, New Jersey, an outskirts of Newark whose nickname was Brick City, and where the Day-Elder Company soon established its factory. This was a good business move since Newark was a fast-growing shipping and industrial center at that time.

Once the Morris Canal connected Newark with the iron and farm area inland and as patent leather production took off, Newark's population grew very quickly. From 136,500 in 1880 it turned into 347,000 by 1910. It was also the location of celluloid production, the first commercially viable plastic invented by John W. Hyatt. Thomas Edison worked in Newark prior to moving to Menlo Park, New Jersey, and Newark was also the center for zinc electroplating. All of this industry helped companies such as Day-Elder, especially with a good workforce and numerous customers.

After World War I Day-Elder trucks were distributed nationally and into Canada. The vehicles were conventional assembled trucks considered of good quality. The trucks were powered by Continental four-cylinder motors and used Timken worm drive. By 1922 Day-

D. E. TRUCKS

Manufactured by

DAY-ELDER MOTORS CORPORATION, Newark, N. J.

Model	J	A	B	C
Capacity	¾ ton	1-1½ tons	1½-2 tons	2½-3 tons
Drive	Worm	Worm	Worm	Worm
Chassis Weight	2,000 lbs.	3,000 lbs.	3,300 lbs.	4,600 lbs.
Chassis Price	$950	$1,495	$1,755	$2,365
Engine	Le Roi	Continental	Continental	Buda
H. P. (S.A.E.)	15.6	19.6	22.5	29
H. P. (Actual)	20	25	28	37
Cylinders	4 en bloc	4 en bloc	4 en bloc	4 en bloc
Bore	3¼"	3¾"	3¾"	4¼"
Stroke	4½"	5"	5"	5½"
Wheel Base	108"	128"	144"	150" and 165"
Tread Front	56"	56"	56"	56"
Tread Rear	56"	56"	56"	58¼"
Tires Front	33x4" Pneu.	34x3"	34x3½"	36x4"
Tires Rear	33x4" Pneu.	34x4"	34x5"	36x7"
Frame—Pressed.				
Front Axle	Sheldon I-beam Elliott knuckle	Columbia I-beam Elliott knuckle	Columbia I-beam Elliott knuckle	Schuler I-beam Elliott knuckle
Rear Axle	Sheldon semi-floating	Hayes semi-floating cast housing	Hayes semi-floating cast housing	Hayes semi-floating, cast housing
Springs Front—Semi-elliptic.				
Springs Rear—Semi-elliptic.				
Carburetor	Schebler Model R	Zenith Model O	Zenith Model O	Zenith Model O
Cooling System	Thermo-syphon	Thermo-syphon	Thermo-syphon	Pump
Oiling System—Combination forced feed and splash.				
Ignition—Magneto.				
Control—Center.				
Clutch	Dry disc	Dry plate	Dry plate	Dry plate
Transmission	Detroit Selective, 3 speeds forward and 1 reverse	Covert Selective, 3 speeds forward and 1 reverse	Covert Selective, 3 speeds forward and 1 reverse	Covert Selective, 3 speeds forward and 1 reverse
Brakes	Internal rear wheels	Internal & external rear wheels	Internal & external rear wheels	Internal rear wheels
Steering Gear	Worm	Screw and nut	Screw and nut	Screw and nut
Equipment—Lamps, horn, jack, tools and governor on Models A, B and C.				

Elder, which also called its trucks D.E., offered 1-ton to 5-ton models, and Buda motors were also available. During the mid-1920s the market stayed fairly steady for Day-Elder, but by 1928 there was a downturn even though the company introduced a model line called "Super Service Sixes" for 1929. For 1930 additional models up to 8-ton capacity were introduced with various improvements and additional choices such as Hercules engines in order to compete with Brockway and other locally popular manufacturers. However, by 1937 the company met its demise as the Depression continued.

DeKalb

Many of the names in this entire review of companies were used by different firms, usually because they are common last or regional names. Therefore, clarification is often needed. In the case of DeKalb, confusion would not be surprising since nine different states have the name for one of their cities or counties, including Alabama, Georgia, Illinois, Indiana, Mississippi, Missouri, New York, Tennessee and Texas.

The DeKalb Wagon Company of DeKalb, Illinois, is the truck-building company that is illustrated here. It was not affiliated with the DeKalb delivery car built in St. Louis, Missouri, in 1915 or another DeKalb organized to build cars earlier in Fort Wayne, Indiana.

Given that information, it must be stated that very little is known about the DeKalb Wagon Company except that it began building trucks in 1914 in an agricultural area about 65 miles away from Chicago. The model line would include 1½-ton to 3½-ton capacity trucks with the engine under the driver's seat. It would appear that four-cylinder Continental engines were used. Chain drive was standard until 1916 when worm drive became optional.

The Model E-2 was a 2-ton model available

in 1918, along with the unusually named Model E-2½. Both were worm drive and used a Fuller three-speed transmission. From all records it may be assumed that manufacturing did not continue after World War I.

DeMartini

In the first two decades of the previous century there were half a dozen small manufacturers of trucks in San Francisco, and in the last year of World War I, George J. DeMartini began production in the city. It is believed that he founded his company earlier as U.S. cities began municipal garbage collection service, but documented truck manufacturing began in 1918. DeMartini had a connection with the military at the San Francisco Presidio, and his first known truck was a 4-ton laundry vehicle for the U.S. Marine Corps. DeMartini assembled it with a Buda motor and a Brown-Lipe transmission. It was fairly long at 160-inch wheelbase, using solid rubber tires.

DeMartini was an inventor and machinist who built his own airplane after working for the Army-Navy Industrial Service. Local refuse haulers were the biggest set of customers for DeMartini, which built standard, conventional, assembled trucks. Many of his early trucks had dump beds, but some trucks were also built as flatbeds for local contractors and as fire trucks. Some of the DeMartini trucks that have been left extant still have the telltale side steps for refuse collection. Most of the DeMartini trucks had open cabs or were C-cabs. In World War I the model line spanned from 1-ton to 3½-ton capacity.

After World War I, DeMartini continued to build trucks for local city services, although he left the drayage dock work to two other local builders: Doane and MacDonald. Buda engines were offered with four-speed Brown-Lipe selective sliding gear transmissions for the steep hills of San Francisco and vicinity.

DeKALB TRUCKS

Manufactured by

DeKALB WAGON CO., DeKalb, Ill.

Model	E-2	E-2½
Capacity	2 tons	2½ tons
Drive	Worm	Worm
Chassis Weight	4,300 lbs.	4,900 lbs.
Chassis Price	$2,100	$2,450
Engine	Continental	Continental
H. P. (S.A.E.)	27.2	27.2
H. P. (Actual)	42	42
Cylinders	4 en bloc	4 en bloc
Bore	$4\frac{1}{8}$"	$4\frac{1}{8}$"
Stroke	$5\frac{1}{4}$"	$5\frac{1}{4}$"
Wheel Base	134" and 146"	136" and 144"
Tread Front	58"	58"
Tread Rear	$58\frac{1}{2}$"	$58\frac{1}{2}$"
Tires Front	$34x3\frac{1}{2}$"	36x4"
Tires Rear	36x5"	36x6"

Frame—Pressed.
Front Axle—I-beam forging.
Rear Axle—Timken floating I-beam.
Springs Front—Semi-elliptic.
Springs Rear—Semi-elliptic.
Carburetor—Master.
Cooling System—Pump.
Oiling System—Forced feed.
Ignition—Magneto.
Control—Left drive, center control.
Clutch—Dry plate.
Transmission—Fuller Selective, three speeds forward.
Brakes—Internal expanding rear wheels.
Steering Gear—Screw and nut.
Equipment—Driver's seat, dash and oil lamps.

DeMARTINI TRUCKS

Manufactured by

DeMARTINI MOTOR TRUCK CO., Inc., 379 Bay St., San Francisco, Cal.

S P E C I F I C A T I O N S

Model	BW 17	CW 17	DW 17	EW 17
Capacity	1 ton	1½ tons	2½ tons	3½ tons
Drive	Worm	Worm	Worm	Worm
Chassis Price	$1,865	$2,400	$2,800	$3,600
Motor				
H. P. (S.A.E.)	22.5	25.6	28.9	28.9
H. P. (Actual)	28 at 1100 R.P.M.	30 at 1000 R.P.M.	32.5 at 1000 R.P.M.	32.5 at 1000 R.P.M.
Cylinders	4 en bloc	4 en bloc	4 en bloc	4 en bloc
Bore	3¾"	4"	4¼"	4¼"
Stroke	5½"	5½"	5½"	5½"
Wheel Base	145"	145"	157"	169"
Tread Front	56"	56"	58"	58"
Tread Rear	58"	58"	58"	66"
Tires Front	36x3"	36x3½"	36x4"	36x5"
Tires Rear	36x4"	36x6"	36x7"	36x6" dual

Frame—Rolled.
Front Axle—I-beam, Elliott.
Rear Axle—Semi-floating.
Springs Front—Semi-elliptic.
Springs Rear—Semi-elliptic.
Carburetor—Stromberg.
Cooling System—Pump.
Oiling System—Forced feed.
Ignition—Magneto.
Control—Left drive, center control.
Clutch—Dry plate.
Transmission—Selective, three speeds forward and one reverse.

Brakes	Two sets internal, rear wheels	One set internal, one set external, rear wheels	Two sets internal, rear wheels	Two sets internal, rear wheels

Steering Gear—Screw and nut.
Equipment—Driver's cab, two oil dash lamps, oil tail lamp, set of tools, mechanical horn, jack, front bumper.

After using dual chain drive, semi-floating worm drive was adopted using Sheldon rear axle and Ross steering gear. Price for a 2-ton Model OV in 1925 was up to $3,200. The Depression greatly reduced orders for trucks and DeMartini built dump beds between 1931 and 1934. In an interview towards the end of his career, George DeMartini stated that he had numerous inventions and original designs during the course of his life but never spent any time on seeking patents.

Denby

There were a number of good reasons to start a motor vehicle manufacturing company in Detroit, Michigan, and that is exactly what the founders of Denby did in 1914. The area was home to the Ottowa Indians under Chief Pontiac until it became Fort Detroit, named after the Detroit River, a name given in 1701 by French founder Antoine de la Mothe Cadillac, as previously mentioned.

Numerous companies were taking advantage of the waterways of the Great Lakes and the local, capable labor force. Ford, Cadillac, and then General Motors, Dodge and Chrysler manufactured cars in Detroit, as did early truck builders. Denby started building trucks in 1914 from ¾-ton to 2-ton capacity with the lightest model selling for $890 at that time. The Type E 2-ton was priced at $1,985. Canvas cab cover, panel body and starting and lighting systems were all optional at extra cost.

By the last year of World War I a 5-ton model was offered, which lasted until 1922, the year before Denby was finally incorporated as a business establishment. During the war model numbers were numerical from the 1-ton capacity Model 12 to the 5-ton capacity Model 210.

In the mid–1920s Denby also built 30-passenger buses up until the stock market crash in 1929. Even though artillery wheels were often used, Denby was also known for its solid disc wheels, which were sturdier, albeit heavier and eventually prone to corrosion. However, in comparison to wood-spoke wheels, they were superior, as well as more expensive. Denby vehicles were powered by Continental engines with a few exceptions that were powered by Hercules motors. By 1930 the Depression hit the company hard almost immediately, and it was the last year of manufacturing.

Denmo

In 1916 the Denneen Motor Company of Cleveland, Ohio, began building commercial vehicles. (Some records show "Deneen" as the spelling of the name, which is erroneous.) What is known is that Denneen did not build any passenger cars.

As much as Cleveland was a hotbed of industrial and, more specifically, motor vehicle development, very little is known about the Denneen Motor Company. Given the fact that the company actually produced only a few trucks, it is one of the most obscure companies in this entire listing.

The Denmo used a 4-cylinder Wisconsin engine, three-speed transmission and Torbensen rear axle. Pneumatic tires were used at the front and solid rubber tires on rear, which was not unusual for light commercial vehicles when the manufacturer tried to get as much capacity as possible. The illustration for the 1917 Denmo seems to show the Model 10 with pneumatic tires in front and solid rubber tires at the rear in a situation where men are sitting in the truck bed for additional traction and the wheels are digging in for an uphill ride.

The fact that Denmo listed a Motometer as equipment it offered with its trucks gives the opportunity to discuss this ubiquitous component of the era's vehicles. In 1912 George H. Townsend, president of the Moto Meter Company, obtained the exclusive rights under

DENBY TRUCKS

Manufactured by

DENBY MOTOR TRUCK COMPANY, Detroit, Mich.

Model	12	13	15	210
Capacity	1 ton	2 tons	3 tons	5 tons
Drive	Internal gear	Internal gear	Internal gear	Internal gear
Chassis Weight	2,300 lbs.	3,900 lbs.	4,500 lbs.	8,725 lbs.
Chassis Price	$1,460	$2,025	$2,525	$4,900
Engine	Continental	Continental	Continental	Continental
H. P. (S.A.E.)	19.6	22.5	22.5	32.4
H. P. (Actual)	25 at 1300 R.P.M.	29 at 1275 R.P.M.	29 at 1275 R.P.M.	40 at 1050 R.P.M.
Cylinders	4 en bloc	4 en bloc	4 en bloc	4 in pairs
Bore	$3\frac{1}{4}''$	$3\frac{3}{4}''$	$3\frac{3}{4}''$	$4\frac{1}{2}''$
Stroke	$5''$	$5''$	$5''$	$5\frac{1}{4}''$
Wheel Base	124"	144"	144"	170"
Tread Front	56"	$56\frac{1}{4}''$	58"	$68\frac{3}{4}''$
Tread Rear	56"	$59\frac{1}{2}''$	64"	65"
Tires Front	34x3"	$36x3\frac{1}{2}''$	36x4"	36x6"
Tires Rear	34x4"	36x6"	36x7"	40x6" dual or 40x12" single

Frame—Pressed steel.
Front Axle—I-beam, drop forging.

Rear Axle	Russell internal gear	Russell internal gear	Russell internal gear	Celfor internal gear

Springs Front—Semi-elliptic.
Springs Rear—Semi-elliptic.

Carburetor	Zenith	Zenith	Zenith	Stromberg
Cooling System	Thermo-syphon	Thermo-syphon	Thermo-syphon	Pump

Oiling System—Splash and forced feed.
Ignition—Eisemann magneto.
Control—Left drive, center control.
Clutch—Dry plate.

Transmission	Detroit Selective, three speeds	Detroit Selective, three speeds	Detroit Selective, three speeds	Warner Selective, four speeds

Brakes—Internal expanding and external contracting, 14 inch drums.

Steering Gear	Ross worm	Gemmer worm	Gemmer worm	Ross worm

Equipment—Two side oil lamps, one tail, seamless gas tank, driver's seat, jack and set of tools and governor.

THE DENMO TRUCK
Manufactured by
THE DENNEEN MOTOR CO., Cleveland, Ohio

SPECIFICATIONS

Model   10
Capacity   1¼ tons
Drive   Internal gear
Chassis Price $1,385
Motor
   H. P. (S.A.E.)   22.5
   H. P. (Actual)   35
   Cylinders   4 en bloc
   Bore   3¾"
   Stroke   5"
Wheel Base   124", 140" $70 extra
Tread Front   56"
Tread Rear   56"
Tires Front   34x4½" pneu.
Tires Rear   34x4"
Frame—Pressed.
Front Axle—I-beam section.
Rear Axle—Floating.
Springs Front—Semi-elliptic.
Springs Rear—Semi-elliptic.
Carburetor—Stewart.
Cooling System—Thermo-syphon.
Oiling System—Forced feed.
Ignition—Magneto.
Control—Left drive, center control.
Clutch—Dry plate.
Transmission—Selective, three speeds forward and one reverse.
Brakes—Rear wheels.
Steering Gear—Worm.
Equipment—Splitdorf-Apple two-unit starting and lighting equipment, horn, spot light, driver's seat, bumper, dash and instrument board assembly, tool kit, speedometer, electric tail light, license bracket, electric front lamps, rain vision windshield, front fenders, spare rim, tire pump, Motometer, Pierce governor.

Boyce patents to manufacture radiator and dashboard type motor temperature indicators. The Motometer was essentially a type of thermometer which actually measured the vapor temperature at the top of the radiator.

These circular shaped devices (sometimes referred to as lollipop shaped) were designed to fit into the detachable radiator cap and be visible from the driver's seat to know when the engine coolant temperature was reaching the boiling point. At that time water was the only fluid that circulated throughout the "water-cooled" engine before "antifreeze" liquids were developed. Systems were not pressurized and ideal temperature was kept around 180 degrees Fahrenheit in order to burn gasoline more efficiently, keeping in mind that for every thousand feet of altitude the boiling point of water dropped two degrees. (At 10,000 feet water boils at 192 degrees Fahrenheit).

Most vehicle manufacturers wanted to have their own emblems and logos prominently perched on the top front of their hoods, so they employed graphic artists at Motometer to design one specifically for them. Motor vehicle dealers and clubs would also have Motometers built with their name or emblem for advertising purposes. By 1927 Motometer employed 1800 people and boasted that 10,000,000 of their gadgets had been sold.

However, as motor vehicle design became more sophisticated, radiators were hidden under front grilles and sheet metal, and the common "hood ornament" that consisted of a Motometer, even if it had wings, arms or other appurtenances, was gradually replaced by a company's own decorative statuette or other adornment. Dashboard mounted "heat indicators," better known as temperature gauges, took the place of Motometers and similar types of temperature sensors for the radiator cap. There was also a problem with theft, as it became common knowledge that the Motometer and radiator cap worth between

$5.00 and $20.00 at that time could be easily unscrewed and absconded with by anyone with a penchant for such dishonest behavior.

Motometer was bought out by National Gauge and Equipment of Wisconsin in 1926. The photo illustration of the Denmo shows a Motometer on the radiator cap of the truck. Whether it had custom Denmo graphics is not visible. The Grant Motor Company bought Denneen in 1917 and produced some trucks called Denmo-Grant. At that time the 35 hp Walker engine was adopted until the H.J. Walker Company was bought after World War I. The entire operation went into receivership in 1922, and that was the end of Denmo and Denmo-Grant.

Detroit Electric

Of all the early battery-powered car builders in America, Detroit Electric was one of the most successful manufacturers. The enterprise had its beginnings as the Anderson Carriage Company, which had been founded at Port Huron, Michigan, and then transplanted to Detroit by William C. Anderson in 1895. He hired engineer George M. Bacon to design an electric vehicle using the Anderson horse-drawn conveyances as its basis, and in 1907 the first horseless carriage built by this company was offered to the public for $1200.

By the end of 1907, 125 Detroit Electrics were built, with another 400 the following year. In addition to the cabriolet-style runabout, enclosed models called Victoria and Coupe were also manufactured, and the numbers of Detroit Electrics built continued to increase, with 1500 for 1910 alone. Anderson bought the Elwell-Parker Company of Cleveland, which produced electric motors and had supplied Baker Electric, a competitor of Anderson.

During this period of automobile manufacturing there were many proponents of battery-powered vehicles, which required no

A N D E R S O N
E L E C T R I C
CAR COMPANY

D E T R O I T
M I C H I G A N

Price	**$3000**
Model 47 Four-Passenger Brougham .	2850
Model 46 Roadster	2500
Model 45 Forward-Drive Brougham . .	2800
Model 44 Victoria	2300
Model 43 Four-Passenger Brougham .	2550

MODEL: DETROIT ELECTRIC "48" DUPLEX DRIVE BROUGHAM

COLOR	Blue, green or maroon.
SEATING CAPACITY . .	Five persons.
BODY:	
LENGTH OVER ALL .	156 inches.
WIDTH OVER ALL .	84 inches.
WHEELBASE . . .	100 inches.
GAUGE	56 inches.
TIRE DIMENSIONS:	
FRONT	34 x 4½ inches (pneumatic); or 36 x 4½ inches (cushion).
REAR	34 x 4½ inches (pneumatic); or 36 x 4½ inches (cushion).

BRAKE SYSTEMS . .	Internal expanding; also magnetic brake.
BATTERY	40 cells, 13 plate.
SPEED	22 miles per hour.
NO. OF FORWARD SPEEDS	Five.
NO. OF REVERSE SPEEDS	Five.
CONTROL	Lever control.
STEERING	Lever.

hand-cranking, priming, stoking, condensation bleeding, ignition system, boiler, exhaust system producing choking clouds of smoke, et cetera. The electric vehicle was simple to operate, clean and quiet. It also had a short range and the slow process of recharging was needed. Battery replacement every couple of years was expensive when the technology was rather primitive.

By 1911 the company was renamed the Anderson Electric Car Company, able to build all major components except such parts as wheels, tires and batteries. A "chainless" direct shaft drive was introduced, making the propulsion system both quieter and more durable. An "underslung" roadster had the looks of the gasoline engine car by using a similar suspension system so that leaf springs were mounted above the chassis rails, giving the vehicle a low, "rakish" look. The issue of range was addressed in a response that the Detroit Electric could travel further than anyone would wish to travel in one day. That may have been the case in 1911 when Detroit Electric introduced a 1-ton delivery van, but with the improvement of road conditions it was not a slogan with which to ride into the future of motorization.

One company-sponsored test showed a Detroit Electric traveling 211 miles on a single charge, yet it was recommended that 80 miles should be the expected maximum. The company marketed its passenger cars specifically to urban females, but there was also a line of taxis. Some of the Detroit Electric cars were assembled in Scotland.

Production dropped from 4660 cars in 1914 to 3000 by 1916. No records of electric car use have been found regarding military operations in Europe. In 1919 the company name was changed to Detroit Electric Car Company. A false hood and mock radiator somewhat contradicted the boast that electric cars were "still the best" in 1920. Commercial vehicles such as milk vans continued to be built in 1922, but by 1927 that market also dwindled, and as the Great Depression took over, the electric vehicle business faded away. By 1938, as one of the longest-surviving American electric vehicle builders, Detroit Electric finally succumbed to the realities of economic stress and customers' preferences.

Detroiter

In addition to the Detroit Electric, Detroit Speedster, Detroit Taxicab and Detroit Steam Car, there was also the unrelated Detroiter, which began in that city in 1912 under the company name of Briggs-Detroit. It stood out by its standard design from all the other vehicles with a Detroit name, in that it was a conventional touring car powered by a 25 hp four-cylinder engine right from the first year of production.

The company was a collaboration of two men: Claude S. Briggs and John A. Boyle, who hired W.S. Lee as chief engineer and Zach C. Barber for sales and marketing in order to compete with the Brush Runabout Company, which is where Claude Briggs had gotten his start.

Displayed at the Detroit Auto Show in January of 1912, the first Detroiter was the Model No. 1 touring powered by a four-cylinder Continental engine. It was what was called an assembled car in that nearly every component was purchased "off the shelf" from the original parts manufacturer/distributor (OEM).

Apparently, the price was right at $850 per copy in competition with the Brush. But after a roadster was introduced in 1914, the long lineup of body styles for 1915 did not prevent a dismal financial condition as liabilities were nearly double the amount of assets. Later in the year the company was bought out by A.O. Dunk of the Puritan Machine Company.

Once the takeover was complete Claude Briggs left immediately, and by the time America entered World War I, he named him-

**BRIGGS-
DETROITER
COMPANY**

DETROIT, MICH.

Price	$900
With electric lighting and electric self-starter . .	1025
Roadster	900

MODEL: DETROITER FIVE-PASSENGER TOURING CAR

COLOR	Body, hood and wheels Raven blue; chassis black.	ARRANGED	Vertically, under hood.
		CAST	En bloc.
SEATING CAPACITY .	Five persons.	BORE	3½ inches.
CLUTCH . . .	Multiple disc.	STROKE	5 inches.
WHEELBASE . .	104 inches.	COOLING . . .	Water.
GAUGE	56 inches.	RADIATOR . . .	Tubular.
TIRE DIMENSIONS:		IGNITION . . .	Jump spark.
FRONT . . .	32 x 3½ inches.	ELECTRIC SOURCE .	High tension magneto and storage battery.
REAR . . .	32 x 3½ inches.		
BRAKE SYSTEMS . .	Double expanding on both rear wheels.	DRIVE	Shaft.
		TRANSMISSION . .	Selective sliding gear.
HORSE-POWER . . .	N. A. C. C. (formerly A. L. A. M.) rating 19.6.	GEAR CHANGES .	Three forward, one reverse.
		POSITION OF DRIVER .	Left side drive and center control.
CYLINDERS	Four.		

Price includes top, top hood, windshield, speedometer and demountable rims self chairman of the executive board with J.S. Kuhn as president. By this time the Detroiter was available with a Perkins 31 hp V-8, which was introduced in 1916, followed by a six-cylinder 45 hp motor for 1917. Another reorganization took place and an auction liquidated all of the company's assets, including remaining cars, parts dies, machinery and factory equipment by the time World War I ended.

Diamond T

One of America's best regarded truck manufacturers began when C.A. Tilt built his first automobile in 1905, but it took another six years before commercial vehicles were built. The famous Diamond T emblem was created by his father, who had a shoe factory. The T was of course for Tilt, and the Diamond stood for quality, which Diamond T trucks represented for five and a half decades, building over a quarter million trucks over the years.

After Tilt had made passenger cars which were placed for sale in Chicago by 1907, a customer asked if Tilt could build a truck, which he did and continued to do so successfully in series by 1911. A few of the first Diamond T trucks used chain drive, along with a Continental four-cylinder motor. Thereafter, shaft-drive was the special feature of Diamond T, and in 1912 the company offered trucks up to 5-ton capacity.

At the time it was common practice to build a four-cylinder motor with a large displacement, which is what the early Diamond T engine represented at 432 cubic inches producing 40 brake horsepower. But the high quality of the motor, transmission, clutch, brakes, axles, radiator and other components did not include planned obsolescence, and the first Diamond T truck was still in service around Chicago in the early 1930s.

For 1914 the 1½-ton Model J still had right-hand steering at a time when many manufacturers were uncertain about the best position for the driver. Right-hand traffic had already been adopted much earlier in the United States for practical reasons, and in part to break from the British authority of laws and conventions at the time of American independence.

DIAMOND T TRUCKS

Manufactured by

DIAMOND T MOTOR CAR CO., Chicago, Ill.

S P E C I F I C A T I O N S

Model	J-5	J-4	J-3	L
Capacity	1 ton	1½ tons	2 tons	3½ tons
Drive	Worm	Worm	Worm	Worm
Chassis Price	$1,485	$1,900	$2,200	$3,300
Motor				
H. P. (S.A.E.)	19.60	27.23	27.23	32.4
H. P. (Actual)	25	28	35	42
Cylinders	4 en bloc	4 en bloc	4 en bloc	4 in pairs
Bore	3½″	3¾″	4⅛″	4½″
Stroke	5″	5″	5¼″	5½″
Wheel Base	132″	154″ and 160″	154″ and 160″	170″ Standard Special to 186″
Tread Front	57¾″	58″	58½″	62″
Tread Rear	58″	58½″	58½″	66¾″
Tires Front	36x3″	36x3½″	36x4″	36x5″
Tires Rear	36x4″	36x5″	36x6″	36x5″ dual
Frame	Pressed steel 4⅞″	Pressed steel 5⅝″	Pressed steel 5⅝″	Pressed steel 7″
Front Axle—Timken.				
Rear Axle—Timken worm.				
Springs Front—Semi-elliptic.				
Springs Rear—Semi-elliptic.				
Carburetor	Rayfield LL-2E	Rayfield LL-3E	Rayfield LL-3E	Rayfield LL-3E
Cooling System	Thermo-syphon	Thermo-syphon	Pump	Pump
Oiling System—Splash.				
Ignition—Bosch magneto.				
Control	Left drive, center control	Left drive, center control	Right drive, center control	Right drive, center control
Clutch—Dry plate.				
Transmission	Selective, three speeds forward, one reverse	Selective, three speeds forward, one reverse	Selective, three speeds forward, one reverse	Selective, four speeds forward, one reverse
Brakes—Internal, rear wheels.				
Steering Gear—Worm and wheel.				

Equipment—Seat, horn, oil lamps, tools, jack, tool box, hubodometer, and front fenders on J-5 and J-4. Governor in addition to above on J-3 and L.

The early Diamond T truck was powered by a four-cylinder Continental motor along with a three-speed Brown-Lipe transmission and a worm-drive Timken rear axle. The heavier 3-ton and 5-ton models still used chain drive at a time when metallurgical advances had yet to allow for high torque transfer. Chain drive was undoubtedly a true and tried method, albeit subject to constant wear problems.

By 1916 the model line included trucks from ¾-ton to 5-ton capacity, and Continental engines were used through 1918. Diamond T opened a new, modern 250,000-square-foot factory in Chicago's north side. The company built fewer than 1000 Model B Liberty trucks on a 1,000-foot progressive assembly line through 1918. (It is believed that the company finished additional Liberty trucks with parts on hand once the war was over). According to records, the U.S. Army ordered an additional 2,000 trucks at the end of the war. The company used "The Nation's Freight Car" as a slogan during World War I partly as a result of limitations in availability of commercial railroad services due to military transports, an additional burden on the private sector.

Surviving the postwar downturn, Diamond T continued to build high-quality trucks through the 1920s. One of the notable equipment offers by 1920 was the "Spring Wheel," which was a solid rubber tire with inner rubber inserts as a type of substitute for pneumatic tires, which were only beginning to catch on and become available for heavier vehicles. Diamond T used four-cylinder Hinkley engines at the time, coupled to three-speed selective sliding transmissions and semi-floating worm drive rear axles. Attention was paid to style, and prices reflected quality, ranging from $2,220 to $5,660 in 1921.

New styling was introduced in 1923 which included a "coupe" cab. A new "high-speed" model was offered using a Hercules motor at a time when other companies advertised various "speed" models of their own. Top speed of 25 mph for a truck was no longer par for the course. Another restyling took place at Diamond T in 1926.

Because this book focuses on the time span before, during and around World War I , the complex history of Diamond T through World War II, and its subsequent merger with Reo in 1966, are not discussed.

Doane

In the early days of motor vehicle manufacturing a company that specialized in a narrow market niche could succeed on a small scale, and such was the case with Doane, which began building trucks in 1916 for the dock work around the huge, busy port of San Francisco. The low-bed trucks were built especially for use by longshoremen, and the company competed for this specific market around the country (and a few for export) with one other similar manufacturer by the name of MacDonald. Both Doane and Mac-Donald trucks had several design features specifically aimed at the stevedore and the dockhand.

The most noticeable feature was the "low-boy" cargo bed, built only sixteen inches off the ground. Neither springs nor axle took up much room under or above the rear of the chassis, and a single chain drive drove the axle manufactured by Doane. The first trucks had a 6-ton rating, but drayage trucks along the piers were often loaded four times that weight. In 1918 a 2½-ton model was offered, powered by a 36.2 Waukesha four-cylinder motor.

Low-bed trucks provided a large capacity for faster, self-propelled drayage, traveling at the speed of a slow jog. Ten miles per hour was considered cruising speed. Both Doane and MacDonald built only a few dozen vehicles per year for several reasons. The utilitarian application was highly specialized, and the

DOANE TRUCKS

Manufactured by

DOANE MOTOR TRUCK CO., 428 3rd St., San Francisco, Cal.

Model	1918	1918
Capacity	2½ tons	6 tons
Drive	Chain	Chain
Chassis Weight	6,200 lbs. with body	10,500 lbs. with body
Chassis Price	$3,500 with body	$5,350 with body
Engine	Waukesha	Waukesha
H. P. (S.A.E.)	29	36
H. P. (Actual)	35	48
Cylinders	4 in pairs	4 in pairs
Bore	4¼″	4¾″
Stroke	5¾″	6¾″
Wheel Base	156″	178″
Tread Front	66″	68″
Tread Rear	77″	96″
Tires Front	36x4″	36x6″
Tires Rear	36x7″	40x6″ dual

Frame—Rolled.
Front Axle—Doane.
Rear Axle—Doane square section.
Springs Front—Semi-elliptic.
Springs Rear   Semi-elliptic   Semi-elliptic and coils
Carburetor—K. Holley.
Cooling System—Pump.
Oiling System—Splash.
Ignition—Magneto.
Control—Right hand steer, left hand control.
Clutch—Dry plate.
Transmission—Brown-Lipe Selective, three speeds forward, one reverse.
Brakes—Jack shaft and rear wheel drums.
Steering Gear—Screw and nut.
Equipment—Body complete including painting, etc.

trucks were of little use in other areas, especially as speeds grew and even cumbersome trucks were expected to keep up with street traffic. Such companies as DeMartini, Doane, Doble, Hewitt-Ludlow, Kleiber and Mac-Donald, all located in San Francisco itself at one time, competed for every niche and stitch of local commercial vehicle work, including delivery, refuse, sewer, firefighting, mail delivery, construction, ambulance, electrical power, telephone, mass transit, funeral, et cetera.

Doane added a rigid six-wheel truck in 1924 with seven forward speeds and three reverse, allowing for a maximum 25 mph. Solid rubber tires were used exclusively through the 1920s and into the mid–1930s. One of the six-wheel trucks was used in conjunction with a four-wheel trailer as a delivery tanker with 4,900 gallons' capacity for Mohawk Oil Company of California. In the late 1930s both Hi-bed and Low-bed trucks were available, as well as six-wheel 10-ton dump trucks.

If anything made these trucks obsolete, it would be such devices as forklifts, conveyor belts, versatile motorized cranes and other forms of automation. But at least ten Doane trucks built in 1916 were still working on the docks in the mid–1950s. Small, light, quick burden carriers would also take part of the market. Custom-building specialty vehicles a few at a time was also very expensive. Back in the 1920s a $3,000 to $4,000 price tag, which was what a Doane commanded, was considered a substantial expenditure. Doane merged with Graham in 1946 after World War II and lasted as a manufacturer until 1948.

Dodge

Among the survivors of the Great War era, the one truck and passenger car builder that stayed in business to this writing was Dodge. The Dodge Brothers, Horace and John, were major suppliers to Ransom Eli Olds of Oldsmobile fame, who bought thousands of complete transmissions from the two machinists. They also built tens of thousands of engines, transmissions and axles for Henry Ford. All four men made huge fortunes, but by the end of 1914 a new make of motor vehicles appeared with a dual triangle emblem that also read "Dodge Brothers," independent of any other company. It only took one year for the Dodge Brothers to be third in size in the American auto industry, having produced 45,000 autos for 1915 alone.

By 1916 the first light truck body was mounted on a Dodge passenger car chassis, and the Dodge truck was born. The Dodge Touring was accepted by General Pershing as his personal staff car, which was named Daisy and used to chase Pancho Villa during the Punitive Expedition in Mexico, a precursor to America's entry into the war in Europe. General Pershing later wrote about how durable his Dodge was, running some 18 hours daily, and he also used Dodge light trucks. The Dodge Brothers coined the term "dependability" and used it in their advertising at the time.

The civilian version of the Dodge truck, in the guise of the screen-side business truck, was also first mounted on the 114-inch chassis, and the military bought over 2,600 screen-side trucks, most of which were floated overseas. Dodge dealers also mounted light truck bodies on Dodge chassis, so that soon there were numerous Dodge trucks out and about across the country. Officially, Dodge did not list its screen-side trucks until 1918. A closed panel delivery was offered to the public by the end of that year. At that point a variety of bodies were available from various sources: farm wagon bodies, ambulances, fire trucks, funeral cars and special delivery trucks among them.

Right after the war ended Dodge introduced a taxicab, which was only produced for two years, and it like the other Dodge vehicles was powered by the well-made Dodge L-head

DODGE BROTHERS COMMERCIAL CAR

Manufactured by

DODGE BROTHERS, Detroit, Mich.

Capacity	½ ton
Drive	Bevel gear
Chassis Weight	2,610 lbs.
Chassis Price	$885
Engine	Dodge Brothers
H. P. (S.A.E.)	24.5
H. P. (Actual)	30—35
Cylinders	4 en bloc
Bore	3⅞"
Stroke	4½"
Wheel Base	114"
Tread Front	56"
Tread Rear	56"
Tires Front	33x4" Pneumatic
Tires Rear	33x4" Pneumatic

Frame—Pressed.

Front Axle—I-beam.

Rear Axle—Dodge Brothers full-floating.

Springs Front—Semi-elliptic.

Springs Rear—Three-quarter elliptic.

Carburetor—Special design.

Cooling System—Pump.

Oiling System—Splash and force feed.

Ignition—Delco Distributor.

Control—Left-hand drive, center control.

Clutch—Dry plate disc.

Transmission—Dodge Brothers Selective, three speeds forward and one reverse.

Brakes—Internal and external.

Steering Gear—Worm.

Equipment—Two electric head lamps with dimmer, electric tail lamp and instrument board lamp, oiled duck curtains for complete enclosure, two wire screens, electric horn, license brackets, tire pump, jack, tool kit, tire carrier with demountable rim.

D O D G E
BROTHERS

D E T R O I T
M I C H I G A N

Price	**$885**
Two-Passenger Roadster	885
Five-Passenger Convertible Sedan	1350
Two-Passenger Convertible Coupe	1350
Five-Passenger Winter Touring .	1050
Two-Passenger Winter Roadster .	1050

DODGE BROTHERS TOURING—5

COLOR	Black	LUBRICATION	Splash with circulating pump	
SEATING CAPACITY. . .	Five			
POSITION OF DRIVER .	Left side	RADIATOR	Tubular	
WHEELBASE	114 inches	COOLING	Water pump	
GAUGE	56 inches	IGNITION	Storage battery	
WHEELS	Wood	STARTING SYSTEM .	Single unit	
FRONT TIRES	32 x 3½ inches	STARTER OPERATED .	Chain to crank shaft	
REAR TIRES	32 x 3½ inches, anti-skid	LIGHTING SYSTEM . .	Electric	
SERVICE BRAKE . . .	Contracting on rear wheels	VOLTAGES	Twelve	
		WIRING SYSTEM . . .	Single	
EMERGENCY BRAKE .	Expanding on rear wheels	GASOLINE SYSTEM . .	Vacuum	
		CLUTCH	Dry multiple disc	
CYLINDERS	Four	TRANSMISSION . . .	Selective sliding	
ARRANGED	Vertically	GEAR CHANGES . . .	Three forward, one reverse	
CAST.	En bloc			
HORSEPOWER	24.03 (N.A.C.C. Rating)	DRIVE	Spiral bevel	
		REAR AXLE	Full floating	
BORE AND STROKE .	3⅞ x 4½ inches	STEERING GEAR . . .	Worm and worm wheel	

In addition to above specifications, price includes top, top hood, windshield, speedometer, ammeter, tire pump, electric horn and demountable rims.

four-cylinder motor that produced 24 hp. The Dodge Roadster was fitted with a box and instantly became a pickup of sorts, and a panel delivery was offered by Dodge Brothers called the Business Car. A tractor-trailer combination featured a Torbensen heavy-duty rear axle, extended frame and custom cab from Colt-Stratton Company of New York. As the newly modified and reinforced Dodge trucks grew in popularity, so too did the model line expand during the 1920s. However, as Dodge reached the number-two spot in the automotive industry in 1920, both John and Horace died, having become somewhat famous for their bar-busting drinking habits. Frederick Haynes became president of Dodge Brothers as their widows became the owners.

The 1919 the Series One commercial vehicles from Dodge were carried over into 1920 before the recession of 1921 forced layoffs of three-quarters of the 22,000 Dodge workforce. Dodge slipped to number three in the industry but quickly rebounded. Dodge acquired Graham Brothers, which became the manufacturer of Dodge trucks by default, and officially by 1924. The history of Dodge, which goes continuously to this day, has included much involvement with military production. For further reading please see *The Illustrated Encyclopedia of American Trucks and Commercial Vehicles* by the author, as well as numerous books on the subject of Dodge history that is beyond the scope of this book.

Dorris

One of the earliest automotive pioneers in America was George Preston Dorris, who began experimenting with motor vehicles circa 1891 and finished at least one gasoline-powered prototype by 1897 in his native Nashville, Tennessee. He teamed up with John L. French the following year and helped organize the St. Louis Motor Carriage Company in Missouri, where Dorris became chief

engineer with a claim to build "Rigs that Run" at a time when not all of them actually did that very well.

Once French moved to Peoria, Illinois, in 1905, his company began to flounder and soon disappeared. Dorris, on the other hand, remained in Nashville, where he built a passenger car by 1906 and a truck prototype in 1911, which used a transmission built by Dorris, along with shaft drive and double-reduction rear axle. The Dorris engine was placed under the seat, as was typical of the time, and the company sold a few of these 2-ton rated trucks.

In 1915 Dorris introduced its Model IAW, which sold a lot better, using the Dorris four-cylinder engine that produced 48 A.L.A.M. horsepower. During this period the company struggled to stay in business, and in 1917 company president H.B. Krenning resigned for personal health reasons. By the end of World War I some 350 of these trucks were sold. Both a 2-ton and 3-ton were also introduced using a Dorris four-cylinder overhead-valve (OHV) four-cylinder engine.

Also in 1918 the Model K-4 was introduced, and the next year the Model K-7 followed. The K-7 was rated at 2-ton and was powered by the Dorris 312 cid OHV engine. George Preston Dorris had numerous patents, six of them for improvements of motor vehicle transmissions, despite the fact that many of his trucks used Muncie four-speed and Warner transmissions. By 1923 the Dorris passenger car was "practically hand-built," as advertising proclaimed, but by 1926 production ended. Truck manufacturing continued until 1928 in a gradual fade-out of the Dorris enterprise.

Dort

As an original partner of General Motors founder William Crapo Durant when "Billy" Durant was still in horse-drawn wagon building back in 1886 in Flint, Michigan, Josiah

THE DORRIS TRUCK

Manufactured by

THE DORRIS MOTOR CAR CO., 4100 Laclede Ave., St. Louis, Mo.

Model	K-4
Capacity	2 tons
Drive	Worm
Chassis Weight	5,000 lbs.
Chassis Price	On application
Engine	Dorris K4
H. P. (S.A.E.)	28.9
H. P. (Actual)	30
Cylinders	4 en block
Bore	$4\frac{1}{4}$"
Stroke	$5\frac{1}{2}$"
Wheel Base	144" or 162"
Tread Front	$58\frac{1}{2}$"
Tread Rear	$58\frac{1}{2}$"
Tires Front	36x4"
Tires Rear	36x7"

Frame—Pressed.
Front Axle—Timken.
Rear Axle—Timken full-floating.
Springs Front—Semi-elliptic.
Springs Rear—Semi-elliptic.
Carburetor—Stromberg M-2.
Cooling System—Pump.
Oiling System—Force.
Ignition—Magneto.
Control—Left drive, center control.
Clutch—Multiple dry disc.
Transmission—Selective, four forward.
Brakes—Expanding, rear wheels.
Steering Gear—Worm and worm wheel.
Equipment—Oil side and tail lamps, speedometer, hand diaphragm horn, oil pressure gauge, complete set of tools, jack, driver's seat complete with spring cushion, Lunkenheimer primer and gasoline tank. Extra charge for governor when ordered.

**DORRIS MOTOR
CAR COMPANY**

S T .   L O U I S
M I S S O U R I

Coupe	. . . .	Prices
Sedan	. . . .	Upon Application
Limousine	. . . . . .	

DORRIS TOURING—1-C-6

COLOR	Optional
SEATING CAPACITY . .	Four
POSITION OF DRIVER .	Left side
WHEELBASE	130 inches
GAUGE	56 inches
WHEELS	Wood
FRONT TIRES	36 x 4½ inches
REAR TIRES	36 x 4½ inches, anti-skid
SERVICE BRAKE . . .	Contracting on rear wheels
EMERGENCY BRAKE .	Expanding on rear wheels
CYLINDERS	Six
ARRANGED	Vertically
CAST.	In threes
HORSEPOWER	38.4 (N.A.C.C. Rating)
BORE AND STROKE .	4 x 5 inches
LUBRICATION	Full force feed
RADIATOR	Tubular
COOLING	Water pump
IGNITION	High tension magneto
STARTING SYSTEM . .	Two unit
STARTER OPERATED .	Gear to fly wheel
LIGHTING SYSTEM . .	Electric
VOLTAGES	Six
WIRING SYSTEM . . .	Single
GASOLINE SYSTEM . .	Vacuum
CLUTCH	Dry multiple disc
TRANSMISSION . . .	Selective sliding
GEAR CHANGES . . .	Three forward, one reverse
DRIVE	Spiral bevel
REAR AXLE	Three-quarters floating
STEERING GEAR . . .	Worm and gear

In addition to above specifications, price includes top, top hood, windshield, speedometer, ammeter, tire pump, electric horn and demountable rims.

**DORT MOTOR
CAR COMPANY**

FLINT, MICHIGAN

Five-Passenger Touring   .
Three-Passenger Roadster } Prices on
Five-Passenger Sedan . . } Applica-
Three-Passenger Coupe . . } tion
Five-Passenger Sedanet . . }

DORT TOURING—11

COLOR	Body, dark green; fenders and hood, black	LUBRICATION	Pump over and splash
SEATING CAPACITY .	Five	RADIATOR	Cellular
POSITION OF DRIVER .	Left side	COOLING	Thermo-syphon
WHEELBASE	105 inches	IGNITION	Storage battery
GAUGE	56 inches	STARTING SYSTEM . .	Two unit
WHEELS	Wood	STARTER OPERATED .	Gear to fly wheel
FRONT TIRES	30 x 3½ inches	LIGHTING SYSTEM . .	Electric
REAR TIRES	30 x 3½ inches, anti-skid	VOLTAGES	Six
SERVICE BRAKE . . .	Contracting on rear wheels	WIRING SYSTEM . . .	Single
		GASOLINE SYSTEM . .	Gravity
EMERGENCY BRAKE .	Expanding on rear wheels	CLUTCH	Cone
		TRANSMISSION . . .	Selective sliding
CYLINDERS	Four	GEAR CHANGES . . .	Three forward, one reverse
ARRANGED	Vertically		
CAST	En bloc	DRIVE	Plain bevel
HORSEPOWER	19.6 (N.A.C.C. Rating)	REAR AXLE	Three-quarters floating
BORE AND STROKE .	3½ x 5 inches	STEERING GEAR . . .	Worm and nut

In addition to above specifications, price includes top, top hood, windshield, speedometer, ammeter, voltmeter, clock, tire pump, electric horn and demountable rims.

Dallas Dort stayed in the buggy business until 1915 when he started his Dort Motor Car Company. Dort hired Etienne Planche as his chief engineer. Planche was an experienced automotive engineer from Europe who had helped Louis Chevrolet design his car under Durant's wing. Dort assembled cars in Canada as the Gray Dort under license to William Gray.

Having registered the trademark "Dort" in 1914, the company had little trouble fending off a lawsuit by the Dart Company of Indiana. The case was thrown out of court, where it was stated the public was wise enough to distinguish between the two similar names which were in fact quite different.

The first two years Dort offered four-cylinder open touring cars. Dort would stick with Lycoming engines until nearly the end, and only in the last year of production a six-cylinder engine manufactured by Falls was offered. In 1917 the company built two closed cars and a "Cloverleaf Roadster" for $695. Rare Army photos show soldier mechanics honing their repair skills on Dort cars during the war. By the end of World War I the model line included Touring, Roadster, Sedan, Coupe and Sedanet, with prices around $1000 across the model line.

By 1919 prices had risen some ten to twenty percent, and perhaps not coincidentally, radiators were styled after Rolls-Royce. In 1920 the Sedanet was dropped when, as one of its best years, Dort produced some 30,000 vehicles, competing closely with his old friend who was building cars under his own name by then: Durant (and Star). It wasn't until 1921 that Dort began building trucks, beginning with a ¾-ton van. Subsequently, the company offered a Light Delivery Car and an Express with steel body. By 1923 solid disc wheels were often standard equipment on Dort cars. Passenger cars and commercial vehicles shared chassis throughout production, which ended in 1924. By 1925 the Dort factory was sold to

A.C. Spark Plug. That year Josiah Dort died after a heart attack while playing golf.

Duplex

An outskirts of the city of Detroit, Charlotte, Michigan, was the site of the founding of the Duplex Power Car Company in 1907, having taken over the defunct auto maker named J.L. Dolson at that location. But Duplex trucks had nothing to do with Dolson, including its designers and engineers, who were newly hired.

In the first year a ¾-ton prototype truck was built with four-wheel-drive. It was powered by a 14 hp two-cylinder engine. With this vehicle as the basis for the design, the Model B was sold successfully until 1915. At that time the company built its Model C, which was rated at 2-ton capacity, and its Model D, which was rated at 3-ton capacity, both of which were powered by a 20 hp four-cylinder motor mounted ahead of the driver.

Just before the United States entered World War I, Duplex introduced a 3⅓-ton truck as the company moved to Lansing, Michigan, where the name was changed to Duplex Truck Company in 1916. Duplex adopted Buda four-cylinder motors in conjunction with three-speed transmissions, using chain drive that allowed direct drive, or 2:1 ratio which translated to a ratio of 64:1 because final drive was by spur and ring gear in the wheels which were carried by dead axles front and rear so the power axles were relieved of carrying the weight of the chassis and payload. Power locks in both front and rear differentials allowed a single wheel to have traction for off-road emergency situations.

Because of the destruction of the company's history records in a flood during 1975, it is not certain when Duplex built two-wheel-drive trucks, but it is known that by 1917 only four-wheel-drive units were being manufactured. During 1917 and 1918 Duplex built

THE DUPLEX TRUCK
Manufactured by
DUPLEX TRUCK CO., Lansing, Mich.

Model	E
Capacity	3½ tons
Drive	Internal gear
Chassis Weight	6,050 lbs.
Chassis Price	$4,000
Engine	Buda
H. P. (S.A.E.)	29
H. P. (Actual)	40 on brake test
Cylinders	4 en bloc
Bore	4¼″
Stroke	5¼″
Wheel Base	130″
Tread Front	60″
Tread Rear	60″
Tires Front	36x6″
Tires Rear	36x6″

Frame—Channel section, pressed.
Front Axle—Duplex I-beam section, reversed Elliott
Rear Axle—Duplex fixed, I-beam section.
Springs Front—Semi-elliptic.
Springs Rear—Semi-elliptic.
Carburetor—Schebler Model R.
Cooling System—Centrifugal pump.
Oiling System—Pressure and splash.
Ignition—Magneto.
Control—Left-hand steering wheel, shifting lever at right.
Clutch—Dry plate.
Transmission—Brown-Lipe Selective, four speeds forward.
Brakes—External service brake at chain case, external emergency at rear wheels.
Steering Gear—Screw and sliding nut.
Equipment—Full set of tools, jack, driver's cab.

trucks for the military, justifying its $400 price increase to "take care of the war tax."

Once the war ended Duplex began building a two-wheel-drive truck called the Limited, which was rated at 2 tons. Pneumatic tires and a different gear ratio allowed for slightly higher speeds, following the market trend for "speed trucks" built by various companies. In 1920 Duplex organized a publicity stunt in which a Limited truck was fitted with four 55-gallon drums and sent on an endurance run around the Indianapolis Motor Speedway. The press covered the event as the truck was driven 935 miles nonstop, which was a new record at the time. A pace car was used to pass coffee to the driver, who was not allowed any pit stops.

As little as the public knows about Duplex trucks, it should be noted that Duplex continued to build numerous models of trucks over the following six decades until the company's demise in 1985.

Durable

The Durable Motor Truck Company was located in Hammond, Indiana, and produced light trucks called the Model B-18 for 1918. Records show that the company actually began the previous year, building its first 1½-ton capacity truck at a time when a number of entrepreneurs believed the war in Europe, already in full effect, would bring government contracts. This did not benefit the Durable Motor Truck Company, which does not appear to have gotten any type of military or government contract.

In 1917 the local press announced that the Durable Motor Truck Company would be "the first vehicle assembly plant in the Calumet Region," which was defined by the rivers of that name. The company's "10 acre complex" included a 16,000-square-foot factory building. Because Hammond lies directly on the border of northern Illinois and north-

ern Indiana, the Durable factory was in the former (West Hammond, Illinois) while the offices were located in the latter (Hammond, Indiana). The press further stated that 100 orders had been placed, which would immediately employ 50 men, and that the local farming community would be the main customer base.

All of these plans seemed to have been cut short, and by the summer of 1918 the only fame Hammond had achieved for the moment was the circus train wreck of June 22 in which 86 people were killed and twice that many injured.

The one distinctive piece of equipment that Durable offered was a Buel whistle, which was an exhaust whistle in lieu of a horn. Via a valve attached to a floor pedal in the cab, the exhaust whistle was blown by redirecting the motor's exhaust fumes through it. The exhaust whistle was often accompanied by an exhaust "cut-out," which redirected the exhaust so as to relieve back pressure to the motor, giving some extra horsepower "which may be valuable in climbing hills," as the maintenance manual stated. It was also used to check if a cylinder was misfiring, using the louder noise for easier comparison.

Whatever plans the organizers of Durable Motor Truck had did not go forward past 1918, due to material shortages, labor shortages and sales that were not forthcoming.

Elcar

"The Car for the Many" was the slogan devised by brothers William B. and George B. Pratt, who first wanted to build a car using their own name, then decided on the name Elcar, which was manufactured by the Elkhart Carriage and Motor Car Company in Elkhart, Indiana. The company's name offered them an opportunity to build horse-drawn wagons as well, which they entirely abandoned after the first Elcar appeared in 1916.

THE DURABLE TRUCK

Manufactured by

DURABLE MOTOR TRUCK CO., Hammond, Indiana

Model	B-18
Capacity	1½ tons
Drive	Worm
Chassis Weight	2,980 lbs.
Chassis Price	On application
Engine	Continental
H. P. (S.A.E.)	25
H. P. (Actual)	35
Cylinders	4 in pairs
Bore	3¾″
Stroke	5″
Wheel Base	125″
Tread Front	56½″
Tread Rear	56″
Tires Front	34x4″
Tires Rear	34x5″

Frame—Pressed steel.
Front Axle—Columbia I-beam section.
Rear Axle—Wisconsin semi-floating.
Springs Front—Semi-elliptic.
Springs Rear—Semi-elliptic.
Carburetor—Stromberg 1¼″ L-B type.
Cooling System—Thermo-syphon.
Oiling System—Combination forced feed and splash.
Ignition—Berling magneto, set spark.
Control—Left-hand drive, center control.
Clutch—Dry plate.
Transmission—Fuller Selective, three speeds forward.
Brakes—Both brakes on rear wheels, emergency brakes internal, service external.
Steering Gear—Screw and nut type.
Equipment—Two side and one rear oil lamp, tool kit, tool box on running board, Buel whistle, driver's seat, oil can and jack.

Elcar

ELKHART
CARRIAGE AND
MOTOR CAR
COMPANY

ELKHART
INDIANA

Price $1295
Four-Passenger Touring Roadster 1295
Five-Passenger Sedan 1795

ELCAR TOURING—D-SIX

COLOR	Body, olive green; running gear, black
SEATING CAPACITY .	Five
POSITION OF DRIVER	Left side
WHEELBASE	116 inches
GAUGE	56 inches
WHEELS	Wood
FRONT TIRES	33 x 4 inches
REAR TIRES	33 x 4 inches, anti-skid
SERVICE BRAKE . . .	Contracting on rear wheels
EMERGENCY BRAKE .	Expanding on rear wheels
CYLINDERS	Six
ARRANGED	Vertically
CAST	En bloc
HORSEPOWER	25.35 (N.A.C.C. Rating)
BORE AND STROKE .	3¼ x 4½ inches
LUBRICATION	Force feed and splash
RADIATOR	Cellular
COOLING	Water pump
IGNITION	Storage battery
STARTING SYSTEM . .	Two unit
STARTER OPERATED .	Gear to fly wheel
LIGHTING SYSTEM . .	Electric
VOLTAGES	Six
WIRING SYSTEM . .	Single
GASOLINE SYSTEM . .	Vacuum
CLUTCH	Dry plate
TRANSMISSION . . .	Selective sliding
GEAR CHANGES . . .	Three forward, one reverse
DRIVE	Spiral bevel
REAR AXLE	Full floating
STEERING GEAR . .	Worm and gear

In addition to above specifications, price includes top, top hood, windshield, speedometer, ammeter, voltmeter, tire pump, electric horn and demountable rims.

During World War I the factory produced ambulance bodies, and in 1918 the Elcar Touring, Sedan and Roadster were available with a four-cylinder or a six-cylinder Continental motor on the same 116-inch wheelbase chassis.

Business continued under the leadership of the two Pratt brothers until 1921, when they decided to sell the whole business to Auburn, Indiana, executives G.W. Bundy, W.H. Denison, A.M. Graffis and F.B. Sears, who changed the name to Elcar Motor Company. Under F.B. Sears as president and A.M. Graffis as chief engineer, the company beat out the Driggs Company for a lucrative contract to build 1000 taxis for the Diamond Taxi Company of New York City. The taxis were built as four-cylinder and six-cylinder versions and had iterations customized as El-Fay, Martel and Royal Martel. Martel was another taxi service company in New York City under Jules Martin, who bought approximately 200 Elcars under the second and third name.

For 1925 Elcar brought out a Model 8-80 with Touring, Roadster and Brougham body styles on a 127-inch wheelbase chassis using a Lycoming straight-eight motor, placing the Elcar among a more extravagant elite, especially once the four-cylinder models were dropped in 1926. When the stock market crash of 1929 arrived there was a desperate attempt to save the company by building a car called the Lever, so named after the engine designed by Alvah Powell. Harry Wahl tried to revive the Mercer using an Elcar chassis in 1930, and a prototype was built at the Elkhart factory, but the company could not avoid receivership by 1931. The factory built a few El-Fay and Allied taxis before it closed down for good the following year as the Great Depression took yet another company into bankruptcy.

Elgin

Among the companies that came into existence during World War I was the Elgin, which first rolled off the assembly line in 1916. Because the founders had been in the watch and clock manufacturing business they announced the Elgin as "The Car of the Hour" and "The Car Built Like a Watch." The tooling of the New Era Motor Car Company was bought and moved from Joliet, Illinois, to Argo, Illinois, where production began, using a six-cylinder motor on a 114-inch chassis in Touring or Roadster guise. The same body styles and engine were continued in 1917 with a two-inch stretch of the wheelbase.

For 1918 Elgin stretched the wheelbase an inch and added a six-cylinder engine, and a sedan was also in the model lineup. A few endurance tests around Illinois proved out the workmanship and reliability of the Elgin, and the company's prospects attracted an increasing number of investors. Generous dividends had been paid to a crowd of stock owners in 1916, and enthusiasm abounded when additional money was handed out in 1920, when sales reached $7,000,000.

After the war, the company had high hopes and big plans, and a new design was introduced in 1922 which incorporated a Cutler-Hammer selective gearbox and dual transverse rear suspension. However, the debilitating postwar recession arrived, and unexpectedly, Elgin was forced to sell a bond issue to raise $500,000 for working capital.

In June of 1923 the company was reorganized as Elgin Motors, Incorporated, and the whole enterprise was moved to Indianapolis, where the former Federal truck factory was occupied. But after the company had built only a few cars in the new location, money woes and internal strife, including lawsuits, shut down Elgin by midyear of 1924.

Emblem (motorcycle)

The Emblem Company began in Angola, New York, which is located on the western end of New York very close to Lake Erie. The

**E L G I N
MOTOR   CAR
C O M P A N Y**

C H I C A G O
I L L I N O I S

Price $1095
Four-Passenger Roadster 1095
Sedan 1645

ELGIN SIX TOURING—SERIES F

COLOR	Body, maroon or dark royal blue; hood, radiator, fenders and running gear, black
SEATING CAPACITY .	Five
POSITION OF DRIVER	Left side
WHEELBASE	117 inches
GAUGE	54 inches
WHEELS	Wood
FRONT TIRES	33 x 4 inches
REAR TIRES	33 x 4 inches, anti-skid
SERVICE BRAKE . . .	Contracting on rear wheels
EMERGENCY BRAKE .	Expanding on rear wheels
CYLINDERS	Six
ARRANGED	Vertically
CAST	En bloc
HORSEPOWER	21.6 (N.A.C.C. Rating)
BORE AND STROKE .	3 x 4¼ inches
LUBRICATION	Splash with circulating pump
RADIATOR	Cellular
COOLING	Thermo-syphon
IGNITION	Storage battery
STARTING SYSTEM . .	Two unit
STARTER OPERATED .	Gear to fly wheel
LIGHTING SYSTEM . .	Electric
VOLTAGES	Six
WIRING SYSTEM . .	Single
GASOLINE SYSTEM . .	Vacuum
CLUTCH	Plate
TRANSMISSION . . .	Selective sliding
GEAR CHANGES . . .	Three forward, one reverse
DRIVE	Spiral bevel
REAR AXLE	Full floating
STEERING GEAR . . .	Worm and gear

In addition to above specifications, price includes top, top hood, windshield, speedometer, ammeter, tire pump, electric horn and demountable rims.

town was named after the nation of Angola in Africa when Quakers lived in this area of New York and were supporting missionary work. The town has always been small; the railroad was built through it in the late 1800s, but it was never a large manufacturing or industrial city. But it didn't take a large company to build a few Emblem motorcycles beginning in 1907.

The first Emblems were single-cylinder with optional clutch or direct drive, the latter being not uncommon in the early days of motorcycle design when a pedal start and engine shut down by stopping was adequate for this type of transportation. V-belt or flat belt was also an option. The standard bicycle chain drive was left intact even when the V-twin was introduced in 1913 which was 1255 cc and produced 10 hp.

By 1916 the Emblem V-Twin was offered as a 12 or 14 hp motor, with an 800 cc twin available in addition to a 600 cc 7 hp one-cylinder motor. After entering racing briefly, Emblem concentrated on the more mundane civilian market during World War I, and a more affordable motorcycle was designed.

In 1917 a 530 cc F-head V-twin was introduced and the price was dropped to $175. With 7 hp this motorcycle could reach 50 mph and was priced as low as the previous single from Emblem. Wheelbase was 52 inches.

The basic Emblem had an Eclipse clutch and was just one speed, but there was a three-speed version also available. A mechanical oil pump was also optional, and the cartridge spring design of the front fork allowed for 2½ inches of travel. But as customers began to prefer larger machines with more hp and weight, the Emblem motorcycle found an export market for a few years before closing the doors permanently in 1925.

Empire

There were two motor vehicle manufacturers in business concurrently by the name of Empire. The Empire Automobile Company of New York, which began in 1912, had nothing to do with this Empire of Indianapolis, Indiana, which got its start in 1909. The four main investors in the latter were James Allison, Carl Fisher, Robert Hassler and Arthur Newby; all of them were to become successful, not by way of the car they began building, but through another project called the Indianapolis Motor Speedway.

Allison would go on to found an aircraft motor manufacturing company under his name. Fisher was founder of Prest-O-Lite, which, among other things, built an explosive gas self-starter for gasoline motors. The other two men were closely associated with National Vehicle Company of Indianapolis, which would outlast this Empire, not to be confused with yet another Empire Motor Company that lasted only for one year in 1896 at Pittsburgh, Pennsylvania.

The first Empire automobiles of 1909 and 1910 clearly reflected their founders' interest in motor sports in that there were only two models: the Model A Roadster and the Model B Sportster, both powered by a 20 hp four-cylinder motor with chain drive and both priced well under a thousand dollars. However, the men involved were preoccupied with their oval racetrack, especially since the first race on a dirt surface was a disaster with numerous accidents occurring during the first race of 1909. The raceway was paved with bricks by December of that year, and henceforth it became home to one of the most well-known and popular 500-mile auto races in the world.

Meanwhile, the Empire appeared only as a Roadster in 1911, now featuring shaft drive designed by Harry C. Stutz, who immediately went on to design and build his own car. Focusing entirely on making the Indianapolis Motor Speedway a success, the owners of Empire sold their company in 1911. Assembly was moved to Greenville, Pennsylvania, where the remaining Empire cars were renamed Fay after the new company president, Frank Fay. But at the same time a new Empire 25 model was also introduced for 1912 as the company moved back to Indiana, this time to Connersville and the wheel company factory of that name.

By July of 1915 the Empire was back in Indianapolis, and what had been called "The Little Aristocrat" was now powered by a four-cylinder Teetor engine or a six-cylinder Continental engine. For 1918 a Sedan, Touring and Roadster were built and prices ranged from $1360 to $1685 with the six-cylinder motor. As World War I ended the Empire was in financial trouble, and for 1919 the Model 72 was built only as a 25 hp six-cylinder touring car with 120-inch wheelbase. That was the last of the Empire.

Erie

There were a handful of companies that built motor vehicles by the name of Erie in the early days of the industry, but they were unrelated to one another. Once the Erie Cycle & Motor Carriage Company of Anderson, Indiana, was finished experimenting with one-cylinder cars and a steam prototype at the turn of the previous century, the Erie Motor Car Company of Painesville, Ohio, also took the name to build cars from 1916 just until 1919. The last year is included here in that the company was in business during the short period covered and spent most of 1918 building E.M.C. trucks for the war effort.

But there was also the Erie & Sturgis Company of Los Angeles, which built a large self-propelled carriage in 1897. Then there was also Erie Truck Manufacturing, actually located in Erie, Pennsylvania, on Lake Erie.

This Erie company began in 1914 and specialized in building trucks rather than passenger cars. Within a year the company offered 1½-, 2-, 2½- and 3½ -ton models which were powered by Continental four-cylinder engines. Chassis were built in several lengths from 144 inches up to 168 inches. Timken axles were used throughout the model line.

Erie remained in production through the war, then survived the shortages and the postwar recession until 1922. For the last year of production only the 2½-ton model was available. As with many other companies, competition was very tough after World War I, and many small companies succumbed in the early 1920s while others roared off into that decade before the Great Depression had its effects.

THE ERIE TRUCK
Manufactured by
ERIE MOTOR TRUCK MFG. CO., Erie, Pa.

S P E C I F I C A T I O N S

Model	G	Specification of other Models on application
Capacity	2-2½ tons	
Drive	Worm	
Chassis Price	On application	

Motor
H. P. (S.A.E.)   27.23
H. P. (Actual)   40 at 1600 R. P. M.
Cylinders   4 en bloc
Bore   4⅛"
Stroke   5¼"
Wheel Base   150"
Tread Front   58"
Tread Rear   58"
Tires Front   36x4"
Tires Rear   36x4" dual
Frame—Pressed Fish Belly, 6".
Front Axle—I-beam section, Timken bearing.
Rear Axle—Full-floating Timken.
Springs Front—2½x44" semi-elliptic.
Springs Rear—3x56" semi-elliptic.
Carburetor—Stromberg.
Cooling System—Pump and cast radiator.
Oiling System—Pump and splash.
Ignition—Eisemann water-proof H. T.
Control—Left drive, center control.
Clutch—Dry plate disc.
Transmission—Selective, three speeds forward and one reverse.
Brakes—Rear wheels, internal expanding.
Steering Gear—Worm and nut.
Equipment—Lamps, tools, and jack.

Evans (motorcycle)

In 1916 the Cyclemotor Corporation was established in Rochester, New York. This was the city where auto companies such as Cunningham, Selden and Sullivan had begun, so the industrial foundation of the area was already in place when Evans began in 1916.

This area was also a hotbed of activity for motorcycle manufacturers. A list of such companies which had their origins in the State of New York between 1900 and 1925 include the following, mostly very obscure and ephemeral makes: Auto-Bi, Autocyclette, Autoped, Barber, Bowman, Buffalo, Canda, Clement, Curtiss, Cyclemotor, Day, De Long, Edmond, Emblem, Erie, Fleming, Gibson Mon-Auto, Hafelfinger, Hercules, Industrial, Keifer, Kulture, Lewis, Maltby, Marvel, MB, Mears, Mesco, Midget Bi-Car, Monarch, Morgan, Moto-pede, Neracar, Nioga, OK, Pam, Pierce, P-T, Regas, Reliance, Ruggles, SDM, Slattery, Spiral, Starlin, Stratton, Thomas Auto-Bi, Tiger, Widmayer, Williams, and Willis. Nearly all of these builders were out of business before America's entry into the Great War.

The Evans was powered by a two-stroke single-cylinder motor with 120 cc. Its output was 1½ hp and weighing 75 pounds it was capable of 40 mph. Wheelbase was 50 inches. Price was $135 in 1918. The engine drove the rear wheel via belt, and the standard bicycle pedal chain was left intact. Although the Evans was only one step up from a bicycle, the frame was specifically made to hold a streamlined gasoline tank. The Cyclemotor Corporation was no longer in production by 1924.

Excelsior (motorcycle)

In addition to Harley-Davidson and Indian, Excelsior was one of the "big three" motorcycle builders originally as this type of vehicle was developed, evolving from bicycles at the beginning of the previous century. Out of dozens of start-up companies before World War I, Excelsior was also one of the three that lasted into the Great Depression, although it did not survive that era.

Only a few years after Indian and Harley-Davidson (1901 and 1903, respectively) began building their two-wheel machines, Excelsior Supply Company entered the market in 1906 in Chicago, Illinois. But the first series production began in 1908 with a 500 cc single-cylinder motorcycle with pressurized oiling

producing 4 hp and 45 mph. It featured belt drive and had a 56-inch wheelbase. The model had been tested thoroughly, and when three examples were entered in the Chicago-Kokomo Reliability Run, all three received a perfect score.

In 1910 the Excelsior V-twin was first introduced, which was powered by an 820 cc motor that at first produced 8 hp and 45 mph top speed. In 1911 the motor was enlarged to 1000 cc with 10 hp and 60 mph capability. Bicycle manufacturer Arnold-Schwinn & Company bought Excelsior that year without making any changes for 1912.

In 1913, under new management and ownership, the company was renamed Excelsior Motor Manufacturing and Supply. Lee Humiston set a new world record of 100 mph on an Excelsior V-twin at a boardtrack in Los Angeles, California. The U.S. Army began buying Excelsior motorcycles in 1913. Ignaz Schwinn instigated the production of a lightweight two-stroke model for 1914. With competition heating up between the top rivals, Schwinn bought out Henderson Motorcycle Company in 1917, continuing it separately from Excelsior, which discontinued its two-stroke V-twin that year.

The Lightweight two-stroke was also discontinued, and now Schwinn's firm began working on the Henderson four-cylinder motorcycle. The Ultra Power Twin of 1918 had a 15 hp motor and was endowed with a three-speed transmission, automatic compression release on the kick starter, and a generator and electric lights. Price was $265 with magneto, and with battery system an extra $30. Only a few Excelsior motorcycles were used by the military, but the green military paint was used after World War I ended due to abundant inventory.

Excelsior continued to compete in racing, with Indian and Harley-Davidson, the main rivals, far outspending Schwinn and his team. Then in 1920 the tragic death of race rider Bob Perry at a test trial greatly diminished Excelsior's and Henderson's racing ambitions. In 1925 the Super-X with 750 cc and 20 hp was to be the last big development at Excelsior even though it was a breakthrough design in Class C racing and prompted Indian and Harley-Davidson to develop their own 750 cc machines.

After the stock market crash the Schwinn family decided that motorcycle production would not be profitable. The Excelsior brand was discontinued, with the exception of an unrelated revival called Excelsior-Henderson in 1998 at Belle Plaine, Minnesota.

Fageol

Among the early designers and builders of motor vehicles, the Fageol Brothers, William B. and Frank R., as little known as they are today, were famous and successful in their own heyday before World War II and even before World War I. They built their first experimental gasoline-powered car in 1900. They moved to Des Moines, Iowa, where they became auto dealers. They then moved to Oakland, California, where the temptation to manufacture their own vehicles took precedence over their ventures.

With the help of Louis H. Bill, who had helped organize the California Motor Company of San Francisco, the Fageol Motors Company was established, and the first vehicle to roll out of the factory in 1917 with a $12,000 price tag was a touring car on a 145-inch wheelbase, powered by a 125 hp Hall-Scott aviation six-cylinder engine. A second car was a roadster with a 135-inch wheelbase. Extravagance was part of the inspiration. However, just as with other companies at the time, World War I was interrupting business in more ways than one.

One of the key players in the company's functioning was Colonel Elbert J. Hall, who was now preoccupied with the war. Material shortages were a key issue by 1917, as was the lack of manpower, and customers were greatly distracted. Many factories were being diverted for war production. Apparently, some of these factors prevented the Fageol brothers from producing more than two prototypes which were shown at the Chicago Automobile Show. Two other prototypes were built, and all of the cars were sold, one of them to Cuba.

At the end of the war the Fageol brothers switched to a more practical approach in manufacturing motor vehicles in the form of farm tractors. The tractors also had the distinctive dorsal hood vents for which Fageol had obtained a patent. The tractors did not sell well, and the Fageol factory began producing trucks, which were conventional, assembled vehicles rated from 2½-ton to 6-ton capacity. Four-cylinder Waukesha engines were used along with Timken axles. Fageol began building its own transmissions.

The Fageol cabs and fenders were rugged but as simple as possible, avoiding compound curves wherever possible. In the 1920s the model line was expanded to include models from 1½-ton to 5-ton capacity with prices from $3,000 to $5,000. In 1921 Fageol introduced its Safety Coach, a low, wide, multi-door bus intended for cross-country service.

Business picked up and the Thomart Motor Company in Kent, Ohio, was acquired for building the 22- and 29-passenger Safety Coach. ACF-Brill built Fageol buses in Detroit under license. Due to the onset of the Great Depression a merger with Los Angeles-based Moreland was planned, but fell through because of heavy financial losses. Fageol was reorganized and survived until 1938, when all of its assets were sold to Sterling of Milwaukee, and then to T.A. Peterman, who again reorganized the company as Peterbilt.

Federal

This company with the big name got its start in 1910 and lasted a half century. Originally, the founder, M.L. Pulcher, began building trucks under the name of Bailey Motor Truck Company in Detroit, which was soon changed as a marketing strategy. He had already organized the Oakland Motor Car Company in Pontiac, Michigan, in 1907. Pulcher used the term "never an experiment" as his advertising slogan for trucks that were reliable if not innovative. The first Federal was rated at 1-ton and was powered by a four-cylinder Continental engine using a three-speed transmission. Price for chassis was $1,800, but Federal also provided stake with cab, plain stake bed and open express body trucks.

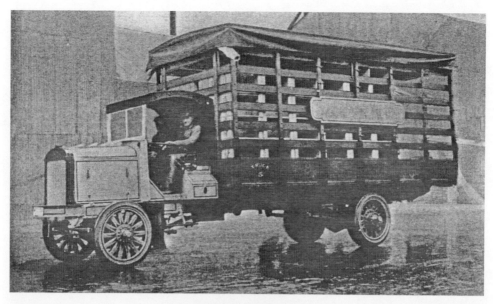

FAGEOL TRUCK

Manufactured by

FAGEOL MOTORS COMPANY, Oakland, Cal.

Model	2½-Ton	3½-4-Ton	5-6-Ton
Capacity Chassis	2½ tons	3½-4 tons	5-6 tons
Drive	Worm	Worm	Worm
Chassis Weight	4,800 lbs.	7,600 lbs.	8,300
Chassis Price	$3,000	$4,000	$5,000
Engine	Waukesha	Waukesha	Waukesha
H. P. (S.A.E.)	28.9	32.4	36.1
H. P. (Actual)	35 at 1100 R.P.M.	40 at 1000 R.P.M.	50 at 1050 R.P.M.
Cylinders	4 in pairs	4 in pairs	4 in pairs
Bore	4¼"	4½"	4¾"
Stroke	5¾"	6¾"	6¾"
Wheel Base	144"—172"	144"—172"—190"	144"—172"—190"
Tread Front	56"	66½"	68⅜"
Tread Rear	58½"	65¾"	69½"
Tires Front	34x4"	36x5"	36x6"
Tires Rear	36x7"	36x5" dual	40x6" dual
Frame	Rolled 6"	Pressed 8"	Pressed 8"

Front Axle—Timken I-beam.
Rear Axle—Timken full-floating.
Springs Front—Semi-elliptic.
Springs Rear—Semi-elliptic.
Carburetor—Zenith L-5.
Cooling System—Pump.
Oiling System—Splash and forced.
Ignition—High Tension magneto.
Control—Left drive, gear levers center.
Clutch—Dry plate.
Transmission—Brown-Lipe Selective, three speeds.
Brakes—Timken Duplex rear.
Steering Gear—Worm and nut.
Equipment—Seat riser and lazy back upholstered in leather, built in tool boxes, side and tail lamps (oil), Stewart mechanical horn, Stewart-Warner vacuum system on 3½ and 5 ton, Fageol patented automatic spring lubrication, roll high grade tools, ratchet screw jack, oil can, wheel wrenches. Chassis finished in priming coats, Fageol olive drab.

FEDERAL TRUCKS
Manufactured by
FEDERAL MOTOR TRUCK CO., Detroit, Mich.

S P E C I F I C A T I O N S

Model	S	M	P	W
Capacity	1 ton	1½ tons	2 tons	3½ tons
Drive	Worm	Worm	Worm	Worm
Chassis Price	On application	On application	On application	On application
Motor				
H. P. (S.A.E.)	19.6	27.2	27.2	28.9
H. P. (Actual)	25	33	33	40
Cylinders	4 en bloc	4 en bloc	4 en bloc	4 en bloc
Bore	3½"	4⅛"	4⅛"	4¼"
Stroke	5⅛"	5¼"	5¼"	5½"
Wheel Base	132"	120" and 144"	144" and 168"	108", 156", 180"
Tread Front	56"	56"	56"	66½"
Tread Rear	58"	58¼"	58¼"	67¾"
Tires Front	34x3" solid or 35x5" pneu.	36x3½"	36x4"	36x5"
Tires Rear	34x4" solid or 35x5" pneu.	36x5"	36x4" dual or 36x7"	36x5" dual or 36x8"
Frame	Pressed	Pressed	Pressed	Rolled
Front Axle—I-beam, Elliott.				
Rear Axle	Semi-floating, square	Full-floating, round	Full-floating, round	Full-floating, square
Springs Front—Semi-elliptic.				
Springs Rear—Semi-elliptic.				
Carburetor	Zenith O4	Stromberg M	Stromberg M	Zenith O5
Cooling System—Pump.				
Oiling System	Forced feed	Pump circulated	Pump circulated	Forced feed
Ignition—Eisemann magneto.				
Control—Left drive, center control.				
Clutch	Dry plate	Cone	Cone	Dry plate
Transmission	Selective, three speeds forward, one reverse	Selective, three speeds forward, one reverse	Selective, three speeds forward, one reverse	Selective, four speeds forward, one reverse

Brakes—Internal, expanding rear wheels.
Steering Gear—Worm and wheel.
Equipment—Seat, front fenders, three oil lamps, jack, horn, oil can, tools, extra demountable rim with pneumatic tires on Model S.

For 1911 the Model C was powered by a 28.9 hp four-cylinder motor using a leather-faced cone clutch and three-speed transmission. This type of clutch was not unusual in this era, but by that time it was antiquated and manufacturers were developing more durable materials which did not rely on leather or fabric facing. The open delivery sold for $2,200. One good idea Federal employed was dual brakes on the rear wheels at a time when most vehicles did not have any front brakes due to linkage design feasibility problems and other complexities before hydraulic systems were incorporated.

"Pulling yourself up with your own bootstraps" was how the press described wheel winches introduced by Federal in 1912 at a time when getting stuck in the mud was a common occurrence. Before World War I began, 1,000 Federal trucks had been manufactured, and with a name like Federal it was no surprise that the U.S. Post Office bought a small fleet. Sales representatives were located across the country for the company, a crucial strategy, with as much competition as there was in this era.

In 1915 Federal introduced its first worm drive truck which was rated at 1½-ton, the axle being provided by Timken-David Brown. This was the Model J, which had an engine governor limiting the truck to 15 mph, normal operating speed for a truck in those days. By 1916 the model line was expanded up to 3½-ton capacity, and the factory was enlarged to keep up with demand. Both chain drive and cone clutches were discontinued.

By the time the U.S. entered the war, Federal introduced models on both ends of the line, with a 1-ton Model S and a 5-ton Model X, so there were five capacities of trucks available, often still referred to as "commercial cars." Federal's motors now had five main bearings and a gear pump for circulating oil, worm drive from Timken-Detroit was provided and driveshafts were tubular to save weight; all important design innovations for durability and efficiency. In 1918 Federal introduced short wheelbase truck tractors for pulling four-wheel and semi-trailers, and this included the Heavy-Duty model rated at 7-ton capacity with semi-trailer. For some reason the five-ton was shown in the photo of the catalog, but neither of the heaviest models were listed.

After World War I the model line remained essentially the same with different designations and prices ranging from $1,900 to $3,475. In 1920 pneumatic tires were introduced on the lightest SD model. The following year a delivery van was offered, basing top speed on the pneumatic five-inch cord tires at a time when this was the limiting factor. By 1923 a total of 27,000 trucks and bus chassis had been built by Federal.

The Federal-Knight became the new offering for 1924. The Knight engine was being accepted by numerous companies by this time and built under license. In 1926 a six-cylinder motor was offered by Federal. Federal stayed in business in the Depression and World War II, finally succumbing to the bottom line in 1959.

Fiat

Although the name "Fiat" is closely associated with a company in Italy by that name, the company's vehicles were built under license in the United States from 1910 to 1918 and were known as American Fiat. Before being assembled at Poughkeepsie, New York, Fiat began building cars and trucks in Torino, Italy, in 1899.

O.H. Keep was the first man to become an importer of Fiat to the United States in 1901, after which the firm of Hollander & Tangeman took over in 1902 under the name of Hol-Tan. The company also marketed a Hol-Tan auto which was actually built by Moon. When the licensing agreement began, Hol-Tan lost the franchise to distribute Fiats to the notion that they would now be built in America.

There was enough confidence about the Fiat designed and first built in Italy that prominent men got in on the licensing agreement, and Ben J. Eichberg, a diamond importer, became president of American Fiat, while the vice-presidency was taken by J.S. Josephs, with the general manager position in the hands of Albert E. Schaaf from Pope-

Toledo. Further listing of personnel included factory manager T.C. Collings from Lozier, and the treasurer was John Laurie Treas, who was also employed by the *Horseless Age Magazine*, a connection that would possibly help with somewhat positive press coverage.

The Poughkeepsie factory specialized in the large Fiat models 53, 54 and 55, although in size they were not consecutive. All were powered by four-cylinder motors in 1910 with a six-cylinder Model 56 exclusively built for the United States market. Every American Fiat sold meant royalties paid to Fiat in Italy. But it was not just a matter of simple assembly in New York. Only a few parts were imported — nearly all were manufactured in the United States, and all cars remained in the U.S., thereby not disrupting exports from Italy to other countries. Therefore, American Fiat was truly an American product, at least for the while.

Armored cars were built as American Fiat model 55 during World War I, and fifty of these were discovered to be sidetracked to England when their chassis were identified after bodies were replaced and the cars sold as passenger vehicles in 1920. Fiats from Italy were imported between 1910 and 1914 before the war began in Europe. It was the disruption of war that ended the importation, not politics, since Italy was on the Allied side in World War I. About one-fourth of the Fiats in the United States during that period were imported, the rest built at the Poughkeepsie factory.

Fiat entered racing in the U.S. as well as in Europe before World War I with the most notable driver being David Bruce-Brown. It was also at this time that Fiat sued several American companies, including Oldsmobile, for infringement of its radiator design. This did not move forward as the war continued and America entered it in full force. By February of 1918 Duesenberg bought the Poughkeepsie factory for its machinery, which was moved

F I A T

501 FIFTH AVENUE
NEW YORK CITY

Price $6500
Seven-Passenger Touring . . . 5500
Seven-Passenger Limousine . . . 6500

FIAT BROUGHAM—E-17

COLOR	Optional		RADIATOR	Cellular
SEATING CAPACITY .	Seven		COOLING	Water pump
POSITION OF DRIVER .	Right side		IGNITION	High tension magneto and storage battery
WHEELBASE	140 inches			
GAUGE	56 inches			
WHEELS	Wood		STARTING SYSTEM . .	Two unit
FRONT TIRES	35 x 5 inches		STARTER OPERATED .	Gear to fly wheel
REAR TIRES	35 x 5 inches		LIGHTING SYSTEM . .	Electric
SERVICE BRAKE . . .	Expanding on rear wheels		VOLTAGES	Twelve
EMERGENCY BRAKE .	Expanding on rear wheels		WIRING SYSTEM . . .	Double
			GASOLINE SYSTEM . .	Pressure
CYLINDERS	Four		CLUTCH	Multiple disc in oil
ARRANGED	Vertically		TRANSMISSION . . .	Selective sliding
CAST.	En bloc		GEAR CHANGES . . .	Four forward, one reverse
HORSEPOWER	42.03 (N.A.C.C. Rating)		DRIVE	Spiral bevel
BORE AND STROKE .	5⅛ x 6¾ inches		REAR AXLE	Semi-floating
LUBRICATION	Splash with circulating pump		STEERING GEAR . . .	Worm and gear

In addition to above specifications, price includes speedometer, ammeter, voltmeter, clock, tire pump, electric horn and demountable rims.

to Elizabeth, New Jersey. Manufacture of Fiats in America was never attempted again, and Fiats continued to be imported into the United States until 1980, when maintenance, repair and supply of parts became too much of a burden on Fiat in Italy.

Ford

One of only a few surviving and truly enduring motor vehicle companies in the United States as of this writing, it was almost single-handedly started by Henry Ford with some financial backing, according to the historical record that has continued for over a century by the very successful Ford company and Ford family. However, there is no dispute that at the age of 33 Henry Ford built his first experimental vehicle in 1896, the Quadricycle, while still in the employ of Thomas Edison. Having seen his neighbor Charles Brady King drive around Detroit in the car he had fabricated earlier in 1896 may well have prompted Ford to complete his own first car in the summer of that same year. Ford had already built and then tested a gasoline motor in his kitchen sink five years earlier.

Half the wall had to be removed for Ford to drive out of his brick garage because the Quadricycle was too large to fit through the door. This is not an apocryphal detail of his early work, but perhaps it indicates that Ford may not have expected his Quadricycle to run. In fact, it did so considerably well, using a two-cylinder four-stroke motor with a combination chain and belt drive.

Henry Ford toured the countryside with his wife Clara and five-year-old son Edsel before another neighbor named Charles Ainsley gave Ford $200 for the Quadricycle. Ford used the money to build his second car, which was finished by early 1898. By that time men with money were paying attention to Ford's efforts, and soon Detroit's mayor William C. Maybury and investor William H. Murphy

joined forces with Henry Ford to form the Detroit Automobile Company, which resulted in the disorganized manufacture of at least eleven cars in addition to a race car which beat Winton at the Grosse Point Race Track in 1901. But the investors that Ford had found did not share his enthusiasm for motor sports, nor did they realize the power of free publicity. By the end of 1901 a new company called the Henry Ford Company was formed with several investors.

Henry Ford's famous mass production factory had yet to materialize, and so, disillusioned with Ford's slow progress, the backers brought in a consultant named Henry Martyn Leland. This apparently gave Ford such a start that he quit the company for a payoff of $900 and an agreement that Leland and his cohorts would not use Ford's name. This was no special burden on Henry Leland as he got into the business of designing and building the Cadillac (and later the Lincoln).

At the same time Henry Ford joined up with Tom Cooper and built two more race cars, one of them being the 999 four-cylinder job that displaced 1153 cubic inches and reached a speed of over 60 mph on a one-mile track at Grosse Pointe in 1903. Barney Oldfield had started as a bicycle racer and would be the first to break the 60 mph and 100 mph records in an internal combustion vehicle.

The year 1903 was also the year Ford established his third company with the investment of coal baron Alexander Young Malcolmson. The first car Ford began to produce in series was the Model A (the first of two Model A cars), which sold for $750. In the first fifteen months 1700 were built and shipped.

However, Ford had a problem. He had not obtained an A.L.A.M. license to manufacture automobiles in the United States under the Selden Patent, which gave a monopoly to the owners, who were also electric vehicle manufacturers (along with royalties being paid to

SPECIFICATIONS

Model	TT
Capacity	1-ton
Drive	Worm
Chassis Price	600
Motor	
H.P.	20
Cylinder	4
Bore	3 ?
Stroke	4
Displacement	176.7 cid
Wheel Base	124"
Tires Front	30" × 3"
Tires Rear	32" × 3½"

Frame — Pressed steel
Front Axle — Drop forged
Rear axle — Ford worm drive
Carburetor — Ford
Cooling system — Thermo-syphoning
Oiling system — Splash
Ignition — Ford magneto
Clutch — Dry disc
Transmission — Two-speed planetary
Brakes — On rear drums
Steering Gear — Ford
Equipment — Electric lighting system, battery, seat, horn, tools.

George Selden, the patentee). Ford had applied and had been denied a license, so he brazenly continued building cars. A.L.A.M. sued, and the ensuing litigation gave Ford plenty of good press for seven years as being the David fighting Goliath.

In the end Ford won, but not until 1911 and not without an appeal. The Ford-Selden litigation has been called the most significant lawsuit in the history of the American automotive industry. Selden and the owners of his patent, closely affiliated with the electric vehicle industry, lost millions of dollars. In addition to that, the electric self-starter was invented and introduced at the same time, greatly diminishing one of the last advantages of electric vehicles.

Ford continued building cars as the Selden lawsuit went on, producing a Model B and a Model C, which were quite different from each other, although the Model C was very similar to the Model A. The Model B used a four-cylinder motor, had shaft drive and was priced at $2000. Playing along with investor Malcolmson's whims, Ford built a two-cylinder Model F in 1905 which sold for $1200, and then a six-cylinder Model K that appeared at the end of that year.

During this period the Dodge Brothers, who were superior machinists and great businessmen, were building many of the major components for Ford, including engines and transmissions. Ford bought out Malcolmson, who wanted to remain in the high-priced field, whereas Ford wanted to focus on a low-priced car. He also began building his own motors and eventually all other components. The first really affordable car that Ford introduced was the Model N, which sold at a lower price than the Curved Dash Oldsmobile, the best-selling car of that period.

By 1906 Ford was selling 8000 cars a year, and 90 percent of them were low-priced models, which were also available as the Model R and Model S in 1907 for $750 and $700, respectively. It was in 1908 that the Model T arrived, perhaps changing the history of the automotive industry, not just in America but around the world. That Henry Ford had been behind the idea of the Model T is no secret, but what is less known is that there were five men who were instrumental in its coming to fruition: metallurgist Childe Harold Wills, entrepreneur Walter Flanders (who would go on to build the E-M-F) and engineers Joseph Galamb, Charles Sorenson and Jimmy Smith.

So many decades later now, the first Model T's specifications may be fairly obscure and forgotten, but in 1908 the 100-inch wheelbase little car was revolutionary with its performance and reliability given its price tag. The L-head four-cylinder motor gave 20 hp and had a simple two-speed planetary transmission which allowed it to reach 45 mph on a good day. It got 25 miles per gallon, which at the time was quite satisfactory. The "Tin Lizzie," as it was affectionately called, didn't get into total mass production until August of 1913, when the moving assembly line was activated at Ford.

As was the case with many wealthy and powerful men, Henry Ford had his enemies and they were not few and far between. His generous $5 per day wages introduced in January of 1914 was in itself enough to infuriate his competitors and other employers in the industry who were not as generous or cavalier. For that year the rest of the entire American auto industry produced 200,000 cars while Ford produced 300,000 Model T's. It was enough to make any rival envious, although Ford's attitudes about controlling labor and his published anti–Semitic views were enough to make him a hated man in various circles as well.

During the war, Ford Model T's were used throughout many countries in various ways from staff cars to ambulances to improvised armored cars. In 1917, as America entered the war, Ford also finally produced a light truck, which was at least partially in response to the numerous after-market kits that were sold to transform the standard Model T into a light truck. Before war's end Ford began building two-man tanks using Model T engines, but the contract was terminated as the war suddenly ended.

Aside from a couple of early ventures to build delivery vehicles, it might be perplexing why Ford would not enter the light truck field for nearly an entire decade after the Model T was introduced. Part of the answer was that there was plenty of competition already building light trucks, and the Model T was selling so well that trying to enter the light truck field was still a gamble. But so many after-market conversion kits were being sold that Ford introduced the Model TT in 1917. It was derived from some of the conversions in that the Model TT, rated at 1-ton, used worm gear shaft drive and had solid rubber tires.

The Model TT also had a larger 10-gallon gas tank and dual brake system along with a longer wheelbase at 124 inches. Ford had produced 100,000 Model TT trucks by the end of 1919. Price started at $600 and dropped to $550 in 1919.

By 1922 one million Model T Fords were manufactured. It was the year Ford would acquire Lincoln. By the end of the model line in 1928 half of all cars in America were Ford Model T make and model, built over the previous twenty years. In 1928 Ford interrupted manufacturing to retool for the company's second Model A. Ford would introduce a flathead V-8 in 1932 and kept prices down to survive the Depression.

Ford's styling changed dramatically during the 1930s, keeping up with the trends of industry and holding on to its market share up to World War II, when it would produce half of all Jeeps, in addition to other major contributions to the war effort.

Henry Ford would live through World War II until 1948, but his son Edsel died five years earlier. After the war Henry II, Edsel's son, took over the helm, helping resurrect and continue the company his grandfather had started. The company's colorful and illustrious history has continued since the early days but from this point is beyond the scope of this discussion.

Forschler

Of the very few motor vehicle manufacturers that existed in Deep South, the Philip Forschler Wagon Company started out in New Orleans, Louisiana. Compared to the Atlantic States, the Northeast and the Midwest, there was not enough industry to support much large-scale manufacturing, and yet there were those entrepreneurs who went ahead despite the odds of success, the advantage being there were few competitors.

By 1914 the Forschler Company was offering 1½-ton and 3-ton trucks powered by four-cylinder motors spring mounted on separate sub-chassis. This was not unusual practice at the time when engine vibration was not inconsiderable and engine mounts could not dampen mechanically-induced shaking. Double chain drive and a three-speed transmission were also fairly typical at the time, although switching to worm-gear shaft-drive was progressive for Forschler in 1917.

As the war ended Forschler was reorganized as the Forschler Motor Truck Manufacturing, Incorporated, staying in New Orleans and supplying local customers with a small number of trucks from ¾-ton to 2-ton capacity. The company was fading fast during the postwar recession, just as with other small companies, but Forschler still listed itself in various catalogs as a manufacturer. That meant that Philip Forschler and his investors were reluctant to file for bankruptcy, but by the end of 1924 manufacturing had ceased for good.

FORSCHLER TRUCKS

Manufactured by

FORSCHLER MOTOR TRUCK MFG. CO., Inc., New Orleans, La.

Model	SO	AO	AXO	BO
Capacity	¾ ton	1 ton	1½ tons	2 tons
Drive	Worm	Worm	Worm	Worm
Chassis Weight	1,500 lbs.	3,200 lbs.	3,600 lbs.	4,200 lbs.
Chassis Price	$1,100	$1,900	$2,200	$2,500
Engine	Le Roi	Continental	Continental	Continental
H. P. (S.A.E.)	17	19.6	19.6	27.2
H. P. (Actual)	22	25	30	35
Cylinders	4 en bloc	4 en bloc	4 en bloc	4 en bloc
Bore	3⅛″	3½″	3½″	4⅛″
Stroke	4½″	5″	5″	5¼″
Wheel Base	120″	138″	138″	142″
Tread Front	56″	56″	56″	56″
Tread Rear	56″	56″	56″	56″
Tires Front	32x2½″	34x3″	34x3″	34x4″
Tires Rear	32x3″	34x4″	34x5″	34x5″

Frame—Rolled channel steel.
Front Axle—I-beam.
Rear Axle—Sheldon semi-floating.
Springs Front—Elliptic and semi-elliptic.
Springs Rear—Quarter and semi-elliptic.
Carburetor—Zenith.
Cooling System—Pump.
Oiling System—Splash and pump.
Ignition—Magneto.
Control—Left drive, center control.

Clutch	Dry plate	Dry plate	Dry plate	Disc in oil
Transmission	Detroit Selective, 3 speeds forward and 1 reverse	Fuller Selective, 3 speeds forward and 1 reverse	Fuller Selective, 3 speeds forward and 1 reverse	Fuller Selective, 3 speeds forward and 1 reverse

Brakes—Enclosed expanding rear axle drum.
Steering Gear—Screw and nut.
Equipment—Set of tools and governor.

Four Wheel Drive and Four Wheel Steer

This short-lived enterprise in Beech Creek, Pennsylvania, that started in 1915 should not be confused with the earlier Four Wheel Drive Company of Rockford, Illinois, which emerged in 1905, nor should be confused with FWD of Clintonville, Wisconsin. At the turn of the previous century many considered it nearly impossible to design an efficient and durable system to drive all four wheels, let alone steer them front and back. The men in Rockford gave up by 1907.

Charles Jeffery, son of Thomas Jeffery of Rambler fame in Wisconsin, oversaw the design of the 2-ton Jeffery Quad in 1913, and it became the contemporary of the Four Wheel Drive (FWD) trucks that appeared in Clintonville, Wisconsin, at about the same time. The Beech Creek truck was the design of machinist Paul J. Smith of Galeton, Pennsylvania.

Smith obtained two patents pertaining to dual drive shafts from a central gear-box and independent fully-floating axles fore and aft. A wealthy lumberman named William H. Ward saw the value of a truck of this type for work in the field and forest and became a major investor. The prototype was completed in 1915 using a 40 hp Pittsburgh four-cylinder engine and a Philadelphia transmission. The entire town of 800 was treated to a demonstration drive and many local men invested in the enterprise. George F. Hess became president after a few changes in the list of affiliated characters.

The 3-ton truck had four-wheel drive and four-wheel steer, the latter of which was built by the DuBois Iron Works. Price was set at $3,950, and two were sold in 1916. In 1918 Beech Creek still advertised its out-of-the-ordinary truck with the long name, and the key players remained as an auto dealership after World War I. The only other four-wheel-drive and four-wheel-steer truck being manufactured in the U.S.A. at the time was the even more obscure Golden West (Robinson) of Sacramento, California. As a builder the Beech Creek Truck and Auto Company was no longer in business after the war.

Franklin

Franklin's claim to fame was its air-cooled engine. It wasn't unusual that the company's name arrived from its key investor, Herbert H. Franklin, a successful owner of a die casting enterprise in Syracuse, New York. But the actual design of the motor was a creation of John Wilkinson, who also found additional financial backing from Alexander T. Brown so that by 1902 a Franklin car was shown to the public.

That an air-cooled engine was employed in the first Franklin Runabout was in line with a number of early auto manufacturers at a time when small motors were employed to power light "horseless buggies." The Franklin engine was also a two-cycle engine with overhead-valve design and was mounted transversely and coupled to a two-speed planetary transmission, very similar to that of the later Ford Model T. The combination of shaft-drive, wood body and full-elliptic spring suspension made the vehicle modern in some ways and not-so-modern in others. As opposed to relying on movement of air stream as the vehicle traveled to cool the engine, a gear-driven fan was used to keep the air moving continuously.

In 1904 the company sponsored a New York-to-San Francisco publicity run, which ended up taking 33 days, beating the Winton record by nearly half the time. By 1905 a commercial vehicle was introduced with the same four-cylinder motor but mounted longitudinally. The Franklin ¾-ton light truck was easily distinguished along with the passenger cars, which sported the same barrel-shaped hoods. The fan was incorporated with the

FOUR WHEEL DRIVE AND FOUR WHEEL STEER

Manufactured by

BEECH CREEK TRUCK & AUTO CO., Beech Creek, Pa.

Model   B
Capacity   3 tons
Drive   Bevel gear
Chassis Price $3,850
Engine
  H. P. (S.A.E.)   28.9
  H. P. (Actual)   32.6
Cylinders   4 in pairs
  Bore   4¼"
  Stroke   5¾"
Wheel Base   132"
Tread Front   56"
Tread Rear   56"
Tires Front   36x6"
Tires Rear   36x6"
Frame—Channel, rolled.
Front Axle—Beech Creek, full-floating.
Rear Axle—Beech Creek, full-floating.
Springs Front—Parallel and transverse, semi-elliptic.
Springs Rear—Parallel and transverse, semi-elliptic.
Carburetor—Kingston.
Cooling System—Centrifugal pump.
Oiling System—Circulating splash.
Ignition—Eisemann high tension magneto.
Control—Right drive, center control.
Clutch—Borg & Beck, dry plate.
Transmission—Selective, six speeds.
Brakes—Double, contracting on transmission; emergency, contracting on rear wheels.
Steering Gear—Screw and nut type, two speeds, patented.
Equipment—Prest-o-lite head lights, oil side and tail lights, hand horn, and complete tool equipment.

**II. H. FRANKLIN
MANUFACTUR-
ING COMPANY**

SYRACUSE
NEW YORK

Price	$2050
Roadster	2000
Four-Passenger Roadster	2050
Sedan	2950
Brougham	2900
Limousine	3200
Town Car	3200
Cabriolet	2850

FRANKLIN TOURING—SERIES 9

COLOR	Brewster green		BORE AND STROKE	3¼ x 4 inches
SEATING CAPACITY	Five		LUBRICATION	Force feed
POSITION OF DRIVER	Left side		COOLING	Air
WHEELBASE	115 inches		IGNITION	Distributor and storage battery
GAUGE	56 inches			
WHEELS	Wood		STARTING SYSTEM	Single unit
FRONT TIRES	32 x 4 inches		STARTER OPERATED	Chain to crank shaft
REAR TIRES	32 x 4 inches, anti-skid		LIGHTING SYSTEM	Electric
			VOLTAGES	Twelve
SERVICE BRAKE	Contracting on transmission drum		WIRING SYSTEM	Double
			GASOLINE SYSTEM	Vacuum
EMERGENCY BRAKE	Contracting on rear wheels		CLUTCH	Multiple disc in oil
			TRANSMISSION	Selective sliding
CYLINDERS	Six		GEAR CHANGES	Three forward, one reverse
ARRANGED	Horizontally			
CAST	Separately		DRIVE	Spiral bevel
HORSEPOWER	25.35 (N.A.C.C. Rating)		REAR AXLE	Semi-floating
			STEERING GEAR	Worm and gear

In addition to above specifications, price includes top, top hood, windshield, speedometer, circuit indicator, clock, tire pump and electric horn.

flywheel in 1910, an inexpensive design used as an effective compromise. The full-elliptic suspension was credited by Franklin's marketers with making the non-dismountable pneumatic tires good for 20,000 miles, if they didn't receive a puncture, which would be a very unlikely non-occurrence at the time.

By 1912 the 1-ton Franklin truck was no longer produced, but the company stayed in the commercial field by producing a taxi, which had the appearance of a Renault. As many, if not most, motor vehicle manufacturers moved away from air-cooled two-cycle engines, Franklin made it a company honor to continue making engineering progress within those constraints. By the time the war began Franklin was using only six-cylinder air-cooled engines which featured aluminum pistons. The company made a point of entering races and economy runs. One such outing in 1917 showed a fleet of 175 Franklin cars averaging 40.3 miles per gallon. By now only limousines stayed in the commercial vehicle side of output at the Franklin factory in Syracuse, while the company built mostly sedans.

As America entered the war, production at Franklin was a healthy 9000 cars a year. Wins at Los Angeles-to-Phoenix and public relations stunts such as a San Francisco-to-Walla Walla, Washington, run using low gear attracted the right kind of attention. But the styling was lagging behind and by 1923 investors, dealers and customers were begging for a new look, which would include a faux radiator, to which Wilkinson was so opposed he resigned in protest. The Franklin for 1925 was called the Series II, and not only included a false radiator but also included a new sport runabout and boattail speedster. The new coachwork stylist was Frank de Causse, whose new designs were built by such coachwork builders as Brunn, Derham, Holbrook, Locke and Willoughby.

Raymond Dietrich took over after de Causse's death in 1928. "Cannonball" Baker took the Franklin 11B on very successful endurance races including Pike's Peak. However, as soon as the stock market crash of 1929 descended on Syracuse, production went from 14,000 cars per year to 2,000 just two years later. Going ahead with plans to build a V-12 car just as the Depression set in was the last gasp for Franklin. A few prototypes were built, which kept the doors open only until 1934.

Fulton

The barrel shape of the hood and oval radiator along with unusual color schemes and decorative advertising made the Fulton truck stand out from the crowd. At first it was built by the Clyde Motor Truck, but within a year of company start-up in 1917 the firm's name was changed to the Fulton Motor Truck Company of Farmington, Long Island, New York.

William F. Melhuish was president of Clyde and then Fulton and planned on building 1000 medium trucks per year. The first was 1½-ton powered by a 36 hp four-cylinder L-head motor and used a three-speed Detroit transmission. Price was $1090 for the first year of manufacture. The distinctive radiator with its large upper flange was also practical in that it had a seven-gallon capacity.

Fulton trucks were not used by the military in World War I. By 1919 the price had increased to $1,850, and a 2-ton model was introduced for $2,350. Fulton built a right-hand steer passenger car in 1920, and although it was intended for export, it remained only as a prototype despite positive press coverage when journalists noticed the car circling around New York City.

Manufacturing faded out in 1923, but the company offered trucks for sale until 1925, possibly units from leftover parts. Prices had been reduced to $1,495 and $2,135, respectively. The Model A was rated at 1-ton and

THE FULTON TRUCK
Manufactured by
FULTON MOTOR TRUCK CO., Farmingdale, L. I., N. Y.

Model	FX
Capacity	1½ tons
Drive	Internal gear
Chassis Weight	3,100 lbs.
Chassis Price	$1,420
Engine	Herchell Spillman
H. P. (S.A.E.)	16.9
H. P. (Actual)	36 to 38
Cylinders	4 en bloc
Bore	3¼″
Stroke	5″
Wheel Base	136″
Tread Front	56½″
Tread Rear	56½″
Tires Front	34x3½″
Tires Rear	34x5″

Frame—Pressed steel channel.
Front Axle—I-beam, Elliott knuckle.
Rear Axle—Russell round section.
Springs Front—Semi-elliptic.
Springs Rear—Semi-elliptic.
Carburetor—Carter LO-1.
Cooling System—Thermo-syphon.
Oiling System—Splash, forced feed to bearings.
Ignition—Magneto.
Control—Left-hand drive, center control.
Clutch—Borg & Beck dry plate.
Transmission—Detroit Gear & Machine Co. Selective, three speeds.
Brakes—Band and shoe rear wheels.
Steering Gear—Screw and nut.
Equipment—Lamps, tool kit and jack.

the Model C was rated at 2-ton, both being powered by four-cylinder motors.

Despite an emphasis on styling and a good reputation for durability, Fulton trucks could not compete with numerous other manufacturers, once the postwar recession took its toll and war surplus trucks took away business from small companies such as this one.

F. W.D.

Usually abbreviated to FWD from Four Wheel Drive, among the most influential and successful early truck builders, which started out as a two-man machine shop, was the Badger Four Wheel Drive Auto Company of Clintonville, Wisconsin (the Badger State), not to be confused with other previously-mentioned "four-wheel-drive" firms.

Otto Zachow and his brother-in-law, William Besserdich organized their automobile company in 1910. Their patents went further in improving on the 4 × 4 concept with double-Y U-joint design mounted in a forged ball. The invention was to propel their company, if not them personally, to fame and fortune.

The first FWD was nicknamed "The Battleship" even though it was a large, open passenger car. But soon large military contracts would arrive as the war in Europe exploded and the Quartermaster Corps was sent to chase Pancho Villa into the Mexican desert. The FWD truck was quickly found to be the best vehicle for off-road work, in addition to the Nash Quad, which had actually been the Jeffrey, until Charles Jeffery sold the company following his father's sudden death.

FWD trucks were sent to Europe in large numbers even before America entered the war. Both France and Britain purchased thousands of the trucks, creating a demand to double production and double it again so that other companies were engaged to build the FWD

Model B truck under license; Kissel, Mitchell and Premier, to be specific. However, in the meantime Zachow and Besserdich had both sold the rights to their patents in order to make ends meet, and they both lost out on the windfall even after attempting a legal suit.

Besserdich went on to help organize the Oshkosh Truck Company and Zachow returned to his machine shop near downtown Clintonville, a small city to this day. There was such a labor shortage during World War I in the central Wisconsin area, women for the first time became test drivers and held many other jobs at FWD.

The FWD was rated at 3-ton capacity and was powered by a four-cylinder Wisconsin engine using a three-speed transmission. By the time the war ended some 15,000 FWD trucks had been produced, the most 4 × 4s produced by any one company at the time in the world. About half of the 30,000 surplus trucks after the war were FWD, so the government either distributed them or sold them to local municipalities and city governments.

FWD trucks made excellent snowplows and were used often in road building. The FWD company thrived on spare and replacement parts during the 1920s while continuing to refine their basic designs. For public relations FWD developed an Indy 500 racing car in 1932 which was four-wheel-drive and powered by a Miller air-cooled V-8. It came in fourth that year but saw little success after that. The FWD racing program ended in 1953 after some Pike's Peak attempts.

FWD became a multi-axle-drive engineering specialty company during the 1950s with such vehicles as the giant Teracruzer intended for the Arctic snow or desert sand. Human refuse and cement trucks also became the specialty at FWD, but what saved the company economically is the purchase of Seagrave fire engines, which keep the factory busy as of this writing.

THE F. W. D. TRUCK

Manufactured by

FOUR WHEEL DRIVE AUTO CO., Clintonville, Wis.

S P E C I F I C A T I O N S

Model   **B**
Capacity   3 tons
Drive   F.W.D. Bevel gear
Chassis Price $4,000
Motor
  H. P. (S.A.E.) 36.1
  H. P. (Actual) 45 at 1100 R.P.M.
  Cylinders 4 in pairs
  Bore $4\frac{3}{4}''$
  Stroke $5\frac{1}{2}''$
Wheel Base 124"
Tread Front 56"
Tread Rear 56"
Tires Front 36x6"
Tires Rear 36x6"
Frame—Pressed.
Front Axle—F. W. D.
Rear Axle—F. W. D.
Springs Front—Semi-elliptic; special design.
Springs Rear—Platform.
Carburetor—Stromberg.
Cooling System—Thermo-syphon with centrifugal pump and high-speed fan.
Oiling System—Force and splash.
Ignition—Magneto.
Control—Right drive, right control.
Clutch—Multiple disc, Hele-Shaw.
Transmission—Selective, three speeds forward and one reverse.
Brakes—External on transmission and rear wheels.
Steering Gear—Screw and nut.
Equipment—Complete set of tools, tool box, oil cans, horn, hub cap, motor and magneto
    wrenches, two oil side and one oil tail lamp.

Gabriel

Cleveland, Ohio, became an industrial center soon after it was settled by the pioneers of the North American continent. It was filled with factories, including one run by a small company, W.H. Gabriel Carriage and Wagon Company, that had been in business since 1851. It became the Gabriel Auto Company and tried to succeed in building cars beginning in 1910. When that didn't go well, even though the Gabriel car was highly reliable according to test results at the time, the company switched to light truck manufacturing in 1913.

With their headquarters in downtown Cleveland, the company officers announced they would also be representatives of K-R-I-T cars and Grabowsky trucks from Michigan. But it was all too tempting to build one's own truck at the time when nearly all the components save chassis rails and sheet metal cabs were available off the shelf from one company or another. Grabowsky was absorbed by Rapid and became part of GM.

In the meantime Gabriel offered a model line of trucks through World War I. which included 1-, 2- and 3½-ton capacities, all powered by different size four-cylinder Buda engines and Brown-Lipe transmissions. At one point a 4-ton truck was listed as the company tried to survive the postwar recession.

Gabriel trucks did not sell well after World War I, and although the company was listed into 1920 only a few of the last vehicles were built that year by this company.

Garford

Garford began as the Federal Manufacturing Company in Elyria, Ohio, building automobile components starting in 1903. Finding success in the new auto industry led the company officers to expand into auto manufacturing. Arthur L. Garford had started Fed-

eral Manufacturing and got into a partnership with Studebaker in Indiana.

With a contract to assemble and sell Studebakers, Garford showed its own two cars in 1907, prompting Studebaker to make legal threats. Garford built New York "taximeter cabs" at a time when the business of "taxicabs," "taxis" and "cabs" was just evolving. Briefly, Garford distinguished its Studebakers from its Studebaker-Garfords, which became just plain Garfords in 1910 when the contract with Studebaker expired.

In 1911 Garford built limousines, and in 1912 the passenger car division was acquired by Willys-Overland. The truck division continued as Garford after 1913 with its own marque and logo. The first Garford trucks were COE design and were rated at 5-ton capacity using a four-speed transmission with dual chain drive. In 1915 the company moved to Lima, Ohio, and was organized as the Garford Motor Truck Company.

By 1916 the model line consisted of 1-, 1½- and 2-ton conventional trucks in addition to the heavier COE types. For 1917 there were also three truck tractors for towing two- and four-wheel trailers. The U.S. military bought Garford trucks during World War I, and some were used for troop transport.

Garford trucks were transformed into half-tracks using Holt crawler components. Also, the Garford factory was contracted to build 1,000 Liberty trucks for the war effort. The company survived the postwar slowdown and dropped its COE trucks by 1920. During that decade Garford made strides in developing better transmissions up to seven-speed with two- or four-speed in reverse gear. A low bus chassis was developed before Relay Motors of Indiana bought out Garford in 1927. Two years later the stock market crash caused business to plummet for Garford, with the name fading out entirely as a vehicle builder by 1933.

GABRIEL TRUCKS
Manufactured by
THE GABRIEL MOTOR TRUCK CO., Cleveland, Ohio
315 Prospect Avenue N. W.

Model	C	E	F
Capacity	1 ton	2 tons	3½ tons
Drive	Worm	Worm	Worm
Chassis Weight	2,800 lbs.	4,300 lbs.	6,500 lbs.
Chassis Price	$1,750	$2,750	$3,750
Engine	Buda	Buda	Buda
H. P. (S.A.E.)	25	30	35
H. P. (Actual)	35	45	55
Cylinders	4 en bloc	4 en bloc	4 en bloc
Bore	4″	4¼″	4¼″
Stroke	5½″	5½″	6″
Wheel Base	136″	156″	180″
Tread Front	58″	58″	66″
Tread Rear	58″	58″	66″
Tires Front	35x5″ Pneu.	35x5″ Pneu.	36x5″
Tires Rear	35x5″ Pneu.	36x6″	36x5″ dual

Frame—Pressed.
Front Axle—I-beam.
Rear Axle—Timken full-floating, round.
Springs Front—Semi-elliptic.
Springs Rear—Semi-elliptic.
Carburetor—Rayfield.
Cooling System—Centrifugal pump.
Oiling System—Forced feed.
Ignition—Magneto.
Control—Left-hand drive, center control.
Clutch—Dry plate.

Transmission	Brown-Lipe Selective, three speeds	Brown-Lipe Selective, four speeds	Brown-Lipe Selective, four speeds

Brakes—Internal rear wheel.
Steering Gear—Worm.
Equipment—Oil side and tail lamps, tool box, tools, jack, pump, horn, seat box and seat, front fenders and governor.

GARFORD TRUCKS

Manufactured by

THE GARFORD MOTOR TRUCK CO., Lima, Ohio.

Model	75B	66B	70B	77B
Capacity	1 ton	1½ tons	2 tons	3½ tons
Drive	Worm	Worm	Worm	Worm
Chassis Weight	3,500 lbs.	4,250 lbs.	4,530 lbs.	7,235 lbs.
Chassis Price	$2,100	$2,500	$3,000	$3,900
Engine	Buda	Buda	Buda	Wisconsin
H. P. (S.A.E.)	22.5	22.5	29	29
H. P. (Actual)	27	27	35	44
Cylinders	4 en bloc	4 en bloc	4 en bloc	4 en bloc
Bore	3¾"	3¾"	4¼"	4¼"
Stroke	5½"	5½"	5½"	6"
Wheel Base	128"	142"	142"	128"
Tread Front	56"	56½"	58½"	62½"
Tread Rear	57¼"	58¾"	60¾"	65"
Tires Front	34x4½" Pneu.	36x3½"	36x4"	36x5"
Tires Rear	36x4"	36x5"	36x7"	40x5" dual

Frame—Pressed steel.
Front Axle—I-beam, reversed, Elliott.
Rear Axle—Timken floating.
Springs Front—Semi-elliptic.
Springs Rear—Semi-elliptic.
Carburetor—Rayfield.

Cooling System	Pump	Pump	Pump	Pump

Oiling System—Circulating splash.
Ignition—H. T. magneto.
Control—Right-hand steer, center control.
Clutch—Dry disc.

Transmission—Brown-Lipe selective, three speeds.				Four speeds

Brakes—Hand internal expanding rear wheel drums, foot internal expanding rear wheel drums.
Steering Gear—Worm and nut.
Equipment—Driver's seat, cushions, curved steel dash with oil lamp set flush in dash front, bumper, complete tool kit, vibrator horn, jack, oil can, oil tail lamp. On Model Model 75-B, one extra demountable rim and tire repair kit.

Gary

Not many companies in the motor vehicle industry were named after their city but Gary Motor Truck Company was one of them. An earlier company by the name of Gary built a taxi in Chicago in 1909 but was not related to this company, and the Gary Automobile Manufacturing Company of 1914 was also not related to this Gary.

The Gary Motor Truck Company began as America prepared to go into World War I, chasing Pancho Villa in the Punitive Expedition into Mexico in 1916. The first Gary trucks ranged from ¾-ton to 2-ton capacity and remained essentially unchanged during the war. By 1918 the model range reached 3-ton capacity.

Surviving the postwar recession, in 1922 the company was reorganized as the Gary Motor Corporation. The company had used Buda motors, whether as a design strategy or as part of the fiscal restructuring along the way. The model line expanded from 1½-ton to 5-ton capacity. Frank Dawson remained as president. Prices were reduced dramatically, which cut into profit for the company and also in the detailing of the vehicles.

At first the price slashing was effective, and by the mid–1920s Gary offered 1-, 1½-, 2½- 3-, 3½- and 5-ton capacity trucks, with chassis for the heaviest Model B50 with 182-inch wheelbase selling at $4,850. Solid rubber tires were universal and conventional layout was standard across the model line. However, Gary did not offer enough to stay competitive, and by 1927 the factory doors were closed permanently.

General Motors Corporation (G.M.C.)

Even though General Motor Corporation became the largest motor vehicle manufacturer in the world at one time, not everyone knows the name or significance of its founder, William Crapo Durant. Durant was a born deal maker who began as a co-owner of the Durant-Dort Carriage Company in Flint, Michigan. While Josiah Dallas Dort went his separate way, Durant began buying up newly created motor vehicle companies such as Buick and Cadillac as well as numerous component manufacturers. He also acquired truck builders Rapid and Reliance by 1908, and after incorporating and consolidating General Motors, he reorganized truck manufacturing in 1911 at Pontiac, Michigan, using the GMC emblem.

The first truck designs were left over from Rapid and Reliance, which used two-cycle engines of two, three and four cylinders. But the new General Motors trucks evolved into a consolidated design as the company went through a turmoil of leadership with the position of president changing hands several times in just three years. Durant remained as vice president and was the one who manipulated the company's real activities.

Between 1912 and 1915 GM built a large model line of electric trucks from 1½-ton to 5-ton capacity. But it soon became apparent that the gasoline engine would be the dominant propulsion system once refining and distributing abundant petroleum fuels and lubricants became an international industry. As efficient as electric motors were even at that time, no company could produce a battery that had anywhere near the energy density of gasoline and other petroleum distillates.

GM dropped its electric vehicle production quite abruptly by 1916. Part of this conclusion was derived from military purchases, which rarely included electric vehicles because there was little time or opportunity to recharge batteries out in the field away from a city's electrical grid.

By 1916 GMC trucks were either ¾-ton or 1-ton capacity and General Motors built many thousands of ambulances for the war effort,

GARY TRUCKS

Manufactured by

THE GARY MOTOR TRUCK COMPANY, Gary, Ind.

Model	F	H	HU	K
Capacity	1 ton	2 tons	2½ tons	3 tons
Drive	Worm	Worm	Worm	Worm
Chassis Weight	3,200 lbs.	4,500 lbs.	4,800 lbs.	6,500 lbs.
Chassis Price	On application	On application	On application	On application
Engine	Buda	Buda	Buda	Buda
H. P. (S.A.E.)	22.5	28.9	28.9	32.4
H. P. (Actual)	30	45	45	52.5
Cylinders	4 en bloc	4 en bloc	4 en bloc	4 en bloc
Bore	3¾″	4¼″	4¼″	4½″
Stroke	5¼″	5½″	5½″	6″
Wheel Base	130″	144″ or 156″	162″	162″ or more
Tread Front	56″	56″	56″	62″
Tread Rear	56″	56″	56″	66″
Tires Front	36x3½″	36x4″	36x4″	36x5″
Tires Rear	36x4″	36x6″	36x7″ DeLuxe	36x5″ dual
Frame	Pressed steel	Pressed steel	Pressed steel	Steel channel

Front Axle—I-beam section, Lemoine type knuckle.
Rear Axle—Sheldon semi-floating.
Springs Front—Semi-elliptic.
Springs Rear—Semi-elliptic.

Carburetor	Stromberg M-1	Stromberg M-2	Stromberg M-2	Stromberg M-3
Cooling System	Thermo syphon	Pump	Pump	Pump
Oiling System	Splash	Forced feed	Forced feed	Forced feed
Ignition	Eisemann	Eisemann	Eisemann G.A.	Eisemann G.A.
	magneto	magneto	Automatic	Automatic

Control—Left-hand drive, center control.
Clutch—Dry plate, multiple disc.

Transmission	Fuller Selective	Fuller Selective	Fuller Selective	Warner Selective,
	3 speeds forward	3 speeds forward	3 speeds forward	4 speeds forward
	and 1 reverse	and 1 reverse	and 1 reverse	and 1 reverse

Brakes—Internal expanding, acting on pressed steel drums on rear wheels.
Steering Gear—Worm and split nut.
Equipment—Open driver's seat, side oil lamps, oil tail lamp, horn or Buell whistle, oil can,
jack, tool box, tool kit and governor.
    Vesta complete electric lighting equipment furnished without delay on any model as
an extra.

G. M. C. TRUCKS

Manufactured by

GENERAL MOTORS TRUCK CO., Pontiac, Mich.

Model	16	21	A—31—B	A—41—B
Capacity	¾ ton	1 ton	1½ tons	2 tons
Drive	Bevel gear	Worm	Worm	Worm
Chassis Weight	2,875 lbs.	3,794 lbs.	4110 lbs. 4150 lbs.	4525 lbs. 4580 lbs.
Chassis Price	$1,395	$1,950	$2,350	$2,690
Engine	Continental	Continental	Continental	Continental
H. P. (S.A.E.)	22.5	22.5	22.5	27.22
H. P. (Actual)	27.50	31	30	35
Cylinders	4 en bloc	4 en bloc	4 en bloc	4 en bloc
Bore	3¾"	3¾"	3¾"	4⅛"
Stroke	5"	5"	5"	5¼"
Wheel Base	132"	136"	130"—144"	144"—158"
Tread Front	56"	58¼"	58¼"	58½"
Tread Rear	56"	58"	58½"	58¼"
Tires Front	35x5" Pneu.	34x3½"	36x3½"	36x4"
Tires Rear	35x5" Pneu.	34x5"	36x5"	36x4" dual

Frame—Pressed.
Front Axle—I-section Elliott.

Rear Axle	Weston-Mott ¾ floating, round	Timken semi-floating, round	Timken full-floating, round	Timken full-floating, round

Springs Front—Semi-elliptic.
Springs Rear—Semi-elliptic.
Carburetor—Marvel automatic.
Cooling System—Pump.

Oiling System	Splash and force	Splash and force	Splash and force	Splash—pressure

Ignition—Magneto.
Control—Left drive, center control.
Clutch—Dry plate.

Transmission	G. M. C. Selective, 3 speeds	G. M. C. Selective, 3 speeds	G. M. C. Selective, 4 speeds	G. M. C. Selective, 4 speeds
Brakes	Internal and external rear wheels	Internal on rear wheels	Internal on rear wheels	Internal on rear wheels

Steering Gear—Screw and nut.
Equipment—Model 16, two oil side lamps, one oil tail lamp, mechanical horn, jack, tire pump, oil can, five instruction books and two spare parts books, tool bag and tools. Models 21, 31, 41, two oil side lamps, one oil tail lamp, mechanical horn, screw jack, oil can, four instruction books and two spare parts books, three tool bags, tools and governor on all models.

especially on the lighter Model 15 chassis powered by a 19.60 hp four-cylinder Continental motor. In the meantime Durant was moved aside from power by GM's bankers, giving him the opportunity to start Chevrolet. Within a couple of years Durant bought controlling interest in General Motors and Chevrolet was suddenly the owner of GMC by 1917 with Pierre Du Pont a major stockholder. The GMC model line changed very little between 1916 and 1920 even after the war ended. In 1920 GM began building its own four-cylinder motors.

As Billy Durant was removed once again from GM, he went on to found Durant Motors and Pierre Du Pont took over as president of GM. General Motors activities throughout the United States and around the globe continued, creating one of the richest and most complex company histories in the world up to the present time.

General Vehicle
(G. V. electric)

As the Vehicle Equipment Company of New York City, the company was a component supplier known as V.E.C. beginning in 1900. This company was started by Robert Lloyd Havemeyer, who had made his fortune in the sugar business and was known as the "Sugar King." He was also a progressive businessman and got his two sons, Hector and Arthur, involved in the new technology of electric power.

By 1906 V.E.C. evolved into the General Vehicle (G.V.) Company, which throughout its relatively short life span concentrated on commercial battery-powered vehicles. There was a relatively large market for electric trucks around New York at the turn of the previous century, and G.V. also specialized in crane trucks to lift safes in tall buildings as well as in manufacturing sightseeing buses.

G.V. also built a Ladies' Phaeton electric

car, and by the second year of vehicle manufacturing, there were nine different models available, which included flatbed trucks and a Chatsworth bus. The trucks were from ¾-ton to 5-ton capacity. Harking back to its component manufacturing days, G.V. produced its own lead-acid batteries while using General Electric motors. Unlike some other electric vehicle builders, which mounted their motors on each wheel or axle, G.V. placed its motors in the center of the chassis and transferred power to the rear wheel via chains.

Under license from Daimler, Germany, G.V. began assembling gasoline-powered trucks in 1913. During the war this relationship was suspended. In 1915 G.V. merged with the Peerless Truck Division of Cleveland, Ohio. But both companies continued to build commercial vehicles using their own names. By 1916 G.V. began building hybrid gasoline-electric trucks which were purchased by the New York Sanitation Department. No matter the diversification, by 1920 G.V. was no longer building any vehicles.

Glide

Peoria, Illinois, was the birthplace of the Glidemobile in 1903. J.B. Bartholomew began earlier when he established peanut and coffee roasters using his own name. He was fascinated with machines and in 1901 he again used his own name to build a gasoline-powered motorcar. By 1904 the name of the 8 hp one-cylinder was simplified to Glide, which was apparently derived from the company's actual address: 210 Glide Street in Peoria.

In 1905 a two-cylinder motor was added, and the following year a four-cylinder engine was available with the Model E. By 1907 the Glide expanded in size, adopting a six-cylinder Rutenber engine, dropping the one- and two-cylinder engines. Popcorn and peanut roasting machinery was mounted on Glide

G. V. ELECTRIC TRUCKS

Manufactured by

GENERAL VEHICLE CO. Inc., Long Island City, N. Y.

S P E C I F I C A T I O N S

Model

Capacity	½ ton	½ ton	1 ton	2 tons
Drive	Chain	Worm	Chain	Chain
Chassis Price	$1,700	$1,950	$2,100	$2,600
Wheel Base	88"	108"	103"	113"
Tread Front	56"	58"	60"	61"
Tread Rear	56"	58"	60"	61"
Tires Front	36x3"	36x3"	36x3½"	36x4"
Tires Rear	36x3"	36x3"	36x3½"	36x3" dual
Frame	Channel, rolled	Channel, pressed	Channel, rolled	Channel, rolled
Speed	12 M.P.H.	12 M.P.H.	10 M.P.H.	9 M.P.H.
Miles (per battery charge)	45	45	45	45
Front Axle	Round	I-beam	Round	Round
Rear Axle	Fixed	Full-floating	Fixed	Fixed

Springs Front—Semi-elliptic.
Springs Rear—Semi-elliptic.

Battery Equip.	44-11 G. V. Lead	44-11 G. V. Lead	44-13 G. V.	44-17 G. V.
	44-9 M. V. I. C.	44-9 M. V. I. C.	44-11 M. V. I. C.	44-15 M. V. I. C.
	60-G6 Edison	60-A5 Edison	60-A6 Edison	60-A8 Edison

Motor—G. E. series.

Steering Gear	Pinion and sector	Semi-irreversible	Pinion and sector	Pinion and sector

Control—Five speeds forward and two reverse.

Brakes—Internal expanding.

Equipment—Mechanical hand horn, tail and head lamps, hubodometer, kit of tools, charging plug with 12 feet of cable.

**THE
BARTHOLOMEW
C O M P A N Y**

PEORIA, ILLINOIS

Price $1495
Four-Passenger Roadster . . . 1495

GLIDE LIGHT TOURING—SIX-40

COLOR	Body, meteor blue or maroon; running gear, black with ivory wheels	BORE AND STROKE .	3⅛ x 5 inches
		LUBRICATION	Splash with circulating pump
SEATING CAPACITY. .	Five	RADIATOR	Tubular
POSITION OF DRIVER .	Left side	COOLING	Water pump
WHEELBASE	119 inches	IGNITION	Storage battery
GAUGE	56 inches	STARTING SYSTEM . .	Two unit
WHEELS	Wood	STARTER OPERATED .	Gear to fly wheel
FRONT TIRES	34 x 4 inches	LIGHTING SYSTEM . .	Electric
REAR TIRES	34 x 4 inches, anti-skid	VOLTAGES	Six
		WIRING SYSTEM . . .	Single
SERVICE BRAKE . . .	Contracting on rear wheels	GASOLINE SYSTEM . .	Vacuum
		CLUTCH	Dry multiple disc
EMERGENCY BRAKE .	Expanding on rear wheels	TRANSMISSION . . .	Selective sliding
		GEAR CHANGES . . .	Three forward, one reverse
CYLINDERS	Six		
ARRANGED	Vertically	DRIVE	Spiral bevel
CAST.	En bloc	REAR AXLE.	Three-quarters floating
HORSEPOWER . . .	23.44		
(N.A.C.C. Rating)		STEERING GEAR . . .	Worm and gear

In addition to above specifications, price includes top, top hood, windshield, speedometer, ammeter, voltmeter, clock, tire pump, electric horn and demountable rims.

chassis, which were considered well built and high quality according to the automotive press of the day. For 1908 Glide built 200 vehicles.

J.B. Bartholomew invested in the motor vehicle industry, helping establish component manufacturers and sinking his own money in the Avery Company, which built farm machinery and vehicles. "Ride in a Glide and then Decide" was one of several advertising slogans that the company relied upon for its sales of fairly large, if not entirely luxurious cars.

In 1911 Glide offered ¾-ton trucks which used shaft drive, but this commercial model line was only continued through the following year. By 1916 only the six-cylinder motor was available. By the time America entered the war Glide was building sedans, roadsters and touring cars. The postwar recession hit the small company hard, and by 1920 it was no longer in business.

Gramm-Bernstein

In the early days of the American motor industry Benjamin Gramm was one of the more active and innovative businessmen involved with commercial vehicle production. Gramm began in Chillicothe, Ohio, when he built his first vehicle, which was steam-powered. He helped form the Gramm-Logan company in 1908 at Bowling Green, Ohio. This company became simply Gramm in 1910 and was moved to Lima, Ohio. The company produced trucks there until 1913, when John Willys bought the enterprise. In the meantime Gramm had begun to collaborate with Max Bernstein, forming the Gramm-Bernstein Company in 1912.

The company built 2- and 3½-ton trucks for the first three years. In 1915 the model line was expanded with a 6-ton model. Benjamin Gramm was an experienced motor vehicle designer, and along with the Selden Company, he helped in formulating the basis of the Class

B Liberty truck for the U.S. Army. During World War I Gramm-Bernstein was one of the companies contracted by the government to assemble about 1,000 Liberty trucks. The civilian model line of the above mentioned Gramm-Bernstein trucks continued to be built as well. Each model had a worm drive system for its rear-axle propulsion.

Gramm-Bernstein continued production after World War I with models ranging from 1-ton to 6-ton. Gramm-Bernstein used great flexibility in its truck designs with the adoption of several motor manufacturers including Lycoming, Hinkley and Continental, and other major components were also supplied by a variety of manufacturers.

In 1926 six-cylinder engines were adopted. At that time Gramm formed a new company with his son W.J. Gramm, as well as R.M. Kincaid. This company became the Gramm-Kincaid Company, again a producer of commercial vehicles. However, Gramm- Kincaid only lasted as a name until R.M. Kincaid left in 1926, at which time the company became Gramm once again. Gramm-Bernstein lasted until 1930, when the stock market crash affected the company's finances drastically. The Gramm company lasted until 1942.

Grant

George D. Grant and Charles A. Grant were brothers in Detroit, Michigan, who decided to go into auto manufacturing in 1913. Joining the two founders was a solid group of men: Secretary-Treasurer David A. Shaw arrived from Simplex Motors, Chief Engineer James M. Howe arrived from Cornell University, factory manager George S. Salzman and production manager George S. Waite both had experience at Thomas and Simplex.

For 1913 the first Grant car was a tiny roadster. The Grant featured a 12 hp four-cylinder engine, a 90-inch wheelbase, three-speed sliding gear transmission and shaft drive. It sold

GRAMM-BERNSTEIN TRUCKS
Manufactured by
GRAMM-BERNSTEIN MOTOR TRUCK CO., Lima, Ohio

S P E C I F I C A T I O N S

Model	W-1	W-1½	W-2	W-2½
Capacity	1 ton	1½ tons	2 tons	2½ tons
Drive	Worm	Worm	Worm	Worm
Chassis Price	$1,650	$2,000	$2,300	$2,700
Motor				
H. P. (S.A.E.)	19.6	22.6	22.6	29
H. P. (Actual)	28.5	32	32	37
Cylinders	4 en bloc	4 en bloc	4 en bloc	4 in pairs
Bore	3½"	3¾"	3¾"	4¼"
Stroke	5¼"	5¼"	5¼"	5¾"
Wheel Base	124"	130"	146"	156"
Tread Front	56"	56"	56"	57"
Tread Rear	57"	61"	62"	62"
Tires Front	34x3½"	34x3½"	34x4"	36x4"
Tires Rear	34x4"	36x5"	34x3½" dual	36x4" dual

Frame—Pressed.
Front Axle—I-section; Elliott knuckle.
Rear Axle—Semi-floating.
Springs Front—Semi-elliptic.
Springs Rear—Semi-elliptic.
Carburetor—Zenith.

Cooling System	Thermo-syphon	Thermo-syphon	Thermo-syphon	Pump

Oiling System—Splash.
Ignition—Magneto.
Control—Left drive, center control.
Clutch—Dry plate.
Transmission—Selective, constant mesh, three speeds forward and one reverse.

Brakes	Two internal on rear wheels	One internal and one external on rear wheels	One internal and one external on rear wheels	One internal and one external on rear wheels

Steering Gear—Screw and nut.
Equipment—Full set of tools, lamps, horn, jack, hubodometer.

GRANT TRUCKS

Manufactured by

GRANT MOTOR CAR CORP., Cleveland, Ohio

Model	Model 10	Model 11	Model 12	Model 15
Capacity	1½ tons	1½ tons	1800 lbs.	2 tons
Drive	Internal gear	Internal gear	Internal gear	Internal gear
Chassis Weight	3,100 lbs.	3,225 lbs.	2,400 lbs.	3,400 lbs.
Chassis Price	$1,490	$1,585	$1,020 with body	$1,790
Engine				
H. P. (S.A.E.)	22.5	22.5	16.9	22.5
H. P. (Actual)	35	35	27	35
Cylinders	4 en bloc	4 en bloc	4 en bloc	4 en bloc
Bore	3¾″	3¼″	3¼″	3¼″
Stroke	5″	5″	5″	5″
Wheel Base	124″	140″	115″	124″
Tread Front	56″	56″	56″	56″
Tread Rear	56″	56″	56″	56″
Tires Front	34x4½″ Pneu.	34x4½″ Pneu.	32x4″ Pneu.	34x3½″
Tires Rear	34x4″ Solid	34x4″	32x4″ Pneu.	34x5″
Frame—Pressed steel.				
Front Axle	I-beam Elliott	I-beam Elliott	I-beam Elliott	I-beam Elliott
Rear Axle—Torbensen I-beam.				
Springs Front—Semi-elliptic.				
Springs Rear—Semi-elliptic.				
Carburetor	Stewart	Stewart	Carter	Stewart
Cooling System—Thermo-syphon.				
Oiling System—Splash-force.				
Ignition—Magneto.				
Control—Left steer, center control.				
Clutch—Dry plate.				
Transmission—Grant-Lees Selective, three speeds.				
Brakes—Internal expanding external contracting on all models.				
Steering Gear	Worm and nut	Worm and nut	Worm and wheel	Worm and nut

Equipment—Models 10, 11, 15—Splitdorf-Apple two unit starting and lighting equipment, spot light, driver's seat, bumper, dash and instrument board assembly, tool kit, speedometer, electric tail light, license bracket, electric front lamps, rain vision windshield, front fenders, spare rim, tire pump, motometer and governor. Model 12—Bijur starting and lighting equipment, express flare board body and canopy top, bumper, spot light, windshield, front and rear fenders, running boards, full dash assembly, speedometer, spare rim.

for $495, and at that price 3000 were sold in 1913 and 1914. Apparently, its small size confused the public into thinking that the Grant was a cyclecar, which it was not. The Grant Company moved to Findlay, Ohio, in November of 1913, occupying the factory of the defunct Findlay Motor Company.

During the period just before World War I the American cyclecar fad involved a number of manufacturers that produced very small, lightweight autos, as the name "cyclecar" would imply. Most of these were powered by small one- and two-cylinder motors and used insubstantial chain drive and motorcycle wheels. What cyclecars were primarily known for was that they were cheap and flimsy. The misconception that the Grant was a cyclecar prompted the company to immediately introduce a larger six-cylinder car on a 106-inch wheelbase for 1915 called the Model S.

What was unusual about the Grant was the one built in Findlay briefly overlapped with the Grant Six, which was built by Harry Elmer in Cleveland, Ohio, in 1912 and 1913. This larger car was discontinued as the Grant of Findlay continued its six-cylinder car, moving to Cleveland in 1916 in a reorganization that claimed production capacity of 35,000 per year, which was never achieved. In fact, only one-eighth of that number were manufactured.

Denmo-Grant trucks were assembled in Cleveland by 1916. As production grew to 10,000 for 1918 and 1919, Grant was engaged in building U.S. Army trailers and munitions for the war effort. As Grant bought the engine builder H.J. Walker Manufacturing, the postwar recession set in and the company's fortunes plummeted, with final factory closure in 1923.

Hackett

One of the few companies that essentially existed only during World War I was the Hackett Motor Car Company of Jackson and Grand Rapids, Michigan. The ephemeral company was founded by Mansell Hackett, who was from England and owned the Disco Starter Company in Detroit, Michigan. His business did well enough that Hackett decided to buy up an automobile company or two that were going bankrupt.

Those companies were not difficult to find. Benjamin Briscoe started the Argo Motor Company in Jackson, Michigan. Its first vehicle was a cyclecar of solid specifications including four-cylinder motor, three-speed transmission and shaft drive. By 1916, due to the waning vogue of the cyclecar phase in America, the Argo became a larger, standard-size car. However, Brisoe sold the entire venture to Hackett late in 1916. At that point the Argo cars continued to be assembled until 1918 with whatever parts were available. At the same time the Hackett was also being manufactured.

The rare Hackett automobile was powered by a G.B. & S. four-cylinder motor and offered as a 1917 model at the end of 1916 for $888 FOB Frederick M. Guy was the engineer behind the Hackett, and although he was the designer of a rotary-valve engine, the Hackett always used a standard poppet-valve four-cylinder engine. The company's fortunes plummeted in 1918 as material shortages affected the entire American industry. Hackett was forced to move to Grand Rapids, Michigan, that year.

For 1919 production resumed in what had been cited as a dozen cars per week. Sales did not keep up with production, and by October of that year a reorganization was attempted, which failed. After producing some two-passenger and three-passenger roadsters, as well as five-passenger touring and "all-season" touring cars, the company ceased production with what is believed to have been a total of 118 Hacketts ever manufactured. The former Hackett factory at Grand Rapids

**HACKETT
MOTOR CAR
COMPANY**

**JACKSON
MICHIGAN**

Five-Passenger Touring . . ⎫ **Prices**
Two-Passenger Roadster . . ⎬ **Upon**
Three-Passenger Roadster . ⎱ **Appli-**
Five-Passenger All-Seasons . ⎭ **cation**

HACKETT FOUR TOURING—A. L.

COLOR	Blue, brown or red	LUBRICATION	Force feed and splash
SEATING CAPACITY .	Five	RADIATOR	Tubular
POSITION OF DRIVER .	Left side	COOLING	Thermo-syphon
WHEELBASE	112 inches	IGNITION	Storage battery
GAUGE	56 inches	STARTING SYSTEM . .	Two unit
WHEELS	Wood	STARTER OPERATED .	Gear to fly wheel
FRONT TIRES	32 x 3½ inches	LIGHTING SYSTEM . .	Electric
REAR TIRES	32 x 3½ inches, anti-skid	VOLTAGES	Six to eight
SERVICE BRAKE . . .	Contracting on rear wheels	WIRING SYSTEM . . .	Single
		GASOLINE SYSTEM . .	Vacuum
EMERGENCY BRAKE .	Expanding on rear wheels	CLUTCH	Dry multiple disc
		TRANSMISSION . . .	Selective sliding
CYLINDERS	Four	GEAR CHANGES . . .	Three forward, one reverse
ARRANGED	Vertically		
CAST	En bloc	DRIVE	Plain bevel
HORSEPOWER . . . . 22.5 (N.A.C.C. Rating)		REAR AXLE	Semi-floating
BORE AND STROKE . .	3¾ x 4¼ inches	STEERING GEAR . . .	Worm and nut

In addition to above specifications, price includes top, top hood, windshield,
speedometer, ammeter, tire pump, electric horn and demountable rims.

continued to produce Lorraine automobiles. Frederick Guy's rotary-valve engine was produced in the Ace Auto plant in Ypsilanti.

Hahn

The Hahn Automobile of Pueblo, Colorado, predated and was not affiliated with the W.G. Hahn and Brothers Company of Hamburg, Pennsylvania. Since the previous century Hahn had built horse-drawn conveyances until 1907, when the company added a line of trucks. For the first couple of years only a few motorized vehicles were assembled by Hahn.

By the end of 1913 the name was changed to Hahn Motor Truck and Wagon Company as it became more obvious that the new form of self-propelled transportation was taking over the market, and yet the company leaders felt that by including "wagon" in their name they were not abandoning their original business intentions. A 1½-ton Hahn chassis for 1914 was priced at $2,400.

Selling commercial vehicles as a chassis, which usually included cowl, fenders and cab with all running gear, was standard practice when most buyers had a special use in mind and hired another company to build the custom body for whatever were their business needs — and there were many dozens of applications from A to Z, as there are to this day.

In 1915 Hahn expanded its model line to five trucks from ¾-ton to 3½-ton capacity. The company also began to build complete fire trucks. In 1916 Hahn adopted worm drive for its truck line, but chain drive was still used for the 5-ton model that was offered in 1918, apparently by special order. Metallurgical limitations still prevented the use of worm drive for higher capacity trucks in which higher torque was required.

After World War I the recession and inflation forced Hahn's prices to increase dramatically, and the name was changed again, finally dropping the "and Wagon" portion, since horse-drawn wagons were now completely eliminated from the model line. Hahn continued to specialize in fire trucks and mobile machine shops for the military. The company began using Ford chassis to build United Parcel Service (UPS) delivery trucks after World War II.

Fire trucks on custom chassis using Waukesha gasoline and Detroit Diesel motors were the mainstay through the 1980s until 1990, when the company closed its doors for the final time.

Hal

After inheriting his father's huge bicycle business in Plattsburgh, New York, Harry Lozier continued the company's quest to find a new direction and new product line. Company superintendent George R. Burwell and engineer John G. Perrin built experimental vehicles as early as 1898. Once motor launches and marine engines were also tried as a business venture, Harry Lozier settled on motorcar production in Cleveland and wanted no expense spared building the Lozier automobile.

After gathering as much information and materials as possible, including entire engines brought from various European manufacturers, Lozier formed a detailed vision of the type of car he wanted to build. By 1905 the Lozier Model B was produced, using a four-cylinder motor on a 115-inch wheelbase. For the best materials and highest quality components, the price was $4500.

At the new motorcar show at Madison Square Gardens, it became clear that the Lozier vehicle would be competing not only with American cars but with the top-level European cars, then considered superior to U.S. built cars, by and large. By 1907 some fifty Loziers were produced in limousine, runabout, touring and landaulet body styles on

HAHN TRUCKS

Manufactured by

HAHN MOTOR TRUCK & WAGON CO., Hamburg, Pa.

Model	C	D	E	F
Capacity	1 ton	1½ tons	2 tons	3½ tons
Drive	Worm	Worm	Worm	Worm
Chassis Weight	3,800 lbs.	4,500 lbs.	5,000 lbs.	6,000 lbs.
Chassis Price	$1,750	$2,000	$2,250	$3,000
Engine	Continental	Continental	Continental	Continental
H. P. (S.A.E.)	40	40	50	50
H. P. (Actual)	30 at 1000 R.P.M.	30 at 1000 R.P.M.	40 at 1000 R.P.M.	40 at 1000 R.P.M.
Cylinders	4 en bloc	4 en bloc	4 in pairs	4 in pairs
Bore	4⅛″	4⅛″	4½″	4½″
Stroke	5¼″	5¼″	5½″	5½″
Wheel Base	136″	142″ and 157″	144″—159″	150″—162″
Tread Front	58″	60″	60″	68″
Tread Rear	58″	60″	60″	68″
Tires Front	36x3½″	36x3½″	36x4″	36x5″
Tires Rear	36x5″	36x6″	36x4″ dual	36x5″ dual

Frame—Pressed.
Front Axle—Timken I-beam.
Rear Axle—Timken worm drive.
Springs Front—Semi-elliptic.
Springs Rear—Semi-elliptic.
Carburetor—Stromberg.
Cooling System—Pump.
Oiling System—Splash and forced feed.
Ignition—Mai.
Control—Left drive, center control.
Clutch—Multiple disc, dry.
Transmission—Brown-Lipe selective, three speeds forward.
Brakes—Duplex on rear wheels.
Steering Gear—Worm sector.
Equipment—Driver's seat, side and tail lights, horn, jack, full set of tools.

HAL MOTOR CAR COMPANY

CLEVELAND, OHIO

Price	**$3600**
Four-Passenger Touring Roadster	3750
Three-Passenger Touring Roadster	3600
Seven-Passenger Limousine . . .	5000
Seven-Passenger Town Car . . .	5000
Six-Passenger Sedan	4750

HAL TWELVE TOURING—25

COLOR	Optional	BORE AND STROKE .	2⅞ x 5 inches
SEATING CAPACITY .	Seven	LUBRICATION	Full force feed
POSITION OF DRIVER .	Left side	RADIATOR	Cellular
WHEELBASE	135 inches	COOLING	Water pump
GAUGE	56 inches	IGNITION	Storage battery
WHEELS	Wood	STARTING SYSTEM . .	Single unit
FRONT TIRES	34 x 4½ inches	STARTER OPERATED .	Gear to fly wheel
REAR TIRES	34 x 4½ inches, anti-skid	LIGHTING SYSTEM . .	Electric
		VOLTAGES	Six
SERVICE BRAKE . . .	Expanding on rear wheels	WIRING SYSTEM . . .	Single
		GASOLINE SYSTEM . .	Vacuum
EMERGENCY BRAKE .	Contracting on rear wheels	CLUTCH	Dry multiple disc
		TRANSMISSION . . .	Selective sliding
CYLINDERS	Twelve	GEAR CHANGES . . .	Three forward, one reverse
ARRANGED	V type, 60 degrees	DRIVE	Spiral bevel
CAST	In threes	REAR AXLE	Full floating
HORSEPOWER	39.68 (N.A.C.C. Rating)	STEERING GEAR . . .	Worm and gear

In addition to above specifications, price includes top, top hood, windshield, speedometer, ammeter, voltmeter, clock, tire pump, electric horn and demountable rims.

two wheelbases, with prices starting at $5,000 and double that for elaborately appointed iterations. Lozier made an enormous investment in auto racing, and it paid off with well-publicized victories, but at the wrong time in history.

Even though Lozier and his cohorts spent lots of effort on developing the best car possible, what's most important is that the market for such an automobile was quickly vanishing on the American landscape. This was primarily due to World War I, even though America was not directly involved in 1914. However, once the war exploded in Europe the industry began to focus on war production for overseas, the spending mood of the general public soured even among the well-to-do, and material and labor shortages soon encroached upon nearly every type of business.

The Lozier cars, with what was thought to be bronze striping by many pedestrians (which was actually 24-carat gold) had fewer and fewer followers no matter the status-seeking that was still in vogue. Lozier Company officers defected, there was a reorganization, and the competition jumped ahead. Lozier decided to fend for himself by going on to build a car using his own initials, "HAL," much in the vein of Ransom Eli Olds and Harry C. Stutz, once they parted ways with their contractually intertwined obligations that induced them to find another name even if it were still based on their own vanity.

The Hal was a "popularly-priced" car, which meant it was a considerable compromise with what the original Lozier aspired to be. However, the Hal, which was built in Cleveland, was still fairly extravagant in its introduction during 1916 as a (Weidley) 12-cylinder car on a 135-inch wheelbase selling for $2100. Lozier himself left the company at the end of the year just before American forces withdrew from Mexico after a long and fruitless chase of Pancho Villa. But Lozier's departure was for private reasons due to health

problems. A. Ward Foote of the Foote-Burt Machine Company of Cleveland took over as president of Hal.

The company continued to suffer material shortages as the country geared up for the world war, and Frank B. Willis became company president late in 1917. Warren G. Harding bought a HAL-Twelve, one of six body styles, including the open-sided Shamrock roadster introduced in 1918. That year bankruptcy was announced. By April the ten remaining unsold Hal cars were auctioned off and the company was no more.

Hall

At least a half dozen motor vehicle manufacturers by the name of Hall were organized before the Lewis-Hall Iron Works began building trucks with the Hall name at Detroit, Michigan, in 1915. Hall assembled conventional trucks in what could be called heavy-duty models at a time when most trucks were under two-ton capacity. There were numerous builders producing commercial vehicles of ½-, ¾-, 1- and 1½-ton capacity. The business philosophy at Lewis-Hall was to build 2-ton, 3½-ton, 5-ton and 7-ton capacity trucks. Each of the models was powered by a Continental motor using a three-speed Brown-Lipe transmission and Timken axles.

As was the case with nearly every truck builder before World War I, trucks over 5-ton still used dual chain drive when worm drive and bevel-gear differentials were not up to metallurgical and bearing strength for the heaviest duty service. However, chain-drive vehicles still needed constant slack adjustment, lubrication, replacement and sprocket repair even if the drive mechanism was easily accessible and required minimal technical knowledge for maintenance. During World War I metallurgy was improved and very few motor vehicles were manufactured after the war using chain drive.

HALL TRUCKS

Manufactured by

LEWIS HALL IRON WORKS, Detroit, Mich.

S P E C I F I C A T I O N S

Model	2-Ton Worm	3½-Ton Worm	3½-Ton Chain	5-Ton Chain
Capacity	2 tons	3½ tons	3½ tons	5 tons
Drive	Worm	Worm	Double side chain	Double side chain
Chassis Price	$2,000	$2,800	$2,800	$3,600
Motor				
H. P. (S.A.E.)	27	45	45	45
H. P. (Actual)	24	32½	32½	33½
Cylinders	4 en bloc	4 in pairs	4 in pairs	4 in pairs
Bore	4⅛"	4½"	4½"	4½"
Stroke	5¼"	5½"	5½"	5½"
Wheel Base	132"	144"	144"	144"
Tread Front	60"	65"	65"	66"
Tread Rear	60"	72"	72"	72"
Tires Front	36x4"	36x5"	36x5"	36x6"
Tires Rear	36x4" dual	36x5" dual	36x5" dual	40x6" dual

Frame—Special rolled.
Front Axle—I-beam, roller bearing head knuckle.

Rear Axle	Full-floating	Full-floating	Rectangular dead	Rectangular dead

Springs Front—Semi-elliptic.
Springs Rear—Semi-elliptic.
Carburetor—Zenith.
Cooling System—Pump.
Oiling System—Circulating splash.
Ignition—Magneto.
Control—Left or right.
Clutch—Dry plate.

Transmission	Progressive, 3 speeds forward, 1 reverse	Progressive, 3 speeds forward, 1 reverse	Progressive, 3 speeds forward, 1 reverse	Progressive, 4 speeds forward, 1 reverse

Brakes—Two on rear wheel, internal expanding.
Steering Gear—Worm.
Equipment—Complete set of lamps, tools and tool kit complete, jack, horn, etc.

World War I had a profound effect on manufacturers in the U.S., and Hall was no exception. For the companies that did not receive large military contracts, especially relatively small companies such as Lewis-Hall, if material shortages, labor force interruptions and market reduction did not kill an enterprise, then the postwar recession took its toll. This was the case with Hall trucks, which continued to be built one at a time through 1922. The fact that a company such as Lewis-Hall was listed in the catalogs of the day along with giant companies did not mean that the small builder was truly competitive, and this was proven out when Hall trucks ceased to be fabricated in 1922.

Harley-Davidson (motorcycle)

It would be difficult to prove that the modern bicycle fad of the 1890s did not have a major influence on motorcycle development at the beginning of the previous century, and that Harley-Davidson was not one of those companies that was a direct outgrowth of that sudden popularity. It would be an especially tough case to make, given that none of the founders of the company were machine designers or engineers in 1903 when Harley-Davidson began as a business in Milwaukee, Wisconsin.

The first Harley-Davidson was only a little more than a motorized bicycle, with a 405 cc single-cylinder four-stroke motor. Horsepower was three and wheelbase was 51 inches, using a bicycle-type loop frame that also held the gasoline and oil tank. Chain drive was used for the pedals, whereas the engine powered the rear wheel using a belt drive.

The Harley-Davidson was improved considerably by 1906 with a leading link front fork and a motor increased in displacement to 440 cc (27 cid). Employee stock options were given to 18 workers in 1907, the year they assembled 153 motorcycles. At that time Walter Davidson was president, his brother William was vice president, with Arthur Davidson sales manager and William Harley chief engineer and treasurer.

"The Silent Gray Fellow" was the company's slogan, and the Harley-Davidson factory entered racing reluctantly, watching its competitors, especially Indian, use this type of competition to their advantage. In 1908

Walter Davidson had gotten a perfect score at the Catskill-New York National Endurance meet, but by the following year Harley-Davidson officially entered racing competition, and sales nearly tripled through 1910.

The first Harley-Davidson V-Twin was produced in 1909, but with design problems only 26 were built before the larger motorcycle reappeared in 1911. The frame had been redesigned to hold the more powerful motor and absorb its vibration, and the Model 7D was now capable of 60 mph at a cost of $300. Harley-Davidson proved itself in England by winning the top three spots at the Isle of Man competition in 1911.

In 1912 the V-Twin now called the Model X8E had eight hp produced by 989 cc. Both chain and belt drive were available. The rear hub-mounted clutch was optional. Roller bearings for the connecting rods and self-aligning ball bearings for the crankshaft were incorporated into the engine design.

In 1913 the single-cylinder 565 cc Model 9A, with a 5-35 motor, which stood for 5 hp and 35 cid, was continued along with the V-Twin. The smaller Harley-Davidson sold for $290 while the price for the V-Twin went up to $350. The U.S. Army began buying Harley-Davidson motorcycles in 1913. Although three-wheel delivery cars were a very small part of

the company's business, the Forecar with 600-pound capacity appeared in 1913. It would be the precursor to the commercial sidecars called Package Trucks. In 1931 the Servi-car was introduced, which had two wheels in back; it would be in production until 1973.

Just as Harley-Davidson's involvement in racing revved up, World War I interrupted the civilian pastime and the company's gray color was replaced by olive drab, supplies of which would last for well over a decade. By rules of the organizers it was stipulated that the racing machines were to be available to the public, if they were not outright production models, but Harley-Davidson priced the 8-valve V-Twin at $1500, discouraging the average privateer racers from buying them up.

The standard motor of the 17-J model, based on the racing iteration but built in series for the general public as well as the military, was rated at 15 hp by 1917 and capable of 3000 RPM. Harley-Davidson production was 8,527 in 1917 for the Model 17-F and 9,180 for the Model 17-J. Both Harley-Davidson and Indian were thoroughly tested during the 1916–1917 Punitive Expedition, in which General John Pershing's forces chased Pancho Villa unsuccessfully after Columbus, New Mexico, was attacked by the renegade revolutionary from Mexico.

Harley-Davidson contributed approximately 15,000 motorcycles to the war effort. which was about the same as Indian. Many of the motorcycles used sidecars, which had various purposes such as to carry personnel, to be used as a mobile machine gun, for courier work, as ammunition vehicles, and some other more unusual purposes such as mini-ambulances. Proving themselves in the field for a variety of auxiliary roles led to the selection of William S. Harley of Harley-Davidson to become the head of the newly-formed Society of Automotive Engineers committee dealing with the standardization of motorcycles built for the military in 1918.

After World War I Harley-Davidson introduced a 6 hp 584 cc Sport V-Twin Model W. It was priced at $335 and was capable of 50 mph. But the 1000 cc and 1200 cc bikes became the so-called signature motorcycles produced by Harley-Davidson with the streamlined Model JD of 1926 an example of a classic design that would remain as the basis of gradually improved large motorcycles for decades.

Harley-Davidson played a major role again in World War II and has continued producing motorcycles in the United States up to this writing. Along the way American competitors dropped out so that by the mid–1960s Harley-Davidson was the only American manufacturer of motorcycles. The company's revival during the 1980s and 1990s has led to its wide-ranging success, but the details of the company's long and colorful history after the Great War are beyond the scope of this discussion.

Harvey

There were more motor vehicle manufacturers named after the city rather than the state in which they resided, and the Harvey Motor Truck Company was one of the former category, named after its city in Illinois. The truck builder started out in 1911 producing 1½-ton and 3-ton capacity commercial vehicles. By the time the United States got bogged down in the Punitive Expedition of 1916–1917, Harvey was also building 5-ton capacity trucks, although there is no record of the military buying the company's vehicles.

By 1918 Harvey was offering 2½-, 3½-, 5- and 10-ton trucks each powered by a Buda motor of different size using a four-speed Brown-Lipe transmission. What was unusual about the heaviest Harvey truck listed was that it was one of the very highest capacity trucks built during World War I as well as the fact that it used worm drive. Comparable trucks such as those built by Mack used chain drive and were not rated that high. Harvey 10-ton trucks used a governor, which was standard equipment, limiting them to twelve mph.

Harvey provided other accessories and tools as standard equipment, which was more than many competitors provided. But such objects as "windshield, side and tail lamps, horn, dash and foot boards," which may have been automatically considered as integral to any vehicle in later years, were all listed by Harvey as extra accessories provided by the manufacturer in 1918.

Harvey survived both the war and the post-war downturns, and by the mid–1920s offered trucks of 2½-ton and 3½-ton capacity which were powered by Buda engines and used Brown-Lipe transmissions, Fuller clutches and Sheldon axles. In 1927 Harvey set out to build a Road Builders' Special in order to compete with Hug, builder of dump trucks for road building. Hug outlasted Harvey by a full decade after Harvey went out of business in 1932.

Haynes

Haynes automobiles began as Haynes-Apperson in Kokomo, Indiana, in 1893 when Elwood P. Haynes used a Sintz marine engine

HARVEY TRUCKS

Manufactured by

HARVEY MOTOR TRUCK CO., Harvey, Ill.

Model	W.F.A.	W.H.A.	W.K.A.	H.T.
Capacity	2½ tons	3½ tons	5 tons	10 tons
Drive	Worm	Worm	Worm	Worm
Chassis Weight	5,300 lbs.	7,700 lbs.	8,600 lbs.	7,700 lbs.
Chassis Price	$2,850	$3,850	$4,600	$4,000
Engine	Buda	Buda	Buda	Buda
H. P. (S.A.E.)	28.90	32.40	32.40	32.40
H. P. (Actual)	40 at 1000 R.P.M.	50 at 1000 R.P.M.	50 at 1000 R.P.M.	50 at 1000 R.P.M.
Cylinders	4 en bloc	4 en bloc	4 en bloc	4 en bloc
Bore	4¼″	4½″	4½″	4½″
Stroke	5½″	6″	6″	6″
Wheel Base	150″	160″	160″	125″
Tread Front	56″	64″	64″	64″
Tread Rear	58″	66″	74″	66″
Tires Front	36x4″	36x5″	36x6″	36x5″
Tires Rear	36x7″	36x5″ dual	40x6″ dual	36x5″ dual
Frame	Rolled 6″	Rolled 7″	Rolled 7″	Rolled 7″

Front Axle—I-beam, Elliott.
Rear Axle—Sheldon semi-floating.
Springs Front—Semi-elliptic.
Springs Rear—Semi-elliptic.

Carburetor	Stromberg M-2	Stromberg M-3	Stromberg M-3	Stromberg M-3

Cooling System—Pump.
Oiling System—Forced feed.
Ignition—Magneto.
Control—Left drive, center control.
Clutch—Dry plate.
Transmission—Brown-Lipe Selective, four speeds.
Brakes—Internal on rear wheels.
Steering Gear—Worm.
Equipment—Driver's cab, windshield, curtains, dash and foot boards, front mud guards, side and tail lamps, horn, jack, full set of tools and governor.

HAYNES
AUTOMOBILE
COMPANY

K O K O M O
I N D I A N A

Price	**$3985**
Four-Passenger Fourdore	2785
Seven-Passenger Sedan	3385
Four-Passenger Coupe	3335
Five-Passenger Touring	2785

HAYNES "LIGHT TWELVE" TOWN CAR—44

COLOR	Haynes blue, beige brown, deep carmine or royal green	LUBRICATION	Full force feed
		RADIATOR	Cellular
		COOLING	Water pump
SEATING CAPACITY. .	Five	IGNITION	Storage battery and distributor
POSITION OF DRIVER	Left side		
WHEELBASE	127 inches	STARTING SYSTEM . .	Two unit
GAUGE	56 inches	STARTER OPERATED .	Gear to fly wheel
WHEELS	Wire	LIGHTING SYSTEM . .	Electric
FRONT TIRES	34 x 4½ inches	VOLTAGES	Six
REAR TIRES	34 x 4½ inches	WIRING SYSTEM . .	Double
SERVICE BRAKE . . .	Expanding on rear wheels	GASOLINE SYSTEM . .	Vacuum
		CLUTCH	Dry multiple disc
EMERGENCY BRAKE .	Expanding on rear wheels	TRANSMISSION . . .	Selective sliding
		GEAR CHANGES . . .	Three forward, one reverse
CYLINDERS	Twelve		
ARRANGED	V type, 60 degrees	DRIVE	Spiral bevel
CAST	In sixes	REAR AXLE	Three-quarters floating
HORSEPOWER . . . . (N.A.C.C. Rating)	36.3		
BORE AND STROKE .	2¾ x 5 inches	STEERING GEAR . .	Screw and nut

In addition to above specifications, price includes windshield, speed-ometer, ammeter, clock, tire pump, electric horn and demountable rims.

to build a tiller-steered auto-buggy, which was completed by the Apperson brothers, who owned the Riverside Machine Shop in the same city. The local paper noted Elwood Haynes driving around the city on July 4, Whether or not the name "Haynes Pioneer" was used at that time is not clear, but much later that became the early car's moniker.

Haynes made claims of being the first American to build an automobile, and whether or not he could prove that, his partnership with the Apperson brothers resulted in the tooling up of their machine shop to build one Haynes-Apperson "auto buggy" or one "motor carriage" approximately every fortnight. By 1898 the Haynes-Apperson two-cylinder motor carriage went into series production. At the end of the year a small factory was leased and production increased to two cars per week. Prices ranged around $1200 to $2000. A Mrs. John Landon claimed to be America's first woman driver when she drove an 1897 Haynes-Apperson around Kokomo the following year.

The Haynes-Apperson won a few notable endurance runs for publicity, which was nearly always the purpose with such automotive spectacles, before Haynes and the Appersons went their separate directions, and both producing their own cars. Before the Haynes-Apperson became the Haynes, a four-cylinder motor was introduced in 1904. For the following year the two-cylinder engine was still available in the Model L and Model M Haynes, and the Model K was now built on a 108-inch wheelbase with the four-cylinder motor.

In 1907 a Haynes survived the Vanderbilt Cup competition in third place, in part prompting advertising that the Haynes 50 hp four-cylinder car was the most powerful shaft-drive automobile built in the United States. The Haynes Model U rode on a 118-inch wheelbase and included a limousine body style for $4750. The Haynes also continued to

grow in size from 1914 onward, with 125-, 127-, 130- and 136-inch wheelbases and a six-cylinder engine arriving in 1913.

By the time America entered the world war, Haynes introduced its V-12 motor, which was modestly rated at 60 hp, then increased to 70 hp. The Light Twelve, as it was called, survived the war and continued to be built through the postwar recession, although it is believed only a total of 650 such cars were fabricated in total during the years 1918–1922. Haynes himself went on a public relations campaign using the claim he was "first in America" to build a car, but by 1923 it mattered little to prospective buyers who still had dozens of other makes with other features from which to choose. No amount of bragging about the make's origins could keep the company afloat, and for 1923 and 1924 the six-cylinder Haynes was the last car built by this allegedly primogenital motor vehicle manufacturer.

Henderson (motorcycle)

Tom and William Henderson were inspired to build motorcycles beginning in 1911 in Detroit, Michigan. The first Henderson Four motorcycle appeared in 1912 and was noted for its long 65-inch wheelbase in addition to the large 7 hp 965 cc four-cylinder motor, which required hand cranking to start. Advertising stated "The long wheelbase of the Henderson ... permits the riders to sit between the wheels, reducing road shocks to the minimum."

For 1912 the horsepower was increased to eight by lengthening the stroke, increasing the displacement to 1065 cc, and improving the manifold. The front fork was improved and a new design was adopted for the rear brake. As with most motorcycles and the four-wheel vehicles of this era, there were no front brakes.

In 1913 the contracting band rear brake was attached to a pedal on the footboard. The

V-Twin used a Schebler carburetor, Bosch ignition and an Eclipse clutch. All of these American-made components were "off-the-shelf," available for any builders who wanted to manufacture a motor vehicle, no matter how many wheels it would have. Price for the 310-pound 1913 Henderson, capable of 55 mph, was $325.

As with so many auto and truck country and world crossings for the sake of publicity, Henderson made headlines in 1913 when Carl Stearns Clancy became the first person to "ride around the world" on a motorcycle, specifically a 1912 Henderson.

The following year Henderson built its Model C, which was a lighter motorcycle with a two-speed rear hub. Advertising lauded the merits of four-cylinder smoothness, compared to the "jerks" of the one- and two-cylinder motorcycle motor. However, weight was up to 310 pounds and the price was up to $295, with an additional $40 for the two-speed version which used a Thor hub. The 1915 Henderson was capable of 70 mph when a Henderson two-speed hub was introduced.

Customers and dealers enjoyed the power and smoothness of the four-cylinder motor but wished for a shorter wheelbase, which was offered in the Model E that was developed in

1914 for 1915 in addition to the Model D. The Model E had a 58-inch wheelbase, which was still a half-foot longer than other comparable motorcycles but shortened by seven inches from the Model D, and prices remained the same.

For 1916 the longer wheelbase Model D was discontinued as prices dropped to $265 for the one-speed and $295 for the two-speed versions. With the difficulties of material and labor shortages once America was entering the Great War, Henderson's dismal financial condition forced the company to sell all assets to Ignaz Schwinn in 1917. The Henderson Model G for that year was the last independently built motorcycle from that make. It featured improvements such as three-speed transmission and better front fork.

Schwinn planned to take on Indian and Harley-Davidson, and the transcontinental record set previously by "Cannonball" Baker was smashed by rider Alan Bedell on a Henderson with a 7-day, 16-hour time that bettered the previous record by four days. The fact that Henry Ford bought a Henderson that year added to other publicity such as Roy Artley's championship of the Canada-to-Mexico run in 1917.

Tom and William Henderson stayed on only until 1919 to get the Henderson set up for production in Chicago at the Excelsior factory that Schwinn had also bought, after which the brothers went on to other projects separately.

Improvements of the Henderson motorcycles continued under Schwinn. The motor was increased in displacement to 1310 cc, which produced 18hp. The final years of 1929 and 1930 were financial debacles for the entire company, and by 1931 motorcycle manufacturing under both the Excelsior and Henderson names were discontinued as Schwinn coasted into the Great Depression building only bicycles by that name.

Hercules

To unravel the mysterious short history of this Milwaukee-based company is a formidable challenge to this day. Various truck and automotive compilations do not even list such a company, and yet the Goodrich Catalog of 1917 clearly presented a photograph and a listing of three models of Hercules trucks "manufactured by the Hercules Motor Truck Company, 606 Linus Street, Milwaukee, Wisconsin." Although in previous motor vehicle history writings this company was said to have no affiliation with the Hercules trucks built in Great Britain and Germany, what is known is that A.O. Smith Company of Milwaukee was listed as a producer of motor vehicle components as early as 1902. By 1903 A.O. Smith took over the Federal stamping plant in Milwaukee, a firm not affiliated with cars or trucks, of which several used the Federal name before World War I, including the large truck manufacturer that existed from 1910 to 1959 in Detroit, Michigan.

The connection with Hercules in England seems to have gotten started when A.O. Smith obtained manufacturing rights to the Wall Auto Wheel, a self-contained motorized wheel similar to the Davis, Dayton and Crocker motorized wheels, each used as a substitute for a front or rear bicycle wheel, or as an attachment for a bicycle.

In the case of A.O. Smith, the company not only sold half a million dollars' worth of such wheels at $60 each using the Smith name along with some improvements, but also got into building a complete buckboard called the Smith Flyer by 1916. The fact that A.O. Smith was manufacturing motor vehicle components under the Hercules name as well as light vehicles in Milwaukee insinuates that it was affiliated with the manufacture of the Hercules Motor Truck.

However, there was a Hercules Motor Truck already in existence by 1913 in South Boston, Massachusetts (not affiliated with the Hercules Motor Car Company of New Albany, Indiana), and this company lasted until 1915 building only a 1-ton express. Could the truck of 1918 illustrated here representing three model listings be a product of that company by the exact same name, transplanted from South Boston? Was it affiliated with A.O. Smith, or was it a brief venture independent of all of these others? As of this writing no concrete answers have been found, but it is certain that such a company existed in Milwaukee and built at least the truck shown in the published photograph.

Hewitt-Ludlow

Two men with the last name of Hewitt preceded the cofounders of this company as motor vehicle makers. Edward Ringwood Hewitt and John Hewitt worked in New York and Chicago, respectively, while the unrelated Edward T. Hewitt and his younger brother William A. Hewitt, along with James Ludlow, started their truck manufacturing enterprise in San Francisco during 1912. San Francisco itself, for all its fame as a colorful, pioneering and touristy peninsula of 49 voluptuous square miles, was also the location of a few truck builders before World War II.

HERCULES TRUCKS

Manufactured by

HERCULES MOTOR TRUCK CO., 606 Linus St., Milwaukee, Wis.

Model	2-Ton	3½-Ton	5-Ton
Capacity	2 tons	3½ tons	5 tons
Drive	Worm	Worm	Worm
Chassis Weight	4,500 lbs.	7,500 lbs.	9,000 lbs.
Chassis Price	$2,800	$3,750	$4,750
Engine	Continental	Continental	Continental
H. P. (S.A.E.)	29.4	33.7	33.7
H. P. (Actual)	47	54	54
Cylinders	6 en bloc	6 in threes	6 in threes
Bore	3½"	3¾"	3¾"
Stroke	5¼"	5¼"	5¼"
Wheel Base	150"	160"	168"
Tread Front	56"	56½"	61"
Tread Rear	56½"	58"	67"
Tires Front	34x4"	36x5"	36x5"
Tires Rear	36x4" dual	40x5" dual	40x6" dual

Frame—Pressed.
Front Axle—I-beam.
Rear Axle—Hercules full-floating.
Springs Front—Semi-elliptic.
Springs Rear—Semi-elliptic.

Carburetor	Rayfield GL-3	Rayfield G-4	Rayfield G-4

Cooling System—Pump.
Oiling System—Splash and forced feed.
Ignition—Dixie magneto.
Control—Left-hand drive, center control.
Clutch—Multiple dry disc.
Transmission—Brown-Lipe Selective, three speeds forward and reverse. 3½-Ton, Midship four speeds.
Brakes—Internal expanding service brake on propeller shaft, hand brake on rear wheels. 3½-Ton, external propeller.
Steering Gear—Worm.
Equipment—Electric starter, generator, storage battery, powerful electric dash lights, electric tail lamp, tools, hubodometer, electric horn, jack, seat with back and cushions.

HEWITT-LUDLOW TRUCKS
Manufactured by
HEWITT-LUDLOW AUTO CO., 901-951 Indiana St., San Francisco, Cal.

S P E C I F I C A T I O N S

Model	1917	1917	1917
Capacity	2—2½ tons	3½ tons	3½ tons
Drive	Worm	Worm	Chain
Chassis Price	$2,550	$3,350	$3,000
Motor			
H. P. (S.A.E.)	22.5	30	30
H. P. (Actual)	30 at 1150 R.P.M.	35 at 1150 R.P.M.	35 at 1150 R.P.M.
Cylinders	4 en bloc	4 en bloc	4 en bloc
Bore	3¾″	4¼″	4¼″
Stroke	5½″	5½″	5½″
Wheel Base	140″	144″ and 156″	144″ and 156″
Tread Front	59″	69″	69″
Tread Rear	59″	69″	69″
Tires Front	36x4″	36x5″	36x5″
Tires Rear	36x7″	40x5″ dual	40x5″ dual
Frame	6″, 10½ lb. Channel	6″, 13 lb. Channel	6″, 13 lb. Channel
Front Axle	I-beam Sheldon Type	I-beam Liggett Type	I-beam Liggett Type
Rear Axle	Hewitt-Ludlow Worm Semi-floating	Semi-floating	Heavy Rectangular Sec.

Springs Front—Semi-elliptic.
Springs Rear—Semi-elliptic, extra heavy.
Carburetor—Stromberg, M2.
Cooling System—Pump.
Oiling System—Splash and forced feed.
Ignition—High tension or dual system optional.
Control—Left drive, center control.
Clutch—Hartford cone.
Transmission—Selective, jaw clutch type, three speeds forward and one reverse.

Brakes	Service, external contracting on drive shaft; Emergency, expanding on rear wheel drum	Service, external contracting on drive shaft; Emergency, expanding on rear wheel drum	Service external contracting on jackshaft; Emergency, expanding on rear wheel drum

Steering Gear—Screw and nut, irreversible.
Equipment—Electric side and tail lights, storage battery, fenders, horn, seat with full upholstery, tool kit.

Hewitt-Ludlow was the earliest of them, and like the others (aside from Doble) assembled entire vehicles using purchased parts from original equipment manufacturers (OEMs), partly relying on the Ralston Iron Works of San Francisco. In the case of Hewitt-Ludlow the engines were from Buda, using worm drive. Capacities were from ¾- ton to 3½-ton, and by 1916 the price started at $1650.

Hewitt-Ludlow gearing and suspension were particularly adapted to the impressive undulations of the city's geography. In addition to a model line that spanned 1½-ton to 5½-ton capacities, Hewitt-Ludlow also began building 6-ton trucks for the U.S. Army for use at the Presidio, among other places on the West Coast, as World War I commenced for the United States. These were used as transporters and also for towing artillery.

Tractor-trailer units were named Hewitt-Talbot in honor of the man who helped develop the "fifth wheel" design, which later became a standard in the industry for use in large articulated trucks that pulled any type of trailer. At the time the concept was called "absolute tracking." In 1926 the Ralston Iron Works, named after Bay Area silver magnate H. Ralston, bought the Hewitt-Ludlow Company, and Edward T. Hewitt continued to build trailers until 1930.

Hollier

Charles Lewis began in the auto industry by building the Jackson automobile in Jackson, Michigan, during 1903. The Jackson went on to greater success without its company president for two more decades as Lewis began building the Hollier car at his own Lewis Spring and Axle Company, also located in Jackson.

Lewis and his engineering staff designed a V-8 motor rated at 40 hp used in the first Hollier Touring Eight model, which rode on a 112-inch wheelbase and was priced at $985

in 1915. However, material shortages during World War I soon depleted the metal stock (among other components) needed to continue casting the engine blocks of the proprietary "Lewis" V-8, and Hollier was essentially forced to adopt a Falls six-cylinder engine, although the V-8 was still available.

Production was ample for a small company, with 3000 units per year up until the end of the war. However, Lewis somehow refused to follow the trend to build closed cars, and his customers were soon left dissatisfied with the offering of only touring and roadster motorcars no matter how sprightly they were powered by a six or an eight. Customers were also confused by the fact that a company by the name of "Lewis Spring and Axle" was building an entire car.

Lewis changed the company's name to Hollier, by this time located in Chelsea, Michigan, a small town in the southern part of the state. With prices steadily climbing to $2000 by 1921, as the postwar recession groaned on, the marketing of the Hollier found fewer and fewer enthusiasts among those interested in an open car undistinguished in its styling and unvaried in its selection of body styles. Holliers no longer rolled off the line in 1922 as the company ended production.

Horner

Wyandotte, Michigan, was a swamp from which Chief Pontiac planned his attacks against white settlers before the city was founded as a river port. The Wyandotte Iron Ship Works were built there in the late 1800s. There was adequate industry and manpower for the Detroit-Wyandotte Company to begin manufacturing Horner trucks in 1913.

At first the company built a 5-ton truck, and by the time war was fulminating across Europe, the model line was expanded to include 1-, 1½-, 2- and 3-ton trucks. What was

**LEWIS SPRING &
AXLE COMPANY**

Price, $1285

C H E L S E A
M I C H I G A N

HOLLIER TOURING—188

COLOR	Dark blue or French gray	BORE AND STROKE	3 x 4¼ inches
SEATING CAPACITY	Five	LUBRICATION	Full force feed
POSITION OF DRIVER	Left side	RADIATOR	Cellular
WHEELBASE	116 inches	COOLING	Thermo-syphon
GAUGE	56 inches	IGNITION	Storage battery
WHEELS	Wood	STARTING SYSTEM	Single unit
FRONT TIRES	34 x 4 inches, anti-skid	STARTER OPERATED	Chain to crank shaft
REAR TIRES	34 x 4 inches, anti-skid	LIGHTING SYSTEM	Electric
		VOLTAGES	Six or twelve
SERVICE BRAKE	Contracting on rear wheels	WIRING SYSTEM	Single
EMERGENCY BRAKE	Expanding on rear wheels	GASOLINE SYSTEM	Vacuum
		CLUTCH	Cone
CYLINDERS	Eight	TRANSMISSION	Selective sliding
ARRANGED	V type, 90 degrees	GEAR CHANGES	Three forward, one reverse
CAST	In fours	DRIVE	Spiral bevel
HORSEPOWER	28.8	REAR AXLE	Full floating
(N.A.C.C. Rating)		STEERING GEAR	Worm and gear

In addition to above specifications, price includes top, top hood,
windshield, speedometer, electric horn and demountable rims.

HORNER TRUCKS

Manufactured by

DETROIT-WYANDOTTE MOTOR TRUCK CO., Wyandotte, Mich.

Model	1918	1918	1918	1918
Capacity	1½ ton	2 tons	3 tons	5 tons
Drive	Worm	Worm	Worm	Worm
Chassis Weight	4,480 lbs.	4,665 lbs.	6,900 lbs.	8,590 lbs.
Chassis Price	$2,650	$2,750	$3,550	$4,750
Engine	Continental	Continental	Continental	Continental
H. P. (S.A.E.)	27¼	27¼	36½	46½
H. P. (Actual)	32	32	43	54
Cylinders	4 en bloc	4 en bloc	4 in pairs	4 in pairs
Bore	4⅛″	4⅛″	4½″	5¼″
Stroke	5¼″	5¼″	5½″	5¾″
Wheel Base	145″	145″	145″	169″
Tread Front	56″	60″	60″	66″
Tread Rear	56″	60″	66″	70″
Tires Front	36x4″	36x4″	36x5″	38x6″
Tires Rear	36x4″	36x3½″ dual	40x4″ dual	42x5″ dual

Frame—Pressed.
Front Axle—I-beam.
Rear Axle—Timken worm full-floating.
Springs Front—Semi-elliptic.
Springs Rear—Platform.
Carburetor—Master.
Cooling System—Pump.
Oiling System—Forced feed.
Ignition—Magneto.
Control—Left.
Clutch—Dry plate.
Transmission—Brown-Lipe-Chapin, three speeds forward and one reverse.
Brakes—Internal.
Steering Gear—Worm.
Equipment—Lamps, horn, tools, metal tool box, driver's seat, cushion, front fenders, foot
    boards and governor.

most unusual about Horner trucks was that all of them used the same 145-inch wheelbase and had Brown-Lipe-Chapin transmissions. Only the 5-ton was longer, first listed at 156-inch, and in 1918 lengthened to a 169-inch wheelbase. By this time the 1-ton was dropped from the lineup.

All Horner trucks were mainly differentiated by the size of their Continental four-cylinder motors. Standard equipment included front fenders, footboards, seat cushion, tools, lamps and governor. At that time nearly every truck had a governor to keep the engine's RPM down, and the vehicle's top speeds were below 18 mph. In 1918 that may have been acceptable, but it was incongruous with the speed of most passenger cars, which could reach two to four times that clip.

It should be noted that at that time there were no high-speed highways or such a thing as a multi-lane "freeway." Trucks were considered motorized wagons and the name "truck" was derived from a horse-drawn conveyance not expected to exceed the speed of a running man. It was the durability and reliability of trucks that were touted as the main superiority of trucks over flesh-and-blood animals.

Most advertising claimed a truck could perform the work of several horses and a couple of men, day and night, without getting sick or sleepy. Even mechanical maintenance of a motor vehicle was less work than the feeding, grooming, harnessing, training, shoeing, resting and fenced pasturing, as well as manure removal, that a horse involved, and several horses or mules were usually needed.

Horner trucks switched from chain-drive to Timken worm drive during World War I. In appearance Horner trucks used what has been dubbed a "Renault"-type hood, but a number of well-known American trucks had the swept-back hood, including International, Kelly and Mack. A hood of this type meant the radiator was behind the motor, which had

its advantages in cooling capacity with the use of a fan. It also provided protection from damage while allowing easy access to the motor itself for maintenance or repair at a time when that type of work was necessary every few thousand miles, which was still less than the needed care of a draft animal. Nevertheless, even with some advanced features Horner trucks were no longer in business after the Armistice was signed in Europe, but it's unknown just how much the war had affected manufacturing and marketing at the Detroit-Wyandotte Company.

Hudson

Hudson was the name of at least ten motor vehicle manufacturers before the Great War. There was only one that continued to stay in business for nearly half a century, and it was the Hudson Motor Car Company of Detroit, Michigan. It was founded by Roy D. Chapin, engineer Howard E. Coffin, George W. Dunham and Roscoe B. Jackson, all of whom had departed from Olds Motor Works, and the first two had built the Chalmers-Detroit and Thomas-Detroit. Production had quickly ramped up to 4000 within one year by 1909.

Having obtained a Selden License to manufacture autos in the yet-unresolved legal dispute that Ford was waging at the time, and having acquired the former factory of Aerocar, the Hudson looked to be a success and quickly fulfilled its promise. The light, quick Hudson Roadster, capable of 50 mph, was a sure-fire hit with a price tag of $900 in 1910.

The 1912 Mile-a-Minute Roadster was the next winner for Hudson. By midyear Hudson had a new factory in Detroit and a new six-cylinder motorcar to show for Coffin's design efforts. It was introduced for model year 1913 at $2450 in touring guise, and as World War I began, a light six was offered for $1560. Hudson was producing 10,000 cars per year, fully utilizing assembly line manufacturing

**HUDSON
MOTOR CAR
COMPANY**

**DETROIT
MICHIGAN**

Price	$3150
Seven-Passenger Phaeton	1950
Four-Passenger Phaeton	2050
Runabout Landau	2350
Four-Door Sedan	2750
Limousine	3400
Limousine Landau	3500
Town Car	3400
Town Car Landau	3500
Full Folding Landau	4250

HUDSON SUPER-SIX TOURING LIMOUSINE

COLOR	Hungarian blue or coach painter's green with black enameled fenders and splash guards	HORSEPOWER	29.4 (N.A.C.C. Rating)	
		BORE AND STROKE	3½ x 5 inches	
		LUBRICATION	Splash with circulating pump	
SEATING CAPACITY	Four	RADIATOR	Cellular	
POSITION OF DRIVER	Left side	COOLING	Water pump	
WHEELBASE	125½ inches	IGNITION	Storage battery	
GAUGE	56 inches	STARTING SYSTEM	Single unit	
WHEELS	Wood	STARTER OPERATED	Gear to fly wheel	
FRONT TIRES	33 x 5 inches, anti-skid	LIGHTING SYSTEM	Electric	
		VOLTAGES	Six	
REAR TIRES	33 x 5 inches, anti-skid	WIRING SYSTEM	Single	
		GASOLINE SYSTEM	Vacuum	
SERVICE BRAKE	Contracting on rear wheels	CLUTCH	Multiple disc in oil	
		TRANSMISSION	Selective sliding	
EMERGENCY BRAKE	Expanding on rear wheels	GEAR CHANGES	Three forward, one reverse	
CYLINDERS	Six	DRIVE	Spiral bevel	
ARRANGED	Vertically	REAR AXLE	Three-quarters floating	
CAST	En bloc	STEERING GEAR	Worm and gear	

In addition to above specifications, price includes windshield, speedometer, ammeter, tire pump, electric horn and demountable rims.

techniques that have often been attributed solely to Henry Ford. In fact, by the time Ford introduced his Model T in 1908, many of the large manufacturers were taking full advantage of the efficient assembly line, allowing thousands of vehicles to roll off the line every year. That meant that in a 250-day work year at least 40 cars were being completed per day, or approximately one vehicle every twenty minutes was finished and ready for dealership distribution in order for there to be 10,000 produced in a single year.

As America's attention was captivated by an invasion of Mexico in search of Pancho Villa, racer Ralph Mulford drove a Hudson Six to a new record of 102.5 mph, and at Sheepshead Bay a 24-hour speed record of 75 mph was set, which remained for the next 15 years. Other successes in races and runs were well publicized to the benefit of sales at Hudson, which sold 25,700 cars for model year 1916.

Because of Hudson's high production output, durability and performance, ambulances began to be custom-built by civic organizations such as the Red Cross using the Hudson Super Six, and a number were floated over to Europe on a humanitarian basis. Hudsons were also built as ambulances and some light trucks for the U.S. Army. The Super Six produced 76 hp from a 289 cid and was available in at least nine body styles for 1918.

Due to the war the Hudson racing team was discontinued in August of 1917. Numerous racing programs were drastically affected across the country during the war effort when automotive speed competitions were deemed frivolous and were discouraged. It's significant to note that as soon as World War I ended, Hudson resumed its racing program, entering the Indianapolis 500, qualifying with several cars and finishing with one in eighth place. Also, in 1919, the boxy Essex was introduced as a lower-priced car to add to Hudson's market share.

Hudson's good fortunes went on for many years, and the company survived the first year after the stock market crash, even if sales were half that of 1929. Sales for 1931 were half again, and in 1933 had plummeted to 2400, but just enough to continue in business. In 1934 sales rebounded to 27,100 when Roy Chapin resumed as president. Hudsons continued to succeed in racing during the 1930s. By the mid–1930s a Hudson convertible could be bought for less than $1000. However, after World War II, management decisions, including a reluctance to develop a V-8, and a merger with Nash to form American Motors, resulted in the end of Hudson as a marque in 1957.

Hupmobile

Adding the word "mobile" to their slightly abbreviated name, Robert and Louis Hupp began producing cars in Detroit during 1909 at their Hupp Motor Car Company. Robert Hupp had already had experience in the business of motorized wheels at Olds, Ford and Regal, with a prototype of his own finished at the end of 1908. The following year the little Model 20 with a 16.9 hp four-cylinder engine was offered for $750, and 1615 people parted with that amount to start the company off on a successful ride for the next three decades.

From the beginning the two brothers chose their partners well — J. Walter Drake was installed as president, Charles Hastings came over from Thomas-Detroit, Otto von Bachelle had built an electric car, Emil Nelson was another engineer, and Edward Denby joined up, later to become Secretary of the Navy. By 1910 production had more than tripled, and by 1911 just over 6000 Hupmobiles were sold.

The 1908 Paris to New York round-the-world car race, facetiously celebrated later in film, prompted Hupmobile to create a round-the-world promotion of their own in 1910.

H U P P
MOTOR CAR
CORPORATION

D E T R O I T
M I C H I G A N

Price, $1250

HUPMOBILE ROADSTER—R

COLOR	Body, Hupmobile blue; hood, fenders and running gear, black	BORE AND STROKE .	3¼ x 5½ inches
		LUBRICATION	Force feed and splash
SEATING CAPACITY. .	Two	RADIATOR	Cellular
POSITION OF DRIVER .	Left side	COOLING	Thermo-syphon
WHEELBASE	112 inches	IGNITION	Storage battery
GAUGE	56 inches	STARTING SYSTEM . .	Two unit
WHEELS	Wood	STARTER OPERATED .	Gear to fly wheel
FRONT TIRES	32 x 4 inches	LIGHTING SYSTEM . .	Electric
REAR TIRES	32 x 4 inches, anti-skid	VOLTAGES	Six
		WIRING SYSTEM . . .	Single
SERVICE BRAKE . . .	Contracting on rear wheels	GASOLINE SYSTEM . .	Vacuum
		CLUTCH	Dry plate
EMERGENCY BRAKE .	Expanding on rear wheels	TRANSMISSION . . .	Selective sliding
		GEAR CHANGES . . .	Three forward, one reverse
CYLINDERS	Four		
ARRANGED	Vertically	DRIVE	Spiral bevel
CAST	En bloc	REAR AXLE	Three-quarters floating
HORSEPOWER . . . 16.9 (N.A.C.C. Rating)		STEERING GEAR . . .	Screw and nut

In addition to above specifications, price includes top, top hood, windshield, speedometer, ammeter, tire pump, electric horn and demountable rims.

After traveling over 48,000 miles through 26 countries the Hupmobile used in the promo returned to a Hupp Motor Company minus one of its founders. Robert Hupp had gotten into such a heated disagreement that he had resigned, and per contractual agreement he could not start another company in the auto industry using his name. Hence, he founded R.C.H. and later Hupp-Yeats, Monarch and Emerson, all without much success, as opposed to the Hupmobile, which continued without Hupp quite handily.

In 1913, 13,650 Hupmobiles were sold. Frank E. Watts would become the chief engineer for the next 26 years. Hupmobiles continued to sell well through World War I under his leadership once Drake had been pressured away from the helm due to his penchant for extravagant models that had few enthusiasts.

In 1917 the Series R was introduced as a smaller, lower-priced car that became popular for nearly a decade. Hupmobile introduced a straight-eight-cylinder flathead engine in 1925. The following year a six-cylinder engine was introduced as the four-cylinder motor was discontinued. Styling got a progressive influence from Amos Northup. In the early 1930s Raymond Loewy was also hired to add pizzazz to the Hupmobile, for which there was only limited opportunity in such things as fender and wheel design. By the end of the 1930s Hupp Motors was in deep financial trouble and no amount of dissecting its manufacturing capabilities or tweaking the styling along the lines of Errett Cord at Auburn could keep the company from bankruptcy in 1942.

Hurlburt

New York City was the location of the Hurlburt Motor Truck Company, which did not produce passenger cars but concentrated only on trucks. At its inception the factory was in Manhattan, moving to cheaper digs in the Bronx by 1915. Hurlburt may have had the advantage of the big city in terms of labor force and a concentration of potential business customers, but the small company also had competitors the likes of Mack in this busy part of the world. But there were local businesses such as Tiffany Studios, Schultz Bread, John Wanamakers, and Loose-Wiles Biscuit Company that bought Hurlburt trucks for delivery work.

The first Hurlburt truck model line consisted of 1-, 2- and 3½-ton capacity. The model line remained essentially the same with the addition of a 5-ton capacity Model 5. Otherwise the models were named 1, 2 and 3, and each was powered by a Buda motor of different power rating. It's notable how the actual engine horsepower corresponded to the horsepower as rated by the earlier Association of Licensed Automobile Manufacturers (A.L.A.M.) or Society of Automotive Engineers (SAE). The 25 hp Buda motor was actually measured at 22.50 with all of its accessories attached, the 38 hp was 28.90, the 45 hp was 32.4 and the 48 hp was 33.75.

What was unusual for the Hurlburt Model 5 of 1918 was that it was powered by a six-cylinder engine. Most trucks of the day used various sizes of four-cylinder motors. All Hurlburts used worm drive of their own manufacture. Standard equipment from Hurlburt included a generator and battery. There was no mention of fenders, floorboards, windshield, seat and cab, which some truck manufacturers did not include in their bare chassis. Even these basic components were built onto the running chassis after purchase, such as the unusual modified C-cab illustrated here.

As with nearly all vehicles of the day, there were no front brakes due to complexity of linkage on wheels that pivoted prior to the advent of hydraulic brakes.

Customer base was expanded to other East Coast states, such as the Harrisburg Manufacturing and Boiler Company of Harrisburg, Pennsylvania. From the catalog listing it

HURLBURT TRUCKS

Manufactured by

HURLBURT MOTOR TRUCK CO., 133rd St. & Harlem River, N. Y., N. Y.

Model	1	2	3	5
Capacity	1½ tons	2 tons	3½ tons	5 tons
Drive	Worm	Worm	Worm	Worm
Chassis Weight	4,300 lbs.	5,600 lbs.	6,400 lbs.	7,800 lbs.
Chassis Price	$2,600	$3,500	$4,150	$5,000
Engine	Buda	Buda	Buda	Buda
H. P. (S.A.E.)	22.50	28.9	32.4	33.75
H. P. (Actual)	25	38	45	48
Cylinders	4 en bloc	4 en bloc	4 en bloc	6 en bloc
Bore	3¾"	4¼"	4¼"	3¾"
Stroke	5½"	5½"	6"	5½"
Wheel Base	136" or 148"	148" or 170"	146" or 170"	156" or 170"
Tread Front	56"	57¼"	57½"	62"
Tread Rear	63"	62¾"	62¾"	64"
Tires Front	34x4"	36x4"	36x5"	36x6"
Tires Rear	34x5"	36x4" dual	36x5" dual	40x6" dual

Frame—Pressed steel.
Front Axle—I-beam Elliot.
Rear Axle—Hurlburt full floating.
Springs Front—Semi-elliptic.
Springs Rear—Semi-elliptic.

Carburetor	Flechter 3AX	Flechter 3AX	Flechter 3AX	Flechter 4AX

Cooling System—Pump.
Oiling System—Forced feed and splash.
Ignition—Magneto.
Control—Left drive, center control.
Clutch—Multiple dry disc.

Transmission	Brown-Lipe Selective, 3 speeds	Brown-Lipe Selective, 3 speeds	Brown-Lipe Selective, 3 speeds	Brown-Lipe Selective, 4 speeds

Brakes—Expanding rear axles.
Steering Gear—Worm and nut.
Equipment—Speedometer, electric side and rear lamps, electric generator and 80 ampere
      hour battery, electric hand lamp, ammeter, horn, complete set of tools in tool box,
      special wrenches, jack, oil gun, oil can and governor.

would appear the Hurlburt six-cylinder 7-ton model did not appear until after World War I, but it was dropped in 1920. In the last two years of Hurlburt's existence a 10-ton model was built, which was available as an articulated six-wheel vehicle. Manufacturing ceased in 1927.

Indian (motorcycle)

Modern bicycle development was highly influential in the evolution of motor vehicles, whether they were two-, three- or four-wheel design. In the case of George Hendee and Oscar Hedstrom, who were bicycle racers, the idea to build motorized bicycles materialized into one of the most well-known manufacturing companies of motorcycles in America.

Hendee was already building Silver King bicycles at Middletown, Massachusetts. The collaboration between the two men resulted in the Hendee Manufacturing Company, which began in 1901. The first Indian "motocycle," which could be considered a motorized bicycle before it was called a "motorcycle," was powered by a 213 cc 1¾-hp single-cylinder engine which was actually integral with the seat post. It was designed by Hedstrom and built by Aurora Automatic Machine Company in Illinois. A diamond-shaped bicycle frame was used for the first seven years of manufacture before racing convinced Hedstrom to use the loop frame design.

The factory for building Indians was located in Springfield, Massachusetts, and production reached 376 units for 1903. Another 200 more than that were built the following year. By 1905 the engine was increased to 213 cc and 2.25 hp. By this time the Indian could reach 25 mph and cost $200.

It was in 1907 that the Indian V-twin engine made its first appearance in the form of a 633 cc four-stroke 4 hp motor, which was still integral to the frame upright tube. The Isle of Man Tourist Trophy was won on an Indian by Teddy Hastings in 1907 before Harley-Davidson entered the race. Indian hired him for a repeat performance, which he accomplished the following year.

French-Canadian Jake DeRosier was the next race-winning Indian rider who made a name both for himself and for the company that sponsored him. His Indian had a 1000 cc motor producing 7 hp, and the special motorcycle weighed only 130 pounds while being capable of 70 mph. The series-produced ver-

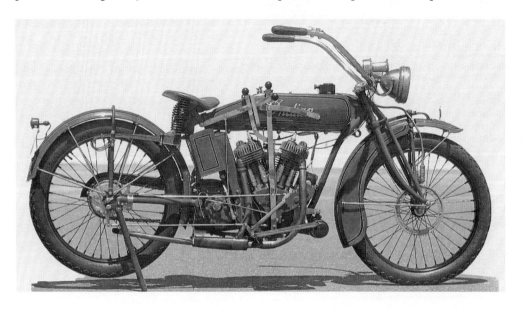

sion sold for $350 in 1908, and the diamond bicycle design would be discontinued in 1909 when the new loop frame series was introduced.

The Indian motorcycle dramatically changed appearance in 1909, primarily due to the new loop frame and the "modern" position of the engine. Motordromes with boardwalk racing tracks were more popular than ever and speeds were near 80 mph with the goal of reaching 100. Riders were banking at 60 degrees, twice as far over as before, and the stress and vibration on the machines were greatly increased, forcing rival companies to optimize the design of their motorcycles through death-defying competition.

The front-fork leaf-spring design that Indian introduced in 1910 remained as a signature component, and overall production reached 6000 that year. A single-cylinder Indian was offered which was powered by a 316 cc motor producing 5 hp. Wheelbase was 56 inches, which was three inches longer than the 8-valve racer of 1911, capable of 100 mph. That year production zoomed up to 20,000.

In 1912 an accident at the New Jersey Motordrome resulted in the deaths of riders Eddie Hasha and Johnnie Albright along with six spectators. It was the beginning of the end of boardwalk racing. Nevertheless, Indian production broke new records, with 32,000 built for 1913. Hedstrom retired when Jake DeRosier died from racing injuries that year. Hendee retired two years later.

In 1915 a three-speed transmission was first introduced by Indian for both its 1000 cc V-Twin and 700 cc single-cylinder F-head bikes. Kickstart and generator were options now. Charles Franklin took the place of Hedstrom as chief engineer, and production concentrated on military orders of the Powerplus, which amounted to 20,000 units for 1917, with only a small portion available to the general public.

After the war it was noted that the company had neglected its civilian customers for a couple of years, allowing Harley-Davidson to make inroads into their share of the market. By 1919 Indian's dominance in sales to civilian customers had been surpassed, and the record production of 1913 would never again be reached. However, the Indian Daytona Twin would dominate racing, winning 14 of 17 national competitions in 1920.

That year the new model called the Scout was introduced by Indian. It was powered by a 600 cc V-Twin producing 11 hp, was capable of 55 mph and cost $325. Sidecar racing gained popularity and Flxible of Loudonville, Ohio, was the largest seller of sidecars. The lighter Scout handled better than the Powerplus and became just as, or even more popular.

The Powerplus was replaced by the Big Chief and the Chief, 1200 cc and 1000 cc motorcycles that used side-valve motors and first appeared in 1923. Police departments bought the two Chief models around the country in direct competition with Harley-Davidson marketing. The light, single-cylinder Prince came out in 1925 with a 350 cc motor producing 7 hp. It was priced at $195.

Under company president Frank Weschler, Indian bought out Ace Motorcycle Company in 1926, producing its own four-cylinder version which displaced 1265 cc. It was called the Indian Ace and sold for $425.

In subsequent years as the Great Depression began, Indian introduced a three-wheel commercial car called the Dispatch Tow, which was used for servicing and maintenance of automobiles. By the mid–1930s the 1200 cc Chief had 34 hp and racing speeds reached 120 mph.

In World War II Indian switched to military production for 1942. Its model 640, based on the Scout with 750 cc, was built for the military. Also, Indian's model 841 was a departure from previous designs in that the V-Twin was transversely mounted and had shaft drive in order to meet military specs.

After World War II Indian struggled to regain a foothold in the civilian market. By 1953 the company as a manufacturer was defunct. Smaller imported motorcycles were marketed under the Indian name and a revival effort with manufacturing in the late 1990s in California also met with a dead end in production of Indian motorcycles.

Indiana

One of the few trucks named for the state in which it was manufactured was the Indiana, and the company was located in Marion beginning in 1911. Indiana used either Waukesha or Rutenber engines. The weakness of the Waukesha motors was in that they were only splash lubricated, which was adequate for most work but had its limitations. Force-feed lubrication became the state of the art as torque and RPM increased.

Styling was not heavily emphasized on Indiana trucks, and Indianas were conventional with hard rubber tires and dual chain drive. Pneumatic tires became optional before World War I, and during the war Indiana built 600 trucks for the U.S. Army. By this time Indiana switched to worm drive, and only the lightest model had a three-speed transmission. Otherwise Indiana used four-speed Brown-Lipe transmissions.

By 1918 Indiana was building its own worm drive rear axle for its lightest 1-ton truck, while the rest of the lineup, including the 5-ton model, were from Sheldon. The factory was assembling 4000 trucks per year by 1920. The model line would include up to 5-ton capacity trucks by 1921, and a 7-ton was added in 1923. That year Indiana switched to Hercules motors for its model line up to 3-ton capacity.

A 2-ton model truck built by Indiana in the mid–1920s used a proprietary engine, making the company one of the most diversified in terms of engine availability. In 1925 a seven-speed transmission was built by Indiana for use in its 7-ton model line. The truck was distinctive with a detachable sloping radiator grille, and the Waukesha engine and rear axle were designed to be easily removable for servicing. A similarly designed 3-ton Indiana truck appeared in 1926.

The following year Indiana became a subsidiary of Brockway but the Indiana name continued. However, because of the Great Depression, Brockway had to sell Indiana in 1932. In the meantime Brockway had introduced the use of Wisconsin and Continental engines, making Indiana associated with five engine manufacturers by this time, plus one of its own. It was after the forced sale by Brockway that White bought Indiana and operations moved to Cleveland, Ohio. A large variety of trucks and commercial vehicles, including step vans, were built in the late 1930s, but by 1939 production came to a halt.

International

Among the earliest and most successful truck builders of all time was International. As International Harvester Corporation (IHC) the company was already in business selling farm machinery in 1902, tracing its origins to Cyrus Hall McCormick, who had patented the horse-drawn reaper in 1847. When the McCormick Harvester Company merged with the Deering Harvester Company, along with three other smaller companies in Chicago during 1902, International Harvester was formed. It became one of the world's largest builders of all types of agricultural farm implements and machinery, including trucks and tractors.

By 1907 the IHC "Auto Buggy" appeared, which was a "highwheeler" in that the motor vehicle used large horse-drawn wagon-type wheels up to 44 inches in diameter. These early IHC vehicles were developed by E.A. Johnson, who began experimenting in 1905

INDIANA TRUCKS
Manufactured by
INDIANA TRUCK CO., Marion, Ind.

SPECIFICATIONS

Model	S	D	R	L
Capacity	1 ton	2 tons	3½ tons	5 tons
Drive	Worm	Worm	Worm	Worm
Chassis Price	$1,385	$2,000	$3,000	$4,000
Motor				
H. P. (S.A.E.)	19.6	27.2	28.9	42
H. P. (Actual)	32	37	35	52
Cylinders	4 en bloc	4 in pairs	4 in pairs	4 in pairs
Bore	3½″	4⅛″	4¼″	5 1/10″
Stroke	5¼″	5½″	5¾″	5½″
Wheel Base	130″	150″	156″	163″
Tread Front	56″	58″	58″	62″
Tread Rear	56″	58″	66″	74⅝″
Tires Front	36x3½″	36x4″	36x5″	36x5″
Tires Rear	36x4″	36x7″	36x5″ dual	40x6″ dual

Frame—Rolled.
Front Axle—I-beam, Elliott.

Rear Axle	Full-floating	Semi-floating	Semi-floating	Semi-floating

Springs Front—Semi-elliptic.
Springs Rear—Semi-elliptic.
Carburetor—Stromberg M.
Cooling System—Pump.

Oiling System	Splash	Forced feed and splash	Splash	Forced feed and splash

Ignition—Magneto.
Control—Left drive, center control.
Clutch—Borg & Beck, dry plate.
Transmission—Selective, three speeds forward and one reverse.
Brakes—Internal expanding on rear wheels.
Steering Gear—Screw and nut.
Equipment—Dash and tail lamps, hand horn, screw jack, oil can, tool box, complete tool
    kit, consisting of tool bag, hammer, monkey wrench, metal screw driver, plyers,
    S wrenches ⅝ to 1, Wescott wrench, cold chisel, small screw driver, center punch,
    punch, cotter extractor, box of cotters, also necessary lubrication instruction
    charts.

INTERNATIONAL MOTOR TRUCKS
Manufactured by
INTERNATIONAL HARVESTER CORPORATION
Sold by
INTERNATIONAL HARVESTER CO. OF AMERICA, Chicago, U.S.A.

S P E C I F I C A T I O N S

Model	F	H
Capacity	1 ton	¾ ton
Drive	Internal gear	Internal gear
Chassis Price	$1,500	$1,225
Motor		
H. P. (S.A.E.)	19.61	19.61
Cylinders	4 en bloc	4 en bloc
Bore	3½″	3½″
Stroke	5¼″	5¼″
Wheel Base	128″	115″
Tread Front	56″ or 60″	56″ or 60″
Tread Rear	56″ or 60″	56″ or 60″
Tires Front	36x3½″	36x3″
Tires Rear	36x4″	36x3½″
Frame	Pressed steel	Semi-flexible

Front Axle—I-beam.
Rear Axle—Round.
Springs Front—Semi-elliptic.
Springs Rear—Platform.
Carburetor—Holley.
Cooling System—Pump.
Oiling System—Forced feed and splash.
Ignition—High tension magneto.
Control—Left drive, center control.
Transmission—Selective, three speeds forward and one reverse.
Brakes—Two internal expanding on rear axle.
Steering Gear—Screw and nut.
Equipment—Model F: High tension magneto, two oil lamps, oil tail lamp, front fenders, horn, and tools. Model H: High tension magneto, front and rear fenders, two gas headlights, Prest-o-lite gas tank, oil tail lamp, horn, and tools.

after the company had already produced tractors in 1889. Manufacturing of IHC highwheelers moved from Chicago, Illinois, to Akron, Ohio, by the end of 1907.

Both passenger and commercial highwheelers were built by IHC from 1907 through The horizontally-opposed two-cylinder engines could be ordered with water cooling (models starting with W) or air cooling (models starting with A). Customers had their preferences based upon the climate of their residence, since water-cooled engines were susceptible to cracking when freezing temperatures occurred. By 1914 the IHC designation was changed to simply International for the company's vehicles.

In 1915 a new series of International truck production ensued with the model line named H, F, K, G and L from ¾-ton to 3½-ton. By this time all but the heaviest had pneumatic tires as an option. For those who wished to have the radiator behind the engine those models used the "Renault" hood, which may have looked somewhat aerodynamic but had little need for it at 15–25 mph. Radiators behind the engine were better protected, gave more accessibility to the engine and were more efficient due to shrouded fans in conjunction with the cooling tubes.

International trucks were used during World War I in various capacities. At this time the company had captured four percent of the truck market amid many dozens of manufacturers. In addition to the 1-ton Model F, one of the best-selling trucks was the Model H, which was ¾-ton capacity, built from 1915 to 1923.

Speed trucks were introduced in 1921 as the entire industry began to incorporate light trucks that could run at 30 mph, which was double that at which the trucks of World War I would travel with engine governors which were used on most trucks except for the lightest ones converted from passenger cars.

International, International Harvester, or IHC as it was sometimes referred to, still exists and produces trucks of all various types and sizes up (as well as all types of machinery) to this writing. The rich and complex history of International has filled and will continue to fill volumes and is beyond the scope of this brief discussion.

Inter-State

Muncie, Indiana, was the location of the company that Thomas F. Hart started up after a contest he held to name his new car. Who came up with the name of Inter-State Automobile Company is not known, but by 1909 production began of a medium-priced four-cylinder passenger car in three body styles: Touring, Runabout and Demi-Tonneau. A Roadster and Torpedo were added for 1910 and 1911.

By 1912 the series was expanded to include the Thirty, Forty and Fifty, divided up between Model 30-A through Model 52. The numeric designations of the series referred to the horsepower of the four-cylinder engines. Prices were now as a high as $3400 for Model 50–52. But finances were not all well at Inter-State by the beginning of World War I and the whole enterprise was sold to F.C. Ball, who was a manufacturer of glass jars and was an investor in Inter-State back in 1909.

Under new management and ownership, Inter-State continued to manufacture passenger cars, and briefly tried its luck with a 38.4 hp six-cylinder engine. With debts cleared, Inter-State now became a modest $1000 car powered by a four-cylinder Beaver engine. More significantly Inter-State developed a Deluxe Delivery commercial car in 1916, listed in 1917 for $850 on a 110-inch wheelbase. Coincidentally, it was rated at 850-pound capacity. For 1918 both the modest passenger cars and a Delivery Wagon were built until May of that year.

At that time the entire factory was converted

INTER-STATE
M O T O R
C O M P A N Y

M U N C I E
I N D I A N A

Five-Passenger Touring .	)	Prices
Four-Passenger Roadster .	}	Upon
Two-Passenger Roadster .	}	Application
800-Pound Delivery Wagon	)	tion

INTER-STATE TOURING—T

COLOR	Blue		LUBRICATION	Splash with circulating pump
SEATING CAPACITY .	Five			
POSITION OF DRIVER	Left side		RADIATOR	Cellular
WHEELBASE	110 inches		COOLING	Thermo-syphon
GAUGE	56 inches		IGNITION	Storage battery
WHEELS	Wood		STARTING SYSTEM . .	Two unit
FRONT TIRES	33 x 4 inches		STARTER OPERATED .	Gear to fly wheel
REAR TIRES	33 x 4 inches, anti-skid		LIGHTING SYSTEM . .	Electric
			VOLTAGES	Six
SERVICE BRAKE . . .	Contracting on rear wheels		WIRING SYSTEM . . .	Single
EMERGENCY BRAKE .	Expanding on rear wheels		GASOLINE SYSTEM . .	Gravity
			CLUTCH	Cone
CYLINDERS	Four		TRANSMISSION . . .	Selective sliding
ARRANGED	Vertically		GEAR CHANGES . . .	Three forward, one reverse
CAST	En bloc			
HORSEPOWER	19.6		DRIVE	Bevel
(N.A.C.C. Rating)			REAR AXLE	Semi-floating
BORE AND STROKE .	3½ x 5 inches		STEERING GEAR . . .	Worm and gear

In addition to above specifications, price includes top, top hood, windshield, speedometer, ammeter, clock, tire pump, electric horn and demountable rims.

for materiel production for the war effort. The interruption in manufacturing was not unusual in that numerous factories across the United States were quickly converted in this way. There was no choice whether or not to cooperate. Uncle Sam was considered a reliable employer so most industry leaders, their investors and stockholders clearly saw the necessity of the conversion to war production, and were expecting compensation to cover all costs.

The surprise was that the war ended suddenly and much sooner than expected. Most prognosticators said World War I would continue into 1919 and possibly longer. Military contracts were immediately canceled, leaving numerous small companies in the lurch, often holding inventories of raw material or partially finished components. That was the death knell for Inter-State, which did not return to manufacturing. The factory was sold to General Motors, which, like other large companies, could absorb the financial shock of contractual cancellations.

Jackson

Not affiliated with Byron Jackson of San Francisco, who built a steam car in 1897, Byron J. Carter, who was also affiliated with steam but in the printing press business in Jackson, Michigan, built a steam automobile in that city during 1899. He had also been in the bicycle business with his father, Squire B. Carter, and a few copies of his steam car were built as the "Michigan" by the Michigan Automobile Company in Grand Rapids of that state.

Byron Carter had patented a steam engine and then founded the Jackson Automobile Company with the financial backing from Jackson bankers George A. Matthews and Charles Lewis. The goal was to build both steam and gasoline cars.

This was realized in series production of the Jaxon Steam and the Jackson Gasoline in 1903 in the form of runabouts which sold for under $1000. The spelling of the steam car was altered for differentiation but the steam car appeared only in 1903. At the turn of the previous century it was still uncertain which method of propulsion, in addition to electric battery power, would be the best, would be most accepted by the public and would have the most widespread infrastructure. Byron J. Carter left his options open at first, but by 1904 the company decided on gasoline and introduced a two-cylinder Surrey.

Byron Carter had another idea that was not quite fully baked and that was the use of friction drive, so when his partners nixed the design he resigned to go build the Cartercar. Carter had an accident involving the kickback of a hand crank starter that broke his jaw, an injury that would take his life (due to medical complications) and was cited by Charles Kettering as one of the inspirations for inventing the electric starter motor.

The Jackson car offered a four-cylinder motor by 1906 and manufactured a high-wheeler by the name of Fuller. Jackson built the Duck for 1913, which was a standard car except it was steered from the rear seat, an innovation that met with less than enthusiastic acceptance. Also that year, a Northway six-cylinder was introduced with better welcome, and a Ferro V-8 arrived for 1916. The Jackson was likened to the Rolls-Royce in appearance if not in price or quality. Charles Lewis left to build the Hollier.

The Jackson Wolverine arrived in 1918, and was very similar to the earlier Sultanic but was powered by a V-8 and had other more modern amenities. The company's factory was retooled for building trucks. This misstep was due in large part to the war, and auto manufacturing did not resume until 1920. Jackson truck production turned out to be an abortion. For 1923 Jackson merged with the Dixie Flyer of Louisville, Kentucky, and National

JACKSON
AUTOMOBILE
COMPANY

JACKSON
MICHIGAN

Price	. . .	$1575
Five-Passenger Touring	. . . .	1495
Four-Passenger Cruiser .	. . . .	1495
Two-Passenger Roadster	. . . .	1495
Seven-Passenger Touring	. . . .	1570
Seven-Passenger Sedan	. . . . .	2195

WOLVERINE VIII FLYER

COLOR	Body, azure blue; running gear, black		BORE AND STROKE. .	3 x 3½ inches
SEATING CAPACITY. .	Four		LUBRICATION	Force feed
POSITION OF DRIVER .	Left side		RADIATOR	Tubular
WHEELBASE	118 inches		COOLING	Thermo-syphon
GAUGE	56 inches		IGNITION	Storage battery
WHEELS	Wood		STARTING SYSTEM . .	Single unit
FRONT TIRES	34 x 4 inches		STARTER OPERATED .	Gear to fly wheel
REAR TIRES	34 x 4 inches, anti-skid		LIGHTING SYSTEM . .	Electric
SERVICE BRAKE . . .	Contracting on rear wheels		VOLTAGES	Six to eight
EMERGENCY BRAKE .	Expanding on rear wheels		WIRING SYSTEM . . .	Single
CYLINDERS	Eight		GASOLINE SYSTEM . .	Vacuum
ARRANGED	V type, 90 degrees		CLUTCH	Dry plate
CAST.	En bloc with crank case		TRANSMISSION . . .	Selective sliding
HORSEPOWER . . . . 28.8 (N.A.C.C. Rating)			GEAR CHANGES . . .	Three forward, one reverse
			DRIVE	Spiral bevel
			REAR AXLE	Floating
			STEERING GEAR . . .	Worm and gear

In addition to above specifications, price includes top, top hood, windshield, speedometer, ammeter, clock, tire pump, electric horn and demountable rims.

of Indianapolis, Indiana, as a new venture called Associated Motor Industries. By the following year all of these makes were no longer in existence.

Jeffery

Thomas Jeffery was a true pioneer in the American automotive industry. He had begun in Chicago with a partner named Philip Gormully building the Rambler bicycle and G&J tires. By 1897 he and his son, Charles, began building experimental tiller-steered one-cylinder motorized vehicles using bicycle wheels. The cars were dubbed "Rambler" after the bicycle that Jeffery was building. Upon Gormully's death the Jefferys sold the bicycle company and got into the business of building motor vehicles in Kenosha, Wisconsin.

After a few iterations with variations of front engine/rear engine, right/left side tiller/steering wheel combinations, the Rambler appeared in series production by 1902. The press praised the little car of which 1500 were built that year, increasing to a production number of 2342 for 1904, which included a two-cylinder version. A four-cylinder version arrived for 1906 and was advertised as "The Right Car for the Right Price," which reflected the starting price tag of $1750. At the time the Rambler was the best-selling car in America, outpacing such rivals as Buick, Ford and Olds. But in April of 1910 Thomas Jeffery suddenly died of a heart attack while on vacation in Italy.

Charles Jeffery took over the company, renaming it "Jeffery" in honor of his father who had left a will designating the company to his family. By 1913 the Rambler was joined by a one-ton four-wheel-drive truck designed for the Army Quartermaster Corps. It was called the Quad, and by 1914 the four-cylinder and six-cylinder cars were called Jeffery. Jeffery also began building commercial vehicles from ¾-ton up to 1½-ton. The Jeffery Quad was upgraded to 2-ton capacity and was powered by a 36 hp four-cylinder Buda engine with four-speed transmission. It also had four-wheel steering and its top speed was 20 mph. Numerous steel-plate-clad versions were built, creating some of the first armored cars in existence, including a double-ended version with drivers at each end for quick escape. Only prototypes of the special Jeffery Quad armored cars were built. However, in the first two years at least 10,600 standard Jeffery Quads were built and many were shipped overseas to England and France before America entered the war.

It was on May 7, 1915, that Charles Jeffery was accompanying some 40 Jeffery Quads on the *Lusitania*. Near the British coast a German submarine torpedoed the passenger ship, and 1198 people perished. Jeffery was one of the 761 who survived. At the age of forty the following year in 1916, he sold the Jeffery company and the Jeffery Quad became the Nash Quad. Prior to the transfer to Nash, Jeffery offered three models of trucks for model year 1917.

Jordan

As advertising manager of the Thomas B. Jeffery Automobile in Kenosha, Wisconsin, Edward S. Jordan married into the Jeffery family and did well for himself. By 1916 he struck out to build his own car in Cleveland, Ohio, when Charles Jeffery sold the Jeffery Company to Charles Nash. By 1917 the Jordan was in series production as an example of a refined assembled car, which was Edward "Ned" Jordan's idea from the start. Off-the-shelf components included a Fedders radiator, Bosch ignition, Gemmer steering gear, Bijur electrical system, Stewart-Warner fuel system, Sparton horn, Brown-Lipe clutch and a 29.4 hp Continental four-cylinder motor. Just under 1,800 model year 1917 Jordan autos (in touring and roadster form) were sold.

JEFFERY TRUCKS
Manufactured by
THE NASH MOTORS CO., Kenosha, Wis.

S P E C I F I C A T I O N S

Model	Quad—4016	All Purpose—2016	Rapid Service—1016
Capacity	2 tons	1½ tons	¾ ton
Drive	Four-wheel, internal gear	Internal gear	Spiral bevel gear
Chassis Price	$2,850	$1,465	$965
Motor			
H. P. (S.A.E.)	28.9	22.5	22.5
H. P. (Actual)	33.9 at 1200 R.P.M.	34.25 at 1600 R.P.M.	34.25 at 1600 R.P.M.
Cylinders	4 en bloc	4 en bloc	4 en bloc
Bore	4¼″	3¾″	3¾″
Stroke	5½″	5¼″	5¼″
Wheel Base	124″ std., 142″ $50 extra	130″ std., 142″ $50 extra	116″
Tread Front	56″	56″	56″
Tread Rear	56″	57″	56″
Tires Front	36x5″	34x4½″ pneu.	35x4½″ pneu.
Tires Rear	36x5″	34x5″	35x4½″ pneu.
Frame—Channel, pressed.			
Front Axle	I-beam, special knuckle	I-beam	I-beam
Rear Axle	I-beam, special knuckle	Fixed I-beam	Semi-floating
Springs Front—Semi-elliptic.			
Springs Rear—Semi-elliptic.			
Carburetor	Stromberg KR2	Stromberg L2	Stromberg L2
Cooling System—Pump.			
Oiling System—Splash and force feed.			
Ignition	Eisemann	Dixie	Dixie
Control—Left drive, center control.			
Clutch—Dry plate.			
Transmission	Ind. clutch, 4 speeds forward, 1 reverse	Selective, 3 speeds forward, 1 reverse	Selective, 3 speeds forward, 1 reverse
Brakes	Contracting on propeller shaft and expanding on four wheels	Contracting on rear wheels, emergency on propeller shaft.	Contracting on rear wheels, emergency on propeller shaft.
Steering Gear	Worm and split-nut on all four wheels	Worm and split-nut	Worm and wheel

Equipment—Side and tail lights, horn, tire chains, tools and jack, electric headlights with dimmers, windshield, driver's seat, hood and cowl, dash with foredoors, extra demountable rims.

THE THOMAS B.
J E F F E R Y
C O M P A N Y
KENOSHA, WIS.

Price $3700

MODEL: JEFFERY SIX LIMOUSINE

COLOR	Green, blue, brown or maroon.
SEATING CAPACITY .	Seven persons.
CLUTCH	Cone.
WHEELBASE . . .	128 inches.
GAUGE	56 inches.
TIRE DIMENSIONS:	
FRONT	37 x 5 inches.
REAR	37 x 5 inches.
BRAKE SYSTEMS .	Double expanding on both rear wheels.
HORSE-POWER . . .	N. A. C. C. (formerly A. L. A. M.) rating 33.7.
CYLINDERS	Six.
ARRANGED	Vertically, under hood.
CAST	In pairs.
BORE	3¾ inches.
STROKE	5¼ inches.
COOLING . . .	Water.
RADIATOR	Vertical tube.
IGNITION	Jump spark.
ELECTRIC SOURCE .	High tension magneto and dry batteries.
DRIVE	Shaft.
TRANSMISSION . . .	Selective sliding gear.
GEAR CHANGES .	Four forward, one reverse.
POSITION OF DRIVER .	Left side drive and center control.

Price includes electric lighting, electric self-starter, speedometer
and demountable rims

**JORDAN
MOTOR CAR
COMPANY**

CLEVELAND, OHIO

Price	.$2375
Seven-Passenger Touring	1995
Four-Passenger Touring	1995
Seven-Passenger Sedan	2750
Town Car	3300
Brougham	3000
Limousine	3500

JORDAN SPORT MARINE

COLOR	Body, green or maroon; running gear, black		LUBRICATION	Force feed and splash
			RADIATOR	Cellular
SEATING CAPACITY. .	Four		COOLING	Water pump
POSITION OF DRIVER	Left side		IGNITION	Storage battery
WHEELBASE	127 inches		STARTING SYSTEM . .	Two unit
GAUGE	56 inches		STARTER OPERATED .	Gear to fly wheel
WHEELS	Wire		LIGHTING SYSTEM . .	Electric
FRONT TIRES	33 x 4½ inches		VOLTAGES	Six
REAR TIRES	33 x 4½ inches		WIRING SYSTEM . . .	Single
SERVICE BRAKE . . .	Contracting on rear wheels		GASOLINE SYSTEM . .	Vacuum
EMERGENCY BRAKE .	Expanding on rear wheels		CLUTCH	Plate
			TRANSMISSION . . .	Selective sliding
CYLINDERS	Six		GEAR CHANGES . . .	Three forward, one reverse
ARRANGED	Vertically		DRIVE	Spiral bevel
CAST	En bloc		REAR AXLE	Semi-floating
HORSEPOWER . . . . (N.A.C.C. Rating)	29.4		STEERING GEAR . . .	Worm and gear
BORE AND STROKE .	3½ x 5¼ inches			

In addition to above specifications, price includes top, top hood, windshield, speed-ometer, ammeter, voltmeter, clock, tire pump, electric horn and demountable rims.

Despite the entry into war by the United States, Jordan sold 5,000 copies for 1918 and was spared any direct involvement in materiel production. That allowed the company to move forward with one of Jordan's most popular offerings for the next decade, the Playboy.

The Jordan Playboy was a hit from the start. The word "playboy" in 1919 had similar connotations to those of decades later and Ned Jordan, considered an expert in creating snappy advertising, made the best of it. His ads pushed the envelope to the point of exciting the Society for the Prevention of Vice into censoring some of them. In what would be considered mildly subtle today, Jordan's ad showing a house at night with one light on in an upstairs bedroom and a Playboy auto parked outside was considered so titillating as to have its provocative illumination airbrushed into dark obscurity by censors.

Nevertheless, with its shiny wire wheels, the Playboy's sporting image at a time when "sports car" was yet to be adopted as common nomenclature was irresistible for enough buyers to make the car a success. Lockheed hydraulic brakes were introduced in 1925, and a straight-eight designed at Jordan was built by Continental. It made the following year the highest production in company history with 11,000 units sold, including a touring, brougham and three sedans in addition to the roadster.

Despite Ned Jordan's personal problems with health and marriage and the company's management troubles, the Jordan enterprise was somehow propelled to produce its best motorcars yet: the Great Line Model Eighty and Model Ninety of 1929, and the Model Z Speedway Ace for 1930, the latter with a guarantee of 100 mph at a price of $5500. But 1929 was the year of the stock market crash, and by 1932 the Jordan, with its famous Playboy, Blueboy and Tomboy, along with other fine models, became yet another manufacturer in the hands of the undertaker. It has been written that of the 65,000 Jordans produced in nearly one and a half decades, 50,000 were still on the road at the beginning of the Great Depression.

Kelly-Springfield

Often referred to as just "Kelly," the Kelly-Springfield Motor Company of Springfield, Ohio, evolved from the Frayer-Miller automobile manufactured by the Oscar Lear Auto Company in Columbus, Ohio. Kelly did not build passenger cars but concentrated entirely on trucks, or commercial cars as they were often called in the early years. Beginning in 1910 Kelly used an air-cooled four-cylinder motor until 1912, when the company switched to a water-cooled unit of its own manufacture.

Kelly was one of the handful of truck builders that adopted what has been called the "Renault" hood, which was swept back due to the fact that the radiator was behind the engine. As already mentioned in describing this matter, there were advantages in cooling efficiency, access to the motor and protection of the radiator itself.

One-, two- and three-ton capacity trucks were available using three-speed transmissions and chain drive. At the time Kelly offered artillery wheels and solid rubber tires as well as express bodies from the factory. The model line was expanded to include 3½-ton trucks by the beginning of World War I.

Just before America entered World War I, one of the largest civilian contracts up to that time was made between Kelly-Springfield and the United States Circus Corporation. The circus placed an order for one hundred 3½-ton trucks to use for transporting its show around the country instead of using the railroad. They may have anticipated the huge traffic of military equipment and vehicles being moved by rail as America prepared to enter the war overseas. The tracks were jammed across the country at a time when interstate highways were yet to be developed.

KELLY-SPRINGFIELD TRUCKS

Manufactured by

THE KELLY-SPRINGFIELD MOTOR TRUCK CO., Springfield, Ohio

Model	K-31	K-32	K-35	K-40
Capacity	1½ tons	1½ tons	2½ tons	3½ tons
Drive	Chain	Worm	Chain	Chain
Chassis Weight	4,590 lbs.	4,685 lbs.	5,200 lbs.	8,285 lbs.
Chassis Price	$2,500	$2,500	$3,000	$3,850
Engine	Kelly-Springfield	Kelly-Springfield	Kelly-Springfield	Kelly-Springfield
H. P. (S.A.E.)	22.50	22.50	22.50	32.40
H. P. (Actual)	30 at 1300 R.P.M.	30 at 1300 R.P.M.	30 at 1300 R.P.M.	46 at 1300 R.P.M.
Cylinders	4 en bloc	4 en bloc	4 en bloc	4 in pairs
Bore	3¾″	3¾″	3¾″	4½″
Stroke	5¼″	5¼″	5¼″	6½″
Wheel Base	144″ Std., 110″, 120″, 168″ Opt.	144″ Std., 112″ 120″, 168″ Opt.	144″ Std., 110″ 120″, 168″ Opt.	150″ Std., 116″, to 208″ Optional
Tread Front	57″	57″	59″	70″
Tread Rear	62″	60″	65″	74″
Tires Front	36x3½″	36x3½″	36x4″	36x5″
Tires Rear	36x6″	36x6″	36x4″ dual	38x5″ or 40x5″ dual

Frame—Pressed channel.
Front Axle—I-section, Elliott type.

Rear Axle	Kelly-Springfield Dead I-beam	Kelly-Springfield Semi-floating	Kelly-Springfield Dead I-beam	Kelly-Springfield Dead I-beam

Springs Front—Semi-elliptic.
Springs Rear—Semi-elliptic.

Carburetor	Zenith L-4, 1″	Zenith L-4, 1″	Zenith L-4, 1″	Rayfield GL4, 1¼″

Cooling System—Centrifugal pump.
Oiling System—Forced feed.
Ignition—Magneto.
Control—Left-hand drive, center control.
Clutch—Cone.
Transmission—Covert Selective, three speeds forward.
Brakes—Internal expanding rear wheels.
Steering Gear—Worm and wheel.
Equipment—Driver's seat, two oil dash side lamps, oil tail lamp, full set of small tools in kit roll, two-ton jack and number of special tools and wrenches, warning signal, mud guards for front wheels connected to running board, hubodometer.

In 1918 the model line was expanded to eight different capacities, from 1½-ton up to 6-ton, although not all were listed in the Goodrich catalog. Kelly introduced worm drive for its lightest model, in essence experimenting with the advanced mechanical design that had yet to be proven for heavy duty use. Dual chain drive for the heavy models remained through 1926. Toward the end of the company's existence Hercules engines were also used. By 1928 Kelly-Springfield was going out of business, and even before the stock market crash of 1929 the company was no longer in manufacturing.

King

Not affiliated with the temporarily contemporary A.R. King Manufacturing Company of Kingston, Ohio, the King auto was built by Charles Brady King in Detroit, Michigan. C.B. King got involved with the horseless buggy early on when he built a four-cylinder car in 1895.

It was not in time for the first Chicago Times-Herald Contest of that year, in which Duryea became world-renowned as America's foremost gasoline-powered motor vehicle. But when King did complete his first car on March 6, 1896, it became the first car driven on the street of Detroit, Michigan, the city that would become a metonym for the American auto. From all accounts Henry Ford was present as a bystander (technically following on a bicycle). King patented his "gas engine for vehicles and launches" and helped Ford obtain some components for his first car of 1896.

After serving as a machinist during the Spanish-American War, King returned and sold his engine manufacturing company to Ransom Eli Olds, after which he produced the Northern auto with Jonathan Maxwell for six years. When the Northern car did not fare well, King traveled to Europe to spend two years learning the art of automotive design.

When he returned he promptly designed and built the four-cylinder King auto, which went into production in Detroit during 1911 with a half-million-dollar capitalization.

King's design was advanced and up-to-date, including an *en bloc* motor (with all four cylinders cast in one section), cantilever suspension springs and left-hand-side steering, at a time when designers and the public were still arguing the merits of either side. The gear-shift lever was placed in the middle of the floor when many vehicles still had levers located on the outside on the running boards, stemming from the horse-drawn wagon traditions of having the brake lever mounted there.

The King looked like a success and by the following year the factory was moved to the former Hupmobile plant in Detroit when that company moved its operations. However, within the same year the enterprise went into receivership, and King was purchased by Artemus Ward, a New York advertising executive who hired J.G. Bayerline as president by 1913.

By the end of 1914 King introduced its own V-8 motor just two months after Cadillac set a milestone for first American production motor of this type. Output reached 3000 cars for King in 1915 as the new V-8 caught a lot of customers' attention at a price tag of $1350 for the Touring. The following year the company also built 3000 autos, but Charles King went off to war, as so many of those in the industry had to do during World War I, especially after conscription was enforced through the Selective Service Act of 1917.

King worked for the Signal Corps, one branch of the U.S. military that was more involved with motor vehicles than others. As far as the fledgling motor aircraft was related to the motor vehicle industry, King was in charge of designing the King-Bugatti aero engine, making use of one of several other talents and capabilities with which he was blessed.

The King company did not continue its success as America entered the war. Sales slid,

KING MOTOR CAR COMPANY

DETROIT MICHIGAN

Price	$2150
Three-Passenger Roadster . . .	2150
Four-Passenger Foursome . . .	2300
Seven-Passenger Sedan	2900

KING EIGHT TOURING

COLOR	Phaeton green	LUBRICATION	Force feed
SEATING CAPACITY .	Seven	RADIATOR	Tubular
POSITION OF DRIVER	Left side	COOLING	Thermo-syphon
WHEELBASE	120 inches	IGNITION	Storage battery
GAUGE	56 inches	STARTING SYSTEM . .	Two unit
WHEELS	Wood	STARTER OPERATED .	Gear to fly wheel
FRONT TIRES	34 x 4 inches	LIGHTING SYSTEM . .	Electric
REAR TIRES	34 x 4 inches, anti-skid	VOLTAGES	Six
		WIRING SYSTEM . . .	Single
SERVICE BRAKE . . .	Contracting on rear wheels	GASOLINE SYSTEM . .	Vacuum
		CLUTCH	Dry plate
EMERGENCY BRAKE .	Expanding on rear wheels	TRANSMISSION . . .	Selective sliding
CYLINDERS	Eight	GEAR CHANGES . . .	Three forward, one reverse
ARRANGED	V type, 90 degrees		
CAST	In fours	DRIVE	Spiral bevel
HORSEPOWER	28.8 (N.A.C.C. Rating)	REAR AXLE	Full floating
		STEERING GEAR . . .	Worm and split nut
BORE AND STROKE .	3 x 5 inches		

In addition to above specifications, price includes top, top hood, windshield, speedometer, ammeter, tire pump, electric horn and demountable rims.

and after the war troubles with material shortages and the recession added to Artemus Ward's departure as president. Charles A. Finnegan bought King's assets for $500,000, paying off all liabilities as the company continued to build only an eight-cylinder car through 1922. Under new management the company was moved to a smaller factory in Buffalo, New York, where 240 King autos were built for 1923. After exporting cars overseas, King sold its last units in England before the company closed down in 1924.

Kissel

A number of early motor vehicle manufacturers built both passenger cars and trucks when the two types of vehicles greatly overlapped in size and design, and Kissel Kar was one of those versatile companies. In 1907, Hartford, Wisconsin, became the city of the Kissel Kar, the name referring to L. Kissel & Sons, who were a large, very well-to-do local family.

As World War I began, among those that assembled the FWD Model B was Kissel Kar. The company was a significant contributor to the war effort in Europe during this period, representing American automotive engineering even if it was on a small scale. Ironically, Kissel Kar was organized by the newly-transplanted German family of L. Kissel and his sons George and Will, who began in farming and soon built their first automobile in 1905. Having made money in the lumber, real estate, grocery and building businesses, by 1907 the Kissel conglomerate decided to go into series auto manufacturing, and the first cars had bodies built by a sleigh manufacturer named Zimmerman in the same part of this snowy country.

The first Kissel Kar featured a four-cylinder motor and shaft drive, quite advanced for the time. By 1908 Kissel light trucks were also being built on passenger car chassis. Numerous models were offered by 1909 from $1350 to $3000 ranging in wheelbase from 107 to 128 inches.

Perhaps through a historical accident in 1908, Herman Palmer, a graduate engineer, was on a tour of Wisconsin, playing cello with a small orchestra. When the train departed from Hartford, the orchestra had one fewer musician. Palmer enthusiastically joined Kissel Kar to pursue a career in automotive engineering. The Kissels were also fortunate to attract J. Frederich Werner to their employment ranks. Werner was an experienced auto designer who had worked for Opel Motor Works in Russelheim, Germany.

With engineering expertise abounding, Kissel introduced a drop frame reaching over both front and rear axles in 1911. And because Kissel's market was largely in areas of cold and rainy weather the company built many enclosed cab vehicles, both cars and trucks.

This was the period when Austro-Hungry was occupying Bosnia-Herzogovina, Croatia, Slovenia and Northern Serbia. The Balkan Wars at the time took their toll during 1912 and 1913. When Austro-Hungry declared war on Serbia in 1914, Kissel Kar was one of the first U.S. companies that began obtaining contracts from European countries for truck-based ambulances. There were connections through Werner, who still had contacts back in Germany. Kissel obtained at least six orders for ambulances, including one for 30 such vehicles from the Serbian government. The ambulances featured "pneumatic tires to provide easy riding for the wounded soldiers," as company literature stated.

The "Kar" portion of the name was dropped to draw focus away from the German background of the company owners and engineers, especially after pro-German sympathizers poured sand into the transmissions of a trainload of FWD trucks, among other vehicles. But the small Kissel company's high-quality vehicles were sought out at least in

KISSEL MOTOR CAR COMPANY

HARTFORD WISCONSIN

Price $2085
Four-Passenger All-Year Sedané   2085
Five-Passenger Open Touring . . 1495

KISSEL HUNDRED-POINT SIX ALL-YEAR SEDAN

COLOR	Body, dark blue; hood and fenders, black; wheels, Dayton grey	BORE AND STROKE .	3¼ x 5 inches	
SEATING CAPACITY. .	Five	LUBRICATION	Force feed and splash	
POSITION OF DRIVER	Left side	RADIATOR	Cellular	
WHEELBASE	117 inches	COOLING	Water pump	
GAUGE	56 inches	IGNITION	Storage battery	
WHEELS	Wood	STARTING SYSTEM . .	Two unit	
FRONT TIRES	34 x 4 inches	STARTER OPERATED .	Gear to fly wheel	
REAR TIRES	34 x 4 inches, anti-skid	LIGHTING SYSTEM . .	Electric	
SERVICE BRAKE . . .	Contracting on rear wheels	VOLTAGES	Six	
		WIRING SYSTEM . . .	Single	
EMERGENCY BRAKE .	Contracting on rear wheels	GASOLINE SYSTEM . .	Vacuum	
		CLUTCH	Cone	
CYLINDERS	Six	TRANSMISSION . . .	Selective sliding	
ARRANGED	Vertically	GEAR CHANGES . . .	Three forward, one reverse	
CAST	En bloc			
HORSEPOWER	25.35 (N.A.C.C. Rating)	DRIVE	Spiral bevel	
		REAR AXLE	Full floating	
		STEERING GEAR . . .	Screw and nut	

In addition to above specifications, price includes windshield, speedometer, ammeter, electric horn and demountable rims.

KISSEL KAR TRUCKS

Manufactured by

KISSEL MOTOR CAR CO., Hartford, Wis.

Model	Flyer	General Utility	Freighter	Heavy Duty
Capacity	¾ ton	1¼ tons	2 tons	3½ tons
Drive	Bevel gear	Worm	Worm	Worm
Chassis Weight	2,500 lbs.	3,600 lbs.	4,700 lbs.	6,900 lbs.
Chassis Price	$1,285	$1,885	$2,575	$3,550
Engine	Kissel	Kissel	Kissel	Kissel
H. P. (S.A.E.)	24	24	28.9	28.9
H. P. (Actual)	32 at 1100 R.P.M.	32 at 1100 R.P.M.	37 at 1200 R.P.M.	37 at 1200 R.P.M.
Cylinders	4 en bloc	4 en bloc	4 en bloc	4 en bloc
Bore	3⅞"	3⅞"	4¼"	4¼"
Stroke	5½"	5½"	5½"	5½"
Wheel Base	135"	152"	168"	168"
Tread Front	56"	56"	57½"	62"
Tread Rear	56"	56"	57½"	66"
Tires Front	32x4" Pneu.	34x3½"	34x4"	36x5"
Tires Rear	32x4" Pneu.	34x5"	36x7"	36x5" dual
Frame	Pressed 4¼"x$\frac{3}{16}$"	Pressed 5"x¼"	Pressed 6"x¼"	Pressed 8"x¼"

Front Axle—I-beam Elliott knuckle.

Rear Axle	Kissel full-floating	Sheldon semi-floating	Timken full-floating	Sheldon semi-floating

Springs Front—Semi-elliptic.
Springs Rear—Semi-elliptic.
Carburetor—Stromberg horizontal.
Cooling System—Pump.
Oiling System—Splash.
Ignition—Magneto.
Control—Left-hand drive, center control.

Clutch	Cone	Dry plate	Dry plate	Dry plate
Transmission	Warner Selective 3 speeds forward	Warner Selective 3 speeds forward	Warner Selective 4 speeds forward	Warner Selective 4 speeds forward
Brakes	Ext. contracting	Int. expanding	Int. expanding	Int. expanding
Steering Gear	Split nut & worm	Split nut & worm	Split nut & screw	Screw and nut

Equipment—Two dash lamps, tail lamp, horn, jack, complete set of tools and Kissel all year cab.

small numbers as an early representation of help from America, especially after the Kissel "All Year Car" of 1913 featured a completely enclosed cab. This was also adopted for Kissel trucks and was available the following year as a removable winter cab mounted with plate glass windows. The severe Wisconsin winters were undoubtedly one source of inspiration for this design, also adaptable within the rainy terrain of northern Europe.

Kissel also featured indirectly illuminated dashboard lights in 1914, which was another innovation just starting to be adopted at that time by manufacturers. After using Beaver engines manufactured in Wisconsin, Kissel developed its own 48 hp six-cylinder L-head motor, which remained in production for 15 years. The Weidley V-12 engine was briefly adopted for some of Kissel's heavier trucks. After producing ambulances, trucks and a few staff cars, Kissel resumed production for the civilian market after the war and continued to stay in the automotive field until the company's final demise as the Great Depression set in by 1931.

Kleiber

Of the handful of motor vehicle manufacturers located in the city of San Francisco itself, the largest company was Kleiber, although it was not the company that survived the longest on the Pacific Coast. Kleiber built both passenger cars and trucks, but the passenger car business was only in its last years and production numbers were small.

Beginning in 1913 Kleiber specialized in building conventional assembled trucks. Paul Kleiber was not a native of San Francisco as has been erroneously reported in various discussions. In fact he arrived from Alsace-Lorraine in 1894 at the age of 25. In the late 1890s he experimented with horseless carriages. He obtained the distributorship for

Gramm trucks after the turn of the century, and went into series production of trucks named after himself in 1914.

The factory, whose building still exists along old rail tracks near the waterfront as of this writing, was built as a 140,000-square-foot brick building that was the largest such structure west of Chicago at the time. Kleiber brought four-cylinder Continental engines and Brown-Lipe transmissions in by rail car and offered 1½-ton to 5-ton models from the beginning. Bosch ignition, Timken worm drive and Ross steering were some of the other OEM components used in assembling the Kleiber trucks.

In 1918 Kleiber also built the 1-ton Model AA, and at the time prices ranged from $2,600 to $5,600 for the heaviest Model D rated at 5-ton capacity. The company survived World War I shortages and the postwar recession. By the mid–1920s the 60 hp Continental Red Seal six-cylinder engine was adopted for some models. By 1928 Kleiber introduced four-wheel hydraulic brakes, a progressive design change at the time. Ten different models of trucks were available that year, and by 1930 the company built its first six-wheel model truck.

Between 1924 and 1929 Kleiber also built passenger cars. As ambitious as the decision was, only 30 passenger cars using the Red Seal engine were produced in 1924 with 175 slated for 1925. "Aristocratic in Appearance" was a marketing misnomer by all known accounts. An 85 hp Continental straight-eight motor was adopted for 1929, but after two prototypes of the car were built the company went under even before the stock market crash of that year.

Klemm

Of the numerous motor vehicle builders listed here Klemm may be one of the most

KLEIBER TRUCKS

Manufactured by

KLEIBER & CO., Inc., Eleventh and Folsom Sts., San Francisco, Cal.

Model	AA	A	BB	B
Capacity	1 ton	1½ tons	2 tons	2½ tons
Drive	Worm	Worm	Worm	Worm
Chassis Weight	4,200 lbs.	4,800 lbs.	5,200 lbs.	5,800 lbs.
Chassis Price	$2,100	$2,500	$2,750	$3,200
Engine	Continental	Continental	Continental	Continental
H. P. (S.A.E.)	22.5	27.2	27.2	32.4
H. P. (Actual)	30	35	35	50
Cylinders	4 en bloc	4 en bloc	4 en bloc	4 in pairs
Bore	3¾″	4⅛″	4⅛″	4½″
Stroke	5¼″	5¼″	5¼″	5½″
Wheel Base	130″	140″	140″	150″
Tread Front	56″	58″	58″	62″
Tread Rear	56″	58″	58″	62″
Tires Front	34x3½″	36x3½″	36x3½″	36x4″
Tires Rear	34x5″	36x5″	36x3½″ dual	36x4″ dual

Frame—Rolled channel.
Front Axle—I-beam.

Rear Axle	Timken semi-floating	Sheldon semi-floating	Timken full-floating	Sheldon semi-floating

Springs Front—Semi-elliptic.
Springs Rear—Semi-elliptic.
Carburetor—Schebler.
Cooling System—Pump.
Oiling System—Splash and forced feed.
Ignition—Magneto.
Control—Right drive, center control.
Clutch—Wet plate.
Transmission—Brown-Lipe Selective, three speeds forward.
Brakes—Rear wheel expanding.
Steering Gear—Screw and nut.
Equipment—Horn, side lamps, tail lamps, jack, complete set of tools and special wrenches.

KLEMM 6-6-60 TRUCKS

Manufactured by

E. R. KLEMM, 1447 W. Austin Ave., Chicago, Ill.

Model	K	L
Capacity	6 to 7 tons	5 to 6 tons
Drive	Chain	Chain
Chassis Weight		
Chassis Price	On application	On application
Engine		
H. P. (S.A.E.)	A. L. A. M. 43.5	A. L. A. M. 43.5
Cylinders	6 in pairs	6 in pairs
Bore	4¼"	4¼"
Stroke	5"	5"
Wheel Base	144" to 187"	144" to 187"
Tread Front	60½"	60½"
Tread Rear	66"	66"
Tires Front	36x6"	36x5"
Tires Rear	40x6" dual	40x5" dual
Frame	1 piece 8" channel	1 piece 8" channel

Front Axle—Timken Detroit.
Rear Axle—Round, 4½" Vanadium.
Springs Front—Sheldon, semi-elliptic.
Springs Rear—Sheldon, semi-elliptic.
Carburetor—Stromberg or Rayfield.
Cooling System—Centrifugal pump and fan.
Oiling System—Wisconsin, oil forced.
Ignition—Bosch duplex system.
Control—Right drive, center control.
Clutch—61 disc, oil clutch.
Transmission—Driggs-Seabury selective, three speeds forward and one reverse.
Brakes—Klemm, rear wheel, expanding.
Steering Gear—Ross screw gears.
Equipment—Steel tool box with three shelves, two electric head lights, tail light, horn, required tools, 36 gallon gasoline tank. Klemm trucks furnished with cab, curtains, windshield and cushions, Klemm hoists and all steel body, and McCanna governor.

obscure of them all. E.R. Klemm of Chicago, Illinois, has been listed as a manufacturer of automobiles when by all evidence not a single car was ever built by his company. Instead, Klemm built heavy trucks and built them very briefly during 1917 and 1918.

The Klemm factory was located in Chicago. Klemm offered two truck models, both of which were considered heavy-duty at the time. In reverse alphabetical order, which was not entirely unusual at the time, the K Model Klemm was rated at 6- to 7-ton while the Model L was rated at 5- to 6-ton. What remains unclear is what distinguished the two models besides the slightly larger wheels for the Model K. They both used Driggs-Seabury transmissions, which were furnished from a somewhat obscure manufacturer also. It appears that they also provided an unusual "wet" oil clutch with what is listed as a 61-disc system. At this time single- and multiple-disc and wet and dry clutches, along with cone and friction drive, were still being used throughout the industry.

All internal-combustion engine motor vehicles needed a clutch of some sort in that the motor needed to work (turn) continuously, unlike electric motors that could be shut on and off without any problems, or steam engines in which the motive energy in the form of superheated water vapor could be diverted out and away, leaving only a hot, white cloud. In this era and for many decades clutches were the weak link in the vehicle power drive train and had to be replaced every few thousand miles.

The two model trucks from Klemm both had eight-inch one-piece channel frames, both had the same wheelbases available, and both were powered by the same engine, which was a six-cylinder Wisconsin motor limited by a McCanna governor. Both trucks had a 36-gallon gasoline tank, which was quite large even for that time and was a selling point in terms of range at a time when there was not a "filling station on every corner." Both used dual chain drive and had brakes only on the rear wheels. It was discovered that this type of braking system on trucks of that size often did not perform adequately.

It's unknown if more than only a handful of Klemm trucks were ever built. Having a listing in the B.F. Goodrich truck catalog did not ensure the manufacturer was not a mom-and-pop operation in 1917. Klemm disappeared as a manufacturer in 1918, most likely as a result of wartime shortages. Very little is known about the company's financial activity or about E.R. Klemm after the war.

Kline

James A. Kline started out in business at Harrisburg, Pennsylvania, as a machinist and bicycle dealer by 1899. The following year he obtained the dealership for Locomobile and built an experimental gasoline car of his own. His dealership also began to carry Franklin and Oldsmobile cars. Being a machinist and having considerable skill in the field of mechanics, by 1905 Kline was hired to redesign the York automobile, which soon became the Pullman automobile.

Switching partnerships in 1909 to include Samuel E. Baily and Joseph C. Carrell, the new company was called B.C.K. and introduced the Kline Kar in 1910 at York, Pennsylvania. The six-cylinder car performed well and won races driven by professional competitors named Jimmy and his son Jimmy, Jr. Following the success of the Kline, a business venture from Richmond, Virginia, bought the B.C.K. enterprise, and James A. Kline joined them. Due to the fact that the car they were about to manufacture was the design and creation of James Kline, the company was called the Kline Motor Car Corporation and a factory was completed at Richmond.

James also designed the four- and six-cylinder engines for his car, which were

**KLINECAR
CORPORATION**

**RICHMOND
VIRGINIA**

Price $1495
Four-Passenger Sport-Tour. . . 1495
Four-Passenger Shamrock . . . 1495
Two- and Three-Passenger
   Runabout 1495
Five-Passenger Sedan 2220

KLINE KAR TOURING—SERIES 6-38

COLOR	Body, dark green; running gear, black	LUBRICATION	Force feed and splash
SEATING CAPACITY. .	Five	RADIATOR	Cellular
POSITION OF DRIVER .	Left side	COOLING	Water pump
WHEELBASE	120 inches	IGNITION	Storage battery
GAUGE	56 inches	STARTING SYSTEM . .	Two unit
WHEELS	Wood	STARTER OPERATED .	Gear to fly wheel
FRONT TIRES	34 x 4 inches	LIGHTING SYSTEM . .	Electric
REAR TIRES	34 x 4 inches, anti-skid	VOLTAGES	Six
SERVICE BRAKE . . .	Contracting on rear wheels	WIRING SYSTEM . . .	Single
EMERGENCY BRAKE .	Expanding on rear wheels	GASOLINE SYSTEM . .	Vacuum
CYLINDERS	Six	CLUTCH	Plate
ARRANGED	Vertically	TRANSMISSION . . .	Selective sliding
CAST.	En bloc	GEAR CHANGES . . .	Three forward, one reverse
HORSEPOWER . . . 25.35 (N.A.C.C. Rating)		DRIVE	Spiral bevel
BORE AND STROKE .	3¼ x 4½ inches	REAR AXLE	Full floating
		STEERING GEAR . . .	Worm and nut

In addition to above specifications, price includes top, top hood, windshield, speedometer, ammeter, electric horn and demountable rims.

manufactured by Kirkham Machine Company in Bath, New York. By 1913 production was up to 1000 Klines a year. Prices ranged from $1750 for the Model 4-30 to $4700 for the Model 6-60 Limousine.

Receivership was initiated in 1915, but the efforts of James "Jimmy" Kline kept the company solvent and it continued on as before the attempt to take over its affairs. According to some records 1917 was a good year for Kline with production at over 1390 cars. But with the sudden end of the war came a sudden recession, and Kline was forced to use Continental engines, making the Kline Kar another assembled vehicle. The company did not drop the "Kar" as Kissel Kar did during the war, discounting the belief that it sounded too German when war was being waged against that enemy. The Kline Kar was out of business by 1924 with a memorable quote from James Kline reverberating over his closed factory: "I'd rather see my children dead than prostituted to cheapness and inferior workmanship."

Knox

A citizen of Springfield, Massachusetts, Harry A. Knox was also a neighbor of J. Frank Duryea at the turn of the previous century. The automotive pioneer greatly influenced Knox to get into motor vehicle development also, so that by 1895 Knox began building experimental gasoline vehicles at his employer's place of business, the Overman Wheel Company. Being a graduate of the Springfield Technical Institute and having completed three cars by 1898, Knox formed the Knox Automobile Company with E.H. Cutler, owner of the Elektron Company, builder of elevators.

Perhaps because A.H. Overman had been discouraged by the experiments with gasoline engines, he had decided to build steam automobiles as Knox began manufacturing three-wheel runabouts in 1900 under his own name. Fifteen were built in 1900 and 100 the following year before 250 were produced in 1902 as a four-wheeler was also introduced, called the Knoxmobile. It was also available in a commercial vehicle form with flatbed or box body.

In 1903 the vehicle was known as the "Waterless Knox." Knox also built buses, some of which were shipped as far away as Japan in 1905, as well as light trucks, and one of them played a significant role that year.

The very first truck competition in the United States took place on May 20 and 21 in 1903. Two of the fourteen entries were from Knox. The 1903 Truck Show was sponsored by the fledgling Automobile Club of America and took place in New York City around Central Park and across the Harlem River. The contest seemed to answer a challenge of the day published by the *Horseless Age Magazine*: "The motor truck must end its purely butterfly existence and be made to assume its share of the world's work, if it is to survive."

Of the fourteen entries one withdrew due to mechanical problems. The rest were powered by various means of propulsion including steam heated by coke, coal, kerosene and gasoline. There were also five powered by a gasoline internal combustion engine and battery-powered electric trucks.

Starting from the Automobile Club of America headquarters at Fifth Avenue and 59th Street, each truck was required to make a 20-mile run to 230th Street and back, leaving the starting line in three-minute intervals. The trucks varied in capacity from 12,000 pounds for a Coulthard steam truck down to the lightest, which was a Mobile rated at 750-pound capacity. The lighter trucks were required to travel an additional 20 miles along the streets of Manhattan.

The lighter of the two Knox trucks, which was rated at ¾-ton, covered the entire route in three hours and thirty-five minutes consuming four gallons of gasoline, an average of 11.3

KNOX TRACTORS
Manufactured by
KNOX MOTORS CO., Springfield, Mass.

S P E C I F I C A T I O N S

Model	35	36 Towing Tractor
Capacity	5 tons and upwards	3 tons and trailers
Drive	Chain	Chain
Chassis Price	$4,500	$5,000
Motor		
H. P. (S.A.E)	40	40
H. P. (Actual)	40 at 1000 R.P.M.	40 at 1000 R.P.M.
Cylinders	4 in pairs	4 in pairs
Bore	5″	5″
Stroke	$5\frac{1}{2}$″	$5\frac{1}{2}$″
Wheel Base	$108\frac{1}{2}$″	$108\frac{1}{2}$″
Tread Front	$57\frac{3}{8}$″	$57\frac{3}{8}$″
Tread Rear	62″	62″
Tires Front	36x4″	36x4″
Tires Rear	38x6″ dual	38x6″ dual

Frame—Channel rolled steel, drilled and hot riveted.

Front Axle—Steel casting with I-beam section $3x3\frac{3}{4}$″.

Rear Axle—Drop forging of rectangular section $2\frac{3}{4}x4\frac{5}{8}$″.

Springs Front—Semi-elliptic.

Springs Rear	Cantilever type	Semi-elliptic

Carburetor—Zenith.

Cooling System—Centrifugal pump.

Oiling System—Forced feed.

Ignition—Eisemann magneto.

Control—Left drive, center control.

Clutch—Dry plate, cork inserts.

Transmission—Selective, three speeds forward and one reverse.

Brakes—Jackshaft, hydraulic brake on rear wheels.

Steering Gear—Screw and nut.

Equipment—Model 35: Trailer platform complete, including upper and lower circles, upper and lower bolster plates and locking bar, two electric side lamps, one electric tail lamp, one dash and electric searchlight, storage battery, complete set of tools, hand-operated horn, Pyrene fire extinguisher, speedometer, cab and side curtains, one extra valve and spring complete, one oil can, four spark plugs with gaskets, four driving chain links, one gasoline oil can, one can of grease and Bijur electric-starting system, two heavy jacks for lifting trailer. Equipment for Model 36 same as Model 35 without trailer platform and jacks for lifting trailer.

miles per gallon. The Knox turned out to be the winner of the contest. The huge Coulthard used an amazing 1,335 pounds of coke and 869 gallons of water to travel 60 miles, while the Waverly electric used $2.50 worth of electricity. The press cited the Knox as "The car that never drinks" because it was powered by a one-cylinder air-cooled four-stroke engine which used pins pressed into the cylinder as opposed to fins used for cooling. This engine was nicknamed "Old Porcupine" due to its appearance. The little truck also had tiller steering and a two-speed epicyclic transmission without reverse gear. Harry Knox drove the winning entry himself.

Due to some mishaps during the New York race, the truck competition in New York was summarized in 1903 by *The Horseless Age* as follows: "A well trained horse will often prevent a collision with an intersecting vehicle, but with the motor vehicle there is no such safeguard, and all safety depends upon the alertness of the driver and his facilities for watching the road in all directions."

Harry Knox left the company abruptly the following year in order to build Atlas vehicles, and his old enterprise began building three-wheel truck tractors for pulling articulated trailers. By 1905 Knox was building trucks up to 3-ton capacity. In 1906 a Knox auto finished the Glidden Tour with a perfect point record, but no thanks to Harry Knox himself, whose departure from the company bearing his name was not amicable.

By 1908 creditors were in control of Knox as the company managed to expand to meet demand even though the Knox car now cost $2500. It was powered by a 30 hp four-cylinder engine on a 102- or 112-inch wheelbase. This was a far departure from the tiny one-cylinder $1000 vehicle that Harry Knox had designed, and in 1911 a six-cylinder engine was also offered, as the Knox limousine reached a price tag of $6000.

As war began in Europe, Edward O. Sutton bought the Knox company for $631,000 and reorganized it as Knox Motors Company. All passenger cars were phased out immediately and Knox, having had success in the commercial field, continued building trucks and fire apparatus. One such vehicle had been delivered to the Springfield Fire Department in September of 1906.

Once Charles Hay Martin, a former employee of Knox, returned to the company under Sutton, he invented the Martin Rocking Fifth Wheel system for attaching a tractor to a trailer. This invention (similar to that of Hewitt-Talbot design) was very successful and helped sell three-wheel tractors called Knox-Martin. These were used to tow what had been horse-drawn fire apparatus when municipal departments were not prepared to purchase entire new self-propelled fire apparatus rigs. Knox trucks from 2- to 5-ton capacity were offered after 1911, and all were forward control design. Knox built sight-seeing coaches and ambulances as well.

By 1915 after Sutton took over, the Knox truck tractors were all four-wheel design for better stability. Charles Martin formed his own company during 1916 to build his "fifth-wheel" system in Chicopee Falls, Massachusetts. After the war Knox merged with the Militor Corporation, also located in Springfield, and the Militor motorcycle was briefly built by the new cooperation. However, the huge, unwieldy bike did not sell and plans to build a passenger car went nowhere. By 1924 Militor and Knox were no longer in business.

Koehler

H.J. Koehler owned sporting goods stores under his own name, so it was no surprise that he began selling autos of various makes, including Hupmobile and Rider-Lewis, as early as in 1898 when operating motor vehicles was still considered more of a sport than as a real means of transportation. Having been closely

KOEHLER TRUCKS

Manufactured by

H. J. KOEHLER MOTORS CORPORATION, Newark, N. J.

Model	K	KT
Capacity	1¼ tons	3-ton Tractor for semi-trailer
Drive	Internal gear	Internal gear
Chassis Weight	3,000 lbs.	3,100 lbs.
Chassis Price	$1,150	$1,550
Engine	Koehler	Koehler
H. P. (S.A.E.)	16.9	16.9
H. P. (Actual)	35	35
Cylinders	4 en bloc	4 en bloc
Bore	3½"	3½"
Stroke	5"	5"
Wheel Base	129"	106"
Tread Front	56"	56"
Tread Rear	56"	56"
Tires Front	34x3"	34x3"
Tires Rear	34x4"	34x5"

Frame—Rolled.
Front Axle—I-beam, inverted Elliott.
Rear Axle—Torbensen internal gear.
Springs Front—Semi-elliptic.
Springs Rear—Semi-elliptic.
Carburetor—Stromberg M.
Cooling System—Thermo-syphon.
Oiling System—Splash and forced feed.
Ignition—Eisemann magneto.
Control—Left drive, center control.
Clutch—Dry plate.
Transmission—M. & M. selective, three speeds.
Brakes—Service, external contracting on rear wheels—emergency, internal expanding in rear wheels.
Steering Gear—Pinion and sector.
Equipment—On Model K—Oil lamps, tools and mechanical horn; on Model K. T.—Cab top, governor on motor, 5th wheel for trailer, oil lamps, tools and mechanical horn.

involved with various makes, Koehler realized he knew enough about the machines to build one of his own, which he accomplished in 1910.

He leased a factory in Bloomfield, New Jersey, and began to go into series production with a 40 hp four-cylinder touring car using a 112-inch wheelbase. The price was $1650 before accouterments and remained through 1913, but just as World War I was about to explode in Europe, Koehler decided that the commercial field would be a surer bet.

Koehler had already used his touring car chassis as early as 1910 to build commercial cars such as a 1,600-pound capacity light truck, van, panel body, express body, stakebed, flatbed and more specifically Plumbers and Contractors Job, Canvas-side, Bakers and Confectioners Body and Furniture Body. The same two-speed planetary transmission as in the passenger car was attached directly to the jackshaft for these lower-geared, slower and heavier-set commercial cars.

The simplicity of these vehicles, along with a forward-control design and vertical steering wheel, harked back to the horse-drawn days, overlapping with the equine form of motive power that had various pros and cons, and from which the term horsepower itself derived.

Koehler introduced its 1-ton Model K in 1916 which would in short time use a Herschell-Spillman four-cylinder motor and had Torbensen internal gear drive. Koehler struggled to survive in the early "Roaring" 1920s with trucks from 1½-ton to 5-ton capacity. However, by 1923 the competition had taken its final toll on Koehler.

Krebs

Even an unusual name such as Krebs coming from one specific region can cause confusion a century later, and J.C.L. Krebs did so if indeed he was the person recognized in *The Motor Age* in the summer of 1901 as having

built an automobile at a machine shop in the city of Ottawa, Ohio. More than a decade later, in 1912, a Krebs Commercial Car Company was organized in Clyde, Ohio, and although it was J.C.L. Krebs who was behind this venture, there was no mention of previous endeavors.

Krebs never built passenger cars, but by 1912 the company was building light trucks using two-cylinder two-cycle engines. By 1915 the model range capacity was from ¾-ton to 3-ton. During World War I Krebs manufacturing was located at the Elmore Manufacturing Company in Clyde, Ohio, once Elmore was absorbed by General Motors, as several other companies were while William Crapo Durant was building his automobile empire. By 1918 the Model 98 was available as a 5-ton capacity truck.

It is unclear if the Krebs Motor Truck Company of Bellvue, Ohio, which existed between 1922 and 1925 was a reincarnation of the Krebs company from Clyde, Ohio. The first one ceased operation before the end of World War I. The second one was renamed Buck in 1925 and lasted until 1927. Most likely, J.C.L. Krebs started over again using his own name, and in the second, better effort the company produced trucks ranging from ¾-ton to 6-ton capacity. The model numbers were similarly named and Timken work drive, Brown-Lipe transmissions and Continental motors were used. In both cases the Krebs enterprises faded away into history.

Lane

Just as the United States found itself reluctantly drawn into the Mexican Revolution when Pancho Villa attacked Columbus, New Mexico, on March 9, 1916, the Lane Motor Truck Company became yet another outfit vying for customers who had dozens of manufacturers from which to choose that year. Even though the Punitive Expedition turned

KREBS TRUCKS

Manufactured by

THE KREBS COMMERCIAL CAR CO., Clyde, Ohio

S P E C I F I C A T I O N S

Model	98	90	60	40
Capacity	5 tons	3½ tons	2 tons	1½ tons
Drive	Worm	Worm	Worm	Worm
Chassis Price	$4,000	$3,250	$2,375	$2,050
Motor				
H. P. (S.A.E.)	32.4	32.4	27.2	27.2
H. P. (Actual)	39	39	32	32
Cylinders	4 in pairs	4 in pairs	4 en bloc	4 en bloc
Bore	4½″	4½″	4⅛″	4⅛″
Stroke	5½″	5½″	5½″	5½″
Wheel Base	160″ and 180″	180″	163″	145″
Tread Front	68″	61″	58½″	58″
Tread Rear	69½″	67″	58½″	58½″
Tires Front	36x6″	36x5″	36x4″	36x4″
Tires Rear	40x6″ dual	36x5″ dual	36x4″ dual	36x5″

Frame—Pressed.
Front Axle—I-beam.
Rear Axle—Full floating.
Springs Front—Semi-elliptic.
Springs Rear—Semi-elliptic.
Carburetor—Zenith.
Cooling System—Pump.
Oiling System—Splash.
Ignition—Magneto.

Control	Right drive	Right drive, right control	Right drive, right control	Right drive, center control

Clutch—Dry plate.
Transmission—Selective, four speeds forward and one reverse.
Brakes—Expanding, rear wheels.
Steering Gear—Screw and nut.
Equipment—Set of tools, jack, horn, gas head lamps, gas tank, oil side and tail lamps.

LANE TRUCKS

Manufactured by

LANE MOTOR TRUCK CO., Kalamazoo, Mich.

Model	F	B	C
Capacity	1½ tons	2½ tons	3½ tons
Drive	Worm	Worm	Worm
Chassis Weight	3,600 lbs.	5,200 lbs.	6,000 lbs.
Chassis Price	$1,850	$2,700	$3,500
Engine	Continental	Continental	Continental
H. P. (S.A.E.)	22.5	29.39	33.75
H. P. (Actual)	25	33	45
Cylinders	4 en bloc	6 en bloc	6 in threes
Bore	3¾"	3½"	3¾"
Stroke	5"	5¼".	5¼"
Wheel Base	135"	150"	160"
Tread Front	56"	58"	63"
Tread Rear	56"	58"	66"
Tires Front	34x3½"	34x4"	36x5"
Tires Rear	34x5"	36x6"	36x5" dual

Frame—Rolled channel.
Front Axle—I-beam.

Rear Axle	Wisconsin semi-floating	Timken full-floating	Sheldon semi-floating

Springs Front—Semi-elliptic.
Springs Rear—Semi-elliptic.
Carburetor—Stromberg.

Cooling System	Thermo-syphon	Pump	Pump

Oiling System—Forced feed and splash.

Ignition—Generator.		Magneto	Magneto

Control—Left steer, center control.
Clutch—Dry plate.

Transmission	Fuller progressive, 3 speeds forward	Covert Selective, 3 speeds forward	Covert Selective, 3 speeds forward
Brakes	Internal and external on rear wheels	Internal on rear wheels	Internal on rear wheels

Steering Gear—Split nut.
Equipment—Cab, windshield, starter, generator, electric lights, electric horn, tools and governor.

out to be more of a dress rehearsal for America's entry into World War I in Europe a year later, there was a surge in truck manufacturing as the American military began buying motor vehicles, and proof of their value and superiority to the horse became more commonly accepted.

The Lane company's small factory in Kalamazoo, Michigan, began building ¾-ton trucks mostly for local use. They were powered by a four-cylinder and six-cylinder Continental engine, depending on the model. The lightest Model F rated at 1½-ton capacity was powered by a four-cylinder Continental engine. It was priced at $1850, whereas the Model B, which was rated at 2½-ton capacity, was priced at $2700 and was powered by a six-cylinder Continental motor. The 3½-ton Model C was priced at $3500 and had a yet larger six-cylinder engine.

Lane trucks exemplified the diverse choice of some of the component sources, which in this case was the manufacturers of axles. In the early days motor vehicle builders could simply buy major components from various companies and assemble their car or truck by building only the chassis and body.

In the case of Lane the Model F used axles from Wisconsin, the Model B had axles from Timken and the Model C used axles from Sheldon. Transmissions were from Fuller and Covert. It may have brought into question the efficiency of maintenance and parts replacement with such a wide selection of original equipment manufacturers (OEMs), but this approach was standard practice and a wide variety of component sources was part of the luxury of American industrial strength. Over the years engine, transmission, body, axle, clutch, radiator, electrical and other component manufacturers were bought out and absorbed into large corporations, becoming proprietary fabricators, no longer able to provide their products simply to anyone who could pay for the parts.

Individual machine shops, such as Dodge Brothers for example, were suppliers for others before becoming complete builders themselves. There was an abundance of independent manufacturers for everything from bolts to complete motors, particularly before and during World War I. However, the postwar recession was a crucible of competition that eliminated many small companies, and Lane was one that did not survive the year 1920.

Lange

The H. Lange Wagon Works began as a horse-drawn wagon builder a decade before announcements were made in September 1909 at Pittsburgh, Pennsylvania, that the company would be going into motor truck manufacturing. The first Lange trucks were built using Gramm-Logan chassis. Gramm-Logan was one of several collaborations between Benjamin Gramm along with his son Willard Gramm and a business and engineering partner such as Logan, Max Bernstein (Gramm-Bernstein), and R.M. Kinkaid (Gramm-Kinkaid), as well as John Willys, the latter of which did not result in a hyphenated truck name. All of these partnerships took place in northern Ohio. Gramm-Logan was the earliest of the collaborations, taking place from 1908 to 1910.

In 1911 Lange began building its own chassis for a 2-ton model truck. The following year the company was reorganized and became the Lange Motor Truck Company. All Lange commercial vehicles were conventional assembled trucks, and the company did not venture into passenger car production.

By 1918 the company offered two models: the 1½-ton C and the 2½-ton B, both powered by four-cylinder Continental engines using chain drive and Cotta three-speed selective transmissions. By the mid–1920s the 22.5 hp Continental J2 motor continued to be used and Brown-Lipe transmissions were

LANGE TRUCKS
Manufactured by
LANGE MOTOR TRUCK CO., Pittsburgh, Pa.
6633-45 Hamilton Ave., near Fifth Ave.

Model	C	B
Capacity	1½ tons	2½ tons
Drive	Chain	Chain
Chassis Price	$1,950	$2,650
Engine	Continental	Continental
H. P. (S.A.E.)	22.5	27.22
H. P. (Actual)	30	35
Cylinders	4 en bloc	4 en bloc
Bore	3¾″	4⅛″
Stroke	5¼″	5¼″
Wheel Base	130″	136″
Tread Front	58″	60″
Tread Rear	58″	60″
Tires Front	36x3½″	36x4″
Tires Rear	38x4″	38x6″

Frame—Rolled.

Front Axle—Lange.

Rear Axle—Lange dead rectangular.

Springs Front—Semi-elliptic.

Springs Rear—Semi-elliptic.

Carburetor—Stromberg type G.

Cooling System—Thermo-syphon.

Oiling System—Splash.

Ignition—High tension magneto.

Control—Left drive, center control.

Clutch—Wet plate.

Transmission—Cotta Selective.

Brakes   External on jackshaft   Internal on rear wheels

Steering Gear—Worm.

Equipment—Side and tail lamps, seat and cushion and governor.

employed with Timken front and rear axles. The 2½-ton Lange used the K-4 Continental engine. By this time a 3½-ton model was added, powered by 32.4 Continental L-4 motor. The company faded out quickly as the Great Depression set in by 1931.

Lansden (electric)

John M. Lansden and partner William M. Little were behind the Lansden. They started out in Alabama with experimental electric cars during 1901 when working at the Birmingham Electric Manufacturing Company. They then moved to Newark, New Jersey, in 1904, and their first electric trucks appeared there that year. The Type 36 Style A had an 87-inch wheelbase and was powered by a ¾ hp DC motor. The entire chassis was fitted with batteries under the flatbed, and final drive was by dual chain. The passenger cars built by Lansden were very similar to the commercial chassis.

In 1906 two more "Style" models were added, which were essentially the same as the Type 36, and in 1907 Lansden offered a ½-ton and 1½-ton. Lansden added a new design that included a long hood where batteries were placed, giving the appearance of a standard gasoline-powered truck, but most Lansdens were still forward control and also had batteries in rows within the frame. Vans were available from 1-ton to 5-ton capacity.

In 1910 a Lansden electric taxicab was introduced, but electric passenger car production was phased out, although a few were built on a custom basis until parts ran out within the following months. John Lansden left the company he had founded in 1911 in order to manage electric truck manufacturing at General Motors, which was gearing up for large production the following year. The Lansden Company moved to Allentown, Pennsylvania, and continued without him.

Under the auspices of Mac-Carr, Lansden began production of a new 5-ton electric truck in 1912. It had a 136-inch wheelbase and was advertised as having the range of fifty miles on a single charge. The truck used alkaline batteries from Thomas Edison, who was experimenting with battery chemicals at a time when lead acid type were the standard design.

In 1914 the company moved to Brooklyn, New York, and stayed in business there through World War I. Lansden was reincorporated at Danbury, Connecticut, after the war. Here the company adopted the use of alkaline Edison batteries exclusively, but by this time it was fairly well accepted that battery energy density could not match that of combustible liquid fuel such as gasoline.

Lansden was one of the few truck companies offering a truck rated at ⅓-ton capacity, which apparently translated to 666.6 pounds. Its lightest Model BB was apparently also available as a ½-ton and used "Direct, Herringbone and bevel gear," which was very unusual. This was a proprietary Lansden spur gear transmission in addition to the controller, which used battery switching for four speeds. Note that Lansden provided an "operating cable" which was used to plug the batteries in for recharging, giving the truck 60 miles of range at 10 to 12 mph top speed for the 1-ton Model M.

General Motors dropped its electric truck manufacturing in 1915, but John Lansden did not return to his old company. Electric vehicle production dwindled throughout the industry during the 1920s, and Lansden faded out during this decade, joining dozens of other defunct electric vehicle companies.

Lapeer

The Lapeer Tractor Truck Company began building short-wheelbase trucks for towing articulated trailers beginning in 1916. The town of Lapeer is located in a rural area in

LANSDEN TRUCKS
Manufactured by
THE LANSDEN CO. Inc., Brooklyn, N. Y.

S P E C I F I C A T I O N S

Model	M	M	M	M
Capacity	750 lbs.	½ ton	1 ton	2 tons
Drive	Bevel gear	Bevel gear	Bevel gear	Bevel gear
Chassis Price	$1,175	$1,500	$1,700	$2,100
Wheel Base	90″	90″	106″	120″
Tread Front	56″	56″	56″	66″
Tread Rear	56″	56″	56″	66″
Tires Front	36x2½″	36x2½″	36x3″	36x4″
Tires Rear	36x3″	36x3″	36x3½″	36x3″ dual

Frame—Cold pressed steel, channel section double heat treated, hot riveted.

Speed	14 to 16 M.P.H.	12 to 14 M.P.H.	10 to 12 M.P.H.	8 to 10 M.P.H.
Miles (per battery charge)	65	60	60	50

Front Axle—Heavy die forged, I-beam type, Timken knuckles, Timken roller bearings.

Rear Axle—Nickel steel, die forged, machine set, fixed, Timken roller bearings.

Springs Front—Chrome Manganese steel, oil tempered, semi-elliptic.

Springs Rear—Semi-elliptic.

Battery Equipment—60 cells Edison, optional 44 cells Exide or other Lead.

Motor—General Electric.

Steering Gear—Inclined post, worm and sector, ball bearing, operating in oil, Lansden special.

Transmission—None employed.

Control—Four speeds forward and two reverse.

Brakes—Service, internal expanding hub. Emergency, armature shaft, contracting band.

Equipment—Hubodometer, Sangamo ampere hour meter, dash and tail lights, horn, operating cable and plug, necessary tools. Boot and body extra.

LAPEER TRUCKS

Manufactured by

LAPEER TRACTOR TRUCK CO., Lapeer, Mich.

Model	A	G
Capacity	3 tons	5 tons
Drive	Internal gear	Internal gear
Chassis Weight	3,050 lbs.	3,400 lbs.
Chassis Price	$1,750	$2,300
Engine	Waukesha	Waukesha
H. P. (S.A.E.)	19.6	19.6
H. P. (Actual)	25	25
Cylinders	4 en bloc	4 en bloc
Bore	3½″	3½″
Stroke	5¼″	5¼″
Wheel Base	90″	90″
Tread Front	56″	56″
Tread Rear	56″	56″
Tires Front	34x3½″	34x5″
Tires Rear	34x3½″	34x3½″ dual

Frame—Rolled.

Front Axle—I-beam.

Rear Axle—Torbensen I-beam.

Springs Front—Semi-elliptic.

Springs Rear—Semi-elliptic.

Carburetor—Stewart.

Cooling System—Pump.

Oiling System—Splash and forced feed.

Ignition—Magneto.

Control—Steer left, gear levers center.

Clutch—Dry plate.

Transmission—Fuller Selective, three speeds.

Brakes—Rear wheels.

Steering Gear—Worm and nut.

Equipment—Oil lamps, horn, tools, driver's cab and governor.

northwest Michigan not far from Flint and Lansing, better known for the automotive industry than Lapeer.

The first 5-ton truck tractors were powered by Wisconsin engines and used a three- speed transmission. The following year Waukesha engines were adopted, and Lapeer offered a 3-ton model in addition to the earlier 5-ton tractor truck. Both trucks used three-speed Fuller transmissions.

Lapeer claimed to be the first truck in the American motor vehicle industry to build completely enclosed cabs as standard equipment. Operating a vehicle that had evolved from horse-drawn wagons, the driver of a "truck," which originally referred to a type of delivery wagon, did not expect to have any protection from the weather, unlike passengers in formal carriages and the long-distance stagecoach or train car. Even taxicab drivers sat outside of the enclosed cab (which could also mean taxicab) but the word "cab" itself was an abbreviation for cabriolet, which was a horse-drawn conveyance for hire in the 1800s. In that sense the etymology of the word "cab" actually indicated a meaning opposite of that which it originally described.

The word "taxi" derived from the Greek word meaning "to charge," and in 1907 taximeter cabs imported from Europe were introduced in Manhattan. But in the days of the open cab or truck C-cab, part of the tradition stemmed from class distinctions, in which the well-to-do were seated inside a protected enclosure while the driver was outside with plenty of room to swing a horsewhip and have full visibility of the road and surroundings, but without the luxury of protection from the weather.

Even on later automobiles of the 1920s and 1930s, a brougham or towncar had the chauffeur's area left uncovered, while the passengers or car's owner sat in the enclosed rear. Truck manufacturers often built their vehicles on the chassis as far back as the cowl and dashboard, providing only a hood and front fenders. The new owner was expected to build his own cab for the driver and body for carrying the cargo.

The early, simple cabs were basic wooden boxes. Before safety glass was invented and accepted into use by the 1930s, plate glass was used for motor vehicle cabs, if there were any glass at all, and it was often considered more dangerous than an open window at a time when there were no seat belts. Being thrown through a plate glass windshield or side window meant certain injury, so an open cab was sometimes safer. Visibility was also better when rear view mirrors were very rarely used.

Companies that bought open-cab or bare-chassis vehicles often added some protection for the driver, especially in northern states with inclement weather during a good portion of the year. By World War I various types of tarps and fabric were used as sheilds in rainstorms, but the driver was expected to provide his own hat and rain gear. A cab such as that provided by Lapeer was considered luxurious up until the Great War. Lapeer succumbed to the postwar recession and competition. By 1920 the company was no longer manufacturing trucks, switching instead to building trailers through that decade until the Great Depression.

Larrabee

H. Chester Larrabee and R.H. Deyo were the founders of the Larrabee-Deyo Motor Truck Company in Birmingham, New York, during 1916. As so many other companies of this particular era, this one started out much earlier building carriages, wagons and sleighs, evolving from the Sturtevant-Larrabee Company.

Larrabees were conventional assembled trucks starting with a one-ton model capacity in 1916, and quickly expanding the model line up to 5-ton capacity by the end of World

LARRABEE TRUCKS
Manufactured by
LARRABEE-DEYO MOTOR TRUCK CO., Inc., Binghampton, N. Y.

S P E C I F I C A T I O N S

Model	M	N	O	R
Capacity	1 ton	1½ tons	2½ tons	3½ tons
Drive	Worm	Worm	Worm	Worm
Chassis Price	$1,500	$2,000	$2,300	$3,100
Motor				
H. P. (S.A.E.)	23	27.2	27.2	32.4
H. P. (Actual)	30	40	40	45
Cylinders	4 en bloc	4 en bloc	4 en bloc	4 in pairs
Bore	3¾″	4⅛″	4⅛″	4½″
Stroke	5″	5¼″	5¼″	5½″
Wheel Base	130″	140″	154″	154″
Tread Front	56″	62″	62″	62″
Tread Rear	56″	62″	62″	66″
Tires Front	34x3½″	36x3½″	36x4″	40x5″
Tires Rear	34x5″	36x5″	36x6″	40x5″ dual
Frame	Channel pressed	I-section integral	I-section integral	I-section pressed

Front Axle—I-section, integral.
Rear Axle—Semi-floating; top worm.
Springs Front—Semi-elliptic.
Springs Rear—Semi-elliptic.
Carburetor—Schebler R.

Cooling System	Thermo-syphon	Pump	Pump	Pump

Oiling System—Splash.
Ignition—Magneto.
Control—Left drive, center control.
Clutch—Dry plate.
Transmission—Selective, three speeds forward and one reverse.

Brakes	Expanding rear wheel	Expanding and contracting rear wheel	Expanding rear wheel	Expanding rear wheel

Steering Gear—Split nut and screw.
Equipment—Seat (full upholstered), gasoline tank and front fenders, set of tools with all necessary special wrenches, wheel puller, hubodometer, warning signal, jack, oil can, two highest grade oil side lamps, one oil tail lamp, number plate holders.
Electric starting and lighting system will be applied to any model at additional cost.

War I, although as with a number of truck companies, not all models were listed. Four-cylinder Continental motors were used throughout the model line, although there was an apparent offer by the company to custom fit any make of engine. At that time most engines were interchangeable in trucks as long as they fit into the chassis, and even if the transmission did not match up bolt for bolt, machinists would quickly mill an adapter plate. In this case the transmissions were from Brown-Lipe and worm drive rear axles were from Sheldon.

Larrabee survived the war and developed the Six-Speed Larrabee-Deyo, which was introduced in 1921. For 1922 a one-ton "speed" truck was offered which used a six-cylinder Continental engine. From all appearances, in terms of models offered during the 1920s, Larrabee prospered. By 1927 a four-speed transmission was available along with spiral bevel rear axles, steel spoke wheels, four-wheel hydraulic brakes, handbrake expanding on the rear drums, electric lights and starter and full instrumentation on the dashboard. By this time most trucks were built with pneumatic tires and Larrabee was one of them.

At that time Larrabee also built a small bus chassis which was offered at $3,900, less than for its 5-ton truck for $4,750. The company also built several hundred "Majestic" taxicabs which were primarily used in New York City. By 1929 production of Larrabee and Larrabee-Deyo trucks, as they were also called, reached 400 units per year, which was a steady business for a small company, with about two vehicles built each work day. But as soon as the Great Depression hit, sales faded out and the company vanished in 1932.

Note that the 1917 illustration of the working Larrabee truck shows that the vehicle does not have a rear bumper, taillights or license plate, and yet the rear tailgate shows plenty of wear, so it is unlikely this is a merely posed photograph.

Lexington

Kinzea Stone was a wealthy horse race promoter in Kentucky who became more promotor by 1909, when he started his motor vehicle company at Lexington. The fresh enterprise moved in 1910 to Connersville, Indiana, where the prospects for manufacturing were far better than in rural Kentucky. By 1911 the company was bought by E.W. Ansted, who was already in the business of manufacturing vehicle axles and leaf springs.

Ansted added to his established business by building the four-cylinder Lexington and the six-cylinder Howard, both cars already designed and ready to be built in series. A Chicago distributor by the name of Howard contracted for the latter car; hence the name of the company became Lexington-Howard. But the contract with Howard was only for four years, and in 1914 the car was discontinued. Four-cylinder engines were phased out by 1916.

The company was reorganized by 1918, remaining in Connersville as the Lexington Motor Company. John C. Moore remained chief engineer from the company's beginning in Indiana until the very end. Moore designed a Lexington called the Thoroughbred Six, which alluded to the company's origins in horse racing country. He was also responsible for the design of the Minute Man Six, alluding to Lexington, even if of a different state. The Skylark Model was joined by the Concord Six in 1924, and the company used an emblem with a American Revolution minuteman holding a musket.

Lexingtons sold well because they performed well, which was proved in 1920 when they placed first and second at Pikes Peak Hill Climb, already famous by that time. Selling well translated to mean six thousand Lexingtons built for that year alone. Production ramped up to a thousand per month in 1921. Some motors were built by Ansted, and a few

LEXINGTON-
H O W A R D
C O M P A N Y

CONNERSVILLE
I N D I A N A

Price $1385
Four-Passenger Convertible
    Coupe 1545

LEXINGTON CLUBSTER—O

COLOR	Blue-black or green; wheels, white	BORE AND STROKE .	3¼ x 4½ inches
		LUBRICATION	Force feed and splash
SEATING CAPACITY .	Four	RADIATOR	Cellular
POSITION OF DRIVER .	Left side	COOLING	Water pump
WHEELBASE	116 inches	IGNITION	Storage battery
GAUGE	56 inches	STARTING SYSTEM . .	Single unit
WHEELS	Wood	STARTER OPERATED .	Gear to fly wheel
FRONT TIRES	32 x 4 inches	LIGHTING SYSTEM . .	Electric
REAR TIRES	32 x 4 inches, anti-skid	VOLTAGES	Six
		WIRING SYSTEM . . .	Single
SERVICE BRAKE . . .	Contracting on rear wheels	GASOLINE SYSTEM . .	Vacuum
EMERGENCY BRAKE .	Expanding on rear wheels	CLUTCH	Dry multiple disc
		TRANSMISSION . . .	Selective sliding
CYLINDERS	Six	GEAR CHANGES . . .	Three forward, one reverse
ARRANGED	Vertically		
CAST	En bloc	DRIVE	Spiral bevel
HORSEPOWER	25.35	REAR AXLE	Full floating
(N.A.C.C. Rating)		STEERING GEAR . . .	Worm and gear

In addition to above specifications, price includes top, top hood, windshield, speedometer, ammeter, tire pump, electric horn and demountable rims.

Lexingtons were badged with that name. E.W. Ansted consolidated all of the component manufacturing under his ownership as United States Automotive Corporation. But when Alanson P. Brush sued Ansted in 1921 for patent infringement on his engine, the bad press was a one-two punch as the postwar recession hit almost simultaneously. Creditors, amongst them the Jacques Manufacturing Company that built some car bodies, sued and accused Ansted of being insolvent.

By 1922 production was down to 3500 cars for the year. Under receivership, the company limped along into 1927, when Auburn took over the factory, and under Errett Lobban Cord, who would also become known for the Duesenberg and the car by his own name, the Lexington was phased out by the end of the year with the last model modestly called the 6-50.

Liberty (auto)

Not to be confused with the Liberty standardized trucks of World War I, among the American motor vehicle companies that were founded as the war expanded in Europe was the Liberty Motor Car Company. It was organized in Detroit during 1916 with $400,000 in capital stock, and in the incorporation papers it was explained the manufacturing was organized "for the purpose of producing a medium-priced car with body refinements as a most attractive feature." That remained to be seen, but not for many years. The company took over the former factory of the R-C-H Corporation of Detroit, which had closed in 1915.

Organizers of Liberty Motor Car were already experienced men in the industry, including the head of the company, Percy Owen, who had been vice president and sales manager of Saxon. Among those joining him from Saxon were Harry F. Ford (no relation to Henry Ford), chief engineer R.E. Cole and

H.M. Wirth in purchasing. James F. Bourquin came from the Paige-Detroit Company and Chalmers, whose financial interests in Saxon had been acquired by Harry Ford.

With a strong financial beginning, the Liberty was aggressively marketed and had its debut at the exclusive Hotel Pontchartrain in 1916. For the rest of the year production reached 730, and by end of World War I, production had reached 6000 in 1919. Around 1917 a few six-cylinder light trucks were built. By 1921 11,000 Liberty cars had been built.

Receivership arrived in January of 1923, and only about 100 cars were built for the entire year. All assets of the company were acquired by the Columbia Motor Car Company, which assembled Liberty cars from leftover parts into 1924. The Budd Wheel Company bought the Liberty factory in 1925.

Liberty (truck)

To clarify the similarity in names, the Liberty 4 × 2 truck built under the auspices of the American armed forces was a culmination of specifications brought together during July of 1917. In August of that year the relatively new Society of Automotive Engineers (SAE) organized 50 engineers in eight groups. A total of 150 companies would build the components using a 424 cid four-cylinder motor, the block for which would be manufactured by Continental, along with a cylinder head from Waukesha.

In October of 1917 a finished prototype was evaluated, and by May of 1918 production was organized for an output of 1000 trucks per month. The "USA" emblem was used on almost all radiators. The fifteen companies that were assigned to do final assembly were Bethlehem, Brockway, Diamond T, Garford, Gramm-Bernstein, Indiana, Kelly-Springfield, Packard, Pierce-Arrow, Republic, Selden, Service, Sterling, U.S. Motor Truck and Velie.

None out of this entire list of companies

**LIBERTY
MOTOR CAR
COMPANY**

**DETROIT
MICHIGAN**

Price	**$1350**
Two-Passenger Roadster	1350
Four-Passenger Roadster	1350
Five-Passenger Sedan	1925
Town Car	2700
Landaulet	2700

LIBERTY SIX TOURING—10-B

COLOR	Body, blue; chassis, black	LUBRICATION	Force feed and splash
SEATING CAPACITY. .	Five	RADIATOR	Cellular
POSITION OF DRIVER .	Left side	COOLING	Thermo-syphon
WHEELBASE	115 inches	IGNITION	Storage battery
GAUGE	56 inches	STARTING SYSTEM . .	Two unit
WHEELS	Wood	STARTER OPERATED .	Gear to fly wheel
FRONT TIRES	32 x 4 inches	LIGHTING SYSTEM . .	Electric
REAR TIRES	32 x 4 inches, anti-skid	VOLTAGES	Six to eight
SERVICE BRAKE . . .	Contracting on rear wheels	WIRING SYSTEM . . .	Single
		GASOLINE SYSTEM . .	Vacuum
EMERGENCY BRAKE .	Contracting on transmission	CLUTCH	Plate
CYLINDERS	Six	TRANSMISSION . . .	Selective sliding
ARRANGED	Vertically	GEAR CHANGES . . .	Three forward, one reverse
CAST.	In sixes	DRIVE	Spiral bevel
HORSEPOWER . . .	25.35 (N.A.C.C. Rating)	REAR AXLE	Semi-floating
BORE AND STROKE .	3¼ x 4½ inches	STEERING GEAR . . .	Worm and gear

In addition to above specifications, price includes top, top hood, windshield, speedometer, ammeter, clock, tire pump, electric horn and demountable rims.

built more than a few hundred Liberty trucks, with Gramm-Berstein and Selden assembling the most at 1,000 each. The unpredicted early Armistice resulted in the sudden cancellation of nearly all military contracts. Some Liberty trucks were assembled from remaining parts in inventory, and the Liberty truck remained in small production numbers for the military.

Many of those companies involved in the war effort did not survive the cancellations, material shortages, postwar recession and oversupply of surplus vehicles. At the same time, the government changed overall procurement policy in a misdirected belief that war would not return; that the Great War was somehow truly going to be the "War to End All Wars."

Lippard-Stewart

The Lippard-Stewart Motor Company, which was located in Buffalo, New York, for all of its short life, was yet another of a handful of companies that used what had been called the "Renault"-type hood. The company began building trucks in 1911, and commercial vehicles is what it built exclusively, with the first model rated at ¾-ton. The following year a complete open cab Panel Delivery was available for $1800 from the factory.

The swept-back hood, which was also used by Mack, Kelly and International for a time, meant that the radiator was behind the engine and drew the hot air away from the motor using motor-driven fans, which exhausted through a vent behind the hood and front fender on each side. This positive air flow was a superior method to relying on air flow created by vehicle speed, which was usually only five to fifteen mph at that time, and engine governors kept top speed not much higher than that. Access to the engine was much better as long as the radiator did not need replacement. At the time engine maintenance and repair were far more common than radiator repair, so in the early days that was advantageous even if sheet metal tooling

LIPPARD-STEWART TRUCKS

Manufactured by

LIPPARD-STEWART MOTOR CAR CO., Buffalo, N. Y.

S P E C I F I C A T I O N S

Model	MW	B	W	H
Capacity	½ ton	¾ ton	¾ ton	1 ton
Drive	Worm	Bevel	Worm	Worm
Chassis Price	$925	$1,500	$1,600	$2,000
Motor				
H. P. (S.A.E.)	16.9	22.5	22.5	22.5
H. P. (Actual)	22	30	30	30
Cylinders	4 en bloc	4 en bloc	4 en bloc	4 en bloc
Bore	3¼″	3¾″	3¾″	3¾″
Stroke	5″	5¼″	5¼″	5¼″
Wheel Base	106″	115″, 125″ & 135″	115″, 125″ & 135″	145″
Tread Front	56″	56″	56″	56″
Tread Rear	56″	56″	56″	58″
Tires Front	33x4″ pneu.	35x4½″ pneu.	35x4½″ pneu.	36x3″
Tires Rear	33x4″ pneu.	35x4½″ pneu.	35x4½″ pneu.	36x5″

Frame—Pressed channel.
Front Axle—I-beam, Elliott.

Rear Axle	Semi-floating	Full-floating	Full-floating	Full-floating

Springs Front—Semi-elliptic.
Springs Rear—Semi-elliptic.
Carburetor—Zenith.

Cooling System	Thermo-syphon	Pump	Pump	Pump

Oiling System—Pump and splash.
Ignition—Magneto.
Control—Left drive, center control.
Clutch—Cone.
Transmission—Selective, three speeds forward and one reverse.

Brakes	Duplex expanding rear wheels	Internal expanding, external contracting	Duplex expanding on rear wheels	Duplex expanding on rear wheels

Steering Gear—Screw and nut.
Equipment—Tool kit, lamps, jacks, instruction books, fenders, etc.

was more complex. Appearance was also a consideration when most trucks had a boxy "coffin"-style hood.

Records show that the U.S. Army bought at least three 1½-ton Lippard-Stewart trucks when Pancho Villa attacked Columbus, New Mexico, in 1915. Suddenly, the government was desperate for rugged motor vehicles during the Punitive Expedition, and these trucks were tested in the rugged conditions of the desert. Continental four-cylinder engines rated at 35 hp along with David Brown worm drive rear axles were used, the latter having the advantage of not being exposed to sand and dirt as chain drive was. Although it appears the U.S. military bought several more Lippard-Stewart trucks, by the end of the war the company was defunct.

Little Giant

Of the lesser-known motor vehicle builders that began just before World War I was the Chicago Pneumatic Tool Company, also known as C.P.T. The company was well known for compressors and pneumatic and electric tools at the very genesis of such tools' existence. C.P.T. was also to build the Little Giant series of trucks in Chicago, Illinois, as well as the C.P.T. truck and the Duntley Commercial.

At that time there were many people in all types of businesses who wanted to get into motor vehicle manufacturing as the gasoline engine and electric motor increasingly and consistently proved their domination over the horse. Hundreds of small businesses sprang up across America trying to cash in either on the latest craze (as some predicted would be the mere outcome of the automobile) or on what would be the next phase of viable personal and commercial transportation.

The C.P.T. was a car built in 1906 using a two-cylinder motor that produced 22 hp and used solid tires. It was built in a series of 50

units that year only as transportation for its traveling salesmen.

In 1910 the Chicago Pneumatic Tool Company got back into motor vehicle manufacturing when the Duntley was designed as a one-ton capacity commercial car. It featured a 20 hp horizontally-opposed gasoline two-cylinder engine, a planetary transmission and shaft drive. "Strong, Simple, Reliable and Efficient" were the only words used in the advertising slogan. It was exported to England as the C.P.T.

In 1912 the name of these commercial vehicles was changed to Little Giant. There were numerous vehicles of this period that used the name "Little" for some reason or another, but these Little Giant trucks were not affiliated with the Little of Amesbury, Massachusetts (1900); the Little of Camden, New Jersey (1911); the Little of Arlington, Texas (1911); the Little of Flint, Michigan (1912 — acquired by William Durant and GM); the Little Cyclecar of Detroit, Michigan (1914); the Little Four Steam of Detroit (1904); the Little Kar of Grand Prairie, Texas (1920); the Littlemac of Muscatine, Iowa (1930); the Little Mystery of Detroit (1929); the Little Princess of Detroit (1913); Little Red Devil of St. Louis, Missouri (1904); or the Little Steamer of Salem, Massachusetts (1900).

The Little Giant trucks were rated at ¾-ton capacity and one-ton capacity by 1915 when the two-cylinder engine was superseded by a Continental four-cylinder, three-speed sliding gear transmission and worm drive. By 1917 the company offered 3½-ton trucks as well, but by 1918 the motor vehicle manufacturing side of the business was abandoned.

Locomobile

Editor and publisher of the *Cosmopolitan Magazine* in Watertown, Massachusetts, John Brisben Walker was the man behind the incorporation of the Locomobile Company of America in 1899. His partner was Amzi

LITTLE GIANT TRUCKS

Manufactured by

CHICAGO PNEUMATIC TOOL CO., Chicago, Ill.

Model	15	16	17
Capacity	1 ton	2 tons	3½ tons
Drive	Worm	Worm	Worm
Chassis Weight	2,950 lbs.	4,500 lbs.	6,200 lbs.
Chassis Price	$1,650	$2,500	$3,450
Engine	Continental	Continental	Continental
H. P. (S.A.E.)	19.6	27.2	32.4
H. P. (Actual)	34 at 2000 R.P.M.	40 at 1500 R.P.M.	45 at 1500 R.P.M.
Cylinders	4 en bloc	4 en bloc	4 in pairs
Bore	3½"	4⅛"	4½"
Stroke	5"	5¼"	5½"
Wheel Base	138"	144"	176"
Tread Front	56"	58"	66¼"
Tread Rear	58¼"	58½"	65¼"
Tires Front	34x3½"	36x4"	36x5"
Tires Rear	34x5"	36x7"	36x5" dual
Frame	Channel section pressed steel 4 9/16 x2x 3/16	Channel section pressed steel 5 11/16 x2½x 3/8	Channel section pressed steel 8x3x 3/8

Front Axle—I-beam section. Thrust bearing on knuckle.
Rear Axle—Timken full-floating.
Springs Front—Semi-elliptic.
Springs Rear—Semi-elliptic.

Carburetor	Schebler Type R 1"	Schebler Type R, 1¼"	Stromberg M-1½
Cooling System	Thermo-syphon	Pump	Pump

Oiling System—Combination pump and splash.
Ignition—Magneto.
Control—Right-hand steer, center control.
Clutch—Dry plate.
Transmission—Warner Selective.
Brakes—Hand and foot, internal duplex on rear wheels.
Steering Gear—Screw and nut.
Equipment—Cab, wind shield and curtains furnished. Governor on Model 17.

**LOCOMOBILE
COMPANY
OF AMERICA**

**BRIDGEPORT
CONNECTICUT**

Price	. . . .	**$5950**
Six-Passenger Touring	. . . .	5950
Four-Passenger Touring	. . . .	6050
Seven-Passenger Limousine	. .	7200
Seven-Passenger Landaulet	. .	7300
Seven-Passenger Berline	. . . .	7400

LOCOMOBILE TOURING—48 SERIES TWO

COLOR	Optional		RADIATOR	Cellular
SEATING CAPACITY. .	Seven		COOLING	Water pump
POSITION OF DRIVER .	Left side		IGNITION	Tandem-dual high tension magneto and storage battery
WHEELBASE	142 inches			
GAUGE	56 inches			
WHEELS	Wood		STARTING SYSTEM . .	Single unit
FRONT TIRES . . .	37 x 5 inches		STARTER OPERATED .	Gear to fly wheel
REAR TIRES . . .	37 x 5 inches		LIGHTING SYSTEM . .	Electric
SERVICE BRAKE . .	Contracting on rear wheels		VOLTAGES	Six
EMERGENCY BRAKE .	Expanding on rear wheels		WIRING SYSTEM . . .	Single
			GASOLINE SYSTEM . .	Pressure
CYLINDERS	Six		CLUTCH	Dry multiple disc
ARRANGED	Vertically		TRANSMISSION . . .	Selective sliding
CAST.	In pairs		GEAR CHANGES . . .	Four forward, one reverse
HORSEPOWER	48.6 (N.A.C.C. Rating)			
BORE AND STROKE .	4½ x 5½ inches		DRIVE	Spiral bevel
LUBRICATION	Force feed and splash		REAR AXLE	Full floating
			STEERING GEAR . . .	Worm and gear

In addition to above specifications, price includes top, top hood, windshield, speedometer, voltmeter, clock, tire pump, electric horn and demountable rims.

Lorenzo Barber, who has been considered the first asphalt magnate when roads were only beginning to be paved. With some backing the two men bought out the Stanley Brothers for $250,000 in 1900 and continued to build steam cars. The new name, however, was Locomobile, which alluded to steam locomotives and not to any Spanish word with which Americans were not familiar. Amzi Barber and John Walker had disagreements from the start, Walker was bought out, and by 1901 Barber moved manufacturing to Bridgeport.

By 1902 4000 "bicycle-frame" steam-powered Locomobiles had been manufactured. From some accounts, they needed to have their water tank filled every 20 miles, but a Locomobile racing car made headlines when it achieved 50 mph, giving the company some good press. In addition to the passenger cars a ½-ton Locodelivery was also built.

Barber's son-in-law, S.T. Davis, Jr., took over as company president. He had already been treasurer of the company and was also president of the Association of Licensed Automobile Manufacturers (A.L.A.M.), a very powerful organization placed in charge of collecting licensing fees from all motor vehicle manufacturers on behalf of the Selden Patent, which would involve one of the most famous litigations in the auto industry when Henry Ford sued A.L.A.M. and eventually won the case.

One of the suppliers of major components for Locomobile was the Overman Wheel Company of Chicopee Falls, Massachusetts. Despite the name, Overman built boilers for steam vehicles as well as water pumps and other parts for Locomobile. Overman also built its own Victor Steam Car, which was discontinued in 1903 as Overman merged with Locomobile, moving its plant to Bridgeport.

The renowned motor vehicle designer Andrew Riker developed a gasoline-powered car at Overman prior to the merger. This was to be the major change in the company's future. The Riker-designed Locomobile was considered "exemplary" by the press and was available as a two-cylinder or four-cylinder car with a pressed steel body and wheel steering at a time when tiller steering and one-cylinder engines were still state-of-the-art.

By 1905 Locomobile cars were becoming famous in various races, with a first place in 1908 when George Robertson won the Vanderbilt Cup in the "Old 16." In 1911 the T-head six-cylinder Model 48 was introduced, which became the flagship for Locomobile for more than a decade. J. Frank de Causse, who has been called a brilliant engineer, organized a custom department which would be responsible for creating extravagant cars owned by the Vanderbilts, William Carnegie and other wealthy people of the era. However, S.T. Davis, Jr., suddenly died in 1915 of cerebral hemorrhage and the company finances were thrown into disarray.

General John Pershing owned Locomobile limousines during World War I which were shipped to France for his official use. The Chief of Staff, General James Harbord, arrived on May 29, 1917, with the first Locomobile limousines, which at the time cost about $7000 to $10,000, bringing accusations of extravagance from the French Parliament.

Such opulence was justified as a need for military prestige and show of leadership. It was pointed out that the large vehicles were less susceptible to gunfire, explosives and disrepair. General Pershing eventually ordered nineteen Locomobiles at those prices and a special Locomobile limousine was also built for him. The Locomobile Special Overseas Limousine, a later development at the end of 1918, had steel disc wheels, but its entire custom body was narrower for "better aerodynamics," along with a V-shaped windshield. It was powered by a T-head six-cylinder motor producing 48.6 hp and rode on a 142-inch wheelbase. General Pershing traveled frequently between his headquarters at Chaumont and various field commands and government offices in Paris using two limousines in case of tire or mechanical failure, and perhaps to thwart an attack.

In 1917 *National Geographic* carried a full-page ad proclaiming, "The Locomobile is the car built in limited quantities and with such extreme carefulness. A production of only Four Cars a Day — for the exclusive class accustomed to the best and not content with compromise." At that time some of the lamps and metal work were the design of Tiffany studios.

Locomobile was also involved in building experimental armored cars based on Model 48 chassis and drive train. The company was also engaged in building the final and most advanced tank design of the war, which was called the Mark VIII. It was a joint venture between the British and American forces. The prototype was assembled by Locomobile in Bridgeport, Connecticut, rolling out September 29, 1918, powered by a Rolls-Royce engine. It was too late, as the war soon ended, and only a pilot series of the Mark VIII tanks were assembled in Scotland.

Despite its productivity during the war, by 1919 Locomobile had used up its credit and went into receivership. A merger under Emlen S. Hare involving Simplex and Mercer did not fare well in 1920. Another consolidation under William Durant in 1922 did not solve the company's problems. The Model 90 and the Junior Eight proved to be inadequate remedies, as was the introduction of a Lycoming straight-eight motor for 1927. A few Locomobiles were built for 1928 and 1929, but the stock market crash took Durant's empire down rapidly, and Locomobile did not get a chance to enter the new decade.

Luverne

Ed Leicher and Fenton Leicher were horse buggy builders in Luverne, Minnesota, where they decided to switch to auto manufacturing in 1904. Their first automobile was from a kit they had bought from A.L. Dyke of St. Louis, Missouri.

It should be noted that Andrew Lee Dyke, who was born in Dykesville, Louisiana, in 1875, had established the first automotive supply company in 1899. His most popular product was a kit to build an entire auto, which included all parts and blueprints, with prices ranging from $600 to $1000, depending on size of the vehicle and whether it had a 5 hp one-cylinder or 12 hp two-cylinder motor. He built demonstration models of his cars, which were sold across the country, and he produced the first electric car west of the Mississippi. After selling his company in 1901, he built a six-cylinder car in 1904 called the Dyke-Britton, after which Andrew Dyke turned to writing and publishing his *Dyke's Gasoline Encyclopedia,* which remained in print for decades and made him a wealthy man.

Meanwhile, back in Luverne, the Leicher brothers, having learned about assembly through their Dyke kit car, built their own car using a Buick engine in 1904 and then continued to manufacture cars with Rutenber or Beaver engines, establishing the Luverne Automobile Company in 1906. The Luverne highwheelers were followed by a conventional four-cylinder car, and touring cars continued after 1910.

The Big Brown Luverne six-cylinder car followed the Montana Special, and in 1912 the company built its first fire engine. Passenger car production ceased in 1916, and Luverne built trucks from then on, including a series that was used in the war effort. In the 1920s the Luverne Motor Truck Company evolved into the Luverne Fire Apparatus Company, and after 1970 it was called the Luverne Fire Equipment Company.

Maccar

Once Jack Mack broke away from his brothers and the Mack Brothers Company of

THE BIG BROWN LUVERNE TRUCK
Manufactured by
LUVERNE AUTOMOBILE CO., Luverne, Minn.

Model	BBL
Capacity	2 tons
Drive	Internal gear
Chassis Weight	3,000 lbs.
Chassis Price	On application
Engine	Golden, Belknap, Swartz Co.
H. P. (S.A.E.)	28
H. P. (Actual)	36
Cylinders	4 en bloc
Bore	$3\frac{3}{4}''$
Stroke	$4\frac{1}{2}''$
Wheel Base	140″
Tread Front	56″
Tread Rear	56″
Tires Front	34x4″ Pneumatic
Tires Rear	34x5″

Frame—Channel steel built-up.
Front Axle—I-beam, roller bearing spindle.
Rear Axle—Torbensen I-beam, internal gear.
Springs Front—Semi-elliptic.
Springs Rear—Semi-elliptic.
Carburetor—Schebler R.
Cooling System—Thermo-syphon.
Oiling System—Splash, constant level.
Ignition—Bosch magneto.
Control—Left-hand drive, center control.
Clutch—Dry plate.
Transmission—Detroit Selective, three speeds.
Brakes—Internal and external on axle.
Steering Gear—Worm.
Equipment—Electric starter and lights, driver's cab, platform stake body or convertible farm truck body.

MACCAR TRUCKS

Manufactured by

MACCAR TRUCK CO., Cliff St., Scranton, Pa.

S P E C I F I C A T I O N S

Model	L	H	M	U
Capacity	1—1½ ton	2½ tons	3½ tons	5½ tons
Drive	Worm	Worm	Worm	Worm
Chassis Price	$2,100	$2,600	$3,250	$4,150
Motor				
H. P. (S.A.E.)	33	44	44	44
H. P. (Actual)	30	40	40	40
Cylinders	4 en bloc	4 in pairs	4 in pairs	4 in pairs
Bore	4⅛″	4½″	4½″	4½″
Stroke	5¼″	5½″	5½″	5½″
Wheel Base	150″	162″	174″	186″
Tread Front	58″	58½″	61″	64″
Tread Rear	58″	60½″	66¾″	71½″
Tires Front	36x4″	36x4″	36x5″	36x5″
Tires Rear	36x5″	36x4″ dual	36x5″ dual	40x6″ dual

Frame—Pressed.
Front Axle—I-beam section, solid K.
Rear Axle—Full floating.
Springs Front—Semi-elliptic.
Springs Rear—Semi-elliptic.
Carburetor—Stromberg, M2.
Cooling System—Pump.
Oiling System—Force and splash.
Ignition—Magneto.
Control—Left drive, center control.
Clutch—Dry plate.

Transmission	Selective, three speeds forward, one reverse	Selective, three speeds forward, one reverse	Selective, three speeds forward, one reverse	Selective, four speeds forward, one reverse

Brakes—Internal on rear wheels.
Steering Gear—Screw and nut.
Equipment—Full set of tools and jack, two side and one rear oil lamp, horn, and spare parts.

Mack truck fame, he joined up with Roland Carr in 1912 to form the Maccar Company in Allentown, Pennsylvania. Maccar built only trucks, which at first were conventional assembled ¾-ton and 1½-ton capacity. Maccar shared its factory with the Webb Motor Fire Apparatus Company and the Lansden Company during 1912 and 1913. But by 1915 Maccar was reorganized and moved into a new factory at Scranton, Pennsylvania. The name changed to the Maccar Truck Company, but both Jack Mack and Roland Carr left for greener pastures. Jack Mack died in a trolley accident in 1924.

For 1915 the Maccar line of trucks ranged from ¾-ton to 2-ton capacity. All were powered by four-cylinder Wisconsin engines. As the United States entered World War I, Maccar expanded its line to include a 3½-ton and a 5½-ton truck, but all still used chain drive before switching to worm drive in 1918. As with so many East Coast truck builders that produced more than prototypes, Maccar provided some of its vehicles to the military.

As the war ended Maccar began developing a new design called the Model M, which was powered by a Continental engine using a Brown-Lipe transmission and Timken worm drive. It was rated at 3½-ton and priced at $4300. In the 1920s Maccar's market expanded but remained primarily in the New England and New York region.

By the mid–1920s Maccar offered six-cylinder engines following the general trend of the industry. Maccar united with Hahn and Selden in 1929. Cast iron radiators and distinctive sheet metal were carried on through the beginning of the Great Depression. Six-wheel trucks were introduced in 1930 and four-cylinder engines were abandoned the following year. The joint venture of Hahn, Selden and Maccar finally met its demise in 1935, with Hahn reorganizing for a much longer ride in the industry.

Mack

Of the earliest truck builders still in existence as of this writing, Mack may be the most famous one. It was founded by five Mack brothers in 1901 when they built their first motor vehicle in the form of a 15-passenger sightseeing bus, which would be fitted with a motor of their own design and manufacture after the first four-cylinder engine was deemed inadequate. Mack was located in New York City, so there was plenty of opportunity for building motorized transport, and a second order for a bus arrived in 1903 once the first bus proved itself.

Mack moved its operations in 1905 to Allentown, Pennsylvania, which seemed to be a wise move in that the new location was much larger. The company also was not paying top dollar for having its factory "downtown," which was becoming unnecessary as the workforce in the new automotive industry expanded across the East Coast, Midwest and Great Lakes Region. But Mack was still building only 50 vehicles per year by 1906.

The Manhattan Bus was the most successful vehicle, and its chassis was soon used to build delivery trucks up to 2-ton capacity. Forward control was phased out during this period, with all Mack vehicles being conventional design within a couple of years. In 1910 Mack was still producing Junior models (left-hand drive) and Senior models (right-hand drive), with the latter up to 7½-ton capacity by 1911. According to some historians, the bulldog trademark was adopted at this time without fanfare, but it was not installed as a hood ornament until two decades later.

In 1911 the Mack Brothers Company was employing 700 people, plus another 75 at their New Jersey engine factory. With output reaching 600 per year, Mack joined up with Saurer Motor Company, which was the American licensee for building Swiss Saurer trucks. Under a holding company called International Motor Company (IMC), not to be confused with International Harvester, both Saurer and Mack continued to be manufactured independently. Hewitt trucks became a third member of IMC in March of 1912, and all three were advertised together. The Mack brothers themselves all left the company with the exception of Willie, who retired from Mack a decade later, but not before starting an

independent company named Mackbilt in 1916. Jack Mack helped form Mac-Carr (Maccar) before he was killed when a trolley hit his car in 1924. Gus and Joseph left the auto industry altogether before World War I. The International Motor Truck Corporation (IMTC) absorbed the earlier IMC and dropped Hewitt.

However, the Mack company acquired the engineering expertise of Edward R. Hewitt and Alfred F. Masury. By 1914 Hewitt had designed the Mack AB, which lasted as a model until 1935. Alfred Masury designed the AC model. Financial difficulties rocked Mack at this time, but the emergence of the two new model lines propelled the company, especially during World War I.

Army records show Mack built 2,563 5½-ton 4 × 2 trucks for the war effort. As the war began in Europe, Mack built a few armored car prototypes on its 2-ton Model AB chassis with .20-inch plate using a 144-inch wheelbase. Powered by a standard 221 cid 45 hp four-cylinder engine, it had worm drive and dual rear wheels with solid rubber. The whole vehicle weighed 9,050 pounds with a Gray-Davis searchlight or two diagonally-mounted machine guns with a curved shield. This type of plate, it should be noted, would only be effective against small arms fire and some shrapnel. A cannon shell as small as 37mm would penetrate this type of shielding, leading to the concentrated effort of developing the armored tank by the military without help from Mack. The Mack armored cars were used for recruiting and parades and never saw action on the ground in Europe.

Some companies did very well as a result of war production. Mack became internationally known for its sturdy "bulldog" trucks, which were even used to transport Renault and Whippet tanks directly on their chassis in an enclosed steel bed. Despite claims that the bulldog icon had already been adopted at Mack, another story has it that the bulldog

MACK TRUCKS

Manufactured by

INTERNATIONAL MOTOR COMPANY, 64th St. and West End ave., N.Y.

Model	AB	AB	AB	AC
Capacity	1 ton	1½ tons	2 tons	3½ tons
Drive	Worm or chain	Worm or chain	Worm or chain	Chain
Chassis Weight	144″ W. B. 4,600	162″ W. B. 5,000	162″ W. B. 5,100	180″ W. B. 8,120
	132″ W. B. 4,350	144″ W. B. 4,900	144″ W. B. 5,000	168″ W. B. 8,070
				156″ W. B. 7,970
Chassis Price	$2,400	$2,800	$3,000	$4,250
Engine	Mack	Mack	Mack	Mack
H. P. (S.A.E.)	25.6	25.6	25.6	40
H. P. (Actual)	31	31	31	48
Cylinders	4 in pairs	4 in pairs	4 in pairs	4 in pairs
Bore	4″	4″	4″	5″
Stroke	5″	5″	5″	6″
Wheel Base	132″ and 144″	144″ and 162″	144″ and 162″	156″—168″—180″
Tread Front	58″	58½″	58½″	68″
Tread Rear	58¼″	58½″	58½″	71½″
Tires Front	36x4″	36x4″	36x4″	36x5″
Tires Rear	36x3½″ dual	36x3½″ dual	36x4″ dual	40x5″ dual

Frame—Pressed steel.
Front Axle—Drop forged I-section.
Rear Axle—Worm: Full-floating. Chain: Dead. Timken bearings.
Springs Front—Semi-elliptic.
Springs Rear—Semi-elliptic.
Carburetor—Stromberg (optional).
Cooling System—Pump.
Oiling System—Circulating gravity feed and splash.
Ignition—High tension magneto.
Control—Left side.
Clutch—Multiple dry plates.
Transmission—Selective, four speeds.
Brakes—Models A. B.; Duplex internal expanding on rear wheels. Model A. C., service
   brake, external type operating on jack shaft, emergency brakes rear wheels, in-
   ternal type.
Steering Gear—Worm and gear.
Equipment—Open metal seat, sliding side-doors, horn, lamps, bumper, spare parts, etc.

name was given to the trucks by British engineers, who arrived in New York in 1917 on a purchasing mission. They immediately ordered 150 of the Model AC Mack, stating, "In appearance these Macks, with their pugnacious front and resolute lines, suggest the tenacious quality of the British Bulldog." The name stayed, although the canine logo wasn't registered until 1921, and as mentioned the hood ornament was installed a full decade later. The controversy over the origins of the bulldog image for Mack remains only as a point of folk history interest in an otherwise insignificant detail of automotive history.

As is often the case during war, technology has often directly accelerated in its development out of sheer necessity. By April of 1917 Goodyear organized a fleet of Mack, Packard and White trucks and embarked on a 740-mile journey to test the new tires from Akron, Ohio, to Boston, Massachusetts, over the Allegheny Mountains. These heights could not be crossed in bad weather without pneumatic tread-pattern tires, which were also capable of withstanding 35 mph on a flat, solid road. Specifically, these tires were called "balloon tires" and were 38×7 in front and 44×10 in the rear.

One of the first problems was the mismatch of the truck's cargo surface area and that of the loading dock. Goodyear used the tandem bogie, which was a non-driven third axle, to solve this problem. Automotive engineer Ellis W. Templin helped in the design of the Goodyear trucks. At this time Harold Gray at B.F. Goodrich and Sidney M. Cadwell at United States Rubber Company were both credited with the discovery of antioxidants for rubber, which further advanced their strength and durability at a time when punctures, ruptures and blowouts were a regular occurrence. The Mack trucks were intrinsic to this truck tire road test and validation.

In 1919 Saurer was dropped by IMTC. In 1922 the company name was again changed to Mack Trucks in order to remove confusion with International Harvester. This was the year of the invention of the refrigeration truck, which was accomplished by R.D. Hatch in San Francisco. He used a Mack truck to install a system using the evaporation of anhydrous ammonia through coiled pipe, which was insulated with ground cork and paper, lining the truck's van body.

Moving beyond the scope of this book, Mack survived the Great Depression, built a line of buses for decades, contributed many thousands of vehicles during World War II, and has continued a successful business history producing trucks of numerous types and sizes as of this writing.

Manly

The Manly Motor Corporation started out in Waukegan, Illinois, a city whose name means "fort," named by local Potawatomi Indians in the 1800s when they ceded all the land to the federal government. It is located north of Chicago near the border of Wisconsin on Lake Michigan. As a small town it was apparently just large enough for a truck manufacturer such as Manly to begin business there in 1917.

An engineer named W. Manly has been recognized as having designed a hydraulic transmission as early as 1909, and the Manly Drive was an earlier company he had started. The Manly Drive transmission was recognized as the first fluid transmission built in the United States, but this design was not put into practical use in motor vehicles until the late 1930s and after World War II when the automatic transmission was first manufactured.

The first three Manly truck models were the 30, 40 and 50, which were 1½-, 2- and 2½-ton capacity, respectively. A reorganization and incorporation in 1918 added the O'-Connell name to the company, although no indication of this is apparent in the listing for

MANLY TRUCKS

Manufactured by

MANLY MOTOR CORPORATION, Waukegan, Ill.

Model	30	40	50	60
Capacity	1½ tons	2 tons	2½ tons	3 tons
Drive	Worm	Worm	Worm	Worm
Chassis Weight	4,500 lbs.	4,900 lbs.	5,400 lbs.	6,300 lbs.
Chassis Price	$2,050	$2,250	$2,600	$3,000
Engine	Waukesha	Waukesha	Waukesha	Waukesha
H. P. (S.A.E.)	22.5	22.5	25.6	28.9
H. P. (Actual)	30	30	33	36
Cylinders	4 en bloc	4 en bloc	4 in pairs	4 in pairs
Bore	3¾″	3¾″	4″	4¼″
Stroke	5¼″	5¼″	5¾″	5¾″
Wheel Base	144″, 156″. 168″	156″ and 168″	156″, 168″, 180″	156″ and 168″
Tread Front	56″	56″	56″	56″
Tread Rear	56″	56″	58″	58″
Tires Front	36x4″	36x4″	36x4″	36x5″
Tires Rear	36x5″	36x6″	40x7″	40x8″

Frame—Pressed.
Front Axle—I-beam.
Rear Axle—Manly, semi-floating.
Springs Front—Semi-elliptic.
Springs Rear—Semi-elliptic.
Carburetor—Zenith.
Cooling System—Pump.
Oiling System—Circulating splash.
Ignition—Eisemann magneto.
Control—Center.
Clutch—Dry. disc.

Transmission	Fuller 3 speed selective	Fuller 3 speed selective	Fuller 4 speed selective	Fuller 4 speed selective
Brakes	External and internal on rear hub	External and internal on rear hub	Internal, rear hub	Internal, rear hub

Steering Gear—Screw and split nut.
Equipment—Driver's seat, front fenders, running boards, three oil lamps, tools, mechanical horn and governor.

that year, which showed that a 3-ton Model 60 was added to the lineup.

All Manly trucks were powered by Waukesha four-cylinder engines and used Fuller three-speed, or in the case of the heavier models, four-speed transmissions. One of the items in the equipment listing was a mechanical horn available with the Manly trucks. In 1918 it was still common to provide a bulb horn for certain vehicles, and one can be seen in the Manly illustration. A mechanical horn was necessary when only a magneto was provided and no battery was used for a lighting and self-starting system.

A century later it is automatically expected that all motor vehicles are provided with an electric horn from the factory. Before World War I it was common to buy an after-market horn or it was optional equipment. There was a large, separate market for their manufacture. Mechanical horns were available as: French horns, which were of the tightly twisted type; chimed horns, which had more than one tone that could be heard at the same time; and dragon horns, were particularly large and loud. Manufacturers boasted of "musical qualities" of the brass instrument-like accessories, and Volier horns imported from France were up to 8 inches in diameter at the bell, and were called "Royal Siren," the equivalent of today's air horn.

There were several electric horn fabricators, such as Sireno and Barco, during the earlier era. In addition there were Husk chimes and gongs, and tri-tone instruments for warning others of impending danger of collision. Klaxon became one of the best known horn makers, and to "lean on the klaxon" became an expression of obnoxious horn blowing by an impatient driver.

Manly suffered business downturn after World War I. It was at least in part due to the postwar recession, but material shortages and weak sales were symptomatic of motor vehicle company failures by 1920, which was the last year for Manly.

Marion-Handley

Marion cars were initially built at Indianapolis, Indiana, beginning in 1904. The first Marions were powered by a Reeves air-cooled four-cylinder engine. A straight-eight-cylinder engine was built for racing the first year of operation. The first two years prices remained at $1500 until the more powerful Model 2, which used a 28 hp four-cylinder engine, appeared in 1906.

Harry C. Stutz, Fred Tone and Robert Hassler all contributed to Marion in engineering details but all departed to start their own automotive businesses, as was the common syndrome of the era. George Schebler built a V-12 roadster in 1908 using a Marion chassis, and Marion continued to attain a reputation as a quality car with a good degree of pizzazz. The following year John North Willys bought controlling interest in Marion.

By June of 1912 the problem of undercapitalization was addressed by reorganizing with capital stock of $1,125,000, which was over tenfold from the initial capitalization. J.I. Handley became Marion's president. He was already president of American Motors Company of Indianapolis (unrelated to the much later company by the same name). However, due to bad debts incurred by Marion, as exemplified by a collections lawsuit in the amount of $4000 by Standard Brass Foundry, Handley was pressured into buying the assets of Marion for $120,000, including John North Willys's portion.

In 1913 the Marion Bobcat became one of the best-known Marion roadsters ever built. It was reasonably priced at $1425. In 1914, J.I. Handley organized Mutual Motors Corporation and bought Imperial Motors of Jackson, Michigan, where Marion was moved; Imperial closed down within a year. Marion acquired the hyphenated Handley name, and the company built Marion-Handley cars beginning in 1916 using a Continental six-

M U T U A L
M O T O R S
C O M P A N Y

J A C K S O N
M I C H I G A N

Price, $1575

MARION-HANDLEY 6-60 TOURING — B

COLOR	Olive green		LUBRICATION	Force feed and splash
SEATING CAPACITY .	Seven		RADIATOR	Cellular
POSITION OF DRIVER	Left side		COOLING	Water pump
WHEELBASE	125 inches		IGNITION	Storage battery
GAUGE	56 inches		STARTING SYSTEM . .	Two unit
WHEELS	Wood		STARTER OPERATED .	Gear to fly wheel
FRONT TIRES	35 x 4½ inches		LIGHTING SYSTEM . .	Electric
REAR TIRES	35 x 4½ inches, anti-skid		VOLTAGES	Six
SERVICE BRAKE . . .	Contracting on rear wheels		WIRING SYSTEM . . .	Single
			GASOLINE SYSTEM . .	Vacuum
EMERGENCY BRAKE .	Expanding on rear wheels		CLUTCH	Dry multiple disc
			TRANSMISSION . . .	Selective sliding
CYLINDERS	Six		GEAR CHANGES . . .	Three forward, one reverse
ARRANGED	Vertically			
CAST	En bloc		DRIVE	Spiral bevel
HORSEPOWER	29.4 (N.A.C.C. Rating)		REAR AXLE	Three-quarters floating
BORE AND STROKE .	3½ x 5¼ inches		STEERING GEAR . . .	Worm and wheel

In addition to above specifications, price includes top, top hood, windshield, speedometer, ammeter, electric horn and demountable rims.

cylinder motor that had been adopted in 1914 with the Model G priced at $2150. Nevertheless, by the end of World War I Marion-Handley was in deep financial crisis, and the company was auctioned off in February of 1919 for $212,000.

Marmon

Indianapolis, Indiana, was the birthplace of several automobile companies, and one of the most successful was Marmon. It was started by Howard C. Marmon, who was a University of California graduate in mechanical engineering. His family owned the Nordyke and Marmon Company in Indianapolis, makers of flour milling equipment. By age 23 Howard C. Marmon had finished his studies in Berkeley and became chief engineer.

Marmon's first car was an experiment for which he designed a V-2 overhead-valve air-cooled motor with multiple-disc clutch and a three-speed selective sliding gear transmission. He also had force-feed lubrication for the engine, which was suspended on a three-point sub-frame with the transmission. The car also had shaft drive, and all in all the design was very advanced for 1902.

The following year Howard Marmon built another car with a V-4 motor and a planetary transmission. Six of the cars were built and some were sold to friends in 1904. Howard Marmon continued to run the operation of Nordyke and Marmon along with his brother Walter, who was in charge of finances. In 1905 manufacturing of autos began, and 25 were built and sold. Subsequently, Marmon built an experimental V-6 and a V-8. The former was not successful, as harmonic vibration had not been resolved for a V-6 engine at that time. The latter engine was mounted on a new 128-inch wheelbase chassis and shown at the New York Automobile Show with a price tag of $5000 but had no buyers.

Marmon's small V-4 was superseded in 1908 with a water-cooled in-line four-cylinder T-head engine and conventional chassis design, and in 1909 the Model 32 became more successful as Nordyke and Marmon continued to make money with flour milling equipment. The first Indianapolis 500 was won by just such a Marmon, driven by Ray Harroun. The car had a long tail, was painted yellow and was called the Marmon Wasp. This car was used as a basis for the six-cylinder Model 48 and smaller six-cylinder Model 41, followed by the Model 34 in 1916. At that point prices ranged from $2950 for a Club Roadster up to $5500 for a Town Car. The Model 34 used aluminum throughout, including cylinder block, entire body and radiator shell, and even such components as pushrods.

Howard Marmon hired Fred Muskovics, Alanson Brush and Samuel B. Stevens, the latter responsible for a cross-country publicity stunt in 1916 in which a Marmon beat the record by 41 hours, which had been set by a V-8 Cadillac. During World War I at least four Marmon touring cars, which were built as five-passenger or seven-passenger open cars, were used as staff cars by the American Expeditionary Forces (AEF). A report from the inspector general, Major James Castleman, Quartermaster Corps of August 7, 1918, stated that Marmon could not supply limousines despite the fact that the American military was ready to buy them at a moment's notice. It was uncertain why Marmon was sold out, but the company survived the war and continued doing business into the 1920s.

In 1924 George Williams, who was the former president of the Wire Wheel Corporation, bought a large portion of stock from Marmon and became its president. Howard Marmon remained vice president and chief engineer. The move increased sales from 2600 per year to 4000 by 1926, but Williams was more interested in the production of quantity

**NORDYKE &
MARMON
COMPANY**

**INDIANAPOLIS
INDIANA**

Price, $3550

MARMON ROADSTER—34

COLOR	Blue, gray or maroon	LUBRICATION	Full force feed
		RADIATOR	Cellular
SEATING CAPACITY	Four	COOLING	Water pump
POSITION OF DRIVER	Left side	IGNITION	High tension magneto
WHEELBASE	136 inches		
GAUGE	56 inches	STARTING SYSTEM	Two unit
WHEELS	Wire	STARTER OPERATED	Gear to fly wheel
FRONT TIRES	34 x 4½ inches	LIGHTING SYSTEM	Electric
REAR TIRES	34 x 4½ inches, anti-skid	VOLTAGES	Six
		WIRING SYSTEM	Single
SERVICE BRAKE	Contracting on rear wheels	GASOLINE SYSTEM	Gravity
		CLUTCH	Cone
EMERGENCY BRAKE	Expanding on rear wheels	TRANSMISSION	Selective sliding
		GEAR CHANGES	Three forward, one reverse
CYLINDERS	Six		
ARRANGED	Vertically	DRIVE	Spiral bevel
CAST	En bloc	REAR AXLE	Three-quarters floating
HORSEPOWER	33.75 (N.A.C.C. Rating)	STEERING GEAR	Worm and worm wheel
BORE AND STROKE	3¼ x 5⅛ inches		

In addition to above specifications, price includes top, top hood, windshield, speedometer, ammeter, clock, tire pump, electric horn and extra wire wheel.

rather than quality. Nordyke and Marmon sold its flour milling business to Allis-Chalmers at the end of 1926, which was a major business transaction for a company that was at the top of that industry, and now the automotive venture was reorganized as the Marmon Motor Car Company.

The result was the Little Marmon of 1927, designed by the renowned Barney Roos of Locomobile, and the all-new motor car, powered by a straight-eight, sold for around $1800, roughly half that of the previous Marmons. Roos left for Studebaker and the Little Marmon disappeared with him, followed by an even lighter and smaller Marmon selling for $1400. By 1929 all six-cylinder models were superseded by straight-eights courtesy of freelancing engineer Thomas J. Little, Lincoln's chief engineer.

The completely redesigned car was called the Roosevelt, and as if anticipating hard times, it was priced at $995. Sales jumped from 14,770 in 1928 to 22,300 in 1929. But the stock market crash sent Marmon sales plummeting to a total of 86 in 1933, the company's last year of production. As a champagne capper in departure, Howard Marmon introduced a 16-cylinder model line for 1931, which was the only Marmon available for the last year of manufacture. The company discontinued manufacturing as so many other great American companies were forced to do in the wake of the Depression.

Master

Master Trucks, Incorporated, began in 1917 in Chicago, Illinois, with the company's headquarters and factory listed at four buildings on Wabash Street. By 1918 the model line consisted of the 2-ton Model M and 2-ton Model O, the latter having a 170-inch wheelbase. There was also the Model T truck tractor, listed at 6- to 10-ton capacity, but it was designed to tow an articulated trailer. The 1918

illustration showing soldiers on and around the Master truck implied that the company obtained a military contract, which was very likely but not well historically documented.

The Master Junior series of trucks appeared after World War I, and between 1921 through 1924 Master built a 21-passenger and a 29-passenger bus chassis. The company survived the postwar recession and expanded its model line as the Master Motor Truck Company.

By 1925 the lightest Master model was called the 11 and was a 1¼-ton capacity truck. It was powered by a 22.5 Buda WTU engine with clutch and transmission from Fuller, and front and rear axles were from Timken. An electrical system was provided by Westinghouse, which was expanding its product lines into the motor vehicle industry while also entering the appliance field and component manufacturing.

The next larger Model 21 was powered by a Buda GBU motor with chassis price at $2,290. There was also a Model 41 with a Buda EBU motor and a Model 51 powered by a 32.4 hp Buda YBU motor, the latter having a 158-inch wheelbase. In addition Master offered a Model 61 rated at 5-ton capacity and a Model 64 rated at 6-ton capacity. The latter was powered by a 36.1 hp Buda ATU motor on a 170-inch wheelbase, which corresponded with the Model O (Long Wheel Base) truck of 1918.

Although 1929 was the year of the stock market crash in America, it appears that the Master Motor Truck Company was defunct by the time of the crash of October 1929.

Maxwell

As a successful sheet metal manufacturer, Benjamin Briscoe became a major investor in early automobile development, and among the early pioneers with which he got involved was Jonathan D. Maxwell, an engineer who had already worked with Ransom Eli Olds

MASTER TRUCKS

Manufactured by

MASTER TRUCKS, Inc., 3132-34-36-38 Wabash Ave., Chicago, Ill.

Model	M	O (Long Wheel Base)	T (Tractor)
Capacity	2 tons	2 tons	6 to 10 tons
Drive	Internal gear	Internal gear	Internal gear
Chassis Weight	4,300 lbs.	4,300 lbs.	4,300 lbs.
Chassis Price	$2,190 f.o.b. Chicago	$2,290 f.o.b. Chicago	$2,450 f.o.b. Chicago
Engine	Buda	Buda	Buda
H. P. (S.A.E.)	28.9	28.9	28.9
H. P. (Actual)	37 at 1100 R.P.M.	37 at 1100 R.P.M.	37 at 1100 R.P.M.
Cylinders	4 en bloc	4 en bloc	4 en bloc
Bore	$4\frac{1}{4}''$	$4\frac{1}{4}''$	$4\frac{1}{4}''$
Stroke	$5\frac{1}{2}''$	$5\frac{1}{2}''$	$5\frac{1}{2}''$
Wheel Base	144″	170″	110″
Tread Front	58″	58″	58″
Tread Rear	58″	58″	58″
Tires Front	34x4″	34x4″	34x4″
Tires Rear	36x6″	36x6″	36x4″ dual

Frame—Pressed.
Front Axle—Timken I-beam.
Rear Axle—Torbensen fixed, I-beam.
Springs Front—Semi-elliptic.
Springs Rear—Semi-elliptic.
Carburetor—Master $1\frac{1}{4}''$.
Cooling System—Pump.
Oiling System—Forced feed.
Ignition—Eisemann G-4.
Control—Left-hand drive, center control.
Clutch—Dry plate.
Transmission—Fuller Selective, three speeds.
Brakes—Internal and external on rear wheels.
Steering Gear—Worm and nut.
Equipment—Tool box, tool kit, three lamps, siren whistle.

Tire Equipment—GOODRICH MOTOR TRUCK TIRES FURNISHED WHEN SPECIFIED.

THE MAXWELL ONE TON TRUCK

Manufactured by

MAXWELL MOTOR COMPANY, Detroit, Mich.

Model	One-ton Truck
Capacity	2000 lbs.
Drive	Timken-David Brown Worm
Chassis Weight	2,385 lbs.
Chassis Price	$985 f. o. b. Detroit
Engine	Maxwell
H. P. (S.A.E.)	21.1
H. P. (Actual)	$33\frac{4}{8}$ by dynamometer test
Cylinders	4 en bloc
Bore	$3\frac{5}{8}''$
Stroke	$4\frac{1}{2}''$
Wheel Base	124″
Tread Front	56″
Tread Rear	56″
Tires Front	32x3″
Tires Rear	32x4″

Frame—Pressed steel.
Front Axle—Forked I-beam.
Rear Axle—Maxwell semi-floating.
Springs Front—Semi-elliptic.
Springs Rear—Semi-elliptic.
Carburetor—K. D. (Special).
Cooling System—Thermo-syphon.
Oiling System—Combined force-feed and splash system.
Ignition—Generator ignition system.
Control—Left-hand drive, center control.
Clutch—Cone type (operating in oil bath).
Transmission—Maxwell Selective sliding gear type, three speeds forward and one reverse.
Brakes—Internal expanding, rear wheel drums (hand and foot).
Steering Gear—Worm and gear.
Equipment—Solid tires (pressed on), seat, front fenders, electric head lights and tail light, electric horn, generator, storage battery 80 ampere-hour capacity, full set of tools.

MAXWELL
MOTOR
COMPANY

DETROIT
MICHIGAN

Price	$ 745
With All-Weather Top	855
Roadster	745
Sedan	1195
Berline	1095

MAXWELL TOURING—25

COLOR	Black	RADIATOR	Tubular
SEATING CAPACITY. .	Five	COOLING	Thermo-syphon
POSITION OF DRIVER .	Left side	IGNITION	Distributor and storage battery
WHEELBASE	108 inches		
GAUGE	56 inches	STARTING SYSTEM . .	Single unit
WHEELS	Wood	STARTER OPERATED .	Gear to fly wheel
FRONT TIRES	30 x 3½ inches	LIGHTING SYSTEM . .	Electric
REAR TIRES	30 x 3½ inches, anti-skid	VOLTAGES	Twelve
SERVICE BRAKE . . .	Contracting on rear wheels	WIRING SYSTEM . . .	Single
		GASOLINE SYSTEM . .	Gravity
EMERGENCY BRAKE .	Expanding on rear wheels	CLUTCH	Cone in oil
CYLINDERS	Four	TRANSMISSION . . .	Selective sliding
ARRANGED	Vertically	GEAR CHANGES . . .	Three forward, one reverse
CAST.	En bloc		
HORSEPOWER . . . . (N.A.C.C. Rating)	21.03	DRIVE	Plain bevel
BORE AND STROKE .	3⅝ x 4½ inches	REAR AXLE	Three-quarters floating
LUBRICATION	Pump over and splash	STEERING GEAR . . .	Worm and gear

In addition to above specifications, price includes top, top hood, windshield, speedometer, tire pump, electric horn and demountable wheels.

and Northern Manufacturing. Briscoe pulled out his money from the Buick company, having lost faith in David Dunbar Buick just as he was designing a winner. He formed a collaboration with J.P. Morgan, who provided another $100,000 in addition to the $50,000 of Briscoe's own to form the new company. By 1905 a factory at Tarrytown, New York, was bought from John Brisben Walker, builder of the Mobile Steamer, to produce the new Maxwell automobile.

The first two-cylinder Maxwells arrived as models H, L, N and S through 1906 when the four-cylinder Model M was introduced, to be carried on through and after 1907. (Maxwell would incorporate a six-cylinder motor only in 1914 during its entire two-decade company history). A special runabout called "Dr. Maxwell," especially marketed to physicians, was very popular before World War I. Company expansion included building factories in New York, Indiana and Rhode Island, and marketing manager *extraordinaire* Cadwallader Washburn Kelsey continued a colorful ongoing public relations program, such as driving up church steps and teeterboard riding, along with set-up police chases, most of which were captured on film for wide dissemination in nickelodeons. Good Glidden Tour showings and other light car race performances helped move sales from 3780 in 1907 to over 20,000 by 1910.

In 1910 Briscoe, who was the main financier of the Maxwell-Briscoe Company and called the shots, formed the United States Motor Company, perhaps modeling himself after William Crapo Durant, in that his own idea of creating an automotive empire like General Motors now included his own takeovers of Stoddard-Dayton, Columbia and Brush. The one ace Briscoe held was in that by acquiring Columbia he also got ownership of the Selden Patent that had been sold to the electric car firm earlier. The Association of Licensed Automobile Manufacturers (A.L.A.M.) was in charge of collecting on the fee which brought in millions of dollars until Henry Ford successfully challenged the Selden Patent, soon resulting in further lawsuits.

The Columbia Mark 84 and Mark 85 were advertised in 1911 with a whole page devoted to the merits of the Selden Patent, but just months later Ford's attorneys would prevail, and the Selden Patent lost most of its validity and all of its allure with millions of dollars in unpaid royalties. Marketing man Kelsey had strongly disputed watering down the model line with various marques, especially at a time when Maxwell was only third behind Ford and Buick in overall sales. He left the company to produce a car under his own name, himself demonstrating some of the megalomanic tendencies of automotive pioneers, and the United States Motor Company went belly-up in 1912. William Durant bought the Tarrytown factory from Maxwell in order to produce the first Chevrolet. Briscoe reorganized as the Maxwell Motor Company and moved operations to Detroit, Michigan.

As World War I began, Maxwell car number 100,000 rolled off the assembly line. Truck production continued as from the beginning, and a few were shipped off to Europe. The company survived the war, but the postwar recession, which really hit by 1920, placed Maxwell near bankruptcy. High volume production also meant huge inventories, so that by 1921, dealers had some 17,000 unsold Maxwells sitting on their lots and in their showrooms.

In 1922 a merger with Chalmers did not rectify the troubles. Walter Chrysler arrived in 1923 and immediately recalled many Maxwell cars in order to make repairs. Reliability vexations were hurting the car's reputation. He also had the Maxwell sparkled up and introduced the Good Maxwell (which may have implied there were also bad Maxwells, as the press pointed out). Chrysler became company president in 1924, introducing a car named after himself. However, as he started Chrysler Corporation in 1925, by 1926 Maxwell was discontinued. Jonathan Maxwell died in 1928 at age 63.

McFarlan

Horse-drawn wagons had been the product of the McFarlan Carriage Company of Connersville, Indiana, since its founding in 1856 by John B. McFarlan, who had arrived from Great Britain. In cooperation with grandson Harry McFarlan, John McFarlan's company progressed into the automotive field, and after the press announced a "motor buggy" to arrive from the company in 1909, in fact a stately and luxurious motor car appeared the following year.

From the beginning in 1910 the McFarlan was powered by a six-cylinder engine on a 120-inch wheelbase with a price tag of $2000. John McFarlan died at age 87 two weeks before the first experimental vehicle rolled off the line, and only 200 McFarlans per year would do so through nearly two decades of production. For that year McFarlan made a name for itself with very good showings at Indianapolis Motor Speedway. From a builder of carriages, such publicity promoted the transformation into the McFarlan Motor Company in 1913.

For the first three years McFarlan offered the buyer a choice of proprietary engines such as Brownell, Buda, Continental and Wisconsin. Just before America entered World War I, McFarlan narrowed the engine choice to the Teetor-Hartley Company. The American Expeditionary Forces (AEF) had one open touring car built by McFarlan, which was a small number indeed, but perhaps proportional to actual production numbers overall.

During the war McFarlan continued to built the Type 127 and the Type 138, both powered by a 48.6 hp six-cylinder engine on a 136-inch wheelbase. Body styles included

Touring, Roadster, Sport, Limousine, Town Car, Knickerbocker Cabriolet, Philadelphia Berline, V Front Sedan, Continental Landau and a four-passenger called the Submarine and Destroyer for 1917 and 1918, respectively, the latter names obviously inspired by battles under and on the seas.

As an exclusive builder of luxury cars where prices had shot up over $6000, McFarlan was little affected by the postwar recession. In 1921 the Twin-Valve Six with triple ignition was introduced using three spark plugs for each cylinder and producing 120 hp. This motor was built by McFarlan, not outsourced. And by this time the Knickerbocker convertible was up to $9000.

Some of Al Capone's lieutenants bought McFarlans for their speed and prestige as Prohibition fueled underground gang activity revolving around smuggling. A total of 235 McFarlans were sold for 1922. By that time even 24-carat gold plating on interior hardware was being used in custom orders. One such example sold for $25,000 to an oil magnate in Oklahoma that year.

A cheaper, slower McFarlan, powered by a Wisconsin motor and introduced in 1924, did not impress the company's clientele and was dropped by 1926. A Lycoming straight-eight motor for 1926 did little for the company's image at a time when Harry McFarlan was ill, with executive partner Burt Barrows suddenly passing and McFarlan himself and the entire company joining him in 1928. The Connersville plant was acquired by Errett Lobban Cord.

Menominee

Named after an Indian tribe, river, and wild rice in Wisconsin, there were at least three motor vehicle manufacturers by this name, but the one that built trucks beginning in 1911 was located in the town of Menominee itself. The small Menominee Truck Company

M c F A R L A N
M O T O R
C O M P A N Y

C O N N E R S V I L L E
I N D I A N A

Price	**$4650**
Town Car	4600
Knickerbocker Cabriolet	5250
Philadelphia Berline	4900
V Front Sedan	4600
Continental Landaulet	4900

McFARLAN SIX LIMOUSINE—TYPE 138

COLOR	Optional	LUBRICATION	Force feed and splash
SEATING CAPACITY. .	Seven	RADIATOR	Cellular
POSITION OF DRIVER .	Left side	COOLING	Water pump
WHEELBASE	136 inches	IGNITION	High tension magneto and storage battery
GAUGE	56 inches		
WHEELS	Wood		
FRONT TIRES	35 x 5 inches	STARTING SYSTEM . .	Two unit
REAR TIRES	35 x 5 inches, anti-skid	STARTER OPERATED .	Gear to fly wheel
		LIGHTING SYSTEM . .	Electric
SERVICE BRAKE . . .	Contracting on rear wheels	VOLTAGES	Six
		WIRING SYSTEM . . .	Single
EMERGENCY BRAKE .	Expanding on rear wheels	GASOLINE SYSTEM . .	Vacuum
		CLUTCH	Dry multiple disc
CYLINDERS	Six	TRANSMISSION . . .	Selective sliding
ARRANGED	Vertically	GEAR CHANGES . . .	Three forward, one reverse
CAST.	En bloc		
HORSEPOWER	48.6 (N.A.C.C. Rating)	DRIVE	Spiral bevel
		REAR AXLE	Full floating
BORE AND STROKE .	4½ x 6 inches	STEERING GEAR . . .	Worm and sector

In addition to above specifications, price includes speedometer, ammeter, clock, tire pump, electric horn and demountable rims.

MENOMINEE TRUCKS

Manufactured by

MENOMINEE MOTOR TRUCK CO., Menominee, Mich.

Model	**H**	**D**	**G**	**J**
Capacity	1½ tons	2 tons	3½ tons	5 tons
Drive	Worm	Worm	Worm	Worm
Chassis Weight	4,150 lbs.	4 525 lbs.	6,300 lbs.	8.200 lbs.
Chassis Price	$2,190	$2,615	$3,580	$4.540
Engine	Continental	Continental	Continental	Continental
H. P. (S.A.E.)	22.5	27.23	32.4	32.4
H. P. (Actual)	32	36	42	42
Cylinders	4 en bloc	4 en bloc	4 in pairs	4 in pairs
Bore	3¾″	4⅛″	4½″	4½″
Stroke	5¼″	5¼″	5½″	5½″
Wheel Base	130″	144″	160″	160″
Tread Front	57¾″	58½″	66″	68⅜″
Tread Rear	58½″	58½″	66″	69½″
Tires Front	36x3½″	36x4″	36x5″	36x6″
Tires Rear	36x5″	36x4″ dual	36x5″ dual	40x6″ dual

Frame—Rolled.
Front Axle—I-beam.
Rear Axle—Timken full-floating.
Springs Front—Semi-elliptic.
Springs Rear—Semi-elliptic.
Carburetor—Stromberg.
Cooling System—Pump.
Oiling System—Combination splash and force.
Ignition—Eisemann.
Control—Left drive, center control.

Clutch	Dry plate, Multiple disc	Dry plate, Multiple disc	Dry plate	Dry plate
Transmission	Brown-Lipe & Fuller 3 speeds selective		Cotta 3 speeds selective	

Brakes—Internal rear wheels.
Steering Gear—Worm and gear.
Equipment—Driver's seat, two running boards, two head lamps, tail lamp, horn, jack, kit of tools, two front fenders. Governor furnished on request.

factory under the ownership of D.F. Poyer was located not far from the birthplace of Four Wheel Drive (FWD) and later Seagrave, but did not build 4 × 4 trucks nor fire engines. Oshkosh and Harley-Davidson also originated nearby.

Menominee started with conventional assembled ¾-ton trucks, which were the only model line until America entered World War I. These early light trucks were powered by a Continental four-cylinder motor with an Eisemann ignition and Stromberg carb along with a three-speed selective sliding gear transmission and Timken worm drive. Prices started at $2080, which would not continue to be competitive as other light trucks such as Chevrolet, Dodge and Ford began to be manufactured in huge numbers.

Trucks such as Menominee were popular in the local vicinity where they were built at a time when brand loyalty was very regional, and marketing and dealership distribution had its limitations. There are no records that Menominee trucks were used in the Punitive Expedition or in Europe during World War I, but production was so small that this would not be out of the ordinary for that size company. This may have been a blessing in disguise, because small companies which were contracted by the military in World War I often had trouble retooling and readjusting back to civilian production, especially once the Armistice was signed, the war suddenly ended and contracts were dropped, leaving material and inventory stranded.

There is very little information about the company's history, but Menominee survived the war and postwar recession so that by 1923 the company expanded its model line from one-ton to six-ton capacity. The one-ton was called the Hurryton. Small 20- and 25-passenger buses were also built. The price for a 132-inch wheelbase cost $1,650 at this time. In 1928 Menominee merged with the Four Wheel Drive Company when the heaviest

Menominee was up to eight-ton capacity. By producing bodies for FWD the company survived in the Great Depression until 1937, when production was discontinued.

Mercer

Mercer County is where the Mercer Automobile Company was born at Trenton, New Jersey, during 1909, with the first automobile completed the following year. The designers behind the project were A.R. Kingston, E.T. George and C.G. Roebling, with unsubstantiated input from Etienne Planche. The first speedster and touring models were powered by an L-head four-cylinder Beaver engine. A Raceabout with a T-head motor appeared in 1911, which was inspired by C.G. Roebling's son Washington A. Roebling II and put into blueprints by engineer Finley Roberston Porter. The 34 hp 300 cid motor along with three-speed transmission with oil-immersed multiple disc clutch added up to a very quick machine. A four-speed transmission in 1913 enhanced the performance even more.

Mercer began entering auto races in 1911, and out of a half dozen, five were won by a Raceabout. The following year Ralph De Palma set eight class world records driving a Raceabout at the Los Angeles Speedway. Another feat covered by the press that same year was the race won by Spencer Wishart at Columbus, Ohio, where he used a Raceabout straight off the showroom floor. Mercer production output was approximately 500 per year during this period, with one-third of the cars being Raceabouts.

On April 15, 1912, Washington Roebling II was one of the victims of the *Titanic* disaster. Two years later Finley Porter resigned and was replaced by Eric H. Delling, who was to design the T-head motor for Mercer. This was a "flat-head" engine with side-valves having intake and exhaust on opposite sides. Delling quit in 1916. Both C.G. Roebling and F.W.

**M E R C E R
AU T O M O B I L E
C O M P A N Y**

Price, $3600

**T R E N T O N
N E W   J E R S E Y**

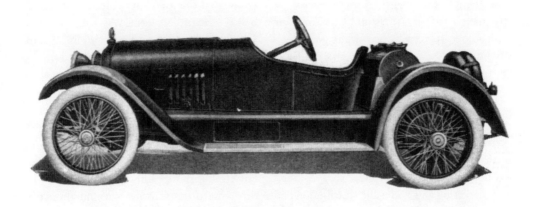

MERCER RACEABOUT

COLOR	Yellow, gray or gunmetal		LUBRICATION	Full force feed
SEATING CAPACITY	Two		RADIATOR	Cellular
POSITION OF DRIVER	Left side		COOLING	Water pump
WHEELBASE	115 inches		IGNITION	High tension magneto
GAUGE	56 inches		STARTING SYSTEM	Two unit
WHEELS	Wire		STARTER OPERATED	Gear to fly wheel
FRONT TIRES	32 x 4 inches		LIGHTING SYSTEM	Electric
REAR TIRES	32 x 4 inches		Voltages	Twelve
SERVICE BRAKE	Expanding on transmission		WIRING SYSTEM	Single
EMERGENCY BRAKE	Expanding on rear wheels		GASOLINE SYSTEM	Vacuum
CYLINDERS	Four		CLUTCH	Dry multiple disc
ARRANGED	Vertically		TRANSMISSION	Selective sliding
CAST	En bloc		GEAR CHANGES	Four forward, one reverse
HORSEPOWER	22.5 (N.A.C.C. Rating)		DRIVE	Spiral bevel
			REAR AXLE	Full floating
BORE AND STROKE	3¾ x 6¾ inches		STEERING GEAR	Worm and gear

In addition to above specifications, price includes windshield, speedometer, ammeter, voltmeter, clock, electric horn and wire wheels.

Roebling died during World War I, although not as a result of enemy action.

Wall Street bankers wrested control of Mercer as the war ended. The new focus was the bottom line under the incoming company president, Emlen S. Hare, who arrived from Packard. Mercer bought into Locomobile and acquired Simplex, at that time calling itself Hare's Motors, which could barely function as a company. In 1921 the company was completely reorganized again and receivership followed in 1923. A Rochester overhead-valve six-cylinder motor was introduced, but production all but ceased by 1924. A few cars were built from leftover parts for 1925. Former Durant executive Harry M. Wahl bought rights to the Mercer name. The reincarnated Mercer arrived as one prototype for the 1931 New York Automobile Show, but it was not meant to be in the throes of the Great Depression, and the famous, popular Mercer was gone forever.

Milburn (electric)

Among those numerous makers of motor vehicles that started out as horse-drawn wagon and buggy builders, the Milburn Wagon Company of Toledo, Ohio, started out in 1848. Rather belatedly, compared to many other companies, Milburn decided to go into auto and truck manufacturing in 1914, and electric vehicles would be the model line. In 1915 Milburn produced 1000 vehicles using a common 100-inch wheelbase for its Light Roadster, Light Coupe and Light Delivery. Price for the delivery was $985, which was $300 less than for the roadster.

Because the vehicles had to be recharged after 60 to 75 miles, Milburn tried to circumvent the shortcoming of battery-powered range problems by placing the battery pack on rollers. "Simply roll out the discharged ones and roll in the freshly charged set.... It makes charging as easy as driving."

This helped sales somewhat at first, but the fact that two sets of relatively expensive batteries were needed for this process was a disadvantage at a time when electric vehicle use was in decline in general. No new technology had been discovered to double the energy density of storage batteries, which was what would be needed to compete with gasoline-powered vehicles capable of twice the range using even a moderate-size fuel tank (with just 10 miles per gallon and a 20-gallon tank the range would be 200 miles).

The Light Delivery was discontinued right after World War I, and a major factory fire in December of 1919 resulted in nearly $1,000,000 in damage with the loss of at least 30 vehicles and parts in inventory. Milburn continued production in buildings of the Toledo University which had been used to train recruits of the Motor Transport Corps during World War I. In 1920 an electric taxicab on a 111-inch wheelbase was produced.

Milburn was recapitalized for $1,000,000 in 1921, when 800 people were employed. However, 600 of them were building car bodies for Oldsmobile. This connection led to the purchase of Milburn by General Motors for $2,000,000 in 1923. Buick took over Milburn, and only a few electric cars were completed before the make was gone permanently.

Mitchell

As did a number of other companies, the Mitchell & Lewis Wagon Company produced horse-drawn conveyances before entering the automotive field. William Turnor Lewis and Henry Mitchell were the men behind the venture in Racine, Wisconsin. By 1901 the Wisconsin Wheel Works, as their bicycle company became to be known, began building the Mitchell motorcycle, which was powered by a 1¾ hp motor. It was not a success, but by 1903 a car powered by a one-cylinder motor was designed and a few were built that year.

M I L B U R N
W A G O N
C O M P A N Y

TOLEDO, OHIO

Price	. . . .	$1885
Sedan	. . . .	2685
Limousine	. . . .	2785
1500-Pound	Delivery	
Chassis	. . . . .	1485

MILBURN BROUGHAM—27

COLOR	Milburn blue		REAR TIRES	32 x 3½ inches, pneumatic
SEATING CAPACITY .	Five		BRAKE SYSTEMS . .	Expanding on rear wheels
BODY:				
LENGTH OVER ALL	138 inches		BATTERY	40 cells, 11 plate
WIDTH OVER ALL .	66 inches		SPEED	23 miles per hour
WHEELBASE	105 inches		NO. FORWARD SPEEDS	Five
GAUGE	56 inches		NO. REVERSE SPEEDS	Two
WHEELS	Wire or wood		CONTROL	Lever operated
FRONT TIRES	32 x 3½ inches, pneumatic		STEERING	Lever

**MITCHELL
MOTORS
COMPANY
INCORPORATED**

**RACINE
WISCONSIN**

Price	**$1250**
Two-Passenger Roadster	1250
Five-Passenger Touring with Demountable Top	1550
Five-Passenger Club Roadster .	1280
Three-Passenger Coupe	1850
Five-Passenger Touring Sedan .	1950

MITCHELL TOURING—D-5-40

COLOR	Body, Mitchell blue; running gear black
SEATING CAPACITY. .	Five
POSITION OF DRIVER .	Left side
WHEELBASE	120 inches
GAUGE	56 inches
WHEELS	Wood
FRONT TIRES	32 x 4 inches
REAR TIRES	32 x 4 inches, anti-skid
SERVICE BRAKE . . .	Contracting on rear wheels
EMERGENCY BRAKE .	Expanding on rear wheels
CYLINDERS	Six
ARRANGED	Vertically
CAST.	En bloc
HORSEPOWER	25.35 (N.A.C.C. Rating)
BORE AND STROKE .	3¼ x 5 inches
LUBRICATION	Force feed and splash
RADIATOR	Cellular
COOLING	Water pump
IGNITION	Storage battery
STARTING SYSTEM . .	Two unit
STARTER OPERATED .	Gear to fly wheel
LIGHTING SYSTEM . .	Electric
VOLTAGES	Six
WIRING SYSTEM . . .	Single
GASOLINE SYSTEM . .	Vacuum
CLUTCH	Cone
TRANSMISSION . . .	Selective sliding
GEAR CHANGES . . .	Three forward, one reverse
DRIVE	Spiral bevel
REAR AXLE	Three-quarters floating
STEERING GEAR . . .	Worm and gear

In addition to above specifications, price includes top, top hood, windshield, speedometer, ammeter, tire pump, electric horn and demountable rim.

The Mitchell Motor Car Company was organized in 1904 and began series production of the B-2 Runabout and B-4 Touring, the numbers referring to number of cylinders. Both air-cooled and water-cooled engines were available, but all models used two-speed planetary transmissions with chain drive. Eighty-two cars were completed that year, but wagons continued to be produced until the end of World War I. Although much has been said about the expansion of the use of motor vehicles of all types during World War I, the military still used thousands of horse-drawn wagons overseas, and many needed to be replaced, in addition to the need for the home market.

Engineer John W. Bates designed the Mitchell cars after experimenting for a number of years. By 1907 Mitchell cars were shaft driven, and air-cooled engines were discontinued. The various branches of the companies under the two founders finally merged as one company under the name of Mitchell-Lewis Motor Company, also producing farm equipment, trucks and buses. The latter two were discontinued after 1908.

Henry Mitchell's son, William Lewis, took over as president and in 1910 the first six-cylinder car was introduced. Production increased from 2940 in 1909 to 5600 in 1910, and in 1912 output reached 6000. In 1913 engineer Rene Petard was summoned from France and hired to design a new T-head engine for the latest Mitchell. However, Lewis inexplicably parted ways with his company and set up shop in Racine with Petard to build a new car called the Lewis. Joseph Winterbottom became president of Mitchell, which was reorganized under that name alone. But being a banker, Winterbottom had other interests and left. Otis Friend took over at the helm in 1916. For that year alone Mitchells were powered by a 29 hp V-8 in addition to the six-cylinder motor.

As the postwar recession sank into the American economy in 1920, the designers at Mitchell took a step forward for which the public was unprepared. At the time the design of standard production cars and trucks for the general market included a very stodgy, square look for the body, radiator and windshield. Mitchell dared to slope the radiator back a tad, and the press immediately pounced on the company with the derogatory moniker of "the drunk Mitchell." The offensive lean was rectified with a vertical radiator immediately for 1921.

Durability runs proved the Mitchell out for further public relations. But the harm was done, and after producing 10,000 Mitchells in 1919, the fallout was that only 2500 were sold in both 1920 and 1921. Mitchells had sold very well during World War I, with 1917 being another banner year when 10,000 Mitchells found new owners. But by 1923 only 100 cars rolled off the assembly line before bankruptcy closed the doors permanently. Nash bought the factory, and remaining parts worth $1.6 million were auctioned off to sit on shelves as replacement components during the Roaring '20s.

Modern

There could have been numerous companies with a name like Modern, but in fact only four such enterprises made an attempt to build motor vehicles. The first was in Chicago in 1911, which makes a case for the presumption that it was probably affiliated with another one registered in that city just three years later. An earlier company actually called Payne-Modern in Erie, Pennsylvania, was not affiliated. The Modern truck shown here, however, was built by yet another company called Bowling Green Motor Car Company in the city by that name located in northern Ohio near Toledo. It was a very small town back in 1911, but manufacturing around the Great Lakes was flourishing,

THE MODERN TRUCK
Manufactured by
THE BOWLING GREEN MOTOR TRUCK CO., Bowling Green, Ohio

S P E C I F I C A T I O N S

Model	30
Capacity	1 ton
Drive	Worm
Chassis Price	$1,500
Motor	
H. P. (S.A.E.)	20
H. P. (Actual)	27
Cylinders	4 en bloc
Bore	$3\frac{1}{2}''$
Stroke	5''
Wheel Base	132''
Tread Front	56''
Tread Rear	56''
Tires Front	$34x3\frac{1}{2}''$
Tires Rear	34x5''

Frame—Pressed, 5'' section.
Front Axle—I-beam, Elliott type.
Rear Axle—Full-floating.
Springs Front—Semi-elliptic.
Springs Rear—Semi-elliptic.
Carburetor—Zenith L-5.
Cooling System—Thermo-syphon.
Oiling System—Splash and forced feed.
Ignition—Magneto.
Control—Right drive, center control.
Clutch—Dry plate.
Transmission—Selective, three speeds forward and one reverse.
Brakes—Internal expanding.
Steering Gear—Screw and nut.
Equipment—Chassis finished in lead, set of oil lamps, tool kit, and jack.

and the Toledo area had its share of entrepreneurs.

Companies such as Bowling Green were so obscure and short-lived that almost no details of the firm's activity remains. From company literature left extant we know that Modern trucks were ½-ton and ¾-ton capacity from the beginning. Both had solid rubber tires and used chain drive, although the heavier truck had optional shaft drive, which was very unusual as an option, as was forward control. The company itself offered a variety of open and closed bodies including express and van types. At some point toward its final span of existence it appears it was reorganized as the Bowling Green Truck Company, clarifying that it did not build passenger cars.

By 1914 a four-cylinder Continental motor was adopted as the standard engine. The model line now also included a one-ton and a 1½-ton capacity truck. The former was chain-driven and the latter had shaft drive. By 1916 a 2-ton and a 3½-ton model were also available. Bowling Green lacked military contracts by 1917, so wartime material shortages limited the company's output to just the 1½-ton capacity Modern, which in appearance did not confirm the name itself. By 1919 Modern trucks were no longer built, the war greatly affecting manufacturing even after it ended, leaving thousands of surplus trucks available to the public at low prices, among other wide-ranging effects.

Mogul

Almost simultaneously two companies were founded with the name of Mogul, and it is not out of the realm of possibility that the one listed in New York City in 1910 moved to Chicago the following year. Upon registering in New York the incorporators were W.L. Waller, C. Monteith Gilpin and James M. Wright, but it's not clear if these were the same men building Mogul trucks in Chicago

the following year. In any case, the Mogul trucks illustrated here were built in St. Louis, Missouri, where very few motor vehicle manufacturers ever set up shop, after Mogul moved from Chicago.

All Mogul trucks were forward control, which would later be called cab-over-engine (COE), but these were open cab design before that moniker was adopted. The first Moguls arrived in 1911. Four-cylinder engines and three-speed transmissions were used throughout the model line, and the specifications for 1917 show a specific comparison between gross and net horsepower output for each of the four models available by that time.

Some records show Mogul built trucks up to 6-ton capacity, but if this was the case they were not available by 1917. Mogul trucks were not extravagant, and optional equipment reflected their modest accouterments. From all evidence 1917 was the last year of production, and although unsubstantiated, wartime shortages and a meager market were probable contributing causes for the company's quick demise.

Moline-Knight

Starting out in East Moline, Illinois, the car company named after its city of origin was founded by W.H. Vandervoort, who was a professor of engineering at nearby University of Illinois when he formed the Vandervoort Engineering Company in 1899 with his classmate Orlando J. Root. Stationary gasoline engines were the company's first product line, which were becoming popular for many different applications in pumping, farming and various industrial uses.

The Moline Automobile Company was incorporated in 1903, with series production commencing in 1904. As with many manufacturers, the alphabetical listing was in reverse, as the Model D was designated for the 12 hp two-cylinder model on an 86-inch

MOGUL TRUCKS

Manufactured by

MOGUL MOTOR TRUCK CO., St. Louis, Mo.

S P E C I F I C A T I O N S

Model	LM	LW	L	T
Capacity	1½ tons	2 tons	2½ tons	3½ tons
Drive	Worm	Worm	Chain	Chain
Chassis Price	$1,600	$2,000	$2,250	$2,550
Motor				
H. P. (S.A.E.)	22.5	27.2	27.2	32.5
H. P. (Actual)	28 at 1200 R.P.M.	35 at 1200 R.P.M.	35 at 1200 R.P.M.	40
Cylinders	4 en bloc	4 en bloc	4 en bloc	4 in pairs
Bore	3¾"	4⅛"	4⅛"	4¼"
Stroke	5¼"	5¼"	5¼"	5½"
Wheel Base	125"	138" to 148"	138" to 148"	165" to 185"
Tread Front	58"	58"	58"	58"
Tread Rear	58"	58"	58"	58"
Tires Front	36x4"	36x5"	36x5"	36x5"
Tires Rear	36x5"	38x4" dual	38x4" dual	38x5" dual
Frame—Pressed steel.				
Front Axle—Timken				
Rear Axle	Timken 6451	Timken 6551	Drop forged	Drop forged
Springs Front—Semi-elliptic.				
Springs Rear—Semi-elliptic.				
Carburetor—Master.				
Cooling System—Pump.				
Oiling System—Splash.				
Ignition—Magneto.				
Control—Left drive, center control.				
Clutch	Dry plate	Dry plate	Wet plate	Wet plate
Transmission—Selective, three speeds forward and one reverse.				
Brakes—Internal expanding.				
Steering Gear—Worm and sector.				
Equipment—Lamp and tools.				

MOLINE AUTOMOBILE COMPANY

EAST MOLINE ILLINOIS

Price	**$1650**
Five-Passenger Touring	1650
Four-Passenger Roadster	1650
Touring Sedan	2280

MOLINE-KNIGHT TOURING—C

COLOR	Body, dark cobalt blue; running gear, black	BORE AND STROKE .	3¾ x 5 inches	
		LUBRICATION	Force feed	
SEATING CAPACITY. .	Five	RADIATOR	Tubular	
POSITION OF DRIVER .	Left side	COOLING	Thermo-syphon	
WHEELBASE	118 inches	IGNITION	Storage battery	
GAUGE	56 inches	STARTING SYSTEM . .	Two unit	
WHEELS	Wood	STARTER OPERATED .	Gear to fly wheel	
FRONT TIRES . . .	34 x 4 inches	LIGHTING SYSTEM . .	Electric	
REAR TIRES	34 x 4 inches, anti-skid	VOLTAGES	Six	
		WIRING SYSTEM . . .	Double	
SERVICE BRAKE . . .	Contracting on rear wheels	GASOLINE SYSTEM . .	Vacuum	
EMERGENCY BRAKE .	Expanding on rear wheels	CLUTCH	Cone	
		TRANSMISSION . . .	Selective sliding	
CYLINDERS	Four	GEAR CHANGES . . .	Three forward, one reverse	
ARRANGED	Vertically			
CAST.	En bloc	DRIVE	Spiral bevel	
HORSEPOWER	22.5	REAR AXLE	Semi-floating	
(N.A.C.C. Rating)		STEERING GEAR . . .	Screw and nut	

In addition to above specifications, price includes top, top hood, windshield, speedometer, ammeter, voltmeter, clock, tire pump, electric horn and demountable rims.

wheelbase while the Model B was the 18 hp four-cylinder car on a 105-inch wheelbase. These were superseded through 1908 with various two-cylinder and four-cylinder models whose designations were consistently out of sequence.

Moline cars won the Chicago Reliability Run more than once, prompting the sales department to adopt the slogan "The Car of Unfailing Service," and reference was made to the "Dreadnought Moline" as a car of real toughness. Succeeding Henry Martyn Leland (founder of both Cadillac and later Lincoln), Vandervoort became the president of the Society of Automotive Engineers (SAE), which took over most activity in the motor vehicle industry after the Association of Licensed Automobile Manufacturers (A.L.A.M.) was disemboweled when Henry Ford won the appeal in 1912 against the owners of the Selden Patent and their legal arm (A.L.A.M.).

The Moline emblem, which featured a battleship up to that time, was now changed to a depiction of Sir Galahad, one of King Arthur's knights. But this was not really happenstance, as Moline adopted the Knight Sleeve-Valve Motor, which was of four-cylinder design at the time.

There were numerous cars that adopted the Knight engine under license before and after World War I, but because there are only three that used this motor during World War I in America (Brewster and Willys being the other two within the 1917–1918 parameters of this book), it's worth delving further into the background of this unique design.

Charles Yale Knight was the designer and patentee of the Knight Sleeve-Valve Motor. According to a paper he presented to the Royal Automobile Club of London in 1908, he began working on his invention in 1903. With financial backing from L.B. Kilbourne, Charles Knight went into production in 1906 calling his automobile the "Silent Knight."

At a time when standard poppet valve grinding was an imperfect science and metallurgical advances did not allow for the level of steel hardening in existence today, lifters and tappets were very noisy and in need of constant adjustment or replacement. The Knight engine did not rely on hardened valves in hardened seats and was known for its quiet, smooth (if complicated) operation. But the poppet valve engine had been already accepted by the motoring public and by nearly all manufacturers. It was also far simpler.

Although the few Knight vehicles that Charles Knight built were successful (57 were built on Garford chassis), proving out his design admirably, no company was willing to chance it on his newfangled motor. Charles Knight obtained British Patent No. 12355 in 1908, the same year Daimler finally bought a license to manufacture Knight engines after rigorous testing. The Daimler 38 went into production using just such a motor. The Knight engine was limited to 2,500 RPM and despite refinements never became a very high performance engine by the nature of its design.

Its disadvantages were primarily in that it was expensive to build. It had a reputation for being difficult to start due to the friction of the sleeve-valves which circumscribed the entire combustion chamber, yet there had to be clearance for vertical movement, usually causing oil consumption and smoky exhaust. Charles Knight received $100 in royalties for every engine sold. Packard unsuccessfully tried to prove the patent invalid. There were those that appreciated its quiet operation and reliability.

Daimler's purchase of a license created a domino effect, and within the next decade American auto builders that bought into the Knight engine "fad," adopting its name as a suffix in their own name, included: Atlas-Knight, Brewster-Knight, Columbia-Knight, Edwards-Knight, Falcon-Knight, Federal-Knight, Handley-Knight, Lyons-Knight,

Moline-Knight, Silent Knight, Stearns-Knight, Sterling-Knight, Stoddard Dayton-Knight, Yellow-Knight and probably the most famous — Willys-Knight.

The medieval Knight name and valiant emblem contributed to marketing schemes of the motor and the cars that were powered by the out-of-the-ordinary powerplant. In 1913 Knight and Kilbourne announced that 26 manufacturers in eight countries were using the sleeve-valve motor design. The Moline-Knight four-cylinder was to be the first sleeve-valve motor cast en bloc and used thermosyphon cooling.

During World War I the Knight engine was rarely if at all used for military operations, and Knight-engine cars and trucks were not sent overseas because it took special know-how to repair and maintain the sleeve-valve motor, and the military tried to make interchangeable parts and standardization a top priority. Moline-Knight ceased manufacturing in 1919. Vandervoort passed away in 1921 at age 53. Root followed in 1928, taking his own life. Even after being used in some aircraft, the Knight engine faded into history by World War II.

Monroe

R.F. Monroe was the president of the Monroe Body Company in what would be a fortuitous location: Flint, Michigan, where William Crapo Durant had started first his horse carriage business, and then his automobile empire. It was where Durant also collaborated briefly with Louis Chevrolet in 1912.

The Monroe Motor Company was organized in August of 1914 in Flint with Durant entering the picture as vice president of the new company. All the stockholders of Monroe were also stockholders of Chevrolet.

The Monroe began production at the Flint factory where Chevrolet had started out, and distributorship was in the hands of Chevrolet dealers. The Monroe was an unremarkable open-body four-cylinder car with a price tag of only $460 at the outset. In 1916 the price went up to $495, and Durant resigned from his position when he quickly lost interest in the company.

Monroe moved to the former Welch factory in Pontiac, Michigan. Capitalization was increased to $1,000,000, and during World War I the Monroe was sold by new Monroe dealers. Apparently, the low price was not enough of an enticement, so by the end of 1918 Monroe was bankrupt. All the assets were bought by the William Small Company of Indianapolis, Indiana. He had been a distributor of Monroe cars. The Pontiac plant was leased to Geneva Motors for production of its Samson tractors, which was a short-lived exercise in misdirected competitiveness.

In Indianapolis, Monroe began building its own engines and now offered a closed sedan body powered by a 35 hp four-cylinder motor on a 115-inch wheelbase chassis for $1850. Louis Chevrolet was hired for his expertise as a consultant in an ironic twist now that Durant went on to produce the car without the man himself. How much influence on design Louis Chevrolet had is not certain, but he did organize seven racing cars with the help of Cornelius Van Ranst, four under the Monroe name and the rest under Frontenac. The effort was a success as Gaston Chevrolet, Louis's brother and once Durant's chauffeur, won the 1920 Indianapolis 500 in a Monroe, which was also the first win for an American car in that race since 1912. But the company did not take full advantage of the spectacular win, and by 1921 William Small was in receivership. With a convoluted ending including purchases by various parties, Monroe auto manufacturing was discontinued by the end of 1923.

Moon

Joseph W. Moon came from a very modest farming background in Ohio. He entered the

M O N R O E
M O T O R
C O M P A N Y

P O N T I A C
M I C H I G A N

Price $995
Roadster . . . 995
Sedan 1850

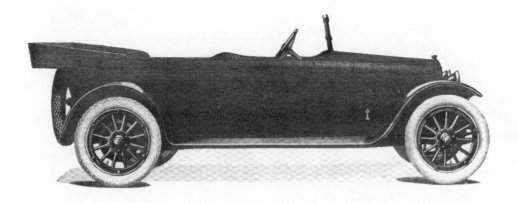

MONROE TOURING—M-6

COLOR	Body, Monroe blue; chassis, black; wheels, white	BORE AND STROKE .	3¼ x 4½ inches
		LUBRICATION	Full force feed
SEATING CAPACITY. .	Five	RADIATOR	Cellular
POSITION OF DRIVER .	Left side	COOLING	Thermo-syphon
WHEELBASE	115 inches	IGNITION	Storage battery
GAUGE	56 inches	STARTING SYSTEM . .	Two unit
WHEELS	Wood	STARTER OPERATED .	Gear to fly wheel
FRONT TIRES	32 x 3½ inches	LIGHTING SYSTEM . .	Electric
REAR TIRES	32 x 3½ inches, anti-skid	VOLTAGES	Six
		WIRING SYSTEM . . .	Single
SERVICE BRAKE . . .	Contracting on rear wheels	GASOLINE SYSTEM . .	Vacuum
		CLUTCH	Dry multiple disc
EMERGENCY BRAKE	Expanding on rear wheels	TRANSMISSION . . .	Selective sliding
CYLINDERS	Four	GEAR CHANGES . . .	Three forward, one reverse
ARRANGED	Vertically	DRIVE	Spiral bevel
CAST	En bloc	REAR AXLE	Semi-floating
HORSEPOWER . . . . (N.A.C.C. Rating)	16.9	STEERING GEAR . . .	Split nut

In addition to above specifications, price includes top, top hood, windshield, speedometer, ammeter, electric horn and demountable rims.

MOON MOTOR CAR COMPANY

ST. LOUIS
MISSOURI

Price, $1195

MOON SIX TOURING—36

COLOR	Body, royal blue; running gear, black	LUBRICATION	Force feed and splash
SEATING CAPACITY. .	Five	RADIATOR	Cellular
POSITION OF DRIVER .	Left side	COOLING	Thermo-syphon
WHEELBASE	114 inches	IGNITION	Storage battery
GAUGE	56 inches	STARTING SYSTEM . .	Two unit
WHEELS	Wire or wood	STARTER OPERATED .	Gear to fly wheel
FRONT TIRES	32 x 3½ inches	LIGHTING SYSTEM . .	Electric
REAR TIRES	32 x 3½ inches	VOLTAGES	Six
SERVICE BRAKE . . .	Contracting on rear wheels	WIRING SYSTEM . . .	Single
EMERGENCY BRAKE .	Expanding on rear wheels	GASOLINE SYSTEM . .	Gravity
		CLUTCH	Dry multiple disc
CYLINDERS	Six	TRANSMISSION . . .	Selective sliding
ARRANGED	Vertically	GEAR CHANGES . . .	Three forward, one reverse
CAST.	En bloc	DRIVE	Spiral bevel
HORSEPOWER . . . . (N.A.C.C. Rating)	19.84	REAR AXLE	Semi-floating
BORE AND STROKE .	2⅞ x 4½ inches	STEERING GEAR . . .	Worm and gear

In addition to above specifications, price includes top, top hood, windshield, speedometer, ammeter, tire pump, electric horn and demountable rims.

horse carriage business in St. Louis, Missouri. Observing the birth of the automobile closely as so many innovators and entrepreneurs of the period did, Moon entered the automobile manufacturing field with a roar, which came from his first car in 1905, powered by a 35 hp Rutenber four-cylinder motor using a three-speed sliding gear transmission and shaft drive, all quite advanced for the time. Brochures touted the Moon as "The Ideal American Car," and the $3000 price tag underscored the class of vehicle that it purported to be. But production was tiny at 45 units for 1906.

The Moon remained pricey until 1910, when the Model 30 was introduced for $1500. It was powered by a slightly smaller 30 hp engine and was two inches shorter in the wheelbase at 110 inches, with the third and largest Moon riding on a 120-inch wheelbase and still priced at $3000. In 1913 Moon introduced a 38.4 hp six-cylinder engine for its Model 65 Five-Passenger Touring, which rode on a 132-inch wheelbase and sold for $2500. For 1916 through 1927 all Moon autos were powered by six-cylinder engines until an eight-cylinder was introduced in 1925. Moon survived World War I without contributing any known vehicles such as staff cars for officers. Right after the war ended, Joseph Moon died, and his son-in-law Stewart MacDonald became president.

In the 1920s Moon tried to keep up with modernization with such things as demountable rims, balloon tires, hydraulic brakes and Rolls-Royce styling. The Continental eight-cylinder 1925 Diana model arrived as a special-order car when all other Moons were six-cylinder. Of these, 13,000 were built for the year, which became Moon's best ever in terms of production output. The Diana metamorphosed into the Aerotype eight-cylinder 8-80 model in 1928.

By 1929 Moon was in deep trouble even before the stock market crash, and entrepreneur Archie Andrews elbowed in for control of the company in order to build the Windsor and Ruxton automobiles. These would have an extremely short production life of about one year as the Great Depression began. The press would later state that it would take two decades to straighten out the financial affairs of the Moon Company. The million-dollar factory at St. Louis was sold for $72,000, and the new owner set out to manufacture matches.

Moreland

Watt Moreland first got experience in designing cars at the Durocar Manufacturing Company before moving to Burbank, California, to start out on his own. In 1909 he unveiled his L-head four-cylinder Moreland car using a four-speed transmission. The Moreland passenger car was produced only in a pilot series of six touring autos to be used by the company executives. Then in 1912 Watt Moreland organized the Moreland Motor Truck Company, and that year 203 trucks were built. Moreland would continue to build prototype passenger cars all the while building trucks. The forward-control trucks were offered as 1½-, 3-, 3½- and 5-ton capacity models powered by either a Hercules or Continental four-cylinder motor.

Just before America's entrance into World War I, Moreland introduced a "gasifier" which allowed low octane distillate fuel to be used. This was already in use for tractors and would prove to be popular with farmers. Moreland did not get involved in wartime production to any large extent primarily because of its location on the West Coast. By 1917 the Moreland factory was producing trucks at Burbank (Los Angeles), where it would remain until the beginning of World War II. Moreland engines were from Continental and Waukesha by 1918, Timken worm drive had been adopted, but all three- and four- speed transmissions were built by Moreland.

MORELAND DISTILLATE MOTOR TRUCKS

Manufactured by

MORELAND MOTOR TRUCK CO., 1701 N. Main St., Los Angeles, Cal.

Capacity	1 ton	1½ tons	2½ tons	4 tons
Drive	Worm	Worm	Worm	Worm
Chassis Weight	2,940 lbs.	4,000 lbs.	5,200 lbs.	7,500 lbs.
Chassis Price	$2,050	$2,750	$3,375	$4,150
Engine	Continental	Continental	Continental	Waukesha
H. P. (S.A.E.)	22.5	27.3	32.5	36.1
H. P. (Actual)	34 at 2000 R.P.M.	40 at 1500 R.P.M.	45 at 1500 R.P.M.	47 at 950 R.P.M.
Cylinders	4 monobloc	4 monobloc	4 in pairs	4 in pairs
Bore	3¾"	4⅛"	4½"	4¾"
Stroke	5"	5¼"	5½"	6¾"
Wheel Base	126"	126" and 150"	144" and 168"	162" and 186"
Tread Front	56"	57¾"	58½"	66½"
Tread Rear	58"	58"	58¼"	65¼"
Tires Front	34x3½"	36x3½"	36x4"	36x5"
Tires Rear	34x4"	36x5"	36x7"	40x5" dual
Frame	Special alloy pressed	Pressed steel	Pressed steel	Pressed steel
Front Axle—Timken I-beam.				
Rear Axle	Timken semi-floating	Timken semi-floating	Timken full-floating	Timken full-floating
Springs Front—Semi-elliptic.				
Springs Rear—Semi-elliptic.				
Carburetor	Ensign or Master			
Cooling System	Thermo-syphon	Centrifugal pump	Centrifugal pump	Centrifugal pump
Oiling System	Plunger pump and splash	Plunger pump and splash	Plunger pump and splash	Pump and splash
Ignition—High tension magneto.				
Control—Left drive, center control.				
Clutch—Multiple disc, dry.				
Transmission	Moreland Selective, 3 speeds	Moreland Selective, 4 speeds	Moreland Selective, 4 speeds	Moreland Selective, 4 speeds

Brakes—Expanding duplex, rear wheels.

Steering Gear—Ross screw and nut.

Equipment—Mechanical horn, full set of tools, including jack, all necessary wrenches, etc. Governor on 4-ton model.

Being one of the very few motor vehicle manufacturers in Southern California, Moreland was successful in building bus chassis, and by 1924 was offering a six-wheel bus chassis which was powered by two six-cylinder Continental engines. This chassis, which had both Westinghouse air brakes and Lockheed hydraulic brakes, was also available as a six-ton capacity truck, although it was more practical as a double-decker bus. However, weight restriction for highways precluded series production.

After 1925 Moreland continued its success, building axles and transmissions. The factory occupied 25 acres, and by 1929, 900 trucks and buses were built for the year. But two years later production dropped to 35 as the Great Depression took its toll.

Negotiations for a merger with Fageol in northern California did not materialize in 1931. Moreland survived and was innovative enough to adopt diesel engines. By the end of the 1930s, Moreland relied mostly on parts sales and repairs rather than vehicle production, and in 1941, as America entered World War II, Moreland would cease all private-sector truck manufacturing.

Nash

As an orphan at six years old in 1872 and a child farm laborer, Charles W. Nash would work his way out of poverty, and this he did by running away to work for William Crapo Durant and his partner J. Dallas Dort at the Durant-Dort Carriage Company. He became the manager by 1895, and in 1908 he became manager of Buick. Two years later he was president of General Motors, organized by William Durant, who would install himself as vice president, a title he preferred to have in nearly all his early companies. But just before America entered World War I, Nash and Durant parted ways.

Nash and another GM expatriate, James Storrow, bought the Thomas B. Jeffery Company midyear in 1916. Charles Jeffery, who survived the *Lusitania* sinking, had inherited his father's company, which built the Rambler car, Jeffery Quad and light trucks, after his father died suddenly in 1914. Charles Jeffery retired after receiving $9,000,000 for the large Nash factory and its entire line of vehicles. The Jeffery Quad continued as the Nash Quad, and this truck was very significant in

NASH TRUCKS

Manufactured by

THE NASH MOTORS CO., Kenosha, Wis.

Model	One-Ton Model 2017	Two-Ton Model 3017	Quad. (2T) Model 4017
Capacity	1 ton	2 tons	2 tons
Drive	Internal gear	Internal gear	Internal gear 4 wheels
Chassis Weight	3,400 lbs.	3,850 lbs.	6,000 lbs.
Chassis Price	$1,495	$1,875	$3,250
Engine	Nash	Nash	Buda
H. P. (S.A.E.)	22.5	22.5	28.9
H. P. (Actual)	27	27	39.5
Cylinders	4 en bloc	4 en bloc	4 en bloc
Bore	$3\frac{3}{4}''$	$3\frac{3}{4}''$	$4\frac{1}{4}''$
Stroke	$5\frac{1}{4}''$	$5\frac{1}{4}''$	$5\frac{1}{2}''$
Wheel Base	130"	144"	124"
Tread Front	$56\frac{1}{2}''$	$56\frac{1}{2}''$	$60\frac{1}{2}''$
Tread Rear	$56\frac{1}{2}''$	$59\frac{1}{2}''$	$60\frac{1}{2}''$
Tires Front	34x3"	34x4"	36x5"
Tires Rear	34x4"	34x6"	36x5"
Frame—Pressed.			
Front Axle—Nash I-beam.			
Rear Axle	Round dead	Round dead	Nash I-beam
Springs Front—Semi-elliptic.			
Springs Rear—Semi-elliptic.			
Carburetor—Stromberg.			
Cooling System—Pump.			
Oiling System—Forced feed and splash.			
Ignition	Delco	Delco	Eisemann
Control—Left drive, center control.			
Clutch—Dry plate disc.			
Transmission	Detroit Selective, three speeds	Detroit Selective, three speeds	Nash Selective, four speeds
Brakes	Service external contracting rear wheels	Service external contracting rear wheels	Service internal and external four wheels
Steering Gear—Worm and nut.			

Equipment—Bijur electric lighting and starting on Models 2017 and 3017; $125 extra on Model 4017. Driver's seat, horn, tools, jack, M. & S. locking differential, and governor all models. Solids bolted or pressed on optional, pneumatics extra.

**NASH MOTORS
COMPANY**

K E N O S H A
W I S C O N S I N

Price **$1295**
Four-Passenger Roadster 1295
Five-Passenger Sedan 1985
Seven-Passenger Touring 1465

NASH TOURING—681

Color	Nash blue, pencilled with gold	Bore and Stroke .	3¼ x 5 inches
Seating Capacity. .	Five	Lubrication	Circulating system
Position of Driver .	Left side	Radiator	Tubular
Wheelbase	121 inches	Cooling	Water pump
Gauge	56 inches	Ignition	Delco system
Wheels	Wood	Starting System . .	Special
Front Tires	34 x 4 inches	Starter Operated .	Gear to fly wheel
Rear Tires	34 x 4 inches, anti-skid	Lighting System . .	Electric
		Voltages	Six
Service Brake . . .	Contracting on rear wheels	Wiring System . . .	Single
		Gasoline System . .	Vacuum
Emergency Brake .	Contracting on transmission	Clutch	Plate
		Transmission . . .	Selective sliding
Cylinders	Six	Gear Changes . . .	Three forward, one reverse
Arranged	Vertically		
Cast	En bloc	Drive	Spiral bevel
Horsepower 29.4		Rear Axle	Semi-floating
(N.A.C.C. Rating)		Steering Gear . . .	Worm and gear

In addition to above specifications, price includes top, top hood, windshield,
speedometer, ammeter, tire pump, electric horn and demountable rims.

World War I, matching only FWD in numbers used overseas as a rugged 4 × 4 in all theaters of war. The Nash Quad was nearly identical to the Jeffery Quad.

With plenty of resources on hand, Charles Nash introduced his own car in April of 1918. It was designed by Erik Wahlberg, who had worked at Durant's Oakland (to be Pontiac) and had thorough knowledge of the Buick motor. The new Nash was also overhead-valve design, and the car featured Hotchkiss drive as well as semi-elliptic suspension. The large Nash factory turned out 10,000 Nash autos for the test of its introductory year, and 27,000 for 1919. In addition to its passenger cars and Quad, Nash produced a standard two-wheel-drive truck.

By the time the postwar recession arrived around 1920, Nash gradually phased out its commercial vehicle model lines so that by 1924 only 203 Nash trucks were built. By 1928 the Nash Quad was discontinued, mostly as a result of its remaining unchanged when the competitors continued to modernize their trucks. By 1930 when the Great Depression began, Nash discontinued its truck production altogether, except for a sedan delivery in 1931 and a short revival during and after World War II in the form of ⅔-ton Army trucks and Nash wreckers from 1947 to 1955, as well as a delivery van in 1951 and 1952.

During the 1920s Nash passenger car production was quite successful. Beginning in 1920, the year that 35,084 Nashes were built, Nash produced the LaFayette. Kenosha, Wisconsin, was the main plant for Nash, but some cars such as the LaFayette were first produced in Indianapolis, then in Milwaukee, Wisconsin. The LaFayette lost $2,000,000 through 1922, but Nash made a profit of $7,600,000 that year on the other cars. These consisted of a baker's dozen models in some ten body styles, with the Series 40 being entirely four-cylinder and the Series 690 being entirely six-cylinder motor powered.

The Ajax was another Nash offshoot in 1925 and 1926, but it was also less than stellar in sales, with about 25,000 produced during this period. The Ajax name was dropped as the Ajax Six became the Nash Six for 1926, the year James Storrow died. Dual ignition got the Advanced and Special models up to 75 mph in 1928. For 1930 Nash introduced the Twin-Ignition Eight. Using conservative monetary policy and keeping debt-to-liability ratio close, Nash actually made a profit of $4,800,000 in 1931 at a time when other companies were crashing financially.

Perhaps going beyond the normal scope of this book, it would be useful to note the importance and size of Nash as an American business entity, which continued for decades despite the dire financial conditions of the Great Depression. By 1932, when American auto production had plummeted to 13 percent of what it was in 1929, Nash made a profit of $1,000,000. Earl McCarty became president of the company as Nash retooled for the revived LaFayette, and Nash lost money for two years as the big changeover took place. George W. Mason took over as president when Nash bought his Kelvinator Company, and Nash again made a solid profit of $3,500,000 in 1937. The efficient and profitable management of Nash could have well been a lesson to so many other auto companies which were folding one after the other. An Ambassador Eight cabriolet designed by the famous Alexis de Sakhnoffsky was an eye-catcher for 1940. With the help of the advanced Nash 600 for 1941, sales went over 80,000 for the year.

Then the Nash factory was converted to build Pratt & Whitney aviation engines during World War II, and after a brief stint with success after the war when the public snapped up anything that was available, Nash got mostly into the small car business, building the Rambler, while its styling lagged behind GM, Ford and Chrysler. A merger with Hudson in 1954 only resulted in both the Nash and Hudson names being dropped by 1958 when only the Rambler was built. Now known as American Motors Corporation, the company would struggle on as the No. 4 of America's "Big Four" for another two decades before collaborating with Renault and then being bought out by Chrysler in 1987, leaving only the "Big Three."

National

Numerous entrepreneurs in America elected to use the name "National" in their hope to establish auto manufacturing, but the only one of significance and series production with that name began in 1900 in Indianapolis, Indiana. L.S. Dow and Philip Goetz were the founders who had been involved with Waverly, a subsidiary of the American Bicycle Company. The following year the National Automobile and Electric Company produced its first car, which was tiller-steered and battery-powered, joining a model line of horse-drawn carriages.

By 1902 the carriage portion of the business was sold, the company was reorganized as the National Vehicle Company, and the following year a pair of gasoline-powered cars were added to the lineup, both a 2-cylinder and a four-cylinder touring version. The following year National built the Model 100 Runabout Long Distance Electric, which featured a brass hood to make it resemble a gasoline-powered car. From the beginning, range was always a limitation for electric vehicles, even if top speed was not, and the energy density of batteries could not match that of liquid petroleum-based fuels. National also built the Park Trap Model 110 and the Piano Box Model 75, among a few others, but they were distinctly in contrast to the Gasoline Model A and Gasoline Model B.

Reorganization once again in 1904 heralded the new name of National Motor Vehicle Company, and by 1906 National electric passenger cars were discontinued under the new president of National, Arthur C. Newby, one of the founders of the Indianapolis Speedway, which would open in 1909. A Rutenber four-cylinder motor powered the National using shaft drive and a three-speed sliding gear transmission. After winning some endurance races, a six-cylinder motor was introduced in 1906, and National cars did well on the dirt track until Indy was paved in 1911. In 1912 National won the Indianapolis 500 with an average speed of 78.22 mph, among several other good showings, but it was the last year of racing for the company.

In 1915 National introduced its V-12 engine in competition with Packard. During World War I a total of 126 National closed cars (sedans and limousines) were sold to the American Expeditionary Forces (AEF), and many of them were powered by the V-12 engine. But once the war ended the V-12 was discontinued. With the advent of the postwar recession, National merged with the Dixie Flyer and the Jackson, becoming known as the Associated Motor Industries in 1922. Clarence A. Earl left Earl Motors to become the new president of National, but the financial situation of the company was so dire, 1924 would be the last year of production.

Nelson & Le Moon

Not to be confused with the E.A. Nelson Motor Car Company of Detroit, Michigan, which appeared later during World War I and built passenger cars, or with earlier Nelson car companies in Connecticut and Iowa, Nelson & Le Moon began in 1910 in Chicago, Illinois. A.R. LeMoon won the Chicago-Detroit-Chicago commercial vehicle run with one of his first trucks, prompting further development of a 1½-ton capacity truck for 1912.

In 1913 a 2-ton and a 3-ton truck were added to the lineup. Dual chain drive was superseded by Timken worm drive for all

**NATIONAL
MOTOR CAR
AND VEHICLE
CORPORATION**

**INDIANAPOLIS
INDIANA**

Price	$2595
Seven-Passenger Touring . . .	2595
Four-Passenger Sport Phaeton .	2595
Seven-Passenger Touring Sedan	3420
Two-Passenger Speedster	2850

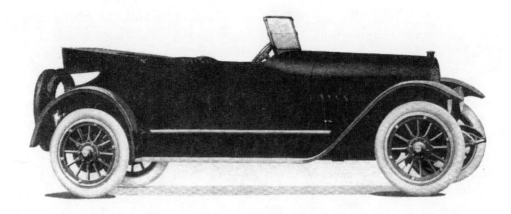

NATIONAL HIGHWAY TWELVE ROADSTER

COLOR	Highway blue or highway gray	LUBRICATION	Force feed
SEATING CAPACITY .	Four	RADIATOR	Cellular
POSITION OF DRIVER .	Left side	COOLING	Water pump
WHEELBASE	128 inches	IGNITION	Storage battery
GAUGE	56 inches	STARTING SYSTEM . .	Two unit
WHEELS	Wood	STARTER OPERATED .	Gear to fly wheel
FRONT TIRES . . .	34 x 4½ inches	LIGHTING SYSTEM . .	Electric
REAR TIRES	34 x 4½ inches	VOLTAGES	Six
SERVICE BRAKE . . .	Contracting on rear wheels	WIRING SYSTEM . . .	Single
EMERGENCY BRAKE .	Expanding on rear wheels	GASOLINE SYSTEM . .	Vacuum
		CLUTCH	Cone
CYLINDERS	Twelve	TRANSMISSION . . .	Selective sliding
ARRANGED	V type, 60 degrees	GEAR CHANGES . . .	Three forward, one reverse
CAST	In sixes	DRIVE	Spiral bevel
HORSEPOWER . . . . 39.68 (N.A.C.C. Rating)		REAR AXLE	Full floating
BORE AND STROKE .	2⅞ x 4¾ inches	STEERING GEAR . . .	Worm and gear

In addition to above specifications, price includes top, top hood, windshield, speedometer, ammeter, tire pump, electric horn and demountable rims.

NELSON & LE MOON TRUCKS
Manufactured by
NELSON & LE MOON CO., Chicago, Ill.

S P E C I F I C A T I O N S

Model	E1	E2	E3	E5
Capacity	1 ton	2 tons	3 tons	5 tons
Drive	Worm	Worm	Worm	Worm
Chassis Price	$1,700	$2,250	$2,950	$4,200
Motor				
H. P. (S.A.E.)	22.5	27.2	32.4	38.5
H. P. (Actual)	30	35	40	50
Cylinders	4 en bloc	4 en bloc	4 in pairs	4 in pairs
Bore	$3\frac{3}{4}''$	$4\frac{1}{8}''$	$4\frac{1}{2}''$	$4\frac{1}{2}''$
Stroke	$5\frac{1}{4}''$	$5\frac{1}{4}''$	$5\frac{1}{2}''$	$6''$
Wheel Base	Optional	Optional	Optional	Optional
Tread Front	56"	56"	60"	64"
Tread Rear	58"	58"	66"	74"
Tires Front	36x3"	36x4"	36x5"	36x6"
Tires Rear	36x4"	36x7"	38x5" dual	40x6" dual

Frame—Rolled channel steel.
Front Axle—I-beam section.

Rear Axle	Full-floating	Full-floating	Full-floating	Semi-floating

Springs Front—Semi-elliptic.
Springs Rear—Semi-elliptic.
Carburetor—Rayfield hot air and hot water jacket.
Cooling System—Pump.
Oiling System—Forced feed and splash.
Ignition—Magneto.
Control—Right drive, center control.
Clutch—Multiple dry disc.
Transmission—Selective, three speeds forward and one reverse.
Brakes—Two sets, internal expanding.
Steering Gear—Screw and nut.
Equipment—Front fenders with steps, oil dash and tail lamps, speedometer or hubodo-
    meter, Stewart hand horn, battery, ammeter, set of tools, tool box.
    Westinghouse electric starting, lighting and generating system $125.00 extra. West-
inghouse electric lighting system $50.00 extra.

models except the heaviest one, as was commonly the case during this time period. The 3-ton Model E5 used a four-speed transmission in 1915 but still used dual chain drive through World War I. So many different makes and types of motor vehicles were built during the World War I era that it was quite possible that Nelson & Le Moon trucks were shipped overseas as the odd unit among hundreds of others before standardization was put into practice, especially before the United States got directly involved in 1917. Prior to that time, companies, charitable organizations and local city governments purchased and then donated light trucks that were quickly transformed into ambulances to be sent to Europe as a humanitarian gesture. But there is no direct evidence that Nelson & Le Moon trucks were utilized in this manner.

In 1918 Nelson & Le Moon introduced a 5-ton truck which was powered by a four-cylinder Buda engine using a four-speed transmission. Continental engines were used exclusively by Nelson & Le Moon until the stock market crash. Surviving the material shortages and postwar recession, by 1925 the company offered 1-, 1½-, 2-, 2½-, 3-, 3½- and 5-ton capacity trucks, all using Brown-Lipe transmissions, Timken front and rear axles, St. Mary's wheels and Ross steering, the latter of which had a large portion of the commercial vehicle industry in the production of this particular vital mechanism.

Only the largest motor vehicle companies manufactured their own steering equipment and axles. Otherwise for the U.S. commercial vehicle industry (and many passenger cars), steering gear was almost entirely built by Ross and six competitors: C.A.S. Products, Columbus, Ohio; Ditwiler, Galion, Ohio; Gemmer, Detroit, Michigan; Saginaw, Saginaw, Michigan; Lavine, Milwaukee, Wisconsin; and Wohlrab, Racine, Wisconsin. In 1927 the "Nelson" part of the name was dropped, and the company became known simply as Le Moon.

Nelson & Le Moon adopted six-cylinder engines in 1928. By 1930 there were 11 models offered by the company, and in 1931 a six-wheel truck was introduced. The company survived into the Great Depression until 1937. Business slowed down for most manufacturers by then, for those still in business, and by this time a motorhome was placed on the market which had been designed and marketed by Brooks Stevens. The motorhome was also used as a portable showroom and office. And Le Moon ventured into building taxicabs for a brief period in order to make ends meet, until a merger with Federal, which became Federal-Le Moon and served only as a dealership. In terms of overall scale of operation it has been estimated that in just a little less than three decades about 3000 Nelson & Le Moon trucks were built.

Netco

As World War I unraveled in Europe, the United States remained neutral and was not directly affected economically at first, so that it was not unusual for such companies as Netco to have a genesis in 1914 when nations were formally declaring war on each other. The New England Truck Company of Fitchburg, Massachusetts, built its first truck in the form of a 1½-ton model powered by a four-cylinder Continental engine. It was worm drive from the beginning and a 2-ton capacity model appeared in 1916.

Netco were conventional assembled trucks as so many commercial vehicles of the era were by definition. The company bought Brown-Lipe transmissions and Timken axles in their assembly of the trucks. The 1918 Model D shown here was by this time the only truck built by Netco, which was not a large company, yet survived for quite a long time compared to so many others that did not.

The Prest-O-Lite tank listed in the extra equipment was used for acetylene lighting,

THE NETCO TRUCK
Manufactured by
NEW ENGLAND TRUCK COMPANY, Fitchburg, Mass.

Model	**D**
Capacity	2 tons
Drive	Worm
Chassis Weight	4,650 lbs.
Chassis Price	$2,800
Engine	Continental
H. P. (S.A.E.)	27.2
H. P. (Actual)	30
Cylinders	4 en bloc
Bore	$4\frac{1}{8}''$
Stroke	$5\frac{1}{4}''$
Wheel Base	144"
Tread Front	$58\frac{1}{2}''$
Tread Rear	$58\frac{1}{2}''$
Tires Front	36x4"
Tires Rear	36x6"

Frame—Pressed channel.

Front Axle—I-beam.

Rear Axle—Timken full-floating.

Springs Front—Semi-elliptic.

Springs Rear—Semi-elliptic.

Carburetor—Zenith L-5.

Cooling System—Pump.

Oiling System—Splash.

Ignition—Magneto.

Control—Left-hand drive, center control.

Clutch—Dry plate.

Transmission—Brown-Lipe Selective, three speeds forward, one reverse.

Brakes—Foot and emergency on rear wheels.

Steering Gear—Worm and nut.

Equipment—Cab, head and tail lights, Prest-O-Lite tank, tools and set of Traction chains.

but it could also be used for starting the engine. At the time even after the advent of the electric-starter motor developed by Charles Kettering at General Motors, introduced in the 1912 Cadillac, there were several somewhat crude methods of starting the internal combustion motor in addition to the hand crank. The spring starter, ignition starter and compressed air starter were three methods, but they were not always reliable. One of the most widely used at the time was the explosive gas method. This was a design which had the most extensive adoption, using an acetylene gas starter. Presto-O-Lite used this method, which involved a hand pump that introduced acetylene gas into the cylinder before a spark exploded it, moving the pistons down and starting the motor. If the motor was in the wrong position this could be a chore.

Netco continued as a company into the 1930s and beyond, surviving the Great Depression. By 1934 models included 2-ton to 10-ton capacity. By 1938 truck manufacturing ceased, but the company remained in business into the 1950s, building industrial and construction equipment.

Niles

The Niles Car and Manufacturing Company was named after the city of its location: Niles, Ohio. The company began building a 1-ton and a 2-ton capacity truck in 1915. But there was also a company in Niles, Michigan, by that name. Most confusing of all was the fact that in 1913, H.A. Wilson and R.G. Adams founded a company in Niles, Ohio, named the Niles Auto & Machine Company, which was not affiliated. Although there is no evidence of any motor vehicle being manufactured by that company (nor by the Niles Automobile Company of 1904 in Evansville, Indiana), its similarity in name to the company that did so beginning in 1915 leads to the assumption that the two men mentioned

above were involved in both enterprises, especially considering that the town of Niles, Ohio, has always been a very small one, reaching a population of 20,000 by the year 2000. Very little is known about the motor vehicle manufacturing at Niles, Ohio.

The year truck manufacturing began in Niles in 1915 was also the year that the McKinley Memorial was erected there in memory of President McKinley, assassinated in 1901. He had been born in Niles in 1843. The town had been founded in 1806 by James Heaton, who started Heaton's Furnace, an iron ore processing plant. The location was then named Nilestown after *Niles Recorder* editor Hezekiah Niles. The town is located in northeastern Ohio in an area now known as the "former industrial belt" after the collapse of the steel industry in the region.

In 1924 major social upheavals punctuated by marches against Catholics by thousands of Ku Klu Klux members and their rivals, Knights of the Flaming Circle, resulted in full-blown rioting for days at a time. Huge tornadoes in 1947 and 1985 destroyed much of the infrastructure in Niles and vicinity, but considering the history of Trumbull County where Niles is located, the truck manufacturing that lasted only until 1920 is of minor historical significance.

Noble

Kendallville, Indiana, located in northeastern Indiana, was never a large town. The region was once part of the industrial belt along the Great Lakes, but the town itself was amid rural surroundings. Nevertheless, the Noble Motor Truck Company got its obscure start in Kendallville in 1917. There were two other earlier companies by the name of Noble which were involved in motor vehicle manufacturing, one in Cleveland, Ohio, and the other in Detroit, Michigan, but they do not seem to be related in any way.

NILES TRUCKS
Manufactured by
THE NILES CAR & MFG. CO., Niles, Ohio

S P E C I F I C A T I O N S

Model	B	E
Capacity	¾—1 ton	2 tons
Drive	Worm	Worm
Chassis Price	$1,275	$1,975
Motor		
H. P. (S.A.E.)	20.5	27.25
H. P. (Actual)	30	40
Cylinders	4 en bloc	4 en bloc
Bore	3½"	4⅛"
Stroke	5"	5¼"
Wheel Base	124"	150"
Tread Front	56"	58½"
Tread Rear	56"	60"
Tires Front	35x5" pneu.	36x4"
Tires Rear	35x5" pneu.	36x7"

Frame—Pressed.
Front Axle—I-beam, Timken.
Rear Axle—Full-floating worm.
Springs Front—Semi-elliptic.
Springs Rear—Semi-elliptic.

Carburetor	Stromberg M-1	Stromberg M-2
Cooling System	Thermo-syphon	Pump

Oiling System—Splash and forced feed.
Ignition—Magneto.
Control—Left drive, center control.
Clutch—Dry plate.
Transmission—Selective, three speeds forward and one reverse.
Brakes—Double internal, rear hubs.
Steering Gear—Worm.
Equipment—Side and front oil lamps, head lights with size B Prest-o-lite tank, reduction valve and instant lighters, hubodometer, tool kit, tool box and all necessary wrenches.

THE NOBLE TRUCK

Manufactured by

NOBLE MOTOR TRUCK CO., Kendallville, Ind.

Model	NW-2
Capacity	2 tons
Drive	Worm
Chassis Weight	4,600 lbs.
Chassis Price	$2,300
Engine	Continental
H. P. (S.A.E.)	27.2
H. P. (Actual)	40 at 1500 R.P.M.
Cylinders	4 en bloc
Bore	$4\frac{1}{8}''$
Stroke	$5\frac{1}{4}''$
Wheel Base	148″
Tread Front	56″
Tread Rear	58″
Tires Front	36x4″
Tires Rear	36x6″

Frame—Pressed.

Front Axle—I-beam section.

Rear Axle—Sheldon semi-floating.

Springs Front—Semi-elliptic.

Springs Rear—Semi-elliptic.

Carburetor—Stromberg M-1.

Cooling System—Pump.

Oiling System—Combination.

Ignition—Magneto.

Control—Left-hand drive, center control.

Clutch—Dry plate.

Transmission—Cotta constant mesh, three speeds forward.

Brakes—Internal, rear wheel drums.

Steering Gear—Screw and nut.

Equipment—Cab, windshield, curtains, De Luxe tires on rear, oil side lamps and tail lamp, horn, tools and governor.

Noble first offered the NW-2, a 2-ton truck powered by a four-cylinder Continental engine and using a three-speed Cotta transmission. Sheldon axles were also incorporated in what was commonly described as a conventional, assembled truck. The company survived World War I and began using Buda six-cylinder engines as early as 1921.

By 1925 the Noble lineup had expanded to include a 1-ton Model A-76, which was powered by a Buda WTU engine with Clark front and Sheldon rear axle. The 1½-ton Model A-21 had a Clark rear axle, but otherwise was very similar to its lighter version. The 2½-ton Model D-51 used a Buda ETU engine and had a wheelbase of 144 inches, which was the same as the Model A-21. There was also a 3-ton Model D-52 powered by an ETU motor, and a 3½-ton Model E-71 powered by a Buda YTU. The heaviest Noble was the 4-ton E-71 and E-72. All Noble trucks used Ross or Levine steering. Prices ranged from $1875 to $4150.

There may have been a connection between the company and Warren Noble, a gynecologist born in Great Britain who arrived in the United States and started a number of motor vehicle concerns. As a doctor transformed into an automotive engineer, he was a consultant for John North Willys beginning in 1914, then Walter Flanders as well as Henry Ford. Later he served as the Supreme Director of Industrialization in the Soviet Union in the 1930s. He died in Amityville, New York, in 1950 at age sixty-five. The Noble Motor Truck Company was one of numerous firms to be quashed by the Great Depression in 1931.

Northwestern

At least three vehicles at about the same time were named Northwestern. One was made in Chicago in 1914 (Northwestern Cyclecar Works) and two others, one illustrated here from the Star Carriage Company, builder of Northwestern trucks, and the other from the Northwestern Automobile Manufacturing Company, both of Seattle, Washington, in 1914. It appears that none of them were related to each other, nor were they in any way affiliated with the Northwestern Furniture Company of Milwaukee, which listed an automobile in their catalog even earlier.

As with so many companies during the genesis of the motor vehicle industry, the Star Carriage Company built horse-drawn conveyances before getting into the truck manufacturing business. Northwestern trucks were conventional assembled trucks that were powered by Continental four-cylinder motors and used Covert three-speed transmissions. It was unusual for Northwestern to use a cone clutch this late in the development of motor trucks, which was at odds with the company slogan "Built for Seattle and Seattle's Hills." The City of Seattle is rather flat, but nearby areas have mountains, although it is uncertain how the use of a cone clutch, which was usually lined with leather or fabric, would be advantageous.

Front axles were from Elliot and rear axles were from Sheldon. In 1918 a 2-ton model was added. Although not illustrated here, Northwestern's competitor was Gersix, slightly better known as a truck manufacturer, which began in 1912 with its first truck, powered by a six-cylinder engine, arriving at the same time as the Northwestern. Gersix became Kenworth in 1923, and is alive and well as of this writing, whereas Northwestern faded out during the Great Depression and closed its doors permanently by 1933.

Oakland

Not related to the City of Oakland, California, in any way, Oakland automobiles were built in Pontiac, Michigan, and their name was eventually changed to that of the Indian chief whose name became another metonym

NORTHWESTERN TRUCKS

Manufactured by

STAR CARRIAGE CO., Seattle, Wash.

Model	W	W-2
Capacity	1½ tons	2 tons
Drive	Worm	Worm
Chassis Weight	4,200 lbs.	4,500 lbs.
Chassis Price	$2,300	$2,600
Engine	Continental	Continental
H. P. (S.A.E.)	27.8	27.8
H. P. (Actual)	42	42
Cylinders	4 en bloc	4 en bloc
Bore	4⅛"	4⅛"
Stroke	5¼"	5¼"
Wheel Base	140"	164"
Tread Front	56"	56"
Tread Rear	58"	58"
Tires Front	34x3½"	34x4"
Tires Rear	36x6"	36x7"

Frame—Rolled.
Front Axle—I-beam, Elliott type.
Rear Axle—Sheldon, semi-floating.
Springs Front—Semi-elliptic.
Springs Rear—Semi-elliptic.
Carburetor—Stromberg G-2.
Cooling System—Pump.
Oiling System—Splash and force.
Ignition—Bosch Magneto.
Control—Left steer, center control.
Clutch—Cone.
Transmission—Covert three speed, selective.
Brakes—Rear wheels.
Steering Gear—Double worm.
Equipment—Three oil lamps, tools and tool box, jack, oil can, etc.

OAKLAND MOTOR CAR COMPANY

PONTIAC MICHIGAN

Price	. . . .	$ 990
Roadster	. . . .	990
Roadster-Coupe	. . . .	1150
Sedan	. . . .	1190
Sedan, Unit Body	. . . . . .	1490
Coupe, Unit Body	. . . . . .	1490

OAKLAND SENSIBLE SIX TOURING—34-B

COLOR	Body, coach green; running gear, black
SEATING CAPACITY. .	Five
POSITION OF DRIVER .	Left side
WHEELBASE	112 inches
GAUGE	56 inches
WHEELS	Wood
FRONT TIRES	32 x 4 inches
REAR TIRES	32 x 4 inches, anti-skid
SERVICE BRAKE . . .	Contracting on rear wheels
EMERGENCY BRAKE .	Expanding on rear wheels
CYLINDERS	Six
ARRANGED	Vertically
CAST.	En bloc with crank case
HORSEPOWER	19 (N.A.C.C. Rating)

BORE AND STROKE .	$2\frac{13}{16}$ x $4\frac{3}{4}$ inches
LUBRICATION	Force feed
RADIATOR	Tubular
COOLING	Water pump
IGNITION	Storage battery
STARTING SYSTEM . .	Two unit
STARTER OPERATED .	Gear to fly wheel
LIGHTING SYSTEM . .	Electric
VOLTAGES	Six
WIRING SYSTEM . . .	Single
GASOLINE SYSTEM . .	Vacuum
CLUTCH	Cone
TRANSMISSION . . .	Selective sliding
GEAR CHANGES . . .	Three forward, one reverse
DRIVE	Plain bevel
REAR AXLE	Full floating
STEERING GEAR . . .	Screw and nut

In addition to above specifications, price includes top, top hood, windshield, speedometer, ammeter, electric horn and demountable rims.

for the city of American cars built by General Motors.

Before those developments took place, Edward M. Murphy and Alanson P. Brush founded the Oakland Motor Car Company. The Oakland name was derived from Murphy's horse buggies named "Oakland." When he met up with Brush, a partnership was formed as the two men pined to enter the new and exciting field of automotive manufacturing. Brush had already designed an automobile with an unusual two-cylinder motor and an oil-immersed planetary transmission which had been rejected by Cadillac.

The Oakland Motor Car Company was organized in 1907, and the new car by that name was shown in January of 1908. But Alanson Brush was already gone from the company, having met sheet metal magnate Frank Briscoe and become his new partner. Briscoe, who had plenty of means, was willing to sponsor yet another automotive venture, this time with the name of Brush attached to it. The new Oakland did not sell well, and Murphy brought out a 40 hp four-cylinder car with three-speed sliding gear transmission for 1909, abandoning Brush's design altogether.

Edward Murphy suddenly passed away in September of 1909 at the age of 44. By this time William Crapo Durant had acquired Oakland as part of his empire building under the name of General Motors. By 1910 Oakland had built nearly 3000 cars and would do so consistently for the next couple of years. Why the company adopted its slogan as "The Car with a Conscience" would be anybody's guess, but its quality was proven through hill climb and endurance contests by such names as "Giant's Despair" and "Dead Horse Hill" in addition to Pikes Peak.

By 1913 Oakland introduced a formidable 334 cid six-cylinder motor of its own which produced 60 hp and was enough to propel a 130-inch wheelbase chassis. Being part of GM, Oakland adopted the new Kettering electric-starter motor that year, which had been introduced at Cadillac the year previous. In appearance, Oakland had its admirers, so that just over 12,000 cars were sold in 1915 when a new V-8, very similar to Cadillac's, was introduced. However, even with the powerful motor no evidence shows that the U.S. Army or the American Expeditionary Forces bought any Oakland cars, and the company did not build trucks. Material shortages and a lackluster market during World War I would put an end to the V-8 motor in 1918.

By that time Alfred P. Sloan took the helm at GM with an accompanying modernization of the Oakland, if only in appearance. But an inspection of manufacturing practices at the factory revealed a very uneven production capacity varying from ten cars one day to fifty the next, depending on assembly line conniptions, which led to the resignation of general manager Fred W. Warner. Coming over from Autocar, George W. Hannum took over in that capacity, and Oakland continued to be produced with only minor changes through 1924.

As the market improved, so did Oakland, with Duco lacquer paint, four-wheel brakes, new six-cylinder L-head motor, automatic spark advance and other refinements, all amounting to a production total of 35,000 cars for that year alone.

Alfred R. Glancy was the new man at Oakland who introduced the idea of the Pontiac, which was intended to be a six-cylinder car selling for the price of a four-banger. The new name and marketing strategy had a phenomenal success, and the Pontiac was soon outshining its parent name. By 1930 there was another V-8 powering the Pontiac, and by the following year the Oakland name was dropped entirely.

Ohio (electric)

Along with the Milburn Wagon Company, Ohio Electric also built vehicles in Toledo,

OHIO ELECTRIC
CAR COMPANY

TOLEDO, OHIO

Price, $2680

OHIO ELECTRIC—44

COLOR	Optional	REAR TIRES	33 x 4½ inches, pneumatic, anti-skid
SEATING CAPACITY .	Five		
BODY:		BRAKE SYSTEMS . .	Double external
LENGTH OVER ALL	148 inches	BATTERY	40 cells, 13 or 15 plate
WIDTH OVER ALL .	67 inches		
WHEELBASE	103 inches	SPEED	26 miles per hour
GAUGE	56 inches	NO. FORWARD SPEEDS	Five
		NO. REVERSE SPEEDS	Three
WHEELS	Wire or wood	CONTROL	Magnetic
FRONT TIRES	33 x 4½ inches, pneumatic	STEERING	Lever

Ohio, at about the same time beginning in 1910. Before actual production ensued, the company was incorporated in 1909 by James Bell Brown, Henry P. Dodge, Rathbun Fuller, Robert E. Lee and Henry E. Marvin, and Ohio Electric actually shared its facilities with Milburn Wagon for the first two years.

Ohio Electric had the female driver in mind, which was somewhat of a rarity at the time, the press coverage of some famous exceptions notwithstanding. Most remarkably, the Ohio Electric built its 1910 coupe, of which 16 were produced that year, using a design that included tiller steering from the back seat. It was explained that in this way the woman driver had "privacy at all times," controlling the car from the rear instead of "in the front like a chauffeur uncomfortably conspicuous." Ohio Electric advertising used the slogan, "The Only Car for the Woman of Refinement Today."

The Ohio Electric also had a patented magnetic solenoid pushbutton brake system, which was also patented as a dual drive system that could be operated from the front or rear seat using a small control disc and switches. In 1915 the company built 300 cars, and production increased to 650 for 1916.

M.V. Barbour became the new company president in 1915 with C.M. Foster in the vice-president position and Herman H. Brand as secretary-treasurer. But George W. Shaw took over the presidency in 1917 as the company struggled to gain any real foothold in the market.

Part of the trouble was with range, from which all electric vehicles suffered. Any car or truck that was battery-powered at the time would be lucky to get 75 miles out of a single full charge. Another problem was top speed, which was 26 mph, as stated in the spec sheet. That may have been safe for the select woman driver, but the vehicle was relegated to short in-town trips and could not be used for any real road trips.

The third problem, rarely addressed, was the styling of Ohio Electrics, which pertained to most of the electric passenger car builders before World War I. The stodgy, vestibule-like car bodies were difficult to foist on customers who had the choice of dozens of low-slung gasoline autos that often resembled racing cars. All in all, by the middle of 1918, Ohio Electric was out of business, and all of the company's assets and machinery were auctioned off at public auction in June for pennies on the dollar.

Old Hickory

With so many companies that had built horse-drawn wagons switching to motor vehicle production, it was not out of the ordinary that even a company such as the Kentucky Wagon Works would move into the field of motor truck production, which they did in 1915. The name would change that year to the Kentucky Wagon Manufacturing Company, still located in Louisville, Kentucky, better known for its horse breeding than motor vehicle manufacturing. A horse known as Sir Barton was the first to win what was to be called the Triple Crown in 1919. Kentucky was better known for its plantations and whiskey distilleries during the early part of the previous century.

In the dispute of horse vs. truck, at the time the press along with the public struggled to accept and justify the new technology which was about to supplant the beast of burden of age-old tradition and membership in human activities. Some journalists of the 1890s and early 1900s extolled the virtues of the new machines of transport which could outperform and outlast the horse, whereas some members of the press criticized motor vehicles for their noise, exhaust stench and "newfangled" complexity.

Many agreed that the horse's own sense of self-preservation could avoid a collision or

THE OLD HICKORY TRUCK
Manufactured by
KENTUCKY WAGON MFG. CO., Louisville, Ky.

S P E C I F I C A T I O N S

Model	M
Capacity	1250 lbs.
Drive	Bevel
Chassis Price	$825
Motor	
H. P. (S.A.E.)	16.9
H. P. (Actual)	23 at 1200 R.P.M.
Cylinders	4 en bloc
Bore	$3\frac{1}{4}''$
Stroke	5″
Wheel Base	112″
Tread Front	56″
Tread Rear	56″
Tires Front	33x4″ pneu.
Tires Rear	33x4″ pneu.

Frame—Rolled.
Front Axle—I-beam Elliott.
Rear Axle—Semi-floating.
Springs Front—Semi-elliptic.
Springs Rear—Scroll-elliptic.
Carburetor—Carter.
Cooling System—Thermo.
Oiling System—Circulating splash.
Ignition—Generator.
Control—Left drive, center control.
Clutch—Cone.
Transmission—Selective, three speeds forward and one reverse.
Brakes—Double on wheels.
Steering Gear—Worm and sector.
Equipment—Dyneto single unit electric starter, Willard battery electric lights and horn,
    speedometer, license brackets, extra tire carrier, one extra rim, seat cushion,

possibly careening over a precipice, but it was difficult to justify the enormous maintenance of the animals, requiring veterinarians, shoers, groomers, trainers, saddlers, breeders and various other services, whereas the motor truck could be maintained and repaired by anyone with some mechanical sense and a few spare parts.

The fact that the internal combustion engine often startled and frightened horses drew little sympathy except in rural areas, since horses could go into an attack of violent reaction and dangerous revolt at any time for numerous reasons based on mere sudden surprise, not just the rattle of a motor. At the same time the conflict between old and new, progress and status quo, drew attention to the enormous and constant task of removing manure in cities, all of them plagued by layers and piles of horses' excrement wherever horse-drawn conveyances and equestrians traveled. In the final analysis there was no doubt who would win the contest between the horse and the motor truck.

Electric vehicles were deemed considerably more acceptable in some communities, and Old Hickory built commercial electrics under the name of Urban, very similar to those built by GMC. The Urban was discontinued in 1918 at a time during World War I when the internal combustion-powered motor truck proved its worth in the crucible of war.

Stateside, the top speed for trucks was 15 mph on the highway, which helped prevent the disintegration of fragile mechanical components. Electric vehicles were popular in some urban areas, requiring no hand cranking and producing no belching exhaust, which the early internal combustion engine could produce ad nauseum. However, recharging expensive lead acid batteries, whose short life added to the time and cost of maintenance, would soon assist with the demise of the electric car and electric truck of the early 20th century. The Kentucky Wagon Manufactur-

ing Company shut down its production line in 1923, without the option of going back to horse-drawn wagons that were considered nearly obsolete by all but the die-hard farmer and rural resident at that time in America.

Old Reliable

The choice to name its new motor vehicle "Old Reliable" was not a bad one by the Henry Lee Power Company of Chicago, Illinois, in 1911. It would be a name that many companies could have used if it were true to the product's reputation, and Old Reliable trucks might have lived up to their name, at least for one and a half decades. The fact that it sounded like "Oldsmobile," one of the three best-selling autos in America at the time, did not hurt either.

Old Reliable trucks started out as fairly large trucks of 3½-ton capacity. The Old Reliable truck was powered by a four-cylinder motor using forward-control design at a time when acceptable appearance was important to the "horseless wagon" so it would resemble the "horse-drawn wagon" it was supplanting.

Old Reliable featured a motor with twin spark plugs per cylinder when magnetos were fairly weak components and spark plug fouling was commonplace. Oil oozed past piston rings easily with fairly loose machine tolerances being the norm in much of motor vehicle manufacturing, compared to that of vehicles built only a decade or two later. Interchangeable parts and components as a general concept had only just been introduced a few years earlier when mass production was adopted and became widespread among such companies as Buick, Cadillac and Ford.

By 1915 the model line was expanded to include trucks from 1½-ton capacity to 7-ton capacity. Lighter models used worm drive while chain drive was still preferred where much more torque was needed. Forward control was still favored until after World War I,

OLD RELIABLE TRUCKS
Manufactured by
OLD RELIABLE MOTOR TRUCK CO., 3921 Michigan Ave., Chicago, Ill.

S P E C I F I C A T I O N S

Model	W-2	W-3	W-4	7-Ton Dump
Capacity	2 tons	3 tons	4 tons	7 tons
Drive	Worm	Worm	Worm	Chain
Chassis Price	$2,450	$3,250	$3,750	$5,000
Motor				
H. P. (S.A.E.)	25.6	28.9	37.7	
H. P. (Actual)	32 at 1000 R.P.M.	39 at 1000 R.P.M.	45 at 1100 R.P.M.	49 at 1000 R.P.M.
Cylinders	4 en bloc	4 en bloc	4 in pairs	4 in pairs
Bore	4″	4¼″	4¾″	$5\frac{1}{10}$″
Stroke	6″	6″	5½″	5½″
Wheel Base	151″	151″	153″	126″
Tread Front	58″	58″	58″	60″
Tread Rear	58″	66″	66″	74½″
Tires Front	34x4″	34x4″	34x5″	36x6″
Tires Rear	36x4″ dual	36x5″ dual	40x5″ dual	40x7″ dual
Frame—Rolled.				
Front Axle—I-beam.				
Rear Axle	Semi-floating	Semi-floating	Semi-floating	Dead
Springs Front—Semi-elliptic.				
Springs Rear—Semi-elliptic.				
Carburetor—Stromberg.				
Cooling System—Pump.				
Oiling System—Forced feed.				
Ignition—Magneto.				
Control	Right drive, center control	Right drive, center control	Right drive, center control	Right drive, right control
Clutch	Dry plate	Dry plate	Dry plate	Wet plate
Transmission	Selective, 3 or 4 speeds forward, one reverse	Selective, three speeds forward, one reverse	Selective, three speeds forward, one reverse	Selective, four speeds forward, one reverse
Brakes	Internal expanding rear wheel	Internal expanding rear wheel	Internal expanding rear wheel	Foot on jackshaft, emergency on rear wheel

Steering Gear—Screw and nut.
Equipment—Horn, electric head and tail lights, complete set of tools, jack and oil can. Gas lights optional on all models except 1½ and 2-ton worm drives.

when conventional layout of the trucks was adopted using a hood and a distinctive radiator guard. Wisconsin four-cylinder engines were used throughout and both front and rear axles were from Sheldon, but the heaviest 7-ton model used a Waukesha motor. Despite its wide range of models, memorable name and fortuitous location, Old Reliable ceased manufacture in 1927.

Oldsmobile

Of the earliest, best known and longest-lived companies in the American motor vehicle industry, Oldsmobile has stood at the top of the list, perhaps living up to its own name before being discontinued as a make. Ransom Eli Olds was behind the successful venture, although he would soon part ways with his early partners and start a second, nearly as successful company using his initials REO. Before he went on to form his second enterprise, Ransom Olds formed the Olds Motor Vehicle Company of Lansing, Michigan, which he started in 1897.

Olds was a true pioneer in the American auto industry, building and driving his first experimental car in 1887, which was a steam-powered three-wheeler. By 1891 he was already making a name for himself with his second steamer, which was featured in *Scientific American*.

In 1896 he built his first gasoline car, choosing this type of propulsion wisely by moving away from the complexity of the two-level energy transfer process of first burning fuel in order to heat water for the formation of steam. The piston and crank design of the internal combustion engine was very similar to that of the steam engine, if not directly based on it, but it eliminated one major step as the fuel itself was combusted inside the cylinder rather than have a piston pushed by steam.

This would prove to be the vital ingredient and the basic physics in the future success of the motor vehicle. Proponents of steam power would somehow overlook this engineering precept for decades, pointing to "clean" steam exhaust while ignoring the fact that some type of fuel still had to be burned, usually very inefficiently, for steam to be formed in the first place.

In May of 1899 Ransom Olds organized the Olds Motor Works with a working capital of $500,000, consolidating his previous ventures, which had produced all of six vehicles up to that time. Samuel L. Smith who had helped fund the Olds Motor Vehicle Company, advanced another $200,000 towards the new company's formation and as majority stockholder became president. Samuel Smith's two sons, having just graduated from college, were soon employed at the new factory in Detroit where Ransom Olds began building a new array of experimental gasoline and electric prototypes, none of which were clearly set up for series manufacturing.

An accidental fire in 1901, which burned most of the Olds factory and the various vehicles in it, led to the concentration on the only vehicle left intact, which was to be known as the "Curved Dash" Oldsmobile. It became the first mass-produced car in America, with 4,000 units completed in 1903, at a time when Winton was building a fraction of that number, Ford and Cadillac were just starting out, and Buick had a year yet before starting its first production of autos.

The 7 hp single-cylinder four-cycle curved-dash Oldsmobile continued to be built in Lansing, Michigan, in 1904, and a two-cylinder motor was introduced in 1905. As with many of the early motor vehicle builders, both passenger and commercial vehicles were built often using the same chassis and engine, which was the case with the 1904 Oldsmobile Box Body Runabout. When the Oldsmobile Company was bought out by William Crapo Durant in 1908, commercial vehicle production was interrupted until after World War I.

**OLDS MOTOR
WORKS**

**LANSING
MICHIGAN**

Price $1467
Sportster . . . 1550
Roadster . . . 1467
Club Roadster. 1467

OLDSMOBILE TOURING—45-A

COLOR	Body, royal green; running gear, black; wheels, natural wood	BORE AND STROKE .	2⅞ x 4¾ inches
		LUBRICATION	Full force feed
SEATING CAPACITY. .	Seven	RADIATOR	Cellular
POSITION OF DRIVER .	Left side	COOLING	Water pump
WHEELBASE	120 inches	IGNITION	Storage battery
GAUGE	56 inches	STARTING SYSTEM . .	Two unit
WHEELS	Wood	STARTER OPERATED .	Gear to fly wheel
FRONT TIRES	34 x 4 inches	LIGHTING SYSTEM . .	Electric
REAR TIRES	34 x 4 inches, anti-skid	VOLTAGES	Six
SERVICE BRAKE . . .	Contracting on rear wheels	WIRING SYSTEM . . .	Single
		GASOLINE SYSTEM . .	Vacuum
EMERGENCY BRAKE .	Expanding on rear wheels	CLUTCH	Cone
		TRANSMISSION . . .	Selective sliding
CYLINDERS	Eight	GEAR CHANGES . . .	Three forward, one reverse
ARRANGED	V type, 90 degrees		
CAST.	In fours	DRIVE	Spiral bevel
HORSEPOWER	26.45	REAR AXLE	Full floating
(N.A.C.C. Rating)		STEERING GEAR . . .	Screw and nut

In addition to above specifications, price includes top, top hood, windshield, clock, speedometer, ammeter, voltmeter, tire pump, electric horn and demountable rims.

In the meantime Oldsmobile crossed the American continent in 1905 as a public relations event and production expanded to 6,500 for the year. The Curved Dash Oldsmobile was now nearly five years old and Samuel, Frederick and Angus Smith wanted to move forward with new products, whereas Ransom Olds was stuck on the idea and success of the early design. However, the Smiths had control over the company both in number and finance, and Ransom Eli Olds departed amid a stormy quarrel to form REO under contractual agreement not to use his last name.

Although the curved-dash Oldsmobile remained in the company catalogue through 1907, it was placed at the back of a brochure that now had a 36 hp four-cylinder automobile on a 106-inch wheelbase, which was more than twice the size of the curved- dash model. But the market was not ready for a $2750 car after the first model had cost $650, and sales plummeted to 1,055 by 1908. It was then that Durant stepped in with $3,000,000 in GM stock and $17,279 in cash, and Oldsmobile became part of GM.

Introduced in late 1908, the new Oldsmobile was bigger and better, but had a price tag of $4,500. Durant focused on selling the smaller models, but Oldsmobile quickly gained a reputation for its largest cars, called the Autocrat, Defender and Limited, each powered by a 707 cid six-cylinder engine and a wheelbase that reached 138 inches by 1911. A four-cylinder "baby Olds" was produced for 1914, and a V-8 appeared in 1916. As America entered the war, sales at Oldsmobile seemed to surge, with 22,600 for 1917 alone.

Billy Durant regained control over GM, but only until November of 1920 when bankers once again took over GM, and Durant went forward with his auto empire using his own money and name, building such vehicles as the Durant, Star and Rugby trucks. After Erwin "Cannonball" Baker drove a new Oldsmobile Six across the country in twelve and a half days during 1924, when all Oldsmobiles became six-cylinder cars, the marque was all but guaranteed to survive for the rest of the century, if no longer than that.

Oneida

As yet another truck company which began production in 1917, Oneida Motor Truck Company started production in Green Bay, Wisconsin, located on Lake Michigan. The first model series consisted of the 1-ton Model A, 1½-ton Model B, 2-ton Model C and 3½-ton Model D. All used Timken worm drive, and all were powered by Continental four-cylinder motors. Transmissions were from Cotta.

The fact that Oneida bought its transmissions from an original equipment manufacturer (OEM) was par for the course at the time when most components were available "off the shelf." In the case of transmissions and clutches the following companies sold their "gearsets" to any and all who wanted to assemble motor vehicles: Borg & Beck in Chicago, Brown-Lipe in Syracuse, Cotta in Rockford, Cover Gear in Lockport, A.J. Detlaff in Detroit, Detroit Gear in Detroit, Dunmore in Reading, Durston in Syracuse, Fuller in Kalamazoo, Grant Lee Gear in Cleveland, Hartford in Connecticut, Hele-Shaw and Merchant & Evans in Philadelphia, Mechanics Machine in Rockford, and Muncie in Muncie, Indiana. These were the major players, but there were also some smaller companies, or the motor vehicle manufacturer built its own, if it was large enough or had the wherewithal.

After the war Oneida added a 5-ton truck, and engines were also available from Hinkley. Axles were also bought from Wisconsin. Oneida got into the agricultural tractor business starting in 1920, and the company built some electric trucks in the early 1920s, but both of these ventures ended within two years.

ONEIDA TRUCKS

Manufactured by

ONEIDA MOTOR TRUCK CO., Green Bay, Wis.

Model	A	B	C	D
Capacity	1 ton	1½ tons	2 tons	3½ tons
Drive	Worm	Worm	Worm	Worm
Chassis Weight	3,785 lbs.	4,150 lbs.	4,525 lbs.	6,300 lbs.
Chassis Price	On application	On application	On application	On application
Engine	Continental	Continental	Continental	Continental
H. P. (S.A.E.)	22.50	22.50	27.23	32.40
H. P. (Actual)	30	30	35	40
Cylinders	4 en bloc	4 en bloc	4 en bloc	4 in pairs
Bore	3¾″	3¾″	4⅛″	4½″
Stroke	5¼″	5¼″	5¼″	5½″
Wheel Base	130″ or 144″	130″ or 144″	144″ or 160″	160″ or 170″
Tread Front	57¾″	57¾″	58½″	66″
Tread Rear	58″	58½″	58½″	65¾″
Tires Front	36x3½″	36x3½″	36x4″	36x5″
Tires Rear	36x5″	36x5″	36x7″ or 36x4″ dual	36x5″ dual

Frame—Rolled.

Front Axle—Timken I-beam section.

Rear Axle	Timken semi-floating	Timken full-floating	Timken full-floating	Timken full-floating

Springs Front—Semi-elliptic.
Springs Rear—Semi-elliptic.
Carburetor—Stromberg.
Cooling System—Pump.
Oiling System—Splash and forced feed.
Ignition—Bosch magneto.
Control—Steering left, levers center.
Clutch—Hele-Shaw wet plate.
Transmission—Cotta Selective type, gears in constant mesh.
Brakes—Internal on rear wheels.
Steering Gear—Ross worm and nut.
Equipment—Driver's seat, two electric headlights, one electric tail light, storage battery, front fenders, two half running boards, tool box, battery box, auto jack, set of tools with roll, hand horn, speedometer.

The company was affected by the postwar recession and was reorganized in 1924. The model line remained essentially unchanged. Bus chassis from 25-seat to 42-seat were also produced in the mid–1920s, and Continental engines were also used. After 1927 Hinkley engines were adopted exclusively. The firm was reorganized once again in 1928 as the Oneida Truck Company. By the time of the Wall Street stock market crash of October 29, 1929, the company was primed for closure. It did just that the following year.

Overland

At the same time that such well-known American makes as Buick, Cadillac, Ford, Indian and Harley-Davidson were starting out, the Overland name was created in Terre Haute, Indiana, by Charles Minshall, president of the Standard Wheel Company, and Claude E. Cox, a newly graduated engineer from the Ross Polytechnic of that city. The following year, in 1903, a 5 hp one-cylinder Overland was built, and once the prototype was deemed acceptable twelve more were built that year.

In 1904 a two-cylinder motor was introduced in addition to the original, and some 24 Overland cars were sold. A delivery van that was tiller-steered was offered right from the beginning using the original chassis and motor with stiffer springs and solid rubber tires, but evidence of actual manufacture of such a vehicle proves that Overland built a series in the form of postal vans in 1908. The Overland had introduced a four-cylinder motor along with steering wheel and shaft drive by 1905. The Standard Wheel factory in Indianapolis became the manufacturing and headquarters for Overland at the end of 1905.

Charles Minshall had a sudden change of heart and withdrew from the venture, which would have left the young Claude Cox in a bind had it not been for David M. Parry, a horse-buggy builder in Indianapolis. In 1906 the Overland Auto Company was organized with Parry as a majority stockholder, but 1907 was a recession year, and it was left to John North Willys to step in and take charge that year. He bought the company's entire output of 47 cars that had been produced in 1906 and ordered 500 more for 1907 with a $10,000 deposit, which at the time was substantial. When no production of the order ensued, Willys was induced to take over the company, and production continued in a circus tent as the temporary assembly department.

For 1909, 465 cars were assembled in such an atmosphere of dire rescue. Claude Cox found the situation unsuitable and departed from the company. John Willys had the wherewithal to purchase the Pope-Toledo factory in Toldeo, Ohio, as well as the Marion Motor Car Company, and he consolidated his manufacturing under the name Willys-Overland. The reorganization successfully led to an increase in production amounting to 15,500 cars in 1910. All automobiles from Willys-Overland now were four-cylinder until 1915, when left-hand drive was made standard at the company and a six-cylinder motor was reintroduced.

As America entered World War I, John Willys went into direct competition with Henry Ford by announcing a four-cylinder Overland for $495 but which had electric starting and lighting. By 1917 Willys-Overland was producing 140,100 cars per year, second only to Ford. Sales were helped by the Knight engine, which was adopted under license in 1914. Profits for Willys-Overland reached $1,000,000 per year during this time. John Willys also became president of Curtiss, the aircraft company which built the "Jenny" series of biplanes used as reconnaissance and trainers during World War I.

A strike at the Toledo plant and wartime shortages meant that the new low-priced Overland did not arrive until 1919. By that

OVERLAND DELIVERY WAGONS

Manufactured by

THE WILLYS-OVERLAND CO., Toledo, Ohio

Model	1200 lb. B. O. E.	90 P. L. D.	90 O. E. X.
Capacity	1,200 lbs. & 2 passengers	800 lbs. & 1 passenger	800 lbs. & 1 passenger
Drive	Spiral bevel	Straight bevel	Straight bevel
Chassis Weight	2,180 lbs.	1,700 lbs.	1,700 lbs.
Chassis Price	On application	On application	On application
Engine	Overland	Overland	Overland
H. P. (S.A.E.)	27.22	18.22	18.22
H. P. (Actual)	35.6 at 1800—no gov.	32 at 2000—no gov.	32 at 2000—no gov.
Cylinders	4 en bloc	4 en bloc	4 en bloc
Bore	$4\frac{1}{8}''$	$3\frac{3}{8}''$	$3\frac{3}{8}''$
Stroke	$4\frac{1}{2}''$	$5''$	$5''$
Wheel Base	$106''$	$104''$	$104''$
Tread Front	$56''$	$56''$	$56''$
Tread Rear	$56''$	$56''$	$56''$
Tires Front	$33x4\frac{1}{2}''$ pneu.	$31x4''$ pneu.	$31x4''$ pneu.
Tires Rear	$33x4\frac{1}{2}''$ pneu.	$31x4''$ pneu.	$31x4''$ pneu.

Frame—Pressed steel, channel section.

Front Axle—I-beam section forged in one piece.

Rear Axle—Overland $\frac{3}{4}$-floating, pressed steel housing.

Springs Front—Semi-elliptic.

Springs Rear	Semi-elliptic	Cantilever	Cantilever

Carburetor—Tillotson.

Cooling System—Thermo-syphon.

Oiling System—Constant level splash with oil pump

Ignition	Battery	Battery	Battery

Control—Left drive, center control.

Clutch—Cone.

Transmission—Overland Selective, three speeds.

Brakes—Service, contracting on rear wheels; emergency, internal expanding on rear wheels.

Steering Gear—Irreversible: worm and full gear.

Equipment—Auto-Lite two-unit, six-volt electric starting and lighting system, with head, tail and dash lamps, and headlight dimmers; ammeter, windshield, magnetic speedometer, oil indicator, electric horn, extra demountable rim, full set of tools, tire repair kit, jack and pump, hood, dash, front fenders and running boards.

**W I L L Y S -
OVERLAND, INC.**

T O L E D O, O H I O

Touring	
Roadster	**Prices Upon**
Touring Sedan . . .	**Application**
Touring Coupe . . .	

OVERLAND TOURING—85-6

COLOR	Body, Brewster green; wheels, cream	LUBRICATION	Force feed and splash
SEATING CAPACITY . .	Five	RADIATOR	Cellular
POSITION OF DRIVER .	Left side	COOLING	Water pump
WHEELBASE	116 inches	IGNITION	Storage battery
GAUGE	56 inches	STARTING SYSTEM . .	Two unit
WHEELS	Wood	STARTER OPERATED .	Gear to fly wheel
FRONT TIRES	32 x 4 inches	LIGHTING SYSTEM . .	Electric
REAR TIRES	32 x 4 inches, anti-skid	VOLTAGES	Six to eight
SERVICE BRAKE . . .	Contracting on rear wheels	WIRING SYSTEM . . .	Single
		GASOLINE SYSTEM . .	Vacuum
EMERGENCY BRAKE .	Expanding on rear wheels	CLUTCH	Cone
CYLINDERS	Six	TRANSMISSION . . .	Selective sliding
ARRANGED	Vertically	GEAR CHANGES . . .	Three forward, one reverse
CAST	En bloc	DRIVE	Spiral bevel
HORSEPOWER . . . . (N.A.C.C. Rating)	25.35	REAR AXLE	Three-quarters floating
BORE AND STROKE .	3¼ x 4½ inches	STEERING GEAR . . .	Worm and gear

In addition to above specifications, price includes top, top hood, windshield, speedometer, ammeter, electric horn and demountable rims.

time the Ford Model T had a self-starter and electric lighting and remained considerably cheaper than the Overland. The postwar recession forced Willys to succumb to Chase Manhattan Bank's taking control and installing Walter Chrysler as president for a $1,000,000 annual salary. Two years later Chrysler left for a similar management job at Maxwell-Chalmers, but in the meantime Willys-Overland was saved and John North Willys was back at the helm, even if it were for a mere $75,000 annual salary (before profit taking and bonuses). Willys-Overland production resumed at high capacity in the early 1920s, but the name was dropped as the Great Depression ensued, leaving only the Willys name for the 1930s. Under that name there was a huge production of jeeps during World War II. Willys-Overland was purchased by Kaiser-Frazer in 1953.

Packard

James Ward Packard got into the design and production of cars as a result of a challenging dare from Alexander Winton in 1897, when Packard bought a Winton automobile and was quite dissatisfied with it. Upon being rebuffed by Winton when confronting him about some of the inadequacies of the car, Packard embarked on building a car with his own name attached to it. He successfully planned to make it superior to that of what would become a rival manufacturer.

Packard built his first car in his family's light bulb and transformer factory at Warren, Ohio, completing and test driving it in November of 1899. A pilot run of five more cars were built that year with the Model A designation and some refinement in details, until the Model B arrived for 1900. The Model B was powered by a 7 hp one-cylinder four-stroke motor using a two-speed planetary transmission, and 49 were completed for the year. The Packard brothers became stockholders of the Ohio Automobile Company, which was organized to build Packards. By the following year, "Ask the Man Who Owns One" became the company slogan and remained so for decades.

Former Winton customers such as John D. Rockefeller switched to Packard, fulfilling the adage that success is the best revenge. James Ward Packard's company would outlive and outproduce Winton by three decades. A one-cylinder Packard called "Old Pacific" was driven by Tom Fetch from San Francisco to New York in 1903 over 61 days, beating a Winton record by two days set the previous month.

The Ohio Automobile Company had been reorganized as the Packard Motor Car Company in 1902, and a year later the firm moved to Detroit, Michigan. By this time the first four-cylinder Packard had appeared just before the move from Ohio. It boasted a 24 hp engine and a 92-inch wheelbase and was priced at $4850, but it was also built in racing form and called the Gray Wolf, driven by Charles Schmidt, who had designed the Model K and its faster race car iteration.

The Model L four-cylinder Packard had a distinctive radiator, the shape of which became a basis for the Packard appearance for decades. In 1906 the T-head Packard motor was introduced, which had the advantage of a "flow-through" combustion chamber but otherwise remained as a flat-head design. By this time three prestigious American auto makes became known as the "Three P's," which included Packard as well as Peerless and Pierce-Arrow.

The first six-cylinder motor at Packard, a T-head, was introduced in 1911. A better if smaller six was offered the following year which had 60 hp but was by far more durable and better performing, with seven main bearings instead of four. Alvan Macauley and Jesse G. Vincent, the latter heading engineering, became executives at Packard at this time and

PACKARD TRUCKS

Manufactured by

PACKARD MOTOR CAR CO., Detroit, Mich.

Model	1-E	$1\frac{1}{2}$-E	2-E	3-E
Capacity	1-$1\frac{1}{4}$ tons	$1\frac{1}{2}$-$1\frac{3}{4}$ tons	2-$2\frac{1}{2}$ tons	3-$3\frac{1}{2}$ tons
Drive	Worm	Worm	Worm	Worm
Chassis Weight	4,500 lbs.	4,640 lbs.	5,100 lbs.	7,000 lbs.
Chassis Price	$2,650	$3,000	$3,400	$4,100
Engine	Packard	Packard	Packard	Packard
H. P. (S.A.E.)	25.6	25.6	25.6	32.4
H. P. (Actual)	28 at 1000 R.P.M.	28 at 1000 R.P.M.	28 at 1000 R.P.M.	35 at 1000 R.P.M.
Cylinders	4 en bloc	4 en bloc	4 en bloc	4 en bloc
Bore	4″	4″	4″	$4\frac{1}{2}$″
Stroke	$5\frac{1}{2}$″	$5\frac{1}{2}$″	$5\frac{1}{2}$″	$5\frac{1}{2}$″
Wheel Base	126″ and 144″	126″ and 144″	144″ and 168″	156″ and 186″
Tread Front	56″	56″	$58\frac{1}{2}$″	$69\frac{3}{8}$″
Tread Rear	$55\frac{1}{2}$″	$55\frac{1}{2}$″	$55\frac{1}{2}$″	66″
Tires Front	34x$3\frac{1}{2}$″	34x$3\frac{1}{2}$″	34x4″	36x5″
Tires Rear	34x6″	34x$3\frac{1}{2}$″ dual	34x4″ dual	36x5″ dual

Frame—Channel section, rolled steel.
Front Axle—Drop forged I-beam section, knuckles inverted yoke type.
Rear Axle—Packard full-floating.
Springs Front—Semi-elliptic.
Springs Rear—Semi-elliptic.
Carburetor—Packard automatic float feed with large cylindrical mixing chamber.
Cooling System—Centrifugal pump.
Oiling System—Forced feed.
Ignition—Magneto.
Control—Left drive, center control.
Clutch—Multiple disc, dry plate.
Transmission—Packard Selective, four speeds forward and one reverse.
Brakes—Service, contracting on propeller shaft drum; emergency, expanding in rear wheel drum.
Steering Gear—Worm and wheel.
Equipment—Odometer, dash and rear oil lamps, mechanical horn, necessary tools in tool box, jack, oil can and can of oil.

PACKARD
MOTOR CAR
COMPANY

DETROIT
MICHIGAN

Price	**$5250**
Seven-Passenger Standard Tour- ing	3700
Seven-Passenger Salon Touring .	3700
Five-Passenger Phaeton	3700
Five-Passenger Salon Phaeton .	3700
Four-Passenger Runabout . . .	3700
Seven-Passenger Landaulet . . .	5300
Four-Passenger Coupe	5050
Six-Passenger Brougham	5300
Seven-Passenger Brougham . . .	5400
Seven-Passenger Imperial Lim- ousine	5450
Chassis	3300

PACKARD LIMOUSINE—3-25

COLOR	.Body, door panels and wheels, Pack-ard blue striped with black; upper and under body, black	BORE AND STROKE .	3 x 5 inches
		LUBRICATION	Force feed
		RADIATOR	Cellular
		COOLING	Water pump
SEATING CAPACITY .	Seven	IGNITION	Storage battery and generator
POSITION OF DRIVER	Left side		
WHEELBASE	128 inches	STARTING SYSTEM . .	Two unit
GAUGE	56 inches	STARTER OPERATED .	Gear to fly wheel
WHEELS	Wood	LIGHTING SYSTEM . .	Electric
FRONT TIRES	35 x 5 inches	VOLTAGES	Six to eight
REAR TIRES	35 x 5 inches	WIRING SYSTEM . . .	Single
SERVICE BRAKE . . .	Contracting on rear wheels	GASOLINE SYSTEM . .	Pressure
		CLUTCH	Dry multiple disc
EMERGENCY BRAKE .	Expanding on rear wheels	TRANSMISSION . . .	Selective sliding
CYLINDERS	Twelve	GEAR CHANGES . . .	Three forward one reverse
ARRANGED	V type, 60 degrees		
CAST	In sixes	DRIVE	Worm bevel
HORSEPOWER	43.2	REAR AXLE	Semi-floating
(N.A.C.C. Rating)		STEERING GEAR . . .	Worm and nut

In addition to above specifications, price includes speedometer, ammeter, clock, tire pump, electric horn and demountable rims.

would remain with the company for many years.

The V-12, called the Twin Six, was introduced in 1915 at only $2600 base price. At least 34 Packard Open Touring cars were used by the American Expeditionary Forces during World War I. Packard was also closely involved in developing and assembling the Liberty aircraft engine. The V-12 was installed in a Packard racing car and broke all records at Sheepshead Bay in 1917. Along with conservative but elegant styling, large and reliable six-, eight- and twelve-cylinder motors helped keep Packard at the top of American auto manufacturing through the 1920s. Packard survived the 1930s as well as World War II, finally succumbing to market pressures in 1958 after merging with Studebaker.

Paige

Also called Paige-Detroit, the auto company was the business venture of Harry M. Jewett, who had made his money in coal sales and distribution during the 1890s in Michigan. When he saw the car that Andrew Bachle had designed and Fred O. Paige was promoting, he decided to enter the burgeoning automotive field and put up the finances for the car's manufacturing. In 1909 he gathered up $100,000 and installed Fred Paige as president, relying on Paige's experience at the helm of Reliance, which had built trucks before acquisition by William Durant and GM.

The 1909 Paige-Detroit was powered by a three-cylinder two-cycle motor, much as Reliance had used. There were a number of companies that still preferred the two-stroke engine due to its simplicity. For light cars as well as motorcycles two-stroke design was used for many decades and up to this writing, but at one time even trucks, including two-stroke diesel motors, and passenger cars were powered by such engines. However, prior to the expiration of the Selden Patent those vehicles were subject to a licensing agreement or fine.

Two-cycle engines have had their own peculiarities, and the 1909–1910 Paige-Detroit was no exception. Harry Jewett was totally disillusioned with the initial design, calling it "a piece of junk." He fired Fred Paige and continued building the Paige car with a four-cycle four-cylinder motor for 1912. Such names as LaMarquise and Brunswick were designated for some Paige models, bringing a glimmer of prestige to the marque. The "Detroit" was dropped, and the Paige was selling well, with over 4600 in 1914, 7700 in 1915 and over 12,400 built in 1916. The first six-cylinder motor was offered in 1915 and after that no smaller engines were offered.

Only one Paige open touring car was known to be used by the AEF during World War I. At that time the company quickly gained the reputation of being a large, reliable and stylish automobile that could easily have become the fourth "P" along with Packard, Peerless and Pierce-Arrow. "The Most Beautiful Car in America" became the company's slogan, even if it was somewhat bombastic.

After the war Paige continued its success, and in 1921 proved its sporty nature when Ralph Mulford drove a Paige 102.8 mph at Daytona Beach, making it a special order model the following year. A model line called the Jewett arrived in 1922 as a smaller car with more modest price tags. The Paige sedan had surpassed the $4000 mark by that time. Sales of Paige and Jewett hit an all-time high for the company in 1923 with a total of just over 45,550 cars. A brochure in 1925 printed by Paige called "43 Ghosts" referred to the number of auto companies that had not survived the postwar recession.

Harry Jewett's fortunes slipped by 1926, and the following year he sold his company to the Graham Brothers. The company was reorganized as Graham-Paige and lasted until 1941.

**PAIGE-DETROIT
MOTOR CAR
COMPANY**

**DETROIT
MICHIGAN**

Price **$1330**
Two- or Three-Passenger Dart-
   moor Roadster 1330
Glendale Cloverleaf 1330

PAIGE LINWOOD TOURING—6-39

COLOR	Brewster green	LUBRICATION	Force feed and splash
SEATING CAPACITY. .	Five	RADIATOR	Cellular
POSITION OF DRIVER .	Left side	COOLING	Water pump
WHEELBASE	117 inches	IGNITION	Storage battery
GAUGE	56 inches	STARTING SYSTEM . .	Two unit
WHEELS	Wood	STARTER OPERATED .	Gear to fly wheel
FRONT TIRES	32 x 4 inches	LIGHTING SYSTEM . .	Electric
REAR TIRES	32 x 4 inches, anti-skid	VOLTAGES	Six to eight
SERVICE BRAKE . . .	Contracting on rear wheels	WIRING SYSTEM . . .	Single
		GASOLINE SYSTEM . .	Gravity
EMERGENCY BRAKE .	Expanding on rear wheels	CLUTCH	Multiple disc in oil
CYLINDERS	Six	TRANSMISSION . . .	Selective sliding
ARRANGED	Vertically	GEAR CHANGES . . .	Three forward, one reverse
CAST.	En bloc	DRIVE	Spiral bevel
HORSEPOWER . . . . 23.44 (N.A.C.C. Rating)		REAR AXLE	Three-quarters floating
BORE AND STROKE .	3⅛ x 5 inches	STEERING GEAR . .	Screw and nut

In addition to above specifications, price includes top, top hood, windshield, speedometer, ammeter, electric horn and demountable rims.

Palmer

In the early days of American auto manufacturing the name Palmer may have created some confusion in that there was first a Palmer car builder during 1899 in Mianus, Connecticut, later resurrected in Cos Cob, Connecticut, in 1914. Then there was a Palmer in Cleveland and Ashtabula, Ohio, in 1906. There was also a Palmer built in Detroit, Michigan, in 1912, and a much larger company called Palmer-Singer of Long Island, New York. Finally, there was the Palmer of St. Louis, Missouri, which was also called Palmer-Meyer and built only trucks from 1912 to 1918.

There was nothing unusual about Palmer and Palmer-Meyer trucks, as they were interchangeably called. The first Palmer was ¾-ton capacity called the Model B, which was a conventional assembled truck using a four-cylinder motor. A stake body delivery wagon, it was priced at $1550. From sales brochure illustrations it appears the Palmer-Meyers were all dual chain drive. For 1914 a 1-ton and 1½-ton model were added to the lineup with L-head four-cylinders motors and unchanged in appearance from the earlier model. Three-speed sliding gear transmissions were used throughout. Shaft-drive was offered in 1915, and all Palmer trucks had solid rubber tires.

For 1917 fenders were listed as optional equipment. For 1917 the 1-ton model used internal gear drive while the 2-ton model was listed with worm drive. Solid rubber tires were also standard. The company did not survive the year 1918.

Palmer-Moore

Automobiles and trucks with the Palmer name accounted for at least five other companies before Palmer-Moore was also added to the list in 1913. The company was listed in Syracuse, New York, and all of the Palmer vehicles were built on the East Coast except the previously mentioned Palmer of Saint Louis, Missouri.

Palmer-Moore only built trucks, with the first two models being a ¾-ton and a 1-ton model. The Model K of 1913 was a four-cylinder truck priced at $1150. What was somewhat unusual was that Palmer-Moore used a "Renault-style" hood, which was also used at the time by such companies as Mack, International and Kelly on some of their models. This "aerodynamic"-looking hood merely signified that the radiator, or two radiators on each side, were behind the engine. As mentioned before, the advantage was the uncluttered and free accessibility to the motor for maintenance, repair or replacement. There was also less probability of damage to the radiator had it been in front at a time when roads were primitive and various rocks and debris which could damage the radiator were much more common.

By 1917 Palmer-Moore offered the 1-ton Model M and the 2-ton Model O. Both had internal gear drive and were powered by four-cylinder motors. Wheelbase was offered up to 160 inches on the Model O. By this time left-hand drive and central controls were the standard in the industry. The motors were built by Buda and were coupled to a three-speed sliding gear transmission, and although not specified they were very likely from Brown-Lipe or Durston, both of which were built in Syracuse. Standard tires were hard rubber, although pneumatic tires were optional. It appears that the material shortages and other exigencies of World War I precluded the company's survival past 1918.

Pan-American

In January of 1917 Pan-American Motors Corporation was founded in Chicago, Illinois, and appeared to be the manufacturer of the Chicago Light Six passenger car. By way of some obscure historical information, it is

PALMER TRUCKS
Manufactured by
PALMER-MEYER MOTOR CAR CO., 5027 McKissock Ave., St. Louis, Mo.

S P E C I F I C A T I O N S

Model	1917	1917
Capacity	1 ton	2 tons
Drive	Internal gear	Worm
Chassis Price	$1,350	$1,975
Motor		
H. P. (S.A.E.)	22.5	27.2
H. P. (Actual)	30	30
Cylinders	4 L-head en bloc	4 L-head en bloc
Bore	$3\frac{3}{4}''$	$4\frac{1}{8}''$
Stroke	$5''$	$5\frac{1}{4}''$
Wheel Base	132"	144" regular
Tread Front	56"	58"
Tread Rear	56"	58"
Tires Front	$34x3\frac{1}{2}''$	$36x3\frac{1}{2}''$
Tires Rear	34x4"	$36x3\frac{1}{2}''$ dual

Frame—Pressed steel.
Front Axle—Drop forged, I-beam.
Rear Axle—Torbenson internal gear, Timken worm.
Springs Front—Semi-elliptic.
Springs Rear—Semi-elliptic.

Carburetor	Stromberg	Stromberg G-2
Cooling System	Thermo-syphon	Centrifugal pump
Oiling System	Constant level splash	Circulating splash

Ignition—Bosch high tension.
Control—Left drive, center control.

Clutch	Multiple disc	Multiple disc, dry plate

Transmission—Selective, three speeds forward and one reverse.

Brakes	Double acting external	Contracting on propeller shaft
Steering Gear	Worm and gear	Worm and full type

Equipment—Model 1917 (1 ton): Side and rear oil lamps, horn, tool kit, jack, and fenders.
Model 1917 (2 tons): Front fenders, horn, one tail and two dash lights, jack, and tool kit.

PALMER-MOORE TRUCKS
Manufactured by
PALMER-MOORE CO., Syracuse, N. Y.

S P E C I F I C A T I O N S

Model	**M**	**O**
Capacity	1 ton	2 tons
Drive	Internal gear	Internal gear
Chassis Price	On application	On application
Motor		
H. P. (S.A.E.)	19.6	27.23
H. P. (Actual)	25	30
Cylinders	4 en bloc	4 en bloc
Bore	$3\frac{1}{2}''$	$4\frac{1}{8}''$
Stroke	$5\frac{1}{8}''$	$5\frac{1}{2}''$
Wheel Base	126″	140″-160″ optional
Tread Front	56″	56″
Tread Rear	56″	56″
Tires Front	34x3″	34x4″
Tires Rear	34x4″	34x6″

Frame—Pressed.
Front Axle—I-beam.
Rear Axle—Dead I-beam.
Springs Front—Semi-elliptic.
Springs Rear—Semi-elliptic.
Carburetor—Zenith.
Cooling System   Thermo-syphon   Pump
Oiling System—Splash and pump.
Ignition—Magneto.
Control—Left drive, center control.
Clutch—Dry plate.
Transmission—Selective, three speeds forward and one reverse.
Brakes—Expanding and contracting on rear wheels.
Steering Gear—Worm and nut.
Equipment—Oil side and tail lamps, tool kit.

THE PAN-AMERICAN TRUCK
Manufactured by
PAN-AMERICAN MOTOR CORPORATION,
Decatur, Ill.

Model	18
Capacity	2¼ tons
Drive	Internal gear
Chassis Weight	5,000 lbs.
Chassis Price	$2,250
Engine	Buda
H. P. (S.A.E.)	28.9
H. P. (Actual)	40
Cylinders	4 en bloc
Bore	4¼″
Stroke	5½″
Wheel Base	150″—160″
Tread Front	56″
Tread Rear	56″
Tires Front	36x4″
Tires Rear	36x6″

Frame—Rolled steel.
Front Axle—I-beam.
Rear Axle—Torbensen fixed I-beam.
Springs Front—Semi-elliptic.
Springs Rear—Semi-elliptic.
Carburetor—Stromberg vacuum.
Cooling System—Pump.
Oiling System—Forced feed.
Ignition—Magneto.
Control—Left side, center control.
Clutch—Dry plate.
Transmission—Fuller Selective, three speeds.
Brakes—Internal expanding, external contracting rear wheels.
Steering Gear—Worm gear.
Equipment—Driver's cab, gas tank, kit of tools.
Tire Equipment—GOODRICH MOTOR TRUCK TIRES FURNISHED WHEN SPECIFIED.

known that a truck model was also built at least in the first three years of the company's short existence. However, the truck was powered by a four-cylinder engine, whereas nearly all the Pan-American passenger cars used a six-cylinder engine.

Within a year of its organization, Pan-American moved to Decatur, Illinois. The company announced it planned to rename its vehicles Decatur, but the passenger car models kept the name American Beauty. The trucks were named after the year of production, which meant that the 2½-ton Model 18 was really the same vehicle as had been built the previous year. Edward Danner became the new company president in July of 1918, by which time about 200 Pan-American cars had been built, almost all of them using a six-cylinder but of different varieties: Continental, Herschell-Spillman or Rutenber. There was also a lower-priced American Beauty by 1919, the year the wartime and postwar effects took hold.

Pan-American began to suffer from the post-war recession, but in addition, Edward Danner announced an auditor found a shortage in the tens of thousand of dollars while company secretary-treasurer W.A. Phares had disappeared in the meantime. The company's board of directors voted to liquidate the company while it was still solvent. In May of 1922 Phares was arrested in Columbus, Ohio, for embezzlement. The ensuing liquidation auction brought only one-fifth of the value of the $100,000 inventory. Machinery and components were bought at bargain prices, including such things as wire wheel sets for one dollar each. After the company had built about 4000 cars and an unknown number of trucks, that auction would be the letdown and final demise of the Pan-American Motors Corporation.

Panhard

It is not clear just what relationship the Panhard Motors of Grand Haven, Michigan,

had with the Panhard built in France in the early years of motor vehicle manufacturing. At the time companies could use names internationally under license, and a number of European brands were assembled in the United States. It is known that Panhard of France purchased a Selden license by 1905 in order to legally assemble their motor vehicles in the United States.

The Panhard of Michigan was built by the Hamilton Motors Company. This company was started by Guy Hamilton after he had briefly built the Gaylord car from 1911 to 1913 in Gaylord, Michigan. He then formed the Alter Motor Car Company in 1915, which lasted until 1917 in Plymouth, Michigan. It was named after C.A. Alter, who was vice president of the company, which built four- and six-cylinder cars very briefly.

Not giving up on automotive ventures, the entrepreneur then built a car named after himself. The Hamilton lasted only through 1917 in Grand Haven, Michigan, where the Alter had moved before financial woes closed the company down. Hamilton Motors also built an Alter truck which was superseded by the Panhard truck.

The fact that Hamilton used Panhard as its name brings about the opportunity to mention the Panhard built in Paris, since the one that existed in the United States was very obscure and lasted only from 1918 to 1919. Rene Panhard and Emile Levassor were the men behind the famous enterprise which acquired the Daimler patent rights in France. As a company, Panhard et Levassor has been listed as early as 1889, building an experimental car in 1891, and in 1893 manufacturing an omnibus and a "waggonnette."

The company entered the Military Trials of 1900 in France, and in 1911 a Chatillon-Panhard military tractor was fabricated. The company built both conventional and forward-controlled commercial vehicles. The Knight Sleeve-Valve engine, which used a

PANHARD TRUCKS
Manufactured by
HAMILTON MOTORS COMPANY, Grand Haven, Mich.

Model	A	B
Capacity	1 ton	1½ tons
Drive	Internal gear	Internal gear
Chassis Weight	3,200 lbs.	3,600 lbs.
Chassis Price	$985	$1,185
Engine	Gray	Gray
H. P. (S.A.E.)	19.6	19.6
H. P. (Actual)	35	35
Cylinders	4 en bloc	4 en bloc
Bore	3¼"	3¼"
Stroke	5"	5"
Wheel Base	125"	130"
Tread Front	56"	56"
Tread Rear	56"	56"
Tires Front	32x3½" Pneu.	32x3½"
Tires Rear	32x3½"	32x4"

Frame—Rolled.
Front Axle—I-beam, knuckle drop forged.
Rear Axle—Torbensen I-beam, full-floating.
Springs Front—Semi-elliptic.
Springs Rear—Semi-elliptic.
Carburetor—Stromberg.
Cooling System—Thermo-syphon.
Oiling System—Forced feed.
Ignition—Generator.
Control—Left-hand drive, center control.
Clutch—Dry plate.
Transmission—Fuller Selective, three speeds forward and one reverse.
Brakes—Internal expanding and external contracting on rear wheels.
Steering Gear—Screw and nut.
Equipment—Electric lights with dimmers, electric horn, tool kit and jack.

double sleeve design, was adopted in 1910. After World War I Panhard of France built armored cars and half-tracks. The Panhard company lasted until 1967, building many types of cars and trucks over the decades.

The Panhard trucks of Grand Haven, Michigan, lasted only through 1919 in the form of a Model A 1-ton capacity and a Model B 1½-ton capacity. The four-cylinder motors were furnished by Gray using Fuller transmissions and Torbensen axles. Guy Hamilton subsequently built the Apex truck until 1921 (which was not related to several much earlier Apex cars), and this appeared to be his final exercise in motor vehicle manufacturing.

Paterson

In competition with the more famous Durant-Dort Carriage Company, from which sprang Durant's General Motors, William A. Paterson also arrived in Flint, Michigan, to build carriages as early as 1869. By 1908 Paterson built an experimental car and soon dropped horse-drawn conveyances entirely from his production line, hiring E.C. Kollmorgen as chief engineer and production manager.

For 1908–1909 the Paterson was a 14 hp two-cylinder car called the Motor Buggy on an 80-inch wheelbase. This Model 14, of which 64 were built through 1909, was superseded by the 1910 Model 30, which featured a four-cylinder motor with the corresponding number of horsepower. Business increased to a production total of 450 for the year.

Nearly all of the Paterson vehicles were touring cars until a Roadster was offered in 1914, and for 1915 a six-cylinder car was introduced. The larger motor also meant better sales, which increased to 900 for that year. By 1916 four-cylinder engines were discontinued. During World War I the company continued to sell conservatively styled well-built cars, and the Paterson also survived the beginning

of the postwar recession. However, in 1921 William Paterson died at the age of 83, and his son was unable to carry the company through the economic downturn in America.

By 1923 Paterson was forced to sell the entire company to Dallas Winslow, who had been a Dodge dealer also in Flint. Although Kollmorgen remained in his position at Paterson, Winslow's success with the Dodge distracted him from the company he had just bought, and the Paterson was out of business by the end of the year 1923.

Peerless

Of the early American companies that had prestige, Peerless was one of the three usually put into this category, in addition to Packard and Pierce-Arrow. This company began by building clothes wringers, then bicycles in the late 1890s before embarking on the manufacture of a motor vehicle in 1900 in Cleveland, Ohio.

The first Peerless cars were the Type B and Type C Motorettes, which were powered by a one-cylinder motor based on the French De Dion engine design. Under Louis P. Mooers, who had built an experimental car in 1897, there was also a 16 hp two-cylinder Type 4 Peerless for 1902–1903 called the Tonneau, a product of what was by then the Peerless Motor Car Company.

It wasn't until later in 1904 that a four-cylinder car on a wheelbase of 104 inches with a price tag of $6000 was introduced. What made the four-cylinder cars exceptional was their modern design, which featured mounting the engine under a front hood and using a fully-floating bevel gear rear axle with shaft drive. The steering wheel folded forward, an uncommon idea until decades later, although not entirely unique. Styling was considered progressive by the automotive press compared to those of other cars at that time.

By 1905 a limousine was also offered, one of

W. A. PATERSON
C O M P A N Y

F L I N T
M I C H I G A N

Price	**$1265**
Seven-Passenger Touring . . .	1295
Four-Passenger Roadster	1295
Five-Passenger Sedan	1795

PATERSON TOURING—6-45

COLOR	Dark blue	LUBRICATION		Force feed and splash
SEATING CAPACITY. .	Five	RADIATOR		Tubular
POSITION OF DRIVER .	Left side	COOLING		Water pump
WHEELBASE	117 inches	IGNITION		Storage battery
GAUGE	56 inches	STARTING SYSTEM . .		Two unit
WHEELS	Wood	STARTER OPERATED .		Gear to fly wheel
FRONT TIRES . . .	32 x 4 inches	LIGHTING SYSTEM . .		Electric
REAR TIRES . . .	32 x 4 inches	VOLTAGES		Six
SERVICE BRAKE . . .	Contracting on rear wheels	WIRING SYSTEM . . .		Single
EMERGENCY BRAKE .	Expanding on rear wheels	GASOLINE SYSTEM . .		Vacuum
		CLUTCH		Cone
CYLINDERS	Six	TRANSMISSION . . .		Selective sliding
ARRANGED	Vertically	GEAR CHANGES . . .		Three forward, one reverse
CAST.	En bloc			
HORSEPOWER . . . . 25.35 (N.A.C.C. Rating)		DRIVE		Spiral bevel
		REAR AXLE		Full floating
BORE AND STROKE .	3¼ x 4½ inches	STEERING GEAR . . .		Worm and nut

In addition to above specifications, price includes top, top hood, windshield, speed-ometer, ammeter, voltmeter, tire pump, electric horn and demountable rims.

PEERLESS TRUCKS

Manufactured by

THE PEERLESS MOTOR CAR CO., Cleveland, Ohio

Model	TC-3	TC-4	TC-5	TC-6
Capacity	3 tons	4 tons	5 tons	6 tons
Drive	Chain	Chain	Chain	Chain
Chassis Weight	6,900 lbs.	7,100 lbs.	8,050 lbs.	8,850 lbs.
Chassis Price	$4,000	$4,150	$4,700	$5,200
Engine	Peerless	Peerless	Peerless	Peerless
H. P. (S.A.E.)	32.4	32.4	32.4	32.4
H. P. (Actual)	40 at 925 R.P.M.	40 at 925 R.P.M.	40 at 925 R.P.M.	40 at 925 R.P.M.
Cylinders	4 in pairs	4 in pairs	4 in pairs	4 in pairs
Bore	$4\frac{1}{2}''$	$4\frac{1}{2}''$	$4\frac{1}{2}''$	$4\frac{1}{2}''$
Stroke	$6\frac{1}{4}''$	$6\frac{1}{4}''$	$6\frac{1}{4}''$	$6\frac{1}{4}''$
Wheel Base	151″ Standard	151″ Standard	151″ Standard	151″ Standard
	174″ long	174″ long	174″ long	174″ long
Tread Front	68″	68″	68″	68″
Tread Rear	$69\frac{1}{2}''$	$71\frac{1}{2}''$	$73\frac{1}{2}''$	$77\frac{1}{2}''$
Tires Front	36x4″	36x5″	38x6″	38x7″
Tires Rear	40x4″ dual	40x5″ dual	42x6″ dual	42x7″ dual

Frame—Rolled.

Front Axle—I-beam, Elliott knuckle.

Rear Axle—Peerless I-beam.

Springs Front—Semi-elliptic.

Springs Rear—Semi-elliptic.

Carburetor—Stromberg G-3.

Cooling System—Pump.

Oiling System—Splash.

Ignition—Magneto.

Control—Right-hand drive, right control.

Clutch—Cone.

Transmission—Peerless Selective, four speeds.

Brakes—Contracting on jackshaft, expanding in rear hub.

Steering Gear—Worm and wheel.

Equipment—Chassis painted in lead. Driver's seat and cushion, hubodometer, two oil dash lamps, one oil tail lamp, horn, 60 ampere hour storage battery, complete set of tools in tool box, 40 inch pinch bar, five-ton jack and governor.

PEERLESS
MOTOR CAR
COMPANY

CLEVELAND, OHIO

Price	**$2990**
Four-Passenger Roadster	2340
Two-Passenger Sporting Roadster	2490
Four-Passenger Coupe	2850
Seven-Passenger Limousine . .	3690
Seven-Passenger Touring	2340

PEERLESS SEDAN—56

COLOR	Peerless green	LUBRICATION	Force feed
SEATING CAPACITY .	Six	RADIATOR	Cellular
POSITION OF DRIVER .	Left side	COOLING	Water pump
WHEELBASE	125 inches	IGNITION	Storage battery and dry cells
GAUGE	56 inches		
WHEELS	Wood	STARTING SYSTEM . .	Two unit
FRONT TIRES	35 x 4½ inches	STARTER OPERATED .	Gear to fly wheel
REAR TIRES	35 x 4½ inches, anti-skid	LIGHTING SYSTEM . .	Electric
		VOLTAGES	Six to seven
SERVICE BRAKE . . .	Contracting on rear wheels	WIRING SYSTEM . . .	Single
EMERGENCY BRAKE .	Expanding on rear wheels	GASOLINE SYSTEM . .	Vacuum
		CLUTCH	Dry multiple disc
CYLINDERS	Eight	TRANSMISSION . . .	Selective sliding
ARRANGED	V type, 90 degrees	GEAR CHANGES . . .	Three forward, one reverse
CAST	In fours		
HORSEPOWER . . . . 33.8 (N.A.C.C. Rating)		DRIVE	Spiral bevel
		REAR AXLE	Semi-floating
BORE AND STROKE .	3¼ x 5 inches	STEERING GEAR . . .	Worm and gear

In addition to above specifications, price includes windshield, speedometer, ammeter, voltmeter, tire pump, electric horn and demountable rims.

the first this early in the industry. Mooers took his Touring car to Ireland for the Gordon Bennet Cup, which made the press and gave Peerless much publicity despite a crash in the race. Subsequently, Mooers hired Barney Oldfield to do the driving. Oldfield had already made a name for himself driving Ford's 999 racer and Winton's Bullets. The new Peerless 60 hp Green Dragon racing car proved that such competition got plenty of press and therefore advertising even if Oldfield's not-so-glamorous public behavior got him fired. Mooers fled the Peerless company at almost the same time, jumping over to Moon as chief engineer in St. Louis, Missouri.

Peerless began competing in the luxury market by 1906, and built 1175 cars, which was about the same number as Packard and Pierce-Arrow at that time. A six-cylinder motor was introduced in 1907 and a V-8 in 1916. During World War I the company's assets were traded so it was unclear who owned Peerless week to week, but the company prospered nevertheless despite the fact that the neither the U.S. Army nor the AEF listed any purchases from the company.

Peerless built trucks only for a few years between 1911 and 1918, which was unusual for luxury auto manufacturers, but in line with other companies such as Pierce-Arrow. All four models in 1918 from 3-ton to 6-ton capacity were powered by the same Peerless four-cylinder engine and used a Peerless four-speed transmission. Peerless continued to build right-hand steer and right-hand shift trucks long after this was no longer considered industry norm.

Despite the capriciousness of the stockholders, Lewis H. Kittredge remained president of Peerless from 1907 through the war. But in 1921 former Cadillac president Richard H. Collins bought Peerless, and there was an exchange of engineers between the two companies. By 1923 production had risen to 5700

cars for the year at Peerless. But that year there was another exodus of engineers, along with Collins's departure. Edward Ver Linden became president of Peerless, and a new lower-priced car arrived in the form of Model 6-70, powered by a six-cylinder engine, that joined the V-8 model.

Despite its success, the V-8 was discontinued in 1928 and superseded with a straight 8 from Continental. Ver Linden departed, leaving vice president Leon R. German to take the helm, but only for a year before James Bohanon took over in that position. The 1930 Peerless was designed by the renowned auto designer Alexis de Sakhnoffsky, but it was completed just as the stock market crash took place. A V-16 Peerless with a Murphy aluminum body was tested at 100 mph in Muroc Dry Lake, but it never had a chance to go into production. Leftover 1931 cars were sold as 1932 models, and Peerless joined the large flock of other companies that met their demise in the Great Depression.

Pierce-Arrow

Historians have nearly always guffawed over the fact that Pierce had its origins in a company that had built bird cages during the 1800s. Heintz, Pierce and Munschauer of Buffalo, New York, was formed in 1865, also producing iceboxes and other household items. George N. Pierce bought out the entire company and added bicycles to the model line in 1896. This was the decade of major changes in bicycle design as the highwheeler was superseded by the modern bicycle design, essentially still used today. When Colonel Charles Clifton was hired as the company treasurer it was he who promoted Pierce to move into auto manufacturing with a steam car prototype built in 1900.

For 1901 and 1902 only one-cylinder Motorettes were built by Pierce-Arrow, and just as with Peerless, the De Dion engine design

**PIERCE-ARROW
MOTOR CAR
COMPANY**

**BUFFALO
NEW YORK**

Price	$6800
Two-Passenger Runabout . . .	5400
Three-Passenger Runabout . .	5400
Two-Passenger Coupe	6400
Three-Passenger Coupe	6400
Two-Passenger Convertible Road-	
ster	6400
Three-Passenger Convertible	
Roadster	6400
Four-Passenger Touring	5400
Five-Passenger Touring	5400
Seven-Passenger Touring	5500
Brougham	6600
Suburban	6800
Landau.	6800
Vestibule Suburban.	7000
Vestibule Landau	7000
Vestibule Brougham	6800
Vestibule Suburban Landau . .	7000

PIERCE-ARROW SUBURBAN LANDAU—48-B-4

COLOR	Optional	RADIATOR	Cellular
SEATING CAPACITY .	Seven	COOLING	Water pump
POSITION OF DRIVER	Right side	IGNITION	High tension magneto and storage battery
WHEELBASE	142 inches		
GAUGE	56 inches		
WHEELS	Wood	STARTING SYSTEM . .	Two unit
FRONT TIRES	35 x 5 inches	STARTER OPERATED .	Gear to fly wheel
REAR TIRES	35 x 5 inches	LIGHTING SYSTEM . .	Electric
SERVICE BRAKE. . .	Expanding on rear wheels	VOLTAGES	Six
		WIRING SYSTEM . .	Single
EMERGENCY BRAKE .	Contracting on rear wheels	GASOLINE SYSTEM . .	Pressure
		CLUTCH	Cone
CYLINDERS	Six	TRANSMISSION . . .	Selective sliding
ARRANGED	Vertically	GEAR CHANGES . . .	Four forward, one reverse
CAST	In pairs		
HORSEPOWER	48.6	DRIVE	Spiral bevel
(N.A.C.C. Rating)		REAR AXLE	Semi-floating
BORE AND STROKE .	4½ x 5½ inches	STEERING GEAR . .	Screw and nut
LUBRICATION	Force feed		

In addition to above specifications, price includes windshield, speedometer, autometer, and demountable rims.

PIERCE-ARROW TRUCKS
Manufactured by
PIERCE-ARROW MOTOR CAR CO., Buffalo, N. Y.

S P E C I F I C A T I O N S

Model	2-Ton	5-Ton
Capacity	2 tons	5 tons
Drive	Worm	Worm
Chassis Price	$3,000	$4,500
Motor		
H. P. (S.A.E.)	25.6	38
H. P. (Actual)	28	42
Cylinders	4 in pairs	4 in pairs
Bore	4″	4⅞″
Stroke	5½″	6″
Wheel Base	150″ and 180″	168″ and 204″
Tread Front	60″	68″
Tread Rear	56½″	64″
Tires Front	36x4″	36x5″
Tires Rear	36x4″ dual	40x6″ dual

Frame—Pressed.
Front Axle—I-section Elliott.
Rear Axle—Full-floating.
Springs Front—Semi-elliptic.
Springs Rear—Semi-elliptic.
Carburetor—Pierce-Arrow.
Cooling System—Pump.
Oiling System—Forced pressure.
Ignition   Magneto   Magneto and battery
Control—Right drive, right control.
Clutch—Cone.
Transmission—Selective, three speeds forward and one reverse.
Brakes—Transmission and hub.
Steering Gear—Screw and nut.
Equipment—Driver's seat, top, dash and footboards; front mudguards, side and tail lamps, speedometer, horn, jack and full set of tools, wood sills clipped to frame for mounting body.

was relied upon to built the first 150 such cars by the end of that year. For 1903 a two-cylinder motor was employed, as was David Fergusson, an engineer from Stearns who would remain for the next two decades. The four-cylinder Great Arrow actually preceded the name of Pierce-Arrow that was officially adopted in 1909, by which time a six-cylinder motor had been introduced two years earlier.

The first Glidden Tour of 1905 was won by a Pierce car driven by Percy Pierce, son of founder George N. Pierce, and the next four runs by that man were won consecutively by Pierce autos. The famous, patented (by Herbert M. Dawley), fender-molded headlight arrived for 1913 at Pierce-Arrow. In World War I the AEF bought one open touring and one limousine from the company, which was not much but enough for some advertising and prestige. The Dual Valve Six was introduced as the war ended, and Pierce-Arrow stayed with the smaller six-cylinder motor even as others offered the V-8 and V-12.

During Prohibition after World War I, Pierce-Arrows were popular with smugglers because of their quiet reliability. The Seligman banking company took over management of Pierce-Arrow at this time and insisted on developing a sleeve-valve engine akin to the Knight motor. Fergusson strongly disagreed and resigned, bringing in Barney Roos, who also did not see eye-to-eye with the bank executives running the company. They in turn hired Charles L. Sheppy in 1921 as chief engineer and advanced Myron E. Forbes to the presidency. He helped develop the smaller L-head six-cylinder Model 80 introduced in 1924. Four-wheel brakes were adopted in 1926. A vacuum booster was also used, which had been developed by Caleb Bragg and Victor Kliesrath, and this device became the basis of power brakes for many years among manufacturers.

By staying with a six-cylinder engine and conservative styling, Pierce-Arrow was losing market share by 1927, and in 1928 Colonel Clifton died. Under Myron Forbes, Pierce-Arrow merged with Studebaker, and for 1929 production shot up to 10,000 for the year. But despite the introduction of a straight-eight motor, Forbes resigned and Albert Erskine of Studebaker took over as president.

A V-12 motor designed by Karl Wise was developed for Pierce Arrow just as the stock market crashed, although the company continued to manufacture cars independently of Studebaker, with the exception of S-P-A (Studebaker-Pierce-Arrow) trucks. Ab Jenkins set new world records at Bonneville with the new V-12, but it was too late. Studebaker was in receivership by 1933 and Albert Erskine committed suicide. Pierce-Arrow regained its independence but not its financial stability during the 1930s when luxury cars, the only product line at the company, were not best sellers. By 1935 only 875 Pierce-Arrows were built, and in 1937 only 137 rolled off the assembly line. The company was auctioned off in 1938.

Pope (motorcycle)

Colonel Albert Augustus Pope was a very successful businessman who started his Pope Manufacturing Company in Boston, Massachusetts. He began manufacturing a high-wheeler bicycle in 1878 which was marketed under the Columbia name. Meanwhile inventor Pierre Lallement had patented a new pedal-driven bicycle in France, and not finding commercial success there, he moved to Ansonia, Connecticut.

Albert Pope got into the process of buying out as many patents on bicycles as he could find, and he defended against any infringements vigorously. Lallement became his employee and Pope bought his U.S. Patent 59,915, which had been issued back on Nov. 20, 1866. Lallement was an expert witness in one infringement lawsuit in 1880, and with

Pope's aggressive push in taking over the American bicycle industry, his company became the leading manufacturer of "modern" bicycles by 1896.

By 1899 Pope had merged with or acquired 45 bicycle manufacturers. Most of the bicycles he built at a time when the new fad was taking over the country were called Columbia, but he also built brands called the American, Cleveland, Crescent, Imperial, Monarch and Tribune.

Along the way Pope gained control of the Electric Vehicle Company of Hartford, Connecticut, which owned the Selden Patent of 1895. Every gasoline-powered vehicle manufacturer had to buy a licensing agreement from the owner of the patent and pay royalties to George Selden. Pope began investing heavily in various auto and truck companies which would produce such motor vehicles as Pope-Robinson (1903–1904), Pope-Toledo (1904–1909), Pope-Tribune (1904–1908) and Pope-Waverly Electric (1904–1908).

Albert Pope died at age 66 in 1909, and his brother, George Pope, took over the business. The businesses that flourished under Albert Pope soon began to fade away under his brother's management or lack thereof. Two years after Albert Pope's death in 1911 the Pope

name was finally applied to motorized bicycles and motorcycles, which were first produced in Hartford before the company moved to Westfield, Massachusetts, in the southwestern part of that state.

The first single-cylinder Pope motorcycle had a motor with 623 cc and was rated up to 8 hp. The motor had an overhead-valve system and a top speed of 50 mph, and was priced at $215. Once Pope moved to the small town of Westfield, known as "Whip City" in the late 1800s for its horse buggy equipment (as well as brick and cigar production), the Pope motorcycle second generation was quite an evolution from the first machines.

The Pope Single's price was dropped to $165 while the V-Twin of 1912 was introduced with a 1000 cc motor and up to 18 hp. Pope entered racing without much success at the peak of motordrome boardwalk racing popularity. In 1914 the V-Twin was offered with a single- or two-speed transmission for $265 and $300, respectively. The Corbin-Duplex rear brake, Eclipse multi-disc clutch, roller-bearing connecting rods, leaf-spring fork and plunger rear suspension made Pope years ahead of its time.

In 1916 a three-speed transmission was introduced, and the price for the V-Twin went down to $275. By 1918, without military contracts, Pope offered only the single- and three-speed V-Twin, the latter of which was capable of 65 mph in stock form. However, material shortages, dwindling sales, labor troubles and other problems related to the war itself forced Pope to close down in 1918. The main factory at Hartford had already been sold to Pratt-Whitney in 1915. The Selden Patent was deemed unenforceable by the courts and Henry Ford, the challenger, was the winner among dozens of other companies which avoided paying millions of dollars in royalties.

Premier

Yet another high-quality auto from the turn of the previous century beginning with the letter "P" was Premier, although it was not placed in the so-called top three. The company was founded by George B. Weidely in Indianapolis. He had built and sold a motor buggy in 1902, and together with Harold O. Smith formed the Premier Motor Manufacturing Company in 1903 when the company's first four-cylinder Runabout went into production. It was water-cooled from the beginning, as Weidely's 1902 prototype had been, and the 16 hp four-cylinder Model A was joined in 1904 by the Model F and the Two-Cylinder Premier, which was available through 1906. The Premier had overhead valves, shaft drive and a sliding gear transmission, making it rather advanced for the time. An oak leaf radiator badge was claimed to be the first automotive emblem in America.

The benefits and superiority of water-cooling vs. air-cooling were still being discussed at the time, and after a racer with such a design was tested unsuccessfully in 1905, air-cooled engines were nevertheless offered in addition to water-cooled motors for 1907 at Premier, but were discontinued for 1908. By 1910 Premier autos had finished the Glidden

Tour with perfect scores. A Premier race car made headlines in 1916. In the meantime George Weidely and Harold O. Smith left to begin building proprietary engines for other motor vehicle manufacturers, and Premier was sold to a concern headed by F.W. Woodruff who reorganized the company as Premier Motor Car.

As America entered the war, Premier entered the market in 1918 with a new advertising slogan that read, "The Aluminum Six with Magnetic Gear Shift." In 1917 the company had adopted a Cutler-Hammer electrically-operated transmission operated by a lever mounted on the steering wheel. This unusual transmission was used until 1920 when a physician named L.S. Skelton took over Premier.

With new debts paid off by the owner, who had made his money in oil investments and was also promoting a car with his name on it, Premier Motor Corporation was about to enter the new decade in good standing. But L.S. Skelton suddenly died in 1921, sending Premier into receivership once again. Frederick L. Barrows took over in 1923 and reorganized the company as Premier Motors, Inc.

Premier began building taxicabs as its new model line in 1923 and did so until 1926, when the whole enterprise was bought by the National Cab and Truck Company of Indianapolis, which closed the business for good almost immediately.

Rauch & Lang (electric)

Of the handful of electric vehicle producers still in business during World War I, Rauch & Lang was one of the most prominent and well regarded. The company began as the Rauch & Lang Carriage Company in Cleveland, Ohio, during 1884. The company was started by German immigrant Jacob Rauch and real estate magnate E.J. Lang, both residing in Cleveland.

**PREMIER
MOTOR
CORPORATION**

INDIANAPOLIS
INDIANA

Price	$2285
Seven-Passenger Touring	2285
Seven-Passenger Limousine . . .	3285

PREMIER FOURSOME—6-C

COLOR	Body, maroon or brown; chassis, jet black	BORE AND STROKE .	3⅜ x 5½ inches
		LUBRICATION	Force feed and splash
SEATING CAPACITY .	Four	RADIATOR	Cellular
POSITION OF DRIVER	Left side	COOLING	Water pump
WHEELBASE	125½ inches	IGNITION	Storage battery
GAUGE	56 inches	STARTING SYSTEM . .	Two unit
WHEELS	Wood	STARTER OPERATED .	Gear to fly wheel
FRONT TIRES	4½ inches	LIGHTING SYSTEM . .	Electric
REAR TIRES	4½ inches, anti-skid	VOLTAGES	Six to eight
		WIRING SYSTEM . . .	Single
SERVICE BRAKE . . .	Contracting on rear wheels	GASOLINE SYSTEM . .	Vacuum
EMERGENCY BRAKE .	Expanding on rear wheels	CLUTCH	Dry plate
		TRANSMISSION . . .	Selective sliding
CYLINDERS	Six	GEAR CHANGES . . .	Three forward, one reverse
ARRANGED	Vertically	DRIVE	Spiral bevel
CAST	En bloc	REAR AXLE	Semi-floating
HORSEPOWER . . . . (N.A.C.C. Rating)	27.34	STEERING GEAR . . .	Worm and gear

In addition to above specifications, price includes top, windshield, speedometer, ammeter, electric horn and demountable rims.

BAKER R & L COMPANY

CLEVELAND, OHIO

Price, $3000

RAUCH & LANG ELECTRIC—BX-7

COLOR	Optional
SEATING CAPACITY .	Five
BODY:	
LENGTH, INSIDE .	64 inches
WIDTH, INSIDE . .	58¼ inches
WHEELBASE	92 inches
GAUGE	56 inches
WHEELS	Wire or wood
FRONT TIRES	33 x 4½ inches pneumatic, or 36 x 4½ inches cushion

REAR TIRES	33 x 4½ inches pneumatic, or 36 x 4½ inches cushion, anti-skid
BRAKE SYSTEMS . .	Contracting on motor and expanding on rear wheels
BATTERY	41 cells, 13 or 15 plate
SPEED	25 miles per hour
NO. FORWARD SPEEDS	Six
NO. REVERSE SPEEDS	Four
CONTROL	Side lever
STEERING	Lever

The carriages they built were luxurious and the company was prospering when it also became a dealer of the Buffalo Electric. Observing how much interest there was in the new self-propelled battery-powered vehicles, Rauch & Lang began building similar vehicles in 1905. Stanhopes, depot wagons and coaches were the first body styles, and by 1907 Rauch & Lang had acquired the Hertner Electric Company, which supplied the electric motors needed for vehicle manufacture.

With the new electric vehicles in addition to horse-drawn wagons, the company continued doing well, building 500 vehicles in 1908 and getting many more orders it couldn't even fill. Worm drive was available by 1912 and bevel gear transmission was also introduced by 1914. Despite patent infringement troubles with Baker Electric, the two companies merged in 1915, trying to improve their standing in the motor vehicle industry in which gasoline-powered vehicles were quickly taking control of the market.

The manufacturer of electric vehicles was now incorporated for $2,500,000 and called the Baker R&L Company, although the cars and some commercial vehicles were popularly known as Baker-Raulang. In 1916 the Baker name disappeared and the Rauch & Lang named returned for all cars. What was most unusual was that tiller steering was available from the back seat, a feature available only from a few electric car builders of the era. The Owen Magnetic was also produced at the Baker R & L factory during World War I, although it was not shipped to Europe for any combat action. As the war ended, about 700 Rauch & Lang electric vehicles were built for 1919.

After the war the company began specializing in coachbuilding for other manufacturers as popularity of electric motive power seriously declined among auto buyers. The one area that still had demand for electric vehicles was in the truck and commercial vehicle field, and a department for such production was set up in 1920. At the same time Ray S. Deering, who had been president of the Stevens-Duryea Company in Chicopee Falls, Massachusetts, bought the passenger car division of Baker R & L, which was reorganized. R&L taxicabs were built by the company beginning in 1923, and both electric and gasoline versions were available.

As demand for electric cars continued to fall precipitously during the 1920s, the company built gasoline-powered taxis until financial woes forced the closing of the manufacturing plant at Chicopee Falls. A prototype of a gasoline-hybrid using a sleeve-valve engine in 1930 was too late to save the company.

Reading-Standard (R-S) (motorcycle)

Beginning in Reading, Pennsylvania, in 1903, the first Reading-Standard motorcycle was a near replica of the Indian motorcycle of 1902, with a single-cylinder Thor 361 cc motor that was integral to the frame, mounted upright under the seat of the diamond-shape bicycle-type frame.

Reading and vicinity had been settled early on before America's Independence, and the Philadelphia & Reading Railroad had been built and incorporated in 1833. Charles Duryea, credited with being one of America's foremost automotive pioneers, had built some of his first vehicles in Reading. Charles Daniels also founded an auto manufacturing company in Reading, building "bespoke" or custom cars there in 1917. The area called Vanity Fair, named in 1911, became a famous clothing producer of Reading.

Meanwhile, the Reading-Standard of 1906 built a side-valve four-cycle motorcycle engine, considered to be the first such design built in the United States. It was built by Charles Gustafson, the chief engineer at R-S, where the first V-Twin arrived in 1908, an

F-head design producing six hp. Paul "Dare-devil" Derkum raced this type of motorcycle in Los Angeles, but R-S did not meet with great success. Gustafson jumped over to Hendee Manufacturing, builders of Indian, where racing was more successful.

By the time World War I was disrupting Europe, R-S offered only two motorcycles in three models: a V-Twin with or without electric lights (Model 17 T and 17 TE, at $275 and $315, respectively), and a single-cylinder model, Model 17 S, for $240. All used side-valve motors, and the 1100 cc V-Twin was rated at 12 hp while the single was rated at 6 hp. In 1917 R-S advertised itself as "The World's Master Motorcycle" and a few were bought by the military for testing. The model line continued into 1918. By 1922 financial troubles in the postwar recession forced R-S into selling out to Cleveland Motorcycles.

Regal

Charles Lambert, J.E. Lambert and Bert Lambert were three brothers who teamed up with engineer Fred W. Haines in Detroit, Michigan, to form the Regal Motor Car Company and begin production of an auto in 1908. Like David Dunbar Buick, the three brothers had made a fortune in the plumbing business and decided to test their luck in motor vehicle manufacturing, which they began with a capital stock of $100,000, also with the help of designer Paul Arthur. A cross-country trek repeated five times from San Francisco to New York in 1909–1910 gained much publicity and the advertisement slogan "the greatest endurance car in the world" after 22,000 miles had been logged with the car still running well and back home in Detroit.

For 1910 an underslung chassis helped sell the Regal "Slugger," as it was dubbed, powered by a four-cylinder motor with pricing from $900 to $1650, the latter on a 123-inch wheelbase. Production continued to rise so that by 1913, 7,500 Regals rolled off the assembly line. Possibly due to its name, the Regal sold very well in Great Britain, although it was also known overseas as the Seabrook Regal Motor Car.

In 1914 a V-8 designed by S.G. Jenks was added to the company's own four-cylinder engine, and capitalization was increased to $3,000,000. However, the shortage of materials that arrived along with World War I put an end to the company in 1918 even though assets of $1,500,000 were more than double the amount of direct liabilities. An entrepreneur named Maurice Rothschild (it is not known if he was related to the family by that

R E G A L
M O T O R C A R
C O M P A N Y

D E T R O I T
M I C H I G A N

REGAL HIGH POWER FOUR TOURING—J

COLOR	Body, blue; running gear, black	BORE AND STROKE	3½ x 4¾ inches
SEATING CAPACITY	Five	LUBRICATION	Force feed and splash
POSITION OF DRIVER	Left side	RADIATOR	Cellular
WHEELBASE	108 inches	COOLING	Thermo-syphon
GAUGE	56 inches	IGNITION	Storage battery
WHEELS	Wood	STARTING SYSTEM	Two unit
FRONT TIRES	30 x 3½ inches,	STARTER OPERATED	Gear to fly wheel
REAR TIRES	30 x 3½ inches, anti-skid	LIGHTING SYSTEM	Electric
		VOLTAGES	Six to seven
		WIRING SYSTEM	Single
SERVICE BRAKE	Contracting on rear wheels	GASOLINE SYSTEM	Vacuum
EMERGENCY BRAKE	Expanding on rear wheels	CLUTCH	Cone
		TRANSMISSION	Selective sliding
CYLINDERS	Four	GEAR CHANGES	Three forward, one reverse
ARRANGED	Vertically		
CAST	En bloc	DRIVE	Plain bevel
HORSEPOWER	19.6	REAR AXLE	Full floating
(N.A.C.C. Rating)		STEERING GEAR	Worm and gear

In addition to above specifications, price includes top, top hood, windshield, speedometer, ammeter, tire pump, electric horn and demountable rims.

name in Europe) bought the Regal company and continued only in repair and parts manufacture, but the Regal as a motor car was finished.

Reo

It must not have been a comfortable situation for a man such as Ransom Eli Olds to quit the company he had founded and upon leaving be told he could not start another auto manufacturing business under his own name. That did not stop him from using his own initials in 1905 and continuing on successfully in Lansing, Michigan. The conflict had been whether or not to continue building the Curved Dash Oldsmobile, which the controlling owners of the Oldsmobile Company wanted to phase out and did so, along with the man who built it.

The New York Auto Show of 1905 had on display the new 16 hp two-cylinder Reo, joined later that year with a one-cylinder model remarkably similar to the curved-dash Oldsmobile. The former went on to successful sales, but the one-cylinder Reo was offered through 1910 almost as if to make a point about the curved-dash car, even though sales of all one-cylinder cars would lag far behind by that time. In any case, Reo soon became equally successful as a company, especially as a four-cylinder model appeared on the market in 1906, the year commercial vehicles were introduced by Reo.

As Oldsmobiles crossed the continent and performed well in the Glidden Tour, an endurance run with possibly the highest press coverage of all such events, Reo took over the number-three level of production after Ford and Buick in 1907. This left Oldsmobile behind until it was absorbed into General Motors. The success of the Ford Model T prompted Ransom Olds to build the 35 hp F-head four-cylinder Reo car of 1909 that sold for $1250. This new edition of the Reo

featured shaft drive, multiple disc clutch, left-hand steering using worm-and-sector steering gear.

The Reo Motor Truck Company was organized in 1910 as a sister company in which Ransom Olds had 51 percent interest. How much real interest Ransom Olds had in trucks could be disputed, but his company built reliable light trucks for many decades, entering heavy truck production in World War II. The Reo Speed Wagon, which appeared in 1915, would be a very popular light truck model also sold as the Hurry Up Wagon, followed by the Power Wagon in 1920. During World War I Reo experimented with light armored cars, which remained in prototype form only, as did every armored car during World War I, with the exception that a few were built in very small numbers that may technically exceed the definition of a prototype.

In 1912 Reo the Fifth arrived, and in advertising Ransom Olds dubbed it "The Car That Marks My Limit." This could have been misconstrued, but it referred to the fact that Ransom Eli Olds wanted this new model to be his "farewell" car, as he himself put it. The main difference was in standardizing the design with central gear control, abandoning the side lever which seemed to have been derived from horse wagon configuration. Ransom Olds shifted his attention to other business interests.

Reo introduced a six-cylinder car in 1916 and offered the "Sheer-Line" body style. During World War I the U.S. military bought Reo trucks for the war effort, and during the war Reo remained lucrative in the private sector as well, building low-priced cars but remaining behind Ford in production numbers. The Hotchkiss replaced the torque tube drive in 1918. For 1919 the Reo factory began building a series of taxis, which remained a profitable new sideline.

By 1920 the T-6 was introduced using a 50

REO TRUCKS
Manufactured by
REO MOTOR CAR CO., Lansing, Mich.

S P E C I F I C A T I O N S

Model	J	F
Capacity	2 tons	¾ ton
Drive	Chain	Spiral bevel
Chassis Price	$1,650	$925
Motor		
H. P. (S.A.E.)	27.2	27.2
Cylinders	4 in pairs	4 in pairs
Bore	4⅛"	4⅛"
Stroke	4½"	4½"
Wheel Base	146"	120"
Tread Front	59"	56"
Tread Rear	63⅞"	56"
Tires Front	36x4"	34x4½" pneu.
Tires Rear	36x3½" dual	34x4½" pneu.

Frame—Channel section, pressed.

Front Axle	Round bar section; yoke type knuckle	I-section—yoke type knuckle
Rear Axle	Fixed, square section	Full-floating

Springs Front—Semi-elliptic.
Springs Rear—Semi-elliptic.
Carburetor—Johnson Model D, 1".
Cooling System—Pump.
Oiling System—Pump, circulated splash.

Ignition	Low tension magneto	Generator

Control—Left drive, center control.
Clutch—Dry multiple disc.
Transmission—Selective, three speeds forward and one reverse.

Brakes	External contracting on jackshafts and rear hubs	External contracting and internal expanding on rear hubs

Steering Gear—Pinion and sector.
Equipment—Model J: Complete equipment, including driver's seat and cab, but without body. Model F: Complete equipment without body, driver's seat, top or windshield.

**REO MOTOR
CAR COMPANY**

**LANSING
MICHIGAN**

Price $1550
Four-Passenger Roadster 1550
Four-Passenger Enclosed Road-
ster 1750

REO TOURING—M

COLOR	Body, golden olive; wheels, brown	LUBRICATION	Pump over and splash
SEATING CAPACITY .	Seven	RADIATOR	Tubular
POSITION OF DRIVER	Left side	COOLING	Water pump
WHEELBASE	126 inches	IGNITION	Storage battery
GAUGE	56 inches	STARTING SYSTEM . .	Two unit
WHEELS	Wood	STARTER OPERATED .	Chain to transmission
FRONT TIRES	34 x 4½ inches		
REAR TIRES	34 x 4½ inches, anti-skid	LIGHTING SYSTEM . .	Electric
		VOLTAGES	Six
SERVICE BRAKE . . .	Contracting on rear wheels	WIRING SYSTEM . . .	Double
EMERGENCY BRAKE .	Expanding on rear wheels	GASOLINE SYSTEM . .	Vacuum
		CLUTCH	Dry multiple disc
CYLINDERS	Six	TRANSMISSION . . .	Selective sliding
ARRANGED	Vertically	GEAR CHANGES . . .	Three forward, one reverse
CAST	In threes		
HORSEPOWER	30.4 (N.A.C.C. Rating)	DRIVE	Spiral bevel
		REAR AXLE	Full floating
BORE AND STROKE .	$3\frac{9}{16}$ x 5⅛ inches	STEERING GEAR . . .	Pinion and sector

In addition to above specifications, price includes top, top hood, windshield,
speedometer, ammeter, tire pump, electric horn and demountable rims.

hp F-head six-cylinder motor, and all Reos were built on a 120-inch wheelbase. The Reo Flying Cloud arrived in 1927. The interconnecting clutch-brake with no hand brake was Ransom Olds's special invention but was complicated, unpopular, and dropped by 1926. The Flying Cloud featured styling by Fabio Segardi, and by this time the model had Lockheed hydraulic brakes on all four wheels. The Wolverine was a lower-priced phenomenon that lasted only through 1928.

After the stock market crash, plans and tooling had already been completed for the Reo Royale, which appeared for 1931. It had a nine-main-bearing straight-eight motor and body styling by Amos Northup set on a wheelbase up to 135 inches in length. By 1934 the company was in such dire financial straits Olds gave up control and plans were made to merge with various luxury car makers. Plans and squabbles aside, Reo could not go forward on talk alone, and 1936 would be its last year of manufacture of passenger cars. Ransom Olds was 70 years old and resigned when his company board and executives decided to go exclusively into truck manufacturing. This they continued through World War II and up to 1967, when Reo merged with Diamond T, becoming Diamond Reo. Ransom Eli Olds died in 1950.

Republic

Not related to the Republic Motor Car Company of Hamilton, Ohio, which overlapped in time but did not build trucks, the Alma Motor Truck Company of Alma, Michigan, was the enterprise that first built Republic trucks beginning in 1912. Starting with ¾-ton conventional assembled trucks, the company was reorganized as the Republic Motor Truck Company in 1914.

By the time America entered World War I, Republic trucks featured Torbensen internal gear drive with models ranging from ¾-ton to 3½-ton capacity. During this period Re-

public was building 10,000 trucks a year, and William Crapo Durant invested in the firm, so that with U.S. military contracts, 30,000 Republic trucks rolled off the assembly line in 1918. Republic trucks for the civilian market were distinguished by their yellow chassis and body and cab colors that were intended to make heads turn.

By 1920 some 70,000 Republic trucks had been sold since 1914. Lycoming and Waukesha engines were adopted through the 1920s. Republic also built bus chassis up to 185-inch wheelbase powered by four-cylinder Lycoming engines. The most popular Republic chassis bus was the 15-passenger at a time when narrow bodies precluded wide seating arrangements and there were 43 different bus chassis on the market. Most of them were from truck builders that offered both bus and truck chassis.

Eaton and Timken worm drive gradually replaced the Torbensen drive in the mid–1920s at Republic. In the second half of the decade, trucks were built with up to 5-ton capacity and bus chassis were for 16, 20, 26 and 32 passengers. By 1927 Republic offered eight truck models and introduced six-cylinder engines, following market trend.

In 1928 Republic bought Linn Manufacturing Corporation, which continued to build half-tracks for construction work under their own name. In 1929 Republic merged with the commercial division of American LaFrance, which continued to build a few trucks under the LaFrance-Republic name through the 1930s with 14 models using the hyphenated name for 1931. This was the year the 240 hp American LaFrance V-12 motor was introduced, which was quite desirable during the 1930s for trucks and fire engines. In 1932 the factory at Alma was shut down but production continued at American La–France. Sterling badge engineered some Republic trucks until the end of production in World War II.

REPUBLIC TRUCKS
Manufactured by
REPUBLIC MOTOR TRUCK CO., Inc., Alma, Mich.

S P E C I F I C A T I O N S

Model	9	10	11	A
Capacity	¾ ton	1 ton	1½ tons	2 tons
Drive	Internal gear	Internal gear	Internal gear	Internal gear
Chassis Price	$750 with express body	$1,095 express or stake body	$1,275	$1,675
Motor				
H. P. (S.A.E.)	16.9	19.6	22.5	27.25
H. P. (Actual)	25 at 1000 R.P.M.	28 at 1000 R.P.M.	32 at 1000 R.P.M.	40 at 1000 R.P.M.
Cylinders	4 en bloc	4 en bloc	4 en bloc	4 en bloc
Bore	3¼″	3½″	3¾″	4½″
Stroke	5″	5″	5″	5½″
Wheel Base	110″	124″	144″	144″
Tread Front	56″	56″	56″	56″
Tread Rear	56″	56″	56″	56″
Tires Front	32x4″ pneu.	34x3″	34x3½″	34x4″
Tires Rear	32x4″ pneu.	34x4″	34x5″	34x6″

Frame—Pressed steel, U type.
Front Axle—I-beam, drop forged.
Rear Axle—Solid I-beam.
Springs Front—Semi-elliptic.
Springs Rear—Semi-elliptic.

Carburetor	Marvel	Stromberg	Stromberg	Stromberg
Cooling System	Thermo	Thermo	Thermo	Pump

Oiling System—Splash and force.
Ignition—Bosch.
Control—Left drive, center control.
Clutch—Dry plate.
Transmission—Selective, three speeds forward and one reverse.
Brakes—Expanding and contracting on transmission.
Steering Gear—Worm and nut.
Equipment—Model 9: Express body, canopy top, windshield, generator, battery, electric lights, tools, electric horn. All other models: tools, oil lamps, head and rear, except No. 10, on which is furnished express or stake body and bow top.

Riker

Andrew Lawrence Riker made a name for himself as a motor vehicle engineer at Locomobile in Bridgeport, Connecticut, after he was hired there in 1902 to design a steam automobile. Locomobile and Riker soon switched to gasoline power and began building one of, if not the most, luxurious car in America. A Vanderbilt first-place win in 1908 proved the car's performance as well, in addition to other excellent placings in endurance runs and races.

By 1916 his successful designs earned him a place in history when the company named all trucks Riker. Riker trucks were built from 1916 through 1921. When Pancho Villa attacked Columbus, New Mexico, in March of 1916, the Army Quartermaster Corps relied on Andrew Riker to design and implement an interchangeable wheel assembly for trucks which used railroad wheels for rapid deployment of vehicles using the tracks along the border where Villa had escaped with his men.

Because Locomobile was considered one of the more luxurious motor cars in America, it followed that Riker trucks were of high quality and equally reliable. Riker trucks used notable bronze castings for transmissions and engine components. Both 3-ton and 4-ton models powered by a Locomobile four-cylinder T-head engine and four-speed transmission on a 150-inch wheelbase were offered through World War I. Prices started at $4600 for the lighter truck in 1918.

Locomobile went into receivership after World War I when the market fell for luxury cars as the postwar recession took its toll. Reorganized under Hare's Motors, Riker trucks lasted as an entity only until 1921. When William Crapo Durant, who was head of General Motors, bought Locomobile the truck division was discontinued.

Roamer

Yet another company that began as World War I was already exploding in Europe was one started by Cloyd Y. Kenworthy, who took his chauffeur's suggestion and called his new car the Roamer. It was a clever name for a car, akin to the Rambler, but it had a much greater significance at the time because it was the name of a then-famous racehorse.

Kenworthy was a distributor in New York for the Rauch & Lang electric car and saw the future in gasoline-powered vehicles. His partners were Karl H. Martin and Albert C. Barley of Wasp and Halladay cars fame, respectively. The Roamer first appeared in 1916. In appearance it was unquestionably a copy of the Rolls Royce, especially in its radiator grille and front clip treatment.

In 1917 the company moved to Kalamazoo, Michigan, from Streator, Illinois. One of the models was powered by a Duesenberg six-cylinder engine from 1918 until 1924, while other models were powered by Lycoming and Continental engines.

"America's Smartest Car" was the company slogan, and whether or not it was true, the Roamer was always a stylish car with sporty lines and a good reputation. During the war only 1500 cars per year were built due to material shortages and market slump. As the market greatly improved in the early 1920s after the postwar recession, Roamer's sales improved once again. A new record set by a Rochester-Duesenberg-powered Roamer in 1921 helped sales. It was driven by L.F. Goodspeed, company chief engineer at the time. It was the fastest unofficial speed of 105.08 mph for a stock chassis car at Daytona Beach.

As an assembled car the Roamer was in the $3000 range, which was considered expensive. Some Canadian investors tried to help the company with additional capital, and some celebrities such as Mary Pickford and Buster Keaton owned Roamers, but even

RIKER TRUCKS

Manufactured by

LOCOMOBILE COMPANY OF AMERICA, Bridgeport, Conn.

Model	B	BB
Capacity	3 tons	4 tons
Drive	Worm	Worm
Chassis Weight	6,850 lbs.	7,100 lbs.
Chassis Price	$3,900 subject to change	$4,050 subject to change
Engine	Riker	Riker
H. P. (S.A.E.)	28.9	28.9
H. P. (Actual)	44	44
Cylinders	4 in pairs	4 in pairs
Bore	$4\frac{1}{4}''$	$4\frac{1}{4}''$
Stroke	6"	6"
Wheel Base	Std. 150"—170"—190"	Std. 150"—170"—190"
Tread Front	60"	60"
Tread Rear	66"	66"
Tires Front	36x5"	36x5"
Tires Rear	36x6" dual	36x6" dual

Frame—Pressed.
Front Axle—I inverted yoke.
Rear Axle—Riker floating.
Springs Front—Semi-elliptic.
Springs Rear—Semi-elliptic.
Carburetor—Ball (Riker Model).
Cooling System—Pump.
Oiling System—Splash and force.
Ignition—Magneto.
Control—Right.
Clutch—Cone.
Transmission—Riker Selective, 4 speeds.
Brakes—Running Contracting on propeller shaft. Emergency, Expanding on rear wheels.
Steering Gear—Screw and nut.
Equipment—Kerosene side and tail lights, hand horn, full set of tools including jack and instruction books, oiling diagram, etc. Spare valve, spark plug; radiator apron and governor.

B A R L E Y
MOTOR   CAR
C O M P A N Y

K A L A M A Z O O
M I C H I G A N

ROAMER TOURING—D-4-75

COLOR	Optional	LUBRICATION	Force feed and splash
SEATING CAPACITY	Four or seven	RADIATOR	Cellular
POSITION OF DRIVER	Left side	COOLING	Water pump
WHEELBASE	128 inches	IGNITION	High tension magneto
GAUGE	56 inches		
WHEELS	Wire	STARTING SYSTEM	Two unit
FRONT TIRES	32 x 4½ inches	STARTER OPERATED	Gear to fly wheel
REAR TIRES	32 x 4½ inches	LIGHTING SYSTEM	Electric
SERVICE BRAKE	Expanding under wheels	VOLTAGES	Six
		WIRING SYSTEM	Single
EMERGENCY BRAKE	Expanding on rear wheels	GASOLINE SYSTEM	Vacuum
		CLUTCH	Dry plate
CYLINDERS	Four	TRANSMISSION	Selective sliding
ARRANGED	Vertically	GEAR CHANGES	Three forward, one reverse
CAST	En bloc		
HORSEPOWER	25.6 (N.A.C.C. Rating)	DRIVE	Spiral bevel
		REAR AXLE	Three-quarters floating
BORE AND STROKE	4 x 6 inches	STEERING GEAR	Screw and nut

In addition to above specifications, price includes top, top hood, windshield, speedometer, ammeter, voltmeter, clock, tire pump, electric horn and extra wire wheel.

before the stock market crash the Roamer was in dire trouble financially. A few were built for model year 1930 before the factory doors were closed permanently.

Rowe

This company was named after Samuel D. Rowe in Waynesboro, Pennsylvania, when the inventor founded the Rowe Motor Company in 1908. Rowe's motor design involved an unusual air-cooled five-cylinder configuration which he installed in a car of his own fabrication but never marketed. He abandoned the effort but returned to the auto industry in 1910, however unsuccessfully. It wasn't until he moved to Coatesville, Pennsylvania, and began to build trucks that he was able to get financially on track.

The first Rowe trucks were powered by a 25 hp five-cylinder water-cooled motor derived from an earlier design. It is unclear what benefits the five-cylinder configuration actually had, but engine vibration may have been one of the elements that were being rectified with this design, and in-line five-cylinder engines (aside from radial engines) were to return decades later at Audi.

Whether or not Rowe's five-cylinder motor was a success is not certain, but all other trucks built afterwards by Rowe were four-cylinder units. In any case, "Rowe Runs Right" was the company slogan. Rowe built trucks up to five-ton capacity and used four-speed transmissions, and just as World War I began the company adopted Wisconsin four-cylinder engines.

In 1917 Rowe moved to Dowington, Pennsylvania, and then to Lancaster in 1918. "Air bag" suspension was used and Rowe built several fire engines. But 1925 was the last year of production as Rowe could not stay competitive. It has been estimated that from 1912 to 1925 a total of 4,500 Rowe trucks and fire engines were built.

Sandow

As nations declared war on each other in Europe, a new truck manufacturer emerged in Chicago, Illinois, by the name of the Sandow Motor Truck Company. This was yet another company which tried to fill the local market of the vibrant, industrialized Great Lake states and Midwest at a time when dozens of entrepreneurs saw the potential of making money by assembling commercial vehicles which did not have to be grandly styled or have great performance but be simply reliable and at the right price.

Sandow survived World War I building trucks with dual chain drive and worm drive from 1½-ton capacity to 3-ton capacity. As with most small commercial vehicle manufacturers, such things as electric lighting and starting were optional. The Sandow tried to distinguish itself with heavy iron bars over the radiator that resembled a fireplace grille using a large casting that had letters as a simple emblem. Fuller clutches and transmissions were adopted. Front axles were from Sheldon and rear axles were from Timken. Tires were solid rubber as standard equipment. Chassis price was $1895 for the 1½-ton model. The 2-ton model used a Hercules motor while the 2½-ton was powered by a Buda engine.

By 1925 Sandow also built a 5-ton model powered by a 32.4 hp four-cylinder Buda engine with a Brown-Lipe transmission. All in all, the company used a mix-and-match philosophy of design most likely adjusting to customers' demands, and in this way stayed ahead of the competition. The 5-ton Model L had a 175-inch wheelbase, so Sandow did not compete with the light truck builders such as Ford, Chevrolet or Dodge. But whether or not the competition was brisk, by 1928, even before the crisis on Wall Street, Sandow was out of business.

ROWE TRUCKS

Manufactured by

ROWE MOTOR MFG. CO., E. Downingtown, Pa.

Model	CDW	CDW	DEW	FW
Capacity	2 tons	2½ tons	3½ tons	5 tons
Drive	Worm	Worm	Worm	Worm
Chassis Price	$2,800	$3,000	$3,400	$4,500
Engine	Wisconsin	Wisconsin	Wisconsin	Wisconsin
H. P. (S.A.E.)	32	32	40	48
H. P. (Actual)	52 at 1400 R.P.M.	52 at 1400 R.P.M.	45 at 1400 R.P.M.	57 at 1400 R.P.M.
Cylinders	4 en bloc	4 en bloc	4 en bloc	4 in pairs
Bore	4″	4″	4″	4¾″
Stroke	5″	5″	6″	5½″
Wheel Base	142″	164″	156″	171″
Tread Front	58″	62″	62″	68″
Tread Rear	58″	62″	62″	68″
Tires Front	34x4″	34x4″	36x5″	36x6″
Tires Rear	36x6″ or 36x3½″ dual	36x7″ or 36x4″ dual	36x5″ dual	40x6″ dual
Frame	6″ built up	6″ built up	7″ built up	8″ built up
Front Axle—I-beam.				
Rear Axle	Sheldon or Timken full-floating	Sheldon or Timken semi-floating	Sheldon or Timken full-floating	Sheldon or Timken full-floating

Springs Front—Semi-elliptic.
Springs Rear—Semi-elliptic.
Carburetor—Ray-Zenith.
Cooling System—Pump.
Oiling System—Force.
Ignition—Bosch, High Tension.
Control—Left drive, center control.
Clutch—Multiple disc.
Transmission—Brown-Lipe Selective, four speeds forward and one reverse.
Brakes—Rabestos 2 steel—rear, internal expanding.
Steering Gear—Irreversible worm and nut.
Equipment—Vibrating horn, tool kit, jack, bonnet wrench, hub wrench and governor.

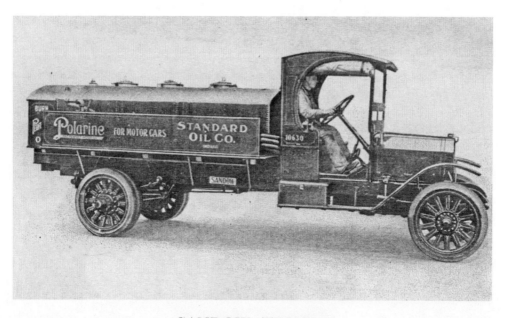

SANDOW TRUCKS

Manufactured by

SANDOW MOTOR TRUCK CO., 3333 W. Grand Ave., Chicago, Ill.

Model	A	B	D	E
Capacity	1 ton	1½ tons	2 tons	3½ tons
Drive	Worm	Worm	Worm	Worm
Chassis Weight	2,850 lbs.	3,300 lbs.	4,400 lbs.	6,000 lbs.
Chassis Price	$1,485	$1,985	$2,650	$3,750
Engine	Continental	Continental	Continental	Continental
H. P. (S.A.E.)	19.5	19.5	27.5	32.4
H. P. (Actual)	34 at 2000 R.P.M.	34 at 2000 R.P.M.	40 at 1500 R.P.M.	45 at 1500 R.P.M.
Cylinders	4 en bloc	4 en bloc	4 en bloc	4 in pairs
Bore	3½″	3½″	4⅛″	4½″
Stroke	5″	5″	5¼″	5¼″
Wheel Base	120″	138″	165″	175″
Tread Front	55⅝″	56″	58½″	63½″
Tread Rear	57″	62″	58½″	64¾″
Tires Front	31x4″ pneu.	34x4″	36x4″	36x5″
Tires Rear	34x4″	34x5″	36x6″	36x5″ dual
Frame	Pressed	Pressed	Pressed	Structural
Front Axle	I bed forged, double lever, base pin	I bed forged, double lever, base pin	I-beam, ball	I-beam, ball
Rear Axle	Sheldon semi-floating	Sheldon semi-floating	Timken full-floating	Timken full-floating

Springs Front—Semi-elliptic.
Springs Rear—Semi-elliptic.
Carburetor—Stromberg.

Cooling System	Thermo-syphon	Thermo-syphon	Pump	Pump
Oiling System—Force and splash.		Force and splash	Pump	Pump
Ignition	Eisemann Magneto	Eisemann Magneto	Bosch Magneto	Bosch Magneto
Control	Left and center	Left and center	Right and center	Right and center
Clutch—Dry plate.				
Transmission	Fuller Selective, three speeds	Fuller Selective, three speeds	Brown-Lipe Selective, three speeds	Brown-Lipe Selective, three speeds

Brakes—Internal, rear wheels.
Steering Gear—Worm.
Equipment—Oil lamp, tools and jack.

Sanford

The Sanford-Herbert Company of Syracuse, New York, began building trucks by the combined name of Sanbert in 1911. The Model J of that year was 1-ton capacity and was priced at $1500. A two-cycle two-cylinder horizontally-opposed motor was mounted under the seat. A two-speed planetary transmission was employed, as was dual chain drive.

A four-cylinder motor was adopted for 1913, and a 1½-ton model was added. Also, a three-speed transmission was adopted, modernizing the Sanbert considerably, although the engine-under-seat layout was continued. This was the year a reorganization of the company resulted in its name's being changed to the Sanford Motor Truck Company.

For 1916 the company built five models from ¾-ton to 2-ton capacity. The engine was mounted ahead of the driver in the so-called conventional position, and worm drive was also adopted. By 1918 the heaviest Sanford truck was the 5-ton Model W-50.

All Sanford trucks were powered by Continental engines by this time. These were bought from Continental Motor Company in Detroit, Michigan. Anyone wishing to build a car or truck had several choices from which to choose when it came to proprietary engines in addition to Continental, including: Buda from Harvey, Illinois; Golden, Belnap & Swartz from Detroit, Michigan; Hercules from Canton, Ohio; Hinkley from Detroit, Michigan; Herschell-Spillman from North Tonawanda, New York; Hall-Scott from Berkeley, California; Lycoming from Williamsport, Pennsylvania; Waukesha from Waukesha, Wisconsin; and Wisconsin engines from Milwaukee, Wisconsin.

Sanford introduced a 1½-ton "speed truck" called the Greyhound in 1923. A bus chassis was also built at this time, although it was discontinued almost immediately. For 1924 six-cylinder engines were adopted for part of the company's truck line. Spiral bevel gear was adopted in 1926, and Sanford's business increasingly relied on production fire trucks. In 1929 pumpers capable of delivering from 350 to 750 gallons per minute were built, and the company survived the early 1930s. However, by 1937 production had faded out entirely. The Sanford make was revived in 1969 in order to build fire apparatus, but by 1989 the company faded out again.

Saurer

It should be noted that Saurer motor vehicles were first designed and built beginning in 1903 in French-speaking Arbon, Switzerland, located on the shores of Lake Constance. The make of Saurer began to be imported into the United States in 1908, which was also the year that Saurer began applying and developing the diesel engine in Europe under the supervision of Rudolf Diesel himself and the Safir Company in Zurich, Switzerland.

Since the use of the diesel engine in America arrived much later, it is appropriate to note here (since there is no other discussion on the subject in this book) that this type of internal combustion motor was invented in Germany by Rudolf Diesel in 1892. The primary difference between the gasoline engine and the diesel engine is that the latter uses high compression for ignition (involving a glow plug for starting) rather than a spark plug needed for each combustion, and the lesser-refined diesel fuel, which is a more crude type of petroleum distillate, is injected at the final stage of compression.

Rudolf Diesel showed his working motor at the 1900 Paris Exposition and the 1911 Paris World's Fair. Just before the beginning of World War I Rudolf Diesel was preparing to show and most likely sell the manufacturing rights of the motor to the British. During the voyage across the Channel, Diesel disappeared

SANFORD TRUCKS

Manufactured by

SANFORD MOTOR TRUCK CO., Syracuse, N. Y.

Model	W-25	W-35	W-50
Capacity	2½ tons	3½ tons	5 tons
Drive	Worm	Worm	Worm
Chassis Weight	5,500 lbs.	6,900 lbs.	7,600 lbs.
Chassis Price	$2,900	$3,600	$4,600
Engine	Continental	Continental	Continental
H. P. (S.A.E.)	27.2	32.4	32.4
H. P. (Actual)	27.2	37	37
Cylinders	4 en bloc	4 in pairs	4 in pairs
Bore	4⅛"	4½"	4½"
Stroke	5¼"	5½"	5½"
Wheel Base	156"	174"	174"
Tread Front	58"	62"	62"
Tread Rear	62"	66"	74⅜"
Tires Front	36x4"	36x5"	36x5"
Tires Rear	36x4" dual	36x5" dual	40x6" dual

Frame—Pressed steel.

Front Axle—Elliott type.

Rear Axle—Sheldon semi-floating.

Springs Front—Semi-elliptic.

Springs Rear—Semi-elliptic.

Carburetor—Stromberg.

Cooling System—Pump.

Oiling System—Circulating splash.

Ignition—Bosch.

Control—Left-hand drive, center control.

Clutch—Dry plate.

Transmission—Warner Selective, four speeds forward and one reverse.

Brakes—Rear wheels, internal.

Steering Gear—Worm and nut.

Equipment—Cab, curtains, horn, two side lamps, one tail lamp, tool box, tools, jack and bumper.

SAURER TRUCKS
Manufactured by
INTERNATIONAL MOTOR CO., New York, N. Y.
64th St. and West End Ave.

Model	L	M
Capacity	5 tons	6½ tons
Drive	Chain	Chain
Chassis Weight	5,900 lbs.	6,900 lbs.
Chassis Price	$4,800	$5,800
Engine	Saurer	Saurer
H. P. (S.A.E.)	30.6	30.6
H. P. (Actual)	37	37
Cylinders	4 in pairs	4 in pairs
Bore	4⅜″	4⅜″
Stroke	5½″	5¼″
Wheel Base	153½″	156¼″
Tread Front	66¼″	66¼″
Tread Rear	66¼″	66¼″
Tires Front	36x5″	36x5″
Tires Rear	42x5″ dual	42x6″ dual

Frame—Pressed steel.
Front Axle—Rectangular yoke on knuckle.
Rear Axle—International Motor Co., fixed.
Springs Front—Semi-elliptic.
Springs Rear—Semi-elliptic.
Carburetor—Saurer.
Cooling System—Pump.
Oiling System—Forced feed.
Ignition—High tension magneto.
Control—Right drive, right control.
Clutch—Cone.
Transmission—International Motor Co. selective, four speeds.
Brakes—Differential contracting, emergency expanding on rear wheels, air brake operated from throttle.
Steering Gear—Worm sector.
Equipment—Extra.

overboard on September 30, 1913, and his body was never found. Diesel engines were used extensively in German submarines subsequently.

Meanwhile, after being assembled by the Quincy, Manchester and Sergent Company in 1909, by 1911 the so-called American Saurer, identical to those vehicles built in France in the form of 4-ton trucks, were now assembled in Plainfield, New Jersey. That same year, when the International Motor Company was formed, Saurer became one of the trucks marketed by this company along with Hewitt and Mack trucks. The Hewitt truck division was sold in 1912 and production ceased in 1914. American Saurer built 5-ton and 6½-ton trucks in 1918, but later that year the make was discontinued. Saurer remained as a company in France until its demise in 1956.

Saxon

Hugh Chalmers, who had built the Chalmers-Detroit in 1908, had been a well-paid executive in the National Cash Register Company. When he decided in 1907 to back auto manufacturers, and motor vehicle development was the latest in industry trends, he would also become the founder of the Saxon Motor Car Company in Detroit, Michigan.

Hiring his Chalmers advertising manager, Harry W. Ford, he began building the Saxon in series December of 1913 with 3000 produced by March of 1914. The Saxon appeared to be another cyclecar during a fad of the period, but upon closer inspection the vehicle turned out to be much more substantial than that. It was powered by a four-cylinder water-cooled Ferro engine (most cyclecars had two-cylinder engines which were often air-cooled) had shaft drive (as opposed to chain drive) and a selective sliding gear transmission (instead of planetary type).

The year 1914 was also the year that Saxon began building a Delivery Car directly based on its passenger car. A Saxon was used in a publicity stunt to christen the Lincoln Highway that crossed the continent in 1914. In 1915 Harry Ford bought out Chalmers's interest and reorganized the company as the Saxon Motor Car Corporation with a move to another factory, which was the former assembly location of the Abbot car in Detroit.

By 1916 Saxon was building 24,000 cars per year. As the U.S. entered the war, Saxon hits its peak production of 28,000 for 1917, all of them six-cylinder cars. Harry Ford died the following year and Benjamin Gotfredson took the helm, but material shortages allowed for only 3425 Saxons to be built for the year. For 1921 an overhead valve four-cylinder engine was introduced, with the six-cylinder motor being discontinued in 1921. C.A. Pfeffer took over as president in 1919 and reorganization took place in 1921. The factory was moved to Ypsilanti, Michigan, but it was too late. Bankruptcy followed in 1922.

Schacht

As with so many of the earliest motor vehicle manufacturers, Schacht built both passenger cars and commercial vehicles. The Schacht Manufacturing Company, builder of horse buggies, was headed by Gustav A. Schacht and assisted by his brother William Schacht. They started building autos in Cincinnati, Ohio, during 1904. The first Schacht was a two-cylinder runabout, joined by a four-cylinder touring car in 1905. Seemingly going backwards in design, Schacht began building only highwheelers in 1907 through 1910, somewhat similar to the highwheelers built by International in Chicago.

By 1909 commercial vehicles began to be built by Schacht in the form of the "Three Purpose Car," which referred to a runabout, family car and delivery car converted from one single vehicle. This was the year the company changed its name to the Schacht Motor Car

SAXON
MOTOR CAR
CORPORATION

DETROIT
MICHIGAN

Price	$ 935
Sedan	1395
Chummy Roadster	935

SAXON SIX TOURING

COLOR	Body, Richelieu blue; wheels, cream; running gear, black	BORE AND STROKE	.	$2\frac{7}{8} \times 4\frac{1}{2}$ inches
		LUBRICATION		Splash with circulating pump
SEATING CAPACITY. .	Five	RADIATOR		Cellular
POSITION OF DRIVER .	Left side	COOLING		Thermo-syphon
WHEELBASE	112 inches	IGNITION		Storage battery
GAUGE	56 inches	STARTING SYSTEM . .		Two unit
WHEELS	Wood	STARTER OPERATED .		Gear to fly wheel
FRONT TIRES	32 x 3½ inches	LIGHTING SYSTEM . .		Electric
REAR TIRES	32 x 3½ inches, anti-skid	VOLTAGES		Six
		WIRING SYSTEM . . .		Double
SERVICE BRAKE . . .	Contracting on rear wheels	GASOLINE SYSTEM . .		Gravity
		CLUTCH		Dry plate
EMERGENCY BRAKE .	Expanding on rear wheels	TRANSMISSION . . .		Selective sliding
		GEAR CHANGES . . .		Three forward, one reverse
CYLINDERS	Six			
ARRANGED.	Vertically	DRIVE		Spiral bevel
CAST	En bloc	REAR AXLE		Semi-floating
HORSEPOWER . . . . (N.A.C.C. Rating)	19.84	STEERING GEAR . . .		Worm and gear

In addition to above specifications, price includes top, top hood, windshield, speedometer, ammeter, electric horn and demountable rims.

G. A. SCHACHT TRUCKS
Manufactured by
THE G. A. SCHACHT MOTOR TRUCK CO., Cincinnati, Ohio
Gest and Evans Streets

Model	2	2½	3½	5
Capacity	2 tons	2½ tons	3½ tons	5 tons
Drive	Worm	Worm	Worm	Worm
Chassis Weight	4,800 lbs.	5,300 lbs.	6,000 lbs.	8,000 lbs.
Chassis Price	$2,950	$3,300	$3,700	$4,700
Engine	Buda	Buda	Buda	Buda
H. P. (S.A.E.)	28.90	28.90	28.90	28.90
H. P. (Actual)	35	35	35	40
Cylinders	4 en bloc	4 en bloc	4 en bloc	4 en bloc
Bore	4¼″	4¼″	4¼″	4¼″
Stroke	5½″	5½″	5½″	5½″
Wheel Base	144″	156″	168″	168″
Tread Front	62″	62″	62″	66″
Tread Rear	64″	64″	64″	68″
Tires Front	36x3½″	36x4″	36x5″	36x5″
Tires Rear	36x6″	36x4″ dual	36x5″ dual	40x6″ dual
Frame	5″ channel steel	6″ channel steel	6″ channel steel	7″ channel steel

Front Axle—I-beam.
Rear Axle—Schacht full floating, round.
Springs Front—Semi-elliptic.
Springs Rear—Semi-elliptic.
Carburetor—Schebler L.
Cooling System—Water with pump.

Oiling System	Splash pressure	Splash pressure	Splash pressure	Force feed and splash

Ignition—Single system—high tension.
Control—Left hand drive, center control.
Clutch—Cone, leather facing with auxiliary springs.
Transmission—Schacht Selective, three speeds forward and one reverse.

Brakes	Internal and external on rear wheels	Internal and external on rear wheels	Internal and external on rear wheels	Internal on rear axle, external on propeller shaft

Steering Gear—Worm.
Equipment—Two oil side lamps, one oil tail lamp, hubodometer, horn, jack, set of tools and governor.

Company, and after building some 8000 autos, the company's name was changed once again to the G.A. Schacht Motor Truck Company in 1913.

From then on only trucks were built. The model line ranged from ½-ton to 4-ton capacity and all were powered by Continental or Wisconsin four-cylinder motors. Hard rubber tires were used exclusively, and the model line included trucks up to 5-ton capacity by 1918.

The company survived the war and postwar recession but narrowed its model line from 2-ton to 4-ton capacity by 1922. Schacht was large enough that it built its own transmissions, axles and many components so it was not considered just an assembler of vehicles. However, some models were purely assembled trucks by 1925, using Fuller clutch and transmission and Shuler front and Wisconsin rear axles.

For 1926 Shacht introduced the Super Safety Coach, which was similar to the Fageol and the Kenworth of the time. The Schacht bus was powered by a six-cylinder motor and used an eight-speed transmission for highway and cross-country work. In 1927 the company merged with LeBlond, becoming the LeBlond-Schacht Truck Company. The next year Armleder Truck Company was absorbed by Schacht, although Armleder trucks continued to be built for eight more years. With power in numbers the company survived into the Depression until 1938.

Scripps-Booth

James Scripps-Booth had money from his newspaper publishing family and became interested in pioneering automobile design. His first effort was in 1912 called the Bi-Autogo. It was a three-seat vehicle with two auxiliary wheels that folded down below 20 mph, making it a combination motorcycle and motor car that could reach 75 mph. It was powered

by an L-head V-8 motor, which predated the V-8 at Cadillac by three years. It also had a compressed air starter and a four-speed transmission. In addition, the hood was covered with 450 feet of copper tubing for use as a radiator. The experimental vehicle made the news but would not be suitable for mass production. The next Scripps-Booth vehicle would be.

The Scripps-Booth Rocket, built in Detroit, Michigan, was a tandem-seat cyclecar that appeared in 1914. A fuel tank at the front resembled a rocket tip, and the prototype was driven from the back seat, which was rearranged for production with front-seat steering. This was not the only car with rear-seat steering, but the others were usually electric cars such as those built by Rauch-Lang. A V-2 air-cooled Spacke motor powered the cyclecar using a planetary transmission and chain drive. The Rocket was priced at $385 and a delivery version called the Packet cost $395. About 400 of these vehicles were built before production ceased in 1914.

That same year the Scripps-Booth Company was formed by James, using his uncle Will Scripps as financier and hiring William B. Stout as designer, the latter who had experience building the Imp cyclecar. James Scripps-Booth had the idea to build a "luxurious light car," and production started in 1915. This was a staggered-seat design for three using a step-down frame, and was called the Model C. A four-cylinder overhead-valve Sterling motor using shaft drive powered the car. A torpedo back, Houk wire wheels and silver radiator shell gave an elegant look to the car that sold for $775. Celebrities such as Reggie Vanderbilt, the King of Spain, the Queen of Holland and Winston Churchill all bought one. A roadster prototype called the Vitesse was powered by a Ferro V-8 motor which gave the car a top speed of 75 mph, but the car was not placed into production.

Instead, the Model D was produced in

SCRIPPS-BOOTH CORPORATION

DETROIT
MICHIGAN

Price $1195
Five-Passenger Touring 1195

SCRIPPS-BOOTH ROADSTER—SIX-40

COLOR	Body, silk green		BORE AND STROKE .	$2\frac{13}{16}$ x $4\frac{3}{4}$ inches
SEATING CAPACITY. .	Three		LUBRICATION	Full force feed
POSITION OF DRIVER .	Left side		RADIATOR	Cellular
WHEELBASE	112 inches		COOLING	Water pump
GAUGE	56 inches		IGNITION	Storage battery
WHEELS	Wood		STARTING SYSTEM . .	Two unit
FRONT TIRES	32 x 4 inches		STARTER OPERATED .	Gear to fly wheel
REAR TIRES	32 x 4 inches, anti-skid		LIGHTING SYSTEM . .	Electric
			VOLTAGES	Six
SERVICE BRAKE . . .	Contracting on rear wheels		WIRING SYSTEM . . .	Single
			GASOLINE SYSTEM . .	Vacuum
EMERGENCY BRAKE .	Expanding on rear wheels		CLUTCH	Cone
			TRANSMISSION . . .	Selective sliding
CYLINDERS	Six		GEAR CHANGES . . .	Three forward, one reverse
ARRANGED	Horizontally			
CAST	En bloc		DRIVE	Plain bevel
HORSEPOWER	19		REAR AXLE	Full floating
(N.A.C.C. Rating)			STEERING GEAR . . .	Screw and nut

In addition to above specifications, price includes top, top hood, windshield, speed-ometer, ammeter, voltmeter, tire pump, electric horn and demountable rims.

Roadster, Coupe and Town Car iterations with the V-8 motor for 1916, with only the Roadster remaining for 1917. The Sterling Motor Company was purchased that year and Scripps-Booth stock went public. But the four-cylinder Model C was having major reliability problems with epithets such as "Scrapps-Bolts" and "Slips-Loose" being bandied about and quoted in the press. The Model G of 1917 used a Chevrolet 490 engine instead of the Sterling motor.

By this time William Durant bought out Scripps-Booth and installed Buick executive A.H. Sarver as president, moving James Scripps-Booth further away from decision making. By 1921 Durant was ousted from General Motors once again, and as Alfred Sloan took over GM, Scripps-Booth was discontinued as a make by the following year.

Selden

On November 5, 1895, the U.S. Patent Office granted George B. Selden a patent on all automobiles. It would lead to one of the largest and most far-reaching litigations in the American automotive industry. Once having obtained the patent, George Selden was in the position of obtaining licensing fees or denying licensing altogether in the United States. His patent was not recognized in Europe, where the Otto internal combustion engine had already been patented and motor vehicles were already being produced.

It was Henry Ford's challenge to the patent, after being rejected for a license, that made history, and his winning the lawsuit on appeal in 1912 meant a monopoly was broken. It was even more significant in that by 1903, when Ford began fighting the Association of Licensed Automobile Manufacturers (A.L.A.M.), the electric vehicle and battery industry (Electric Vehicle Company in particular) was in possession of the Selden patent, limiting and preventing free competition in the market-

place. The fact that Ford was using a four-cycle motor did not invalidate the Selden patent, which relied on the Otto two-cycle motor, but the patent was deemed unenforceable by the judge presiding over the case.

While the court case dragged on, Selden himself got into auto and truck manufacturing. He hired E.T. Birdsall after incorporating the Selden Motor Vehicle Company in 1906 at Rochester, New York, taking over the existing Buffalo Gasoline Motor Company. The Selden auto was a four-cylinder unit with 109-inch wheelbase and cost an average $2500. In 1911 Selden not only lost the power of his patent, but a factory fire set him back months of production before it was rebuilt with insurance money.

In 1912 Frederick A. Law was hired as designer and superintendent, and in 1913 Selden entered the commercial vehicle market. The following year was the last for passenger car production at Selden. During World War I Selden was one of the companies contracted by the government to build the Class B Liberty truck. Civilian truck manufacturing included 1-, 2- and 3½-ton capacity conventional trucks. Many were exported. Right after the war the company was reorganized as the Selden Truck Corporation. George Selden died in 1923, leaving much of his company to his family.

Numerous truck models followed during the 1920s, with a six-cylinder model arriving in 1928. In 1929, even before the stock market crash, Selden was forced to merge with Hahn Motor Truck Corporation of Allentown, Pennsylvania. A few trucks with either name were built from 1930 to 1932 before the Selden name was dropped and Hahn began concentrating on fire apparatus vehicle manufacturing.

Service

Beginning in 1911 the Service Motor Car Company began building light trucks at

SELDEN TRUCKS
Manufactured by
SELDEN TRUCK SALES CO., Rochester, N. Y.

SPECIFICATIONS

Model	G	TL	JC	JWL
Capacity	¾ ton	1¼ tons	2 tons	2 tons
Drive	Worm	Worm	Internal gear	Worm
Chassis Price	$985	$1,700	$2,000	$2,250
Motor				
H. P. (S.A.E.)	15.6	19.6	22.5	27.2
H. P. (Actual)	19	26	28	36
Cylinders	4 en bloc	4 en bloc	4 en bloc	4 en bloc
Bore	3⅛"	3½"	3¾"	4⅛"
Stroke	4½"	5"	5¼"	5¼"
Wheel Base	110"	126½"	150"	150"
Tread Front	56"	56"	56"	56"
Tread Rear	56"	58"	58½"	59½"
Tires Front	32x3½" pneu.	34x3"	36x4"	36x4"
Tires Rear	33x4" pneu.	34x3"	36x6" or 36x3" dual	36x6" or 36x3" dual

Frame—Pressed.
Front Axle—I-beam, knuckles heat treated alloy steel.

Rear Axle	Semi-floating	Full-floating	Fixed	Full-floating

Springs Front—Semi-elliptic.
Springs Rear—Semi-elliptic.

Carburetor	Schebler R	Stromberg M-1	Stromberg M-1	Stromberg M-1
Cooling System	Thermo-syphon	Thermo-syphon	Pump	Pump

Oiling System—Circulating splash.
Ignition—Magneto.

Control	Right drive, center control	Right drive, center control	Optional drive, center control	Optional drive, center control

Clutch—Dry disc.
Transmission—Selective, three speeds forward and one reverse.

Brakes	Expanding on rear wheels	Expanding on rear wheels	Exp. and cont. on rear wheels	Exp. and cont. on rear wheels

Steering Gear—Worm and nut.
Equipment—Models TL, JC, JWL: Three oil lamps, horn, jack and set of tools, driver's seat.
    Model G: Three oil lamps, jack, tools, tire pump, tire repair kit and extra demountable rim.

SERVICE TRUCKS

Manufactured by

SERVICE MOTOR TRUCK CO., Wabash, Ind.

Model	220	240	270	300
Capacity	1 ton	2 tons	3½ tons	5 tons
Drive	Worm	Worm	Worm	Worm
Chassis Weight	3,350 lbs.	4,900 lbs.	6,500 lbs.	8,535 lbs.
Chassis Price	$1,900	$2,750	$3,600	$4,600
Engine	Buda	Buda	Buda	Buda
H. P. (S.A.E.)	19.6	28.9	28.9	32.4
H. P. (Actual)	26	37	37	48
Cylinders	4 en bloc	4 en bloc	4 en bloc	4 en bloc
Bore	3½"	4¼"	4¼"	4½"
Stroke	5⅛"	5½"	5½"	6"
Wheel Base	137"	160"	171"	171½"
Tread Front	58"	58½"	66¾"	68⅞"
Tread Rear	58"	58½"	65¼" or 66¾"	69½"
Tires Front	34x3"	36x4"	36x5"	36x6"
Tires Rear	34x4"	36x7"	36x5" dual	40x6" dual
Frame—Pressed.				
Front Axle—I-section Elliott.				
Rear Axle	Timken semi-floating	Timken full-floating	Timken full-floating	Timken full-floating
Springs Front—Semi-elliptic.				
Springs Rear—Semi-elliptic.				
Carburetor	Stromberg MB-1	Master	Master	Master
Cooling System	Thermo-syphon	Pump	Pump	Pump
Oiling System	Splash	Pressure	Pressure	Pressure
Ignition—Magneto.				
Control—Left drive, center control.				
Clutch	Multiple disc	Dry plate	Dry plate	Dry plate
Transmission	Fuller Selective, 3 speeds	Brown-Lipe Selective, 3 speeds	Brown-Lipe Selective, 4 speeds	Brown-Pipe Selective, 4 speeds

Brakes—Internal expanding on rear wheels.

Steering Gear—Worm and nut.

Equipment—Two oil dash lamps, one oil tail lamp, jack, set of tools, oil can, mechanical horn, running boards, front fenders, bumpers and driver's seat with cushions, chassis painted two coats of gray lead, and governor on all models except No. 220.

Wabash, Indiana. The first Service trucks were powered by a four-cylinder Continental engine using an early-design friction transmission and chain drive. Friction transmissions functioned by having a large roughly-surfaced flywheel and a drive pinion that moved from near the center to the outer diameter, thereby changing the RPM of the pinion. However, the friction itself tended to make for a short life of the relatively simple mechanism.

By 1917 the model line included one-ton to five-ton, each powered by Buda four-cylinder engines. Both three-speed and four-speed transmissions with Timken worm drive were used. The company survived the postwar recession and in 1923 reorganized as Service Motors Incorporated. At that time the lightest Service truck was the 2500-capacity Model 25 powered by a Buda four-cylinder engine using Brown-Lipe clutch and transmission. Front axle was from Shuler and rear axle was from Eaton. Service built trucks that were heavier than the ½-ton to 1-ton light trucks built in enormous numbers at low cost by such companies as Chevrolet, Dodge and Ford.

In 1927 Service bought out Relay and the whole new operation was moved to Lima, Ohio. Both Service and Relay trucks were built side by side and were essentially the same except that Service trucks used worm drive and Relay used internal gear drive. Another difference was that Service used steel disc wheels and Relay used artillery wheels. By 1928 Service built a total of 80 trucks. By 1933 neither brand of truck was in production.

Signal

Located in Detroit, Michigan, the Signal Motor Truck Company began production in 1913. Signal trucks were first powered by side-valve four-cylinder motors using three-speed transmission and dual chain drive. The first model had 1½-ton capacity. Signal did not build any passenger cars, as so many truck companies of the early years did, switching and experimenting between light commercial vehicles and various small autos. Open and closed bodies such as stake trucks and vans were built through 1914 using the first chassis design.

In 1915 Signal expanded to include 1-, 2- and 3-ton capacity trucks. All Signal trucks continued to use dual chain drive. For 1916 worm drive was also offered and finally superseded chain drive. Service built right-hand drive and left-hand drive trucks through World War I. Part of the reason was for export to Great Britain, which also brings up the opportunity to discuss briefly the background of right- and left-hand drive.

Much has been written about the origins of passing another horseman going in the opposite direction toward the right for safety reasons when swords were carried and shields were worn on the left side because everyone was expected to be right-handed. When America was a British colony people still passed to the left side as in England. But after the Revolutionary War, Americans wanted to differentiate themselves from their old oppressors and adopted right-side traffic, which also corresponded with the right-hand traffic of European allies. There were also practical, logical reasons.

In order to hold the reins in the right hand and keep them closer in line with the center of the wagon, the driver would sit to the left of the front seat. In order to see better up ahead, it was logical to drive on the right side. As wagon ruts and wagon trails became roads, people followed one another and developed the tradition of driving and riding on horseback to the right. This was especially true with Conestoga wagons and other wagons that required two or more horses. Horse-drawn wagons were best guided from the left, allowing a clear view ahead but only when driven on the

SIGNAL TRUCKS
Manufactured by
SIGNAL MOTOR TRUCK CO., Detroit, Mich.

S P E C I F I C A T I O N S

Model	F	H	J	M
Capacity	1 ton	1½ tons	2 tons	3½ tons
Drive	Worm	Worm	Worm	Worm
Chassis Price	$1,550	$1,800	$2,250	$3,000
Motor				
H. P. (S.A.E.)	22.5	27.23	27.23	32.4
H. P. (Actual)	25	30	34.5	42.5
Cylinders	4 en bloc	4 en bloc	4 en bloc	4 in pairs
Bore	3¾″	4⅛″	4⅛″	4½″
Stroke	5¼″	5¼″	5¼″	5½″
Wheel Base	120″ and 144″	120″ and 144″	150″ and 180″	168″ and 204″
Tread Front	56″	56″	58″	66″
Tread Rear	58″	58″	58″	68″
Tires Front	34x3″	34x3½″	34x4″	36x5″
Tires Rear	36x4″	36x5″	36x4″ dual	40x5″ dual

Frame—Pressed steel.
Front Axle—Timken I-beam.
Rear Axle—Timken, David Brown; full-floating.
Springs Front—Semi-elliptic.
Springs Rear—Semi-elliptic.
Carburetor—Stromberg.
Cooling System—Centrifugal pump.
Oiling System—Splash with pump circulation.
Ignition—Magneto.
Control—Right or left drive, center control.
Clutch—Dry plate.
Transmission—Selective, three speeds forward and one reverse.
Brakes—Two sets on rear wheels, internal expanding.
Steering Gear—Worm and nut.
Equipment—Driver's seat, front fenders, steps, tool box, oil side lamps, horn, jack and set of tools.

right side of the road. Also, it was easier to turn one's back to the left and protect one's back with a revolver or rifle in case of an attack because most people were right-handed, or were expected to be. The etymology of "being right" and acting as "the right hand" came from the intolerance of being left-handed.

In the U.S. the first laws requiring right-side driving were enacted during 1792 in Pennsylvania, 1804 in New York and 1813 in New Jersey. Once the Ford Model T of 1908 was introduced as a right-side-drive (left-hand steering) vehicle, decreed so by Henry Ford himself, the ubiquitous Model T, soon to comprise half of all vehicles in North America, was an important factor in establishing right-drive and left-side steering wheel. For delivery purposes right-side steering has been left intact to this day for certain applications such as postal vehicles, which has to do with the safety and convenience of the driver constantly exiting and entering the vehicle for delivery work.

Signal added a 4-ton capacity truck in 1918, but the material shortages and postwar recession took their toll on the company. Only the 1½-ton Model F was built up to 1923, the last year of manufacture for Signal.

Simplex

The year 1907 was pivotal in the history of the Simplex Automobile Company. That year Herman Broesel, who was a textile importer, decided like so many others that he wanted to get into the suddenly exploding motor vehicle manufacturing market. He bought the S&M Simplex Company of New York City, which began production of an auto that year designed by Edward Franquist. The Simplex Toy Tonneau of 1907 and 1908 was powered by a 50 hp four-cylinder motor and sold for $5500. The cars were powerful enough that a model called the Speed Car came in sixth in the first Indianapolis 500.

With powerful motors and wheelbases of 124-inch to 127-inch in 1909, Simplex soon found a well-to-do customer base which had an appreciation for the custom coachwork by such companies as Brewster, Demarest, Healey, Holbrook or Quinby. Shaft and chain drive were offered by 1911 with prices approaching $6300.

In 1912 Herman Broesel died and his sons, having inherited the company, sold the assets of the Simplex company to New York investors Goodrich, Lockhart and Smith, part of the company being involved in tire manufacturing. At the end of 1912 the Simplex company also became owners of the Crane Motor Car Company, builders of luxury cars in Bayonne, New Jersey.

With the purchase came Henry Crane, who was well versed in auto manufacturing. All his factory equipment, as well as his newly-designed six-cylinder motor production machinery (casting, lathe and milling operations), were moved in 1915 to New Brunswick, where Simplex had established itself in 1913. The six-cylinder motor was adopted, and the company continued to command prices of up to $7500 for its 1916 seven-passenger Simplex Crane Model 5 Touring model built on a 144-inch wheelbase. In addition, the four-cylinder Model 50 on a 137-inch wheelbase was priced as low as $4600. The Rockefellers owned two Simplex-Crane touring cars, as they were called, by this time.

In 1916 the Simplex Automobile Company was purchased by Wright-Martin Aircraft Corporation, where Hispano-Suiza aircraft engines were produced during World War I. Automobile production was suspended after only 467 Simplex motorcars had been built since 1915 Wright-Martin was not interested in auto production even after the war ended, but a few remaining Simplex cars were assembled through 1920. Henry Crane bought the Simplex assets in 1922 after Emlen S. Hare had his chance at company resurrection along with

**SIMPLEX
AUTOMOBILE
COMPANY**

755 FIFTH AVENUE
NEW YORK CITY

Price, Chassis, $7000

SIMPLEX-CRANE LIMOUSINE

COLOR	Optional	BORE AND STROKE	4⅜ x 6¼ inches
SEATING CAPACITY	Seven	LUBRICATION	Force feed
POSITION OF DRIVER	Left side	RADIATOR	Cellular
WHEELBASE	143½ inches	COOLING	Water pump
GAUGE	56 inches	IGNITION	High tension magneto and storage battery
WHEELS	Wood		
FRONT TIRES	36 x 4½ or 35 x 5 inches		
		STARTING SYSTEM	Two unit
		STARTER OPERATED	Gear to fly wheel
REAR TIRES	37 x 5 or 35 x 5 inches, anti-skid	LIGHTING SYSTEM	Electric
		VOLTAGES	Twelve
SERVICE BRAKE	Contracting on drive shaft	WIRING SYSTEM	Double
		GASOLINE SYSTEM	Pressure
EMERGENCY BRAKE	Contracting on rear wheels	CLUTCH	Single plate in oil
		TRANSMISSION	Selective sliding
CYLINDERS	Six	GEAR CHANGES	Four forward, one reverse
ARRANGED	Vertically		
CAST	In threes	DRIVE	Spiral bevel
HORSEPOWER	45.94	REAR AXLE	Full floating
(N.A.C.C. Rating)		STEERING GEAR	Worm and sector

In addition to above specifications, price includes speedometer, ammeter, voltmeter, clock, tire pump, electric horn and demountable rims.

Mercer and Locomobile, but the Crane-Simplex never got a chance to be produced due to various financial obstacles.

Standard (auto)

There were so many companies in America organized to produce automobiles using the name Standard they are too numerous to list. The one listed here arrived in 1914 having already been in business building railway cars in Butler, Pennsylvania. A large new factory began production of a six-cylinder touring car on a 126-inch wheelbase in 1914, priced at $2100. A straight-eight motor was introduced in 1915 as a roadster or touring car. The company used "Monarch of the Mountains" as its slogan. (Standard Trucks were built by another, separate company next in the listing here.)

By 1917 only the eight-cylinder car was being produced. Even though America was finally drawn into the war in Europe with great uncertainties on the horizon, Standard sold 2500 for 1917. But the material shortages, financial pressures, and lack of confidence in the marketplace caused sales to plummet for Standard, as it did with many other companies, as a direct or indirect result of the war.

At the beginning of 1921, as the postwar recession lagged on, Standard Steel Car Company, which still produced railway cars, announced that it was "popularizing the Standard product." Don C. McCord, who had been with American Mercedes and was now head of the Bankers' Commercial Security Company, was placed in charge of reorganizing Standard. The Standard Steel Car Company sold off its auto division, which became the Standard Motor Car Company in 1923. Despite announcements of various kinds, Standard autos were no longer manufactured.

Standard (truck)

In 1912 the Standard Motor Truck Company, not affiliated with Standard autos listed above, began building trucks in Detroit, Michigan. The company used Continental engines throughout its production history. Continental engines were manufactured in Detroit, as were Timken axles adopted by Standard.

Detroit was a hotbed of motor vehicle development, becoming a metonym for the auto industry. An entire collection of major component manufacturers was concentrated around Detroit. In addition to the two important companies cited above, other Detroit motor vehicle component manufacturers included: Golden, Belknap & Swartz, as well as Hinkley, builders of engines; Zenith, builders of fuel systems and carburetors; Detroit Gear, as well as Dodge, both independent suppliers of transmissions, and the latter also of steering gear; A.J. Detlaff Company and Detroit Gear, builders of transmissions and clutches; Universal Products, makers of U-joints; Russell, builders of front and rear axles; Gemmer, builders of steering gear; and Detroit Panel, Disteel Company, and Kelsey, all three manufacturers of wheels.

Standard used chain drive until 1920. Through World War I Standard trucks were up to 5-ton capacity. The company was reorganized and called Fisher-Standard, but only some of the trucks were called Fisher-Standard. There were a half dozen companies named Fisher, but they were all organized for the manufacture of passenger cars. There were dozens of companies at the beginning of the previous century which were organized for the manufacturing of motor vehicles that adopted the name Standard. Some of these companies tried their hand at producing assembled cars, which meant buying ready-made components from suppliers.

In addition to the carburetor and fuel

STANDARD
STEEL CAR
COMPANY

PITTSBURGH
PENNSYLVANIA

Price	$2450
Seven-Passenger Limousine . . .	4000
Seven-Passenger Sedan	3500
Four-Passenger Roadster	2450
Two-Passenger Roadster	2450
Three-Passenger Coupe	3500

STANDARD EIGHT TOURING—G

COLOR	Blue, green or beige	LUBRICATION	Full force feed
SEATING CAPACITY . .	Seven	RADIATOR	Cellular
POSITION OF DRIVER	Left side	COOLING	Water pump
WHEELBASE	127 inches	IGNITION	High tension magneto
GAUGE	56 inches	STARTING SYSTEM . .	Two unit
WHEELS	Wood	STARTER OPERATED .	Gear to fly wheel
FRONT TIRES	34 x 4½ inches	LIGHTING SYSTEM . .	Electric
REAR TIRES	34 x 4½ inches, anti-skid	VOLTAGES	Six
SERVICE BRAKE . . .	Contracting on rear wheels	WIRING SYSTEM . . .	Single
		GASOLINE SYSTEM . .	Vacuum
EMERGENCY BRAKE .	Expanding on rear wheels	CLUTCH	Plate
CYLINDERS	Eight	TRANSMISSION . . .	Selective sliding
ARRANGED	V type, 90 degrees	GEAR CHANGES . . .	Three forward, one reverse
CAST	In fours	DRIVE	Spiral bevel
HORSEPOWER	33.8 (N.A.C.C. Rating)	REAR AXLE	Semi-floating
BORE AND STROKE .	3¼ x 5 inches	STEERING GEAR . . .	Worm and gear

In addition to above specifications, price includes top, top hood, windshield, speedometer, ammeter, clock, tire pump, electric horn and demountable rims.

STANDARD TRUCKS
Manufactured by
STANDARD MOTOR TRUCK CO., Detroit, Mich.

Model	70	65	85
Capacity	2 tons	3½ tons	5 tons
Drive	Worm	Worm	Worm
Chassis Weight	4,380 lbs.	6,280 lbs.	6,850 lbs.
Chassis Price	$2,575	$3,350	$4,250
Engine	Continental·	Continental	Continental
H. P. (S.A.E.)	27.23	32.40	32.40
H. P. (Actual)	35 at 1050 R.P.M.	40 at 1000 R.P.M.	40 at 1000 R.P.M.
Cylinders	4 en bloc	4 in pairs	4 in pairs
Bore	4⅛″	4½″	4½″
Stroke	5¼″	5½″	5½″
Wheel Base	140″	158″	158″
Tread Front	58″	64″	66″
Tread Rear	58″	65¼″	73″
Tires Front	36x4″	36x5″	36x6″
Tires Rear	36x6″	36x5″ dual	40x6″ dual

Frame—Rolled channel.
Front Axle—I-section, Timken.
Rear Axle—Timken full-floating.
Springs Front—Semi-elliptic.
Springs Rear—Semi-elliptic.
Carburetor—Schebler R.
Cooling System—Centrifugal pump.
Oiling System—Splash.
Ignition—High tension magneto.
Control—Left-hand drive, center control.
Clutch—Dry plate.
Transmission—Selective, sliding gear.
Brakes--Internal expanding.
Steering Gear—Screw and nut.
Equipment—Oil lamps, full set of tools, jack, governor, steel seat and dash assembly, cushion and lazy back.

system provided by Schebler for Standard trucks, fuel systems at that time were manufactured by several companies, such as: Benecke & Kropf in Chicago, Illinois; Briscoe in Pontiac, Michigan; Carter in St. Louis, Missouri; Detroit Lubricator in Detroit, Michigan; Ensign in Los Angeles, California; Holley in St. Louis, Missouri; Johnson in Detroit, Michigan; Marvel in Flint, Michigan; Stromberg in Chicago, Illinois; Tillotson in Toledo, Ohio; and Zenith in Detroit, Michigan.

Every company had the luxury of buying finished components for the motor vehicles they were building, and depending on the percentage of purchased parts, the car or truck would be considered an "assembled" vehicle. This mattered more with passenger cars, since the buyer wanted to stand out from the rest of the pack, which was huge at the time and constituted dozens of makes.

Ready off-the-shelf components included engines, transmissions, clutches, radiators, axles, wheels, truck bodies, fuel systems, electrical systems, lights, gauges, universal joints, steering gear, chain and sprockets and batteries, in addition to nuts, bolts and other small items. Anybody with the ability to build a chassis, suspension, hood, cowl, seats and fenders could build a car or truck during this era, and many did, as listed in this book.

Standard was a big enough company to survive the postwar recession. By 1925 the company introduced a model called the Fisher Fast Freight, which eliminated the "Standard" part of the name apparently for the sake of alliteration. The 1-ton was called the Fisher Junior Express. There was also the Fisher Mercantile Express 2-ton, Fisher Heavy Duty Six 3½-ton capacity model and a 28-passenger bus called the Standard AK. Most of the trucks and buses Fisher-Standard built were marketed with either or the combination of names around Michigan or in Canada. The Great Depression finally took its toll on the company in 1933.

Stearns

F.M. Stearns set his son up with a machine shop at their home in Cleveland after making a considerable amount of money in the stone quarry business. His son, Frank Ballou Stearns, used the shop to build a gasoline-powered car in 1896. F.B. Stearns and Company was organized in 1898 with the help of the Owen Brothers, also of Cleveland. By 1901 there were about 50 Stearns vehicles which had been completed without any single series of motor vehicle being announced. By that time the Owen Brothers went off on their own, and the Stearns father-and-son team began building their own company's model line.

Stearns cars were modern compared to others in that by 1901 they were no longer tiller-steered, had a sliding gear transmission by 1902, a magneto by 1904 and four-speed transmissions by 1905. Left-hand steering was introduced in 1905 but dropped immediately and only reintroduced in 1914. This early period was still fraught with uncertainties as to the basic integrity of various designs which included the quandary of using left- or right-hand drive, tiller or wheel steering, cone or disc (wet and dry) clutch, the merits of friction drive, brake systems of various design and a multitude of other component configurations, including ignition and electrical systems. (See Signal for further discussion of right- and left-side steering).

The slogan of the Stearns company was "Runs Like a Deer." Whether or not this phrase got new buyers to stand in line is uncertain, but the fact that Stearns stock cars won some endurance runs and races without building purpose-built race cars got plenty of press attention. A win at Brighton Beach which took 24 hours and 1253 miles in 1910 made some headlines. Stearns cars were not low-cost, with $5000 an average for the four-cylinder models and up to $7500 for the six-

**F. B. STEARNS
COMPANY**

CLEVELAND, OHIO

Price	**$2575**
Cloverleaf Roadster	2575
Coupe	3200
Coupe Landaulet	3200
Limousine	3875
Limousine Brougham	3875
Landaulet	3985
Landaulet Brougham	3985
Chassis	2050

STEARNS TOURING—SK-8

COLOR	Body, Roman green; wheels, cream; fenders and hood, black	BORE AND STROKE .	3¼ x 5 inches
		LUBRICATION	Force feed and splash
SEATING CAPACITY. .	Seven	RADIATOR	Cellular
POSITION OF DRIVER .	Left side	COOLING	Thermo-syphon
WHEELBASE	125 inches	IGNITION	Storage battery
GAUGE	56 inches	STARTING SYSTEM . .	Two unit
WHEELS	Wood	STARTER OPERATED .	Gear to fly wheel
FRONT TIRES	35 x 4½ inches	LIGHTING SYSTEM . .	Electric
REAR TIRES	35 x 4½ inches, anti-skid	VOLTAGES	Twelve
		WIRING SYSTEM . . .	Single
SERVICE BRAKE . . .	Contracting on transmission shaft	GASOLINE SYSTEM . .	Vacuum
		CLUTCH	Dry multiple disc
EMERGENCY BRAKE .	Expanding on rear wheels	TRANSMISSION . . .	Selective sliding
CYLINDERS	Eight	GEAR CHANGES . . .	Three forward, one reverse
ARRANGED	V type, 90 degrees	DRIVE	Spiral bevel
CAST	In fours	REAR AXLE	Semi-floating
HORSEPOWER	33.8	STEERING GEAR . . .	Worm and gear
(N.A.C.C. Rating)			

In addition to above specifications, price includes top, top hood, windshield, speedometer, ammeter, electric horn and demountable rims.

cylinder models in 1909, the year the Baby Stearns arrived for around $3200.

Production at Stearns had a steady rise, from 240 in 1908 to 1000 by 1911. The Stearns "white line radiator" design was patented, perhaps unnecessarily since its unique distinction would probably not be copied by any other company anyway. More importantly, Stearns was the first company to adopt a Knight engine license in the United States. (More on the Knight engine under Moline-Knight). Once the licensing agreement was in place Stearns used no other engines but. Four-cylinder Knight engines were offered through 1913, and a six-cylinder sleeve-valve engine was offered in 1914.

One of the more innovative approaches in marketing at the time was devised for the Light Four, the first modestly priced Stearns at $1750 in 1914. Advertising addressed potential buyers as "Mr. Substantial Citizen," a slogan perhaps much ahead of its time in terms of blending the plebeian with the elite, not unlike later efforts in creating a comfortable if not wealthy middle class exemplified and symbolized by the cars those buyers drove. It may have worked for Stearns only briefly, especially since a V-8 superseded the six-cylinder motor the following year in 1916, when 4000 Stearns rolled off the assembly line in Cleveland.

But not all was well for Stearns, especially for Frank B. Stearns, who retired in 1917 after an announcement of bad health at age 37. The presidency of Stearns was taken over by George W. Booker. The company continued on its production path as if nothing had changed, and the war and postwar recession had little noticeable impact on the Stearns company, which was the exception rather than the rule. In 1920 the four-cylinder Stearns was reintroduced, and a six-cylinder motor came back in 1923.

Despite its pricey image while wooing moderate-income buyers, Stearns remained a prestige car even after the company was bought by John North Willys in 1925, the most profitable year for Stearns. It remained an independent marque among the Willys-Overland acquisitions, and an in-line sleeve-valve eight-cylinder motor was introduced in 1927, having been designed under the jurisdiction of newly-hired J.F. Trumble. The car was known to be able to reach 100 mph and could be bought for just under $5000 in 1928, or just under $6000 for one with a 145-inch wheelbase.

The end of Stearns was almost as dramatic as the grand automobiles that had been manufactured by the company for some three decades, depending on what would be considered the first vehicle of this make. Just as John North Willys bought Stearns for about $10 per share, the stock market crash took place at the end of 1929, rendering the shares of Stearns about one-eightieth (1/80) of their previous value.

Although having retired from Stearns due to health problems, Frank Ballou Stearns was alive and well, designing a new two-stroke diesel engine which he built in his home machine shop and then sold to the United States Navy. John Willys North became an ambassador and Frank Ballou Stearns turned his interests to organic farming, living well until his death in 1955, despite his previously announced poor health.

Stegeman

The Stegeman Motor Car Company was a builder of a fairly advanced model line of trucks, considering it was a fairly small company which began doing business in 1911 around Milwaukee, Wisconsin. The specific region in Wisconsin was host to a multitude of motor vehicle companies, including Case, FWD, Harley-Davidson, Jeffery, Kissel, Menominee, Mitchell, Nash, Sterling, Winther, and Wisconsin, plus numerous component

STEGEMAN SIX TRUCKS
Manufactured by
STEGEMAN MOTOR TRUCK CO., Milwaukee, Wis.
606 Linus Street

S P E C I F I C A T I O N S

Model	1½-Ton	2½-Ton	3½-Ton	5-Ton
Capacity	1½ tons	2½ tons	3½ tons	5 tons
Drive	Worm	Worm	Worm	Worm
Chassis Price	$1,900	$2,500	$3,000	$4,000
Motor				
H. P. (S.A.E.)	29	29	34	34
H. P. (Actual)	40	40	50	50
Cylinders	6 en bloc	6 en bloc	6 in threes	6 in threes
Bore	3½"	3½"	3¾"	3¾"
Stroke	5¼"	5¼"	5¼"	5¼"
Wheel Base	150"	144" standard 162" long	156"	170"
Tread Front	56½"	56½"	61"	61"
Tread Rear	56½"	56½", 58" Special	65"	69"
Tires Front	34x3½"	34x4"	36x4"	36x5"
Tires Rear	36x5"	36x4" dual	40x5" dual	40x6" dual

Frame—Pressed.
Front Axle—I-beam.
Rear Axle—Full-floating.
Springs Front—Semi-elliptic.
Springs Rear—Semi-elliptic.
Carburetor—Rayfield.
Cooling System—Pump.
Oiling System—Splash and forced feed.
Ignition—Magneto.
Control—Left drive, center control.
Clutch—Multiple dry disc.
Transmission—Selective, three speeds forward and one reverse.
Brakes—Foot brake expanding on propeller shaft; hand, expanding on rear wheels.
Steering Gear—Irreversible worm and nut.
Equipment—Electric starter, powerful electric dash head lights, electric tail light, tools,
    hubodometer, electric horn, jack, seat with back and cushions.

manufacturers including Wisconsin axles and engines along with other parts and accessories.

Perhaps that is why it was not surprising that yet another company came into existence, by the name of Stegeman, building commercial vehicles from ¾-ton up to 5-ton. All models used hard rubber tires, as was most common for truck applications in the early days. The chain drive was offered in a fully enclosed oil bath for an extra $150. This may have been somewhat costly at the time, but it most likely had its own good selling points in that a greased open drive chain picked up an endless gummy amalgam of sand, pebbles and dirt that greatly reduced its life span.

Stegeman used shaft drive early on and the lighter models were available with pneumatic tires. By the time America was immersed in World War I the Stegeman company offered electric start and six-cylinder engines. Also, a 7-ton model was offered with a fully-floating worm drive rear axle fabricated by Stegeman. Electric lighting and an electric horn were offered on all models.

Whether material shortages contributed to the demise of the company can only be surmised, but by end of 1918 the Stegeman Motor Car Company was no longer in the business of manufacturing. There is no indication that this Stegeman ever produced passenger cars.

Stephens

The entry of the United States into World War I in Europe did not impede the Moline Plow Company of Freeport, Illinois, from manufacturing automobiles starting in 1917. The company had begun in Moline in 1870 to build horse-drawn wagons. It was founded by G.A. Stephens, after whom the automobile was named. The company announced a drop in demand for buggies with production of the Salient Six Touring beginning in 1917, priced at $1150. It had a partial top cover at the rear in the style of a perambulator.

The early models were powered by a Continental six-cylinder motor, but with wartime shortages a Root and Vandervoort engine was adopted in 1918. The Stephens car was built in an unusual array of four-, five- and six-passenger Touring models plus one Victoria model in 1919, with prices reaching $2000.

John North Willys bought controlling interest of the company that year, but production of the Stephens automobile remained undisturbed. In 1920 the Moline Plow bought out Root and Vandervoort, but because farm machinery purchases were very low during the postwar recession, the engine and auto division was reorganized separately as the Stephens Motor Car Company in 1922.

For 1923 Stephens autos had a new look and had new series designations which encompassed Model 10 and Model 20. Sedan, Touring Sedan, Roadster and Touring were the four body styles, although it wasn't certain why the shorter-wheelbase Model 10 six-cylinder car was more powerful (by two hp) than the longer-wheelbase Model 20. That year 4400 Stephens cars were built, one of the best years ever for the company, and yet discontinuation of auto production was announced in 1924, the last year for Stephens autos as the company refocused on farm implement production. The press divulged that over seven years of production, 24,900 Stephens cars were produced.

Sterling

Of the half-dozen motor vehicle companies with the name of Sterling, this company began in Milwaukee, Wisconsin, in 1916 and built only trucks. There was also another Sterling which gained some fame when William Durant and his partner J. Dallas Dort formed a company by that name in Flint, Michigan, but no manufacture followed.

World War I had a direct impact on this company in that it began as the Sternberg

MOLINE PLOW
C O M P A N Y

S T E P H E N S
M O T O R
B R A N C H

M O L I N E
I L L I N O I S

Price	. . . .	**$1485**
Three-Passenger Roadster	. . .	1485
Five-Passenger Sedan	. . . . .	1985
Four-Passenger	. . . .	1550

STEPHENS SALIENT SIX TOURING—75

COLOR	Body, black or green; chassis, black; wheels, ivory		BORE AND STROKE . .	3¼ x 4½ inches
			LUBRICATION	Full force feed
			RADIATOR	Cellular
SEATING CAPACITY . .	Five		COOLING	Thermo-syphon
POSITION OF DRIVER .	Left side		IGNITION	Storage battery
WHEELBASE	118 inches		STARTING SYSTEM . .	Two unit
GAUGE	56 inches		STARTER OPERATED .	Gear to fly wheel
WHEELS	Wood		LIGHTING SYSTEM . .	Electric
FRONT TIRES	32 x 4 inches		VOLTAGES	Six to eight
REAR TIRES	32 x 4 inches, anti-skid		WIRING SYSTEM . . .	Single
SERVICE BRAKE . . .	Contracting on rear wheels		GASOLINE SYSTEM . .	Vacuum
			CLUTCH	Dry multiple disc
EMERGENCY BRAKE .	Expanding on rear wheels		TRANSMISSION . . .	Selective sliding
CYLINDERS	Six		GEAR CHANGES . . .	Three forward, one reverse
ARRANGED	Vertically		DRIVE	Spiral bevel
CAST	En bloc		REAR AXLE	Full floating
HORSEPOWER	25.35 (N.A.C.C. Rating)		STEERING GEAR . . .	Worm and gear

In addition to above specifications, price includes top, top hood, windshield, speedometer, ammeter, tire pump, electric horn and demountable rims.

STERLING TRUCKS

Manufactured by

STERLING MOTOR TRUCK CO., Milwaukee, Wis.

S P E C I F I C A T I O N S

Model	2½-Ton	3½-Ton	5-Ton	7-Ton
Capacity	2½ tons	3½ tons	5 tons	7 tons
Drive	Worm	Worm	Worm	Chain
Chassis Price	$2,800 Std. W. B.	$3,400 Std.	$4,500	$5,250
	$2,925 Sp. W. B.			
Motor				
H. P. (S.A.E.)	22.5	22.5	32.5	32 5
H. P. (Actual)	40	45	52	52
Cylinders	4 in pairs	4 in pairs	4 in pairs	4 in pairs
Bore	4¼"	4¼"	4¾"	4¾"
Stroke	5¾"	6¾"	6¾"	6¾"
Wheel Base	156"	158" Std., 192" Sp.	168"	168"
Tread Front	56"	60"	62⅝"	64"
Tread Rear	56"	66"	74"	77⅜"
Tires Front	36x4"	36x5"	36x5"	36x6"
Tires Rear	36x4" dual or	36x5" dual	40x6" dual	40x7" dual
	36x7"			

Frame—Pressed, wood sill inlay.
Front Axle—I-beam, Elliott.

Rear Axle	Semi-floating	Semi-floating	Semi-floating	Double side chains

Springs Front—Semi-elliptic.
Springs Rear—Semi-elliptic.
Carburetor—Holley, type H.
Cooling System—Centrifugal pump.
Oiling System—Splash and pump.

Ignition	Eisemann H. T.	Eisemann H. T.	Eisemann dual	Eisemann dual
	magneto	magneto	H. T. magneto	

Control—Left drive, center control.
Clutch—Multiple dry disc.

Transmission	Sliding selective,	Individual jaw	Individual jaw	Individual jaw
	3 speeds forward,	clutch, 3 speeds	clutch constantly	clutch constantly
	1 reverse	forward, 1 reverse	in mesh	in mesh
Brakes	Both sets double	Both sets double	Both sets on	Jackshaft and
	rear wheels	rear wheels	rear wheels	rear wheels

Steering Gear—Screw and nut.
Equipment—Steel cab with top, storm curtains, truck type windshield, hubodometer, jack, full set of tools, one piece oil lamps.

Motor Truck Company in 1916, but due to anti–German sentiments, the name was quickly changed to Sterling. The company started out building trucks from ¾-ton to 7-ton capacity. All models had four-cylinder motors and worm gear drive, except the heaviest model, which still used dual chain drive. The four motors that were available were from 30 hp and 138 cid to 52 hp and 478 cid.

Sterling trucks were of high quality and featured windshields, electric headlights and oil side lamps as standard equipment when other truck builders offered them as optional equipment. One of the distinguishing details for Sterling trucks was their widely-spaced hood louvers. During World War I Sterling assembled a total of 479 Liberty Class B trucks for the military, in addition to production of the earlier trucks for the civilian market. This involvement in World War I military truck production makes it opportune to describe just what the Liberty Class B truck actually was.

A lack of standardization during the period 1914–1916, when the U.S. contributed materially to the war before entering it, resulted in a chaotic number of various truck makes and millions of spare parts to support them as they were shipped to the Allies in Europe. By July of 1917 the military submitted specifications for a standardized 4 × 4 truck to the newly-formed Society of Automotive Engineers (SAE). The engine was to be a 424 cid four-cylinder type of which Continental manufactured the block, Waukesha the cylinder heads and Hercules the pistons. Fifteen truck manufacturers would assemble the Liberty B, and production began in January of 1918. After just over 9,300 were assembled, the Armistice was signed and the contract for the remainder of the order for 43,000 was canceled.

Just after World War I the Hayssen family took over the company with Robert G. Hayssen becoming the president. Ernst M. Sternberg became vice president with Frank Luick as secretary-treasurer. In 1922 Sterling obtained a patent on a wood insert system for the vehicle frames which had been designed by William Sternberg. This "inlay" system strengthened the steel frames without additional welding or corrosion and was fairly low cost.

Just before the stock market crash of 1929 Sterling issued $1,800,000 in stock, which was intended to pay off bank loans, accounts payable and factory mortgage. The company's move was timed in such a way that a move was made to buy out LaFrance-Republic Company in 1931, in order to introduce new cabs and a more modern look for Sterling's trucks. LaFrance-Republic was already a company created by a merger out of necessity due to the Great Depression, and its inventory was sold off over the next few years. The Sterling F Series were badged as LaFrance-Republic until 1942.

However, due to failure to meet dividend requirements in preferred stock at the end of 1931, the Hayssen family took over the company and Ernst M. Sternberg took over as president once again, with William Sternberg installed as vice president. The company was reorganized in Wisconsin in 1933, with old stock replaced by new shares at a ratio of six to one. Continuing through the difficult 1930s and producing trucks through World War II, Sterling finally succumbed in 1951 when it was bought out by White Corporation.

Stevens-Duryea

J. Frank Duryea and brother Charles E. Duryea have been cited as America's gasoline vehicle pioneers, with development beginning in 1893. Both brothers had been involved with the bicycle industry, but Frank was particularly driven to complete an experimental car which was tested in Springfield, Massachusetts, during 1893. The second Duryea car was entirely built by Frank. It was the winner of the

S T E V E N S -
D U R Y E A
C O M P A N Y

CHICOPEE FALLS
MASSACHUSETTS

Price	**$5800**
Two-Passenger Roadster . . .	4550
Three-Passenger Coupelet . .	5000
Five-Passenger Touring . . .	4550
Five-Passenger Landau Phaeton	5200
Five-Passenger Demi-Berline .	5750

MODEL: STEVENS-DURYEA "C-SIX" LIMOUSINE

COLOR	English purple lake, mulberry red, lakelet green, visible blue or sapphire blue.	ARRANGED	Vertically, under hood.
SEATING CAPACITY .	Seven persons.	CAST	In pairs.
CLUTCH	Multiple disc.	BORE	$4\frac{5}{16}$ inches.
WHEELBASE . . .	131 inches.	STROKE	$5\frac{1}{2}$ inches.
GAUGE	56 inches.	COOLING	Water.
TIRE DIMENSIONS:		RADIATOR	Cellular.
FRONT	37 x $4\frac{1}{2}$ inches.	IGNITION	Jump spark.
REAR	37 x $4\frac{1}{2}$ inches.	ELECTRIC SOURCE .	High tension magneto and storage battery.
BRAKE SYSTEMS . .	Contracting and expanding on both rear wheels.	DRIVE	Shaft.
		TRANSMISSION . .	Selective sliding gear.
HORSE-POWER . . .	N. A. C. C. (formerly A. L. A. M.) rating 44.8.	GEAR CHANGES . .	Three forward, one reverse.
		POSITION OF DRIVER .	Right side drive and right hand control.
CYLINDERS	Six.		

Price includes electric lighting, self-starter, speedometer and demountable rims.
Wire wheels extra

Chicago Times-Herald Race in 1895, carrying brother Charles as a passenger.

However, with cooperation fading in and out between the two brothers, it was Charles Duryea who organized America's first company with the intent to manufacture gasoline motor vehicles. It was called the Duryea Motor Wagon Company and was located back in Springfield. Thirteen Duryea vehicles were built and one was entered in the 1896 London-to-Brighton contest, in which Frank was first to arrive at the finish line. Production was moved in 1898 to Peoria, Illinois, where three-wheelers were produced by the brothers, who did not agree on the future of their company and went separate ways. Frank remained and joined up with the Stevens Arms and Tool Company, hence formation of the Stevens-Duryea Company in 1901.

In the meantime, Charles Duryea tried his luck in Los Angeles, California, with the Henderson Horseless Carriage Company, which went no further before Charles hooked up in Reading, Pennsylvania, forming the Duryea Power Company. This company built tiller-controlled three-wheelers, with steering, gear change and accelerator all managed by one stick. According to statements made by Charles Duryea, he "detested the steering wheel."

Further efforts through 1917 by Charles Duryea involved numerous partnerships and various efforts, much of which were results of experiments with motorized buggies, the Duryea Roller Drive, a cyclecar and various patents. His manufacturing efforts ended in 1917, but he remained involved in writing and historical documentation of the auto industry until his death at age 76 in 1939.

Meanwhile, the Stevens-Duryea Company, along with Frank Duryea, the actual basis for information in general about the Duryea Brothers in this specific discussion, continued with a two-cylinder Runabout through 1905 when a four-cylinder Touring was added back

in Chicopee Falls, Massachusetts. A three-speed transmission was used from the beginning of series production, and in 1906 a 50 hp six-cylinder car was introduced featuring shaft drive.

From then on the Stevens-Duryea would be considered a high-quality conservatively-styled car even if slogans such as "Twentieth Century Hustler" were used in 1906, undoubtedly with a different meaning than might be inferred today.

Stevens-Duryea grew its reputation on large sedans and limousines before World War I, with prices reaching $6300 by 1915. However, financial troubles and disagreement as to product line caused closure of both the Duryea auto production line and the Stevens armament division. Westinghouse bought out the entire company in order to produce war materiel during World War I, but in 1919 some of the former Stevens-Duryea executives, along with Ray S. Deering and Thomas L. Cowles, reacquired the whole company and reorganized in 1919 as Stevens-Duryea, Incorporated.

The Stevens-Duryea Six was reintroduced with 80 hp after World War I. Also, under Ray Deering, the Baker R&L firm was purchased to build Rauch & Lang electric taxis. Receivership of the entire company followed, which included inventory of some 200 cars, about half of which were pre-owned and reconditioned. A year later Ray M. Owen of Owen Magnetic bought Stevens-Duryea. By 1924 production was resumed, but because the Stevens-Duryea had not changed since 1920, orders dwindled down to nothing by 1927, when the company closed for good.

Stewart

After leaving the Lippard-Stewart Company of Buffalo, New York, Thomas R. Lippard, along with his previous partner, started the Stewart Motor Corporation in the same

STEWART TRUCKS

Manufactured by

STEWART MOTOR CORPN., Buffalo, N. Y.

SPECIFICATIONS

Model	3	4	6
Capacity	1 ton	1½ tons	¾ ton
Drive	Shaft	Shaft	Internal gear
Chassis Price	$1,390	$1,485	$795
Motor			
H. P. (S.A.E.)	19.60	19.60	14.40
H. P. (Actual)	36	30	27
Cylinders	4 en bloc	4 en bloc	4 en bloc
Bore	3½"	3½"	3"
Stroke	5⅛"	5⅛"	4¼"
Wheel Base	118"	140"	110"
Tread Front	56"	56"	56"
Tread Rear	56"	56"	56"
Tires Front	34x3½"	34x3½"	32x4" pneu.
Tires Rear	34x4"	34x5"	32x4" pneu.

Frame—Pressed.
Front Axle—I-beam.
Rear Axle—Internal gear.
Springs Front—Semi-elliptic.
Springs Rear—Semi-elliptic.
Carburetor—Zenith.
Cooling System—Thermo-syphon.
Oiling System—Splash and force.
Ignition—Magneto.
Control—Left drive, center control.
Clutch—Dry plate.
Transmission—Selective, three speeds forward and one reverse.
Brakes—Expanding and contracting, rear wheel.
Steering Gear   Screw and nut   Screw and nut   Worm and gear
Equipment—Model 4: Seat, tools, jack, side and tail lights, mechanical horn, and bumper.
      Models 3 and 6: Glass windshield, mechanical horn, tools, jack, side and tail lights, bumper.

city. So as not to infringe on the name they began with, their new Stewart firm also produced trucks concurrently in the same area under only a slightly different name until Lippard-Stewart went out of business in 1919.

The first Stewart trucks were nearly indistinguishable from those of Lippard-Stewart, using the so-called Renault hood and being powered by a four-cylinder Continental engine. Starting with a ¾-ton model, the trucks had a three-speed transmission and Timken bevel drive.

In 1914 the U.S. Navy bought Stewart trucks in the form of ambulances, some of which were deployed around Washington, D.C. That year a light bus was also built, with the help of the National Body and Top Corporation, and passenger cars were built for 1915 and 1916, powered by six-cylinder Continental motors. The Renault hood was also used for the passenger cars, but they were soon discontinued.

In 1916 both pneumatic tires and the electric starter motor, the latter invented some four years earlier at GM, were introduced at Stewart. The Series 2 trucks were replaced by the Series 3 and Series 4, which were 1-ton and 1½-ton, respectively. A ½-ton was offered by 1917 with an express body.

In 1918 Stewart built trucks up to 2-ton capacity, and it appears that some customers ordered chain drive, although that was not the standard design. Ads stated "One Stewart truck supplants 10 horses." According to a number of tests and studies, that may have been quite accurate, depending on the type of work performed.

After World War I Stewart introduced yet another heavier truck in the form of a 3½-ton model. Engines were supplied from various builders including Buda and LeRoi. An expansion program increased the production potential to 10,000 trucks per year. With 345 distributors in 27 countries, the production number was not out of proportion to the sales

potentials. Despite a coal strike and a railroad strike in 1920, adding to the troubles of the postwar recession, production at Stewart more than doubled at the time.

Late in 1921 a "speed" truck was added to the model line in response to a market trend which had already been established by such vehicles as the Reo Speed Wagon. These light trucks all had pneumatic tires and were geared so that the top speed was over 30 mph, whereas before top speed was governed to be under 20 mph. The Stewart speed truck sold for $1395. By this time the Stewart factory was 500,000 square feet and about 400 people were employed by the company.

Stewart built 18- and 25-passenger buses in the mid–1920s, and in 1926 six-cylinder motors were introduced. Stewart also introduced Lycoming straight-eight motors in 1931 along with 10-wheel trucks. The company survived the Great Depression with notable restyling during the late 1930s. However, all production ended in 1941.

Studebaker

The Studebaker brothers entered the horse-drawn wagon manufacturing business in 1852, and this mode of transportation was built by the company until 1920. The company supplied wagons to the Union Army during the Civil War, and the enterprise was incorporated as Studebaker Brothers Manufacturing Company in 1868. John M. Studebaker's son-in-law, Frederick Fish, began experimenting with horseless buggies in 1897. By 1902 the company began producing electric vehicles, which were mostly designed by Thomas Edison.

In 1903 twenty-nine electric vehicles were sold, and by 1913 1,841 Studebaker electrics were built before the company discontinued battery-powered vehicle production. Studebaker truck production with up to 4-ton capacity began in 1903. A collaboration with

STUDEBAKER TRUCKS
Manufactured by
STUDEBAKER CORPORATION, Detroit, Mich.

S P E C I F I C A T I O N S

Model	Panel	Station Car	Ton Express	Ton Bus
Capacity	½ ton	½ ton	1 ton	1 ton
Drive	Bevel gear	Bevel gear	Bevel gear	Bevel gear
Chassis Price	$850	$850	$1,200	$1,200
Motor				
H. P. (S.A.E.)	24.03	24.03	24.03	24.03
H. P. (Actual)	40	40	40	40
Cylinders	4 en bloc	4 en bloc	4 en bloc	4 en bloc
Bore	3⅞"	3⅞"	3⅞"	3⅞"
Stroke	5"	5"	5"	5"
Wheel Base	112"	112"	125"	125"
Tread Front	56"	56"	56"	56"
Tread Rear	56"	56"	56"	56"
Tires Front	34x4" pneu.	34x4" pneu.	35x5" pneu.	35x5" pneu.
Tires Rear	34x4" pneu.	34x4" pneu.	35x5" pneu.	35x5" pneu.

Frame—Pressed channel section.
Front Axle—Forged I-beam section.
Rear Axle—Floating.
Springs Front—Semi-elliptic.
Springs Rear—¾-elliptic   ¾- elliptic   Semi-elliptic   Semi-elliptic
Carburetor—Schebler.
Cooling System—Pump.
Oiling System—Splash.
Ignition—Generator, storage battery.
Control—Left drive, center control.
Clutch—Cone.
Transmission—Selective, three speeds forward and one reverse.
Brakes—Expanding and contracting rear axle.
Steering Gear—Worm and worm wheel.
Equipment—Motor-driven horn, speedometer, cowl, lamp, lighting switch, oil pressure
      gauge, battery indicator, self-starter.

Garford in Elyria, Ohio, to build gasoline cars continued until 1908. At first a two-cylinder motor was used until a four-cylinder was introduced in 1905. Further involvement with internal combustion vehicles continued with the marketing of Everett-Metzger-Flanders (E-M-F), then the Flanders 20 car, and then the takeover of E-M-F and the formation of Studebaker Corporation in 1911.

Studebaker began building its own monoboc six-cylinder engines in 1913, in fact pioneering the design in the U.S. along with Premier. The car was a success and sold well as Albert Russell Erskine took over the vice-presidency in 1915. Large numbers of Studebakers were supplied for the war effort, including at least 130 open touring staff cars for the AEF. The engineering department was run by the consulting team of Carl Breer, Owen R. Skelton and Fred M. Zeder during the war. The team designed the first postwar Studebakers before helping Walter Chrysler with his new car. By 1920 all Studebakers were powered by six-cylinder motors.

Although Studebakers were well designed and rugged, the engineering department in the early 1920s was not very progressive. As certain companies such as Packard began introducing four-wheel brake systems, Studebaker took out full-page magazine advertising calling such innovations "Unsafe." Yet by 1926 Studebaker adopted four-wheel brakes, as did many other companies in the late 1920s. It was soon deemed that two-wheel brake systems were unsafe.

Under Erskine, at South Bend Studebaker experimented both with new styling and with a new lower-priced car named after him. He let go the Zeder-Skelton-Breer team and hired Delmar G. Roos when the engineering consultants objected to his idea of a new eight-cylinder motor. The new straight-eight and styling from Ray Dietrich was successfully brought together for 1928 as the Studebaker President, even if the Erskine was not a hit.

Both the Studebaker Dictator and Commander models were entered in various races, and their winning records brought publicity and sales. But the stock market crash brought with it a whole variety of ills for Studebaker.

The purchase of Pierce-Arrow in 1928 proved to be a mistake, and the formation of S-P-A, which was to build only trucks, did not go off when the half-baked move to buy White proved to be a great mistake as well. The Rockne was introduced in 1932 and was also a failure, punctuated only by the death of Knute Rockne in an airplane crash. By March of 1933 Studebaker went into receivership, and four months later Albert Erskine committed suicide. Paul Hoffman and Harold Vance took over the helm at the company, selling off Pierce-Arrow for an even $1,000,000.

The two men brought Studebaker out of receivership in 1935 and the company was in stable financial shape when World War II started. Studebaker provided heavy trucks in World War II and rebounded after the war. However, after its belated merge with Packard, the company faded out of existence in the early 1960s with the sporty Avanti as its last hurrah and a factory in Canada as its last place of actual production.

Stutz

Harry C. Stutz was engaged in experimenting with cars from the turn of the previous century when he left Ohio and arrived in Indianapolis, Indiana, in 1903. Stutz worked for several auto firms and developed a transaxle type of transmission, which was designed to be mounted at the rear, eliminating the need for a differential.

By 1910 he organized his own company, which manufactured automotive components. He built a racing car and entered it into the Indianapolis 500 that year. Driven by Gil Anderson, it placed 11th, which was good enough for publicity, and helped form the Ideal Motor

STUTZ MOTOR CAR COMPANY

INDIANAPOLIS
INDIANA

Price	$2750
Four-Passenger Bulldog Special .	2650
Two-Passenger Roadster	2550
Bearcat	2550

STUTZ BULLDOG SPECIAL—SERIES S

Color	Elephant gray, maroon or blue		Lubrication	Force feed and splash
Seating Capacity. .	Seven		Radiator	Cellular
Position of Driver .	Right side		Cooling	Water pump
Wheelbase	130 inches		Ignition	Double distributor
Gauge	56½ inches		Starting System . .	Single unit
Wheels	Wire		Starter Operated .	Gear to fly wheel
Front Tires	32 x 4½ inches		Lighting System . .	Electric
Rear Tires	32 x 4½ inches		Voltages	Seven to eight
Service Brake . . .	Expanding on rear wheels		Wiring System. . .	Double
Emergency Brake .	Expanding on rear wheels		Gasoline System . .	Pressure feed
			Clutch	Cone
Cylinders	Four		Transmission . . .	Selective sliding
Arranged	Vertically		Gear Changes . . .	Three forward, one reverse
Cast.	En bloc		Drive	Plain bevel
Horsepower . . . . 30.63 (N.A.C.C. Rating)			Rear Axle	Three-quarters floating
Bore and Stroke .	4⅜ x 6 inches		Steering Gear . . .	Worm and gear

In addition to above specifications, price includes top, top hood, windshield, speedometer, ammeter, voltmeter, electric horn and extra wire wheel.

Car Company. Stutz began building a very similar car for sale on the open market. It used a 389 cid 50 hp four-cylinder T-head Wisconsin motor with the Stutz transaxle design. The Stutz was a right-hand-steered car, and amid the Toy Tonneau, Roadster and Touring body styles was also the Bearcat, for which Stutz would become most well known.

In 1912 a six-cylinder motor was introduced which helped win 25 out of 30 races entered that year. There were rumors that the clutch springs were intentionally so stiff women couldn't drive the Bearcat, but that was not intentional. A special race car of 1915, using a single overhead cam 16-valve engine built by Wisconsin, would power the latest bare-bones racer, part of the "White Squadron" Stutz racing team which competed with Mercer at the time.

Stutz remained a right-hand-steered car through World War I until 1921. In 1915 Cannonball Baker drove a Stutz Bearcat across the continent from San Diego to New York in eleven days, 7 hours and 15 minutes, setting a new record. By the time America entered the Great War in 1917, Stutz was building 2200 cars per year. The previous year was when Harry Stutz decided to build his own motor, per the earlier T-head design. The ensuing public stock offer in 1916 allowed an investor to buy controlling interest in Stutz. Now Alan A. Ryan had more to say about Stutz than Stutz himself, and the founder of the company left to build another car named the H.C.S., using his initials as Ransom Eli Olds did.

By 1922 Ryan was broke and Bethlehem Steel magnate Charles M. Schwab took over Stutz. He organized the introduction of a new overhead-valve six-cylinder motor that produced 70 hp, but the Stutz Bearcat was soon discontinued. In 1925 Frederick E. Moskovics became president of Stutz with the intent of changing the company's image to one of luxury rather than racing reputation. The Stutz

Vertical Eight, referring to the new engine with underslung worm drive, arrived in 1926. Styling was now the focus at Stutz, and European names such as Biarritz, Monte Carlo and Versailles were some of the chosen model names. The Stevens Cup of 1927 was won by a Stutz, which was awarded the AAA Stock Car Champion, proving that speed had not been abandoned at Stutz either.

The following year the Stutz Black Hawk averaged 106.53 mph at Daytona, making it the fastest stock production car built in the United States. But by 1929 Stutz discontinued sponsoring factory racing after the death of its driver Frank Lockhart while he was attempting a land speed record at Daytona. And both a patent infringement lawsuit instigated by Scripps-Booth regarding the underslung worm drive, as well as a breach of contract lawsuit brought by Weidley for termination of a motor manufacturing agreement, put the Stutz company in a precarious position just before the stock market crash.

Moskovics quit and Edgar S. Gorrell took over, bringing in the new DV-32 Stutz Bearcat for 1932, which had a dual-overhead cam and four valves per cylinder providing 156 hp and capability of better than 100 mph. The Super Bearcat followed, but the Great Depression all but precluded sales, and over the period of five years up to 1935, only 1500 Stutz cars were sold. The company was forced to switch its entire motor vehicle production to building the Pak-Age-Car, which was a light delivery van. It would take a couple more years for insolvency to go through the courts, relegating the Stutz name to history.

Sullivan

Not related to the Sullivan Manufacturing Company located nearly simultaneously in St. Louis, Missouri, for the purpose of building motor vehicles, the Sullivan Car Company of Rochester, New York, which began in 1910,

SULLIVAN TRUCKS.

Manufactured by

SULLIVAN MOTOR TRUCK CORP., Rochester, N. Y.

Model	F	E
Capacity	1½ tons	2 tons
Drive	Worm	Worm
Chassis Weight	3,500 lbs.	4,500 lbs.
Chassis Price	$2,150	$2,600
Engine	Buda	Buda
H. P. (S.A.E.)	22.5	27.23
H. P. (Actual)	25	35.5
Cylinders	4 en bloc	4 en bloc
Bore	3¾″	4⅛″
Stroke	4½″	5½″
Wheel Base	129″	150″
Tread Front	56″	58″
Tread Rear	59″	60″
Tires Front	36x3″	36x4″
Tires Rear	36x5″	36x6″

Frame—Pressed steel.
Front Axle—I-beam Elliott.
Rear Axle—Timken semi-floating, pressed housing.
Springs Front—Semi-elliptic.
Springs Rear—Semi-elliptic.
Carburetor—Holley automatic.

Cooling System	Thermo	Pump

Oiling System—Combination splash and force.
Ignition—Magneto.
Control—Left drive, center control.

Clutch	Cone	Dry plate
Transmission	Covert Selective, three speeds	Brown-Lipe Selective, three speeds

Brakes—Internal—rear wheels.
Steering Gear—Screw and nut.
Equipment—Three oil lamps, horn and complete set of tools. Governor furnished at extra cost.

at first built light motorized delivery wagons that included platform stake trucks. These were powered by two-cylinder horizontally-opposed motors with a two-speed planetary transmission. Solid rubber tires were standard and capacity was 800 pounds.

By 1912 Sullivan introduced ½-ton and ¾-ton capacity truck models, still using solid rubber tires and chain drive. For 1914 a 1-ton model was manufactured, and two years later a 2-ton truck was added to the model line, which was powered entirely by four-cylinder Buda engines along with Brown-Lipe transmissions and Timken worm drive. Sullivan trucks were apparently rugged enough that some were built as tankers. Nearly all trucks of this era before and during World War I used engine governors. Sullivan offered one as optional equipment, which was somewhat unusual but was probably meant to keep the base FOB price as low as possible. It was not stated which type of governor was available, but there were a few possibilities.

At the time the most commonly used engine governors were of two types: the centrifugal engine governor and the intake speed flow, in addition to the clutch governor for protecting the mechanism rather than limiting speed. The centrifugal type was much more common and used fly-ball design, which had diametrically opposed metal balls that swung out on a rotating shaft using swivel linkage. This design was derived from steam locomotives but was improved and streamlined for the smaller gasoline engine. It could be attached via a flexible or solid shaft from the engine, a wheel or the transmission, the latter being rarely used.

The purpose of the engine governor was to limit either the vehicle speed and/or the engine speed. The vehicle speed governor was used to limit the top vehicle speed while the engine governor prevented racing the motor when changing gears, in neutral or when releasing the clutch, which would essentially also limit the top vehicle speed. This was very important when engine RPM was a serious limitation and usually had to be kept considerably below 2000, particularly on commercial vehicles. Engines designed for racing that were capable of 3000 RPM increased in number during the 1920s and 1930s as bearing, metallurgy, valve train, piston weight, engine balancing and other elements of design were improved.

The most common intake governor was usually mounted between the intake manifold and the carburetor, limiting the amount of fuel mixture into the engine. The Simplex single-drive governor used a shaft to control both the engine and vehicle speed, whereas the Duplex-drive governor could control either the engine or vehicle speed.

A variation on the shaft-driven centrifugal engine governor was the Monarch type governor, which was actuated by the speed of the ingoing fuel mixture and therefore was not connected mechanically to the vehicle. This had its advantage of simplicity and disadvantage of a lack of positive instantaneous operation. There was also a Pierce type clutch governor based on a large dashpot which was used to govern the clutch in order to protect its structural integrity. The transmission driven governor was rarely used but had been invented. Governors have been used to the present day to prevent engine wear, wasteful gasoline consumption and going over speed limits.

The Sullivan Motor Company did not survive the year 1923 in the postwar recession. It does not appear that Sullivan manufactured any passenger vehicles.

Thor (motorcycle)

Aurora, Illinois, was the location of the Aurora Automatic Machinery Company, where motorcycle engines were built for Indian from 1902 until the contract expired in 1907. The company also built similar engines for

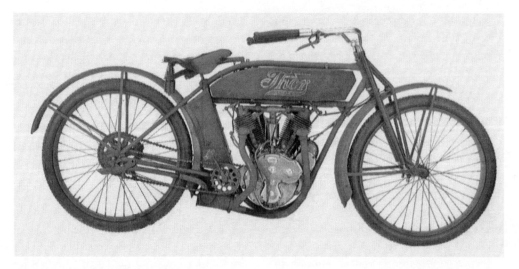

Manson, Racycle, Rambler, Reading-Standard and Warwick, all motorized bicycle and motorcycle manufacturers.

Aurora was in the highly industrialized northeastern region of Illinois, where in 1856 the Chicago, Burlington & Quincy Railroad had been founded. Numerous manufacturing companies settled in the area, relying on the supply of steel and an abundant skilled labor force of European descendants.

In 1907 the company began building its own motorcycles under the name Thor. The Thor Single 243 cc motor produced 3 hp using a 56-inch wheelbase. The motorcycle weighed 165 pounds and was capable of 40 mph. It sold for $210. The four-link fork was unique and an elegant design but was redesigned for better performance the following year.

Having built engines for so many other companies, Aurora intended for its motorcycle to give others competition in racing, and in 1915 Bill Briers came in second place to Indian motorcycle rider Glenn Boyd at the Dodge City 300 in Kansas.

By 1910 the Thor V-Twin was a new proprietary engine with 1190 cc, up to 9 hp by 1914, and was offered with a single- or two-speed transmission. By the following year financial troubles set in and Thor introduced its last

new bike. This was a 15 hp V-Twin with a 58-inch wheelbase which sold for $285. A single-cylinder model was also available, but by 1917 the company was being acquired by the Standard Salvage Company of Detroit, Michigan, and Thor disappeared later that year.

Tiffin

The Tiffin Wagon Works was located in Tiffin, Ohio. The company began building gasoline commercial vehicles in 1913, which was inauspicious due to the fact that the following year the area suffered one of the worst floods in modern history as the Upper Mississippi devastated Seneca County where Tiffin was located. Of the dozen factories that were damaged, the Tiffin Wagon Works managed to survive.

Tiffin built 1200-pound capacity conventional assembled trucks, as well as 2-ton forward control trucks, both with dual chain drive. By 1916 the company listed the ¾-ton Model A, 1-ton Model G, 2-ton Model M, 5-ton Model S and 6-ton Model SW. All models used Buda four-cylinder motors and dual chain drive.

One of the pieces of optional equipment that was offered by Tiffin during World War I was called the "lazy back." This was just an

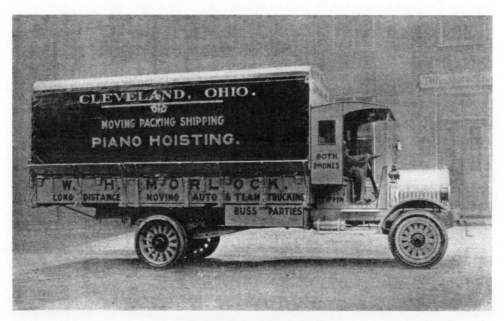

TIFFIN TRUCKS

Manufactured by

THE TIFFIN WAGON CO., Tiffin, Ohio

Model	A	AW	GW	MW
Capacity	¾ ton	1 ton	1½ tons	2½ tons
Drive	Internal gear	Worm	Worm	Worm
Chassis Weight	2 575 lbs.	3,040 lbs.	3,750 lbs.	4,640 lbs.
Chassis Price	$1,190	$1,550	$1,970	$2,700
Engine	Continental	Continental	Continental	Continental
H.P. (S.A.E.)	19.6	19.6	22.5	27.23
H.P. (Actual)	25	25	30	35
Cylinders	4 en bloc	4 en bloc	4 en bloc	4 en bloc
Bore	3¼"	3¼"	3¾"	4⅛"
Stroke	5"	5"	5¼	5¼"
Wheel Base	110"	112"	135"	144"
Tread Front	56"	56"	56"	60"
Tread Rear	56"	56"	61"	60"
Tires Front	35x4½" Pneu.	34x3"	36x3½"	36x4"
Tires Rear	35x4½" Pneu.	34x4"	36x5"	36x3½" dual

Frame—Pressed steel.
Front Axle—I-beam.

Rear Axle	Russell dead, round	Sheldon semi-floating, round	Sheldon semi-floating, round	Timken full-floating, round

Springs Front—Semi-elliptic.
Springs Rear—Semi-elliptic.
Carburetor—Schebler R.

Cooling System	Thermo-syphon	Thermo-syphon	Pump	Pump

Oiling System—Splash forced feed.
Ignition—Magneto.
Control—Left drive, center control.

Clutch	Cone	Dry plate	Dry plate	Cone
Transmission	Detroit Selective, 3 speeds forward and 1 reverse	Detroit Selective, 3 speeds forward and 1 reverse	Warner Selective, 3 speeds forward and 1 reverse	Covert Selective, 3 speeds forward and 1 reverse

Brakes—Rear wheels.
Steering Gear—Screw and nut.
Equipment—Seat, seat frame cushion, lazy back, three oil lamps, jack, horn, and tool kit.

ordinary cushion for the driver's back on the front seat, but in some cases, such as for this company, it was considered an extra. What would later be considered unthinkable in their absence, comfortable seats, especially in commercial vehicles, were considered a luxury. In addition such things as cabs (let alone enclosed cabs), windshields, heaters (let alone air conditioning) and other amenities would only later become standard equipment over decades.

The fact that a seat cushion would be called a "lazy back" was one indication how primitive driver and passenger accommodations were. During this period some trucks were so stiff in their suspensions, drivers needed to use what they called "kidney belts" to support their lower back as the vehicles bounced mercilessly across the terrain.

By 1917 electric starting was standard equipment on Tiffin trucks, with oil, acetylene and electric lamps optional. By 1921 Tiffin listed models with capacities of 1½-ton, 2½-ton, 3½-ton, 5-ton and 6-ton. As was the case with so many companies the postwar recession affected the company's business and production fell. Only the two largest truck models were offered for 1922 and 1923, but how many were actually built before Tiffin discontinued manufacturing altogether cannot be verified.

Trabold

Located in Johnstown, Pennsylvania, Trabold Truck Manufacturing Company began in 1911. Cambria County, where Trabold was located, was a region of industry which had gotten its start by way of the Pennsylvania Main Canal and a railroad system that helped boost steel production, whose peaking out would later be the culprit of a larger downturn of the area. But back at the turn of the previous century the Johnstown area had a population of some 75,000, considerably larger than even today.

In 1898 Adam G. Trabold started out experimenting with motor vehicles around Johnstown. The area's availability of steel and machinery as well as expertise was conducive for motor vehicle development, as with many cities around the Great Lakes. By 1905 Trabold built a second vehicle and started a dealership. In 1911 Trabold built a forward-control truck powered by a four-cylinder Buda engine. Within the following year the Trabold trucks were of conventional design but still used Buda engines.

It may be noted that forward-control design was a derivative of horse-drawn wagons on which drivers sat high up at the very front to access reins for the horses. But with a motor vehicle, sitting on top of the engine meant noise, vibration and more complicated linkages for clutch and transmission controls. Later use of forward-control would be called cab-over-engine (COE), a design that was specifically meant to save space and reduce the length of trucks, in many cases due to overall length restrictions for large trucks.

Trabold switched from chain drive to bevel gear drive around 1915, but customers could specify which type of drive they wanted. Shaft drive using worm, bevel and internal gears were still considered complicated and beyond most mechanics' knowledge, however more durable and efficient they were. Chain drive was very easy to repair or replace, but the metal links of the chain would stretch and were open to the ever-prevalent road dirt that required readjustment or repair. Heavy trucks still used chain drive at the time before metallurgical advances would eventually allow shaft drive for all motor vehicles.

Trabold reorganized in 1922 as the postwar recession had its effects, and the company became simply Trabold Motors Company, still in Johnstown. Then the company moved to Ferndale, Pennsylvania, in 1924. The following year Trabold was assembling approximately two trucks per week. These were 1½-

TRABOLD TRUCKS
Manufactured by
TRABOLD TRUCK MFG. CO., Johnstown, Pa.

S P E C I F I C A T I O N S

Model	T24	T45	H	HW
Capacity	1 ton	1 ton	2 tons	2 tons
Drive	Internal gear	Internal gear	Chain	Worm
Chassis Price	$975	$1,075	$2,000	$2,100
Motor				
H. P. (S.A.E.)	19.60	19.60	29	29
H. P. (Actual)	32	32	45	45
Cylinders	4 en bloc	4 en bloc	4 en bloc	4 en bloc
Bore	3½″	3½″	4¼″	4¼″
Stroke	5⅛″	5⅛″	5½″	5½″
Wheel Base	124″	145″	136″	136″
Tread Front	56″	56″	62″	62″
Tread Rear	56″	56″	62″	62″
Tires Front	36x3″	36x3″	36x4″	36x4″
Tires Rear	36x3½″	36x4″	36x6″	36x6″

Frame—Rolled channel.
Front Axle—I-beam.

Rear Axle	Internal gear	Internal gear	Solid rectangular	Worm

Springs Front—Semi-elliptic.
Springs Rear—Semi-elliptic.
Carburetor—Stromberg.

Cooling System	Thermo	Thermo	Pump	Pump

Oiling System—Splash.
Ignition—Magneto.
Control—Left drive, center control.
Clutch—Dry plate.
Transmission—Selective, three speeds forward and one reverse.
Brakes—On rear wheels.
Steering Gear—Worm and sector.
Equipment—Side and tail lamps, tool kit, jack.

ton (3000 lbs) and 2½-ton (5000 lbs) capacity. By 1929 Trabold was experiencing a financial crisis punctuated by the stock market crash. The manufacturing of trucks quickly faded out, but the company survived until 1960 building truck bodies.

Trojan

The Trojan Carriage Woodwork Company got its start in Toledo, Ohio, with a product described by its specific name before the company moved to Cleveland in the same state and turned to motor vehicle manufacture. The company specialized in commercial vehicles without delving into passenger car production when the first model arrived in 1914 in the form of a ¾-ton capacity truck. By 1916 a 1-ton model was added, and both were powered by four-cylinder engines.

Even though worm drive was used, the Trojan was a very basic design even for its era. The Model 26 and 27 for 1917 were both rated at 1-ton and varied only in wheelbase with the prices of $1500 and $1600 representing the difference. Electric lighting and starting were apparently not offered on the Trojan trucks, and engine cooling was still by thermosyphoning.

Before the universal adoption of water pumps on water-cooled engines, thermo- syphoning was a method of cooling the motor that relied on the coolant to rise into the upper radiator tube by way of high heat and then flow into the radiator. Upon descending by gravity as it cooled in the radiator tubes, the water would return into the engine block through the lower radiator tube. This was a slow process, so a belt-driven fan was needed for additional air to pass through the radiator, especially considering most trucks ran at walking speed and were governed to between 12 and 16 mph, so wind chill alone could not be relied on for cooling.

Furthermore, the height of the radiator had to be both higher at top and at bottom than the engine's water jackets. The height of the water had to be higher than the inlet tube; otherwise the coolant would be exposed to a hot air "bubble" and boil without the needed circulatory flow. The shape of the radiator needed to be rather narrow and tall for the entire effect to work, thereby dictating the shape of the vehicle. Any use of an added sealant in the radiator would plug up the whole system. Many drivers tried to find the best compromise by using corn meal to plug up a leak without closing off the syphoning effect. The entire method of thermosyphoning was abandoned and vehicles that were using this system by World War I were considered primitive. The only savings was in the lack of a water pump because the belt drive for the fan was already in place, but sealing the bearings of the water pump with the use of primitive packing relying on string and rubber was the obstacle in switching over to the universal adoption of the water pump.

Trojan was a small company and all the more susceptible to the wartime material shortages and then the postwar recession. Without military contracts and with plenty of competition in the region, the company was only listed until 1920, with manufacturing likely ceasing the previous year.

Union

Besides the Union Motor Truck Company of Philadelphia, Pennsylvania (1901–1904), the Union Automobile Manufacturing Company of St. Louis, Missouri (1905), and the Union Motor Truck Company of San Francisco, California (1912–1914), there was also the Union Motor Truck Company of Bay City, Michigan, that pertains to the text here. Known for shipbuilding and lumber industry, Bay City is located in the "crease" of Michigan on Lake Huron and the Saginaw River.

The first Union truck was the Model B,

TROJAN TRUCKS
Manufactured by
THE COMMERCIAL TRUCK CO., Cleveland, Ohio

S P E C I F I C A T I O N S

Model	26	27
Capacity	1 ton	1 ton
Drive	Worm	Worm
Chassis Price	$1,500	$1,600
Motor		
H. P. (S.A.E.)	18	18
H. P. (Actual)	30	30
Cylinders	4 en bloc	4 en bloc
Bore	$3\frac{3}{8}''$	$3\frac{3}{8}''$
Stroke	5''	5''
Wheel Base	120''	146''
Tread Front	56''	56''
Tread Rear	58''	58''
Tires Front	36x3''	36x3''
Tires Rear	$36x3\frac{1}{2}''$	$36x3\frac{1}{2}''$

Frame—Pressed.
Front Axle—I-beam, U type.
Rear Axle—Semi-floating.
Springs Front—Semi-elliptic.
Springs Rear—Semi-elliptic.
Carburetor—Stromberg, Model M1.
Cooling System—Thermo-Syphon.
Oiling System—Splash and pressure feed.
Ignition—Magneto.
Control—Left drive, center control.
Clutch—Dry plate.
Transmission—Selective, three speeds forward and one reverse.
Brakes—Expanding inside drum.
Steering Gear—Screw and nut.
Equipment—Full set of tools, hand horn, two oil side lamps, oil tail lamp.

THE UNION TRUCK

Manufactured by

UNION MOTOR TRUCK CO., Bay City, Mich.

Model	B
Capacity	2½ tons
Drive	Internal Gear
Chassis Weight	4,750 lbs.
Chassis Price	$2,075 with cab
Engine	Wisconsin
H. P. (S.A.E.)	25.60
H. P. (Actual)	45
Cylinders	4 en bloc
Bore	4″
Stroke	6″
Wheel Base	152-176″ optional
Tread Front	56″
Tread Rear	56″
Tires Front	39x4″
Tires Rear	39x6″

Frame—Pressed.
Front Axle—I-beam, drop forged.
Rear Axle—Russell, round.
Springs Front—Semi-elliptic.
Springs Rear—Semi-elliptic.
Carburetor—Schebler ''R.''
Cooling System—Thermo-syphon.
Oiling System—Force feed.
Ignition—Magneto.
Control—Right hand, center control.
Clutch—Dry disc.
Transmission—Fuller Selective, three speeds forward.
Brakes—External contracting and internal expanding.
Steering Gear—Screw and nut.
Equipment—Lamps, tools, curtains, Duplex Governor.

which was at 2½-ton capacity. This remained the only model for several years through World War I without any substantial changes. It was powered by a four-cylinder Wisconsin motor using a Fuller three-speed transmission and a bevel gear rear axle.

The Union company survived World War I without any apparent involvement in production for the war effort, most likely due to the fact that this was a very small company not set up for any large-scale manufacturing. It was the type of enterprise often driven out of business during this period, for reasons such as material shortages and lack of skilled labor as men went off to war. Then the postwar recession often took its toll, as well as labor strikes, but Union stayed in business and introduced a 4-ton and 6-ton capacity model line of trucks in 1921. The following year Union built a small bus.

Some records show a 1½-ton Model E with a 150-inch wheelbase introduced about the time the company began having major financial problems. The Model E was powered by a four-cylinder Continental 6M engine using a Fuller clutch and transmission. In 1924 the company listed its 2½-ton truck as models FLW, FV, FWC and FW, each powered by a Wisconsin TAU engine. The Indestructible Wheel Company provided the Union with its wheels. The models had the same capacity but differed in axles, which were from Walker, Shuler, or Clark, and wheelbases were different.

Equipment included an engine governor. Although the simplex and duplex terminology would be used generically, it also referred to the Duplex Engine Governor Company of Brooklyn, New York. Union ceased manufacturing after 1925, although it was still listed for that year.

United

Grand Rapids, Michigan, known as "Furniture City" at one time, was the location of the United Motor Truck Company, which began manufacturing in 1915. It should not be confused with the National United Service Company of Detroit, Michigan, which built passenger and light delivery cyclecars by the name of National at the same time. There was also the United Horse Subduer Company of New York City; United Motor Company of New York City; United Auto Company of Newark, New Jersey; United Motor Corporation of Pawtucket, Rhode Island; United Motor & Vehicle Company of Boston, Massachusetts; United Motors Company of Camden, New Jersey, and United Motors Company of Chicago, Illinois. All of these were in existence before World War I and perhaps proved that using the name "United" was a popular choice, even if none of these companies ever actually manufactured a motor vehicle in spite of the fact they were each organized to do so. There was yet another company named the United Products Corporation in Grand Rapids, Michigan, organized to build cars and trucks, which never got started. The only company so named that got into the actual building of motor vehicles during the Great War, namely trucks, was the United Motor Truck Company, illustrated here.

The first United trucks were 1½-, 3- and 5-ton models. These were conventional assembled trucks each powered by a four-cylinder Continental engine. The lightest truck had worm drive, as did one of two 3-ton models, proving once again that chain drive and shaft drive were still both contending for acceptability, especially in the minds of customers who either did not trust shaft (worm or bevel gear) drive, or preferred to perform the continual but familiar maintenance on chain drive.

The company was reorganized in 1916 as the United Motors Company. It continued manufacturing during and after World War I, and in 1922 was reorganized again as the United Motors Products Company (apparently

UNITED TRUCKS
Manufactured by
UNITED MOTORS CO., Grand Rapids, Mich.

S P E C I F I C A T I O N S

Model	BSW	CSW	DSW	ESW
Capacity	2 tons	3½ tons	4 tons	5 tons
Drive	Worm	Worm	Worm	Worm
Chassis Price	$2,250	$2,900	$3,200	$3,900
Motor				
H. P. (S.A.E)	27.2	32.4	32.4	36.1
H. P. (Actual)	40 at 1500 R.P.M.	50 at 1500 R.P.M.	50 at 1500 R.P.M.	62 at 1700 R.P.M.
Cylinders	4 en bloc	4 in pairs	4 in pairs	4 in pairs
Bore	4⅛″	4½″	4½″	4¾″
Stroke	5¼″	5½″	5½″	5½″
Wheel Base	144″ (168″ opt.)	144″ (168″ opt.)	144″ (168″ opt.)	144″ (168″ opt.)
Tread Front	62½″	66″	66″	66″
Tread Rear	64½″	70″	70″	74⅝″
Tires Front	36x4″	36x5″	36x5″	36x6″
Tires Rear	36x4″ dual	36x5″ dual	36x6″ dual	40x6″ dual

Frame—Rolled channel.
Front Axle—I-beam.
Rear Axle—Semi-floating, round, worm.
Springs Front—Semi-elliptic.
Springs Rear—Semi-elliptic.
Carburetor—Stromberg.
Cooling System—Pump.
Oiling System—Forced feed.
Clutch—Multiple dry disc.
Ignition—Magneto.

Control	Left drive, center control	Left drive, center control	Right drive, center control	Right drive, right control
Transmission	Selective, three speeds forward, one reverse	Selective, three speeds forward, one reverse	Selective, three speeds forward, one reverse	Selective, four speeds forward, one reverse

Brakes—Double expanding axle.
Steering Gear—Worm.
Equipment—Two oil side lights, oil tail light, horn, oil can, jack, tool kit, special axle wrenches.

not related to the company mentioned above with a similar name). Truck production continued through the 1920s until the company was acquired by Acme in 1927 and the model line was merged with the new parent company in Cadillac, Michigan. The United name was phased out by the time the Great Depression got underway.

Universal

The Universal Truck Motor Company began in Detroit, Michigan, in 1910. It should be noted that at least thirteen other companies using the "Universal" name were organized to build motor vehicles, all of them prior to World War I, in the following cities: East Orange, New Jersey; Pittsburgh, Pennsylvania; New York City; Chicago, Illinois; San Francisco, California; Detroit, Michigan; Martinsburg, West Virginia; Buffalo, New York; Madison, Wisconsin; Wilmington, Delaware; Denver, Colorado; New Castle, Indiana; and Washington, Pennsylvania. According to some sources, the Universal Truck Motor Company that was in existence during the Great War did not begin production until 1911.

Right from the beginning Universal built a mid-range capacity truck in the form of a dual chain-driven 3-ton forward-control model with a wheelbase of 132 inches. It was powered by a four-cylinder motor and was joined in 1913 by a 1-ton and a 2-ton model. The lightest truck used shaft drive and was upgraded to 1½-ton capacity in 1916. The other two models remained the same.

What was noteworthy about the Universal was that as a small company it listed its own engines, transmissions and axles, which was very unusual at a time when there was an excellent selection of original equipment manufacturers (OEMs) across America. The Universal 32 hp four-cylinder engine was used in the Model G 1½-ton, whereas a purportedly weaker Universal 30 hp four-cylinder engine was used in the Model D 2-ton capacity truck. This may have been a typographical error, but it was not unusual to have truck models listed out of alphabetical sequence in relation to their size and capacity.

The Universal engine had splash lubrication, which meant that the main, cam and piston rod bearings received oil only through immersion and the splash effect of rotation. This was a simpler and cheaper method of motor lubrication which was phased out in the decade after World War I because it precluded higher RPM and higher torque and it led to higher frictional wear. With the addition of a gear-driven oil pump, which was the most common design, oil was pumped through a series of internal arteries which lubricated key points under pressure. But splash lubrication continued to have its proponents through the 1920s.

Also, as was the case with many commercial vehicles of the era, lighter models used shaft drive while heavier models remained chain-driven. This was essentially the result of inadequate metallurgical alloying and hardening of steel, which would greatly improve as a result of World War I and during the next few decades, especially during World War II. Universal trucks ceased to be produced right after World War I due to the postwar recession, although the company was listed until 1920.

U.S.

The United States Motor Truck Company was organized in Cincinnati, Ohio. With such a name it is perhaps not especially surprising but still worth noting there were sixteen other companies using the name "United States" in their own name, fifteen of them prior to World War I, and all were organized for the purpose of manufacturing motor vehicles. Trucks with the "USA" emblem during

UNIVERSAL TRUCKS
Manufactured by
UNIVERSAL SERVICE CO., Detroit, Mich.
1120 Grand River Avenue

S P E C I F I C A T I O N S

Model	A	D	G
Capacity	3 tons	2 tons	1½ tons
Drive	Chain	Chain	Worm
Chassis Price	$3,400	$2,800	$1,950
Motor			
H. P. (S.A.E.)	25.6	25.6	22.5
H. P. (Actual)	30	30	
Cylinders	4 in pairs	4 in pairs	4 en bloc
Bore	4″	4″	3¾″
Stroke	5½″	5½″	5½″
Wheel Base	132″	132″	130″
Tread Front	64″	64″	64″
Tread Rear	67″	67″	67″
Tires Front	36x5″	36x4″	34x3½″
Tires Rear	36x4″ dual	36x4″ dual	34x5″
Frame—Rolled channel steel.			
Front Axle	I-beam	I-beam	Timken
Rear Axle	Fixed rectangular sec.	Fixed rectangular sec.	Full-floating
Springs Front—Semi-elliptic.			
Springs Rear—Semi-elliptic.			
Carburetor	Zenith O4	Zenith O5	Zenith O4
Cooling System—Pump.			
Oiling System—Constant splash.			
Ignition—Magneto, Eisemann G.			
Control	Right drive, right control	Right drive, right control	Left drive, center control
Clutch	Dry multiple disc	Dry multiple disc	Single dry plate
Transmission—Selective, three speeds forward and one reverse.			
Brakes	Emergency, expanding shoe type; Service, contracting shoe type	Emergency, expanding shoe type; Service, contracting shoe type	Service and emergency expanding type
Steering Gear	Ross	Ross	Lavine
Equipment—Side and tail lamps, horn, tool box, and tool kit.			

U. S. TRUCKS

Manufactured by

THE UNITED STATES MOTOR TRUCK CO., Cincinnati, Ohio

S P E C I F I C A T I O N S

Model	H	J	K	E
Capacity	2 tons	3½ tons	5 tons	2 tons
Drive	Worm	Worm	Worm	Chain
Chassis Price	On application	On application	On application	On application
Motor				
H. P. (S.A.E.)	27.2	32.4	36.1	27.2
H. P. (Actual)	35	40	45	35
Cylinders	4 en bloc	4 in pairs	4 in pairs	4 en bloc
Bore	4⅛″	4½″	4¾″	4⅛″
Stroke	5¼″	5¼″	6¼″	5¼″
Wheel Base	144″	162″	168″	144″
Tread Front	59″	62″	62″	59″
Tread Rear	60″	67″	73″	62½″
Tires Front	34x4″	36x5″	36x5″	34x3½″
Tires Rear	36x4″ dual	40x5″ dual	40x6″ dual	36x3½″ dual
Frame—Rolled.				
Front Axle—I-beam, Elliott.				
Rear Axle	Semi-floating	Semi-floating	Semi-floating	Fixed
Springs Front—Semi-elliptic.				
Springs Rear—Semi-elliptic.				
Carburetor—Float feed.				
Cooling System—Pump.				
Oiling System—Splash, circulating.				
Ignition—Magneto.				
Control	Left drive, center control	Left drive, center control	Right drive, center control	Left drive, center control
Clutch—Cone.				
Transmission—Selective, three speeds forward and one reverse.				
Brakes	Internal, rear wheels	Internal, rear wheels	Internal, rear wheels	Compression on jackshaft, expanding in rear wheels
Steering Gear	Screw and nut	Screw and nut	Screw and nut	Worm and nut

Equipment—Three oil lamps, kit of tools, jack, special starting battery, hubodometer, extra small parts.

World War I were Liberty trucks built specifically as military vehicles for the war effort using independent manufacturers which were organized by the U.S. government and SAE to create a standardized 4 × 2 truck (see Liberty). Using "United States" in a private company's name may have been patriotic, and this company made use of that tactic in its advertising, but it did not guarantee high quality of product or truly successful sales and marketing.

The first U.S. truck was built in 1909 and was powered by a 20 hp horizontally-opposed two-cylinder motor. Capacity was listed as 1-ton and 1½-ton for the two versions in the first model line. In 1912 the company's first four-cylinder truck was built, which included a forward-control 1½-ton truck and a conventional 3-ton truck.

By 1916 U.S. listed 3½-ton, 4-ton and 5-ton capacity trucks using chain drive or worm drive, depending on capacity and customer specifications. After the war, production slowed but resumed during the 1920s with an expansion of the model line in 1922 to include 1½-ton to 7-ton models. Continental and Hinkley engines were adopted, along with Fuller clutches and transmissions, Sheldon rear axle, and Shuler front axle. Only the heaviest models used Brown-Lipe transmissions and Sheldon rear axle. The 7-ton Model T was powered by a four-cylinder Buda engine.

That the U.S. truck had a hub odometer brings up the subject of this invention, which was used first in ancient times by counting the revolutions of a wagon or chariot wheel and multiplying by its circumference. The first manufactured automotive speedometer for general use was built by Thorpe & Salter in London in 1902. In 1906 the Baldwin Chain and Manufacturing Company sold its Monitor Recorder, which made a record of a truck's daily stops, starts and speed by combining a clock with a speedometer/odometer. The hub odometer was attached to the truck's rear axle hub, hence its name, and it used a magnet to trip a recorder for the distance traveled. The speedometer mechanism necessitated a more complex technology.

By 1912 the Sears-Cross Company offered its "Commercial Spedindicator," which showed speed up to 35 mph as well as trip and total mileage. This information was vital for any type of commercial delivery or hauling work to understand efficiency and optimize profit, whereas the passenger car's speedometer/odometer was more important to show off top speed to help with staying within the speed limit, as well as to show the extent of the vehicle's use.

There were essentially four types of speedometers in the early days of motoring. The centrifugal design was derived from steam engine technology and the fly-ball governor, which used diametrically opposed metal balls that swung out on a rotating shaft using swivel linkage with centrifugal force.

The hydraulic design used a vertical tube of mercury or other heavy liquid with a hydraulic screw driven off the vehicle's engine, transmission or axle. The miniature centrifugal pump that was created in this manner moved a float on top of the liquid, or just the liquid itself, whose top edge was then calibrated visually with some type of graticule or lined ruler. A pneumatic design of the speedometer/odometer, called the Van Sicklen type, used air pressure against a light vane attached to a dial.

The magnetic, or mechanical, speedometer/odometer was the most complex but also the most accurate. This design is based on a permanent magnet that is spun inside a housing. Driven by a cable, the magnet creates magnetic currents, and the housing is forced lightly in the direction of the spin while held back by a spring, thereby giving a readout. This type was built by such companies as American, Every-Ready, Jones, Perfection,

Smith and Warner (Stewart-Warner) during this era. The latter company would have 90 percent of the market after World War I. It would take years before magnifying lenses and tiny light bulbs were incorporated to become a standardized part of the speedometer/odometer so that they would be actually easily visible to the driver in daylight and at night.

It appears the United States Motor Truck Company remained in business and manufactured trucks on a relatively small-scale basis, but the Wall Street stock market crash and ensuing Great Depression put an end to the enterprise entirely by 1930.

Velie

The Velie Carriage Company made the transition from horse-drawn to motor-driven vehicle production in 1909 at Moline, Illinois, after being in business building the former type of vehicles since 1902. William Lamb Velie was the man behind the name and the company, and by 1911 Velie was also producing commercial vehicles.

Moline, located in northwestern Illinois, was better known as the headquarters for John Deere, but before that it was also home to the Moline Wagon Company and the Moline Auto Company, known for building the Moline-Knight before World War I. The fact that Velie was located in the same city as that of the headquarters of John Deere was more than a coincidence. William Velie's mother, Emma Deere, financed the Velie venture, and her father had already made quite a name for himself when he invented the self-scouring plow in 1848, moved his business to Moline, and subsequently made a fortune building farm implements, equipment and tractors.

The first Velie cars were carried in the John Deere catalog. There were 1,000 built, and these were powered by motors supplied by the American and British Manufacturing Com-

pany. The Velie firm switched to Lycoming engines, and in 1911 the company was building its own motors when the first Velie truck was produced. That year a Velie came in 17th out of 46 cars in the second Indianapolis 500, which was good enough for promotional purposes.

Emma Deere's investment paid off as Velie became a success, selling about 3500 cars per year, plus a number of trucks. William Velie built a 46-room mansion in Moline. By 1915 a Continental six-cylinder car was introduced, which included a muffler bypass "to be used as a warning signal," the advertising explained, but was also good for street racing.

During World War I Velie did well on government contracts and was reorganized with a $2,000,000 capitalization. Velie was one of the assemblers of Liberty trucks, although the 455 built by the company were hardly enough to count a profit since the contract was canceled as soon as the Armistice was signed, and smaller companies stuck with material and parts inventories for various military projects ending up suffering. Many companies worked toward the war effort on a break-even level in any case.

The Velie featured a Presto Tank as optional equipment, which could be used both for its lights and as a Presto self-starter. After the war Velie once again entered racing, with company executives knowing full well that it was one of the best ways of promoting their product. Velie showed its superiority at the annual Pikes Peak contest, and by 1920, 9000 Velies rolled off the line. Even in the early 1920s, as the recession lagged on, Velie sold 5000 cars per year with an engine built in its own factory.

After a bout of illness when engineer Herbert Snow and "efficiency expert" Edwin McEwen took over, William Velie's health returned and he installed his son Will Jr. as vice-president. In 1928 a straight-eight motor was offered, but on October 28 that year William

VELIE MOTORS CORPORATION

MOLINE
ILLINOIS

Price **$1850**
Seven-Passenger Touring . 1595

VELIE SPORT CAR—39

COLOR	Blue or maroon	LUBRICATION	Pump over and splash
SEATING CAPACITY. .	Four	RADIATOR	Cellular
POSITION OF DRIVER .	Left side	COOLING	Water pump
WHEELBASE	124 inches	IGNITION	Storage battery
GAUGE	56 inches	STARTING SYSTEM . .	Two unit
WHEELS	Wood	STARTER OPERATED .	Gear to fly wheel
FRONT TIRES	33 x 4½ inches	LIGHTING SYSTEM . .	Electric
REAR TIRES	33 x 4½ inches, anti-skid	VOLTAGES	Six
SERVICE BRAKE . . .	Contracting on rear wheels	WIRING SYSTEM . . .	Single
EMERGENCY BRAKE .	Expanding on rear wheels	GASOLINE SYSTEM . .	Vacuum
		CLUTCH	Dry multiple disc
CYLINDERS	Six	TRANSMISSION . . .	Selective sliding
ARRANGED	Vertically	GEAR CHANGES . . .	Four forward, one reverse
CAST.	En bloc	DRIVE	Spiral bevel
HORSEPOWER	29.4 (N.A.C.C. Rating)	REAR AXLE	Three-quarters floating
BORE AND STROKE .	3½ x 5¼ inches	STEERING GEAR . . .	Worm and gear

In addition to above specifications, price includes top, windshield,
speedometer, ammeter, voltmeter, electric horn and demountable rims.

VELIE TRUCKS
Manufactured by
VELIE MOTORS CORPORATION, Moline, Ill.

Model	25-A	26-A
Capacity	1½-2 tons	3½ tons
Drive	Worm	Worm
Chassis Weight	4,800 lbs.	6,800 lbs.
Chassis Price	$2,750	$3,600
Engine	Continental	Continental
H. P. (S.A.E.)	27.2	32.4
H. P. (Actual)	35	45
Cylinders	4 en bloc	4 in pairs
Bore	4⅛"	4⅛"
Stroke	5¼"	5½"
Wheel Base	135" and 150"	160" and 172"
Tread Front	58½"	62"
Tread Rear	58½"	66¾"
Tires Front	36x4"	36x5"
Tires Rear	36x7"	40x5" dual

Frame—Pressed steel.
Front Axle—Timken I-beam, roller.
Rear Axle—Timken full-floating.
Springs Front—Semi-elliptic.
Springs Rear—Semi-elliptic.
Carburetor—Stromberg.
Cooling System—Pump.
Oiling System—Splash and force.
Ignition—Bosch High Tension.
Control—Right drive, center control.
Clutch—Dry plate.
Transmission—Brown-Lipe Selective, four speeds.
Brakes—Internal, rear wheels.
Steering Gear—Worm and wheel.
Equipment—Top and curtains, seat and cushion, headlights and Presto Tank, side and tail lights, jack, oil cans, tools, hand horn, bumper, tool box, governor. Stewart Vacuum feed system and hubodometer.

Velie suddenly died of an embolism. On March 29, 1929, his son died of a heart attack. John Deere took over the factory, and that was the end of Velie even before the stock market crash at the end of October of 1929.

Vim

As a trade name VIM was not an abbreviation of anything specifically. It was created by the Touraine Company of Philadelphia, Pennsylvania, in 1913. The company was already building a newly-badged Nance passenger car under the Touraine name with Harold B. Larzelere steering the enterprise. The Touraine was a six-cylinder auto, but Touraine also built a cyclecar in 1914 using the VIM name. Since neither the six-cylinder nor the two-cylinder VIM was selling, the company began building the Vim truck in 1913. The three letters were often, but not always, all capitalized.

The first model was a 1½-ton truck powered by a four-cylinder Northway engine which had a cone clutch and bevel drive. This was an usual combination in that the former was a design from earlier days, yet it remained in use even after World War I, while the latter was a more advanced type of mechanism. The cone of the cone clutch itself was made of sheet metal but the area of contact was lined with leather, or later with fabric of properties similar to leather. A series of usually six spring-loaded buttons or "studs" called "clutch leather expanders" mounted in a bolt circle under the leather or fabric kept the leather stretched flat out against the contact surface and allowed gradual engagement. There was a clutch brake to keep it from spinning freely when released.

If a cone clutch grabbed too quickly and the vehicle jerked, the leather expanders needed adjustment. The clutch leather would eventually dry out within a few thousand miles and begin either to grab or to slip. The maintenance manual recommendation was to "rub a little neatsfoot" on the leather to soften it. This type of terminology, let alone the technology, is now an obscure and forgotten detail of the automotive past but very significant from an historical and curiosity point of view. Neatsfoot was a light, pale grease or oil made by boiling the joints and shin bones of cattle. It was used as a light lubricant and dressing for leather.

The cone clutch mechanism was essentially open to the outside air for access in application of such things as neatsfoot and the maintenance or replacement of the cork or rubber lining of the clutch brake, prior to fully enclosed clutches. It therefore was highly susceptible to being contaminated with engine oil, grease, and road grime, and was not expected to last very long. Hence, the replacement of the clutch was a regular maintenance problem, and a few thousand miles for a clutch was considered a normal life span. Single plate and multiple disk clutches were more commonly used by World War I, and the single plate asbestos-lined clutch would eventually emerge as the most durable design, with the asbestos being superseded by less virulent material only in recent years.

Vim sold about 13,000 trucks a year by 1916. The company also provided at least fourteen types of bodies, from flatbeds to furniture vans and everything in between. By 1918 a 1½-ton and a 3-ton model were offered, and both were powered by an engine built by what was now called the Vim Motor Truck Company, a name which had been adopted in a reorganization during 1915.

Once World War I had ended the company switched back to buying Continental and Hercules engines. This was most likely due to material shortages and high costs of building one's own engines at a time when "off-the-shelf" motors were available across the land. In 1921 the Standard Steel Car Company took over Vim and soon sold off all of the assets.

VIM TRUCKS

Manufactured by

VIM MOTOR TRUCK COMPANY, Philadelphia, Pa.

Model	21	22	23
Capacity	½ ton	1½ tons	3 tons
Drive	Bevel gear	Worm	Worm
Chassis Weight	1,900 lbs.	4,400 lbs.	6,000 lbs.
Chassis Price	$845	$2,750	$3,550
Engine	Vim	Vim	'Vim
H. P. (S.A.E.)	14.4	22.5	28.9
H. P. (Actual)	22	36	46
Cylinders	4 en bloc	4 en bloc	4 en bloc
Bore	3"	3¾"	4¼"
Stroke	4½"	5½"	5½"
Wheel Base	108"	142"	150"
Tread Front	56"	56"	57"
Tread Rear	56"	58"	60"
Tires Front	31x4" Pneu.	36x4"	36x4"
Tires Rear	31x4" Pneu.	36x6"	36x4" dual

Frame—Pressed steel.
Front Axle—I-beam.

Rear Axle	Three-fourth floating	Semi-floating	Semi-floating

Springs Front—Semi-elliptic.
Springs Rear—Semi-elliptic.

Carburetor	Zenith	Zenith truck	Zenith truck
Cooling System	Thermo-syphon	Pump	Pump
Oiling System	Splash	Forced feed	Forced feed

Ignition—Dixie magneto.
Control—Left-hand.

Clutch	Cone	Dry plate	Dry plate
Transmission	Selective, three speeds	Selective, four speeds	Selective, four speeds
Brakes	Internal expanding and external contracting rear wheels	Double internal expanding rear wheels	Double internal expanding rear wheels

Steering Gear—Worm.

Equipment—Model 21—Dash, windshield, five lamps, tools, horn and accessories. Models 22 and 23—Oil lamps, horn, tools, jack, tank and seat. Model 21 has 14 bodies on standard chassis.

Walker Balance Drive (electric)

In 1906 the Automobile Maintenance & Manufacturing Company of Chicago, Illinois, began manufacturing electric commercial vehicles using the name Walker Balance Gear. This name described the design in that an electric motor was mounted in each of the four wheels. This was a very common practice for electric vehicle design in the early days, with Ferdinand Porsche showing a car at the Paris Show of 1900 using this type of technology. Because they were simply connected by flexible wires to the batteries and controller, the motors on the front wheels swiveled to steer the entire vehicle. No transmission, differential or driveshaft was needed, greatly simplifying the entire machine.

But in order to reduce the cost of the electric trucks and make the drive mechanism even simpler, Walker began using one single DC motor mounted between the rear wheels using internal gear drive. Walker also built a gasoline-electric hybrid vehicle at the time, but it was not successful, most likely because it did not fit into either category of electric or internal combustion technology for which there were separate and somewhat divisive proponents.

In 1912 the company was reorganized as the Walker Vehicle Company in Chicago. Five models ranging from 750-pound to 3½-ton capacity were available. All used the single rear axle motor, the smallest of which was 3.5 hp with gear ratio reducing RPM so that speed was no higher than 8 mph.

As internal combustion vehicles quickly gained popularity and the infrastructure for their domination grew and flourished, some electric vehicle builders attempted to make their cars and trucks look like gasoline-powered vehicles, and Walker was one of them. The ½-ton Walker Electric had a hood that was strictly decorative in order to blend in to the appearance of standard gasoline trucks.

All Walker electrics were forward-control with a huge battery box suspended under the chassis. In 1929 the design was further manipulated to resemble gasoline trucks, and that may have helped Walker remain in business into the 1930s. There were electric vehicle enthusiasts all along, and some applications such as local delivery work benefited from the low cost, simplicity and clean, quiet service of electric trucks. Walker trucks were available in up to 7-ton capacity from 1929.

Towards the end of the use of electric road vehicles, Walker again turned to hybrid technology, calling the design Walker Dynamotive. Four-cylinder Waukesha or six-cylinder Chrysler engines were used to drive a large 15-kilowatt generator that was attached at the bell housing which powered the single electric motor at the rear axle. These trucks were 1-ton and 1½-ton capacity, respectively. The advantage was higher speed and range, while the omission of a standard clutch, transmission and driveshaft kept simplicity as part of the design.

Many of the Walker electric trucks up to 5-ton capacity were exported to Great Britain during the 1930s. There they found acceptance among such industries as dairy delivery vehicles, working early mornings very quietly, with nary a puff of exhaust, and at low speed in light traffic. They were also used around airports with the advantage of safety around highly volatile aviation fuel. But the low cost of petroleum and energy density of gasoline would eclipse electric vehicle technology for decades, and Walker was one of the last companies in America in the pre–World War II era to build this type of road vehicle when the company ceased production in 1942.

Walter

New York City would be the location of the successful company that William Walter

WALKER ELECTRIC TRUCKS

Manufactured by

Walker Vehicle Company, 531-545 W. 39th St., Chicago

Model	K	L	D	N
Capacity	1 ton	2 tons	3 tons	5 tons
Drive	Walker Balance Drive	Walker Balance Drive	Walker Balance Drive	Walker Balance Drive
Chassis Weight	2,500 lbs.	3,700 lbs.	4,700 lbs.	6,300 lbs.
Chassis Price	$1,900	$2,300	$2,650	$3,300
Wheel Base	96" or longer	110" or longer	130" or longer	144" or longer
Tread Front	56"	56"	56"	62"
Tread Rear	56"	56"	56"	62"
Tires Front	34x3½"	38x4"	36x5"	36x7"
Tires Rear	36x4"	38x6"	38x4" dual	38x6" dual
Frame—Rolled channel.				
Speed	14 M. P. H.	13 M. P. H.	12 M. P. H.	10 M. P. H.
Miles	40 to 75	40 to 70	40 to 60	40 to 60

Front Axle—I-section, drop forged steel axle, vanadium steel drop forged knuckles.

Rear Axle—Walker Vehicle Co. hollow steel, enclosing motor and differential, drop forged vanadium steel stub axles.

Springs Front—Semi-elliptic, chrome-vanadium steel.

Springs Rear—Semi-elliptic chrome-vanadium steel.

Battery Equipment—Edison or Lead optional.

Motor—Series.

Steering Gear—Ross differential screw.

Transmission—Walker balance drive.

Control—Five speeds forward and five reverse.

Brakes—External and internal, both on rear wheel drums.

Equipment—Electric dash and tail lights, odometer, ampere-hour meter, safety switch, hand horn, charging plug and receptacle, fenders, kit of tools.

THE WALTER FOUR WHEEL DRIVE TRACTOR TRUCK
Manufactured by
MILWAUKEE LOCOMOTIVE MFG. CO., Milwaukee, Wis.

S P E C I F I C A T I O N S

Model	M-O
Capacity	10 tons, 2 on tractor, 8 on trailers
Drive	Spur gear on four wheels
Chassis Price	On application
Motor	
H. P. (S.A.E.)	30.7
H. P. (Actual)	42
Cylinders	4 en bloc
Bore	$4\frac{3}{8}''$
Stroke	6"
Wheel Base	108"
Tread Front	64"
Tread Rear	64"
Tires Front	40x4" dual
Tires Rear	40x4" dual

Frame—Rolled.

Front Axle—Rectangular, steering knuckle carries enclosed driving gear and pinion.

Rear Axle—Rear axles are same as front and interchangeable.

Springs Front—Semi-elliptic.

Springs Rear—Semi-elliptic.

Carburetor—Float feed.

Cooling System—Pump.

Oiling System—Constant level splash with pump.

Ignition—Magneto.

Control—Left drive, center control.

Clutch—Cone.

Transmission—Selective, four speeds forward and one reverse.

Brakes—One foot, one hand, both acting on all wheels.

Steering Gear—Worm and full worm gear, steer all four wheels.

Equipment—Tools, jack, and oil lamps.

founded after settling on Staten Island when he immigrated from Switzerland in 1883. He imported a car from Europe in 1898 and realized he could make a number of improvements. He used his American Chocolate Machinery Company facilities on Manhattan to build a four-wheel two-cylinder car in 1899. After three years of tinkering with the car he placed in on the market as the Waltmobile.

The following year (1903) he built a four-cylinder car which now had 24 hp, double that of the first Waltmobile, and the name was changed simply to Walter. In 1904 Walter introduced a new car at the New York Auto Show which was very well accepted. It featured a steel frame with aluminum body, a spring clutch, wheel steering, shaft drive and three-speed selective sliding gear transmission. The 30 hp four-cylinder motor was an H-head design, with overhead intake valves, all advanced for 1904.

All of these cars were still being built at his chocolate machinery factory until 1905 when the Walter Automobile Company was formed, after about 150 Walter cars had already been completed. French engineer Etienne Planche came onboard at this time. With more powerful 40 hp and 50 hp motors for 1906, the company adopted the slogan "The Aristocrat of American Motordom." That year the entire Walter auto operation was moved to a former brewery in Trenton, New Jersey. Planche made connections with C.G. Roebling and in 1909 the Walter car became the Mercer after Walter defaulted on $24,000 worth of bonds. William Walter began building commercial vehicles back at the chocolate factory in Manhattan.

Walter 4 × 4 trucks would appear within a couple of years from the old Walter factory, and by 1914 the Walter, with its Renault hood, was marketed primarily as a military vehicle and for municipal uses. Walter built its own four-cylinder motor and it became a valuable part of the Allied arsenal during World War I along with the Nash Quad and the FWD, although built in fewer numbers than the other two main 4 × 4 trucks.

After the war during the recession, the Walter switched to Waukesha engines, and the company moved to a new factory on Long Island in 1923. Walter pioneered setting the engine ahead of the front axle for better overall weight distribution, something that would be emulated by FWD and Oshkosh.

The varied and colorful history of the Walter company continued for many decades. As with other companies whose history deserves an entire chapter or tome, the entire history of Walter is beyond the scope of this book. It was one of the very few American motor vehicle companies that lasted beyond the Great Depression.

Watson

The Watson Wagon Company was a builder of horse-drawn conveyances in Conastota, New York, a village among hamlets, as defined by local designations. Located near Lenox in Madison County in central New York, the word Conastota derived from the Iroquois Indian name meaning "cluster of pines," which was an indication of just how small this location was, yet it became a community in which a truck manufacturer began in 1917. A small workforce and adequate supply of parts and materials must have been present despite this area's being better known as the "mucklands" of poorly drained soil where by that time some 200 farms were growing onions.

One of the innovations of the Watson company was the design and manufacture of what was called a "Trucktractor." This name would stick as a description for highway trucks that pulled trailers, and this is what the "Trucktractor" was as early as 1917. The "tractor" was a conventional assembled truck with a short chassis where a small platform contained a

WATSON TRACTOR TRUCKS

Manufactured by

WATSON WAGON CO., Canastota, N. Y.

S P E C I F I C A T I O N S

Model	Tractor	5-ton Dumping Trailer	5-ton Platform Trailer
Capacity	5 tons	5 tons or 120 cu. ft.	5 tons
Drive	Worm	Worm	Worm
Chassis Price	$3,600	$4,000	$3,900
Motor			
H. P. (S.A.E)	32.4	32.4	32.4
H. P. (Actual)	45 at 1500 R.P.M.	45 at 1500 R.P.M.	45 at 1500 R.P.M.
Cylinders	4 in pairs	4 in pairs	4 in pairs
Bore	$4\frac{1}{2}''$	$4\frac{1}{2}''$	$4\frac{1}{2}''$
Stroke	$5\frac{1}{2}''$	$5\frac{1}{2}''$	$5\frac{1}{2}''$
Wheel Base	80''	$135\frac{1}{2}''$	115''
Tread Front	61''	61''	61''
Tread Rear	$64\frac{3}{4}''$	60''	60''
Tires Front	34x4''	34x4''	34x4''
Tires Rear	36x5'' dual	52''x5''x1'' steel	39''x5''x1'' steel
Frame	Channel 6x10½ per ft.	Channel 6x10½ per ft.	Angle 3''x5''x⅝''

Front Axle—Timken I-section, roller bearing knuckle.

Rear Axle	Timken round full-floating	Timken 3'' sq.	Timken 2¾'' sq.

Springs Front—Semi-elliptic.
Springs Rear—Semi-elliptic.
Carburetor—Zenith Model L1½'', fixed jet.
Cooling System—Centrifugal pump.
Oiling System—Constant level splash.
Ignition—Bosch magneto, dry cells for starting.
Control—Right drive, center control.
Clutch—Dry plate.
Transmission—Brown-Lipe selective, four speeds forward and one reverse.
Brakes—Emergency and service, internal expanding.
Steering Gear—Gemmer worm and sector.
Equipment—Speedometer, horn, side lights, tail light, tool box, tools.

swivel coupling to attach to a towed tractor with two or more wheels. The so-called fifth wheel was not invented by Watson, but the company used a very similar mechanism to that of the Knox-Martin and Hewitt-Talbot.

The Watson truck was powered by a four-cylinder Continental motor and used a Brown-Lipe four-speed transmission and Brown-Lipe clutch. Timken worm drive was used and solid rubber tires were mounted on artillery wheels with duals on the back. The parabolic radiator and crescent cab were characteristic of Watson. The frame extended in front to create a bumper. This truck was rated at 5-ton tow capacity.

After World War I the company became the Watson Products Corporation. The company built semi-trailers mostly for construction purposes using steel wheels with solid rubber. By 1920 1½-ton and 3-ton trucks were offered by Watson. Switching to left-hand drive, the company also adopted Buda motors. The front bumpers were spring-loaded instead of being directly part of the frame. Watson was reorganized in 1923, but by 1925 financial woes got the better of the company.

Westcott

The Westcott Carriage Company, which got its start in 1896 at Richmond, Indiana, was one of dozens of companies that would make the transition into building motor vehicles. Since the 1890s the Richmond area, which is on the border of Ohio in the center of Indiana, had become home to a considerable industrial activity that would eventually produce such cars as the Rodefeld, the Davis, the Pilot and the Crosley. The Wayne Works, also located there, was the builder of horse-drawn "kid hacks," precursors to school buses, which became a long-lasting series for Wayne.

In 1909 Burton J. Westcott decided he wanted to go into automotive manufacturing and built a gasoline motor buggy that year.

But the following year he ventured forward quickly by building a 40 hp four-cylinder touring car while changing the name of his enterprise to Westcott Motor Car Company. Production quickly rose to three cars per day. Wescott entered the Indianapolis 500 in 1911 in which the driver, Harry Knight, purposely crashed his Westcott to avoid running over another contestant. Positive publicity abounded from that event. Two years later the huge flood of Dayton, Ohio, provided another heroic opportunity when Westcott cars were used for rescue and relief work.

In 1916 Westcott switched to six-cylinder Continental engines to the exclusion of other engines, and the company moved to Springfield, Ohio, where Burton Westcott became mayor in 1921. Fewer than 1850 Westcott cars were built each year and the company did not build commercial vehicles. Westcott made an early introduction of four-wheel brakes as well as balloon tires in 1924, but even such innovations did not prevent receivership as the company owed some $825,000 to various vendors and suppliers, prompting chief engineer J.H. Tuttle to leave the company. The tragedy of bankruptcy in 1925 might have been a large reason why Burton Westcott died at age 57 in January of the following year.

White

In partnership with William L. Grout, Thomas H. White was involved with building sewing machines beginning in 1859 in Orange, Massachusetts. In 1866 the White Sewing Machine Company was moved to Cleveland, Ohio, and roller skates and bicycles were added to the product line. Thomas White had four sons, Thomas II, Rollin, Walter and Windsor, the last an inventor of a flash boiler, but all of whom got involved in building the company's first four steam vehicles that appeared in 1900. By the following year three steam vehicles were being built per week by the

WESTCOTT MOTOR CAR COMPANY

SPRINGFIELD OHIO

Price	**$1940**
Five-Passenger Touring	1940
Four-Passenger Cloverleaf Roadster . .	1890
Sportster	2290
Seven or Five-Passenger Convertible Sedan	2790
Four-Passenger Coupe	2790

WESTCOTT TOURING—SERIES 18

COLOR	Body, gray, blue or green; running gear, black		BORE AND STROKE .	3½ x 5¼ inches
			LUBRICATION	Force feed and splash
SEATING CAPACITY. .	Seven		RADIATOR	Cellular
POSITION OF DRIVER .	Left side		COOLING	Water pump
WHEELBASE	125 inches		IGNITION	Storage battery
GAUGE	56 inches		STARTING SYSTEM . .	Two unit
WHEELS	Wood		STARTER OPERATED .	Gear to fly wheel
FRONT TIRES	35 x 4½ inches		LIGHTING SYSTEM . .	Electric
REAR TIRES	35 x 4½ inches, anti-skid		VOLTAGES	Six
			WIRING SYSTEM . . .	Single
SERVICE BRAKE . . .	Contracting on rear wheels		GASOLINE SYSTEM . .	Vacuum
EMERGENCY BRAKE .	Expanding on rear wheels		CLUTCH	Dry multiple disc
			TRANSMISSION . . .	Selective sliding
CYLINDERS	Six		GEAR CHANGES . . .	Three forward, one reverse
ARRANGED	Vertically		DRIVE	Spiral bevel
CAST.	En bloc		REAR AXLE	Semi-floating
HORSEPOWER	29.4 (N.A.C.C. Rating)		STEERING GEAR . . .	Worm and wheel

In addition to above specifications, price includes top, top hood, windshield, speedometer, ammeter, clock, tire pump, electric horn and demountable rims.

**THE WHITE
MOTOR
COMPANY**

CLEVELAND, OHIO

Price	**$5000**
Limousine . .	**6200**
Cabriolet . .	**6400**
Landaulet. . .	**6200**
Chassis . . .	**3900**

WHITE SIXTEEN-VALVE FOUR TOURING—GM

COLOR	Optional	LUBRICATION	Full force feed
SEATING CAPACITY	Seven	RADIATOR	Cellular
POSITION OF DRIVER	Left side	COOLING	Water pump
WHEELBASE	137½ inches	IGNITION	High tension magneto
GAUGE	56 inches		
WHEELS	Wood	STARTING SYSTEM	Two unit
FRONT TIRES	35 x 5 inches	STARTER OPERATED	Gear to fly wheel
REAR TIRES	35 x 5 inches	LIGHTING SYSTEM	Electric
SERVICE BRAKE	Contracting on rear wheels	VOLTAGES	Twelve
		WIRING SYSTEM	Double
EMERGENCY BRAKE	Expanding on rear wheels	GASOLINE SYSTEM	Vacuum
		CLUTCH	Plate
CYLINDERS	Four	TRANSMISSION	Selective sliding
ARRANGED	Vertically	GEAR CHANGES	Four forward, one reverse
CAST	En bloc		
HORSEPOWER	28.9 (N.A.C.C. Rating)	DRIVE	Spiral bevel
		REAR AXLE	Semi-floating
BORE AND STROKE	4¼ x 5¾ inches	STEERING GEAR	Worm and sector

In addition to above specifications, price includes top, top hood, windshield, speedometer, ammeter, clock, tire pump, electric horn and demountable rims.

WHITE TRUCKS

Manufactured by

THE WHITE COMPANY, CLEVELAND, OHIO

Model	GBBE	TBC	TAD	TCD
Capacity	$\frac{3}{4}$ ton	$1\frac{1}{2}$-2 tons	3 tons	5 tons
Drive	Bevel gear	Bevel gear D. R.	Chain	Chain
Chassis Weight	2,960 lbs.	4,150 lbs.	6,765 lbs.	8,000 lbs.
Chassis Price	$2,300	$3,300	$4,100	$5,000
Engine	White	White	White	White
H. P. (S.A.E.)	22.5	22.5	22.5	28.9
H. P. (Actual)	30	30	30	45
Cylinders	4 en bloc	4 en bloc	4 en bloc	4 en bloc
Bore	$3\frac{3}{4}$"	$3\frac{3}{4}$"	$3\frac{3}{4}$"	$4\frac{1}{4}$"
Stroke	$5\frac{1}{8}$"	$5\frac{1}{8}$"	$5\frac{1}{8}$"	$6\frac{3}{8}$"
Wheel Base	$133\frac{1}{2}$"	$157\frac{1}{2}$" Opt. $145\frac{1}{2}$"	163"	169"
Tread Front	56"	$58\frac{9}{16}$"	$64\frac{3}{8}$"	$64\frac{3}{8}$"
Tread Rear	56"	$62\frac{1}{4}$" C dual	$66\frac{1}{2}$" C dual	$70\frac{3}{4}$" C dual
Tires Front	$34x4\frac{1}{2}$"	$36x4\frac{1}{2}$" Pneu.	36x5"	36x5"
Tires Rear	$34x4\frac{1}{2}$"	36x4" dual or 36x7"	40x5" dual	40x6" dual
Frame	Heat treated pressed alloy steel	Heat treated pressed alloy steel	I-Beam	I-Beam
Front Axle	I-beam drop forged	I-beam drop forged	Square section drop forged jack-shaft and rear axle	

Rear Axle—White type.
Springs Front—Semi-elliptic.
Springs Rear—Semi-elliptic.
Carburetor—White, aspirating.
Cooling System—Pump.
Oiling System—Force, gravity and splash.
Ignition—High tension magneto.

White team, which mostly consisted of the four brothers. The first White truck was built in 1901.

One of the innovations adopted in White steamers was the use of condensers "in order to avoid the appearance of steam in crowded traffic, where they are certain to be used," as was explained in company literature. Most White vehicles were light delivery wagons, but in 1902 a heavier prototype was built. Pneumatic tires were introduced, but hard rubber tires and steel wheels were used for trucks and road-building vehicles. Shaft drive was introduced in 1903.

By 1904 a bus chassis was manufactured amid several other commercial vehicles. The following year White was the only automobile of any type in the inaugural of Theodore Roosevelt, who would drive a White steamer in Puerto Rico in 1907, becoming the first American president to drive a car. The heaviest production White was a 3-ton truck produced in 1906, when approximately 1500 vehicles per year were being built by White. Thomas White concentrated on sewing machines as his sons built motor vehicles.

The first gasoline vehicle from White appeared at the end of 1909 for model year 1910. This was also the year that the popularly elected President William Howard Taft (with a 100-year record for voter turnout) organized the first White House fleet, which comprised several cars, including one White steamer. John D. Rockefeller and Buffalo Bill Cody were owners of White autos at this time. White quickly transformed its production over to gasoline-powered vehicles in 1911, the same year taxicabs became a product line for White. The company then entered into a collaboration in 1912 with Riddle funeral cars.

Thomas White passed away in 1914 and a subsequent reorganization took place in 1916, as White Motor Company. This meant that Windsor White remained president with Walter White as vice president. In 1918, after

building 18,000 passenger cars, half steam and half gasoline, White switched solely to commercial vehicle and truck production. As World War I began in Europe, White got into large contracts with the U.S. military, so that from the time Pancho Villa attacked Columbus, New Mexico, on March 9, 1916, White would provide 18,000 one-ton and three-ton trucks for the Quartermaster Corps and AEF, in addition to 409 White Open Touring used as staff cars during 1917 and 1918.

As a large company White had the opportunity not only to build in quantity but also had the wherewithal to manufacture specialty vehicles, such as the sightseeing buses that first appeared in 1917 at Yellowstone National Park. The City of San Francisco would use White buses beginning in 1918 before the war ended. Other cities soon adopted this type of bus, and due to widespread acceptance and success, the design would eventually be also built by several competitors.

White became a dominant manufacturer of trucks by the time World War I ended, so despite overall economic downturns after the war, White continued to produce large numbers of commercial vehicles through the 1920s. White introduced seat comfort innovations in their buses during the 1920s, and the White "Six" arrived in 1926.

A.E. Bean became president of White in 1931. The company survived the Great Depression in part by absorbing the Indiana Truck Corporation in 1932, sold off by Brockway. Then White merged with Studebaker and continued building trucks under the newly-formed Studebaker-Pierce-Arrow (S-P-A) truck division, but finances were so uncertain the entire relationship quickly fell apart.

For 1932 White sold a total of only 2,138 vehicles, leading to major layoffs in the workforce. Somehow the company survived the miserable economic times of the 1930s and became a major contributor during World

War II, building half-tracks and armored cars. Eventually, White would merge with Sterling and Freightliner in 1951 (soon selling off Freightliner), acquire Reo in 1957 and Diamond T in 1958, and eventually would become part of the White-GMC-Autocar and Volvo conglomerate of badges and mergers in which the White name would finally be lost entirely as a truck manufacturer by 1995.

White Hickory

As was the story with several companies in the United States, White Hickory was a very small builder of trucks, a company which got its unlikely start during 1917 at Atlanta, Georgia. The Model H appears to be the only truck built by this assembler, which lasted as an independent enterprise for only four years in total.

Perhaps most remarkable is the fact that White Hickory was the only motor vehicle manufacturer in Georgia during this entire period. This rarity extended to Alabama, Florida, Kentucky, Louisiana, Tennessee and other Southern and Plains states where even light motor vehicle manufacturing was not a common type of business over a half-century after the Civil War. The South remained a farm and trade region of the United States as the North became ever more industrialized, especially on the East Coast and along the Eastern Seaboard north of the Carolinas and Virginias.

As illustrated here, White Hickory, the name referring to a type of wood, used a Continental motor with Eisemann magneto ignition. It's significant to note that magneto ignition was still the most common method of supplying a spark to ignite the fuel mixture in an internal combustion engine even as World War I would become the crucible of innovation, especially in motor vehicle technology.

Mechanical distributors would gradually supplant the magneto as storage batteries became commonplace and necessary for electrical lighting, which supplanted oil and acetylene gas lights. As is implied by the name, the high-tension magneto was usually based on two or three pairs of magnets in which a rotating armature along with primary and secondary windings created enough voltage for the spark plug to ignite the fuel mixture. Ignition systems at the time were available from over two dozen independent companies in addition to Eisemann of Brooklyn, New York.

White Hickory expanded its model line to include a 2½-ton and 3½-ton capacity truck model for 1921, but the postwar recession was too much for the company to sustain any manufacturing business whatsoever by 1922.

Wichita

Wichita Falls, Texas, was the logical location of the Wichita Falls Motor Company. However, it would be easy to confuse this company with the Wichita of Kansas, which had its own Wichita Motor Company, reportedly for a brief time in 1914. However, the actual falls on the river have not existed since they were destroyed in the flood of 1886, and a more recent artificial reconstruction that recirculates water for visiting tourists nearby can hardly be considered a genuine phenomenon.

M. McKeirnan was the designer behind the Wichita vehicles in Texas, and he had an invention that made his trucks a little different from the rest. A single lever attached to the steering wheel controlled the spark, throttle, clutch and transmission. This complex unit was first tested on a Maxwell auto before Wichita trucks went into production in 1911.

The most unusual aspect of the Wichita company was that it was possibly the first motor vehicle manufacturer in America which was organized and directed by a woman, namely Mrs. Nettie C. McIntyre, who hailed from Denver, Colorado. She was also the

THE WHITE HICKORY TRUCK

Manufactured by

WHITE HICKORY WAGON MFG. CO., Atlanta, Ga.

Model	H
Capacity	1½ tons
Drive	Worm
Chassis Weight	3,565 lbs.
Chassis Price	$2,200
Engine	Continental
H. P. (S.A.E.)	22.5
H. P. (Actual)	36
Cylinders	4 en bloc
Bore	3¾"
Stroke	5"
Wheel Base	144"
Tread Front	58½"
Tread Rear	58½"
Tires Front	36x3½"
Tires Rear	36x5"

Frame—Pressed steel.

Front Axle—Timken drop forged I-beam.

Rear Axle—Timken David Brown worm, full-floating.

Springs Front—Semi-elliptic.

Springs Rear—Semi-elliptic.

Carburetor—Stromberg.

Cooling System—Centrifugal pump.

Oiling System—Combination force feed and splash.

Ignition—Eisemann magneto.

Control—Left steer, center levers.

Clutch—Dry disc.

Transmission—Fuller Selective, three speeds forward, one reverse.

Brakes—Duplex internal, rear wheel.

Steering Gear—Ross worm and nut.

Equipment—Oil lamps—front and tail, horn, tools and driver's seat.

WICHITA TRUCKS
Manufactured by
WICHITA FALLS MOTOR CO., Wichita Falls, Texas

S P E C I F I C A T I O N S

Model	Q	R	L	O
Capacity	5 tons	2½ tons	1½ tons	3½ tons
Drive	Worm	Worm	Worm	Worm
Chassis Price	$3,850	$2,350	$1,800	$3,250
Motor				
H. P. (S.A.E.)	32.4	22.2	19.6	32.4
H. P. (Actual)	40	32	No governor	40
Cylinders	4 in pairs	4 en bloc	4 en bloc	4 in pairs
Bore	4½"	3¾"	3½"	4½"
Stroke	5¾"	5¼"	5"	5¾"
Wheel Base	165"	144"	118"	165"
Tread Front	56"	56"	56"	56"
Tread Rear	74⅝"	56"	56"	66"
Tires Front	38x6"	36x4"	36x3"	36x5"
Tires Rear	38x6" dual	36x7"	36x5"	36x5" dual

Frame—Pressed.

Front Axle—I-beam, Elliott type knuckle.

Rear Axle—Semi-floating.

Springs Front—Semi-elliptic.

Springs Rear—Semi-elliptic.

Carburetor—Stromberg G-1.

Cooling System	Pump	Pump	Thermo-syphon	Pump

Oiling System—Forced feed.

Ignition—Bosch.

Control—Right drive, center control.

Clutch—Cone.

Transmission—Selective, three speeds forward and one reverse.

Brakes—Internal expanding rear wheel drum.

Steering Gear—Worm and nut.

Equipment—Two gas side lights, oil tail light, horn, oil can, tool kit, acetylene gas tank.
        Also seat and cushion.

principal stockholder of Wichita Falls Motor Company.

The primary market at first for Wichita was oil field work before it built vans and buses. Before World War I Wichita built 1-ton and 2-ton capacity trucks with right-hand steering. By the time America entered the war Wichita expanded its model line to include trucks from 1½-ton to 5-ton capacity. All of them were powered by a Waukesha motor of one cid or another.

In 1920 Wichita introduced a utility car referred to as the "oil field tool pusher." Powered by a 50 hp four-cylinder engine, with a wheelbase of 127 inches, it was designed to carry three persons and 1000 pounds of oil field equipment. The unusual combination truck and passenger vehicle sold for $2150. This was the era of oil field discoveries in Texas which helped propel the entire American auto industry through cheap and abundant quantities of petroleum that literally gushed out of the ground in this entire part of the country. The oil sold for a "couple of bits" a barrel at one point during this period of vast exploitation before large scale depletion set in.

Aside from this utility car, Wichita did not build passenger cars. The company exported its trucks to Mexico and China in addition to dozens of countries across the globe. The single-lever control system was popular with drivers, simplifying operation at a time when starting and controlling a truck took considerable strength and skill. The company's slogan was "The Sun Never Sets on Wichita." However, once the Great Depression took hold, Wichita Falls Motor Company only lasted until 1932.

Wilcox

Minneapolis, Minnesota, was the location of the H.E. Wilcox Motor Car Company. John F. Wilcox and Maurice Wolfe were also partners in the enterprise that began in 1910. The latter organizer already had experience when he began building the Wolfe car in 1906 before joining up with Wilcox and Wilcox. The passenger cars under the Wilcox name which appeared from 1910 to 1913 had either air-cooled or water-cooled engines depending on customer demand, which was often undecided. The Carrico air-cooled engine was discontinued before the passenger cars were entirely dropped as well.

There had been two earlier companies, organized in Plainfield, New Jersey, and Chicago, Illinois, both named Wilcox but without further evidence of manufacture. At first the Wilcox commercial vehicle produced in Minneapolis was in the form of a delivery car and was based on the Wolfe passenger car that appeared in 1910.

Then a 1-ton and 3-ton truck were offered, the latter chassis also used to build a bus. Within three years before World War I Wilcox Trux, as the company was now called, was the largest producer of commercial vehicles in Minneapolis, but competition was not heavy in this part of the United States.

In 1918 Wilcox offered six capacities of trucks from ¾-ton to 5-ton. In addition to Buda and Continental four-cylinder engines Wilcox also began building its own motors. Bus chassis also became a product line for Wilcox in the early 1920s, and these were powered by a six-cylinder Continental motor geared for high-speed (60 mph), long-distance travel.

In 1925 the Northland Transportation Company ordered 39 of the 29-passenger buses, and these were badged as Northland. H.E. Wilcox sold the entire Wilcox firm, which now produced more buses than trucks in 1926. The Motor Transit Corporation was formed that year as a holding company for Greyhound bus lines, and those buses were briefly known as Will buses before the Wilcox enterprise soon faded out of existence.

WILCOX TRUCKS

Manufactured by

H. E. WILCOX MOTOR CO., Minneapolis, Minn.

Model	S	X	Q	P
Capacity	1 ton	1½ tons	2 tons	3½ tons
Drive	Worm	Worm	Worm	Worm
Chassis Weight	2,800 lbs.	4,200 lbs.	4,700 lbs.	6,330 lbs.
Chassis Price	On application	On application	On application	On application
Engine	Continental	Wilcox	Wilcox	Wilcox
H. P. (S.A.E.)	22.5	29	29	29
H. P. (Actual)	32 at 1500 R.P.M.	40 at 1100 R.P.M.	40 at 1100 R.P.M.	40 at 1100 R.P.M.
Cylinders	4 en bloc	4 in pairs	4 in pairs	4 in pairs
Bore	3¾"	4¼"	4¼"	4¼"
Stroke	5"	5"	5"	5"
Wheel Base	128"	144"	150"	154"
Tread Front	56"	58"	58"	58"
Tread Rear	56"	58⅝"	58⅝"	66"
Tires Front	35x5" Pneu.	36x4"	36x4"	36x5"
Tires Rear	35x5" Pneu.	36x5"	36x3½" dual	36x5" dual

Frame—Pressed.

Front Axle—I-beam section.

Rear Axle—Sheldon semi-floating.

Springs Front—Semi-elliptic.

Springs Rear—Semi-elliptic.

Carburetor—Stromberg.

Cooling System	Thermo-syphon	Pump	Pump	Pump

Oiling System—Splash.

Ignition—Magneto.

Control—Left drive, center control.

Clutch	Dry disc	Cone	Cone	Cone
Transmission	Brown-Lipe Selective, 3 speeds	Wilcox Selective, 3 speeds	Wilcox Selective, 3 speeds	Wilcox Selective, 3 speeds

Brakes—Internal rear wheels.

Steering Gear—Worm.

Equipment—Driver's seat, electric lights and battery or Prest-o-Lite, horn, hubodometer, tail light, complete set of tools, jack. Extra demountable rim with chassis equipped with pneumatic tires and governor.

Willys (Willys-Overland, Willys-Knight)

John North Willys started out as a sporting goods salesman in Elmira, New York, at the turn of the century. He got started with the Overland car in 1907, and eventually put his own name on motor vehicles in 1914. The Willys of that year was the Willys-Knight, which was to use the Knight sleeve-valve motor until the Great Depression.

Out of some fifteen companies that acquired a licensing agreement from inventor Charles Knight, Willys would become the largest builder of the somewhat unusual powerplant, manufacturing as many of the engines as the other fourteen American companies combined. However, John Willys's acquisition of the Knight license was by way of buying out the Edwards Motor Car Company, which had already acquired the Knight engine license. The plant was moved (along with its founder H.J. Edwards) to the former Garford factory in Elyria, Ohio, which John Willys had also bought, along with the Gramm Motor Car Company. The latter would be instrumental in building trucks and commercial vehicles.

At the time when all gasoline engines were noisy (especially before hydraulic valve lifters, advanced vibration dampers, counter-balancing and improved engine compartment insulation), the Knight engine was considered quieter and less apt to need valve replacement after a few years of use.

For the first model year of 1915 the Willys-Knight was a four-cylinder car that was available as a Roadster or Touring with K-17 and K-19 designations. It was in 1916 that a poppet-valve six-cylinder Continental motor was introduced for the Willys, remaining for only three years. Prices across the board fell by half to an average $1200, depending on the body style, which now included a Coupe and Limousine for the Willys-Knight.

A sleeve-valve V-8 arrived for 1917. Few if any Knight-engine vehicles made it overseas for the war effort, mostly due to the need for specialized mechanics who were familiar with the Knight engine, as well as a whole collection of different replacement engine parts.

For 1918 Willys offered four-, six- and eight-cylinder cars in several body styles. Once the war ended this model line was continued despite material shortages, but prices remained steady or even dropped to offset the large inflation during the recession of this period.

John Willys had purchased the Duesenberg factory in Elizabeth, New Jersey, which stretched his company's finances to the limit. By 1921 only four-cylinder Willys-Knight autos and light trucks were offered in the model line. The engineering consultant team of Zeder-Skelton-Breer had taken their share of the business, and Chase Manhattan Bank finally stepped in to manage the Willys company by installing Buick president Walter Chrysler at the helm. The Elizabeth factory was auctioned off along with the Willys Six, which would be the basis for the first Chrysler car.

Willys increased sales from 50,000 in 1921 to 200,000 by 1925. The Knight engine was very popular, but the lower-priced Overland autos accounted for most of the profits that were posted by that time. Along with the new line of six-cylinder motors introduced in 1925, the Lanchester vibration damper was an impressive component detail for buyers.

Willys bought out Stearns-Knight in Cleveland, continuing production under that name until the stock market crash. The Falcon-Knight introduced in 1926 was a lower-priced car to add to the lineup, and even once the Great Depression took hold, John Willys kept sales humming and profits stacking up. Willys became the first American ambassador to Poland as his vice president Linwood A. Miller took over in March of 1930.

WILLYS-OVERLAND, INC.

TOLEDO, OHIO

Touring . . . . . . ⎱
Club Six . . . . . . ⎰ Prices Upon
Touring Sedan . . . ⎰ Application

WILLYS SIX TOURING—89

COLOR	Body, olive green; wheels, cream	LUBRICATION	Force feed and splash
SEATING CAPACITY. .	Seven	RADIATOR	Cellular
POSITION OF DRIVER .	Left side	COOLING	Water pump
WHEELBASE	120 inches	IGNITION	Storage battery
GAUGE	56 inches	STARTING SYSTEM . .	Two unit
WHEELS	Wood	STARTER OPERATED .	Gear to fly wheel
FRONT TIRES	33 x 4½ inches	LIGHTING SYSTEM . .	Electric
REAR TIRES	33 x 4½ inches, anti-skid	VOLTAGES	Six to eight
		WIRING SYSTEM . . .	Single
SERVICE BRAKE . . .	Contracting on rear wheels	GASOLINE SYSTEM . .	Vacuum
		CLUTCH	Cone
EMERGENCY BRAKE .	Expanding on rear wheels	TRANSMISSION . . .	Selective sliding
CYLINDERS	Six	GEAR CHANGES . . .	Three forward, one reverse
ARRANGED	Vertically		
CAST	En bloc	DRIVE	Spiral bevel
HORSEPOWER	29.4	REAR AXLE	Three-quarters floating
(N.A.C.C. Rating)			
BORE AND STROKE .	3½ x 5¼ inches	STEERING GEAR . . .	Worm and gear

In addition to above specifications, price includes top, top hood, windshield, speedometer, ammeter, tire pump, electric horn and demountable rims.

In 1933 the Willys Model 77 was one of two lowest-priced cars in America at just $335 for the Coupe, which was in direct competition with the tiny American Austin. In May of 1935 John Willys suffered a heart attack and died in August of that year. His company had survived receivership, and by bidding competitively, would produce about half of all the Jeeps for World War II before the Willys name became history.

Wilson

The J.C. Wilson Company was located in Detroit, Michigan, and began by building horse-drawn wagons as so many other car companies did. Wilson trucks first appeared in 1914 in the form of 2-ton models that were chain driven. Wilson was one company that received a contract with the U.S. military by 1917 when a 1-ton and a 3-ton model were added by Wilson. This may have been an indication of a departure from the reliance on horses by the military, but only a very gradual one.

When the British entered World War I on August 4, 1914, their first major shipment to France was 60,000 horses and 1,200 trucks. Later the same year Canada shipped 7,000 horses and 133 trucks. Clearly, the motor truck was yet to become a truly recognized means of viable transport for troops, ammunition, artillery and equipment.

There were six primary reasons why motor transport was not in the forefront at the beginning of World War I:

1. The motor truck was still unproven and unreliable as a mode of transportation.
2. Nobody was certain which would be the best fuel to choose: electricity, steam or gasoline power.
3. Roads were primitive or nonexistent.
4. Hundreds of small manufacturers offered a confusing array of machines and components, none of which were interchangeable.
5. Railroads crisscrossed the European Continent as well as across America.
6. People were familiar with the equine and the iron horse, but not with motors which required maintenance and repair work.

The horse was still relied upon to plod through the mud and snow carrying soldiers or pulling a wagon or artillery piece. But the European military command soon began to see the advantage of the steel machine over the flesh-and-blood animals. Wilson introduced a 3⅓-ton and a 5-ton truck for 1918, both offered with four-speed Brown-Lipe transmissions and Timken worm drive.

What few trucks were built for the military by Wilson in 1917 and 1918 also demonstrated that the use of the gasoline-powered truck would become finally recognized as the most effective method of transportation. But using a motley collection of dozens of different manufacturers, some of them relatively small and obscure such as Wilson, would lead to chaos in the maintenance, repair and parts departments of the military motor pool before standardized trucks called "Liberty" trucks were designed and placed into production, albeit too late for the actual war effort. But Wilson was in such poor financial condition that the small company, despite military contracts, was out of business by 1925.

Winther

Martin P. Winther was an engineer working for the Jeffery Company in Wisconsin, and after that firm was sold to Charles Nash, Winther had the means to start his own company in 1917 to produce commercial vehicles. The Winther Motor Truck Company began in the somewhat similar-sounding Winthrop Harbor, Illinois. From the beginning the Winther trucks were conventional, assembled trucks up to 6-ton capacity.

As the war ended the Winther factory

WILSON TRUCKS

Manufactured by

J. C. WILSON CO., Detroit, Mich.

Capacity	1 ton	2 tons	3½ tons	5-6 tons
Drive	Worm	Worm	Worm	Worm
Chassis Weight	2,900 lbs.	4,500 lbs.	6,800 lbs.	7,500 lbs.
Chassis Price	$1,650	$2,550	$3,250	On application
Engine				
H. P. (S.A.E.)	19.6	27.2	32.4	32.4
H. P. (Actual)	25	35	40	40
Cylinders	4 en bloc	4 en bloc	4 in pairs	4 in pairs
Bore	3½″	4⅛″	4½″	4½″
Stroke	5″	5¼″	5¼″	5¼″
Wheel Base	124″	144″	160″	160″
Tread Front	56″	58″	66″	66″
Tread Rear	56″	59″	74″	74⅝″
Tires Front	35x5″ Pneu.	36x4″	36x5″	36x6″
Tires Rear	35x5″ Pneu.	36x4″ dual	36x5″ dual	40x6″ dual
Frame	Pressed	Rolled channel	Rolled channel	Rolled channel
Front Axle—I-beam.				
Rear Axle	Full floating, worm	Semi-floating, worm	Semi-floating, worm	Semi-floating, worm
Springs Front—Semi-elliptic.				
Springs Rear—Semi-elliptic.				
Carburetor—Float feed.				
Cooling System	Thermo-syphon	Pump	Pump	Pump
Oiling System—Forced feed and splash.				
Ignition—Magneto.				
Control—Left drive, center control.				
Clutch	Dry plate	Cone	Dry plate	Dry plate
Transmission	Selective, three speeds	Selective, three speeds	Selective, four speeds	Selective, four speeds

Brakes—Two sets expanding on rear wheel drums.

Steering Gear—Worm.

Equipment—Seat and cushions, tools, steel tool box, front fenders, horn, running boards, two front and one tail light (oil), wheel puller.

WINTHER TRUCKS

Manufactured by

WINTHER MOTOR TRUCK CO., Winthrop Harbor, Ills.

Model	48	68	88	108
Capacity	2 tons	3 tons	4 tons	5 tons
Drive	Internal gear	Internal gear	Internal gear	Internal gear
Chassis Weight	5,300 lbs.	6,400 lbs.	7,600 lbs.	8,300 lbs.
Chassis Price	$3,000	$3,600	$4,200	$5,000
Engine	Wisconsin T. U.	Wisconsin T. U.	Wisconsin U. U.	Wisconsin A. U.
H. P. (S.A.E.)	25.6	25.6	28.9	36.1
H. P. (Actual)	38	40	45	50
Cylinders	4 en bloc	4 en bloc	4 en bloc	4 in pairs
Bore	4″	4″	$4\frac{1}{4}$″	$4\frac{3}{4}$″
Stroke	6″	6″	6″	$5\frac{1}{2}$″
Wheel Base	150″	150″	156″	162″
Tread Front	$58\frac{1}{2}$″	$66\frac{1}{2}$″	$66\frac{1}{2}$″	$68\frac{3}{8}$″
Tread Rear	58″	66″	63″	63″
Tires Front	36x4″	36x5″	36x5″	36x5″
Tires Rear	36x7″ or 36x4″ dual	36x10″ or 36x5″ dual	40x10″ or 40x5″ dual	40x12″ or 40x6″ dual
Frame—Structural steel.				
Front Axle	Timken 1540 B I-section	Timken 1630 B I-section	Timken 1630 B I-section	Timken 1730 B I-section
Rear Axle	Clark Rud forged load carrying member	Clark round	Clark forged rectangular section	Clark forged rectangular section

Springs Front—Semi-elliptic.
Springs Rear—Semi-elliptic.
Carburetor—Master.
Cooling System—Pump.
Oiling System—Gear pump.
Ignition—Eisemann magneto.
Control—Right hand drive, center control.
Clutch—Dry disc.
Transmission—Brown-Lipe selective, sliding gear.

Brakes	Rear axle	Rear Axle	Rear axle	Rear axle

Steering Gear—Screw and nut.
Equipment—All models have starting and lighting equipment as optional at additional
    cost, Bijur system used, also governor.

moved to larger facilities in Kenosha, Wisconsin, changing names to the Winthrop Motor Truck Company. And yet the truck's name remained Winther as a collaboration took place with an engineer named Marwin who designed a four-wheel-drive system. Therefore, all Winther-Marwin trucks were 4 × 4s. Winther company advertising claimed that the U.S. Navy used their trucks, although it wasn't clear what that meant in terms of quantity of production. Winther and Winther-Marwin trucks were all powered by Wisconsin engines using Borg & Beck clutches and Cotta three-speed or four-speed transmissions. Most axles were internal gear from Celfer.

In 1920 the company entered the passenger car market but this did not meet with success and the project was canceled almost immediately. In 1921 a reorganization took place, and the name of the company became Winther Motors Incorporated. The model line was expanded to include 1-ton up to 7-ton trucks with prices ranging from $2700 up to $4700. The heaviest truck model would use a Herschell-Spillman engine and transmissions were now from Brown-Lipe, Fuller and Warner. Internal gear axles were from Clark, Midway or Torbensen, along with Timken front axles.

As much variety and engineering went into Winther and Winther-Marwin trucks, the company was beset by financial problems. For the last year of production another reorganization resulted in a name change to Winther-Kenosha. In 1927 the company's assets were sold to H.P. Olsen, and manufacturing was discontinued entirely by the following year.

Winton

Alexander Winton has been considered one of the pre-eminent pioneers in American motor vehicle development and manufacturing. Winton was born in Scotland and arrived in the United States in 1884. He established the Winton Bicycle Company in Cleveland in 1891. By 1896 he had built his first gasoline-powered automobile prototype. The Winton Motor Carriage Company was founded in March of 1897. His second car was powered by a 10 hp two-cylinder motor which he proved at the horse-racing Glenville Track at Cleveland, attaining a speed of 33.6 mph, which was considered very impressive.

During the summer of 1897 Winton and his shop partner William A. Hatcher drove in another experimental two-cylinder car from Cleveland to New York City, making headlines. That type of publicity allowed Winton to sell all three of his first cars almost immediately. By the end of the following year he had sold twenty-two autos. James Ward Packard bought the twelfth Winton, developing his own from the perceived inadequacies of this one, while Winton established the first production line of auto manufacturing in America. Winton has been credited with building the first truck in the United States, which was completed in 1898. For 1899 he had sold nearly 100 "motor carriages."

Winton's company consisted of Thomas W. Henderson, vice president; George H. Brown, secretary-treasurer; and first engineer Leo Melanowski who recommended Winton hire a man named Henry Ford as a mechanic. Winton decided against hiring the man whom he believed was not qualified, although Henry Ford had already built his first vehicle in 1896 called the Quadricycle.

By 1899 Winton made a second trip to New York City in one of his cars, this time accompanied by Cleveland journalist Charles Shanks, who would become advertising manager for Winton. Shanks repeatedly used the term "automobile" and as other newspapers picked up the story, so the word became immediately popularized at a time when "autobain," "motorcycle," "gasoline buggy" and "horseless carriage" were used interchangeably.

THE WINTON COMPANY

CLEVELAND, OHIO

Price	**$4500**
Four-Passenger Touring	3500
Five-Passenger Touring	3500
Six-Passenger Touring	3500
Seven-Passenger Touring . . .	3500
Runabout	3500
Full Four-Door Limousine . .	4750
Sedan	4750
Limousine Landaulet	4750
Coupe	4500
Coupelet	3750

WINTON SIX LIMOUSINE—48

COLOR	Optional	LUBRICATION	Force feed
SEATING CAPACITY. .	Seven	RADIATOR	Cellular
POSITION OF DRIVER .	Left side	COOLING	Water pump
WHEELBASE	138 inches	IGNITION	High tension magneto
GAUGE	56 inches		
WHEELS	Wood	STARTING SYSTEM . .	Two unit
FRONT TIRES	37 x 5 inches	STARTER OPERATED .	Gear to fly wheel
REAR TIRES	37 x 5 inches	LIGHTING SYSTEM . .	Electric
SERVICE BRAKE . . .	Contracting on rear wheels	VOLTAGES	Six
		WIRING SYSTEM . . .	Single
EMERGENCY BRAKE .	Expanding on rear wheels	GASOLINE SYSTEM . .	Vacuum
		CLUTCH	Dry multiple disc
CYLINDERS	Six	TRANSMISSION . . .	Selective sliding
ARRANGED	Vertically	GEAR CHANGES . . .	Four forward, one reverse
CAST	In pairs		
HORSEPOWER . . . . 48.6 (N.A.C.C. Rating)		DRIVE	Spiral bevel
		REAR AXLE	Full floating
BORE AND STROKE .	4½ x 5½ inches	STEERING GEAR . . .	Worm and gear

In addition to above specifications, price includes speedometer, ammeter, voltmeter, clock, tire pump, electric horn and demountable rims.

The Electric Vehicle Company, having bought the Selden patent five years prior, decided that Winton would be a fine example as the first company to be charged with infringement. Winton did not fight the patent and bought a license from the Association of Licensed Automobile Manufacturers (A.L.A.M.). The mechanic that Winton had refused to hire, Henry Ford, balked at complying with the Selden patent, and after much legal wrangling, including Ford's filing of a history-changing appeal after losing, the Selden patent was deemed unenforceable. Henry Ford also beat Winton in racing during 1901.

Winton built race cars called Bullet No. 1 and Bullet No. 2, the first being driven by Alexander Winton himself, the second driven by Barney Oldfield. No. 2 was powered by two horizontally stacked four-cylinder motors in 1904, technically becoming the first eight-cylinder car in America. Meanwhile Winton autos made headlines again in 1903 when Dr. H. Nelson Jackson and his chauffeur Sewell H. Croker drove from San Francisco to New York just for the publicity and on a bet.

For 1905 Winton offered a shaft-drive four-cylinder auto called the Model C, even though the hood was shaped like the letter "D," a continuing distinguishable feature of Winton cars. The following year Winton sold its first 20 hp two-cylinder commercial van to the Goodrich Motor Tyre Company in England. According to company records sales reached 1100 in 1907, which was also the year that the company introduced its first three- and four-speed sliding gear transmissions and a six-cylinder motor. The planetary transmission and all the other motors built by Winton were superseded from that point. In 1909 Winton introduced a compressed air starter, which could also be used for pumping the tires. He believed in the superiority of this type of starter, but after demand was made very clear, he finally gave in with an electric starter in 1915. By 1916 Winton was producing 2450 cars per year. During World War I Winton supplied heavy equipment and load carriers for the military. But after the war, despite the fact that the Winton factory was kept busy for the war effort, and perhaps due to Alexander Winton's own stubbornness, the company began losing money. Alexander Winton lost almost all of his $5,000,000 fortune by the time the Great Depression caught up with him. In 1932 he died with barely $50,000. The Winton as an automobile ceased to exist in 1924. The factory continued to build diesel engines.

Wisconsin

Baraboo, Wisconsin, was the location of the Wisconsin Motor Truck Works, which began in 1912 and was not affiliated with the better known builder of engines by that name. Although the state of Wisconsin was the location of many motor vehicle builders and automotive components in the early years, there were only two other companies by that name that attempted to produce vehicles, one in 1899 and one in 1914, both in Milwaukee and both lasting for only one year. Neither were affiliated with the Wisconsin Motor Truck Works, which lasted considerably longer.

The company moved from the small town of Baraboo, in Sauk County in central Wisconsin, to Sheboygan, located on the eastern edge of Wisconsin on Lake Michigan, in There the ¾-ton trucks which were the first model line of the company were briefly continued in what was now called Myers Machine Company. There the new line of 2-ton trucks was introduced.

By the end of the war the Myers Machine Company was reorganized once again and moved to Loganville, Wisconsin, which was very close to Baraboo but even smaller with only a few hundred residents. Very much in innovative and independent Wisconsin

WISCONSIN TRUCKS

Manufactured by

MYERS MACHINE COMPANY, Sheboygan, Wis.

Model	B-1918	C-1918	E-1918
Capacity	1½ tons	2½ tons	5 tons
Drive	Worm	Worm	Worm
Chassis Weight	3,400 lbs.	4,780 lbs.	11,000 lbs.
Chassis Price	$1,650	$2,500	$5,000
Engine	Waukesha	Waukesha	Waukesha
H. P. (S.A.E.)	19.61	25.60	36.15
H. P. (Actual)	36	33	50
Cylinders	4 en bloc	4 in pairs	4 in pairs
Bore	3½″	4″	4¾″
Stroke	5¼″	5¾″	6¾″
Wheel Base	136″	156″	160″
Tread Front	56″	56″	56″
Tread Rear	56″	56″	75″
Tires Front	34x3½″	36x4″	36x6″
Tires Rear	34x4″	36x6″	40x6″ dual
Frame	Pressed steel	Pressed steel	Rolled channel

Front Axle—I-beam.
Rear Axle—Sheldon semi-floating.
Springs Front—Semi-elliptic.
Springs Rear—Semi-elliptic.

Carburetor	Master—1″	Master—1¼″	Master—1¼″

Cooling System—Pump.
Oiling System—Splash and forced feed.
Ignition—Magneto.
Control—Left-hand drive, center control.
Clutch—Dry plate.

Transmission	Fuller Selective, three forward, one reverse	Fuller Selective, three forward, one reverse	Cotta Selective, three speeds forward, one reverse

Brakes—Internal—rear wheels.
Steering Gear—Screw and nut.
Equipment—Cab, windshield, curtains, oil side and tail lamps, jack, tools and governor.

tradition, this distant rural location once again proved that, perhaps with the blacksmith connections, a small company could survive as a builder of motor vehicles in the early years simply by assembling components such as engines, clutches, transmissions, axles and other significant parts manufactured around the United States and brought to a remote shop without the need of a big factory, highly skilled workers or even an engineering department.

Wisconsin trucks continued to be built up to 5-ton capacity in the early 1920s. Engines were provided by "original equipment manufacturers" (OEMs) such as Herschell-Spillman, Continental and Waukesha. The Myers Machine Works acquired the Six Wheel Truck Company of Fox Lake, Wisconsin, yet another small town, located in Dodge County about halfway to Sheboygan. This acquisition gave Myers Machine the blueprints for the six-wheel Super-Traction truck, which were used to build a bus chassis. A simpler four-wheel chassis bus was also listed in 1925, but Myers Machine Works along with its acquisitions faded away permanently by 1926.

Witt-Will

One of the very few motor vehicle ventures organized around Washington, D.C., was the Witt-Will Company, Incorporated, which began doing business in 1911. As was the formula for a number of early companies, especially those setting out to build commercial vehicles, Witt-Will assembled conventional and forward-control trucks using four-cylinder Continental motors and Brown-Lipe transmissions with a choice of Timken worm or Timken bevel rear axles.

There is no indication that Witt-Will built trucks for the military during the Great War, but it did survive the material shortages and the postwar recession. However, the company's proximity to the White House proved

to be a boon for some federal contracts as a transport truck. By 1920 the Witt-Will had not changed much and capacity remained from 1½-ton to 5-ton. Six-cylinder engines were introduced by 1927. The two-ton capacity Model P used a 27.2 hp Continental engine with a Brown-Lipe transmission and Ross steering gear. Archibald wheels still carried solid rubber tires.

Motor vehicle assemblers during this era had a choice of manufacturing their own wheels, or buying them straight "off the shelf" from several independent companies which in addition to Archibald in Lawrence, Massachusetts, included; Auto Wheel in Lansing, Michigan; Bimel in Portland, Indiana; Budd in Philadelphia, Pennsylvania; Clark in Buchanan, Michigan; Dayton in Dayton, Ohio; Detroit Panel in Detroit, Michigan; Disteel in Detroit, Michigan; Hayes in Jackson, Michigan; Hoopes in West Chester, Pennsylvania; Indestructible Wheel in Lebanon, Indiana; Interstate Foundry in Chicago, Illinois; Jones & Phineas in Newark, New Jersey; Kelsey in Detroit, Michigan; Michigan Malleable Iron in Detroit, Michigan; Motor Wheel in Lansing, Michigan; Muncie in Muncie, Indiana; Northern Wheel in Alma, Michigan; Prudden in Lansing, Michigan; Royer in Aurora, Indiana; Schwartz in Philadelphia, Pennsylvania; Smith and Day in Syracuse, New York; St. Marys in St. Marys, Ohio; Standard Wheel in Terre Haute, Indiana, Van Wheel in Oneida, New York; Walker Axle in Chicago, Illinois; Wayne in Newark, New Jersey; and Whitcomb in Kenosha, Wisconsin.

In the late 1920s the Witt-Will 4-ton Model A had a 172-inch wheelbase and was powered by a 36.1 hp Continental B5 engine. This was the longest wheelbase chassis from Witt-Will and was also used on the heaviest 5-ton capacity model. The unusual components of this latter model were its Westinghouse ignition and Smith and Day wheels.

WITT-WILL TRUCKS

Manufactured by

WITT-WILL CO., Inc.,; 52 North Street, N E., Washington, D. C.

Model	W-D-1-18	W-D-2-18
Capacity	1 ton	2 tons
Drive	Worm	Worm
Chassis Weight	3,500 lbs.	4,550 lbs.
Chassis Price	$2,000	$2,650
Engine	Continental	Continental
H. P. (S.A.E.)	30	27.20
H. P. (Actual)	22.5 at 1000 R.P.M.	35 to 40
Cylinders	4 en bloc	4 en bloc
Bore	$3\frac{3}{4}''$	$4\frac{1}{8}''$
Stroke	$5\frac{1}{4}''$	$5\frac{1}{4}''$
Wheel Base	122"	144"
Tread Front	$58\frac{1}{2}''$	$58\frac{1}{2}''$
Tread Rear	$58\frac{1}{2}''$	$58\frac{1}{2}''$
Tires Front	$36x3\frac{1}{2}''$	$36x3\frac{1}{2}''$ or 4"
Tires Rear	$36x4''$	$36x7''$ or $36x3\frac{1}{2}''$ dual

Frame—Pressed steel.
Front Axle—Timken I-beam.
Rear Axle—Timken full floating.
Springs Front—Semi-elliptic.
Springs Rear—Semi-elliptic.
Carburetor—Zenith L.
Cooling System—Pump.
Oiling System—Forced feed and splash.
Ignition—Eisemann high tension magneto.
Control—Left drive, center control.
Clutch—Dry plate.
Transmission—Brown-Lipe selective, three speeds forward, one reverse.
Brakes—Internal, expanding on rear wheel drums.
Steering Gear—Worm and sector.
Equipment—Side and tail lamps, full kit of tools.

The 5-ton model was priced at $4500 for running chassis. With federal contracts fading out and the stock market crash taking its toll, by the end of 1929 Witt-Will ceased truck manufacturing but continued on a small scale in building auxiliary equipment on the chassis of other truck makes into the 1930s before fading out entirely.

Woods (electric)

The Woods Motor Vehicle Company got an early start in vehicle manufacturing in Chicago, Illinois, during 1899. It was not affiliated with another electric vehicle company in New York by the same name, but it was organized to compete with the giant Electric Vehicle Company of that city.

Woods was capitalized with $10,000,000, and the principals of the company were August Belmont, Samuel Insull and "Standard Oil magnates and investors from Toronto," which would somewhat dispel the notion that all purveyors of petroleum automatically invested in internal combustion technology.

The company was named after Clinton E. Woods, whose patents the company had bought with the notion that he would also manage the company, but after a reorganization in 1901 Clinton Woods left to become an auto dealer. Some claims have been made that a Woods electric, which was known to have been shipped to the manager of the Honolulu Iron Works, was the very first motor vehicle used in Hawaii.

With new president Louis Burr, who had arrived from the Kimball Company, Woods began to manufacture about 500 vehicles per year by 1902, which included a Hansom taxicab called Style 11. Woods used one electric motor as part of its rear axle for propulsion, and that year a hood was used to cover the battery pack in front. Gasoline-electric hybrid cars were built from 1905 to 1907. This type of vehicle was not well understood or ac-

cepted by the general public, satisfying neither gasoline nor battery proponents, and Woods discontinued the hybrid design in 1908, at least temporarily, before it was adopted once again a decade later, and by others a century later.

Prices for Woods electrics ranged around $3000 at that time, which was considered moderate in the field of electric cars, but it was still about double for similar sized gasoline-powered cars. The lackluster sales before World War I induced Woods to reintroduce its gasoline-electric hybrid cars in 1916, which were called Woods Dual Power. But even with a gasoline engine, top speed was specified as 35 mph.

A rare "see-through" illustration from the American Technical Society published in 1917 is possibly the best way to show the overall layout of the Woods Dual Power "hybrid-electric" design, considered the "state-of-the-art" almost exactly 100 years later and employed by several major motor vehicle manufacturers around the world at the time of this writing.

One of the cited advantages of the electric power-train was that by using a potentiometer-type controller there was an "infinite" number of speeds forward and reverse, referring to the incremental steps from zero to top speed, instead of employing the simpler battery-switching method, which created a number of set voltages and corresponding speeds. But despite these advantages, new "rakish" styling and extended range, the Woods Dual Power Model 54 was the last offering, as the company went out of business even before the end of World War I.

Zeitler & Lamson

Named for their founding entrepreneurs of which little personal information is known, Zeitler & Lamson started out in Chicago, Illinois, in 1914. Conventional, assembled trucks

WOODS DUAL POWER—54

COLOR	Green or blue		BRAKE SYSTEMS . .	Expanding on rear wheels
SEATING CAPACITY .	Four			
BODY:			BATTERY	24 cells, 11 plate
LENGTH OVER ALL	102 inches			
WIDTH OVER ALL .	59 inches		SPEED	35 miles per hour
WHEELBASE	124½ inches		No. FORWARD SPEEDS	Infinite
GAUGE	56 inches			
WHEELS	Wood		No. REVERSE SPEEDS	Infinite
FRONT TIRES	34 x 4 inches, pneumatic		CONTROL	Finger levers and pedal
REAR TIRES	34 x 4 inches, pneumatic		Steering	Wheel

ZEITLER & LAMSON TRUCKS
Manufactured by
ZEITLER & LAMSON TRUCK CO., Chicago, Ill.

S P E C I F I C A T I O N S

Model	1½-ton	2½-ton	3½-ton	5-ton
Capacity	1½ tons	2½ tons	3½ tons	5 tons
Drive	Worm	Worm	Worm	Worm
Chassis Price	$1,850	$2,450	$3,150	$4,150
Motor				
H. P. (S.A.E.)	25.6	25.6	36.5	41
H. P. (Actual)	41	55	65	75
Cylinders	4 en bloc	4 en bloc	4 in pairs	4 in pairs
Bore	4″	4″	4¾″	5 1/10″
Stroke	5″	6″	5½″	5½″
Wheel Base	Optional	Optional	Optional	Optional
Tread Front	56″	56″	58″	59″
Tread Rear	58″	60″	61″	61″
Tires Front	36x3½″	36x4″	36x5″	36x6″
Tires Rear	36x5″	36x7″	40x5″ dual	40x6″ dual
Frame	Pressed 5¾″	Pressed 5¾″	Structural channel 7″	Structural channel 8″
Front Axle	Sheldon D 343	Sheldon 3 FA 10	Sheldon 4 FA 20	Sheldon 5 FA 30
Rear Axle	Sheldon W 10	Sheldon W 21	Sheldon 30	Sheldon W 50

Springs Front—Semi-elliptic.
Springs Rear—Semi-elliptic.

Carburetor	Stromberg M 2	Stromberg M 2	Stromberg M 3	Stromberg M 3

Cooling System—Pump.
Oiling System—Forced feed.
Ignition—Bosch magneto and Atwater Kent igniter.
Control—Left drive, center control.

Clutch	Borg & Beck, dry, 10″	Borg & Beck, dry, 12″	Borg & Beck, dry, 12″	Borg & Beck, dry, 12″

Transmission—Three speeds forward and one reverse. Gears always in mesh.
Brakes—Internal expanding.
Steering Gear—Worm and nut.
Equipment—Electric lights, generator, duplex governor, hubodometer.

from 1-ton to 5-ton capacity in one-ton increments were available from the beginning. All of them were powered by four-cylinder Continental engines. Chassis prices ranged from $1550 to $4150. Production was interrupted in 1917 when the Lamson portion of the partnership withdrew, and the new pair of manufacturers became King-Zeitler for 1919 once the war ended. A few Zeitler and Lamson chassis were built as fire engines.

Besides the magneto purchased "off the shelf" from American Bosch in Springfield, Massachusetts, and the Atwater Kent Igniter in Philadelphia, Pennsylvania, motor vehicle manufacturers had a variety of electrical systems from which to choose, which they could simply assemble into their product line no matter what type of auto or truck they were building.

The other companies that provided electrical systems as original equipment manufacturers (OEM) in this period were: Allis-Chalmers in Milwaukee, Wisconsin; Apollo in Apollo, Pennsylvania; Auto-Lite in Toledo, Ohio; Ericsson in Buffalo, New York; Connecticut Electric in Meriden, Connecticut; Dayton in Dayton, Ohio; Eisemann in Brooklyn, New York; Gray & Davis in Boston, Massachusetts; Kokomo in Kokomo, Indiana; K.W. Ignition in Cleveland, Ohio; Leece-Neville in Cleveland, Ohio; North East Electric in Rochester, New York; Owen Dyneto in Syracuse, New York; Prest-O-Lite in Indianapolis, Indiana; Remy in Anderson, Indiana; Robert Bosch in New York City; Scintilla in New York City; Simms in Orange, New Jersey; Splitdorf in Newark, New Jersey; Wagner in St. Louis, Missouri; Westinghouse in Springfield, Massachusetts; and U.S. Light & Heat in Niagara Falls, New York.

King-Zeitler's model line in the new decade consisted of ¾-ton to 5-ton, much as it was before specializing in commercial vehicles, only with no known production of any passenger cars. In the early 1920s a bus chassis was also offered. Continental four-cylinder motors continued to be used, and Brown-Lipe transmissions and clutches with Timken axles were the standard equipment.

In 1924 the ¾-ton was discontinued and the model line continued as before with only minor changes. Prices also remained about the same as a decade earlier, with $4,525 for the 5-ton, which was powered by a 36.1 hp Continental B5 engine. This was known as the Model 90. All of the trucks used Bimel wheels. Even in the late 1920s the heaviest model was still available only with solid rubber tires. By the time of the stock market crash there was no longer any demand for King-Zeitler motor vehicles.

Abbreviations

AEF . . . . American Expeditionary Forces

A.L.A.M. . . . . Association of Licensed Automobile Manufacturers

cc . . . . cubic centimeters

cid . . . . cubic inch displacement

C.T. . . . . Commercial Truck

COE . . . . cab over engine

D.C. . . . . direct current

e.g. . . . . *exempli gratia* (for example)

GM . . . . General Motors

hp . . . . horsepower

IHC . . . . International Harvester Corporation

IMTC . . . . International Motor Truck Company

Jr. . . . . Junior

mm . . . . millimeter

mph . . . . miles per hour

N.A.C.C. . . . . National Automobile Chamber of Commerce

OEM . . . . original equipment manufacturer

PACCAR . . . . Pacific Car and Foundry Corporation

RPM . . . . revolutions per minute

SAE . . . . Society of Automotive Engineers

S.P.C.A. . . . . Society for the Prevention of Cruelty to Animals

UPS . . . . United Parcel Service

V.E.C. . . . . Vehicle Equipment Company

Bibliography

Automobile Engineering, Vol. I–V. American Technical Society. 1917.

Barker, Ronald, and Anthony Harding. *Automobile Design.* SAE, 1970.

Beaumont, W. Worby. *Industrial Electric Vehicles and Trucks.* London: Charles Griffin, 1920.

Brokaw, H. Clifford, and Charles A. Starr. *Putnam's Automobile Handbook.* G.P. Putnam's Sons, 1918.

Brown, Roland, and Mac McDiarmid. *The Ultimate Motorcycle Encyclopedia.* Hermes House, 2002.

Crimson, Frederick W. *International Trucks.* Motorbooks. 1995.

Dowds, Alan. *Encyclopedia of Motorcycles.* San Diego, CA: Thunder Bay Press, 2007.

Dyke, A.L. *Dyke's Automobile and Gasoline Engine Encyclopedia.* Chicago: The Goodheart-Willcox, 1917 (4th ed.), 1925 (14th ed.), 1945 (20th ed.).

Edwards, John. *Auto Dictionary.* Los Angeles: HP Books, 1993.

Georgano, G.N. *The Complete Encyclopedia of Commercial Vehicles.* Osceola, WI: Motorbooks International, 1979.

_____. *The Complete Encyclopedia of Motorcars.* New York: E.P. Dutton, 1970.

Graham, Frank. *Audels New Automobile Guide.* New York: Theo Audel, 1943.

Gunnell, John. *Standard Catalog of American Cars 1946–1975.* Iola, WI: Krause Publications, 1992.

_____. *Standard Catalog of American Light Duty Trucks.* Iola, WI: Krause Publications, 1993.

Henshaw, Peter. *Illustrated Directory of Tractors.* Osceola, WI: Motorbooks International, 2002.

Hicks, Roger. *The Encyclopedia of Motorcycles.* San Diego, CA: Thunder Bay Press, 2001.

Homans, James E. *Self-Propelled Vehicles.* New York: Theo Audel, 1907.

Illustrations and Specifications. New York: National Automobile Chamber of Commerce, 1918.

Kimes, Beverly Rae, and Henry Austin Clark. *The Standard Catalog of American Cars 1805–1942.* Iola, WI: Krause Publications, 1989.

La Schum, Edward. *The Electric Truck.* New York: U.P.C. Books, 1924.

Lewerenz, Alfred S. *Antique Auto Body for the Restorer—Brass Work.* Arcadia, CA: Post Motor Books, 1970.

Maxim, Hiram Percy. *Horseless Carriage Days.* New York: Harper, 1937.

Miller, Denis. *The Illustrated Encyclopedia of Trucks and Buses.* New York: Mayflower, 1982.

Motor Trucks of America. Akron, OH: B.F. Goodrich, 1917 (vol. 5), 1918 (vol. 6).

Mroz, Albert. *The Illustrated Encyclopedia of American Trucks and Commercial Vehicles.* Iola, WI: Krause Publications, 1996.

Purdy, Ken W. *1904 Handbook of Gasoline Automobiles.* New York: Chelsea House, 1969.

Shacket, Sheldon R. *The Complete Book of Electric Vehicles.* Domus Books, 1979.

Tragatsch, Erwin. *The New Illustrated Encyclopedia of Motorcycles.* Chartwell Books, 2000.

Wagner, James K. *Ford Trucks Since 1905.* Crestline, 1988.

Wakefield, Ernest H. *History of the Electric Automobile.* Warrendale, PA: Society of Automotive Engineers, 1994.

Wise, David Burgess. *The Illustrated Encyclopedia of the World's Automobiles.* Secaucus, NJ: Chartwell Books, 1991.

Index

Numbers in *bold italics* indicate pages with illustrations.